TRAFFICKING WITH DEMONS

TRAFFICKING WITH DEMONS

MAGIC, RITUAL, AND
GENDER FROM LATE
ANTIQUITY TO 1000

MARTHA RAMPTON

CORNELL UNIVERSITY PRESS
Ithaca and London

Copyright © 2021 by Cornell University

All rights reserved. Except for brief quotations in a review, this book, or parts thereof, must not be reproduced in any form without permission in writing from the publisher. For information, address Cornell University Press, Sage House, 512 East State Street, Ithaca, New York 14850. Visit our website at cornellpress.cornell.edu.

First published 2021 by Cornell University Press

Library of Congress Cataloging-in-Publication Data

Names: Rampton, Martha, author.
Title: Trafficking with demons : magic, ritual, and gender from late antiquity to 1000 / Martha Rampton.
Description: 1st edition. | Ithaca [New York] : Cornell University Press, 2021. | Includes bibliographical references and index.
Identifiers: LCCN 2018040254 (print) | LCCN 2018041264 (ebook) | ISBN 9781501735301 (pdf) | ISBN 9781501735318 (epub/mobi) | ISBN 9781501702686 (cloth)
Subjects: LCSH: Magic—Europe—History—To 1500. | Magic—Religious aspects—Christianity—History of doctrines—Early church, ca. 30–600. | Magic—Religious aspects—Christianity—History of doctrines—Middle Ages, 600–1500. | Women in Christianity—Europe—History—Early church, ca. 30–600. | Women in Christianity—Europe—History—Middle Ages, 600–1500.
Classification: LCC BF1589 .R36 2019 (print) | LCC BF1589 (ebook) | DDC 133.4/3094—dc23
LC record available at https://lccn.loc.gov/2018040254 LC ebook record available at https://lccn.loc.gov/2018041264
ISBN 978-1-5017-8520-7 (pbk.)

To my husband, Steve, and our friends Simone, Jack, Ernie, and Hallie

Contents

Acknowledgments ix

Introduction 1

Part 1: Studying Magic

1. Magic and Its Sources in Late Antiquity and the Early Middle Ages 23
2. Demons of the Lower Air 63

Part 2: Breaking In: Christianity in Classical Rome

3. Ritual, Demons, and Sacred Space 87
4. A Thousand Vacuous Observances 107
5. Maleficium and Traffic with the Dead 146
6. The Screech Owl, the Vampire, the Moon, and the Woman 164

Part 3: Traffic with Demons: Post-Roman Europe

7. *Sub Dio* 189
8. Victimless Magic and Execrable Remedies 214
9. The Awesome Power of the Woman's Craft 248

Part 4: Skepticism: The Carolingian Era

10. Placemaking and the Natural World 273

11. Superstition and Divination Questioned 295
12. Women's Magic Challenged 313
13. Magic, Women, and the Carolingian Court 342
14. Magic and *Materia Medica* 360
    Conclusion 384

Bibliography 395
Index 451

Acknowledgments

The author of an undertaking such as this, which has grown and mutated many times over two decades, accumulates a long list of people to whom she is indebted. I hesitate to start that list for fear of leaving out people who should be included, but the greater wrong would be to omit mention of so many who have inspired, advised, prodded, and supported me along the way. Thomas F. X. Noble, who was there at the inception of the project, lent his wisdom and guidance throughout the process and carefully read more than one draft of the book. My interest in magic was first piqued when I took a course from H. C. Erik Midelfort at the University of Virginia; I am indebted to him, Anne J. Schutte, and Peter S. Baker for reading a very early iteration of this work and recommending that I continue my research. I was able to do that, in part, thanks to the University of Virginia Graduate School of Arts and Sciences and the Corcoran Department of History, which awarded me a duPont Fellowship.

I am thankful to Glenn Olsen, who was my mentor when I was a masters student at the University of Utah. I was an undergraduate when I first met Glenn, and he encouraged me to pursue a graduate degree and gave me the confidence to do it. My thanks go out to friends and colleagues who have read portions of this book or listened to more than one paper on the subject of early medieval magic. I have benefited greatly from conversations over the years with some of the finest thinkers in early medieval studies. Among those scholars are Courtney Booker, Marty Claussen, Lynda Coon, Makye de Jong, Paul Dutton, Emlyn Eisenach, Matthew Gabriele, Valerie Garver, Pat Geary, Kelly Gibson, Matthew Gillis, Eric Goldberg, Anne Latowsky, Amy Livingstone, Rob Meens, Jinty Nelson, and Andy Romig, all of whom have shown interest in my research and have engaged me at various points with questions and observations that clarified my thinking. Lynda Coon generously read a full draft of the book and gently nudged me to make changes that have resulted in a much improved final product. I am grateful to Aaron Greer, associate professor of anthropology at Pacific University, who helped guide me through the labyrinth of ritual theory.

ACKNOWLEDGMENTS

I am also indebted to the anonymous readers of the manuscript who invested so much time in helping me work through what I wanted to say and how I might better communicate my ideas. Mahinder Kingra of Cornell University Press, and his predecessor, Peter Potter, have been marvelous to work with. Mahinder and the production team at Cornell can only be described as long-suffering, and I cannot imagine more skillful or thorough editors than I had in Eric Levy, Glenn Novak, and Karen Hwa. I wish to thank them all publicly for their patience, kindness, and sense of shared purpose in bringing this work to fruition.

Pacific University awarded me several grants that provided funds to facilitate my research. This book would never had been possible without the assistance of the stellar staff of the Tim and Cathy Tran Library at Pacific University. Their success at ferreting out rare and obscure electronic sources in this era of COVID-19 has been nothing short of miraculous.

My greatest debt of gratitude goes to my colleague and husband, Steve R. Smith, whose support at all stages of the growth of this book has been herculean and whose love has kept me going and made the whole thing seem worthwhile.

TRAFFICKING WITH DEMONS

Introduction

> Have you believed what many women, turned back to Satan, believe and affirm to be true, [that is] you believe that in the silence of the quiet night when you have gone to bed, your husband lying at your side, you are able bodily to go out through closed doors and, with others deceived by similar error, can traverse spaces of the earth and, without visible arms, can kill people baptized and redeemed by the blood of Christ, and eat their cooked flesh, and in place of their heart put straw or wood or any such thing, and when they are eaten, make them alive again to give them intervals of life?
>
> —Burchard of Worms, *Decretum*

In the early eleventh century, Bishop Burchard of Worms (d. 1025) penned the above canon condemning a fantasy that misguided women of his parish held dear, and still palpable nearly a millennium later is the bishop's dread of women who thought they could change the natural order of things and debase all that was good through magic and esoteric rites.[1] The specter of loosed women escaping the confines of the marital bed to work grisly rituals in league with Satan speaks to the three threads that are woven throughout this book. First and foremost, this study is about magic, which was embedded within the foundational assumptions of society and informed the vocabulary through which people understood the cosmos, divinity, and their own Christian faith. This work examines the multifaceted dimensions of magic, the encounters between Christianit(ies) and

---

1. When primary quotations come from English translations, the Latin generally is not provided in the notes. Burchard of Worms, *Decretum* 19.5.170, 2:446: "Credidisti quod multae mulieres retro Satanam conversae credunt et affirmant verum esse, ut credas inquietae noctis silentio cum te collocaveris in lecto tuo, et marito tuo in sinu tuo jacente, te dum corporea sis januis clausis exire posse, et terrarum spacia cum aliis simili errore deceptis pertransire valere, et homines baptizatos, et Christi sanguine redemptos, sine armis visibilibus et interficere, et decoctis carnibus eorum vos comedere, et in loco cordis eorum stramen aut lignum, aut aliquod hujusmodi ponere, et commestis, iterum vivos facere, et inducias vivendi dare? Si credidisti, quadraginta dies, id est carinam in pane et aqua cum septem sequentibus annis poeniteas."

paganism(s), and the intersections between magic, ritual, and gender in late antique Christendom and the early medieval Latin West.[2] The book begins with the development of the church in the first century and ends with the writings of Bishop Burchard of Worms, the last great synthesizer of canonical prescripts on magic and superstition in the Carolingian era.[3]

Despite striking continuities in the understanding of magic from the late classical age throughout the early Middle Ages, there were also key changes. From the first century through the eighth, although categories were reshuffled to some extent, the specifics of magic practice and the general assessment of it remained largely consistent. However, transformations in power structures, an increasingly centralized orchestration of Christian ceremony, and reevaluations of women's roles changed the estimation of magic in the Carolingian era. Within the early Christian world and post-Roman Europe, magical acts were crimes that injured others and sins that imperiled the individual. In the Carolingian period, although the classifications of magic were essentially unaltered, there was a discernable shift in focus such that suppression of idolatry, superstition, and the magic arts became part of a wholesale imperative of cultural authority and public policy.[4] By around the year 1000,

---

2. In late antiquity and the early Middle Ages, no single, standard understanding or practice of Christianity existed. There were core tenets, but as J. M. H. Smith (*Europe after Rome*, 220–39) observes, the religion "managed to localize itself in a multitude of cultural contexts" (224). See also Brown, *Rise of Western Christendom*, 13–17; Noble and J. M. H. Smith, *Early Medieval Christianities*, xvi–xvii; Rousseau, "Late Roman Christianities," 21. On "paganism(s)" (also "polytheism[s]") see Robinson, *Who Were the First Christians?*, 1–13; Brown, *Rise of Western Christendom*, 58–60; Palmer, "Defining Paganism"; I. Wood, "Pagan Religion and Superstitions," 264; Fox, *Pagans and Christians*, 31. By "West" I mean western Europe and England, roughly as they are currently conceived geographically. The first unit of this book is devoted to the early development of Christianity in the Levant as the church was taking shape within Jewish and pagan cultural milieus. I leave off discussion of the Greek East after approximately 400 when Latin Christendom had absorbed the theology and organization of the Eastern Church and was in the process of developing its own religious and political traditions.

3. See Nelson ("Society") for a discussion of an older historiographic tradition that puts a breach between the Carolingian age and the Gregorian reform movement of the eleventh century. Currently, the position that the end of the first millennium was a historical watershed has been challenged when the notion is applied with a broad brush. Cushing ("Law and Reform") disputes the "Fourier model" of the development of canon law in favor of a discourse in which continuity between the early and high Middle Ages is more impressive than the change (quotation 36). See also Leyser, "Review Article"; Faulkner, *Law and Authority*, 248–52; G. Austin, *Shaping Church Law*, 235–39; Hummer, *Politics and Power*, 1–8.

4. On the constructs of "public/private" and "the state," see Goldberg, *Struggle for Empire*, 207–8; Airlie, "Aristocracy," 93–97; Wormald, "Pre-modern 'State,'" 188–89; Innes, *State and Society*, 254–59; Althoff, *Spielregeln der Politik*, 126–53. All caution that the terms "public/private" and "the state" must be conceived according to their own "inner logic" (Innes, *State and Society*, 254) and in specifically early medieval contexts. Nelson ("Kingship and Empire") argues that although the Carolingian dynasty was underpinned by identification with the church, that did not undercut the concept of statehood.

discourses had changed. Magic had been tamed, and within the thought-world of the elite it was perceived to be largely ineffective, as were the rituals that attended it and the women who practiced it.

In the first Christian millennium, magic was thought to play a natural role within the functioning of the universe and existed within a rational cosmos hierarchically arranged according to a "great chain of being."[5] Magic amounted to traffic with demons of the lower air that were part of the physical order and inhabited the atmosphere between the moon and the earth.[6] Interactions with those demons occurred in highly formalistic, ritual settings and on a routine and casual basis. One of the reasons magic was so pernicious in the eyes of the church was that it relentlessly entrenched itself both in the sacral and the quotidian behaviors even of well-intentioned Christians.[7] The tension between Christian practice and magic behavior was fierce in the first century, and it continued throughout the early Middle Ages as atavistic forms of magic mutated and found sanctuary in the daily habits of Christian peoples and new paganisms entered Europe with their own forms of magic.

Control over magic equated to power, particularly when ritual and symbols (clusters of meaning and the building blocks of ritual) entered the mix. The word "power" can be envisioned in two ways. One denotes power to accomplish an aim; the other suggests power over others for the purpose of directing behaviors or beliefs.[8] Ritual is formative and empowers those involved in it because through the ritualizing process, meaning is fashioned and values or "truths" that inform and direct everyday reality are worked out in ritual space. Following from Jacques Derrida's concept of *"différance,"* the process of signification in a ritual act is deferred beyond the rite as such and

---

5. Struck, "Poet as Conjurer," 128–29; Janowitz, *Icons of Power*, 120–21, 126; Lovejoy, *Great Chain of Being*, 24–66. In general, only intellectuals would have articulated the concept of the "chain of being" per se; nevertheless, for all segments of the medieval population, magic was integral to the normal workings of the universe.

6. Though not synonymous, the terms "magic," "superstition," "pagan/paganism," and "idolatry" overlapped and at times were applied indiscriminately for similar kinds of behavior. The important differences between the words will be explained throughout the book as they become germane. The term "devil" and "demon" were used interchangeably in late antique and early medieval parlance; when I mean "devil" to refer to Satan, I capitalize the word (the Devil).

7. When I use the word "church" I am referring to the institution (ever mutating) and its collective personnel (secular clergy, regular clergy, and missionaries) but am not assuming that they had a unified voice or a tightly coordinated organization, particularly before the ninth century. On this subject see Costambeys, Innes, and MacLean, *Carolingian World*, 85–86, 122–25; de Jong, "Ecclesia and the Early Medieval Polity," 115–22; Wormald, "Pre-modern 'State,'" 189.

8. Lefebvre, *Production of Space*, 10–11; French, *Beyond Power*, 505–6; Lukes, "Power and Structure."

moves into the daily world of the actors, because, as Roy Rappaport argues, ritual is *"the* basic social act."[9] Through ritual, a person or group makes statements or tries on attitudes, which, though initially metaphorical, affect assumptions about the non-ritualized world of everyday experience. Symbols speak a language that is internalized holistically and emotionally. They create a rhetoric difficult to counter by intellectualized arguments because they define the world at a deeply intuitive level.[10] Symbols are ambiguous, fuzzy, porous, malleable, and, as Paul Ricoeur says, tenacious. Through ritual, symbols are reinforced deeply within the psyches of the participants who ingest them.[11]

The architects of the Christian system and those who proselytized the gospel understood ritual in a way not at odds with modern theorists, although there was no contemporary term that connotes what we mean by "ritual."[12] Late antique and early medieval ecclesiastics knew that magical rituals had the potential of reinforcing a "reality" (albeit in Christian eyes a sham reality) counter to the vision of the world the church constructed and resistant to its logic. Magical ritual structured sacred beliefs and cultural conduct, creating an environment in which worldviews were both mirrored and molded. To put it in Pierre Bourdieu's terms, ritual had the capacity to "create appearances and belief, to confirm or transform the vision of the world and thereby action in the world, and therefore the world itself."[13] Augustine, bishop of Hippo Regius in North Africa (d. 430), articulated this same concept when he said that it is necessary to give visible sacrifice to God because acts and words used in worship are symbols and signs that reinforce deeper realities. "When praying to and praising [God], we offer the same things in the heart that our words signify."[14] Because of ritual's potency, it was critical that the church shape the semiotic lexicon of the people whom it served and defuse pagan and demonic magical rites and symbols that were in danger of providing

---

9. Derrida, "Structure, Sign and Play"; Rappaport, *Ecology, Meaning and Religion,* 174. Emphasis in original.

10. Hausmann, Jonason, and Summers-Effler, "Interaction Ritual Theory"; Muir, *Ritual,* 2–6.

11. Ricoeur, "Symbol Gives Rise"; Koziol (*Begging Pardon and Favor,* 303) writes, "Symbols may take their meaning through projection and inversion; but people do not project and invert them in order to give them meaning."

12. Petersen, "Carolingian Music," 19.

13. Bourdieu, "Symbolic Power," 117. To put it in MacMullen's terms (*Second Church,* 101), "forms *were* content." Emphasis in original.

14. Augustine, *De civitate Dei* 10.19, 1:293 "Quocirca sicut orantes atque laudantes ad eum dirigimus significantes voces, cui res ipsas in corde quas significamus offerimus." Augustine wrote *The City of God* (ca. 413–426) to refute pagan accusations that Rome was sacked (410) due to the imperial adoption of Christianity.

meaning at odds with Christian truths. The church understood that ritual possessed the power to create conviction.

Early Christian leaders also understood that managing ritual and the symbols that store ritualized meaning was a way of claiming authority, or "power over." For Michel Foucault, power relationships are worked out through action, so in order for a given party to manipulate belief or exercise control it must structure the "field of action of others,"[15] and that is what the church sought to do by hindering particular rites in favor of others. Catherine Bell argues that ritual "is a strategy for the construction of particular relationships of power. . . . Those who control ritualization are in command of a particularly powerful form of objectification."[16]

Archbishop of Constantinople John Chrysostom (d. 407) understood that the Kalends of January was a pagan holiday of some importance to his congregation in Antioch, but rather than ask them to sit out these special days of feasting, drinking, and merrymaking, he urged his parishioners to forego their traditional rituals and set the day aside to give thanks to God.[17] In a similar vein, the letter of the Roman bishop Gregory the Great (d. 604) to Abbot Mellitus (d. 624), who became the third archbishop of Canterbury, reveals a solid grasp of how structuring the "field of action of others" redirects behaviors and beliefs. The bishop suggests that if the Anglo-Saxons could be persuaded to introduce Christian symbols and sacred objects, such as holy water and relics, into their pagan spaces, they "will be able to banish error from their hearts and be more ready to come to the places they are familiar with, but now recognizing and worshipping the true God."[18] Because early churchmen and churchwomen appreciated ritual's power, control of it was one of the most strategic battles waged for a Christian view of the world, especially given the fact that most people were not likely to encounter or comprehend theological arguments, either written or spoken.[19]

---

15. Foucault, "Subject and Power" (quotation 221). See also Bloch, "Symbols, Song, Dance."

16. Bell, *Ritual Theory, Ritual Practice*, 202, 211. Geertz (*Interpretation of Cultures*, 93–94, and "Religion as a Cultural System," 7–8) explains that ritualized cultural patterns are models of and models for reality.

17. Maxwell, *Christianization and Communication*, 154–57.

18. Bede, *Bede's Ecclesiastical History* 1:30, 106–7: "Dum gens ipsa eadem fana sua non uidet destrui, de corde errorem deponat, de Deum uerum cognoscens ac adorans, ad loca quae consueuit familiarius concurrat." There is an argument to be made that Gregory projected the architecture of Mediterranean cults onto Anglo-Saxon pagan shrines which were not necessarily enclosed in a temple. Be that as it may, the important point is that Gregory appreciated the power of ritual and symbols. See A. Fulk, "Patriarchal Rituals"; Markus, *Gregory the Great and His World*, 177–87.

19. Benko (*Pagan Rome*, 47) says it well when he explains that in the early church, Christianity was appealing "more as a distinct way of life than as a set of doctrines."

Scholars have long recognized that those who grew the early church were thoroughly (sometimes alarmingly) conversant with pagan worship, but older generations of social scientists misinterpreted the reasons why. Many concluded that the similarity between magic and religious ritual objects, ceremonies, and vocabularies resulted in the failure of Christians to distinguish magic from religion; however, most scholars now agree that the opposite was true.[20] Christian thinkers denied the equivalence of demonic/pagan and Christian symbolism but recognized the similitude, and for that reason they were able to juggle the two artfully because Christians and pagans drew from the same storehouse of symbols; they worked with the same raw material to articulate their religious systems. The Christian challenge was to imbue familiar symbols with altered meaning and to make clear how the same object, ceremony, or speech act could draw on different sources of power—one demonic and deleterious, the other godly and salvific. Christian and demonic/pagan activity often shared a ritual form, but they differed in substance, and so the early church was vigilant that the people under its care avoid the very mistake many historians have made in confusing magic and religion.

An analysis of women and their exercise of magic is central to the argument of this book. Virtually all historians accept uncritically that medieval women had a particular facility with magic. For example, David Herlihy writes that "women in early medieval society retained a special affinity to the magical arts." Richard Kieckhefer says, "While there is no reason to think that women alone practiced magic, both pagan and Christian writers ascribed it primarily to them." Pierre Riché observes that "women were always thought to be particularly disposed toward sorcery," and Jeffrey Russell claims that "already [by 800] the witch was . . . more often a woman than a man."[21]

Although throughout the first millennium women were perceived to be, by their very nature, predisposed to engage in disruptive and antisocial magical conduct, a thorough assessment of the early Christian and medieval evidence demonstrates that in fact, women were never considered to be the primary custodians or practitioners of the magic arts. Female magic

---

20. For examples of the older view see Betz, et al., *Religion Past and Present*, s.v. "Magic—Church History"; Thomas, *Religion and the Decline*, 27–57; Singer, *From Magic to Science*, 168–88; Grattan and Singer, *Anglo-Saxon Magic and Medicine*, 6–7; M. Murray, *Witch-Cult*, 9–11.

21. Herlihy, *Opera Muliebria*, 39; Kieckhefer, *Magic in the Middle Ages*, 39; Riché, *Daily Life*, 184; J. B. Russell, *Witchcraft*, 62. From J. Crawford ("Evidences for Witchcraft"), in England, women were rarely condemned for practicing magic until continental prohibitions were absorbed into the English penitentials in the tenth century.

was generally relegated to the domestic sphere, while magic carried out in or pertaining to public spaces tended to be male dominated; by the Carolingian period, this was almost exclusively the case.[22] Women had specialties, which included love magic, healing rites, birth magic, and several nocturnal and chthonic rites, but even in these areas women did not exercise a monopoly.

The perception of women's magic mutated beginning in the mid-eighth century as the Frankish lands of western Europe and Anglo-Saxon England were brought under increasingly well-articulated authority. "The holy," expressed through popular religious practices, monastic movements, and ecclesiastical conventions, came under scrutiny. In the process, activities of holy women were increasingly curbed in the organizational structure of the church. Religious influence, which women once accessed through pilgrimages to Rome, governance of double monasteries, ministering to the sick, preparation of the dead for burial, and working miracles, diminished.[23] This mind-set that women were peripheral in ecclesiastical affairs and, appropriately so, paralleled views about women's inability to control the occult through magic. The Carolingian reformers created an idealized picture of women as largely passive and vulnerable, but particularly when it came to spiritual matters, and magic was a spiritual matter. Given this, most Carolingian sources demonstrate a persistent disinclination to credit the efficacy of female magical power. The constriction of opportunities for women as spiritual specialists occurred simultaneously with changing perceptions of the gender of magic, and I suggest that among the elite, the same forces that narrowed women's religious options had a comparable effect on the belief in female sorcery.

Although they were by and large uninterested in the subject, when Carolingian authors did turn their pens to women trafficking with demons, it is possible to detect opposing semiotic systems in conflict as ecclesiastics attempted to neutralize the power of what were, to them, implausible,

---

22. For a discussion of the construct of "public/private" in late antiquity see Bowes, *Private Worship, Public Values*, 1–17, 217–26; Salzman, *Making of a Christian Aristocracy*, 138–77. See also note 4 above. On the gendering of domestic space see Rezeanu, "Relationship"; Löw "Social Construction of Space."

23. Garver (*Women and Aristocratic Culture*, 8–9) argues that "ecclesiastical leaders believed laywomen should focus on the domestic sphere, explaining how they should best be wives, mothers, and heads of households and estates.... In the early ninth century reformers began to spell out that role more clearly." There was clerical opposition to women's involvement in public affairs if that engagement did not further the interests of the home. Garver also indicates that "strict claustration represented more than empty rhetoric" (15). See also J. M. H. Smith, "Gender and Ideology," 51–54; Schulenburg, "Strict Active Enclosure"; T. Cramer, "Defending the Double Monastery," 60–91.

alien, or threatening rituals (and the symbols that mediate and give rituals shape) in which women acted autonomously in the realm of the sacred. Churchmen feared rites that could nurture a worldview in which women reassumed an "illegitimate" spiritual potency that Carolingian culture had systematically eroded. Religious and secular authorities were determined to neutralize myths of female power, such as Burchard of Worms's nightmarish portrayal of wives freed from the marriage bed wreaking havoc in the heavens. The establishment sought to destroy a matrix of pagan symbols that had the potential to promote concepts of women's majesty outside the liminal space in which they were incubated. This was because, as Catherine Bell writes, "ritual systems do not function to regulate or control the systems of social relations, they *are* the system."[24]

The timeframe covered by this book is broad and the project ambitious. It treats magic, ritual, and gender from the perspective of varied disciplines and more than one historical era. I can by no means claim to be an expert on all of them, and because of this there are likely to be errors and scant justice done to particular topics, despite my best efforts to avoid them. That having been said, I have confidence in the argument of the work and have made the decision that missteps on some details (though regrettable) do not negate the value of a comprehensive, synthetic study. The long early Middle Ages is the period in European history least studied by scholars of magic, and a full appreciation of early medieval culture and society is not possible without bringing magic into the equation. Although late antiquity has not suffered the same neglect as the five hundred years following it, a discussion of late antique Christian magic comprises a portion of the book because in order to appreciate early European magic, a grounding in the intellectual, religious, and cultural landscape of the late Roman world is essential.

Late antiquity formed a bridge between the classical era and the early Middle Ages and is the period in which the building blocks of the early medieval world can be found.[25] Late antique culture flowered roughly from 200 CE and continued until about 450, when the inheritors of the western

---

24. Bell, *Ritual Theory, Ritual Practice*, 130. Emphasis in original.

25. In this brief overview of the background to the historical periods covered in this book, references are kept to a minimum. Even streamlined notes on the scholarship of the sweeping panorama of a thousand years of history would overwhelm the text. I refer readers to comprehensive studies, such as Higham and Ryan, *Anglo-Saxon World*; McKitterick, *Charlemagne*; Blair, *The Church in Anglo-Saxon Society*; Brown, *Rise of Western Christendom*; Costambeys, Innes, and MacLean, *Carolingian World*; J. M. H. Smith, *Europe after Rome*; Wickham, *Framing the Early Middle Ages*; I. Wood, *Merovingian Kingdoms*.

Roman Empire accommodated themselves to post-Roman societies where classical traditions, customs of national ethnic groups, and the Christian religion in its various configurations were homogenizing.

The most defining cultural development of late antiquity was the rise of the church and the formulation of Christianity. As people of the Mediterranean world converted, their enthusiasm for Christianity and its heroes and heroines—martyrs, saints, and holy persons—was grafted onto a time-honored devotion to most all things Roman. Gradually, however, Christian sites, such as churches and tombs of the dead, dimmed the allure of the Roman city. The most zealous devotees of the new faith fled to the desert—the anti-city—and took up residence in caves, thereby registering a radical critique of the very assumptions of the classical dream which averred that humans are perfectible through the state.[26] Due to the labor of committed Christians, including missionaries, the urban clergy, and noblewomen,[27] the religion spread steadily through Egypt, the Levant, and northern Europe in the fourth and fifth centuries. Although numbers are frustratingly difficult to tie down, a scholarly estimate is that in 313, when Emperor Constantine (d. 337) legalized Christianity, there were approximately five to six million adherents in the empire. A century later, the number of Christians had grown to thirty million.[28]

Monastic communities were essential in sustaining the conversion of Europe because they acted as hubs for those seeking to serve the church and as centers for the development and dissemination of doctrine. Communities such as those at Ligugé (ca. 360), Marmoutier (ca. 372), Lérins (ca. 410), and Marseille (ca. 415) attracted men who wished to live ascetic lives dedicated to God. Women's religious communities also flourished during these centuries. John Cassian (d. ca. 435), the monk instrumental in introducing eastern notions of monasticism to the West, founded a female house in Marseille around 415.[29]

The most momentous kingdom to emerge from the late antique dissolution of western Roman sovereignty was carved out by the Frankish dynasty of the Merovingians. Their ascension began with Clovis I (d. ca. 511), who

---

26. Brown, *Cult of the Saints*, 50–85; Brown, *Making of Late Antiquity*, 54–58. For the classical dream see Cochrane, *Christianity and Classical Culture*, 82–124.

27. On the role of women in converting Europe see Nolte-Wolf, "Conversio und Cristianitas"; Scharer, "La conversion des rois." Salzman (*Making of a Christian Aristocracy*, 138–77) challenges the argument that noble Roman women played a conspicuous role in conversion.

28. Robinson, *Who Were the First Christians?*, 1–4; Wilken, *First Thousand Years*, 75–76; MacMullen, *Second Church*, 101–4, 111–14.

29. Melville, *World of Medieval Monasticism*, chap. 1; Brown, *Rise of Western Christendom*, 110–13.

united various Germanic tribes under his militaristic leadership and helped lay the groundwork for the Franks' coexistence and eventual assimilation with the Gallo-Roman population of Gaul.

When Clovis died, he followed the Frankish pattern of inheritance and divided his expansive kingdom among his sons. The four princes had considerable trouble agreeing on the boundaries between kingdoms, and 250 years of partible inheritance resulted in recurrent fratricidal warfare over lands and titles. Although the early Merovingian period is often characterized as brutal and chaotic, recent assessments demonstrate that beneath the territorial conflicts the rudiments of Roman civilization remained in place, there was a steady spread and elaboration of Christianity, and by the seventh century, the sense of a common "Frankishness" began to form.[30] This new polity reached its zenith in the seventh century under Kings Clothar II (d. 629) and Dagobert I (d. 639), during which time the Merovingian achievements were particularly evident. Monasticism thrived;[31] the kings established alliances with bishops, extended political suzerainty, assembled armies, levied taxes, appointed dukes, wrote legal codes, and instituted law courts. Most important, the clear outlines of an evolving, distinct and rationalized medieval civilization became perceptible.[32]

---

30. Reimitz, *History, Frankish Identity*, 1–20; Hen, *Culture and Religion*, 21–42, 251–53; I. Wood, *Merovingian Kingdoms*, 322–24; Riché, *Carolingians*, xvii–7; Geary, *Before France and Germany*, 151–78. Bouchard (*Rewriting Saints and Ancestors*, 87–105 [especially 99–103]) demonstrates that a Carolingian strategy for bolstering the legitimacy of their dynasty was to disparage their predecessors. Documents produced by the Carolingians about the Merovingians, on which scholars are dependent, present Merovingians in an unflattering light.

31. In the post-Roman kingdoms of Europe and England, new communities were established at a brisk pace, particularly by the upper nobility. Caesarius of Arles, who began his religious career as a monk at Lérins, established a convent for his sister within the walls of Arles in southern France (ca. 510). Benedict of Nursia founded the historic monastery at Monte Cassino (ca. 529) in central Italy. The Frankish queen Radegund started a monastery for women in Poitiers (ca. 552) that was inspired by Caesarius's rule and became one of the most celebrated female houses of its time. Other influential communities were the monasteries at Corbie in the Somme Valley (ca. 660), Chelles near Pairs (ca. 658), and Remiremont in Alscace (620). In Britain, the first houses were instituted in Scotland, Wales, and Cornwall in the fifth and sixth centuries and in the south by Archbishop Augustine of Canterbury after his arrival from Rome in 597. Monastic life emerged in Ireland as a consequence of Saint Patrick's ministry there. Among the most noteworthy houses were the double monastery of Kildare (fifth century) begun by Bridget, a daughter of the royal house, and Derry started approximately 546 under Columba, the Irish missionary to Scotland. In 630, Eanswith, daughter of King Eadbald of Kent founded the first monastery for women in England at Folkestone. One of the most famous Anglo-Saxon houses was the Whitby double monastery (657) in Yorkshire. See Melville, *World of Medieval Monasticism*, chap. 2; I. Wood, "Reform and the Merovingian Church"; Bouchard, *Rewriting Saints and Ancestors*, 193–203; McNamara, *Sisters in Arms*, 91–119; Schulenburg, "Women's Monastic Communities," 210–13; Meyer, "Queens, Converts and Conversion," 103–16.

32. Brown, *Rise of Western Christendom*, 55–57; Kaiser, "Königtum und Bischofsherrschaft," 83–98.

After the death of Dagobert, the Merovingian eminence began to fade as a succession of short-lived, mediocre kings and ambitious, competitive noble families fractured the kingdom. A definitive loss of authority and regnal competency was evident by the end of the civil war in 719, and the dynasty was eclipsed by the rising Carolingian house, headed by its eponym, Charles Martel (d. 741), a military mastermind and shrewd politician. The political fiction that the Merovingians governed Gaul was abandoned when Charles's son, Pippin III (d. 768), endorsed by Pope Zacharias (d. 752), maneuvered his way to the throne in 751.

Pippin's son, the great Charlemagne (d. 814), continued his father's military expansion and organizational policies. In the last decades of the eighth century, under Charlemagne's direction, a coalition of the ecclesiastical and secular leadership of western Europe designed a reform agenda for the betterment of the Frankish lands and began the process of imposing a level of conformity in the areas of religion, law, the military, education, marriage, inheritance, liturgy, and public behavior. "Carolingian" can refer narrowly to the ruling families of western and central Europe from the mid-eighth through most of the tenth century, but the term does not map neatly onto any narrowly defined lineage or specific territorial borders. It generally has a broader connotation of the political, religious, and cultural life lived during the reign of Carolingian kings. An even more wide-ranging denotation of the term draws in the late tenth and early eleventh centuries, when European society advanced along the lines set out by Carolingian reformers, even after Carolingian political power had splintered or disappeared.[33]

The reform movement, which was the bedrock of the Carolingian agenda, was an all-embracing enterprise with roots in Celtic and Anglo-Saxon ecclesiology. Christianity reached Roman England in the first centuries after the death of Jesus and was present in Ireland by about 400, which predates Saint Patrick's (fl. fifth century) arrival on the emerald shores. Patrick was kidnapped from his home in Britain as a young boy and enslaved in Ireland, where, after his escape, he was instrumental in establishing an ecclesiastical structure. The traditional view holds that the oxygen of church revival originated in Ireland and England, then breathed life into the continental church as Celtic and Anglo-Saxon monks, pilgrims, and missionaries (along with their manuscripts) migrated to Europe. This view fails to take into account the vibrancy of the Merovingian church, but it remains true that in the seventh century, itinerant monks such as the Irish Columbanus (d. 615) and his companions, founded pivotal monasteries in Gaul and Lombardy (most

---

33. McKitterick, *Charlemagne*, 292–380; McKitterick, "Legacy of the Carolingians."

notable at Luxeuil and Bobbio) that recruited religious from the upper nobility. These *peregrini* worked together with continental bishops, monks, and monarchs to further the development of Christianity in Gaul.[34]

By 410, Britain found itself outside the protection of the retreating Roman imperial polity, and the Romano-Britons were left to fend for themselves. In the mid-fifth century, German peoples from Saxon tribes began migrating to Britain, some looking for farmland, some as mercenaries, some as freebooting warriors. These migrations lasted for about a century and a half, and over a period of approximately fifty years the new peoples gained control of the lowlands of England. Relatively few written sources are extant that explain the process by which the Anglo-Saxons settled in and came to rule the Romano-Britons, and those we do have are Latin and portray the Anglo-Saxons as full-blooded invaders and conquerors. The archaeological evidence is richer than the written word and confirms a dramatic decline of centralized administration and Roman culture after 410. In the wake of this decline came a reversion to paganism, a linguistic evolution from Latin and Gaelic to Old English (at least in the lowlands), and the emergence of the Anglo-Saxons as the ruling class.[35]

In 596, Gregory the Great sent Augustine (d. 604), the soon-to-be first archbishop of Canterbury, and a delegation of missionaries to convert King Æthelbert of Kent (d. 616) to Roman Christianity, and the events of England once again became part of the European record. England was slowly and erratically evangelized as the monarchies of its seven kingdoms embraced the new religion, although periodic reversions to paganism were common.[36] The historical developments of the church and Christian society in England and on the Continent were not identical, but there were many parallels. The sources attest to an energetic cross-fertilization of ideas and exchange of written works across the channel in the seventh through eleventh centuries, and a robust scholarship has demonstrated the close intellectual and spiritual affinities, as well as some political similarities, between the inhabitants of England and those who came under the authority of the Carolingians.[37]

---

34. O'Hara, *Columbanus*, 4–19; Gasparri, "Columbanus, Bobbio and the Lombards"; Meens, *Penance*, 71; I. Wood, *Missionary Life*, 25–28; Boniface, *Letters of Saint Boniface*, ix–x. Angenendt, *Monachi Peregrini*.

35. Higham and Ryan, *Anglo-Saxon World*, chaps. 1, 2.

36. Ibid., chap. 3.

37. M. Wood, "'Stand Strong'"; Eastwood, *Ordering the Heavens*, 6; Wormald, "Pre-modern 'State,'" 188; Story, "Charlemagne and the Anglo-Saxons"; Delen et al., "*Paenitentiale Cantabrigiense*"; McKitterick, "England and the Continent"; Bullough, *Carolingian Renewal*, 272–96. On insular penitentials on the Continent see Meens, *Penance*, 70–100, 158–64; Kottje, "Überlieferung und Rezeption."

Powerful reform-minded bishops such as Wilfrid of Northumbria (d. ca. 709) struck out against secularized monasteries and worked to bring Anglo-Saxon practice in line with Roman usage. Kings Æthelbald (d. 757) and Offa (d. 796) of the kingdom of Mercia had priorities similar to those of Charlemagne, and the political and cultural bonds between the kingdoms tightened in the late eighth century. The Mercian dynasty expanded the territorial and political hegemony of Mercia, held councils, and increased the number of bishoprics and archbishoprics.[38] The tenth-century English and continental churches, enthralled with the spirit of renewal and sharing a vision of how it should look, worked together to operationalize reform.

Pope Leo III (d. 816) crowned Charlemagne the Holy Roman Emperor on Christmas Day in 800, and the Frankish kingdom became an empire. Charlemagne's son, Louis the Pious (d. 840), continued his father's program of secular and religious renewal, but the events of the ninth century successfully challenged the unity of his realm. Emperor Louis followed Frankish custom and assigned different portions of his patrimony to his three sons, but Frankish elites were encouraged to conceive of the empire as a single entity. The oldest son, Lothar (d. 855), inherited his father's imperial crown. The two other sons (Louis the German [d. 876]) and Charles the Bald [d. 877]) were to act as sub-kings over given regions of the federation. The failure of Louis's sons to make their father's vision of "brotherly cooperation" a political reality worked to undermine the cohesiveness of the Carolingian Empire.[39] In the ninth century, Europe, which was already fissiparous due to family feuding, was beset by a devastating series of Viking invasions from the north, Magyars from the east, and Berbers/Arabs from the south. Regionalism prevailed, and the separate nations of modern Europe began to take shape out of the once vast domain of Charles the Great.

In England the Viking invasions were prolonged and severe, but the balance began to tip in favor of the Anglo-Saxons with King Alfred the Great's (d. 899) victory over a large Danish army at the battle of Edington in 878. Alfred and his descendants from Wessex consolidated their authority over other English kingdoms and created a strong monarchy in the south of England supported by the nobility and the church.[40]

In 911 the last Carolingian king of East Francia died, and in 987 the West Frankish line of the Carolingian dynasty came to an end. In both East and

---

38. Higham and Ryan, *Anglo-Saxon World*, 179–231; Wormald, "Age of Offa," 106.
39. On the ideal of a united *regnum* see Costambeys, Innes, and MacLean, *Carolingian World*, 16–19; de Jong, *Penitential State*, 27–28; Goldberg, *Struggle for Empire*, 148–56.
40. Higham and Ryan, *Anglo-Saxon World*, 232–83.

14 INTRODUCTION

West Francia, nobles elected non-Carolingian rulers. East Francia experienced a brief "Ottonian Renaissance" under the Saxon kings initiated by Otto I's (d. 973) marriage to Adelaide of Italy (d. 999) in 951 and his subsequent coronation as emperor by Pope John XII (d. 964) in 962. Intellectuals in Ottonian Europe had been nurtured on the Carolingian vision and furthered the reform work that began in the ninth century. Changes in the political sphere did not cause significant discontinuities in popular or learned culture. The Carolingians transmitted corrected versions of Old and New Testament texts, patristic biblical exegeses, treatises for use in schools, guides to discipline and the religious life, liturgical materials, practical manuals, legal collections, histories, poetry, and the concept of a model library, properly stocked with materials necessary for Christian learning.[41]

By around 1050, Europe powered by the achievements of the Carolingian *renovatio*, was shifting gears. Thinking began to change regarding church hierarchs, ecclesiastical administration, organization of land tenure, and political structures. Along with these transformations, perceptions about the concept of magic metamorphosed. For a millennium, ruling bodies had suppressed errant folk practices and struggled to corral the concept of magic by determining what exactly trafficking with demons amounted to. In the centuries after 1000, the concept of magic shattered like the glass of a windshield which retains its basic coherence while forming new surface patterns. Magic came to encompass anything from a plot element in a romance narrative to the fuel for heresy trials.

Throughout the political vicissitudes of the early Middle Ages, magic was a lived reality, and the fundamentals were consistent from the earliest Christian period to the end of the Ottonian era. Traffic with demons was rooted in daily life in myriad ways and was a serious threat to the thoroughgoing Christianization of Europe's peoples. Understanding the mechanics, efficacy, and gender of magic brings into relief the processes of social and intellectual evolution in the early Middle Ages.

Chapter 1 of this book addresses definitions and historiography, loosening some of the terminological knots that have bedeviled the terms "magic" and "ritual." It also serves as an essay on materials pertaining to this study. My methodology is to amass a critical body of evidence, without claiming that

---

41. MacLean, *History and Politics*, 1–18; *Ottonian Germany*, 1–16; Schneidmüller, "Widukind von Corvey"; Hlawitschka, "Die Herrscher der Ottonenzeit"; Contreni, "Carolingian Renaissance," 756; Nelson, "Kingship and Empire," 77–81; Semmler, "Das Erbe der karolingischen Klosterreform."

all of it contributed equally to contemporary perceptions of magic. Some sources were well known in their time, some not, but the perspective contained in any given text provides a piece of the puzzle even if the text was not widely distributed. I often line fictional works up with other sorts of evidence in order to examine perceptions. When discussing in the same voice, for example, a Roman novel, a seventh-century law code, and a lead tablet found in a fifth-century cemetery, I am not confusing "actual" practices (inasmuch as we can know what is real from any text) with literary imagination. Instead, I am looking for cultural conceptions of magic that are manifest in various types of written records—fictional or otherwise.[42]

Chapter 2 considers demons and their place in late classical and early medieval cosmologies. This discussion is not sequential or linear, nor does it focus on texts in situ; rather, it accommodates a high level of generalization and acts as a large canopy covering material from across a broad spectrum of time and space in order to clarify terms and assumptions that informed an understanding of magic throughout the first millennium. In the Christian mental universe, demons were at the very center of all magic, so much so that magic itself equated to traffic with demons. As this book demonstrates, any active involvement with demons—from blatantly honoring pagan idols, to eating meat cooked at pagan shrines, to casting spells—was magic, even if the persons involved were not intentionally trafficking.

In parts 2, 3, and 4, magic, ritual, and gender are approached chronologically, broken down into three eras: the early Christian,[43] the Merovingian, and the Carolingian.[44] Periodization is always tricky because history does not unfold in neat units, and people do not experience their lives in discrete epochs. Given that, I am not apologetic about organizing the book the way I have, because a nuanced periodization is necessary and all but inescapable. Every chapter harks back to material in previous units and foreshadows issues to come so as to highlight links across the first millennium while

---

42. On aligning fictional and non-fictional sources see O'Gorman, "Detective Fiction."

43. By "early Christian era" I refer to the first through the fifth centuries when Christianity and the imperial Roman government were in a dynamic relationship—at times antagonistic, at times synergetic. In part 2, I focus on the development and growth of the church from its inception thorough late antiquity. Because an understanding of magic in late Rome also requires delving into pagan texts (sometimes extensively), where appropriate I bring them to the service of my argument.

44. At times in this work I use the term "Merovingian era" to refer to events that occurred during the same period in the British Isles, Visigothic Spain, and Lombard Italy. Although political and social circumstances in Gaul, Britain, Spain, and Italy differed, what can be said about magic is largely uniform. For the "Carolingian era" see pages above.

exploring change over time. Each unit covers the myriad sorts and uses of magic—how it was viewed, discussed, categorized, and (to the extent that the sources allow) practiced. Over the course of ten centuries, the scope of "the magical" mutated and grew. There were both progression and permanence as to what constituted magic, what types were thought to be the most toxic, how people encountered the magic arts, and how church and secular authorities sought to structure those encounters.

Broadly speaking, trafficking with demons can be divided into seven types.[45] Although my taxonomy is inevitably overdrawn (as taxonomies tend to be) and there was impressive imbrication, lack of precision, and evolution in the way nomenclature was used, the classificatory system that follows is more than a bricolage created from bits and pieces of data from disparate sources; it paints a coherent portrait of the kinds or aspects of magic practiced in the first millennium. It is etic, while at the same respecting the historical actors' categories.

First is idolatry. In the polytheistic cultures of the ancient world, idolatry constituted the institutionalized veneration of deities—both state-sponsored and familial. But for Christians, those deities were devils, and worship of them through their idols amounted to traffic with demons. Although all magic was at base idolatrous because it acknowledged the power of demons in some way, Christian thinkers of the primitive church differentiated between the formal worship of false gods and other kinds of magical trafficking. However, in the post-apostolic period, the connotation of idolatry broadened as theologians folded an assortment of activities into the concept of idolatry—a concept Christians already accepted as blasphemy. Over time, the term "idolatry" became increasingly oblique, blurry and subtle. As Bernadette Filotas notes, by the early Middle Ages idolatry denoted a "body of customs." It became a watchword for any sort of trafficking with demons and activities thought to be pagan or simply irreligious.[46]

Second, divination and theurgy were in essence pseudo-sciences devoted to mystical, celestial ascent or clairvoyance by means of soothsaying, astrology, lots, and dreams, all of which drew on the abilities of demons.[47]

---

45. Definitions of "types" is very basic here with just enough description to establish a baseline. Because the nuances of the terms in my taxonomy mutate over time, each of the seven categories of trafficking with demons is elaborated upon in various contexts over parts 2, 3, and 4.
46. Filotas, *Pagan Survivals*, 69.
47. On theurgy see Johnston, "Riders in the Sky."

Third, *goetia* is a classical Greek term referring to conjuring for various purposes; some of them were lofty, and some were tawdry. Closely allied to goetia is the Latin *maleficium* which was the word used in the Middle Ages to indicate self-serving and intentionally harmful manipulation of the magic arts.

Fourth, superstition consisted of unexceptional misdeeds or witlessness of individuals, who may or may not have been aware that their actions were demonic. The term implied false or distorted religion, excessive anxiety about the profane affairs of daily life over which people ought not to attempt control, and undue curiosity that gave demons entrée to the unwary and led them to irrational behaviors—or worse, idolatry.[48] Allied to superstition was a brand of magic best labeled as "tricks" (conveyed by Latin terms such as *ludus, ars, praestigia,* and *dolus*). Tricks pertained to dramaturgic displays of magical virtuosity intended to impress an audience and aggrandize the conjurer's own prestige or influence. Performers of magical stunts were not primarily interested in venerating demons, but their histrionics depended on demonic aid and played to the superstitious proclivities of their audiences. Another more insidious kind of tricksters were arch-demons, such as Satan or the Antichrist, whose trickery was considerably more noxious than the attention-getting trafficker in hoaxes.

Fifth, *stria* refers to an inscrutable airborne creature, and *lamia* is a term for a bloodsucking vampire. Each has a long and chilling tradition cloaked in obscurity. They make appearances in various genres from antiquity throughout the Middle Ages, and because of their protean natures, various other female-identified beings were accreted to them.

The sixth category involves healing, which was by no means a subset of magic per se in the early Middle Ages, but demons do appear in the *materia medica* as the cause of disease, disease itself, and sometimes the cure. Among the medical treatments recorded, magical remedies or prophylactics that depend on demons for their efficacy are common.

The seventh category entails love and birth magic, which shared characteristics with maleficium, superstition, and healing. Love magic refers to procedures designed to inflame or squelch romantic/physical attraction, and birth magic sought to stimulate fertility and its opposite, infertility, and to effect abortion.

---

48. Filotas (*Pagan Survivals*, 16–18) discusses the background, nuances, and evolution of the word "superstition." However, she omits mention of magic or the demonic dimensions of the concept which were fundamental to churchmen's and churchwomen's objections. Fatuous superstitious observances led the unwary to traffic with demons.

Thinking on magic was not monolithic, even in a given time and place; authors analyzed practices in different ways and used terms or accepted concepts inconsistently.[49] A person of authority might label a practice "forbidden" and append it to the corpus of existing proscriptions without particular concern about standardization, redundancy, or contradiction. Further, behaviors were fluid and flexible in the daily world of a given era and could at one time be classed in several ways. Categories were not exclusive; the borders between one type of magic and another were unstable. And of course, how various practices might be classified was rarely a concern of the people engaged in the magic arts and only sometimes of interest to those who sought to eradicate them. Particular magical procedures entered a given society's field of vision in some periods more than in others. For example, those in the apostolic age had first to combat overt idolatry, whereas in the Merovingian era, superstition was a more persistent problem.

Although throughout the first millennium there was no hierarchy of types of magic or magical practitioners per se, some were intrinsically less pernicious or objectionable than others. There was a difference between the herbal healer and the malicious *maleficus/malefica*—between the migrant trickster and the simple country farmer clinging to pre-Christian traditions. Theologians and pastors realized that the itinerant magician sought to deceive by devilish tricks, while the peasant often acted from ignorance. They recognized that calculations of the *mathematicus* were hoary and erudite, and the conjurations of the local spellbinder sprang from the waywardness of the unlettered.

Words such as superstition (*superstitio*), pagan (*paganus*), idolatry (*idolatria* or *cultura idolorum*), gentile (*gentilis*) heathen (*ethnicus* or *gens*), necromancy (*necromantia*), juggling/tricks (*praestigia/praestigiae*), and so forth were slippery, nebulous, overlapping, and indiscriminately applied to behaviors that looked very much alike. In the ninth century, a group of fifteen sermons was collected and erroneously attributed to Saint Boniface (d. 754). Sermon six captures the blending of terminology typical of writings throughout the first millennium. "That which is called sacrilege is the worship of idols. And all the sacrifices and divinations of the pagans are sacrileges; so in the same way sacrifices of the dead or dead bodies, or over

---

49. Jolly, Raudvere, and Peters (*Witchcraft and Magic*, 3–5) arrive at the same conclusion when they say that magic is not an absolute category but a matter of perception in a given time period. See also Bailey, "Meanings of Magic"; Filotas, *Pagan Survivals*, 222–38.

their tombs, or auguries, or amulets of herbs, or sacrifices over stones or at springs or trees or to Jupiter or Mercury or to the other pagan gods, all these things are demonic."[50] As Pseudo-Boniface demonstrates, regardless of the nuances in terminology, the common denominator among all the expressions of magic was trafficking with demons.

---

50. Pseudo-Boniface, *Sermones* 6.1, col. 855: "Sacrilegium quod dicitur cultura idolorum. Omnia autem sacrificia et auguria paganorum, sarilegia sunt, quemadmodum sunt sacrificia mortuorum defuncta corpora, vel super sepulcra illorum, sive auguria, sive phylacteria, sive quae immolant super petras, sive ad fontes, sive ad arbores, Jovi vel Mercurio, vel allis diis paganorum, quae omnia daemonia sunt."

❧ Part 1

Studying Magic

Chapter 1

Magic and Its Sources in Late Antiquity and the Early Middle Ages

> If someone accuses a girl or free woman who is under the guardianship of another of being a harlot or a sorceress, and he seems clearly to have blurted out this accusation due to intense fury, then he can offer an oath with his twelve oath helpers [character witnesses] confirming that he accused her of this abominable crime in anger and not with sure knowledge. For these idle and thoughtless words that he should not have spoken, he will pay twelve *solidi* [gold coins] and be exonerated.
>
> —*Laws of the Lombards*

Modern scholars have taken up the history of magic because of its importance to the study of theology, heresy, medicine, rural culture, marginal populations, gender, and juridical processes. The European witch persecutions of the fifteenth through eighteenth centuries have drawn attention to elemental aspects of social and cultural dynamics. For similar reasons, monographs on medieval magical beliefs and witchcraft have proliferated over the last fifty years, but comparatively few studies focus on magic specifically in the early Middle Ages.

"Magic" is a muddled term. Scholars have defined it as anything from "other people's rituals" to "a preternatural control over nature" to "any rite which does not play a part in organized cults."[1] The word is multidimensional, value laden, chameleonlike, and tinted by variable cultural and historical factors. Just establishing how the term ought to be understood has become an intellectual project in its own right. Arriving at a precise definition of magic is not an easy task, due to the breadth and changeability of the beliefs and practices this transmorphous and elusive word connotes.

---

1. Janowitz, *Magic in the Roman World*, i; Flint, *Rise of Magic*, 3; Mauss, *General Theory of Magic*, 24.

For the most part, definitions of magic are either overly nebulous—meant to conform to phenomena that played out over several centuries—or based on archetypes abstracted and collated from many diverse and incomparable cultures or contexts. Historians, philosophers, and social scientists, grappling for a definition since the mid-nineteenth century, have struggled with the overlapping functions of magic, science, and religion in human culture.

The impulse of an older generation of anthropologists, of which Edward Burnett Tylor (d. 1917) and James Frazer (d. 1941) were important voices, was to disentangle magic, science, and religion, assigning each to a separate stage of development and hierarchizing them according to a scheme of intellectual and moral evolution.[2] In his monumental work *The Golden Bough*, Frazer formulates a method for distinguishing magic from religion that was normative for some time, both for anthropologists and for historians. Frazer argues that whereas religion supplicates supernatural powers, magic seeks to compel them. Magicians assume they can manipulate cosmic forces if they perform the required rites. Religion admits its impotence and its dependence on the will of personages or forces it cannot control.[3] This differentiation between magic and religion is riddled with problems. Neither anthropologists nor historians are able to discern with certainty the state of mind of those who interact ritually with the preternatural. Further, elements of coercion and petition are often present at once in a single act. A supplicant who vows to go on a pilgrimage in exchange for a cure may well view the interaction as binding on the patron saint of the shrine.[4] And a faithful Christian praying with the promise from John 14:14 in mind might take as contractual Jesus's promise, "If in my name you ask me for anything, I will do it."[5] In response to the weakness in Frazer's model, Émile Durkheim (d. 1917) and Marcel Mauss (d. 1950) advocated putting to one side individual or collective motivation behind magical ritual and concentrating on the rites themselves within the context of other social phenomena.[6]

---

2. For a full discussion see Tambiah, *Magic, Science, Religion*, 42–83.
3. Frazer, *Magic Art*, 220–43. See also Graf, *Magic*, 27, 34–35; G. Shaw, "Theurgy: Rituals"; Petzoldt, "Magie und Religion."
4. Head, *Hagiography*, 11–16.
5. Christian graveside veneration of sainted martyrs could slip into transactional exchanges. For example from MacMullen (*Second Church*, 86), early fourth-century petitioners "ask the saints to 'bear in mind' So-and-So . . . to insure a safe voyage or good luck to their favorite in the races."
6. Durkheim, *Elementary Forms*, 8–18; Mauss, *General Theory of Magic*, 18–24, 141.

Like anthropologists, historians are obliged to confront the important questions of exactly how to identify magic and decipher its operation within a complex of corresponding societal constructions such as religion and science.[7] The concept and exercise of magic did not remain fixed across the medieval centuries, yet scholars have sometimes generalized about medieval magic based on factors that more accurately reflect later European experience. For example, Jeffrey Russell writes, "The most useful heuristic is to accept the fifteenth-century scholastic and Inquisitorial definition of the witch as classical and then look back through the Middle Ages for the components of that definition, seeking their origins, their development, and the process of their eventual amalgamation."[8] This teleological methodology is particularly characteristic of the approach to the early medieval centuries. Authors not primarily interested in the early Middle Ages have tended to mine its texts for antecedents to later developments in magic and witchcraft and to treat the first millennium of the Christian era as a seedbed for subsequent beliefs and patterns of behavior.[9] Generalizations that hold up in succeeding periods have been applied uncritically to the early medieval experience, presupposing that mutable societal constructs can be measured by a static heuristic and that a pattern can be lifted from its historical framework without distortion.

Many scholars have moved to an excessively inclusive definition of magic—so broad that it amounts to an abdication of definition. They make magic the basis of religion and early science and associate the term with all those things moderns remotely connect with the occult, the weird, or the unscientific. As elements of "the magical," authors have pulled in a wide range of disparate behaviors such as the laying-on of hands for curing the sick and typological exegeses of scripture. Peter Schäfer uses the word to denote "primitive hocus-pocus or abracadabra," and Hugh Trevor-Roper famously calls magical beliefs "the mental rubbish of peasant credulity and feminine hysteria."[10] Under one rubric a wide variety of activities is subsumed, including what clearly seem to be expressions of orthodox devotion such as sacred ceremony and prayerful adulation.[11] Naomi Janowitz takes a

---

7. Bailey and Copenhaver, "From the Editors"; Segal, "Hellenistic Magic."
8. J. B. Russell, *Witchcraft*, 23.
9. For example see Cohn, *Europe's Inner Demons*, ch. 1.
10. Schäfer, *Hidden and Manifest God*, 165; Trevor-Roper, *European Witch-Craze*, 41.
11. Kern-Ulmer, "Depiction of Magic"; Versnel, "Some Reflections"; Flint, *Rise of Magic*, 3–12; Schäfer, "Jewish Magic Literature"; Weltin, "Concept of *Ex-Opere-Operato* Efficacy"; Thorndike, *History of Magic*, 1:2, 5–6, 385–99.

particularly bold position in arguing that the word's "pejorative use in the past" renders it so tainted that it is unserviceable, and she holds that scholars should forswear definitive labels.[12]

The task of establishing a definition is made yet more daunting by the fact that even in a given historical period, there are several vantage points from which magic might be considered: (1) the varying viewpoints of the medieval observers/recorders as preserved in texts, (2) the outlooks of those who participated in magical acts (such an emic view usually can be gleaned only imperfectly from texts that nonparticipants wrote), and (3) the conjecture of present-day interpreters.[13] Given this, should we punctiliously align our sights with those people who used or censured magic, or can scholars legitimately assign labels to medieval behaviors and beliefs according to definitions that take into consideration modern experience? To draw a parallel, in studies of medieval medicine, historians identify diseases that the people of the time would not have been able to name and that, for all intents and purposes, did not exist for them. Many approach magic in the same way. They bring to the conversation contemporary terminology, metrics, and classifications that were not articulated in the given period, discussing the world in terms their medieval subjects would not have comprehended. Ought we, then, endeavor to observe magic through the eyes of a medieval individual, or can we legitimately defer to a twenty-first century gaze?

The answer is that we will inevitably do a bit of both. The questions we moderns frame about magic can only come from contemporary sensibilities and ways of organizing knowledge. Historical study is never disinterested; the very process of reading a text is interactive, uniting past and present. However, in order for history to be a meaningful and humane exploration of the lives of people who lived and died before us, we need to train our voices to tell their stories. Scholars' definition of magic ought to be indexed, as far as possible, on the realities of the medieval people who lived with it, recognizing that if we could drill down through any moment in time we would see that magic was a stew of multiple notions, customs, beliefs, and behaviors. Though the project of defining magic is labyrinthine, forsaking it is perilous. If we abandon the term to the vagaries of

---

12. Janowitz, *Icons of Power*, xiv. See also Janowitz, *Magic in the Roman World*, 1–13.
13. See Theuws's ("Introduction") discussion of Fredrik Barth's term "disordered society" (4) by which Barth critiques the model of the homogeneous society. Marvin Harris, "Emics and Etics Revisited," 48–54; Bourdieu, *Outline of a Theory*, 1–22.

contemporary impressions, we are in danger of misreading medieval culture and those who peopled it.¹⁴

Augustine laid out an explanation for the relationship between human beings and the preternatural that both incorporated earlier thinking and formed the basis for the Christian understanding of magic for the Middle Ages (and beyond). Miracles are allowed by God and wrought by faith, not incantations and spells. Marvels not performed for the honor of God are illicit sorcery accomplished by the deceitful tricks of malignant demons. The stunts of demons are easily discernible from true miracles of the godly because demons demand that sacrificial homage be made to themselves, whereas saints credit their miraculous powers to their maker and contend that all worship is owed to God alone.¹⁵ Augustine made clear that magic encompassed all exceptional phenomena that have no reference to God and are beyond the limits of human power.¹⁶ He made no distinction between "high" forms, such as Egyptian *scientia*, and "low" forms, such as wisewomen's spells. He wrote that people "attempt to distinguish between those condemned because they are given to the illicit arts, whom the common people call *maleficos* (people who are said to be involved with *goetia*). Others they want to see as laudable who engage in theurgy. Yet both groups are tethered

---

14. On this approach see Buc (*Dangers of Ritual*, 226–27): "One should master a culture's grammar, but not think thoughts none of its members ever thought."

15. Augustine, *De civitate Dei* 10.8–12, 1:280–87; 10.16, 1:289–91; 10.19, 1:293–94; 10.26–27, 1:300–303; Augustine, *De doctrina Christiana* 2:23, 96–101. See Origen (*Contra Celsum* 1.68, 62–63) on magic as self-serving. Origen composed *Contra Celsum* (ca. 248) for recent converts and those unfamiliar with the religion in order to counter Celsus's scathing anti-Christian track called *The True Word* (175–177 CE). See Frede, "Origen's Treatise *Against Celsus*." Augustine wrote *De doctrina Christiana* (397–426) to direct clergy on how best to understand, teach, and defend scriptural truth. The work was widely influential throughout the Middle Ages. Throughout Augustine's works, although he often refers to the pursuits of demons as *magia*, he does employ *mira* or *miracula* when referring to the pursuits of both demons and agents of God, but he is clear that the two are different. For example see *De civitate Dei* 10.8, 1:280: "Facere quaedam mira permissi sunt, ut mirabilius unicerentur! Illi enim faciebant veneficiis et incantationibus magicis quibus sunt mali angeli, hoc est daemones dediti." *De divinatione daemonum* 4.8, 606: "Quod vero non solum quaedam daemones futura praedicunt, verum etiam quaedam mira faciunt, pro ipsa utique sui corporis excellentia." See also Brown (*Making of Late Antiquity*, 11–23): "In this period, 'divine power' came to be defined with increasing clarity as the opposite of all other forms of power" (11).

16. Augustine, *De civitate Dei* 10.12, 1:286: "Verum quia tanta et talia geruntur his artibus, ut universum modum humanae facultatis excedant. . . . [Sunt] malignorum daemonum ludibria et seductoria inpedimenta, quae uera pietate cauenda sunt, prudenter intellegantur?" Augustine (*De utilitate credendi* 16.34, 43) distinguished two types of miracles: "Miraculum uoco quicquid arduum aut insolitum supra spem uel facultatem mirantis adparet. . . . Sed rursus haec in duo diuiduntur: quaedam enim sunt, quae solam faciunt admirationem, quaedam vero magnam etiam gratiam benevolentiamque conciliant."

to the fallacious rites of demons working under the guise of angels."[17] Following Augustine's lead, intellectuals throughout the first millennium held that magic involved traffic with demons, and they proscribed it on that basis.[18]

Given "traffic with demons" as the working definition of early Christian magic, formidable challenges remain: (1) What constituted trafficking? (2) What beings were demonic? (3) Did the scholarly understanding of magic differ from that of the nonliterate, and if so, in what ways? (4) To what extent can we decipher actual practices from constructed artifacts—in other words, texts? The answers to these questions were not univocal or static, because over the late antique and early medieval centuries, conceptions of magic changed shades as behaviors were folded into or strained out of the classification of demon worship. Sorting out some of these transformations is the work of parts 2, 3, and 4 of this book.

What Is a Witch?

In his ethnographic research on the magical customs of the Congolese Azande, E. E. Evans-Pritchard (d. 1973) distinguished two types of magical practitioners: the sorcerer and the witch. The sorcerer is an ordinary person (male or female) who, through manipulation of mechanical rites, is able to perform acts of "white" (beneficial) or "black" (harmful) magic. The witch, on the other hand, is one endowed with inherent, insidious magical abilities (often inherited). This person is usually a female able to work her malfeasance with or without ritual incantations, imprecations, spells or charms. She can harm merely by evil intent.[19] Some scholars criticize the overzealous application of these classifications, which homogenizes archetypal patterns that differ in studies dealing with peoples other than the A-zande.[20] But if

---

17. Augustine, *De civitate Dei* 10.9, 1:281: "Conantur ista discernere et inlicitis artibus deditos alios damnabiles, quos et maleficos uuglas appellat (hos enim ad goetian pertinere dicunt), alios autem laudabiles uideri uolunt, quibus theurgian deputant; cum sint utrique ritibus fallacibus daemonum obstricti sub nominibus angelorum."

18. For a few examples across the centuries, Isidore of Seville, *Etymologiarum* 8.9.3, vol. 1; Raban Maur, *De magicis artibus*; Regino of Prüm, *De synodalibus causis* 2.371, 355; Burchard of Worms, *Decretum* 10.40–45, *PL* 140, cols. 839–44.

19. Evans-Pritchard, *Witchcraft, Oracles, and Magic*, 56–64; Evans-Pritchard, "Sorcery and Native Opinion"; Evans-Pritchard, "Witchcraft (*Mangu*)." For societies in which Evans-Pritchard's distinction between the witch and the sorcerer has been attested see Jones, "Boundary to Accusations," 321; Macfarlane "Definitions of Witchcraft"; Marwick, "Some Problems"; Wilson, "Witch Beliefs"; Krige, "Social Function of Witchcraft."

20. In *Witchcraft and Religion* (80), Larner says of witchcraft across cultures, "One clear factor, which emerges from the empirical work so far done, is that the lowest common denominator is very low and that divergences are very great." See also Thomas "Relevance of Social Anthropology," 52.

we take their warning into account and treat Evans–Pritchard's definition as a suggestive model and not a procrustean bed, it is valid and useful to distinguish between people who use magic and people who are magical. This distinction holds in numerous cultures around the world; likewise, when dealing with the early modern European experience, it is reasonable, with some modification, to use the term "sorcerer" for someone who uses demons, and "witch" for heretical individuals contractually committed to Satan, in whose name they are obligated to commit acts of maleficium.

Evans-Pritchard's distinction is not germane within the early medieval paradigm where the intellectual construct of "the witch" did not exist if we understand the word according to either Evans-Pritchard's definition or its use in the early modern period.[21] Virtually all descriptions of early medieval people engaging in various sorts of magic demonstrate that they drew on the power of demons, but the magic was mechanical—realized by the calculated use of words, herbs, ointments, powders, or rites—or it was inadvertent, as when people wore amulets of bones to protect themselves on a journey. When an interaction, such as a spell or healing charm, was completed or the amulet was discarded, the practitioners were unchanged. They had transgressed religious and (in some cases) secular law, but had not become servants of the Devil.

Although there is no single Latin equivalent of the term "witch," the word is broadly and inaccurately used in some translations of early medieval texts. The English words "witch" (etymologically derived from the Anglo–Saxon term *"wicca"*) and "witchcraft" only came into common parlance in Tudor/Stuart England as umbrella terms referring to a variety of practices and practitioners, such as wisewomen, finders, healers, scientists, and Catholics.[22] Medieval writers discriminated among types of magical specialists, many of whom had a singular métier and a particular terminology. For example, a *tempestarius* raised storms, and a *mathematicus* was essentially an astrologer; however the nomenclature for those caught up in trafficking became less differentiated as time went on. None of the early medieval words that refer to magical practitioners communicate the sense of persons who had fundamentally altered themselves. Whereas by around 1400 a witch was someone who made a pact with Satan and was guilty of heresy even if a specific act of maleficium had not been carried out, none of this was true of the early

---

21. Levack, *Witch-Hunt*, 27–56.
22. Bremmer, "Magic *and* Religion," 268 (emphasis in original); Peters, *Magician*, 168–69; Thomas, "Relevance of Social Anthropology"; J. Crawford, "Evidences for Witchcraft." On the word *Hexe* see Franck, "Geschichte des Wortes Hexe." On *wicca* see Meaney, "Aelfric and Idolatry," 121–22.

medieval sorcerer.[23] There is ample evidence in the early Middle Ages of magic, superstition, paganism, and sorcery (in short, traffic with demons), and magical acts were dangerous, feared, sacrilegious, and condemnable, but practitioners themselves were just that: practitioners, malefactors, not people with altered natures—that is to say, not witches.

In 1957, S. F. Nadel made the observation that "no sensible anthropologist" would ask about religion and magic in the abstract; rather, he or she would examine the part played by particular practices within a given social system.[24] Historians have come to that point as well. In the early Middle Ages, magic did not function as an isolated and freakish phenomenon on the margins of society. Because it was integrated into virtually all aspects of life, its study is central to understanding the early European past. This book approaches magic by paying attention to the distinctiveness of the first Christian millennium in the West and examining magic's operation within a complex of societal structures.

What Is Ritual?

Nadel's assessment of magic is no less true of ritual acts—also framed by their placement among other cultural variables. Over the last half century, studies about ritual behavior have burgeoned as scholars in more and more fields are finding it a useful tool for cultural analysis.[25] Classical and medieval history are no exceptions. Historians study late antique and early medieval ritual because the people of the times recognized it as a meaningful form of collective dialogue. Formalized, symbolic interaction was fully and self-consciously developed, finely nuanced, and masterfully exploited.[26] Because

---

23. Bailey, "From Sorcery to Witchcraft." Boureau (*Satan the Heretic*, 68–92) documents the development of the pact in late medieval Europe. Peters (*Magician*, 168–70) sees the first "witches" emerging around 1400. See Zeddies (*Religio et sacrilegium*, 199–279) who places magic from the fourth through the seventh centuries in the context of heresy more than I would. By and large, heresy is intellective, and magic is active.

24. Nadel, "Malinowski," 189. See also Markus, "Augustine on Magic," 375–76.

25. In modern scholarship, ritual is more than a class of behaviors and an object of study; it constitutes a methodology. However, given the considerable imprecision as to the nature of this methodology and the ever-widening application of the word "ritual" to describe a certain type of experience, Bell observed in 1997 (Bell, *Ritual Theory, Ritual Practice*, 3) that "the term [ritual] is long overdue for an extended critical thinking." Pössel ("Magic of Early Medieval Ritual," 114) warns that "'ritual' has developed (or rather, maintained) a conceptual fuzziness; meaning very different things to different scholars, it has, in some cases, become little more than an in-itself symbolic and demonstrative label indicating the presence of anthropologically and theoretically informed approaches." This inexactitude, in my view, in no way invalidates "ritual" as a legitimate modality of analysis.

26. Buc (*Dangers of Ritual*, 9) writes, "Rituals, then, are a complicated point of entry into early medieval political culture, precisely because of the importance the culture attached to solemnities."

the role of ritual was abundantly manifest, scholars increasingly appreciate the extent to which it gives us access to the past.

Ritual studies are central to an understanding of magic because Christian theologians reacted the way they did to magic, in part, because of the ritualistic form it often took—a form that had the ability to communicate meaning beyond the context of the rite itself. Not all magic was ritualistic,[27] but much of it was, and the ritual dimension of some types of magic posed a threat to the Christian imperative.

There is no tidy consensus among scholars or across disciplines as to exactly what ritual is. Many would agree that it is rule governed, symbolic, instrumental, and targeted behavior, but a cross-cultural or global construct of the word is not possible. As is true of magic, a universal template for defining ritual has limited hermeneutic benefit.[28] It is not a clear and distinct category of human activity; rather it should be considered in terms of nuanced contrasts with other kinds of conduct.[29] Still, at its most basic level, ritual always involves externalization—that is, action, and specifically action informed by intention. Clifford Geertz best characterizes ritual with two words: "consecrated behavior."[30] Another uncompromising aspect of ritual is that it is formulaic. This is so much the case that for some the rigidity renders it as empty formalism devoid of meaning. But in fact much of the vitality of ritual lies in its absolute dependability. Stanley Tambiah maintains

---

They were too momentous for the depictions *not* to be highly crafted" manipulated or forged (emphasis in original). See also Warner, "Ritual and Memory."

27. Nor is all ritual magical (Janowitz, *Icons of Power,* xiv–xv). Koziol (*Begging Pardon and Favor,* 289–324) discusses the ordinary nature of ritual expression. "Early medieval rituals," he writes, "were also a natural part of life" (294–95). Hauck ("Rituelle Speisegemeinschaft") discusses ritual involved in the common meal.

28. See Rollo-Koster, review of *Dangers* on the pitfalls of using "attemporal" models to define ritual.

29. Bell, *Ritual: Perspectives and Dimensions,* 3–9, 21, 47–49, 69–72; Muir, *Ritual,* 1–11; Kertzer, *Ritual, Politics, and Power,* 8–11; Tambiah, "A Performative Approach to Ritual"; Goody, "Against 'Ritual'"; Douglas, *Natural Symbols,* xiii–xv. Foucault (*Power and Knowledge,* 245) refuses to develop an ahistorical theory of rituals of power but discusses them in terms of how they operate within specific contexts, arguing that power works itself out within the interdependence of societal relationships.

30. Geertz, *Interpretation of Cultures,* 112; Geertz, "Religion as a Cultural System," especially 28. See also Schilderman (*Discourse in Ritual Studies,* xiii): "Ritual is a framework of interpretive actions per se!"; Theuws, "Introduction," 8. Pössel ("Magic of Early Medieval Ritual," 117) writes, "The real difference between an 'instrumental' and a 'symbolic' act, between washing one's hands in order to clean them, and washing them although they are already clean, is in the mind, not in the action." I take issue with Pössel's analysis, because within a ritualized environment, action creates intention as often as it mirrors it. Action and intention are symbiotic; they are in a processual relationship not a sequential one.

that the repetitive patterning of ritual, or "ritual involution," is the very key to its efficacy, and (I add) to its creativity.[31]

Ritual enlists a particular type of highly symbolic communication that has the potential to connect social life and the individual. The resultant "social dramas" can create an interval in which participants (and sometimes observers) are integrated in a controlled collective environment, which, for all its predictability is still "antistructural" and inventive. The rules and norms of ordinary social life are suspended, at least for the moment, in a show of solidarity, and the actors and observers understand their behaviors as intensely laden, even metaphorical. Although the identity these "cultural performances" creates among participants is symbolic, not empirical, and relatively brief, the bonds can be lasting. As Catherine Bell says, "The group enters into a dialogue with itself about itself."[32] According to Durkheim's social solidarity thesis, ritual exerts a type of control though promotion of consensus and its psychological ramifications.[33] Ironically, a ritual setting can foster at any given time both entrenchment of social norms and the opposite, cultural evolution. And just as "social dramas" affirm the basis of belonging and connect those who do fit in, they also, by logical extension, identify the outsider, that is to say, the "other."

For medieval historians, the term "ritual magic" has come to refer to bookish or learned rites of a pseudoscientific nature.[34] This characterization is not applicable to the early Middle Ages, so for the purposes of this work I use "ritual" to indicate symbolic, expressive, and encoded action that is set apart from ordinary activity; and this includes personal and private as well as communal and public rites.[35]

Symbol and ritual are not synonymous, but all rituals involve the structured and performative manipulation of oral, positional, or gesticular symbols; artifacts can function as iconic signs as well. For Clifford Geertz, symbols embody patterns of meaning and constitute the stuff of human

---

31. Tambiah, "A Performative Approach to Ritual," 149–53. From Davis ("Theories of History," 38), "Tradition can be a form of discovery and innovation." See also Theuws, "Introduction," 8–12.

32. Bell, *Ritual: Perspectives and Dimensions*, 120. For ritual as "social drama" and "cultural performance" see Turner, *Schism and Continuity*, 91–94; MacAloon, "Introduction: Cultural Performances." See Douglas's (*Natural Symbols*) discussion of how the individual exists within a grid of determinative social factors.

33. Durkheim, *Division of Labor in Society*, 39–69, 396–409.

34. Examples are Fanger, "Christian Ritual Magic"; Kieckhefer, *Forbidden Rites*, introd.; and Kieckhefer, *Magic in the Middle Ages*, 116–75.

35. Bell, *Ritual Theory, Ritual Practice*, 3–9, 69–74; Kertzer, *Ritual, Politics, and Power*, 9. See Koziol (*Begging Pardon*, 7–8, 316): "Where there is neither ambiguity nor contradiction, no spiritual or social conflict either within the event or on it edges, there is no longer ritual. There is only ceremony" (quotation 316).

"creatural viability"; "they give meaning . . . by shaping themselves to [reality] and by shaping it to themselves." Geertz claims that culture itself is a historically transmitted pattern of meanings embodied in symbols. "Religious symbols," he says, "provide a cosmic guarantee not only for [people's] ability to comprehend the world, but also, comprehending it, to give a precision to their feeling, a definition to their emotions which enables them, morosely or joyfully, grimly or cavalierly, to endure it." Culture itself is a collection of shared meanings and values that are "transmitted by symbols."[36] Pierre Bourdieu uses the term "structured structures" to explain how humans create a reality through symbols' intellective function.[37]

An important question in the conversation about ritual behavior as it pertains to magic regards the rationality of ritualism. The nineteenth-century English anthropologist Edward Burnett Tylor contended that "primitives,"[38] with their animistic approach to reality, are irrational because they think ritual has the ability to effect change in the world; they mistake "an ideal for a real connexion"—the rain dance brings rain. In a similar vein, the Scottish anthropologist James Frazer viewed magic as an irrational or "prelogical" approach of "primitive" peoples to their natural circumstances. They mistakenly thought their rituals were causal and that the association of two objects by virtue of resemblance or contagion meant that action to one object would affect another object like it or near to it.[39] According to the Frazerian scheme, when humans came to recognize their inability to manipulate the world through magical ritual, they progressed to a state of religion, then to science.[40] Frazer's peers Bronisław Malinowski (d. 1942) and E. E. Evans-Prichard provided a corrective to his position by pointing out that there is a kind of thinking particular to ritualistic settings where the "primitive" grammar of ritual is remarkably practical in that symbolic associations and ceremonial displays are not meant to "work" in a Western scientific sense, but

---

36. Geertz, "Religion as a Cultural System," 8, 13; Geertz, *Interpretation of Cultures*, 87–125 (quotations 99, 104). See also Janowitz, *Icons of Power*, xviii–xxv; Warner, "Ritual and Memory"; MacAloon, "Introduction: Cultural Performances," 2.

37. Bourdieu, "Symbolic Power," 113.

38. On early anthropologists' use of "primitive" to refer to the populations they studied see Dozier, "Concepts of 'Primitive.'"

39. Tylor, *Primitive Culture*, 112–21 (quotation 116). Frazer, *Magic Art*, 52–219. Dependence on resemblance is called "sympathetic magic." Dependence on contiguity is called "contagious magic," and it works on the principal that a person can be helped or harmed if a sorcerer performs rites on items that once belonged to that person, such as fingernails, hair, clothing, and so forth.

40. Frazer, *Magic Art*, 220–43. Responding to Frazer's legacy, see Glosecki, *Myth in Early Northwest Europe*, xviii–xxii; Tambiah, *Magic, Science, and Religion*, 51–64; Lévy-Bruhl, "On Primitive Mentality," 85–91.

ritual has value as an agent for social cohesion.[41] The rain dance does not bring rain, but it marks the rainy season or alleviates group anxiety about the vicissitudes of the weather. Ritual helps nature work. The French philosopher and ethnographer Lucien Lévy-Bruhl (d. 1939) and his school took the argument further. They too rejected the notion that the mentality of "primitives" was an infantile form of logic and proposed that the "mystical mentality" evident in "primitive" belief in the causality of ritual is a fully mature, but radically different, mode of thinking from that credited in the West. It is driven, not by formal logic, but by laws and relations of participation. Lévy-Bruhl argued that "primitive" cultures lack cognitive categories for classical reasoning, but because they are "consubstantial" with the natural world, they understand causation in a direct, participatory fashion. In other words, their rain dance is a constitutive part of the natural yearly cycle that includes rain in the rainy season.[42]

Whereas Lévy-Bruhl's "primitives" were above all mystical and Malinowski's were quintessentially practical, Geertz held that people slip between the two planes with ease. Symbol and ritual activity are seldom just sacred or just profane; rather, they are mixed and only assume their purity when outside observers (such as anthropologists and historians) force categories to facilitate theoretical constructs. Although ritual informs day-to-day experience, in ordinary life people do not operate on the highly symbolic stratum induced by ritual performance. This is the case whether those rituals are numbingly predictable or spontaneous and emotional.[43] So when a man says, "I am a parakeet," he does not mean it literally (he does not try to mate with other parakeets), nor is the statement simply symbolic; rather, the man is "shot through with parakeetness," which reveals itself literally in ritual settings. When not in a ritual context, he might be of the clan of the parakeet—still a parakeet in the background of his reality, but that background can be foregrounded in an instant, especially within the liminal space created in ritual.[44] The same might be said of the early medieval rustics who donned animal skins and danced through the villages on the Kalends of January. It is doubtful these peasants saw themselves as stags when they were out plowing the

---

41. Tambiah, *Magic, Science, Religion*, 51; Malinowski, "Magic, Science and Religion," 25–36.

42. Lévy-Bruhl, *How Natives Think*, 431–47. See also Tambiah, *Magic, Science, Religion*, 84–90; Tambiah, "Magic Power of Words."

43. Mary Douglas (*Natural Symbols*, xvi) notes that ritual does not always express itself with passionate effervescence. "The Catholic rituals I know are not conducive to the arousing of emotion which Durkheim seemed to think is the function of ritual."

44. Geertz, *Interpretation of Cultures*, 112–23 (quotation 121); Geertz, *Religion as a Cultural System*, 37–38. See also Summers-Effler, *Laughing Saints*, 167–68; Glosecki, *Shamanism*, 36–39, 53–67. Lévy-Bruhl, *How Natives Think*, 54–87, 73–76.

fields or sitting by the hearth, but they took on the quality of "stagness" in the Kalends rituals (or so clerics feared).[45]

Indicative of the general move in the social sciences to interpret ritual as reasonable and purposeful, Ludwig Wittgenstein (d. 1951) redirected magic ritual theory when he argued that humans use magical symbols and rituals in the same way; they are metaphorical and expressive, not contributory, and the use of ritual magic does not represent an evolutionary stage but a mode of human expression that occurs in all cultures, irrespective of their degree of sophistication or modernity. In a similar vein, Kenneth Burke in his *Grammar of Motives* says that ritual magic is not bad science, but rhetorical art, which operates not on nature but on the people who manipulate it.[46] Still some contemporary anthropologists and historians tend to separate magical ritual action into (1) the instrumental or pragmatic and (2) the symbolic or expressive, and to interpret the first as practicable and the later as illogical, and in so doing miss the point.[47] This is particularly true in the study of pre-modern medicine where ritual acts give range to a holistic approach and provide space for integration of the "pragmatic" and the "symbolic."

Liminality is a crucial term for understanding ritual. Victor Turner developed (and other scholars readily adopted) this concept, which describes the status of persons who move over the threshold (*limen*) from one stage of life to another, or from profane into ritualized experience. A modern example is the period surrounding pregnancy and the birth of a child when society indulges with a wink all kinds of odd and anomalous behaviors on the part of the parents. Within the liminal zone, status becomes ambiguous and indeterminate; a person is "neither here nor there" but is "betwixt and between all fixed points of classification," and regular rules and expectations are suspended.[48] The liminal state is transitional, characterized by disorientation and creative ambiguity where one's sense of identity is open to reinterpretation. Liminality is unpredictable; societal coding might be undermined and multiple alternative programs generated resulting in personal or group worldmaking transformations. Because of the uncontrolled environment of the liminal state, all societies hedge it in with special taboos

---

45. See chapter 7 on the Kalends of January.
46. Wittgenstein, *Remarks*, 1–18; Burke, *Grammar of Motives*, 564–68. Sax (*Ritual and the Problem of Efficacy*, 3–16) would agree with Burke, but he goes further in maintaining that an aspect of ritual's efficacy is (1) its nonrationality and (2) that "the ends seem disproportionate to the means" (5).
47. Bell, *Ritual Practice, Ritual Theory*, 71; Tambiah "Magic Power of Words"; Bourdieu, *Outline of a Theory* 174–76.
48. Turner, *Dramas, Fields, and Metaphors*, 232; Turner, *Forest of Symbols*, 93–111.

and durational and spatial restrictions.[49] Ritual space is porous because it is liminal, and into it a multitude of contraries can seep and combust creating a new viability. In ritual, thought and action, symbol and theater, profane and sacred meet, interact, and reconcile, even if that reconciliation is unstable.

Ritual acts do more than speak; they act upon the world. Edmund Leach rightly observes that "symbolic behavior not only 'says' something, it also arouses emotion and consequently 'does' something."[50] Sacred symbols and rituals synthesize a people's ethos such that a group develops a sense that its way of living and feeling is the only natural way given the contours of reality. The metaphysic worked out in ritual creates congruence between itself and ordinary life so that the two sustain one other, each borrowing authority from the other. So powerful is the reality created within ritual space, that it sometimes elaborates new systems at the expense of existing affiliations,[51] and therein lay the trouble for the medieval church.

Scholarship on ritual as a hermeneutic tool for navigating the intricacies of early medieval culture has not been without controversy, and the publication of Philippe Buc's *Dangers of Ritual* in 2001 enlivened the debate. Buc's provocative thesis is that historians can never truly retrieve ritual phenomena as they played out in the past because we can only know them from texts which are so profoundly mediated by their authors' biases and partisan agendas as to make ritual acts opaque. Buc argues that "for the early Middle Ages and most of late antiquity, simple access to a ritual as historical fact is impossible if by 'fact' one understands 'event.'"[52]

Buc further asserts that historians have vulgarized anthropological models and slapped them onto early medieval evidence in a futile attempt to gain that access that Buc claims is beyond our grasp. "Ultimately, there can be

---

49. MacAloon, "Introduction: Cultural Performances," 3; Turner, "Liminality."
50. Leach, "Magical Hair," 147. Like Leach, Mauss (*General Theory of Magic*, 19) argues that "rites are eminently effective; they are creative; they *do* things." Emphasis in original.
51. Geertz, "Religion as a Cultural System," 3–4. From J. Z. Smith (*To Take Place*, 75), "Novelty may give clarity to elaborate syntagmatic relations at the cost of impoverishing associative relations."
52. Buc, *Dangers of Ritual*, 248. For much the same view see Pössel ("Magic of Early Medieval Ritual") and Ricoeur ("Model of the Text") who holds that "the world is the ensemble of references opened up by texts" (96). Once performed, a given action (such as a ritual) or "speech event" (93) becomes a fixed text, and it is the scribe who injects that text with meaning or "world propositions" (114) beyond the event itself. By extension, writing about ritual is always implicitly a process of subordination of the object action to the subject interlocutor. See also Roach (*Kingship and Consent*, 201) who observes that "Émile Durkheim long ago observed, a society is constituted not only by its individuals and their environment, but also by the representations (literary and otherwise) it creates of itself."

no anthropological readings of rituals depicted in medieval texts."[53] Buc is particularly critical of positivist and functionalist social-science theories, and he questions those who claim that ritual's function is to create consensus, societal cohesion, and "communitas" (to use Victor Turner's term).[54]

There are a few sticking points in Buc's impressive "essay" which have been adroitly pointed out by several of the book's reviewers.[55] I will discuss two of these difficulties that are relevant to my thinking about ritual. First of all, Buc's argument is circular. He claims that "struggles within Carolingian political culture occurred more through depictions of ceremonies than through their actual performance."[56] But how can he verify this assertion if he cannot trust his sources? If the historicity of all rituals is masked by textuality, the past is a nihilist black hole, and we cannot know anything about "actual performance." Rituals and contemporaries' writings about them were not dichotomous; they grew from the same soil and each informed the other. An artfully deconstructed text can lead us to the historical "event," or at least take us in the vicinity of it. Second, Buc sets up a strawman in his polemic on social scientists who use functionalist theories as modalities of analysis. Virtually all scholars have abandoned a ridged functionalism in favor of post-modern cultural anthropology of the sort pioneered by Clifford Geertz.

Buc demonstrates how thoroughly early medieval reports of solemnities were contextually conditioned, and his plea that scholars respect the text in its own right is a good reminder that we can only see historical ceremony through the prism of the artifact, that is the text, which is constructed from authorial goals and objectives. But every interpretive theory brought to the service of historical investigation must be buttressed with concrete examples and supporting primary evidence. It is curious, therefore, that

---

53. Buc, *Dangers of Ritual*, 4. Pössel ("The Magic of Early Medieval Ritual," 115) expresses the same sentiment when she says that writers often apply the term "ritual" too broadly and uncritically and that historians must do more than assume the explanatory value of anthropological theories. They must also demonstrate the validity of the models within the particularities of a given historical situation. From Ferngren (*Medicine and Health Care*, 8), "The methods of social anthropology need to be kept on a leash and used to complement—not to replace—the textual-philological historical method."

54. Turner, *Dramas, Fields, and Metaphors*, 231–71; Turner, *Ritual Process*, 109–11; Koziol ("Review Article," 368) neatly characterizes the functionalist argument as "the assumptions that a society is an organism that always seeks homeostasis and that rituals 'function' to minimize conflict and return the society to equilibrium."

55. Nelson, review of *Dangers of Ritual*; Walsham, review of *Dangers of Ritual*; Koziol, "Review Article"; Rollo-Koster, review of *Dangers of Ritual*. For Buc's response to these reviews see "Monster and the Critics."

56. Buc, *Dangers of Ritual*, 58.

Buc singles out narratives of ritual as particularly dangerous when all historical documents are affected by the disposition of the narrator or scribe to a greater or lesser degree. Ritual does not pose a special case. When Buc claims that historians cannot encounter texts the way an anthropologist might read a ritual in front of him, he implies that a single and true understanding of the raw data of a medieval ritual would be possible if only we could witness it firsthand, which is not accurate. The researcher is always external to the ritualized occasion and must peer at it through binoculars. The anthropologist's field notes, no less than a saint's vita (for example), impose a coherence on a given ceremony that it may never have had. In short, all observers, whether on site or separated by millennia interpret ritual second-hand.[57]

Buc declines to define ritual (a term he wishes to abandon) except to extend his willingness to accept the modern, commonly understood use of the word. A definition would have been helpful, however, to establish the extent to which his remarks are relevant to ritual as discussed in my book. Buc's point of reference is staged ceremonial orchestrated by hierarchs—royal, comital or ecclesiastical. However, not all ritual behavior was public or ceremonial, and Buc does not address intimate, private, or clandestine rites that often characterize magic activity. This is not to criticize Buc's choices; it is just to say that the warnings in *Dangers of Ritual* are not directly germane to magic rites. The scrutiny and healthy suspicion of textual information that Buc urges is no less important for analysis of private magic than it is for communal pageantry. The difference is that magic is rarely meant to be socially cohesive or communitarian, nor is it portrayed that way in historical sources. On the contrary, it is most often self-serving and disintegrative.[58]

---

57. See Booker (*Past Convictions*, 22–24) on authorial subjectivity in Carolingian chronicles. Theuws, "Introduction," 10–11. From Bell (*Ritual: Perspectives and Dimensions*, 62), scholars compare "rites to texts, arguing that both needed to be 'decoded' in order to determine their real meaning." Geertz observes (*Interpretation of Cultures*, 452) that "the culture of a people is an ensemble of texts . . . which the anthropologist strains to read over the shoulders of those to whom they properly belong." From Ricoeur ("Model of the Text," 103), "The meaning of an event is the sense of its forthcoming interpretations, the interpretation by contemporaries has no particular privilege in this process."

58. It is my view that "ritual" appropriately describes intimate, small group or solitary rites, which puts me at odds with Wils ("From Ritual to Hermeneutics," 258) when he claims that "the reasons for creating a ritual can be varied, but always they are significant experiences that concern not the individual as such but the individual as part of a collective that is either undergoing the same experiences or at least is affected by them. Consequently a 'private ritual' is a contradiction in terms." I also question Hausmann, Jonason, and Summers-Effler ("Interaction Ritual Theory," 322)

Sources on Late Antique and Early Medieval Magic

When examining almost any aspect of late antique or early medieval cultural life, the historian must come to terms with the paucity of materials; this is especially true when dealing with magic.[59] Because it was illegal and forbidden by secular and ecclesiastic lawgivers, people who dealt in the magic arts or indulged in putatively pagan-like conduct rarely left written accounts of their activities, but those who condemned the practices did. Data is overwhelmingly from the pens of the learned strata of male society, and so it is this group whose voices are strongest in this book. This is not to say that elite, masculine views captured in writing were so thoroughly privileged as to be inaccessible or incomprehensible to the masses.[60] Those practicing magic and those writing about it shared the same *Weltanschauung*. There may have been interpretive discrepancies in the minds of the common parishioner and the pastor who imposed penance for singing chants over herbs, for example, but there was no impermeable societal or ideological wall separating the two. The popular and the learned existed in what Karen Jolly calls "overlapping and interacting spheres."[61] Similarly, Richard Kieckhefer correctly argues that in reference to magic "the distinction between 'popular' and 'elite' cultures can usefully be subordinated to a more nuanced and fluid distinction between 'common tradition' and various specialized traditions." In his view, magic's essential components were comparable wherever it occurred.[62] In her scrutiny of pastoral literature, Bernadette Filotas also concludes that beliefs about magic and paganism were not fixed in any particular social or educational class, but rather were shared at all levels of early medieval society.[63] Even when the mindset of folks in one social grouping differed from that of another, people (on the whole) operated within a common discourse

---

when they assert (too categorically) that ritual's "emotional energy" to create social bonds requires at least two interactants.

59. In this section on sources, notes are minimal, because applicable references are supplied throughout the book as each subject becomes relevant.

60. Stock's work on literacy (*Implications of Literacy*, 3–11, 88–92) has shown that the inability to read and write does not preclude a type of cultural literacy by which the uneducated gain knowledge of texts they have never seen. For insights on the interplay of orality and literacy in Carolingian culture see Geary, "Oblivion"; Mordek, "Kapitularien und Schriftlichkeit"; McKitterick, *New Cambridge Medieval History*, 3–12; Dienst, "Zur Rolle von Frauen."

61. Jolly, *Popular Religion*, 173. For popular/elite in early Christianity see Momigliano, "Popular Religious Beliefs."

62. Kieckhefer, "Specific Rationality," 814, 832–36 (quotation 833); Kieckhefer, *Magic in the Middle Ages*, 56–94.

63. Filotas, *Pagan Survivals*, 2–11, 357–60. I avoid the term "pagan survivals" in light of Markus's observation (*End of Ancient Christianity*, 9) that myriad survivals from the pagan past were purely

community and understood the terms of their disagreement in the same way. Though perhaps not seeing eye to eye, people shared an understanding of the terms of the debate. For instance, a rustic may deny that her unsanctioned home cure to correct infertility was magical, but she would understand that magic itself was devilish. Despite variation, the visible elite and the anonymous commoner held sufficient assumptions in common from a range of possibilities to form a flexible, but ultimately coherent, position on what constituted the magic arts.[64]

The perspective on magic varies from source type to source type. Each genre had its own public, objectives, and methods of dissemination that largely determined the ways or extent to which its authors approached the topic of magic. A particular statement can be misunderstood if the reader does not take into consideration the conventions of each document category and the way it approaches magic. For example, in her translation of the Lombard laws, Katherine Fischer Drew observes, "The Lombard kings approached the subject [of witchcraft] in an enlightened manner, practically denying the existence of this occult science and providing protection against random accusations of witchcraft."[65] The Lombard legal canon that begins this chapter would seem to be a case in point. However, although the canon does provide protection against random accusations, that was not due to an enlightened or skeptical attitude toward sorcery; rather it was a function of the purpose of the law codes.

Although it would be inaccurate to say that each class of texts constructs its own "magic," the norms of a given genre determine what a source is likely to reveal. This means a depiction of magic at street level, so to speak, can be teased out of some texts more than others. For instance, manuals of penance deal with personal and domestic sorcery, such as the use of ligatures and abortifacients, and because they are often explicit in portraying the exact behaviors they forbid, readers get a glimpse of contemporary magical practices. On the other hand, council and legal records tend to be both terse and conventional in regard to magical activity; they sketch only its broad

---

secular and passed into medieval culture without any stain of superstition. Also Künzel ("Paganisme," 1056–57) rightly notes that "pagan survivals" are more profitably seen as adaptations and continuities.

64. Rembold (*Conquest and Christianization*, 188–91, 197–99), Kahlos ("Early Church," 148–49), and Palmer ("Defining Paganism") argue that paganism and magic were simply Christian constructs meant to establish "a clear dichotomy: the Christians and the other" (Rembold, 191) and "Christian 'alterity motifs'" (Palmer 425). This polemical discourse was at work, to be sure, but as I argue above, Rembold's, Kahlos's, and Palmer's is a limited understanding of the operation of magic in the first millennium and denies reality and agency to those who did practice the magic arts.

65. *Lombard Laws*, 247n55.

contours and do not elucidate how those who practiced magic might have understood the economy of their worldview. This makes thick emic description difficult.

Despite the relative silence of magical practitioners themselves, the sources for the study of magic and its relationship to ritual and gender are abundant and varied, because references to them, whether brief or extended, are found in virtually all categories of literature. Often it is all but impossible to squint between the lines of a given text to see the variegated world of real time magical practices and rituals, but luckily, some etic sources describe them in enough detail that an authentic positioning is possible. The best chance we have of comprehending magic is to bring into phase, side by side, as many sources as possible, letting the more vocal texts fill in the gaps of the laconic ones, and that is what this book does.

I organize the evidential materials for the study of magic in the first millennium into four categories: (1) pastoral, polemic, and didactic works (penitentials, sermons, homilies, letters, learned treatises, and intertestamental writings); (2) legal records (law codes, capitularies, canons of church councils); (3) narrative sources (histories, annals, chronicles, hagiography, and creative literature); and (4) medical materials.[66]

Pastoral, Polemic, and Didactic Works

Pastoral, didactic, and polemic works were meant to instruct, inform, or persuade on a plethora of topics, and magic is laced throughout them. This category of sources contains written materials that are valuable companions to proscriptive sources because they disclose cultural and societal mandates for specific situations.

Penitentials

Penitentials are lists of sins and their concomitant penances that guided confessors in their task or acted as juridical reference books.[67] Because books

---

66. For an extensive and enormously helpful annotated bibliography on councils, capitularies, penitentials, sermons, letters, law codes, and miscellaneous early medieval sources dealing with magic, see Filotas, *Pagan Survivals*, 361–86.

67. The bibliography on penitential literature is vast. Classic and more recent significant works include Meens, *Penance*; Körntgen, "Canon Law and the Practice of Penance"; Firey, *New History of Penance*; Gaastra, "Penance and the Law"; Hamilton, *Practice of Penance*; Meens, "Frequency and Nature"; de Jong, "What Was Public?"; Körntgen, *Studien zu den Quellen*; Kerff, "*Libri paenitentiales*"; Frantzen, *Literature of Penance*; Kottje, "Überlieferung und Rezeption"; Kottje, *Die Bussbücher*

of penance address both religious and lay, they are a rare source for bringing into focus the personal and domestic spheres of all classes and genders of Europeans and shedding light on the full spectrum of magic and ritual. Because they are graphic and, taken as a whole, exhaustive in their endeavor to provide confessors with as much information as possible about parishioners' transgressions, the penitentials open up a panorama of behaviors. This is so much the case that Bishop Theodulf of Orléans (d. 821) warned that "the priest ought not question [the penitent] about all sins on the chance that when he has gone away from him, by the prompting of the Devil, [the penitent] might fall into some sin that he previously did not know about."[68] In an oblique way, Theodulf demonstrates that the nonliterate were privy to the elites' perceptions of magic as laid out in the manuals of penance. Also, before the tenth century the penitential process was largely didactic, and the confessor expounded the nature of a given offense for the benefit of the repentant sinner.

Recent research on penance suggests that there was considerable diversity in its application in the early Middle Ages. Penance was imposed in a variety of locales, from court to monastery to village; it was adapted to local needs; and both public and private penance were practiced throughout the early Middle Ages. Communal penance was generally reserved for the grave sinner and could not be repeated, but private penance was available to all Christians for even minor trespasses and could be revisited regularly. The handbooks of penance were developed for the confidential form of penance, although it is not entirely clear how they were used.[69]

In clerical circles, particularly during the Carolingian era, there was some opposition to the penitentials, which were thought to be corrupted, idiosyncratic, and unsupported by ecclesiastical authority or precedent.[70] Despite

---

Halitgars von Cambrai; Vogel, *Les "Libri paenitentiales"*; Pierce, "Frankish Penitentials"; *Irish Penitentials*; Vogel, *La discipline pénitentielle*.

68. Theodulf of Orléans, Second Capitulary 14, 176: "Ideo non debet eum sacerdos de omnibus interrogare, ne forte, cum ab illo recesserit, suadente diabolo in aliquod crimen de his, quae antea nesciebat, cadat."

69. Meens, *Penance*, 80, 118–23; de Jong (*Penitential State*, 232–34) argues that Carolingian clerics reinvented what they claimed to be a "pristine" form of penance to be applied when the sin was public. Wagner, "Cum aliquis," 201–2, 216; Hamilton, *Practice of Penance*, 38–44, 72–76; de Jong, "What Was Public?"; Meens, "Historiography"; Frantzen, *Literature of Penance*, 1–18.

70. Ebbo's letter to Halitgar, bishop of Cambrai: *Ep.* 2, 616; Chalon-sur-Saône (*Concilium Cabillonense*) 38, in *MGH Conc. aevi Kar.* 2.1, 281; Council of Paris (*Concilium Parisiense*) 32, 633. On Carolingian clerics' objections to the penitentials see Meens, *Penance*, 130–39; Meens, "Historiography"; Hamilton, *Practice of Penance*, 6; Kottje, *Die Bussbücher Halitgars von Cambrai*, 204–12. From Meens (*Penance*, 111–18), the episcopal appraisal of penitentials was diverse and regional; the most ardent objection to manuals of penance came from Tours, Chalon, and Reims.

their censure, the handbooks were useful to priests, abbots, and abbesses, who needed convenient reference guides to advise wrongdoers who wished to confess. Carolingian reformers, realizing that the books could not be suppressed, began to produce their own penitentials that they felt were better aligned with the canonical practices of the early church. Even so, canons of earlier manuals crept back in as it became clear that the needs of simple priests were not being met by the more sanitized reform penitentials.[71] Several influential bishops stipulated that every priest must be familiar with the manuals of penance.[72]

Penitential books were at times resistant to modernization because ecclesiastical compilers, who readily borrowed both ideas and exact phraseology from extant documents, were apt to be reverential when dealing with authoritative texts and were hesitant to impose changes. As a result, the penitentials contain material copied from generation to generation. Authors often used inherited and archaic vocabularies that mask local activities taking place at the time of composition. That having been said, there are detectable differences in the contents of given penitentials compiled over the medieval centuries. A variety of factors drove modification in penitential literature, making the books valuable to the historian of magic as a barometer of change over time. For example, Thomas Charles-Edwards argues that "the Disciple," who compiled the English *Penitential of Theodore* (ca. 700), initiated changes, "not out of ignorance of traditional rules but merely because pragmatic compromise with the values of lay society was inescapable."[73] Pinpointing changes in traditional prohibitions permits a rare, real time glimpse into the intimate lives of men and women—their quotidian behaviors, folkloric superstitions, and private rituals.

---

71. Burchard of Worms, *Decretum* 19, *Argumentum*, PL 140, col. 949; Meens, "Frequency and Nature," 39–47; de Jong, "Power and Humility," 32–24. See Halitgar of Cambrai's *Poenitential Romanum* (in *Die Bussbücher*, 1:465–89) as an example of a notable reform Carolingian penitential. On Haltigar's penitential see Meens, *Penance*, 130–39 (quotation 137). Also from Meens (*Penance*, 132–34), Raban Maur, one of the preeminent intellectuals of the Carolingian reform era, wrote two penitentials (*Poenitentiale ad Heribaldum Antissiodorensem* and *Poenitentium liber ad Otgarium*) in response to questions from fellow bishops on matters of penance. On abbesses administering penance see Muschiol, "Men, Women," 210–11.

72. Frantzen, "Significance," 412–13; Devailly, "La pastorale en Gaule," 40–41. Fournier and Le Bras (*Histoire des collections canoniques*, 347–50) document that Theodulf of Orléans, Rudolf of Bourges, and Hincmar of Reims required that confessors under their direction be familiar with the *libri poenitentiales*.

73. Charles-Edwards, "Penitential of Theodore," 170. The *Penitential of Theodore* was not compiled by the archbishop himself but by a *discipulus umbrensium* who received information about Theodore's views on penance secondhand (ibid., 141–43). See Meens (*Penance*, 88–100) on Theodore's penitential. The extant copies were concentrated in and around the monastery of Lorsch. See also Jurasinski, *Old English Penitentials*, 204–5; Frantzen, *Literature of Penance*, 63–69.

Bishop Burchard of Worms, a pivotal figure in the development of canon law, is central to the study of magic and ritual in the early Middle Ages. Burchard was bishop of Worms during the reigns of Emperors Otto III (d. 1002) and Henry II (d. 1024), and he was involved in the project of church reform promoted by the German kings who fashioned themselves successors to Charlemagne. Between 1012 and 1023, with the help of Bishop Walter of Speyer (d. 1027) and the monk Olbert of Gembloux (d. 1048), Burchard collected a vast array of conciliar and penitential canons and aggregated them into a compendium entitled the *Decretum* (ca. 1020). This magnum opus of canon law is a radical regrouping and reinterpretation of earlier texts. Although Burchard edited this compilation of documents on church governance and law for the purpose of aiding the clergy under his direction, the impact of the work went far beyond Burchard's own diocese. The *Decretum* was regarded as authoritative in the West for more than a century. Burchard's work is divided into twenty books; book nineteen (called *Corrector sive medicus*) is penitential in nature was designed to be exemplary. Most of the *Decretum's* dicta about female magical ritual are found in the *Corrector*. Burchard borrowed liberally from a variety of earlier penitentials. However, several of the canons regarding sorcery and superstition are new with the *Decretum* and most certainly describe contemporary behaviors or urban legends about those behaviors.[74]

Sermons, Homilies, and Letters

Sermons, homilies, and letters open a window to the concerns and beliefs of the clergy and what they thought was important for laypeople to understand, although extant sermons and homilies are frequently formulaic and in some ways a stilted facsimile of the live originals that were often delivered in the vernacular.[75] Sermons were meant to instruct and correct myriad

---

74. G. Austin, *Shaping Church Law*, 15–31, 53–74, 235–39; Filotas, *Pagan Survivals*, 371; Körntgen, "Canon Law"; G. Austin, "Jurisprudence"; J. Müller, "Die Kirchenrechtssammlung"; Hamilton, *Practice of Penance*, 34–44; Hartmann, "Burchards Dekret." For manuscripts and studies of the *Decretum* see Kéry, *Canonical Collections*, 133–55; Hoffmann and Pokorny, *Das Dekret*; Fransen, "Le Décret"; Vogel, "Pratiques superstitieuses"; Fournier and Le Bras, *Histoire des collections*, 371–77, 454–56; Fournier, "Le Décret."

75. For late antiquity see Maxwell, *Christianization and Communication*, ch. 3, 118–24. For the Middle Ages see Diesenberger, Hen, and Pollheimer, *Sermo Doctorum*; Hummer, *Politics and Power*, 133–37; O'Malley, "Introduction: Medieval Preaching," 2; L. Martin, "Two Worlds," 28–29; Amos, "Preaching and the Sermon"; Barré, *Les homéliaires carolingiens*, 1–30. The 813 Council of Tours (*Concilium Turonense* 17, in MGH *Conc. aevi Kar.* 2.1, 288) stipulates that sermons be delivered in the Roman

behaviors of all classes of the lay population,⁷⁶ so like the penitentials, sermons and homilies are detailed sources for information on magic, ritual, and private life. Sermons exposed common people to bookish concepts of magic. A good example is the sermons of Bishop Caesarius of Arles (d. 542) which were circulated widely and replicated promiscuously throughout the early Middle Ages. Caesarius himself gave a copy of the sermons to virtually every bishop, priest, and deacon who traveled through his city (on the Rhône River in the Provence region of southern France), and he sent copies to several bishops as far away as Spain and Italy, urging them to read the sermons out loud in their local churches. The impact of Caesarius's sermons is inestimable in that his catalogue of magical pagan behaviors came to be a handy set-piece in manifold texts over the first millennium.⁷⁷

The epistolary genre (*ars dictaminis* or *ars dictandi*) was a specialized branch of rhetoric that developed in antiquity,⁷⁸ flourished among early Christians, and became more formalized in the early Middle Ages. In the ancient and medieval worlds, letters were not strictly a private form of communication between two individuals, but were similar to sermons in that they were circulated, often collected into volumes, and published. Only the educated wrote letters, but in the early church, epistles were often read out to whole congregations.⁷⁹ By the early Middle Ages, although letters were widely shared in elite, familial, and clerical circles, their contents were less accessible to the lay public than they had been in late antiquity, in part because of changed demographics.⁸⁰

---

vernacular or in German so all could more easily understand what was said. (Et ut easdem omelias quisque aperte transferre studeat in rusticam Romanam linguam aut Thiotiscam, quo facilius cuncti possint intellegere quae dicuntur.)

76. See Timmermann ("An Authority") on Carolingian sermons. See also Filotas, *Pagan Survivals*, 61. From *Blickling Homilies*, xviii–xxii, in late tenth-century England, sermons were delivered to monastic and lay audiences.

77. On Caesarius and his impact see Grig, "Caesarius of Arles"; Brunner, "Publikumskonstruktionen"; Klingshirn, *Caesarius of Arles*, 273–86; Caesarius of Arles, *Saint Caesarius of Arles*, 1:xvii–xxv.

78. Wilken, *First Thousand Years*, 28–30; Camargo, *Ars dictaminis, ars dictandi*, 29–30.

79. From Cross and Livingstone (*Oxford Dictionary*, s.v. "Clement of Rome, St."), *1 Clement* of Clement of Rome was regularly read in churches. See Bowes (*Private Worship, Public Values*, 97, 160) on letter writing among late antique Christian aristocrats.

80. Heidecker, *Divorce of Lothar II*, 41; Garrison, "Letters"; Mathisen, "Epistolography." An exception in the Merovingian era is found in Gregory of Tours's *Decem libri historiarum* (2.3, 40–42) where he speaks of Bishop Eugenius's letter being read to the "people of the city" (*civibus*). Dutton (*Charlemagne's Mustache*, 144) posits that in the constellation of literate Carolingians, the term "secret letter" may have referred to missives meant to be read by the receiver only. This suggests that epistles were normally quasi-public documents.

Learned Treatises and Intertestamental Writings

The learned treatise, although not a genre of writing per se, describes the major literary output of the patristic age and of several major thinkers of the Carolingian era. Learned treatises are exposés on topics of doctrine or policy directed toward a highly educated readership. They provide the most discursive information we have on sorcery in the first millennium.

Bishop Isidore of Seville's (d. 636) *Etymologies*, although not a treatise, is a foundational work along the same lines; it is the Spanish bishop's attempt to encyclopedize all human knowledge. Isidore's work contains extensive sections on magic, superstition, and demonology, which reflect the thinking of his day,[81] and because the text was revered and referenced throughout the Middle Ages, Isidore's understanding of magic was hegemonic.

Discussion of magic in early Christian and medieval treatises drew liberally from the pseudepigrapha, apocrypha, and intertestamental writings (ca. 400 BCE to ca. 30 CE) spuriously attributed to biblical and apostolic personages. Among the most influential of these works in the early church were the books of Enoch. Enoch is listed in Genesis as the son of Jared and great-grandfather of Noah (Gen. 5:18–29). The Enochic corpus is replete with millenarian predictions, discussion of the origins of magic, and prophecies about the Antichrist. It was so esteemed in the early Middle Ages that some considered Enoch's books to be canonical.[82]

Legal Texts

Law Codes

Roman law in the late antique West was not comprehensively systematized until the Christian Emperor Theodosius II (d. 450) commissioned an imperial legal code.[83] It is a valuable source on governmental regulations of magic in late antiquity. The successor states to the western empire adopted aspects of Roman law (including the very notion of codified, written rulings) and

---

81. Isidore of Seville, *Etymologiarum*, bk. 8.
82. From Nickelsburg (*1 Enoch 1*, 100–101), Enoch is mentioned in the New Testament Epistle of Jude (14), the *Second Epistle of Peter*, the *Letter of Barnabas*, and the works of Justin Martyr, Athenagoras, Irenaeus of Lyon, Pseudo-Clement of Alexandria, Tertullian, Crypian, Origen, Lactantius, and others. On Enoch as a motif in early Christian and early medieval thinking see VanderKam, "1 Enoch, Enochic Motifs"; E. Green, "Enoch, Lent."
83. Honoré, *Law in the Crisis of Empire*, 97–175; Contreni, "Carolingian Renaissance," 749; Arjava, *Women and Law*, 8–23; Matthews, "Making of the Text." On the composition and circulation of the *Theodosian Code* see Sirks, "Sources of the Code"; and Turpin, "Law Codes."

modified it where necessary. Post-Roman vulgar law codes blend the *Theodosian Code* (438) and provincial legal practices.[84] The resultant statutes are the source of many references to magic that appear in Merovingian codes but not in Roman law books. Although the legal texts that inheritors of the western Roman Empire produced were patterned after Roman law as it operated in the fifth and sixth centuries, they were in no sense interpreted or applied uniformly across the West. In his *History of the Lombards*, the Italian Benedictine monk and historian Paul the Deacon (d. ca. 799) summarizes the state of law in post-imperial Europe by criticizing "the laws of the Romans whose prolixity was so excessive that the discrepancies rendered them useless."[85]

Secular codes of the Merovingian, Carolingian, Visigothic, Lombard, and Anglo-Saxon kings help color in the portrait of early medieval magic, but as with each document type, the sort of information it is possible to derive from the laws is very particular. The earliest codes tend to restrict themselves to cases of personal injury, slander, theft, or property damage. Their major goal was to control antisocial conduct, obviate feuds, and secure the peace by ensuring that aggrieved families or individuals were duly compensated based on an index of fines calibrated on the social class of the offended party. Throughout the first centuries of the early Middle Ages, the utilitarian purpose of the laws means that we do not hear much about magic unless it is the criminal means of causing harm to others. In other words, legal documents focus more on maleficium than on other types of magic, such as superstition and idolatry. The Carolingians supported customary law and upheld legal codes developed in the Merovingian period—with some emendation. These adjustments are instructive as to how Merovingian assumptions about magic were evaluated in Carolingian legal circles.[86]

---

84. R. Collins, *Early Medieval Spain*, 24–31; I. Wood, "Code in Merovingian Gaul"; I. Wood, "Administration, Law, and Culture," 67–71; I. Wood, "Disputes," 8–10; Levy, "Vulgarization of Roman Law."

85. Paul the Deacon, *Pauli historia Langobardorum* 15, bk. 1, 63: "Leges quoque Romanorum, quarum prolixitas nimia erat et inutilis dissonantia." I will not deal with the Justinian law code because, although the *Corpus Iuris Civilis* was promulgated under Justinian in 529–534, it was not influential outside Italy until the twelfth century.

86. *Capitulare Aquitanicum* 10, in *MGH Cap.* 1.18, 43: "Ut omnes homines eorum legis habeant, tam Romani quam et Salici, et si de alia provincia advenerit, secundum legem ipsius patriae vivat"; *Capitulare Missorum* 5, in *MGH Cap.* 1.25, 67: "Et per singulos inquirant, quale habeant legem ex nomine"; *Responsa misso cuidam data* 2, in *MGH Cap.* 1.58, 145; *Capitulare missorum generale* 26, in *MGH Cap.* 1.33, 97; and *Conventus in villa colonia* 3, in *MGH Cap.* 2.254, 255; *Annales Laureshamenses* 35 (802), 38–39. Faulkner, *Law and Authority*, 1–8, 48–52; Costambeys, Innes, and MacLean, *Carolingian World*, 187; Contreni, "Carolingian Renaissance," 749; Mordek, "Recently Discovered Capitulary Texts," 448–51; McKitterick, *Carolingians and the Written Word*, 40–60; Nelson, "Dispute Settlement," 47.

The codes, though a valuable source for the study of magic, must be used with caution. For one thing, it is not clear how they functioned in the kingdoms for which they were constructed or how many people would have been privy to them. Patrick Wormald suggests that some of the *leges* acted to a large extent as talismans or antiquarian repositories of inherited wisdom and statements of royal/imperial ideology. Julia Smith also interprets the codes as conceptual rather than "a description of social reality."[87] On the other hand, Rosamond McKitterick argues that the laws operated more or less as recorded in the codes. There is also evidence from other sources that the law codes had practical application. Thomas Faulker suggests that the nature and role of law codes in the Carolingian period were variable, but they were rarely an indicator of ethnicity.[88]

Capitularies

The most significant legal apparatus of the Carolingian period was the capitularies, which are legislative and administrative rulings or decrees spanning the mid-eighth century to the early tenth century.[89] The Carolingian capitularies and later Anglo-Saxon codes are shot through with a Christian perspective and aim to do more than redress crimes. Collectively, they provide a blueprint for a godly society, and in so doing, touch on the full spectrum of sorcery and magical ritual traditions.[90] Many capitularies are imbedded in minutes from lawmaking assemblies, and in some cases, copies were kept in private collections or used as *aides-mémoire* by the *missi dominici* (king's agents) who promulgated legal rulings throughout the kingdom (later the empire).[91] Counts were directed to read out the contents of the capitularies to those answerable to them. An 803 capitulary to the *missi dominici* orders them to make certain that people of all social ranks understand the

---

87. Wormald, "*Lex scripta*"; J. M. H. Smith, *Europe after Rome*, 122. Lambert (*Law and Order*, 1–24) holds that "laws are a much more useful category of evidence than most recent historians have imagined" if they are assiduously studied within their historical and cultural contexts.

88. McKitterick, *Frankish Church*, 1–21, 42–44. Faulkner, *Law and Authority*, 248–52. For insight on the workings of Merovingian law see A. Murray ("Immunity") who discusses an edict of immunity Lothar II issued in 614; Anderson, "Roman Military Colonies"; Fouracre, "'Placita,'" 29. I. Wood ("Disputes," 11) points out that *Pactus legis Salicae* makes sense in a small face-to-face community, whereas the *Burgundian liber constitutionum* reflects the legal needs of a mixed, urbanized society.

89. Mordek, "Kapitularien und Schriftlichkeit"; Nelson, *Charles the Bald*, 9; McKitterick, *Carolingians and the Written Word*, 25–37.

90. From Contreni ("Carolingian Renaissance," 748–51), "Law also was fundamental to Christian notions of right order and the proper maintenance of society" (748).

91. Schmitz, "Capitulary Legislation," 425–28; Mordek, *Kirchenrecht und Reform*, 189.

regulations recently enacted.[92] This evidence aside, scholarly views differ as to what kind of exposure the capitularies actually received, and by extension, how widely regulations regarding magic were known or how ardently they were enforced.

The evolution of Anglo-Saxon law did not differ significantly from its counterpart on the Continent. The earliest law code was produced in the vernacular under King Æthelbert of Kent (d. 616) and was inspired by "a code of law after the Roman manner," meaning it was written.[93] The aggregate of legal prescripts, both criminal and civil, includes topics such as tariffs, oaths, punishments, property, family law, church administration, preservation of the peace, and magic. As in the continental legal tradition, earlier laws focus on crimes and their compensatory fines, but laws from the mid-eighth century on are less strictly custom-based and reflect an evolution of centralizing royal and ecclesiastical bodies that sought to impart a design for an unequivocally Christian society.[94]

In short, law codes are particularly useful in providing information on specific types of maleficium, while capitularies and late Anglo-Saxon jurisprudence broadened to encompass idolatry, superstition, and any other magic that threatened the morals of Christian communities.

Canons of Church Councils

Over the late antique and early medieval centuries, church councils addressed magic and paganism to some extent, inasmuch as they arbitrated on a full range of ecclesiastical, social, and spiritual matters, but canon law is relatively and surprisingly laconic on the subject of magic.[95] Where it does speak, the range of magical activities that Merovingian, Carolingian, Visigothic, Italian, and Anglo-Saxon councils condemned is uniformly conventional—restating proscriptions from patristic literature and councils prior to themselves. Canons primarily contain information on communal idolatrous transgressions, such as celebrations honoring pagan deities, cultic rituals, divination, and

---

92. *Capitulare missorum* 19, in *MGH Cap.* 1.40, 116. See also *Capitula de functionibus publicis* 5, in *MGH Cap.* 1.143, 295; *Commemoratio missis data* 3, in *MGH Cap.* 1.151, 309.

93. Bede, *Bede's Ecclesiastical History* 2.5, 150–51: "decreta illi iudiciorum iuxta exempla Romanorum." See *Die Admonitio generalis* (47–63) for the influence of King Offa's council of 786 on Charlemagne's major capitulary. The General Admonition is a set of eighty-two canons meant to ensure correctness and uniformity in all aspects of the liturgy, teaching, and monastic discipline.

94. Lambert, *Law and Order*, pt. 1, "Foundations of the Anglo-Saxon Legal Order"; Wormald, *Making of English Law*, 29–108, 477–83.

95. From Filotas (*Pagan Survivals*, 45), from 511 to 695, only about six percent of the canons from Gallican councils deal with paganism and superstition.

acts of public magic such as raising storms. There is almost no mention of private infractions or maleficium. As with the penitentials, canonists' use of standardized formulas to describe contemporary situations makes it difficult (but not impossible) to establish the extent to which a given council was responding to perceived threats of recurring magic in its own period. This ambiguates efforts to analyze change over time in both the perceptions about magic and the actual practice of it.

Conciliar activity intensified in Carolingian Europe, and, particularly after the mid-eighth century,[96] secular Frankish jurisprudence and conciliar legislation came more and more to resemble each other. Church and secular councils often met jointly or the king presided at synods. Ecclesiastical decisions were attached to capitular records, and secular law was informed by church decrees. For example, several capitular pronouncements start with wording such as, "Our most pious lord king decreed, with the assent of the holy synod . . ." and "It is established by the lord king and the holy synod that bishops establish justice in their own parishes."[97] The same was true in England and Visigothic Spain, where kings were customarily present at church councils. Because of this synergy, fusion of ecclesiastical decrees and royal pronouncements was frequent.[98]

Narrative Sources

HISTORIES

The biblical aphorism "Let us now praise men of renown"[99] summarizes the motivation behind both classical and Christian histories, the purpose of which was to establish oversize models of virtue and vice in order to

---

96. Conciliar records are extant from 220 synods held between the years 721 and 904. For an overview of Carolingian councils and a careful exposition on each synod see Hartmann, *Die Synoden der Karolingerzeit*, 1–36. Note that Hartmann's section on magic and pagan survivals is short (447–49), reflecting church councils' lack of attention to such subjects. From the Frankfort Capitulary of 794 (*Synodus Franconofurtensis* 20, 53, in *MGH Cap.* 1.28, 76, 78), we know that bishops and priests were expected to be acquainted with the canons.

97. *Synodus Franconofurtensis* 4, in *MGH Cap.* 1.28, 74: "Statuit piissimus domnus noster rex, consentienti sancta synodo." Ibid., 6, 74: "Statutum est a domno rege et sancta synodo, ut episcopi iustitias faciant in suis parroechiis." See Halfond, *Archaeology*, 213–19; Hartmann, *Kirche und Kirchenrecht*; de Jong, "*Ecclesia* and the Early Medieval Polity," 122–31; Vollrath, *Die Synoden*, 403–13; Hartmann, "Laien auf Synoden."

98. For England see Cubitt, *Anglo-Saxon Church Councils*, 39–59. In the case of Visigothic law, P. King (*Law and Society*, 23–51) argues that Recceswinth's laws are underpinned by Catholic ideology and that the notion of the king as the enforcer of laws was thought to be pleasing to God.

99. "*Laudemus viros gloriosos.*" Biblia sacra, Book of Ecclesiasticus 44.1.

demonstrate the value of the first and the pitfalls of the second. Because histories and annals in late antiquity and the early Middle Ages were about notable public events such as wars, monarchies, and high-level church affairs, magic tends to appear when it affects the workings of secular or church governance. Historical texts vary significantly in terms of the extent to which they consider magic, but when they do so, men are involved in activities such as weather magic, cultic rituals, and divining. Women are portrayed as false prophetesses under the influence of demonic forces or trafficking in love magic, maleficium, and magic poisonings. Although female magic tended to be domestic and not the kind of activity that, for the most part, commanded notice in historical works, when their facility with amatory sorcery or poisons (for instance) affected public figures and events, it did become a topic of the genre. Histories and annals reveal how writers perceived magic in situ and can function as a microscope to examine how magic in proscriptive sources such as penitentials, laws, and conciliar canons operated. Unlike penitentials and sermons, which were produced by the educated but tailored for average people, histories and annals were written by and for elite, hieratic, monastic, and court audiences.

There was a difference over time in terms of the types of magic that featured as publicly significant. Unlike classical pagan histories, those of the early church allowed demons onto the historical stage as agents of false religion and illusory divination. But as Arnaldo Momigliano observes in reference to the Merovingian era, "the devils seem to have respected the classical distinction of literary genres. They established themselves in biography, but made only occasional irruptions into the field of *annales*."[100]

Matthew Innes and Rosamond McKitterick propose that a new concept of history writing developed in the Carolingian period that "amounts to an historical revolution" in terms of range, quantity, and the significance.[101] Still, Carolingian historians did not differ from classical or Merovingian writers in terms of the role magic plays in their works. When references to magic appear in histories, chronicles, and annals, then, they pertain to matters of civic concern or provide an explanation for events of communal

---

100. Momigliano, "Pagan and Christian Historiography," 90–93 (quotation 93). See also Muhlberger, *Fifth-Century Chroniclers*, 1–6, 271–74; Graus, "Hagiographie und Dämonenglauben"; McCormick, *Les annales*, 11–21.

101. Innes and McKitterick, "Writing of History," 193. See also Contreni, "Carolingian Renaissance," 751–53; Morse, *Truth and Convention*, 158–62; McKitterick, *Carolingians and the Written Word*, 238; Fleischman, "On the Representation"; Fredegar, *Fourth Book*, introd. See de Jong ("Empire as Ecclesia") on Raban Maur's use of exegesis as *historia*.

importance.[102] Although most histories do not have a great deal to say about magic, there is considerably more of it in Merovingian texts than in the histories the Carolingians produced. In itself, this does not attest to an increased skepticism on the part of the Carolingians, but rather to a more refined sense of genre.

Hagiography

Hagiography is a body of literature about the saints: their lives, suffering, deaths, deeds, postmortem miracles, cults, and the translation of their relics from place to place. It is a rich source for the study of magic, ritual power, and gender, inasmuch as the plots of the vitae often revolve around contests between competing forms of spiritual dominance. The saints formed the front line against paganism, magic, and unbelief, and they fought those battles armed with rival rites and symbols. Peter Brown is spot-on when he observes that "saints positively needed sorcerers" in order to prove their bone fides as spiritual gladiators.[103] Hagiography was a space where women were able to take center stage. Biographers frequently reminded the consumers of their writings that God does not "award the starry kingdom only on men, who are expected to enter the fight; even women win the prize for their valor."[104]

From the beginning, hagiography was a genre shared by a wide audience. It became the habit in monasteries across Christendom to mark the day of a given saint's death on a calendar in order to honor that saint annually. Vitae were produced to accompany these commemorative celebrations, and sections of the biographies were incorporated into liturgies and used extensively as devotional and educational aids—initially for religious, and eventually for lay communities.[105] This gave the laic exposure to clerical

---

102. Humphries, "Chronicle and Chronology"; Muhlberger, *Fifth-Century Chroniclers*, 1–6, 271–74.
103. Brown, *Making of Late Antiquity*, 22. See also Graus, "Hagiographie und Dämonenglauben."
104. Gregory of Tours, *De beata Monegunde* preface, in *Liber vitae partum*, 286: "Qui non solum viris legitime decertantibus, verum etiam feminis in his proeliis faborabiliter desudantibus siderea regna participat."
105. See Justin Martyr (*Apology on Behalf of Christians* 67.3–4, 259) on the public reading of the "memoirs of the apostles." Often called *The First Apology* (between 155–157 CE), Justin Martyr's petition is an apologetic work addressed to Emperor Antoninus Pius. From Gibson ("Carolingian World," 631–32), except for the upper-classes, Carolingian-era laity were less exposed to saints' lives than Merovingian laity had been. Also see Abou-El-Haj, *Medieval Cult of Saints*, 8–9. For the broad and varied audience for Merovingian hagiography see Van Uytfanghe, "L'hagiographie et son public." For early medieval popular access to hagiography, which decreased in the Carolingian era, see Lifshitz (*Norman Conquest*, 14–16).

interpretations of the dangers of demons and prophylactic measures to be taken against them. Some saints' cults were intensely local such as that of Acca of Hexham in Northumbria (d. ca. 740), and other holy persons were venerated throughout the Christian world, such as Antony, the desert saint (356). Although they were not strictly uniform, sacred biographies provided a commonality in the message people received about magic from community to community.

Hagiography is grounded in very particular conventions and can only be used with attention to those conventions, but its modes and purposes are, as Ian Wood writes, a "multiplicity" and it is "an infinitely flexible medium." Vitae were written to inspire emulation and perpetuate the memory of the saints, but they could also be "history . . . liturgy, theology, edification and propaganda."[106] One characteristic of sacred biographies is that sequences of events or reliable bibliographical references are often subordinate to an aura of timelessness in which mundane minutia is glossed over. Saints' biographies are "suprahistorical"; to quote Margot King, "The saint inhabits an atemporal world that is shot through with eternity."[107] However, the minutia is important to the historian. Hagiographical texts provide entrée into lived experience—not by virtue of the deeds of the super-sized saints, but through the unembroidered details that are incidental or inconsequential to the central, encoded narrative. For example, from the vita of Genovefa (d. 512) we learn that the young woman owned property and hired reapers to harvest her crops. This tidbit is instructive for scholars but tangential to the moral of the

---

106. I. Wood, "Use and Abuse," (quotations 93, 108–9). At some level, the differentiation between history and hagiography is arbitrary; on this see Gibson, "Carolingian World." Lifshitz ("Beyond Positivism") argues that history and hagiography do more than overlap; there is no distinction between them and the very notion of genre ought to be discarded. Lifshitz claims that the construct of "hagiography" was a nineteenth-century political and ideological tool. She criticizes scholars of the last one hundred years who (she claims) use empiricism as the yardstick for differentiating histories from sacred biographies. This assertion is an overgeneralization and does not take into account the scholarship on hagiography since Peter Brown's groundbreaking work. It is the case that both historiography and hagiography are "moralizing" (100) and that hagiography is a type of history set in a particular framework, but Lifshitz argues that there is no demarcation between saints' lives and what moderns might consider history proper because both were authored by the same persons, include miracles and the "supernatural," and draw on the Bible for inspiration and content. She ignores the different audiences, narrative structures, archetypes, breadth, and conventions that differentiate the two forms of writing. Further, women are more frequent and dominant players in hagiography than they are in histories, and magic operates quite differently in sacred biographies than it does in annals and histories.

107. King, s.v. "Hagiography," in Strayer, *Dictionary of the Middle Ages*. See also Patlagean, "Ancient Byzantine Hagiography," 111–12. From I. Wood ("Use and Abuse," 109), despite the genre's variability it is "first and foremost . . . a spiritual genre, dependent largely on Biblical models."

vignette in which the information is embedded; the point being that because of her prayers, Christ diverted a storm from the saint's fields.[108]

The striking similitude of holy biographies within a given cultural milieu was purposeful, because the goal of each life was to demonstrate the ways in which every saint shared in the meaning of Christ and the unified communion of saints. Further, the sameness of the saints' lives is due to the fact that hagiographers borrowed readily from one another and relied on biblical language and motifs. Due to the genre's dependence on traditional *topoi* and varied layers of borrowed material, ascertaining shifts in the understanding of magic through hagiographic sources is a creative enterprise. The vast literature on rewriting saints' lives tends to corroborate Robert Bartlett's conclusion that although hagiography "was a tough genre ... preserving distinctive features over the centuries," when vitae were reworked from one period to another, they assumed the values and stylistic concerns contemporary to the redactor. In other words, a ninth-century reworking of the magical elements in a hagiographic narrative inherited from the sixth century tells as much about ninth-century demonism as it does about sixth-century sorcery.[109]

Not every vita was as popular as the next or reached the same audience, but hagiography was a body of writing shared among all classes of people—read out loud in monasteries and at public festivals and captured in illuminations, stone, and glass at local churches and cathedrals. Vitae are important to the study of magic because hagiography was ubiquitous and cross-cultural, and, taken as a whole, sacred biographies shed light on virtually all categories of magic. Further, the genre is generous in yielding descriptions of magical rites, because one of the major goals of hagiography is to demonstrate the valor of the saints in their fight against evil and unbelief, and in numerous hagiographic texts those contests unfolded within the arena of ritual.

Creative Literature

"Creative literature" here means fictionalized works, poetry, hymns, and panegyrics produced to delight, flatter, entertain, commemorate, lament,

---

108. *Vita Genovefae* 50, 235–36. Palmer, *Anglo-Saxons*, 21–29.

109. Bartlett, "Rewriting Saints' Lives," 598. For entry into the vast scholarship of Carolingian hagiography see Gibson's impressive bibliography in "Carolingian World." Gibson demonstrates that hagiography surged in the eighth, ninth, and tenth centuries, but most of the saints venerated lived centuries earlier. For a useful discussion of how to interpret hagiography see Schoolman, *Rediscovering Sainthood*, chap. 3. See also Fouracre and Gerberding, *Late Merovingian France*, 37–42; Magennis, "'Listen Now All'"; J. M. H. Smith, "Problem of Female Sanctity"; Gehrke, *Saints and Scribes*, 1–11; Head, *Hagiography*, 20–57; Patlagean, "Ancient Byzantine Hagiography."

stir the emotions, or (in the case of satire) critique. Some creative literary texts cross genres in that the subject is historical but the prose is lyrical, and many plot elements are embroidered or completely fictional. As with every text, the interpretation of the information is dependent on the nature of the source. Each sort of creative literature is tied to a long tradition and fashioned by its own past.

The literature of the Merovingian and Carolingian eras was similar in many ways to that of late antiquity, and it was enriched by vernacular narratives. The themes were drawn from classical, biblical, and pre-Christian Celtic and German folklore.[110] Likewise, the prose style and linguistical elements were indebted to Roman and Latin influences and employ vulgarisms intended to make some pieces accessible to a varied, non-clerical audience. A good example of the fusion of Latin literature and German popular traditions is the epic poem *Waltharius*. Tales of Walter of Aquitaine, the legendary Visigothic king, are interspersed with classical references, especial from Vergil's *Aeneid*. There existed robust public audiences—both clerical and lay—that avidly consumed creative works. These audiences dwelt in villages and at court and religious centers, and they either read or listened to poems, *plancti*,[111] panegyrics, and heroic fiction.

Poetry was a vehicle for teaching, and polemizing. Virtually all the literary prose giants of the Carolingian era were poets as well.[112] Charlemagne's biographer Einhard (d. 840) tells us that Charlemagne himself transcribed and committed to memory "barbarous and ancient songs" (*barbara et antiquissima carmina*).[113] Magical elements appear in literary texts over the first millennium and are casually interwoven in the materials, reflecting the natural integration of magic in late antique and early medieval cultures.

Medical Materials

Herbal medical material provides a trove of information on magic and ritual; however, because of their practical nature, herbal texts are stingy when it comes to giving up the clues they hold about illness and wellness. Herbal *materia medica* discloses scant overt curative theory and articulates virtually

---

110. C. Edwards, "German Vernacular Literature." "The vernacular was viewed as a pagan and therefore a tainted idiom" (ibid., 142).

111. *Plancti* are poetic laments on tragic events or the death of a particular person; they were numerous in the Carolingian period and generally meant for a lay audience.

112. Contreni, "Carolingian Renaissance," 753–56; Garrison, "Emergence of Carolingian Latin Literature"; McKitterick, *Carolingians and the Written Word*, 227–35.

113. Einhard, *Vita Karoli Magni* 29, 33.

no explicit philosophical, metaphysical, or theological assumptions. One result is that the authors do not identify elements in the texts as demonic or magical when they seem clearly to be so if the reader compares the mechanics of the cures to magical procedures in other sources.[114]

In the classical period, the word *medicina* could refer to both *artes mechanicae* (practical) and *scientia* (theoretical),[115] and that bifurcation continued into the early Middle Ages. Medicine was considered a craft, like woodcarving, plowing, or butchering, but at the same time (though in different circles) texts circulated that were undergird by classical theory.[116] John Riddle has drawn up a list of three aspects of medieval medicine that demonstrate a continuation of healing practices from the Roman period. Medicine in the Latin West was non-institutionalized and informal, many experimental advances were not committed to writing but are evident in drug therapies, and a gap existed between theory and practice that minimized theory.[117] The similarity between ancient and early medieval therapeutics is that healing was not restricted to the specialist. Good health depended on maintaining a holistic approach to life: moderation, restraint, and spiritual purity. This ideal of the lay physician continued into the fourth century when Oribasius (d. ca. 400), a Greek medical author and doctor to Emperor Julian (d. 363), wrote, "It is desired, or really a necessity, that everyone should study medicine from youth alongside other fields and hear its principles, so that they can become good advisors in everything that is related to public safety."[118] It is this informality and marginalization of theory (particularly in herbals) that confronts the historian trying to understand how transmitters of the medical texts understood magic in the *materia medica*.

---

114. Siraisi, *Medieval and Early Renaissance Medicine*, 1–13.

115. From the fourth century BCE, medicine was perceived to be both a philosophy and a skill. Aristotle (*Treatise* 3.11, in *Politics of Aristotle*, 149–150) distinguished the practitioner who "makes up the medicines" from the theoretician "who understands the science." See Seneca (*Ep.* 88, 2:348–76) for the classical differentiation between *artes* and *scientia*. The Romans tended to slight learned theory and avoid abstract discussions of the body. Pliny (*Natural History* 29.8, vol. 8 [418], 192–201) complained that in Rome medicine as *scientia* was insufficiently studied, and as a result, practitioners were dangerous to the public.

116. For example, from Isidore of Seville, *Etymologiarum* bk. 4, especially 4.5.1, vol. 1: "Sanitas est integritas corporis et temperantia naturae ex calido et humido, quod est sanguis, unde et sanitas dicta est, quasi sanguinis status"; ibid., 4.13.1, vol. 1: "Quaeritur a quibusdam quare inter ceteras liberales disciplinas medicinae ars non contineatur. Propterea, quia illae singulares continent causas, ista vero omnium"; ibid., 4.9.3–7, vol. 1: "Pharmacia est medicamentorum curatio. . . . Contraria enim contrariis medicinae ratione curantur."

117. Riddle, "Theory and Practice," 158–59.

118. Oribasius, *Oribasii collectionum medicarum reliquiae* 3.164, 4:139, cited in Scarborough, *Roman Medicine*, 125. See also Getz, *Medicine*, 5.

MAGIC AND ITS SOURCES

Several sources provide evidence of practicing doctors at European courts and in urban centers,[119] but the monastery was the setting for most of the curative activity of the early Middle Ages, both in terms of healing and for transmission of texts. Monks and nuns did more than apply medicines made from ancient recipes; they developed new drugs and improved on the old, altering classical formulas for local use. The populace came to monasteries for treatment, and lay and clerical healers labored together. There is every reason to believe that most women and men were familiar with medical practices at some level, and several herbal recipes direct the sick to act as their own physicians. It is likely, therefore, that the average person was exposed to and carried out recommendations that involved magical procedures.[120]

During the ninth century, the perception of therapeutics began to change. Medicine was not originally part of the *quadrivium* that the Roman authors Martianus Capella (d. ca. 420) and Boethius (d. c. 524) developed; however, within the Carolingian educational program, the inclusion of medicine in the liberal arts became standard, and medicine was recognized as a theoretical discipline. As John Contreni points out, the Carolingians' major contribution to medical science was that they made "the study of medicine, like the study of the liberal arts, intellectually respectable."[121] However, it is important to stress that the new respectability of medicine as a discipline did not prompt revision of utilitarian medical texts or an eradication of the magical elements in them.

Though theoretical treatises were limited to an educated readership, a class of medical literature that circulated widely in early medieval Europe was collected descriptions of ailments and their cures. In this aggregation of texts are herbals, zootherapeutical cures employing animal parts or substances, and assortments of prayers, chants, and charms. The herbal is a practical handbook—a pharmacopoeia—which is generally arranged using a plant name as a rubric under which are listed the ailments for which the plant

---

119. Leja, "Sacred Art," 1–2; Riddle, "Theory and Practice," 166n36; Riché, *Education and Culture*, 69–71, 142–43, 252–53. From Gregory of Tours (*Decem libri historiarum* 8.31, 398), Fredegund kept experienced doctors in her household. Also, ibid., 5.14, 209. On the court of Alfred the Great see Asser, *Medieval Life of King Alfred* 74, 32–33. See also Eigil, *Vita S. Strum* 24, 377. See Nokes ("Several Compilers," 74) on the emerging "portrait of a body of professional leeches" in Anglo-Saxon England.

120. Contreni, "Masters and Medicine"; M. L. Cameron, "Bald's *Leechbook*." From Everett ("Manuscript Evidence," 119), Cassiodorus advised his monks to learn the properties of herbs and "perform the compounding of drugs punctiliously."

121. Contreni, "Masters and Medicine" (quotation 268).

is a remedy.[122] Various redactions and excised portions of the Greek physician Dioscorides's (d. 90 CE) herbal were the most influential of the manuals of applied medicine in the medieval world. His herbal, *De materia medica*, sports a long lineage of works similar to it reaching back into antiquity, and by the sixth century it had been translated into Latin. Drug prescriptions of Dioscorides and the works of Oribasius and the Roman *medicus* Galen (d. ca. 200) were conveyed in individual treatises or incorporated into larger collections.[123]

The magic and ritual incorporated into the *materia medica* present an interpretative challenge because of the nature of the texts. They are practical, not didactic; they are manuals, not treatises. Magic as such is rarely mentioned, but it is implied as the cause of disease and also at times employed as therapy. So, to interpret magic in herbal literature, we must put it in apposition to expressions of magic from other contemporary sources.

Textual Borrowing

Those who peopled late classical and early medieval Europe were mistrustful of novelty; they valued authority, timelessness, and convention—often slavishly. The desire to position texts within a reputable tradition meant that authors borrowed liberally from other written sources, often without attribution.[124] This practice complicates the work of historians wishing to understand change over time. The problem is exacerbated when information in a text is not easily verifiable by evidence external to that text, as is often the case with reference to magic. The question then becomes to what extent might our data on popular culture, and magic specifically, be a collection of desiccated borrowings from one authoritative text to another that fail to represent lived experience? It is my view that we are in danger of distortion if our default is to distrust information about ordinary people

---

122. Baader, "Die Anfänge."

123. Predecessors to Dioscorides (all of whom lived in the fourth and fifth centuries) were Sextus Placitus, Marcellus Empiricus of Bordeaux, and Cassius Felix. Theodorus Priscian, physician to the emperor Gratian, wrote a simple alphabetical herbal entitled *De virtutibus pigmentorum vel herbarum aromaticarum*. Much of it is based on Galen's work with plants.

124. What we in the modern world might call forgery was, in the medieval past, generally respect, humility or a strategy of legitimization. Writings are often unsigned or attributed to a personage the author wished to honor or emulate. See G. Austin "Jurisprudence" on forgery in Burchard of Worm's *Decretum*. Bouchard (*Rewriting Saints and Ancestors*, 1–2) notes that medieval societies were "traditional," not because they were unchanging, but because tradition carried "enormous moral and legal weight."

because we get it through an elite clerical lens or because descriptions of it are so frequently stock.

Too often magical practice is held to a more stringent standard of proof as to its credibility than other sorts of behavior. For example, Rudi Künzel suggests a taxonomy of nine criteria for determining whether a textual description of pagan religious survivals was based on first-hand observation. He asserts that in order to accept the verisimilitude of a practice (1) a similar behavior must be described in a text of a different genre; (2) it must be non-stereotypical but listed amid stereotypical descriptions of commonly described behaviors; (3, 4) the same practice must be described in the same locality in two independent texts separated by a significant interval of time, and there must be differing interpretations in those texts of the same practice; (5) a new detail which is plausible must be added to the description of a traditional behavior; (6) the terminology describing the behavior must employ a vernacular term; 7) the purpose of the text (for example, baptismal vows) must be designed for a specific group (8) the more stereotypical a document is the less likely it is to have recorded genuine behaviors; (9) there must be an element in the text that is a distortive Christian interpretation (like a fairy being labeled a demon).[125]

Künzel's litmus test is overly rigorous and puts an undue burden of proof on aspects of early medieval popular culture. Pierre Payer correctly asks why a historian would not doubt the reality of a workaday sin such as murder or theft, but is skeptical of behaviors that seem improbable to us.[126]

Positions vary widely as to how much a given source reflects actual observation. Bernadette Filotas is overly cautious when she says that handbooks of penance "rarely offer insights into popular culture. The majority relied on earlier models passed from monastery to monastery, and show little response to actual situations."[127] The implication is that the very fact of borrowing is evidence that the behaviors were not "actual." It is just as likely that models were passed down over time and across Europe because clerics needed guidance in responding to "actual situations," even if the language they used was traditional—even mimetic. Yitzak Hen goes one step beyond Filotas and argues that not just penitentials, but "the vast majority of magical practices mentioned in our ecclesiastically biased sources are not only repetitive ad nauseam but also somewhat irrelevant to the context in which

---

125. Künzel, "Paganisme," 1060–62.
126. Payer, *Sex and the Penitentials*, 12–14.
127. Filotas, *Pagan Survivals*, 357. Filotas's assessment of sources other than the penitentials is more optimistic: "Nevertheless, certain differences show that in part at least [authors] based themselves on their own observations of the behaviour of their contemporaries."

they were supposedly performed."[128] Hen sets aside even the stringent criteria that Rudi Künzel charts.[129] To accept Hen's assessment, is to conclude that intellectuals mindlessly transferred devitalized data from text to text for centuries. Borrowing was an accepted, common, and necessary practice (not "ad nauseum," to use Hen's words).[130] Reliance on models does not preclude contemporality, nor, for that manner, is it a foregone conclusion that when a new element emerges in a list of oft-repeated practices that the added information is credible and contemporaneous by virtue of its novelty. Guidelines are useful, but determining whether a text describes a relatively honest facsimile of historical reality is less science and more art. In the end, textual evidence must be evaluated one element at a time.

Gendered Language

An awareness of the gendered bias of the primary texts is central to my methodology. Evaluating the extent to which various sources expressly target the behaviors of women is complicated by several factors. One is that the Latin use of the grammatical masculine when referring to groups of all men or groups of mixed gender makes it difficult to determine whether particular references include women as well as men. Further, there is a basic male-centeredness in the thinking and rhetoric of the period such that the generic human being was perceived to be male. The following examples come from the penitentials, but the phenomenon is not unique to them. The subject of a particular penitential canon is not always obvious. Many canons address "anyone" (*quis*), which could include women. Often requirements or prohibitions begin with the second-person plural: "you," as in *fecisti* (have you done?) or *credidisti* (have you believed?), in which case the contents of the canon could refer to men only, to women only, or to men and women. We know from some of the prefaces to the penitentials that the books were

---

128. Hen, "Early Medieval West," 187 (quotation). For a less absolute appraisal of the relationship of written sources to actual practice see Hen, *Culture and Religion*, 167–72.

129. From Lawrence-Mathers ("Problem of Magic," 100), Anglo-Saxon penitentials "do genuinely address issues perceived as both current and real"; Theuws argues ("Introduction," 6), "Many actions are of an habitual character, hence repetitive, but not for that reason without meaning, nor performed unreflectively." From Gurevich (*Medieval Popular Culture*, 37), penitentials were "practical guides." From Frantzen (*Literature of Penance*, 56), real sins really confessed provided the source material for Anglo-Saxon handbooks of penance.

130. Meens ("Magic," 286) correctly argues that descriptions of magic rites derive from a "literary tradition" and may not attest to the continuance of the rite, but borrowed language does indicate a perceived and "enduring" need for material from the derivative text. I add that virtually all medieval texts derive from a "literary tradition."

MAGIC AND ITS SOURCES   61

written with laymen and laywomen in mind.[131] For that reason, we might assume that if a canon begins *si quis* (if anyone), the sin it describes could be committed by men or women. However, frequently canons that begin as gender neutral and seemingly speak to an audience of men and women are clearly addressing men only, inasmuch as they refer to sexual crimes against women, activities involving wives, and so forth. For example, canon 35 of the Irish *Penitential of Finnian* (sixth century), begins, "If one of the laity is converted to the Lord from his evil actions who has previously committed all kinds of evil deeds, such as fornication . . . he shall do penance for three years . . . and not remain with his wife." Although this canon appears to pertain to all laity, for the author, the male is normative.[132]

When writers mean a penance to be specific to women, they make that apparent. For instance, canon 2.17 of the Irish *Penitential of Cummean* (between 650–700) imposes a penance of one year on bread and water for a cleric who commits fornication, and adds, "also a virgin" (*sic et virgo*). The *Old Irish Table of Commutations* (late eighth century) says, "There is hardly a single layman or laywoman who has not [had] some part in manslaughter." The penitential authors, perhaps subconsciously, seemed to have had only men in mind unless they specifically named women in their comments.[133] This deference to the male is standard in virtually all categories of texts.

An accurate picture of magic in the late antique and early medieval West requires coaxing out and piecing together information from as many sources as possible. It is only by this method that we can view the full panorama of magic and understand how those who left written witness and those who did not write perceived and practiced magic. The nonliterate population constituted an audience for some of the written sources, such as sermons, letters, hagiography, literary works, and medical materials, and their lives and views are also reflected in other sources to which they would never have had direct

---

131. One example is *Poenitentiale Theodori* preface, in *Councils and Ecclesiastical Documents*, 3:176–77: "Multi quoque non solum viri, sed etiam feminae de his ab eo inextinguibili feruore accensi sitim hanc ad sedandam ardenti cum desiderio frequentari huius nostri nimirum saeculi singularis scientiae hominem festinabant."

132. *Poenitentiale Vinniai* 35, in *Die Bussbücher*, 1:506–7: "De laicis si quis ex malis actibus suis conversus fuerit ad Dominum et omne malum antea egerit, i.e. fornicando . . . III annis peniteat . . . et non maneat cum uxore sua." See Meens (*Penance*, 45–61) on Finnian's and Cummean's penitentials, which are two of the earliest handbooks of penance.

133. *Paenitentiale Cummeani* 2.17, 114; *Old Irish Table of Commutations* 8, 278–79, both in *Irish Penitentials*. Another example is *Poenitentiale Theodori* 14.2 in *Councils and Ecclesiastical Documents*, 3:187: "Digamus poeniteat I annum, IV et VI feria et in tribus XLmis abstineat se a carnibus, non dimittat tamen uxorem."

exposure, such as learned treatises and histories. Any given "magic" is colored by the conventions and functions of the kind of text that recorded it. Silences in a particular written work can be deceptive, in that the failure of a source type to address a certain kind of magic does not necessarily indicate indifference or skepticism, but may be a function of genre. A vast array of materials must be used in the investigation of magic because magic does not restrict itself to any one category of texts, so interwoven was it with the entire fabric of early Christian and medieval life.

🌀 Chapter 2

Demons of the Lower Air

> Antony went out to the tombs that were situated some distance from the village. He charged one of his friends to supply him periodically with bread, and he entered one of the tombs and remained alone within, his friend having closed the door on him. When the enemy could stand it no longer—for he was apprehensive that Antony might before long fill the desert with the discipline—approaching one night with a multitude of demons he whipped him with such force that he lay on the earth, speechless from the tortures.... [But Antony said,] "If you are able, and you did receive authority over me, don't hold back, but attack. But if you are unable, why, when it is vain, do you disturb me? For faith in our Lord is for us a seal and a wall of protection." So after trying many strategies, they gnashed their teeth because of him, for they made fools not of him, but of themselves.
>
> —Athanasius, *Life of Antony*

This account from Bishop Athanasius of Alexandria's (d. ca. 373) paradigmatic fourth-century vita of Saint Antony opens a widow onto the world of the early Christian demon, here playing the role of foil to the saintly hermit.[1] This chapter takes a close-up look at demons such as those who plagued Antony in the stark Egyptian desert. I aggregate materials from a broad spectrum of time and space in order to tease these sublunary creatures out of the sources and to explain the circumstances under which humans' collaboration with demons constituted magic. Although there were shifts in beliefs about magic from the patristic period across the early medieval centuries, the concept of "the demon" was remarkably stable throughout the first thousand years of the Common Era.

---

1. Athanasius, *Life of Antony* 8–9, 37–39. Athanasius wrote Antony's vita in the mid-fourth century while himself an exile in the desert. The text was translated into Latin shortly after the author's death, and it was widely influential within the world of early Christianity (and after) both in the Greek East and Latin West.

Demons had a very specific place in late antique and early medieval cosmology. Christianity developed in a world with a well-articulated understanding of a multilayered and hierarchical universe that was, above all, animated. Most inhabitants of the ancient pre-Christian Fertile Crescent and Levant envisioned cosmic energy as sentient. The essence of physical, spiritual, and ethical awareness rested in a host of living beings, varying in their degree of corporeality.[2]

By the first century CE, virtually all pagan philosophic schools challenged or rejected the idea of anthropomorphic deities.[3] Most intellectuals were convinced of a supreme intelligence or intelligences that ordered the universe and—according to many thinkers—created it. The Roman Platonist Apuleius of Madaura (d. ca. 170) expounds this position in his *Apology*. He writes, "Who is that king: the cause and reason and first origin of all natural things, the ultimate father of the soul, the eternal protector of all the living, the perpetual creator of his world. But he works without labor, he preserves without care, he fathers without reproducing. He knows no limitation of space or time or change, and few can conceive and none can articulate the extent of his power."[4] Philosophers such as Apuleius interpreted stories of the deities' negative emotions, such as rage, jealousy, and lust, metaphorically and imagined the gods and goddesses of Olympus as aspects of or subordinates to a supreme deity, who was often envisioned as the sun.[5]

Along with the supreme being, and in a pyramidal relationship to it, there existed a multitude of vital forces. Neoplatonic philosophers viewed the universe and its constituent parts as a finely calibrated hierarchy of "means" connecting polar extremes and yoking together opposites through a series of intermediaries. This relationship was analogized as a "great chain of being," about which the Roman Platonist Macrobius (fl. 400 CE) wrote, "From the Supreme God even to the bottom-most dregs of the universe, there is one tie,

---

2. G. Shaw, "Theurgy: Rituals"; Brown, *Making of Late Antiquity*, 9.
3. For example Cicero, *De natura deorum* 1.25–36, 68–101; Alcinous, *Handbook of Platonism* 15.2, 25; Augustine, *De civitate Dei* 8.5, 1:221–22.
4. Apuleius of Madaura, *Apulei apologia* 64: "Quisnam sit ille basileus, totius rerum naturae causa et ratio et origo initialis, summus animi genitor, aeternus animantum sospitator, adsiduus mundi sui opifex, sed enim sine opera opifex, sine cura sospitator, sine propagatione genitor, neque loco neque tempore neque vice ulla comprehensus eoque paucis cogitabilis, nemini effabilis." Apuleius wrote the *Apologia* for his own defense (158/159 CE), when he was tried for employing the magic arts. See also Augustine, *De civitate Dei* 8.1, 1:216–17; 8.5–6, 1:221–24 where he states that the wisest pagan philosophers agree that God created the visible world and every creature in it.
5. MacMullen, *Paganism*, 73–94; Augustine, *De civitate Dei* 4.11–12, 1:108–10.

binding at every link and never broken. This is the golden chain of Homer which . . . God ordered to hang down from the sky to the earth."[6]

Toward the top of the hierarchy, close to the almighty, were the great demons (also called angels), some of whom took the form of planets, which was a general term for heavenly bodies that included the sun and moon.[7] These beings existed in the upper air that was brilliant with light—they were intelligent, living beings who were exalted physically and morally. The element that dominated in the upper air was fire (or for Aristotle [d. 322 BCE], ether), the most excellent of the four elements. It was the abode of godlike creatures and heroes. The possibility of humans achieving astral immortality was a tenet of late antique Jewish and pagan sects.[8] As the Emperor Julian lay dying in 363 CE, he rebuked the mourners who surrounded his deathbed, saying, "It [is] unworthy to mourn for a prince who was called to union with heaven and the stars."[9]

According to Neoplatonic thinking, other demons, those of the lower air—the space between the earth and the moon—were less exalted in their disposition than the beings constituting the planets and stars. They were positioned between humans and gods and were at times viewed as something akin to guardian angels guiding people through life's vicissitudes.[10] All humans had these sentinel demons assigned to them at birth to help direct their courses. When speaking of the impending death of Emperor Constantius II (d. 361 CE), the Roman historian Ammianus Marcellinus (d. ca. 395)

---

6. Macrobius, *Commentary* 14.15, 145.

7. *Books of Enoch*, 7–22. From Irenaeus of Lyon (*Against the Heresies* 5.2, 1:34), the Gnostic Valentinus claimed that Paradise was a powerful angel above the third heaven. Irenaeus wrote the five books of *Adversus haereses* in Greek (later translated into Latin) at the request of his friend (most likely a bishop) in order to arm his readers against Gnostic theologies. On the sun and moon as planets see Eastwood, "Astronomy of Macrobius," 124–30; for heavenly bodies see Brown, *Rise of Western Christendom*, 145.

8. Justin Martyr, *Justin, Philosopher and Martyr*, 62; Janowitz, *Magic in the Roman World*, 70–82.

9. Ammianus Marcellinus, *History* 25.3.22, 2:500–501: "Humile esse, caelo sideribusque conciliatum lugeri principem dicens." On pagan notions of the astral afterlife see Justin Martyr, *Apology on Behalf of Christians* 21.2–3, 133–35; Janowitz, *Icons of Power*, 64–65. From Brown (*Cult of the Saints*, 1–22), the rise of Christianity and its focus on the anthropomorphized dead severed the relationship between the deceased and the stars.

10. According to Brown (*Making of Late Antiquity*, 75), the mixing of elements in demons made them anomalous creatures—confusing and dangerous, responsible for disorder and disruption in human social relations. See also Janowitz, *Magic in the Roman World*, 33–35; Johannessen, *The Demonic*, 54–55; Brakke, *Demons*, 10–13; G. Shaw, *Theurgy and the Soul*, 8–9; Brown, *Cult of the Saints*, 51; Nock, "Paul and the Magus," 314. Jews and Christians also had a belief in guardian angels; Peter's angel led him from prison when Herod had him arrested (Acts 12:6–17). From D. Martin ("When Did Angels," 675n63), the mid-second-century collection of visions called *The Shepherd of Hermas* (Mandate 6) says that each person has a righteous and a wicked angel.

explained that the emperor knew disaster was about to strike because he could no longer see his familiar spirit or angel.[11]

Like the human being, the demon was a synthetic entity, but with exaggerated characteristics. Demons participated in both the divine and the profane, linking the upper air and earth. They were akin to the gods because they shared in their immortality, but they were also subject to obnoxious, irrational cravings.[12] Demons were corporeal, though of a material much lighter than and superior to the human form—more like that of the greater demons of the upper air. These devils of the lower air could move faster than mortals, read thoughts, and slip in and out of spaces impossible for the human body to occupy. They could inhabit the bodies of "rapacious wild beasts and other very evil animals."[13] Owing in part to these capabilities, demons were the agents of magic. Apuleius shared Plato's (d. ca. 348/347 BCE) belief that "in the middle space between gods and humans, there are certain divine powers with a composite nature that govern all divinations and the miracles of magicians." And Alcinous, a Greek Platonic philosopher of the second century CE wrote, "There are, furthermore, other divinities, the daemons, whom one could also term 'created gods.' . . . To their administration the whole sublunar and terrestrial sphere has been assigned. . . . From them derive omens and presages, dreams and oracles, and all artificial divination performed by mortals."[14] The ancients held that divination was a worthy and legitimate use of demonic power but that magic was an ignoble and, if harmful, a criminal employment of the "airy" creatures. Over the course of the second century CE, demons came to be more and more identified with perversity, deception, and their earthly nature.[15]

A parallelism was thought to exist between the macrocosm (God and his universe) and the microcosm (the individual human). Marcus Manilius, a poet and astronomer in the early first century CE, elucidated this relationship

---

11. Ammianus Marcellinus, *History* 21.14.2, 2:166–67.

12. Augustine, *De civitate Dei* 8.14–17, 1:230–35; 10.11, 1:284; 10.27, 1:301–3. Augustine notes that according to Apuleius, the demons of the lunar and sublunar regions are disturbed by passions, unlike the higher gods such as the sun, moon, and other luminaries in the ether (301). For a thorough discussion of Augustine on demons see ibid., bk. 9. See also Markus, "Augustine on Magic," 378–79.

13. Augustine, *De divinatione daemonum* 3, 603–5; Tertullian, *Apologeticum* 22–23, 1:128–33; Origen, *Contra Celsum* 4.92, 257 (quotation); Minucius Felix, *Octavius* 26–27, 43–47. *Octavius* (n.d.) is a fictional dialogue between a pagan and Christian elucidating and defending Christianity for an educated non-Christian audience.

14. Apuleius of Madaura, *Apulei apologia* 43: "Inter deos atque homines natura et loco medias quasdam divorum potestates intersitas, easque divinationes cunctas et magorum miracula gubernare." Alcinous, *Handbook of Platonism* 15.1–2, 25.

15. Johannessen, *The Demonic*, 46–50; Brown, *Making of Late Antiquity*, 18–20, 25.

when he said, "Why wonder that men can comprehend heaven, when heaven exists in their very beings and each is in a smaller likeness the image of God himself?"[16] The Roman statesman and intellectual Cicero (d. 43 BCE) held that godhood bears the same relationship to matter in the universe as the human soul bears to the human body. According to this view, the macrocosmic world soul mediates between the pure being of god and the sensible plane. In the human microcosm, the intelligent soul both comprehends the divine and has an animal element that condemns it to temptation by the passions.[17]

Those who perceived the universe in Neoplatonic terms, however, represented only a narrow slice of the ancient world's population. In the first three centuries of the Common Era, the religious tableau was a variegated mosaic reaching up and down the social register. A multitude of spiritual systems flourished, including traditional public cults of the Etruscan/Greco-Roman gods and goddesses, with the cult of the emperor added in the early first century. The anthropomorphized deities of the Roman pantheon may have seemed hackneyed to Neoplatonists, but judging by epigraphic evidence and the persistent fervor with which Christian writers vilified them, it is safe to assume that traditional gods and goddesses maintained their credibility and worth for many, including some educated people who comprised the audience for Christian apologetics.[18] Also in the mix were snatches of pre–Roman ancestor devotion, hearth deities, the worship of the solar god Sol Invictus (especially in the military),[19] Judaism in its many sects, Gnostic creeds, a plethora of Eastern mystery cults in continual mutation and adaptation to new locales, and diverse forms of Christianity. One thing each of these belief systems had in common with philosophic schools and with each other was the knowledge that an inexorable aspect of the universal scheme included demons.[20]

Valerie Flint contends that the church "rescued" demons from late antique cosmology. She argues that demons "were one of the features of the old pre-Christian magical world most enthusiastically transferred," and

---

16. Manilius, *Astronomica* 4, 292–95 ; Lindberg, *Beginnings of Western Science*, 139.
17. Cicero, *De natura deorum* 2.7–8, 140–45; 2.30–35, 194–211.
18. Ehrman, *Lost Christianities*, 95–12; MacMullen, *Paganism*, 62–73, 112–30; Weltin, "Concept of *Ex–Opere–Operato* Efficacy."
19. Berrens, *Sonnenkult und Kaisertum*, 9–15, 184–204; R. Smith, *Julian's Gods*, 163–78.
20. K. King, *What Is Gnosticism?*, 5–19; Betz, *Gottesbegegnung und Menschwerdung*, 1–43; Brown, "Sorcery," 131. For demons in Judaism see Werblowsky and Wigoder, *Oxford Dictionary of the Jewish Religion*, s.v. "Demons."

that "if demons had not existed it would have been necessary to invent them."[21] Flint's argument would turn Christian theology into sociology. The church did not "rescue," salvage, or in any way fabricate the creatures of the middle air; they simply were known to exist. Far from making decisions about beliefs within a vacuum suspended above the world that engendered them, Christian cultures were enclosed within the same "natural" system as their religious competitors, and that system included demons, miracles, and magic.[22]

Christians did, however, rethink the role of demons. Unlike most other ancient cults, in which demons could be agents for good or ill, in the Christian scheme demons were by definition evil.[23] Justin Martyr (d. ca. 165), a Platonic philosopher and advocate for the infant church was born in Roman Palestine. He addressed a tract to the Roman senate that has come to be called *The Second Apology*.[24] It lays out the seminal explanation of the role of demons in Christian thought—inspired by Hellenistic Jewish belief as expressed in the books of Enoch, the Book of Jubilees (5, 7, 10), and other pseudepigrapha (ca. 300 BCE to ca. 300 CE).[25] The sons of God "succumbed to intercourse with women, and begot children—who are called demons. They then went on to enslave the human race to themselves, partly through magical changes . . . partly through instruction about sacrifices and incense and libations—things they have needed ever since they were enslaved by passions and desires. And they sowed amongst human

---

21. Flint, *Rise of Magic*, 127–72 (quotations 157, 102). J. A. Smith (*Ordering Women's Lives*, 89–90) and Baker ("Shadow of the Christian Symbol") adopt Flint's appraisal of demons and "Christian magic." For a critique of Flint's argument see Hen, "Early Medieval West," 193–98; Rampton, "Gender of Magic," 32–36; Kieckhefer, "Specific Rationality"; A. Murray "Missionaries and Magic."

22. For a comprehensive discussion of the Neoplatonic view of demons and its influence on patristic thinkers (particularly Eusebius) see Johannessen, *The Demonic*, 43–74; Janowitz, *Magic in the Roman World*, 27–46. Brown ("Sorcery," 122) writes, "Nor is it certain that the religious and intellectual changes of Late Antiquity greatly changed the basic attitude of ancient men to sorcery."

23. Augustine, *De civitate Dei* 9.19, 1:269; G. Shaw, *Theurgy and the Soul*, 9–15.

24. For a full discussion of the apologetic texts, their audiences, and legacy see *Justin, Philosopher and Martyr*, 3–77.

25. From *Complete Books of Enoch* (6–7, pp. 25–29), the myth of the angels' fall from heaven is first mentioned in *1 Enoch* 1–36 (*Book of the Watchers*) which teaches that two hundred fallen angels, called Watchers, lusted after and raped the daughters of man, from whence were born "evil spirits" who led humans to sacrifice "to demons as gods" (quotations 19.1–3, 38). Reed ("Trickery") discusses the impact of the Enochic *Book of the Watchers* (third or second century BCE) on the Christian understanding of the angelic descent myth in Genesis 6:1–4 that persisted until the early fifth century. See also Johannessen, *The Demonic*, 65–70; D. Martin, "When did Angels"; *Complete Books of Enoch*, 1–22. Some writers, such as Augustine (*Quaestionum in Heptateuchum* 1.3, 2), held that the Nephilim were ordinary humans—offspring of the rebellious Seth (the son of Adam and Eve) who mated with the children of his brother Cain. Augustine held that the word "giant" (*gigantes*) should be interpreted as "strong" not as an oversized monster.

beings murders, wars, adulteries, licentiousness, and every kind of evil" (cf. Gen 6:1–4). The progeny of the fallen angels and human women were the Nephilim (meaning giants), and Justin took a bold leap by claiming that the pagan gods, all of them, were, in fact, the Nephilims' offspring who still haunt the earth.[26]

The North African theologian Tertullian (d. after 220) elaborated on Justin's explanation by drawing from the Enochic *Book of the Watchers* where the Nephilim teach their human consorts "charms and sorceries, the cutting of roots, and the uses of plants." Exploiting female "vanity," the giants provided their wives with jewels, makeup, and "the power of spells" (*incantationum vires*). So just as sin entered the world through women (all "Eves"), so did magic.[27]

Augustine held that the beneficent beings with fiery bodies that the Platonists mistook for virtuous demons were really the angels of the upper air. His interpretation differed from Justin Martyr's in that he identified the demons of the lower air, not as the gigantic children born of angels and human women, but as the rebel angels who fought alongside and suffered the same fate as Lucifer (also Belial, Beelzebub, the Devil, Satan, and the "Day Star" [Isa. 14:12]). Once an archangel, because of overweening pride and envy of God, Lucifer was cast out of heaven after he mounted a colossal war against virtuous forces led by the archangel Michael (Rev. 12:7–9). Pride itself came to be seen as a surefire path to the vice of magic because of its centrality in the perversion of the fallen angels.[28]

There was inconsistency in the understanding of what the damned angels' role in salvation history was after the fall. The *Book of Nicodemus* (after 555), which Philip Almond claims "was perhaps the most influential and authoritative of all early Christian writings" except for the New Testament Gospels themselves, discusses the harrowing of hell. In this narrative, Jesus, after his resurrection, descended to Hades to unloose the chains of the

---

26. Justin Martyr, *Second Apology* 4.3–4, 283. For a discussion of the evolution of the Christian understanding of the Devil and the fallen angels see Almond, *Devil*, 1–15; Pseudo-Clement, *Recognitions*, 1.29, 85; Pagels, "Social History of Satan." The *Recognitions* is a fictional account of one Clement (perhaps a reference to Clement I, bishop of Rome) who travels with the apostle Peter throughout the eastern Mediterranean preaching the gospel. The monk Rufinus translated the work into Latin in the late fourth century.

27. *Complete Books of Enoch* 7.1–6, 29; Tertullian, *De cultu feminarum* 1.1–2, 1:343–46; 2.10, 1:364–66; idem, *De idolatria* 4.2, 2:1103–4. For Tertullian's Enochic source see Nickelsburg, *1 Enoch 1* 8.1–3, 188; 9.6–9, 202. See also Almond, *Devil*, 4–5; Elliott, "Tertullian."

28. Augustine, *De civitate Dei* 11.15, 2:336. See Martin of Braga, *Pride* 5, 45–46; Alcuin, *De virtutibus et vitiis* 23 (cols. 630–31), 27 (cols. 632–33). Alcuin wrote *De virtutibus et vitiis* (799/800) for Guy, Charlemagne's designated margrave in Brittany; Alcuin was concerned that Guy may become vainglorious due to his military success.

righteous souls who had lived before him and lead them out of the shadowy cavern. Satan was then bound with irons and cast into the abyss of hell where he oversaw doomed sinners who were mercilessly tormented by devils. There Satan will remain until Christ's second coming. This account does not square with the narrative that Satan and his demonic angels reside in the air above the earth, and the discrepancy vexed demonologists throughout the early Middle Ages.[29]

Irrespective of differing theories on the origin of demons, there was consensus in the belief that pagan deities were actually demons of the lower air. Patristic theologians took their cue from the Psalms: "For all the gods of the peoples are idols" (Ps. 96.5), and from Saint Paul: "What pagans sacrifice, they sacrifice to demons not to God" (1 Cor. 10:20).[30]

Christians demonized the pantheons of Mediterranean cults, and as their religion spread across Europe, in a process of *interpretatio Romana*, Celtic, Germanic, and Norse deities and lesser (or "non-obvious") beings such as fairies, goblins, satyrs, and *pilosi* (hirsute creatures) were folded into the genera of "demons."[31] David Frankfurter makes an astute observation that applies to Christian expansion. He writes that hegemonic religions tend to systematize demonology, with the effect that village-level evil or mischievous beings, such as spirits, sprites, and elves, are cut away from their local and idiosyncratic contexts, caught up, redefined, abstracted, and incorporated into larger ideologies that claim "*greater* authority over spirits. . . . In this process, demons get collected from their local domains and ambiguous intentions, abstracted in lists, polarized as uniformly hostile, and speculatively combined with opposing gods or angels."[32] In this way, the demonology that developed in the Near East and Mediterranean became normative in western European intellectual orbits as Christianity spread.

Christian thinking, both in the patristic era and throughout the early Middle Ages, was in accord with that of the ancients in viewing the air between heaven and earth as the abode of demons. At the end of the first millennium Bishop Burchard of Worms said, "Unclean spirits who slipped from the

---

29. Almond, *Devil*, 56–61 (quotation 57).

30. Justin Martyr, *Apology on Behalf of Christians* 5.1–2, 88–91; Origen, *Contra Celsum* 3.29, 146–47; 3.34, 150–51; 3.37, 153–54; Augustine, *Enarrationes in Psalmos* 95.5, 1347–48.

31. Shaw, *Pagan Goddesses*, 37–48; Cadotte, *La romanisation des dieux*, 1–19; Ando, "Interpretatio Romana"; Spickermann, "Interpretatio Romana?" On "non-obvious" beings see Lewis, "Popular Christianity," 262. On satyrs and *pilosi* see Isidore of Seville, *Etymologiarum* 8.11.103, vol. 1; Burchard of Worms, *Decretum* 19.5.103, 2:432.

32. Frankfurter, *Evil Incarnate*, 13–19 (quotation 19). Emphasis in original.

heavens rove about between the sky and the earth."[33] The terrestrial atmosphere was greatly inferior to the ether or the heavens; it was murky and "heavy," to quote the preeminent Greek theologian Origen of Alexandria (d. ca. 253) and his acolyte Eusebius (d. ca. 339).[34] Prudentius (d. ca. 405), a fourth–century poet, said of the middle air, "It is with the spirits of darkness that we contend night and day, which bear rule over the damp and heavy clouded air [cf. Eph. 6.12]. All this middle region . . . which stretches between the heavens above and the earth beneath . . . upholds the government of diverse powers and is the gruesome seat of wicked rulers under the command of Belial."[35]

Demons of the middle air could impede the progress of souls ascending to the celestial kingdom as the Northumbrian theologian and scholar the Venerable Bede (d. 735) affirmed in his discussion of Saint Fursa (d. ca. 650). This Irish monk had been taken into the heavens at the point of death and made privy to the galactic panoramic. According to Bede, Fursa saw "the fierce onslaughts of the evil spirits who, by their manifold accusations, wickedly sought to prevent his journey to heaven, but they failed utterly for he was protected by angels."[36] Within the same genre of "voyages of the soul," in the late 670s a monk named Barontus (d. c. 720) from St. Peter monastery at Longoreto near Bourges fell unconscious for a day and a night, and two grotesque demons came to carry him to hell. However, Angel Raphael grasped Barontus's soul and with it rose to the gates of Paradise. Four more demons joined the original two and harassed the monk as he ascended. As Barontus and Raphael passed by hell, they could not see much because of the "dark vapors and dense fumes rising from within." The account was recorded by one of Barontus's fellow monks and was widely circulated among Carolingian clergy.[37] A generation later, Boniface, archbishop of Mainz and "Apostle to Germany" (d. 754), narrated a similar account of a

---

33. Burchard of Worms, *Decretum* 20.49, PL 140, col. 1031: "Immundi spiritus, qui e coelo aethereo lapsi sunt, in hoc coeli terraeque medio vagantur."

34. Origen, *Exhortation to Martyrdom* 6.45, 188; Eusebius, *Preparation for the Gospel* 5.2, 1:180: Daemons "dwell about the earth and underground, and haunt the heavy and cloudy atmosphere over the earth."

35. Prudentius, *Origin of Sin*, 240–41.

36. Bede, *Bede's Ecclesiastical History* 3.19, 270–71: "Vidit . . . maxima malignorum spirituum certamina, qui crebris accusationibus inprobi iter illi caeleste intercludere contendebant, nec tamen, protegentibus eum angelis, quicquam proficiebant." See Carozzi (*Le voyage de l'âme*, 99–138, 679–92) for an analysis and edition of *Vita Sancti Fursei*. Visionary literature developed and expanded in the early seventh century (ibid., 185–86). See also Meens, *Penance*, 82–88; Moreira, *Dreams*, 155–58; Fox, *Pagans and Christians*, 97.

37. *Visio Baronti* (quotation 17, 390: "Sed non vidimus, quid intus ageretur propter tenebrarum caliginem et fumigantium multitudinem"). See Hen, "Structure and Aims"; Meens, *Penance*, 85–87;

monk at the monastery of Wenlock who described a vision of a man taken up into the heavens, where he saw angels and demons vying for the souls of the dead.[38]

Death by martyrdom, however, eased the soul's passage through the throngs of demons, and the church father, John Chrysostom (d. 407), bishop of Constantinople, contended that the smoke from burning Christians actually cleared up the miasma a bit. "The smoke ascending [from burning martyrs] suffused the air and asphyxiated all the demons flying around in it. The fumes drove the Devil away and cleaned up the very air itself."[39] Devils also found prayers sung out in unison odious. When Bishop Basil of Caesarea (d. 379) sought to cancel the debt of a young man who had bartered his soul to the Devil, he pressured Satan to return the contractual letter by having his congregation send loud prayers into the air, as Satan could not tolerate the sweet sound of sanctity.[40]

The Christian message was unequivocal that all magic was iniquitous because it depended on the aid of devils, and trafficking with demons was the essence of magic—on this there was no disagreement.[41] As to what constituted trafficking, that was more inchoate. The phrase "the Devil is in the details" applies doubly to early Christian and medieval magic, for although there were multifarious dealings between people and demons, they were

---

Carozzi (Le voyage, 154–58), the author of the Visio Baronti, had some affiliation with Fursa or his Gallic foundation.

38. From Boniface (Die Briefe 10, 7–15), an unknown author recounts demons "hunting souls through the air as they ascended from the prison of the body, and dragging them away to tortures" (Egredientes de corporali ergastulo animas in aere continuo inhianterque persequi et ad tormenta trahere aspexit). See also ibid., 115, 248. From Letters of Saint Boniface (167n1), this letter appears in one manuscript only. For an overview of Boniface's life and works see ibid., introd.

39. John Chrysostom, Sermon 71, in Acta primorum martyrum, 537: "Fumus in altum ascendens aerem occupavit; daemones per aerem volantes sussocabat onmes, diabolum abigebat, et ipsam naturam aeris abstergebat."

40. Cited by Hincmar of Reims, De divortio Lotharii regis, Responsio 15, 210–12. From ibid. (209nn32–33), the account of Bishop Basil was known to Himcmar through Jerome's On Illustrious Men.

41. The following are some examples of this position on demons across the early medieval centuries: (1) Tertullian, Apologeticum 22–27, 1:128–39; 46, 1:160–62; (2) Origen, Contra Celsum 2.51, 105–6; (3) Minucius Felix, Octavius 26, 44–45: "Magi quoque non tantum sciunt daemonas, sed etiam, quicquid miraculi ludunt, per daemonas faciunt; illis adspirantibus et infundentibus praestigias edunt"; (4) Lactantius, Divine Institutes 2.14–17, 159–66; (5) Augustine, De civitate Dei 10.8, 1:280: "Illi [magi] enim faciebant ueneficiis et incantationibus magicis, quibus sunt mali angeli, hoc est daemones"; (6) John Cassian, Conférences 7.14–23, 258–66; (7) Hincmar of Reims, De divortio Lotharii regis, Responsio 15, 210: "Maleficus vero dixit ad eum: 'O homo, ego in istud non praevaleo, sed si vis, mitto te ad meum procuratorem diabolum et ipse preficiet tuam voluntatem'"; (8) Aelfric of Eynsham, De falsis diis, in Homilies of Aelfric, 2:667–724.

not all sorcerous. What, then, were the exact features of the relationship between the demon and the human that constituted a magical interaction? Although there was consensus that magic involved trafficking with demons, there was no method in late antiquity or the early Middle Ages for determining exactly what behaviors were demonic. Both secular and ecclesiastical bodies issued condemnations of magic that were very specific in laying out the nature of the behaviors they proscribed, but no mechanism existed by which a definitive, binding stance on demonology could be formulated and prohibitions emerging from that position enforced.

Yet, even given this ambiguity, the notion was firm that magic occurred when human beings, by some action on their part, lured or beckoned demons (deliberatively or unwittingly) in such a fashion that their powers could be exploited. Behavior that called demons' abilities into play, not the intention of the human actor, was the substance of magic. It was possible for humans to entice demons without knowing it, as was frequently the case when people took part in activities that resembled pagans rites—rites through which, regardless of the participants' state of mind, they were invoking demons' powers to cure illness, bring rain, incite passion, and so forth. Augustine writes in *The City of God* that demons are attracted by "various kinds of stones, plants, woods, animals, songs, and rituals. In order to get these things from humans, first they seduce them by the shrewdest of cunning. . . . hence the origin of magicians and the magic arts."[42]

It was possible to arouse demons simply by feasting on meat sacrificed in cultic ceremonies because the offering of burnt flesh and oozing blood that demons so craved initiated a contract by which they were willing to do humans' bidding. Origen asserted that the denizens of the lower air were "riveted to blood and burnt-offering and magical enchantments"—an observation that became common wisdom henceforth throughout the early Middle Ages.[43] Bishop Isidore of Seville drew on this tradition in his explanation of how humans lured demons, that feasted on the smoke, the incense, and the odor of blood rising into the clouds from the animal sacrifices of pagan ceremonies. "For demons are said to love blood," Isidore wrote, "and

---

42. Augustine, *De civitate Dei* 21.6, 2:767: "per varia genera lapidum, herbarum, lignorum animalium, carminum rituum. Ut autem inliciantur ab hominibus, prius eos ipsi astutiassima calliditate seducunt. . . . unde magicae artes earumque artifices extiterent."

43. Origen, *Contra Celsum* 8.62, 499. See also ibid., 3.29, 147; 3.37, 153. This is an inversion of the narratives in Exodus (29:18; 29:25) and Leviticus (1:9; 4:31; 8:21) where the Eternal thrives off the sweet smell of sacrifice. From Johannessen (*The Demonic*, 48), the belief that demons took nourishment from the blood and flesh of sacrificial animals is a pre-Christian notion. Augustine (*De civitate Dei* 10.19, 1:293–94) adds that demons desire divine honors more than the odor of dead victims.

therefore whenever necromancy is practiced, gore is mixed with water so demons are called more easily by the gore of the blood." In his own time, the Carolingian scholar Raban Maur (d. 856) repeated this commonplace in his short treatise on the magic arts.[44]

The boundary between unintentional trafficking and sinful transgression was inexact. People knowingly and willingly submitted to devils when they succumbed to temptation, but that was not magic because sinners (simply by virtue of being sinners) were not in a position to exploit demons' capabilities. For example, the Iberian theologian Paschasius of Dumium (fl. mid–sixth century) told of an abbot and his encounter with a demon who was pleased because he had successfully coaxed one of the monks into overeating. The demon told the abbot, "I have one friend; he is on my side; whenever he sees me anywhere he comes to me as quick as the wind."[45] The ravenous monk in this story is in voluntary collusion with the demon, but even so, Paschasius is not implying that any magic has transpired. It is more a matter of the errant monk's succumbing to temptation rather than his drawing on the power of the demon. Devils tempted people, who all too often capitulated, and although the opportunity to capitalize on human frailty pleased demons, wayward offenders did not actually engage in trafficking. Furthermore, whereas "sin" could be intellective or behavioral, magic always involved action of some sort on the part of the human being. In other words, magic was never solely cerebral.

Late antique and early medieval demons, and human association with them, differed significantly from the early modern conception that involved "the pact." By the late Middle Ages, a defining aspect of witchcraft was the pact with Satan whereby individuals turned over their wills to the Devil and promised to adore him and join his diabolical coterie in exchange for spectacular powers, or even minor favors.[46] Although there is some mention of pacts in late classical and early medieval materials, they are of a different nature than the pact as it evolved by the fifteenth century. The earlier pact was transactional, more like a contract negotiated between a demon (not necessarily Satan) and a human for the purpose of achieving a specific advantage, and both parties to the agreement had rights. The demons' contractual obligations were to accede to specified requests. The humans were

---

44. Isidore of Seville, *Etymologiarum* 8.9.11–12, vol. 1: "Nam amare daemones sanguinem dicitur. Ideoque quotiens necromantia fit, cruor aqua miscitur, ut cruore sanguinis facilius provocentur." Raban Maur, *De magicis artibus*, cols. 1097–98.
45. Paschasius of Dumium, *Questions and Answers* 8, 121.
46. On the pact see Levack, *Witch-Hunt*, 33–37.

to perform particular rites, and they were often expected to relinquish the soul at death—not to join Satan's terrestrial corps. The deals were binding only for the duration of specific transactions. As Jeffrey Russell points out, in the early Middle Ages, demons and humans bargained on a "relatively equal basis." Alain Boureau speaks of pacts before the thirteenth century as "weak pacts" because, with the help of prayer and the intercession of saints, they could be abrogated.[47]

One of the most frequent kinds of commerce between humans and demons came in the guise of possession and dreams, but humans possessed by devils or troubled by them in their sleep were not themselves considered sorcerous; they were innocent victims.[48] John Cassian explained that possession results "not from a lessening of the soul but from the weakness of the body." The early Christian writer Lactantius (d. ca. 320) describes the bane of possession in graphic detail. "Because these spirits are slender and hard to grasp, they work themselves into people's bodies and secretly get at their guts, wrecking their health, causing illness, scaring their wits with dreams, unsettling their minds with madness."[49] Jerome (d. 419/420), the great Latin theologian, wrote a biography of Saint Hilarion (d. ca. 371) in which the holy anchorite exorcizes an officer of Emperor Constantius's (d. 361) guard who had been plagued with a demon from childhood. The devil, that was tabernacled in the officer's body, forced his prey to howl at night, groan, and gnash his teeth.[50] A hundred years later the Gallic bishop Caesarius of Arles made clear the difference between possession and trafficking with demons. "It is certain, brothers, that a man can hardly be found who sees an unfortunate person vexed by the Devil and is not frightened and terrified. However, by way of piety and perfect charity we ought to fear less and pray more for

---

47. Augustine, *De doctrina Christiana* 2.23.89, 98–99: "So all the specialists in this kind of futile and harmful superstition, and the contracts, as it were, of an untrustworthy and treacherous partnership established by this disastrous alliance of men and devils, must be totally rejected and avoided by the Christian." (Omnes igitur artifices huius modi vel nugatoriae vel noxiae superstitionis, <et> ex quadam pestifera societate hominum et daemonum quasi pacta infidelis et dolosae amicitiae constituta, penitus sunt repudianda et fugienda Christiano); J. B. Russell, *Witchcraft*, 144; Boureau, *Satan the Heretic*, 73.

48. "Innocent" may be a bit too strong. There was a sense among some that those who were possessed or haunted in their dreams may have left themselves vulnerable to assault due to some misdeed or errant thought. Be that as it may, possession and the demonic penetration of dreams did not amount to trafficking with demons. Pseudo-Clement (*Recognitions* 4.16, 138; 4.30, 141) says that even to eat or drink immoderately can result in demonic possession. For an overview of dreaming from the second to the seventh centuries see Le Goff, *Medieval Imagination*, 193–231.

49. Cassian, *Conférences* 7.12, 256: "Nec enim per aliquam animae deminutionem, sed per corporis debilitatem"; Lactantius, *Divine Institutes* 1.14, 161.

50. Jerome, *Life of Saint Hilarion* 22, 308.

that person."⁵¹ In other words, Caesarius considers demoniacs to be helpless against the Devil's harassment. They are not responsible for his attacks, nor is the victim guilty of practicing magic.

Describing a possessed individual in eighth-century England, Bede extends the same nonjudgmental compassion. A guest harassed by an "unclean spirit" came to Abbess Aethelhild's (fl. late seventh century) monastery in the province of Lindsey. He began to gnash his teeth and foam at the mouth while his limbs were twisted by paroxysmal thrashing. Those near him sought help from the abbess, who, according to Bede, "opened the monastery door and went out with one of the nuns to the man's dwelling, where she called a priest and asked him to come with her to the patient. When they reached the place they found a crowd there, all trying in vain to hold the possessed man down and to restrict his convulsive movements. The priest pronounced exorcisms and did all he could to soothe the madness of the wretched man."⁵²

As in the case of the hypothetical man possessed in Caesarius's sermon, Abbess Aethelhild's guest was very much entangled with a demon, but as prey, not as one bargaining or trafficking. A similar example from the Carolingian era involves King Charles the Fat (d. 888). According to the ninth-century East Frankish *Annals of Fulda*, in 873 an unclean spirit entered the prince, and he became so spastic that his friends could hardly restrain him. The chronicler wrote that "the king and all who were with him were exceedingly mournful and wept." Once maneuvered into a church, Charles regained control.⁵³

The *Penitential of Theodore* differentiates between magic and demon possession, suggesting that in the case of possession, people are not responsible for their actions and therefore are not guilty of maleficium. The section entitled "On vexations by the devil" (*De vixatis a diabulo*) explains how best to aid

---

51. Caesarius of Arles, *Sermones*, Sermon 79.1, 1:325–26: "Certum est, fratres, quia vix invenietur homo, qui cum infelicem personam taliter vexari a diabolo viderit, non expavescat et metuat: ratio tamen religionis et perfectae caritatis hoc habeat, ut minus timere, et pro illo amplius orare deberemus." See Barthélemy ("Devils in the Sanctuary") on possession and conceptions of mental illness.

52. Bede, *Bede's Ecclesiastical History* 3.11, 248–49. See Uszkalo, "Rage Possession."

53. *Annales Fuldenses* 873, 77: "Rex autem et omnes, qui cum illo erant, vehementer contristati lacrimas fuderunt." See also *Annales Bertiniani* 873, 121–25; *Annales Xantenses* 873, 30–33. For an interpretation of this event as a ritual gone awry see "Ritual Misunderstanding" where MacLean analyzes the event as an awkward political strategy. Although MacLean does not discuss why Charles selected demonic possession as a means to his ends, given the contemporary understanding of possession, the decision had the effect of exonerating the king from full responsibility. Hincmar of Reims says of possession (*Ep.* 187, 196), "There is customarily no madness without a demon" (Quoniam mania esse non solet absque daemone).

a person afflicted by possession; article five reads, "One who is possessed of a demon is allowed to have stones and herbs without using an incantation." The stones and herbs are medicinal, but the incantation is magical. The author deals with magic or idolatry in a separate section of the penitential, "On the worship of idols" (*De cultura idolorum*), where those interacting with demons are guilty of sinful collusion. In other words, the author distinguishes between traffic with demons and the violation of persons penetrated by them. The penitential called *The Judgment of Clement* (between 700 and 750) stipulates, "If anyone is troubled by a devil and kills himself, it is permitted to pray for him"; that is to say, the person is blameless.[54] One possessed by a demon was crazed or unwell, but that person was innocent of using magic in any fashion.

In the first millennium, "the witch" as a construct had not developed, but the role the witch plays in many societies around the world, past and present, was assumed by "the demon." David Frankfurter observes that there is a mythic need to imagine malevolence on a universal scale and to see evil as a conspiracy that will emerge time and time again as a response to otherness. It is human nature to construct boundaries between "us" and a monstrous other. Virtually every culture imagines a being that is the embodiment of evil—a being responsible for mysterious or inexplicable malice and misfortune.[55] These creatures are intrinsically malevolent and antisocial; they desire blood, shape-shift, copulate promiscuously, control the weather, operate in the spirit world, sicken victims, fly, and are always to be feared.[56]

In the early medieval period, characteristics that many cultures attributed to witches were projected, not onto human agents, but onto demons. Augustine held evil spirits complicit in damage to crops, flood, famine, draught, disease, possession, accidents, and deaths of small children.[57] In his *Differences*, the Spanish bishop Isidore of Seville provides an exhaustive catalogue of demons' sinister misdeeds. "Demons are impure spirits, subtle and peripatetic, able to suffer in spirit (mentally rational), with airy bodies, eternal in time, enemies of humanity, and wishing to do harm. They are swollen

---

54. *Poenitentiale Theodori* 2.10.1–5, 3:197–98 (quotation 2.10.5, 3:198): "Demonium sustinenti licet petras et holera habere sine incantatione"; ibid., 2.15.1–5, 3:189–90; *Judicium Clementis* 12, 3:227: "Si quis vexatus est a diabolo et semet ipsum occidit, licet orare pro eo." All in *Councils and Ecclesiastical Documents*. On the *Judicium Clementis*, see Meens, *Penance*, 102–4.

55. Frankfurter, "Introduction," *Evil Incarnate*.

56. For a collection of nearly fifty motifs of witch-like beings common to societies around the world see J. B. Russell, *Witchcraft*, 13–16.

57. Augustine, *De civitate Dei* 22.22, 2:842–45.

with pride, ingenious in deceit, always devising new frauds. They agitate the senses, feign emotion, upset life, disturb sleep, bring disease, terrify the mind, distort limbs, oversee the drawing of lots, and fake oracles by creating illusions. They induce passion and pour heat on desire. They hide in sacred images. When called, they come, lying with the appearance of truth. They change into various shapes; sometimes they transform themselves into the image of angels."[58]

Demons did not require the complicity of mortals in order to cause mayhem. For example, the *Annals of Fulda* describe an unusual encounter between a villager and a demon. In the Bavarian village of Kempten, an evil spirit makes itself known by throwing stones, banging on walls, locating lost objects, starting fires, destroying crops, and exposing the clandestine fornication of a local priest. The demon fixes its animosity on a particular villager. Whenever this hapless man enters a building, the demon ignites a fire, and soon virtually all the structures in the village are reduced to cinders. The villager is ostracized and forced to live in a field outside of town with his family. Even when the ill-treated man successfully undergoes the ordeal of hot iron to prove his innocence, the demon does not stop.[59] Local priests cannot control the devil, although they try to expel him with the aid of relics, crosses, and holy water.

A similar account of a rogue demon occurs in Alcuin's *Life of Willibrord*. In the town of Trier in western Germany, a wicked spirit infests a household where it causes havoc by throwing food, clothing, and other household good into the fireplace. At one point the demon snatches the a young son from his parents arms and casts him into the fire. As in the case of the devil of Kempton, no priest is able to drive the demon from the home, and in the end the house is devoured in flames.[60] In both cases, the spiteful demons inflict their malice without seeking some exchange or advantage. Given the

---

58. Isidore of Seville, *Liber differentiarum [II]* 2.14, 29–30: "Daemones sunt inpuri spiritus, subtiles et uagi, animo passibiles, [mente rationales,] corpore aerei, tempore aeterni, humanitas inimici, nocendi cupidi, superbia tumidi, fallacia callidi, semper in fraude noui. Commouent sensus, fingunt affectus, uitarn turbant, somnos inquietant, morbos inferunt, mentes terrent, membra distorquent, sortes regunt, praestigiis oracula fingunt, cupidinem amoris inliciunt, ardorem cupiditatis infundunt, in consecratis imaginibus delitescunt; inuocati adsunt, uerisimilia mentiuntur, mutantur in diuersis figuris, interdum in angelorum imaginibus transformantur."

59. One form of trial by ordeal was a judicial practice whereby a suspected malefactor grasped hot iron, and if, by God's grace, the wound was healed in three days, the accused was innocent—otherwise, guilty. For a discussion of trial by ordeal and its sociological basis see Hyams, "Trial by Ordeal."

60. *Annales Fuldenses* 858, 51–52 ; Alcuin, *Vita Willibrordi* 22, 133. Alcuin (d. 804) was a preeminent scholar and clergyman in the court of Charlemagne. Saint Willibrord (d. 739) was a Northumbrian missionary who is known as the "Apostle to the Frisians."

fact that the devils of Kempton and Trier acted independently, these incident were *not* cases of village magic; magic required the participation of a human actor.

The most dangerous antagonist to the holy person in early hagiography is not another human, but demons with whom confrontations are more menacing than the conjuration of any magician. This motif is firmly established in Athanasius's seminal vita of Antony and remains a feature of hagiography, to a greater or lesser extent, through the early Middle Ages.[61] In his work on the relationship between demons and early Christian monks, David Brakke discusses the importance of demons to the desert hermit's self-definition. In a sense, demons became the passions—pesky and troublesome—and according to Brakke, they "provide[d] a language of alterity by which monks could differentiate themselves from other people and from aspects of their selves that obstructed their relationship with God and each other."[62] Brakke's observation takes us back to the beginning of this chapter, where we left Antony languishing in his tomb, exhausted but triumphant—his passions and appetites rendered impotent. The same theme animates Jerome's biography of the desert father Hilarion, Antony's acolyte. "One night," Jerome writes, "he began to hear the wailing of infants, the bleating of flocks, the lowing of oxen, the lament of what seemed to be women, the roaring of lions, the noise of an army. . . . He understood that the demons were disporting themselves, and falling on his knees he made the sign of the cross on his forehead. . . . . and suddenly before his eyes, the earth was opened and the whole array was swallowed up."[63] The rite of passage for desert saints was the ability to withstand the assaults of demons; such heroism defined them. Both Antony and Hilarion passed the test, and because of that, they became spiritual superstars.

Despite the fact that the demons of Kempten and Trier caused no end of trouble for householders and the local communities, generally early medieval demons, including Satan himself, were relatively harmless. In the visionary voyage of Barontus discussed above, the juvenile and willful demons refused to accept Saint Peter's judgment, although he had addressed them

---

61. Athanasius, *Life of Antony* 1–43, 30–64.
62. Brakke, *Demons*, 150–56 (quotation 156). For a useful discussion of Antony's experience in the desert see ibid., 23–47. See also Wiśniewski, *Pagan Temples*, 121. Vos ("Demons Without and Within") explores whether demons were agents of change in saints' biographies and asks if demons pushed protagonists to reach their holy status or, as Brakke claims, did they simply put the saints' fully-realized spiritual resolve to the test? I find Vos's argument in favor of the former view the more compelling.
63. Jerome, *Life of Saint Hilarion* 6, 304.

politely. Peter becomes so irritated with the quarrelsome demons that he clouts them over the head with his keys. Having been duly punished, the devils retreat.[64]

It is not surprising that the sainted gate-keeper of heaven easily dispatched the unruly demons, but humans too could dominate easily the fallen angels who had little chance of success in any given contest with saints or bishops, or even against average Christians who properly utilized prophylactic rituals such as crossing themselves. People who appropriately solicited divine help could nearly always prevail. At times, demons were even so pathetically outdone that they appeared despondently childlike, almost pitiable in their ineptitude.

Athanasius assures his acolytes that demons' strength is chimeral. "They also make crashing sounds and laugh madly, and hiss. But if one should pay no attention to them, they cry out and lament as though vanquished." Jerome paints a vivid picture of unhinged demons frantically pursuing Hilarion in vain as he is sailing among the Cyclades islands. "He heard the voices of unclean spirits shouting in all directions from towns and villages, and running in crowds to the shore." In the same source, Hilarion finds a devil trapped in a brass plate. "The devil began to howl and confess. 'I was compelled, I was carried off against my will.' The old man answers, 'Your strength must be great indeed, if a bit of thread and a plate can keep you bound.'" When the Italian monk Benedict of Nursia (d. 547) replaced a sanctuary of Apollo with a chapel at Monte Cassino, the devil was enraged. "Flames darted from his mouth and eyes. . . . He screamed saying, 'Benedict, Benedict,' and when he got no response, then immediately he added, 'You are cursed not blessed. What do you want with me; why do you torment me like this?'"[65] Edward Peters rightly observes that the motif often brought to bear in early medieval hagiography whereby a saint is tempted by and easily subdues demons (including Satan, whom he describes as "clumsily brutal, occasionally stupid, and often bungling") made demons familiar and manageable.[66]

---

64. *Visio Baronti* 12, 386–87.

65. Athanasius, *Life of* Antony 26, 51. On the same theme see ibid., 6, 35; 24, 49; 28, 52–53. Jerome, *Life of Saint Hilarion* 42, 313–14; 21, 308; Gregory the Great, *Dialogues* 2.8.12, 168–170: "Qui in eum ore oculisque flammantibus saeuire uidebantur. . . . Nam cum clamaret, dicens: 'Benedicte, Benedicte,' et eum sibi nullo modo respondere conspiceret, protinus adiungebat, 'Maledicte, non Benedicte, quid mecum habes, quid me persequeris?'"

66. Peters, *Magician*, 91–92. Quotation from *Witchcraft in Europe*, 10. See also J. B. Russell, *Lucifer*, 156–57.

Although all late antique and medieval people recognized the reality of demons and sorcery, they were in no sense preoccupied with them, nor did magical dealings necessarily constitute or imply liminality. This was partly because of demons' relative incompetence and partially because sorcery and magic were commonplace, natural—one more effort on the part of the forces of evil to tempt humankind.[67] Its normalcy can complicate the task of the historian in identifying magic in the sources. At times a text may hint that a behavior or substance is magical without providing descriptive details, because magic was so ordinary—not particularly noteworthy in itself. For example, imputations of pagan superstitions often implied demonic intercourse or magic, but not always. John Chrysostom complained, "To allow a boy's hair to grow long on his neck is to make him feminine like a girl . . . the result of pagan superstition." Similarly, in 793 the Carolingian scholar Alcuin (d. 804) reproached King Æthelred of Northumbria (d. 796) because his subjects sported pagan haircuts, beards, and clothing. Neither John Chrysostom nor Alcuin had traffic with demons in mind; it was more the case that tags such as superstition and paganism were terms of abuse indicating unsuitable behavior.[68]

Almost invariably, historians writing about Christian magic and the demons who facilitated it treat them as supernatural phenomena, but this characterization misses the mark; both were preternatural and superhuman, but not supernatural.[69] Only God, the creator of natural law, was thought capable of meddling with that law. Magic was akin to a marvel, an extraordinary but explicable circumstance within the natural order. It operated through the agency of demons, that possessed abilities mystifying to humans but integral to the inherent makeup of the demonic creature itself. For example, Athanasius claimed that magicians might appear to know the future because the demons on whom they rely have aerial bodies, lighter than any earthly creature, and can traverse vast reaches at an instant and thereby witness an event in a distant part of the world, such as a storm, and report it to the magicians, making them seem prophetic when in fact

---

67. Jolly, Raudvere, and Peters, *Witchcraft and Magic*, 26. J. Russell observes ("Archaeological Context of Magic") that magic was not a perversion of religion but a common daily occurrence, so, by extension, it was not liminal.

68. MacMullen, *Christianizing the Roman Empire*, 79; Alcuin, *Ep.* 16, 43.

69. For example, Ludwikowska, "Uncovering the Secret," 83; Ferngren, *Medicine and Health Care*, 5; Hall, *Elves in Anglo-Saxon England*, 11; Maguire, "Magic and Money"; A. Murray, "Missionaries and Magic," 189–203; Flint, *Rise of Magic*, 157, 226; *Anglo-Saxon Leechbook III*, 10; J. B. Russell, *Witchcraft*, 20. Leyser ("Angels, Monks, and Demons") makes the same argument in regard to angels. If not a day-to-day presence, they were not an extraordinary feature of the cultural landscape.

nothing supernatural has taken place. In the same vein, Augustine explained that God controls the entire created order, which includes devils. Demons give the impression that they are supernatural because, for example, they will at times "predict that which they themselves are planning to do," or "before they make a prediction they read the future through natural signs which the senses of humans cannot read." Only angels can truly foretell the future, because they share in God's wisdom; demons can just "guess at temporal matters from temporal matters."[70] Athanasius's and Augustine's position was adopted by virtually all Christian exegetes who wrote about magic in late antiquity and the early Middle Ages. Raban Maur articulated this point well when he said that magicians, with the help of demons, appear to change the shape of things, but it is in reality the natural operation of the elements.[71]

Not only were demons (and the magic they facilitated) within the natural order, but the actions of demons were possible through divine permission, and demons were allowed to work only within the parameters God assigned to them. At times God himself used devils to test human beings.[72] Caesarius of Arles told his parishioners that the Lord could give devils permission to injure and sicken Christians as a test to see whether they would turn to magicians for the superficial cures they provide. He assured his hearers, "The Devil is not able to hurt [you] . . . unless he receives his power from God."[73]

One of the most common ways in which God connected with his creation was through astrological, meteorological, or seismographic phenomena. When Augustine discussed the error of astrology he left room for the legitimacy of portents, which, he argued, do not cause events to occur but simply

---

70. Athanasius, *Life of Antony* 31–32, 54–56. Augustine, *De civitate Dei* 9.22, 1:269: "Daemones autem non aeternas temporum causas et quodam modo cardinales in Dei sapientia contemplantur, sed quorundam signorum nobis occultorum maiore experientia multo plura quam homines future prospiciunt; dispositiones quoque suas aliquando praenuntiant. . . . Aliud est enim temporalibus temporalia et mutabilibus mutabilia coniectare eisque temporalem et mutabilem modum suae uoluntatis et facultatis inserere, quod daemonibus certa ratione permissum est." Augustine, *De divinatione daemonum* 3–6, 603–11. See also Tertullian, *Apologeticum* 22, 1:128–30. On the physicality of demons see Johannessen, *The Demonic*, 49–55.

71. Raban Maur, *De magicis artibus*, cols. 1097, 1101–2.

72. Augustine, *Contra Julianum Pelagianum* 4.7.38, cols. 757–58; Augustine, *De divinatione daemonum* 1–2, 599–603.

73. Caesarius of Arles, *Sermones*, Sermon 54.3–4, 1:237–38: "Et illud ante omnia scitote, quod nec vos ipsos nec eos qui ad vos pertinent, nec animalia vestra, nec reliquam substantiam vel in parvis rebus diabolus potest laedere, nisi quantum a deo potestatem acceperit" (quotation 238). See also Raban Maur, *De magicis artibus*, col. 1101.

forewarn of certain occurrences, "showing the created world at the service of the creator." A heavenly body that foretold the future was a microphone, not a proximate cause, and had nothing to do with demonic prognostication. Throughout the period, men and women believed that unusual happenings in the upper air portended important events on earth.[74]

The principle that the entire physical world, including inanimate objects, participated in the divine unity accounts for the belief that stones, jewels, herbs, and metals held clues to occult knowledge. All nature was in sync—in sympathy—and because even the lowest earthly elements had a place on the great chain of being, people believed it was possible to reach the divine from any point on the continuum uniting heaven and earth. The notion of sympathy among elements was held to be a scientific maxim.[75] Origen's philosophical work, *Peri Archôn*, has the sun sighing, "It would be better if I were dissolved to be with Christ, far better," and the fourth-century novel *The Recognitions* of Pseudo-Clement explains that the natural world is so in concert with its creator that the sun grieves to shine its light on the wicked. An anonymous tenth-century lectionary contains a homily in which the very elements recognize the creator and lend themselves to his mission. The sky sends a star; the sea allows Jesus to walk upon it; and at his death the sun darkens, stones break, and the earth quakes.[76]

In short, Christians inherited a coherent, rationalized understanding of the universe from their pagan predecessors, and they altered it very little. One of the most significant changes was that pagan deities became demons of the lower air and were by nature evil. Late antique people (pagans and Christians) and the men and women of early medieval Europe took the possibility of interaction with the occult for granted because it followed the inner logic of existing physics and metaphysics. It was a natural, reasonable extension of the human being's placement within the cosmos.

So why was magic, or the instigation of an alliance with one of God's demonic creatures, so egregious? It was because this communion was a perversion of the relationship that should exist between humans and the divine:

---

74. Augustine, *De civitate Dei* 10.13, 1:287: "mirabilibus rerum signis et motibus apparebat ad eandem legem dandam creatori servire creaturam." See chap. 8 on Gregory of Tours and portents.

75. Janowitz, *Icons of Power*, 109–17. Sympathy was thought to be a "natural" force acting mutually on particles of matter, drawing them together.

76. Origen, *Peri Archôn* 7.5, cited in Brown, *Making of Late Antiquity*, 70; Pseudo-Clement, *Recognitions* 5.27, 149–50. See Bremmer ("Pseudo-Clementines") on the texts' provenance, authors, and manuscript tradition. For the lectionary see Thorndike, *History of Magic*, 1:478.

God or one of his angelic or saintly hosts. Why would Christians seek succor from a creature when God had given them access to the greater power of the creator? The Greek theologian Clement of Alexandria (d. ca. 215) voices this thinking in his exposé on the errors of paganism entitled *Exhortation to the Heathen*. "Let none of you worship the sun, but set his desires on the Maker of the sun; nor deify the universe, but seek after the Creator of the universe." Augustine says much the same in *The City of God*. "Even earthly things themselves ought to be sought from none except the one true God who has power over all things." And Caesarius of Arles chided those who venerated the moon, asking, "Since [the moon] serves rational humans by the command of God, why does man insult God by paying fatuous obeisance to [the moon]?"[77] The transgression at issue in dealing with demons was the affront it implied to God's majesty.

---

77. Clement of Alexandria, *Exhortation* 4, in *Writings of Clement of Alexandria*, 190; Augustine, *De civitate Dei* 10.25, 1:299: "Quid huic tamen utile fuerit etiam ipsa terrena non nisi ab uno vero Deo quaerere, in cuius potestate sunt omnia"; Caesarius of Arles, *Sermones*, Sermon 52.3, 1:231: "cum illa homini rationabili exhibeat deo ordinante servitium, homo illi ad iniuriam dei stultum reddit obsequium?" See also Audoin, *Vita Eligii* 2.16, 707.

PART 2

Breaking In

Christianity in Classical Rome

Chapter 3

Ritual, Demons, and Sacred Space

> It is certainly a monstrous evil that the holy sites should be marred by sacrilegious abominations . . . The place by the oak which is known as Mamre, where we understand Abraham made his home, has been completely spoiled, Eutropia said, by superstitious persons. Idols fit only for absolute destruction have been set up beside it, she explains, and an altar stands nearby, and foul sacrifices are constantly conduced there. . . . [Acacius is directed] that without delay such idols as he may find on the aforementioned site be consigned to the flames, [and] the altar completely demolished . . . He is to have built on the spot a basilica worthy of the catholic and apostolic Church.
>
> —Eusebuis, *Life of Constantine*

In the Christian writings of the first few centuries of the Common Era, discussions of magic were embedded in the larger struggle to articulate the contours of the new faith and defend its theology. The effort to define and distinguish the infant religion compelled Christians to examine the entire fabric of pagan belief, and in that process demonology was a central focus. Pagan competition and forms of opposition (although never unified) drove Christian discourse on traffic with demons and determined the shape apologetics would take. The continual battle the religion waged against magic was in part a conflict over control of cultural symbols and their meanings. The church opposed magic on theological grounds, certainly, but also because it often emerged in ritualistic settings which provoked and preserved, in a virulent form, a worldview at odds with Christianity.

Modern scholarship rightly stresses the imbrication and integration of late Roman civilization and early Christian subcultures. The two were both syncretic and symbiotic. Christianity grew from the soil of pagan thought and was a product of the rich traditions of the Greco-Roman world. Pagan and Christian rituals were homologous; they shared a common rhythm, and they responded to and mirrored one another. However, although the church used the raw materials of pagan culture in forming religious symbols, it consciously altered the signification of familiar objects and rites so as to inculcate new patterns of meaning through them.[1]

Christians understood the power of ritual behavior all too vividly, as they were the victims of judicial violence for their refusal to participate in pagan festivals and sacrifices to idols and were themselves accused of rites involving anti-social behavior such as "unbridled sex and eating human flesh."[2] The nascent communities fostered a deep and full-bodied lexicon of symbols, but they were suspicious of excessive, ostentatious ritual and vacillated between adapting themselves to the dominant culture (at first Jewish, later Roman) and remaining aloof from it. Justin Martyr said of non-Christian sacraments, "The Creator of this world . . . does not need blood, and libations, and incense; we who praise him, to the best of our ability by a word of prayer and thanksgiving for everything we eat, . . . have learnt that this is the only honor worthy of him."[3]

Sometimes Christian rituals were imitative of and sometimes antipodal to pagan rites, and primitive Christians were acutely aware that they were involved in a confrontation of competing ritual systems. It was not easy, however, for them to disparage Jewish and pagan ceremony altogether, because the surface structure of their own ritual forms and key symbols were often very similar. Again and again through the period I examine, writers were explicit that Christian ceremonial was often like pagan rites in its external forms, but differed in substance. And if, as Geertz claims, religion expresses itself "in an oblique and figurative manner that which cannot be stated in a direct and literal one,"[4] then Christian evangelists were wise to engage in a campaign to define meaning encoded in ritual in order to control this very potent form of communication and cultural performance. The architects of the new religion sought to retain the contours of accustomed and efficacious rites and to continue the use of familiar signifiers (symbols) while repositioning that which was signified. Origen of Alexandria gives voice to this approach in his response to the pagan philosopher Celsus (fl. 180) when he says, "[You put] together in one category things which really fall into two different categories. Just as a wolf is not of the same species as a dog, even if it seems to have some similarity in the shape of its body and its bark . . .

---

1. Brown, *Rise of Western Christendom*, 52–92; MacMullen, *Second Church*, 69–94.
2. See also Minucius Felix, *Octavius* 9, 12–14; De Ste. Croix, "Why Were Christians Persecuted?"; Fox, *Pagans and Christians*, 419–92.
3. Justin Martyr, *Apology on Behalf of Christians* 13.1, 109. *Octavius* (n.d.) is a fictional dialogue between a pagan and Christian elucidating and defending Christianity for an educated non-Christian audience.
4. Geertz, *Interpretation of Cultures*, 91; Geertz, *Religion as a Cultural System*, 5.

so also what is accomplished by God's power is nothing like what is done by sorcery." Augustine reiterates Origen's viewpoint when he contrasts Christian miracles to demonic wonders. "Although, it is true that certain of these miracles seem equal to some of those worked by the saints, the ends served by each are different, and scrutiny shows that our miracles are incomparably superior."[5]

Noticing the similarities between magical and religious rituals in the early church, some scholars have concluded that there was no clear distinction between magic and religion, when what is actually the case is that there was often little difference in the ritualistic signs through which each communicated meaning.[6] Justin Martyr claimed that demons anticipated proper Christian sacraments and instituted them among pagans and Jews before the birth of Jesus so as to make Christian rites seem derivative of pagan rituals, particularly those used to exalt the Persian sun god Mithra.[7] Athanasius recognized that the formalistic use of names could be demonic in some circumstances, but insisted that using the name of Jesus ritualistically dispelled magic. Athanasius did not take issue with the sacral use of symbols (such as names), but he substituted one signified (Jesus) for another (demonic deities). Bishop Cyril of Jerusalem (d. 386) contrasted the sanctifying effect of baptismal words on water to futile pagan invocations over animal sacrifices.[8] These and other thinkers reveal Christians struggling to formulate a message on the use of ritual per se and groping for some sort of compass to direct them in telling a new story with traditional semiotic material.

Part of the problem was that a thoroughly Christian vocabulary of ritual worship that could replace pagan customs took time to develop and percolate through the population. The formulation of the earliest Christian rituals took place in a hostile environment—often in a reactive mode—within the bosom of Jewish ceremonial and the shadow of mystery cults and pagan rites that included demonic elements.[9] However, there were no clear guidelines

---

5. Origen, *Contra Celsum* 2.51, 105. See also ibid., 1.68, 63: "[Celsus] compares the stories about Jesus with tales of magic. They might have been comparable if Jesus had done his miracles, like magicians, merely to show his own powers." Augustine, *De civitate Dei* 10.16, 1:290: "Quaedam uero etsi nonnullis piorum factis uideantur opere coaequari, finis ipse, quo discernuntur, incomparabiliter haec nostra ostendit excellere."

6. Arthur, *"Charms"* (at times); Jolly, *Popular Religion*; Flint, *Rise of Magic*.

7. Justin Martyr, *Apology on Behalf of Christians* 54.1–10, 219–25; 62.1–2, 243; 66.4, 256–59.

8. Athanasius, *De incarnatione* 30, 208–9: "No demon endures that name but, as soon as he hears it, takes to flight." See also ibid., 47–50, 252–61; Cyril of Jerusalem, *Catechesis* 3.3, in *Works of Saint Cyril*, 1:109–10. Also, on early Christian polemics contrasting Jewish ritual and Christian baptism see Ferguson, *Baptism*, 266–75.

9. Pagels, *Beyond Belief*, 10, 14, 19–25.

for those Christians borrowing elements from pagan rites in formulating their own rituals as to what activities should be considered magical, outside of the basic premise that magic depended on traffic with demons. Constant vigilance was necessary to assure that familiar and seemingly innocuous practices, which might be masking the mischief of devils, not be introduced into the rites of the new faith. The epistle called *Didache* (also *The Teaching of Twelve Apostles*), an anonymous first-century Greek text—perhaps the earliest extant Christian writing on sacramental rituals—was read out to the people of Corinth from time to time. The epistle was composed before behavioral norms were standardized, and it establishes the correlation between magic, astrology, and idolatry. "My child, do not become a diviner, / since (this) is the path leading to idolatry; / nor an enchanter, / nor an astrologer, / nor a purifier, / nor (even) wish to see these things, for, from all these, idolatry is begotten." Because the church demonized pagan deities as devils, behaviors that resembled veneration of them amounted to *idolatria*, that is, trafficking with demons. Origen wrote that magic is "wrought by evil daemons who are enchanted by elaborate spells and obey men who are sorcerers."[10] Within this context of competing belief systems, female aspects of the holy were up for negotiation. There was no room for goddesses in the monotheism of the new faith, and many ritualized behaviors from the pre-Christian era by which women honored deities of woods, hearth, and home were censored in the religion's reevaluation of the sacred.

Catherine Bell observes that ritual "can act as a medium able to embody the contradictions, tensions, and ideals of a community trying to be born."[11] As Christians worked to articulate a vocabulary of ritual that would demarcate the infant creed, they were faced with the problem of originality. Innovation was not highly valued in the ancient world, especially when it touched systems of beliefs and morals.[12] The widely-read Roman satirist Lucian of Samosata (d. after 180) mocked Christians for their "wondrous lore" and "new cult." Judaism's antiquity secured for the religion Rome's begrudging toleration, a forbearance the empire was not willing to extend to the upstart, novel Christianity.[13] Barbara Myerhoff articulates the problem of inventing

---

10. *Didache* 3.4, 8–9. See Jefford ("Introduction") on the background of *Didache*. Origen, *Contra Celsum* 2.51, 106. See also Tertullian, *De idololatria* 9, 2:1107–9. In the *Book of Watchers* (*Complete Books of Enoch, 1 Enoch* 8.1–4, 30), the demon Baraqijal taught humans astrology and Kokabel imparted the mysteries of the constellations.

11. Bell, *Ritual: Perspectives and Dimensions*, 231.

12. MacMullen, *Paganism*, 2–4.

13. Lucian of Samosata, *Passing of Peregrinus* 11, 13. Ehrman, *Lost Christianities*, 254–57; Horbury, "Jewish-Christian Relations," 318.

new rites. People are reluctant to see ritual as a product of contemporary imagination or necessity because ritual's efficacy is tied to the fantasy that it is timeless. Rituals, she says, should reflect "the underlying, unchanging nature of the world," and if we "catch ourselves making up rituals, we may see all our most precious basic understandings, the precepts we live by, as mere desperate wishes and dreams."[14] Christians found themselves, then, walking a tightrope between the familiar/time-honored/trustworthy and the innovative.

Jewish converts of the apostolic age integrated fresh rituals and the sacred services of their ancestral culture, but by the end of the first century, the apostle Paul's (d. ca. 63 CE) insistence that the church be universal prevailed, and exclusive and highly demanding rites such as circumcision and exacting food restrictions were, for the most part, abandoned. More and more, Christianity separated itself from the orthopraxic Jewish religion and emphasized orthodoxy, that is basic belief in Jesus. Christians were scornful of Hebrew ceremonial and became leery of restrictive rites that might keep would-be converts outside the fold.[15]

Philippe Buc observes that the notion of ceremony as vain and empty is very old in the Western world, and casting the rituals of others as artificial and meaningless has often been a factor in a given group's construction of self.[16] Justin Martyr used Hebrew scripture to characterize Jewish ritual as barren and shallow. His *Dialogue with Trypho*, for which the target audience was most likely those newly converted from Judaism, captures the birth pangs of the primitive church as it struggled to find a conceptual space for the infant religion. He writes that God instituted rites such as fasting, animal sacrifice, circumcision, and keeping the Sabbath in response to the Jews' hardness of heart. Jewish ritual, he claims, exists as a result of sin, and the new covenant, written in Christ's purifying blood, abrogated much of God's original covenant with Moses. Justin pits Christian baptism against Jewish ceremonies, and Christians' more liberal dietary practices against Mosaic

---

14. Myerhoff, "Death in Due Time," 151–53 (quotation 152). See also Wils, "From Ritual to Hermeneutics." Bell (*Ritual: Perspectives and Dimensions*, 224–25, 237) notes that analyses like those of Myerhoff and Wils have been critiqued, especially in light of recent history. Nonetheless, for the late antique world, their insights are valid. See also Geertz, *Interpretation of Cultures*, 142–69.

15. Justin Martyr (*Apology on Behalf of Christians* 67, 259–63) set the stage for the abandonment of many Jewish usages and their replacement with simple Christian rites; *Letter of Barnabas* 9–11, 204–10. The *Letter of Barnabas* (late first/early second century), which deals with interpretation of Old Testament scripture, is an enigmatic text of which the authorship, provenance, and genre are uncertain. Ferguson, *Baptism*, 266–75; Gager, *Kingdom and Community*, 135–40.

16. Buc, *Dangers of Ritual*, 225–26, 251–52. See also MacMullen, *Second Church*, 95–96.

food prohibitions.[17] He claims that the Jews fail to understand that circumcision is a sign or symbol only, not an obligatory rite of passage. The more excellent circumcision, he says, is that of the heart. "Circumcise, therefore, the foreskin of your heart."[18] Justin intuitively heeds Myerhoff's warning about "making up rituals" by drawing on Isaiah, Jeremiah, David, and Zechariah to demonstrate that Christian ritual is not new but embedded in Hebrew scripture, which, Justin claims, Christians understand better than the Jews themselves do.

Although Christian leaders wanted it clear that their religion was distinct from its Jewish progenitor, the situation was slightly different in regard to classical paganism. The message was that Christianity was different, but not too different. This was especially the case as Roman aristocrats and intellectuals began to join the movement.[19] The earliest texts depict Christians struggling to legitimize their practices and beliefs by claiming they were not bizarre and alien, but that they were essentially in line with the values and the sacral observances that every Roman already accepted. For example, Christian critique of burnt offerings and the emphasis on inner sacrifice was consistent with an emerging position among pagan philosophers that deities were not attracted to blood and cooked fat. Justin Martyr went as far as to say that worthy pagans, such as Socrates, were for all intents and purposes Christians. In an effort to demonstrate the veracity of the afterlife, Origen drew on classical examples of pagans who lived on after death. Peter Brown points out that "a lively process of the borrowing of rituals between pagans and Christians appears to have taken place in both directions. Pagan communities borrowed Christian signs and rites. The sign of the Cross would be made at sacrificial banquets. The names of Christian angels and saints would be shouted at the solemn toasts around the table." But establishing correspondences was a double-edged sword. Christians ardently sought toleration from their pagan neighbors, but at

---

17. Justin Martyr, *Dialogue with Trypho* 5, p. 91; 11, 13, 14, pp. 101–15; 20, 22, pp. 131–37. See also Rajak, "Talking at Trypho." From Horbury ("Jewish-Christian Relations," 323–27, 345), Justin Martyr was worried about newly converted Christians Judaizing. Pseudo-Clement echoes Justin Martyr's words (*Recognitions* 1.39, 88) when he claims that baptism was instituted in place of animal sacrifice—purification comes from the wisdom of God, not the blood of beasts.

18. Justin Martyr, *Dialogue with Trypho* 15, 113–17.

19. MacMullen, *Second Church*, 98–104. From Bowes (*Private Worship, Public Values*, 49), the upper echelons of Roman society were becoming Christian as early as the early to mid-second century. Fox *Pagans and Christians*, 609–81.

RITUAL, DEMONS, AND SACRED SPACE

the same time it was critical that they distinguish themselves in order to convince pagans that the way of the Lord was better.[20]

In their inception, Christian rituals were suggestive rather than prescriptive or exacting; their value was not incumbent on precise forms and formulas. The Eucharistic rite varied from setting to setting in the apostolic period. The Acts of the Apostles (19:5) and Justin Martyr speak of baptism in the name of Jesus or the Holy Spirit and not according to a Trinitarian formula.[21] Paul insisted that the converts of Ephesus be baptized "in the name of the Lord Jesus" and receive the "Holy Spirit." The Ephesians replied that they had previously received baptism from John the Baptist and exclaimed, "We have not even heard that there is a Holy Spirit" (Acts 19:1–5). Prayer was also fluid and informal in the first Christian centuries; Clement of Alexandria said prayer should be "engaged in walking, in conversation, while in silence, while engaged in reading and in works ... in every mood." Tertullian urged Christians to pray together often, but beyond this he was vague.[22]

Feasting was a centerpiece of communal life in late antiquity that posed a challenge for Christians; the fare at community meals was historically flesh from the slaughter of animals used in cultic worship. The apostle Paul first equated eating meat served at pagan ceremonial feasts to demonism. "What pagans sacrifice, they sacrifice to demons and not to God. I do not want you to be partners with demons.... You cannot partake of the table of the Lord and the table of demons" (I Cor. 10:20–21). Pagans fully appreciated the significance of cultic offerings in shared feasting, because when Roman officials apprehended Christians, they forced them to eat of the sacrificial offerings or face punishment. Once Christianity was legalized, Paul's warning continued to find purchase in Cyril of Jerusalem's instructions to catechumens. He forbade them to eat the food that was hung up in pagan temples and at festivals because it was "defiled by the invocation of abominable demons."[23]

---

20. Justin Martyr, *Apology on Behalf of Christians* 13.1, 108–9; 46.2–3, 200–201. See Origin (*Contra Celsum* 2.16, 81–83) on life after death. From Janowitz (*Icons of Power*, 1–18), Porphyry held that it was demons, not gods, that fed on animal sacrifices and libations. Iamblichus's view was similar to Porphyry's, but he approved animal sacrifice for the gods of the lower, material world. See also G. Shaw, *Theurgy and the Soul*, 13–17, 149–51; Brown, *Rise of Western Christendom*, 153–54.

21. Hippolytus, *On the Apostolic Tradition*, introduction; Jefford, "Introduction." Meens (*Penance*, 15) says it well in his remarks on rituals in the early church: "Diversity was the norm and unity mostly a rhetorical construction." Weltin, "Concept of *Ex–Opere–Operato* Efficacy," 76–77. The treatise called *Apostolic Tradition* was written about 220 in Rome and was one of the first and most widely accepted of the "Church Orders" (organized set of rules). It reflects a period in church history when there was no centralization from community to community.

22. Phillips, "Prayer in the First Four Centuries," 38–46 (quotation 38), on Tertullian, 46.

23. Cyril of Jerusalem, *First Lecture on the Mysteries* 7, in *Works of Saint Cyril*, 2:157. From Pseudo-Clement (*Recognitions* 2.71, 116; 4.36, 143), admonition against "partak[ing] at the table of demons,"

CHAPTER 3

The sources amply attest that the struggle against idol worship was incremental and frequently frustrated by setbacks. Nominally Christianized peoples vacillated between the new religion and the cults of their ancestors. Newly minted converts tended to revere their new god by forms of worship that had pleased the old gods, and long-established ordinary Christians continued practices that resembled conventional Roman religious rites. The church struggled with entrenched vestiges of pagan idolatry deeply imprinted in rituals. Ramsey MacMullen speaks of two forms of Christianity and the tensions that arose between them shortly after persecutions ended in the early fourth century. One form was "the choice of the Establishment, principally the clergy, in-city," and the second form was "for everybody else." Each population "had different ideas about the language of gesture and voice that one should use toward the divine, its style or propriety; different ideas about the reality of relations with the dear departed; and their own sense of what were the best answers for ordinary people." Customary habits such as lighting candles at tombs and exalting "unlicensed" holy people were condemned.[24]

Many of the central issues of the pre-Constantinian church shifted once the religion was legitimized by the Edict of Milan in 313. Although pagan practices persisted among Christians, the attention of ecclesiastics focused on organizational matters and core questions of Christology, or the nature of the divine in Jesus. In the doctrinal conflicts of the fourth and fifth centuries, magic and demonology did not loom large. This is not to say that Christian thinkers had reached agreement on idolatrous magic; quite the opposite was true. Because magic was not a chief concern during the era of the ecumenical councils, Christian positions on it were diverse, idiosyncratic, and largely unexamined by larger juridical church bodies.

The legalization of Christianity in 313 involved more than bans on particular pagan beliefs and behaviors (which became obsolete in urban centers and aristocratic villas during the fourth century); it intensified a wholesale effort at authorizing a program of Christian rites born in the first century. Imperial governmental policy increasingly favored Christian interests under Emperor Theodosius I's (d. 395) emperorship, and by the late-fourth century, organized worship of demons in an institutionalized fashion was well in decline throughout the major cities of the empire. Roman Christian regimes

---

which implied consuming "blood, or a carcass which is strangled" and other foods offered to demons, became a common motif in Christian literature. Peter would not eat with Clement because Clement was unclean by virtue of the fact that he was not baptized. Wilken, *First Thousand Years*, 69.

24. MacMullen, *Second Church*, 107.

enabled restrictive legislation against pagan cults, such as closing temples, confiscating property, disbanding priesthoods, withholding government subsidies, and prohibiting public sacrifice to the gods. The Christian emperor Theodosius II's legal text, the *Theodosian Code* designates capital punishment for those who carry out nocturnal sacrifice to demons, invoke them with incantations, or engage magic in preparation for funeral rites.[25]

In addition to shaping the imperial legal apparatus, a major drive of the church was to tailor the people's daily behaviors and viewpoints to the new creed. A key figure in this enterprise was Augustine of Hippo, who turned his attention to the quotidian superstitious practices of Christians. As the project of Christianization unfolded, it became evident that there were layers upon layers of demonic habits that would have to be peeled away. Even basic states of mind or internal dispositions of the soul, such as curiosity, pride, or covetousness, created fertile ground in which demonic subversion could germinate.[26]

Sacred Space and Nature Worship

The question of place was prominent among the issues that emerged for Christians crafting a new identity and a way to express that identity through ritual. The new place of worship had to be one where demons did not feel welcome. When Christians established sacred sites, loci of ritual, they were often in blatant spatial competition with pagan competitors whose numinous locales were, for the most part, in the natural world. Although Near Eastern and Mediterranean religions were temple oriented, with a sophisticated conception of enclosed ceremonial, the common person did not, as a rule, enter the hallowed domain, and most popular ritualistic religious activity took place in the fields or outside the temple precinct—in short, out of doors.[27]

---

25. Theodosian Code 16.10.7, 473; 9.16.7, 238. From Goodman ("Temples"), from 397 to 425, laws facilitated temple demolition in order to provide building materials for civic projects and to starve out pagan cults, particularly in the countryside. However literary accounts of the conversion of pagan temples to Christian churches were often propagandistic fabrication or embellishments; most temples "crumbled undisturbed, were demolished for practical reasons or were converted to new functions" (quotation 188). See also Alan Cameron, Last Pagans of Rome, 39–75; Errington, Roman Imperial Policy, 233–59.

26. On curiosity, pride, and covetousness as understood in the context of idolatry and magic see Rampton, "Gender of Magic," 170–76. See also Tertullian (*De idololatria* 11, 2:1110) who equates covetousness to idolatry.

27. Wilken, *First Thousand Years*, 11–13; J. Z. Smith, *To Take Place*, 47–73. See S. Collins (*Carolingian Debate*, 5–13) for a historiography of sacred space in the Christian tradition.

The earliest Christian meeting places were ad hoc, in catacombs and private dwellings (often elite women's homes),[28] but once the religion was legalized, the question of appropriate sacred space became pressing as Christians sought a model that bespoke their theology and collective sensibilities. An early response to this situation was partially worked out when the newly emerging Christian power elite embraced Jerusalem as a model of the sacral. In the two decades after legalization, the first Christian emperor, Constantine I (d. 337), and his mother, Helena (d. ca. 328), traveled to Jerusalem, "the navel of the universe," to visually establish themselves in the cradle of the Christian faith through dramatic displays of ritualistic state theater.[29]

At the beginning of this chapter, we saw Emperor Constantine directing Acacius to burn idols and demolish an altar near the holy oak at Mamre. "Out with the old and in with the new" was a neat and common propagandistic literary leitmotif of the newly official church. In *The Life of Constantine*, the Christian historian Eusebius talks about the importance of protecting Christian memory in the Holy Land and reclaiming the space Emperor Hadrian (d. 138) and a "tribe of demons" had defiled by building a temple to Aphrodite, an "impure demon," over Christ's tomb, and proffering "foul sacrifices there upon defiled and polluted altars."[30] Christian myth was projected onto the terrain, and conversely, the Holy Land infused Christian ritual with a clear and distinctive topographical metaphor, a locus—to be less mapped out than evoked—that was transportable through the liturgy, and, as Jonathan Smith puts it, charted onto the "newly invented Christian year."[31]

Robert Nisbet notes that the first formulation of dramatic cultural change occurs in multivocal symbols and metaphors, which include fully

---

28. Examples are Mary (Acts 12:12); Lydia, a patron for the church at Philippi (Acts 16:14–15); Priscilla, who with her husband was a significant figure in Corinth. (Acts 18:2–3). The same pattern is present in the Pauline corpus. Paul called Phoebe a "benefactor" of the church in Cenchrea (Rom. 16:2). Lewis, "Popular Christianity"; Clark, "Early Christian Women," 23–24. On "house-churches" see Hippolytus, *On the Apostolic Tradition*, 41–42. On catacombs and "house-churches" see MacMullen, *Second Church*, 69–87.

29. Sozomen, *Ecclesiastical History* 1.2–4, 52–57; Eusebius, *Life of Constantine* 41–43.3, 137–38; Iogna-Prat, *La Maison Dieu*, 29–47; Congourdeau, "Jérusalem et Constantinople"; Wilken, *Land Called Holy*, 82–100; Hunt, *Holy Land Pilgrimage*, 6–49.

30. Eusebius, *Life of Constantine* 3.26, 132. See also ibid., 3.25–56, 132–56 on the destruction of pagan holy sites. See Fleischer ("Living Rocks") for Edenic vegetative motifs in early churches. On Eusebius and demons generally see Johannessen, *The Demonic*. On Eusebius see Walker, *Holy City, Holy Places?*, 22–31.

31. J. Z. Smith, *To Take Place*, 74–95 (quotation 90). In *Holy City, Holy Places?* (35–50), Walker contrasts Bishop Cyril of Jerusalem and Eusebius on their respective theologies of place and demonstrates that the notion of Jerusalem as both a holy site and a sacred symbol was not univocal. From Markus (*End of Ancient Christianity*, 139–55), resistance to the notion of Christian holy space was palpable well until the late fourth century.

known components that take on new meaning by their positioning within the metaphor. Similarly Paul Dutton observes that "when metaphors change we should watch carefully, for an entire world of perception and ideas may have changed with them."[32] Although many of the cultural components of the new religion were traditional, the foundational metaphors of Christianity and paganism were different, in competition, and at odds. The pagans' meaningful metaphors were grounded in the natural world. The Christians' root metaphor, on the other hand, was a city: the heavenly Jerusalem, an anagoge for the terrestrial Jerusalem.

Concurrent with Constantine and Helena's imperial visits to the Holy Land, ecclesiastical influence found footing at saints' shrines, particularly in the West. Peter Brown identifies the dissimilarity between Christian and pagan approaches to the grave. For pagans it was a feared, polluted, and haunted space from which the living recoiled. Early Christians fashioned a new kind of hallowed place where the dead and the living commingled, and these shrines were protected from the infiltration of the insidious demonic powers swirling around pagan tombs because they were enclosed by the vault-like supervision of the church.[33]

Like the shrines of the saints, the church building became a symbol for a new vision of worship. The core of Christian religious activity transpired under a roof in a sanctified interior space constructed by human hands. It was more than just a different location from those frequented by pagan celebrants and inhabited by their demonic deities. It was a new concept of place particular to Christianity—delineated, cleansed of demons, consecrated to that special creator god who does not inhere in his creation (trees, rocks, springs) and should not be worshipped through it. Nothing filled demons with dread and kept them at bay like a sanctified church. The motif of demons fleeing in terror from a consecrating bishop was familiar in late antiquity, when the fight against idolatry was a matter of openly confronting pagan cults. Gregory the Miracle-Worker (d. ca. 270), a student of Origen who lived in north-central Turkey, prayed at the local temple, and the next morning the temple warden could not induce a lingering demon to enter.[34] Christian structures were fortifications against demons and those who would traffic with them.

---

32. Nisbet, *Social Change and History*, 3–11. Dutton, *Politics of Dreaming*, 258. See also Pagels, *Beyond Belief*, 109–13.

33. MacMullen, *Second Church*, 104–6; Brown, *Cult of the Saints*, especially 1–49.

34. *Letter of Barnabas* 16, 216–18; Kilde, *Sacred Power, Sacred Space*, 14–37; MacMullen, *Christianizing the Roman Empire*, 59–60 (for Gregory).

Very early in the church's history, the guardianship of the altar—the focal point of the sanctified internal space—became increasingly male gendered, and shrines and churches were perceived as spheres of masculine authority. Deaconesses were an exception; these women were (possibly) ordained and exercised duties similar to those of their male counterparts. But the office started to lose favor by the fourth century, particularly in the West.[35] By the late first century, the process began of corralling ritual and allocating it to male religious specialists who authorized correct procedures. It was important (to some) that ecclesiastics monopolize the fine art of designating the authentic "signified" relative to a whole range of cultural signs. Bishop Ignatius of Antioch (d. ca. 100) stressed that the functionary who must mediate the efficacy of ritual for the group was the bishop. "See that you follow the bishop, even as Jesus Christ does the Father. . . . Let no man do anything connected with the Church without the bishop. . . . [The] Eucharist, [must be administered] . . . either by the bishop, or one to whom he has entrusted it. Wherever the bishop shall appear, there let the multitude (of the people) also be."[36] Kim Bowes points out that by the early third century, the church was shifting its dependence from systems of patronage and family politics, in which women were important brokers, and operating within communities that were led by a singular authority centered on the bishops.[37]

A particularly brazen form of sorcery for pagans and Christians was manipulation of the weather. For example, in *Natural Questions* the Roman Stoic and statesman Seneca (d. 65 CE) derides the people of Cleonae who perform blood sacrifices to avert a storm and believe that "instantly those clouds turned away, once they had tasted a bit of blood." The uneducated "believed that rain could be both attracted and repelled by incantations." The naturalist philosopher Pliny the Elder (d. 79 CE) claimed that charms could compel lightening to strike and that any deviation from the ritual could result in death by electrocution.[38] Christians also held that weather magic was possible, but it was a particularly grave affront to Christian sensibilities

---

35. MacMullen *Second Church*, 89; Muschio, "Men, Women," 203–6. The question as to whether the diaconate as a church office was open to women is hotly debated and too broad for even a cursory treatment of it here. The following sources will give the reader entrée into the literature. Epiphanius of Salamis, *Panarion*, "Collyridians" 3.6, 3:638. Macy, *Hidden History*, 23–88; *Women in Early Christianity*, 62–68; Eisen, *Women Officeholders*, 158–98.

36. Ignatius of Antioch, "Epistle to the Smyrnaeans" 8, 89–90. See Phillips ("Prayer in the First Four Centuries," 48–56) for evolving Christian prayer ritual.

37. Bowes, *Private Worship, Public Values*, 161–88.

38. Seneca, *Natural Questions* 4b.6–7, 67–68; Pliny, *Natural History* 28.4, vol. 8 (418), 10–13. Ammianus Marcellinus (*History* 23.5.9–12, 2:338–41) attests to a special kind of "advisory" divination that prohibits or prescribes a particular course of action.

because of the wariness with which the church approached the outdoors and because of the abusiveness of those who sought to appropriate the prerogatives of God to control the natural world. According to the Book of Enoch, it was the evil demon Ezekiel who taught humans "the knowledge of the clouds."[39] Throughout the Old Testament, God uses weather to discipline his people or to frustrate their enemies. In Jeremiah, God demands that the children of Israel recognize that only he and not the false gods can send rain (Jer. 14:22). One of Jesus's first miracles was to quell a tempest on the Sea of Galilee, causing his disciples to ask, "Who then is this, that he commands even the winds and the water, and they obey him?" (Luke 8:22–25 [quotation 25]. Also Matt. 8:23–27; Mark 4:35–41). When those other than saints or holy men and women, through whom God operated, attempted to influence the weather (whether they succeeded or not), they were appropriating powers over which they had no legitimate claim.[40]

Christian-influenced Roman law forbade weather magic and legislated against magicians, enchanters, conjurers of storms (*malefici, incantantores, immissores*), and others who, through invocation of demons, threw men's minds into confusion. However, the code exempted as innocent those procedures the unlearned undertook to ensure rain, as they most likely were not intentionally colluding with demons, but rather acting out time-honored rituals that enabled them to participate in natural processes.[41] There was no question in Theodosian legislation as to whether humans had the ability to control the elements—they certainly did. The law ignored the peasants and their ineffective rituals and targeted those who were actually able to alter the climate. The concern over the mischief that *malefici, incantantores*, and *immissores* caused was a practical one.

In Roman antiquity, then, Christians and pagans agreed that weather magic was possible. Because this and other sorceries were practiced out of doors, worshippers, who were vulnerable to temptation in the natural environment, were assured safety when swaddled within the four walls of a church. Within the protected space, demons were banished, worship could be supervised, and misconduct such as conjuring storms was not possible. Whereas some pre-Christian rites were hard to peg as distinctly pagan because they were so generic to spirituality (such as prayer or supplication),

---

39. *Book of the Watchers* 8.1–4 in *Complete Books of Enoch*, 30. From Nock ("Paul and the Magus," 309), Simon Magus was reputed to control the weather magically. Latin terms for weather magicians are *tempestarius/tempestaria, emissor, immissor*.

40. Hilarian was one of those holy people who channeled God's power to roil and quell storms (Jerome, *Life of Saint Hilarion* 32, 40).

41. *Theodosian Code* 9.16.3, 237.

the stipulation that proper worship take place indoors was cut and dried. If not easy to enforce, at least the concept was easy to explain: venerating demons took place in a natural setting; the true God was worshipped in a church.

Singing, Dancing, Juggling

An aspect of pagan religiosity that stood in stark opposition to Christian worship involved physical and psychic ecstasy at outdoor public ceremonies. In the classical Mediterranean world there had long been mild disapproval or unease about exuberance or emotive display in religious observance. Ramsay MacMullen argues that upper-class Romans tended to disdain the emotionalism of mystery religions and the degree of physical abandon concomitant with their liturgies, especially that characteristic of Eastern sects.[42] Seneca, for example, wrote that the dancing and howling of Eastern priests smacked of dementia.[43] Despite the elites' contempt for tumultuous spectacles, they were abundant and beloved by the general populations of imperial Rome.

Rites of physical and emotional enthusiasm were not restricted to women, but they were, in large measure, gendered "female," because women were prominent in them, and/or because they were in the service of female deities. This made such displays particularly objectionable. The hair-trigger tendency for a woman to lapse into her basal, excitable, and sexual nature was a source of societal disorder that needed controls, not encouragement. Nearly two hundred years before the birth of Jesus, the Roman senate showed its distaste for intoxicated ebullition in its condemnation of the female-centered Bacchanalian rites, and that prejudice continued into the Common Era.[44] The Roman poet Juvenal's (fl. 127 CE) *Sixth Satire* lampoons women's orgiastic rituals for the goddesses Bellona and Cybele, which were accompanied by howling herds dancing with sexual recklessness. Plutarch (d. ca. 120 CE), a Roman biographer and essayist, said of a "wife" that it is becoming for her "to worship and to know only the gods that her husband believes in, and to shut the front door tight upon all queer

---

42. MacMullen, *Paganism*, 75–80. Romans' and Christians' shared attitudes on physical indulgence in ritual were also applied to sexuality in general, but Christians pushed the pagan Roman ideal of self-control to a new level by embracing celibacy. See Cooper, *Virgin and the Bride*, 45–67; Brown, *Body and Society*, chaps. 1, 4. See Milanezi's discussion ("Pratiques et censures") of laughter as manic, Dionysian madness.

43. MacMullen, *Paganism*, 44, 64.

44. Livy, *History of Rome* 39.15, 246–51. See Bowes, *Private Worship, Public Values*, 196–97; Graf, *Magic*, 49.

rituals and outlandish superstitions. For with no god do stealthy and secret rites performed by a woman find any favour."[45]

Assyrian satirist Lucian of Samosata (d. after 180 CE) described the rites of the Syrian goddess Atargatis, including scenes of male genital self-mutilation, cross-dressing, and riotous celebration. In his treatise *On Dance*, he records details of festivals for Atargatis, Isis, and Phrygian Cybele, which consist of frenzied yelling and whirling as associates hold out the begging bowl. The ceremonies for Anatolian Ma included men dancing half naked, whirling, flailing until blood flowed, and finally self-castration. At Delos, the sacrificial offering itself was made amid wild dancing, hymns, pipes, and nocturnal processions.[46]

In Apuleius's novel, *Metamorphoses*, the protagonist, Lucius, describes in tones of disgust typical of second-century elites the eunuch charlatans steering the statue of the Syrian Goddess around on the back of a donkey for the sake of profits from bogus fortune telling, goaded "into a demented quickstep" by the reed pipe. The goddess's devotees cry out "with frantic-sounding, discordant howls. They put their heads down and for a long time whipped their necks around slickly and whirled their loose, long hair. At intervals, they attacked their own flesh with their teeth, and at last each took the double-edged sword he carried and cut up his own arms." Worship at Hekate's shrine often involved gladiatorial games, music, dramatic presentations, and dancers, and Artemis's shrine in Nanaia had a small theater for dancing and singing.[47] Interestingly, both of these goddesses had a particular association with magic throughout the Middle Ages and into the early modern era.

The architects of the coalescing church found themselves in agreement with Roman elites on the question of orgiastic ritual and women's disproportionate affinity toward libertine emotionalism.[48] Christian prejudice against ritual singing, dancing, and juggling was conditioned by two factors. First, as indicated above, particularly upper-class Christians inherited the Roman

---

45. Juvenal, "Against Women" lines 511–41, in *Satires of Juvenal*, 84–85; Plutarch, "Advice to Bride and Groom," in *Moralia* 19, 310–11.

46. Lucian of Samosata, *On the Syrian Goddess*, 77–78. Lucian's writings were widely known in his own day; more than eighty works are extant.

47. Apuleius of Madaura, *Golden Ass* 8.27, 180. *Metamorphoses* (also called *The Golden Ass* [*Asinus aureus*]) is the only Latin Roman novel that survives in its entirety. It is a story of a man who is magically transformed into an ass. It puts the lower classes of the empire under the microscope, including their religious practices and proclivities to vulgar superstition. On Hekate, Nanaia, and similar aspects of pagan worship see MacMullen, *Paganism*, 18–25, 43.

48. There are some references to ecstasy and speaking in tongues in the New Testament by men and women, such as Acts 19:6, but the new church did not emphasize that particular tradition.

elitist aversion to excesses.⁴⁹ Second, the Old Testament, in its denunciation of temple prostitution and other gentile practices, provided a model for spurning worship that depended on female sensuality and bacchanalian ferocity. It was not so much that ecclesiastics frowned on rituals involving singing, dancing, and juggling because women took a prominent role in them, but male writers of the period—pagan and Christian— disdained wildness that implied lack of control, and they were conditioned to associate that unruliness with women.

The cults that were most extreme in their frenzy and reliance on women (as priestesses, devotees, or the sectarian deity) were those Eastern mystery religions with which pagans conflated Christianity in its early history; and Christianity itself was, of course, an import from the Levant. This was a time when the church was fighting a life-and-death struggle to define and promote itself as different from a multitude of Gnostic and other micro-cults and philosophical belief systems, particularly from the eastern portions of the empire.⁵⁰ One way of making itself distinctive from its competitor mystery religions was to reject bawdy, Dionysian conduct and to align itself with the more restrained Roman tradition, which happened naturally as more and more of the Roman upper class assumed leadership of the church. Christianity spurned the physical mutilation, debauchery, and lack of restraint associated with eccentric Eastern deities, fertility goddesses, and their aficionados.⁵¹

The concern of theologians in the pan-Christian intellectual environment of late antiquity went deeper than a fear of impropriety; singing, dancing, and juggling smacked of the demonic. This is clear in Tertullian's *Apology*, where he describes demons "performing many miraculous juggling tricks." The author of the *Recognitions* made the relationship between unrestrained behavior and demonism explicit. "By this means [drinking, banquets, music] power was given to the demons to enter into minds of this sort, so that they

---

49. Justin Martyr (*Apology on Behalf of Christians* 27.4, 155–57) wrote of the incest performed at the pleasure of Cybele, "mother of the gods." MacMullen, *Second Church*, 107–8; Benko, *Pagan Rome*, 62–74.

50. Pagels, *Adam, Eve, and the Serpent*, 57–77. Robinson notes (*Who Were the First Christians*, 6–12) that in defining the new religion, apologists colored a "flattened portrait of polytheism" (12) and ignored its nuances.

51. Augustine, *De civitate Dei* 6.10, 1:181–83; 24, 1:37–38; Tertullian, *Apologeticum* 35, 1:144–47. The highly-placed clergy took the commitment to eschew leud display up a notch from the staid behavior enjoined on the Roman elite. The canons of the 363 to 364 Council of Laodicea (53–55, in *Seven Ecumenical Councils*, 156–57) stipulate that clergy may dine at weddings, but not clap their hands or "dance or leap." They were forbidden to attend plays or "club together for drinking entertainments." Pseudo-Clement, *Recognitions* 4.13, 4.16, 4.18, pp. 137–38; 4.30, p. 141.

seemed to lead insane dances and to rave like Bacchanalians."⁵² Such ritual displays were enticing because they intensified the experience or encounter of those who participated in them, imprinting on the very bodies of the actors a liberating release into interior psychic states on which demons could prey. Christian ritual worship could not be allowed to mimic rites that had traditionally attracted and pleased demonic deities, and thereby risk transference of a pagan worldview beyond the ritual into daily experience. So Christians took up the complaint of their more conservative contemporaries who disparaged the likes of the goddess Cybele's priests and the devotees of Anatolian Ma.

The ancient correlation between music and sorcery is evident in the etymology of the Latin word *cantare* (sing), which is also the root of the word "enchantment" (*incantatio*), and the Roman *vates* (bard) could be a simple songster or a sorcerous soothsayer. Bishop Irenaeus of Lyon (d. ca. 200) boasted that the highest level of language is hymns, and he contrasted "pure" Christian prayer to heathen song, which he called "incantations"; in so doing he conflated pagan music and magic.⁵³ Clement of Alexandria in the third century and John Chrysostom in the fourth equated the musicians, dancers, and mimes of the pagan holy mysteries with prostitutes. Chrysostom wrote, "Demons congregate where there are licentious chants."⁵⁴ Basil of Caesarea, Ambrose of Milan (d. 397), Pseudo-Clement, and Augustine all expressed consternation at dancing, hand clapping, singing, and piping, particularly in ritualistic performative settings. Bishop Basil reproved Christians who pranced in the chapels of Caesarea, and in Syria, other clerics tried to suppress dancing at weddings and hand clapping or piping along with hymns that took place even inside the church building—conduct that Ambrose called "pagan." Dancing in the fashion of the heathen was discouraged, but if people had to dance, they should only shuffle their feet and avoid "happy glances."⁵⁵ Because ceremonies at pagan shrines could be immoderately demonstrative, with drinking, dancing, eating, and singing, when early Christians celebrated too much at the tombs of the dead with memorial

---

52. Tertullian, *Apologeticum* 23, 1:130: "multa miracula circulatoriis praestigiis ludunt." Pseudo-Clement, *Recognitions* 4.13, 137.

53. Irenaeus of Lyon, *Against the Heresies*, 32.5, 2:24–27.

54. Clement of Alexandria, *Exhortation to the Heathen*, in *Writings of Clement of Alexandria*, 26–33; John Chrysostom, "Exposition of Psalm 41," 14.

55. Basil of Caesarea, *Saint Basil Exegetic Homilies* 14, 213. On Ambrose see MacMullen, *Christianizing the Roman Empire*, 74–76. Pseudo-Clement, *Recognitions* 4.13, 137; Augustine, Sermon 280.6, col. 1283. Augustine was partially motivated by a desire to draw a distinction between Catholic and Donatist ceremony at the graves of the dead. MacMullen, *Second Church*, 95–114 (quotation 107). See Elm von der Osten, "'Perpetua felicitas,'" 283–85.

picnics, Augustine became nervous about how similar their behavior was to that of the idolatrous pagan worshippers. He urged Christians to establish a different pattern of religious observance.[56]

Regardless of the intention of the celebrants or the content of the songs, demon worship was imprinted on the ritual forms themselves. As Ramsay MacMullen writes, "Festive conduct . . . [was] by no means only part of a good time; but it [was] non-Christian."[57] Many such antics, made worse by the fact that they were "womanish," were the techniques used to worship demons and so came to be seen as anti-Christian or demonic.

Christians did not disallow all music; on the contrary, there is a solid tradition of Christian song. But it was very different from the kind of singing that was considered idolatrous. In Matt. 26:30 and Mark 14:26, Jesus sings a hymn with his disciples, and Paul exhorts the Colossian and Ephesian congregations, "In your hearts sing psalms, hymns, and spiritual songs to God," and "Sing psalms and hymns and spiritual songs" (Col. 3:16; Eph. 5:19). Communal singing of psalms is stipulated in the *Apostolic Tradition*, and it was not restricted to the religious community.[58] *Cantare* is also the term used to describe the delivery of the Mass, so the word itself could be cleansed of its pagan connotations within the confines of Christian holy space.

However, although simple song was safe enough, there was particular suspicion about overly aesthetic melodies or the use of instruments in church.[59] Augustine struggled with the sensuousness of music to the point that he sometimes "wished that every melody of the sweet chants to which the psalms of David are set be removed from [his] ears and from the church itself." He praised Bishop Athanasius of Alexandria "who asked that the reader of the psalm perform it with so little inflection of the voice that it was closer to speaking than to singing."[60] Writers such as Clement of Alexandria

---

56. From MacMullen (*Second Church*, 108–109), Ambrose shared the Hipponian bishop's concern that memorial picnics at burial sites (both underground and at open-air cemeteries) were too like non-Christian habits. At the heart of this trepidation was the fear of what Löw calls ("Social Construction of Space," 120) the potential of emotionally charged locales to become expressions of liminal "pluralities" and "overlapping relations."

57. MacMullen, *Christianizing the Roman Empire*, 76. See also MacMullen, *Second Church*, 108, 153n85.

58. Hippolytus, *On the Apostolic Tradition*, 136.

59. John Chrysostom, "Exposition of Psalm 41," 13–16.

60. Augustine, *Confessionum* 10.33.50, 181–82: "Aliquando autem hanc ipsam fallaciam immoderatius cauens erro nimia seueritate, sed ualde interdum, ut melos onme cantilenarum suauium, quibus Dauidicum psalterium frequentatur ab, auribus meis remoueri velim atque ipsius ecclesiae, tutiusque mihi uidetur, quod de Alexandrino episcopo Athanasio saepe mihi dictum commemini, qui tam modico flexu uocis faciebat sonare lectorem psalmi, ut pronuntianti uicinior esset quam canenti."

and Eusebius found themselves apologizing for Old Testament musicians, and allegorizing their use of instruments in services. Clement insisted that the human voice was the instrument most pleasing to God. "Leave the pipe to the shepherd, the flute to the men who are in fear of gods and intent on their idol worshipping. Such musical instruments must be excluded from our wingless feasts. . . . Moreover, King David the harpist . . . urged us toward the truth and away from idols. So far was he from singing the praises of daemons that they were put to flight by him with the true music. . . . [Jesus] scorned those lifeless instruments of lyre and cithara." Eusebius said much the same. "We render our hymn with a living psalterion and a living cithara with spiritual songs. The unison voices of Christians would be more acceptable to God than any musical instrument."[61]

Since instrumental music is amply testified in the Old Testament as a form of worship indulged by some of the most praiseworthy of personages (such as King David [fl. 1000 BCE]), the prejudice against instruments seems to have been due to a reaction against contemporary pagan ritual usage rather than an inheritance from Jewish scripture. Music could be an important means by which to venerate the divine, but it had to be used gingerly, especially when accompanied by instruments, so as never to harness the wrong kind of spiritual power. By changing ritual form from open air theatrical extravaganzas with crass instruments, to the simple harmonizing of human voices in consecrated houses of worship, music was wrested from demons and Christianized.

In the early church, combating the veneration of false gods (demons in disguise) was the first order of business for the new religion, because comportment with them amounted to idolatry—that is to say, magic. But even when commerce with devils ceased in formal, cultic settings, traffic with demons was so etched on some ritual forms of traditional Roman worship that either new rites had to be developed or the symbolic content of old rituals reframed. The clergy sought to save meaningful and familiar ritual forms when it seemed possible to redirect the symbolic content. However, some behaviors were so thoroughly saturated with messages counter to Christian truths that they could not be reformed.

Christians created a new kind of space where demons dared not tread and in which continuity with old rites and the worldview they stored were

---

61. Clement of Alexandria, *Instructor* 62, in *Fathers of the Second Century* 130; Eusebius, *Commentary on Psalms* 91:2–3, in Mitchell, *Songs of Ascents*, 223. See also Valerian, Homily 10.5, in *Saint Peter Chrysologus*, 368.

thwarted. The enclosed hallowed space provided a clean slate on which a new story could be written in the language of ritual. Church leaders disallowed orgiastic, sexualized displays, which demons loved where women were major participants, but they approved hymns and chanted masses. The new religion did not reject, wholesale, age-old notions of the proper approach to deity. In fact, in many cases Christian worship aligned itself in form and tone with traditional somber customs of Roman worship, but the symbolic content making up the pagan rituals was redirected, and the aspects attractive to demons were filtered out.

CHAPTER 4

A Thousand Vacuous Observances

> Something instituted by humans is superstitious if it concerns the making and worshiping of idols . . . or if it involves certain kinds of consultations or contracts about meaning arranged and ratified with demons, such as the enterprises involved in the art of magic. . . . Other examples are these: treading on the threshold when you pass in front of your own house; going back to bed if you sneeze while putting on your shoes; returning inside your house if you trip up while leaving it; or, when your clothing is eaten by mice.
>
> —Augustine, *On Christian Doctrine*

For Augustine, vacuous observances took myriad forms. Some were trivial such as fearing a sneeze; some were more pernicious such as attempting to foresee the future, but all "involved the art of magic" (*magicarum atrium*).[1] The archaic Greeks coined the word *mageia* to denote the ancient craft of the *magi* (wise men, seers, or fire-priests) of Persia.[2] Famous in antiquity for divination, they could read the stars and interpret oracles, numbers, the flight or cry of birds, the direction of smoke from sacrifices, the weather, the whinnying or sneezes of horses, monstrous births, dreams, patterns in water, and the fall of lots. Possibly because of the fame of the magi, the East was the land of mystery and magic that conjured

---

1. Augustine, *De doctrina Christiana* 2.20.74–77, 90–93: "Superstitiosum est quidquid institutum est ab hominibus ad facienda et colenda idola pertinens vel ad colendam sicut deum creaturam partemve ullam creaturae vel ad consultationes et pacta quaedam significationum cum daemonibus placita atque foederata, qualia sunt molimina magicarum atrium. . . . Hinc sunt etiam illa: limen calcare cum ante domum suam transit, redire ad lectum si quis dum se calciat sternutaverit, redire domum si procedens offenderit, cum vestis a soricibus roditur plus tremere suspicionem futuri mali quam praesens damnum dolere."

2. Fowden, *Empire to Commonwealth*, 24–36. From Nock ("Paul and the Magus," 308–23), the magi were Zoroastrian priests from the Median tribe of ancient Persia who carried out the daily ceremonies of fire worship. By the fifth century BCE, the magi—once esteemed—came to be seen as quacks.

images of Egypt, Chaldea, and wondrous lands beyond.[3] Ammianus Marcellinus, familiar with the East from his military service, wrote of Egypt as the well of esoteric knowledge where the ancient philosopher Anaxagoras (d. ca. 428 BCE) was taught to predict meteorological storms and foresee earthquakes by the feel of mud.[4] Thessaly also had a special allure, and, no doubt for that reason, Apuleius set his novel *Metamorphoses*—full of exotica and bewitchment—in that place where "the enchantments used in witchcraft, which the whole world sings of to the single tune of notoriety, had their birth place."[5] By the first century BCE, *mageia* had become a term of abuse associated with impiety, pernicious curiosity, and possible criminality. *Mageia* was replaced by *theurgia* which denoted mystical or learned dealings with the gods.[6]

Divination

Divination was a centerpiece of ancient Mediterranean religion and the technique through which humans came to know the will of the divine.[7] Secrets of the natural order were encoded in its parts, and the priestess's or priest's job was to download that message through the proper management of ritual. Divination was not only licit; it was a criterial feature of Roman worship. Humans could approach deities because of the "sympathy" between the world and the realm of the gods, whose divine *esse* infused the earthly plane. That *esse* was occult, but it could be engaged through the proper rites. Ammianus Marcellinus penned a succinct explanation of the concept behind the practice of reading signs in the flight of birds, the entrails of beasts (*aruspicina*), the words of the sibyls (female seers), thunder, lightning, dreams (*oneiromantia*), and "the gleam of a star's train of light" (*itidemque siderum sulci*). He said, "The spirit pervading all the elements . . . makes us also sharers in the gifts of divination and the elemental powers, when propitiated by

---

3. Brakke, *Demons*, 130; Bremmer, "Birth of the Term"; Janowitz, *Magic in the Roman World*, 9–13; Graf, *Magic*, 169; G. Shaw, *Theurgy and the Soul*, 7, 238; MacMullen, *Paganism*, 122.

4. Ammianus Marcellinus, *History* 22.16.219–22, 2:306–7. In the late antique mystical/theological hermetic text called *Asclepius* (in *Hermetica*, 81) the author speaks of Egypt as "an image of heaven . . . the temple of the whole world." In the thinking of many Christians, the esoteric author Hermes Trismegistus was contemporary to Moses.

5. Apuleius of Madaura, *Golden Ass* 2.1, 21.

6. Ammianus Marcellinus, *History* 26.3.1–6, 2:580–85; Janowitz, *Magic in the Roman World*, 9–13; Graf, *Magic*, 20–24. From Janowitz (*Icons of Power*, 5), the first use of "theurgia" was by Nicomachus of Gerasa in the early first century CE.

7. Jennings, "Divination and Popular Culture," 193–95. I am using the term "divination" to refer to any type of foresight, clairvoyance, or ability to predict the future, and not just its specialized, professional use in formal religion.

divers rites."[8] Clearly, Ammianus Marcellinus held that specific rituals were integral to obtaining occult knowledge.

In the late Roman period, few rejected the possibility that the secrets of the gods, especially concerning the future, could be coaxed out of them if the proper procedures were followed, and the art of augury elicited an awesome respect, partially because those who knew the future had formidable political leverage.[9] Largely because of this, the pagan Romans foreshadowed early Christians' anxiety about divination by recognizing a fine line dividing its legitimate function and its unlawful use. Emperor Augustus (d. 14 CE) had divinatory books burned or buried. Classical writers were so critical of excesses in the practice that in order to defame him, Emperor Julian's detractors alit on the charge that he used "evil arts for divining future events" (*malivoli praenoscendi futura pravas artes assignant*), including extracting embryos from women's wombs in occult rites. Ammianus Marcellinus devoted several chapters of his history to Emperor Valentinian's (d. 375) purge of diviners, whose foreknowledge put them in a position to undermine the state.[10]

Late antique Neoplatonists distinguished common, vulgar divination from the more sublime use of theurgy, the goal of which was to comprehend deity by transcending the profane. The second-century Hellenistic mystery-poem *Chaldean Oracles* is sensitive to the abuse of signs used in a magical fashion and was a manual, of sorts, for the Neoplatonists.[11] Although the Syrian philosopher Iamblichus (d. ca. 330) disdained the crude ritualistic exploitation of cosmic "sympathy" to effect trifling and self-serving outcomes, he insisted that ritual was elemental to aligning oneself with the gods and achieving spiritual illumination. Proclus (d. 485), called "the

---

8. Ammianus Marcellinus, *History* 21.1, 2:90–97 (quotation 21.1.8, 2:92–93). Also on hydromancy, in his trial for magic (*Apulei apologia* 42) Apuleius told the judge of a boy who foretold the future while gazing at an image of Mercury in a bowl of water.

9. Graf, *Magic*, 4. Contrary to the vast majority of pagans, Cicero (*De divinatione*, in *De senectute*, 222–539) was skeptical of the veracity of divination; see particularly book 2, 370–539.

10. Suetonius, *Deified Augustus* 31, 196–97. Ammianus Marcellinus, *History* 21.1.7, 2:92–93. Despite Ammianus Marcellinus's regard for Julian, he felt that the emperor was "superstitious rather than truly religious" (*superstitiosus magis quam sacrorum legitimus observator*); ibid., 25.4.17, 2:510–11. From R. Smith (*Julian's Gods*, 91–113, 219–20), Julian was a devotee of Neoplatonic mysticism, and Ammianus's view reflects the ambivalence many Romans felt toward theurgic rituals. On occult rites see ibid., 219–20. See also Bowes, *Private Worship, Public Values*, 46–48.

11. *Chaldean Oracles* is a mystical poem written in the latter half of the second century that was significant to Neoplatonists. See *Chaldean Oracles*, 1–46 for a full discussion of the text. The oracles were allegedly delivered by deities (often Hekate) and spoken through the mouths of mediums or animated statues. Johnston, "Riders in the Sky"; Lewy and Tardieu, *Chaldaean Oracles*; Fox, *Pagans and Christians*, 196–98.

Successor," was one of the most significant classical philosophers. He shared the unease about the shallow use of ritual and was suspicious of its binding nature. For both men, the essence of magic was coercion, extravagance, and frivolous ritualism. Theurgia was worthier and more splendid. The correct inner disposition, along with somber rites, objects, and appropriate spoken words, was the fitting preparation for approaching God. In order to animate statues and initiate the process of mystic ascent, Neoplatonists depended on sacred stones, metals, gems, herbs, and papyri inscribed with Homeric verses. Iconic sounds such as hissing, clucking, and popping were also key. Porphyry (d. ca. 304 CE), from Tyre in the Roman East, was more puristic than other Neoplatonic philosophers. He believed that any dependence on rites was a drawback to transcendence, and he judged even theurgy to be a lesser form of interaction with divinities because of its ritualism and the characteristics it shared with magic.[12]

The first Christians were obliged to address the issue of divination early in the church's construction. What was to be their view of vaticination, with its long and respectable pedigree in classical Near Eastern sects? The answer was slow to develop and halting once it emerged, as is reflected in various Christian texts. Positions on theurgy were diverse as theologians struggled to determine exactly which divinatory behaviors were actually demonic. Divination's appearance in sacred works added to the confusion. In the Old Testament, God's work is furthered through the aid of diviners and augurs, as in the story of Balaam (Num. 22–24). Astrological divination also plays a pivotal role at various points in the New Testament narrative. For example, astrologers appear in a positive light in Matthew (2:1–11) when the magi see the star of Bethlehem. They travel to Judaea to praise the new king, thereby playing their part in salvation history as instruments of the divine plan.

The Theodosian law code reflects the imprecision in the new religion's stance. It combines the Christian abhorrence for the sin of magic, traditional Roman dread of those who would strive to wield political power by seeing the future, and reverence for time-honored sacred ritual. One of these concerns is often counterpoised against the others, depending on the view of a given authority. Warnings against diviners and their meddling in political affairs are not uncommon in Roman pagan texts, but the authors

---

12. Janowitz, *Icons of Power*, 5–18; From Struck ("Poet as Conjurer," 123–25), Iamblichus thought divination by numbers better than animal sacrifice; G. Shaw, *Theurgy and the Soul*, 5, 11–17, 234, 241; Iamblichus, *Les mystères d'Égypte* 3.15–17, 118–24. Consistent with modern theorists, Iamblichus defined ritual as "action" opposed to thought (ibid., 2.11, 96).

of the *Theodosian Code*, armed with a Christian bias, were emboldened to engage the language of the new religion. A series of statues Constantine I issued impose severe penalties for divination because of its demonic nature. They stipulate that no soothsayer (*haruspex*) or pagan priest (*sacerdos*) shall approach the threshold of any person, even in friendship, on pain of being burned alive, and the code declares that "the inquisitiveness of all for divination shall cease forever." Any augur (*haruspex*), astrologer (*mathematicus*), seer (*vates*), or diviner (*hariolus*) is to be exiled, subjected to the "torture horse" and "iron claws," or executed because his or her activities involve the invocation of demons. Constantine would crush divination of any sort because of its dependence on demons, and he categorically prohibits magicians peddling their trade at private dwellings. However (in seeming contradiction) he allows augurs to practice their "art" publicly. "We do not prohibit the ceremonies of a bygone perversion to be conducted openly."[13] The customary Roman dread of secrecy and political subversion drive the severity of the penalty for magic. A law instigated in 371 under Emperor Valentinian I reflects the same ambiguity. He condemns magic, including astrology, without reservation and assigns "the supreme penalty" to its practitioners, but hieratic prognosticatory practices are allowed. "I judge that divination [*haruspicina*] has no connection with cases of magic, and I do not consider this superstition (*religio*) or any other that was allowed by our elders to be a kind of crime. . . . We do not condemn divination, but we do forbid it to be practiced harmfully."[14] Although a Christian and particularly repressive when it came to magic, Valentinian reflects the older Roman stance on formal public augury—tolerating the practice unless it was performed maliciously. The stated reason for this enactment was to protect "the common safety." In other words, the rationalization for anti-magic legislation was grounded both in moral and practical considerations.

Some Christian thinkers used the term theurgia in a manner comparable to their Neoplatonic neighbors. Dionysius the Areopagite, a fifth-century Christian mystic theologian (fl. 500) even called the Eucharist "theurgy" and agreed with (most) Neoplatonists that material talismans were necessary to communicate with heaven.[15] However, for the most part, fortune telling drew the opprobrium of Christian writers, who would agree with

---

13. *Theodosian Code* 9.16.1–12, 237–39.
14. Ibid., 9.16.9, 238. On purging of magicians under Valentinian see Ammianus Marcellinus, *History* 28.1, 3:86–121; 29.1–2, 3:186–233.
15. G. Shaw, "Neoplatonic Theurgy," particularly 595–99.

Eusebius that oracles are "the deceits and sleights of wizard-men."[16] Augustine shunned divination because of its idolatrous underpinnings, dubious trustworthiness, and presumptuous affront to the creator God, who was ineffable, did not constitute simply the sum of the parts he had fashioned, and could not be known or reached through his creation. The unease about theurgy is significant because of what it says about the Christian stance on magic and ritual. Many shared both the philosophers' enthusiasm and their apprehension about divination, but the piece that tipped the scales against theurgy was not the principle behind the phenomenon of spiritual ascent per se,[17] but the fact that it necessitated rites which had the potential of summoning demons. Despite Neoplatonists' restraints on worship that required gawdy observances and their attempts to separate theurgia from common magic, Augustine was explicit that both *goetia* and theurgia were "deceptive rites of demons" in masquerade as angels, and the work of "wicked spirits creating deceitful illusions."[18]

God did reveal his intent to human beings through dreams and chosen prophets, prophetesses, and saints, but that communication did not hinge on rituals.[19] In fact, it was contaminated by them, in part because they depended on human initiative. God's interaction with his people was his prerogative; it was simple and direct. By the fifth century, virtually all Christian intellectuals had come to see theurgy as just another form of illegitimate prognostication with all the pitfalls of a perverse understanding of the relationship between God and the material world.

At times divination was private and relatively unceremonious, as in theurgic ascent, dream analysis, or seemingly chance events (as when Emperor Constantius II saw his future in the body of a headless corpse). But even when divinatory rites were practiced within a small group of deeply pious mystics, Christian teachers considered those rites pernicious because they combined the perverted power of ritual with the evil influence of demons. Whether public or private, divination posed a political and a spiritual threat.

---

16. Eusebius, *Preparation for the Gospel* 4.2–3, 2:145–52; 5, 2:194–252; MacMullen, *Paganism*, 176n56.

17. For example, Enoch, much admired by patristic writers, ascended to the tenth heaven (*2 Enoch*, in *Complete Books of Enoch*, 119–31).

18. Augustine, *De civitate Dei* 10.9, 1:281: "ritibus fallacibus daemonum obstricti sub nominibus angelorum"; ibid., 10.10, 1:283: "malignorum spirituum cavenda et detestanda fallacia."

19. There are many examples both in the Hebrew Bible and the New Testament. For example, God warns Abimelek to give up Abraham's wife, Sarah (Gen. 20:3); God speaks to Jacob in a dream promising him land and progeny (Gen. 28:10–14); God instructs Mary and Joseph to take Jesus to Egypt (Matt. 2:13).

Astrology

The study of the skies provided the earliest peoples with important knowledge about practical matters such as the agricultural year and the directions of the compass. In addition, the heavenly bodies were thought to afford prophetic or predictive data concerning the character and destiny of human beings. In the ancient world, astrology was among the most common techniques for predicting the future; it was a branch of learning that depended on precise mathematical calculations arrived at by specialists called *genethliaci* or *mathematici*. However, in the centuries surrounding the development of Christianity, several pagan philosophers began to question the reliability of astrological erudition and to scoff at the notion that astrology was a tool for glimpsing the future.[20] As with other forms of divination, early Christian thinkers who inherited the cosmological science that included the divinity of the stars were left to sift through ancestral views in order to ascertain what the proper Christian thinking on astrology ought to be.[21] Opinions were idiosyncratic, and there was no one, clear voice on the topic—that is until Augustine spoke in the early fifth century.

The question as to whether astrology constituted magic was knotty, due in part to its role in the Bible. Pseudo-Clement's *Recognitions* refutes the claims of the *mathematici*, while at the same time asserting that Abraham was an astrologer able to recognize God the creator in the stars.[22] As discussed above, it was through astrological skill that the three magi understood the meaning of the star announcing the birth of the Christ child (Matt. 2:2). Several patriarchs, such as Ignatius of Antioch, Tertullian, Origen, and Athanasius, held that the astrological skills of the magi were indeed magical, but on this one Christmas Eve, benign. God indulged the wise men's sorcery so that the birth of the king might be announced. According to this interpretation, the efficacy of astrological divination ended when the magi followed the star of Bethlehem; a new era had dawned, and the birth of Christ nullified all wisdom of the celestial bodies.[23] This account, in effect, requires the uncomfortable proposition that demons, through stellar magic, made the celestial manifesto of Jesus's birth intelligible to the magi.

---

20. Cicero, *De natura deorum* 2.3–4, 129–35. Others critical of astrology were the Greek Skeptic Carneades (d. ca. 129 BC), the Roman satirist Lucian of Samosata (d. after 180 CE), the Roman sophist Favorinus (fl. ca. 160 CE), and Sextus Empiricus (fl. ca. 200 CE).

21. The Jewish books of Enoch (*Books of Enoch*, 7–22), which Christians revered, convey a positive approach to the knowledge and esoteric significance of the stars.

22. Pseudo-Clement, *Recognitions* 1.32, 86 (Abraham); 10.11–12, 195–96.

23. Ignatius, "Epistle to the Ephesians" 19, 57; Tertullian, *De idololatria 9*, 2:1107–9; Origen, *Contra Celsum* 1.60, 54–55; Athanasius, *Life of Antony* 79, 88.

The archbishop of Constantinople John Chrysostom denied that the star of Bethlehem was related to the science of astrology. Rather, it was simply a sign—a virtue that took on the form of a star so the learned magi could decrypt its meaning. Some church fathers argued that the magi were simply acknowledging the Old Testament prophecy of Balaam, the Amavite augur who predicted "a star shall come out of Jacob, and a scepter shall arise out of Israel" that would rule the nations of the world (Num. 24:17). In other words, the prophecy of the star of Bethlehem came from God, and the magi were simply acknowledging a portent, not reading the future in the stars.[24] This explanation exonerates the magi from using magic, removes the taint of sorcery from the story in Matthew, and denies the functionality of stellar magic.

Some Christian thinkers, such as Tertullian, did not agree that astrology was ineffectual, even after the birth of Jesus. They held that astrological predictions, although often dependable, were dangerous because they were realized through the agency of demons. In fact, Kokabel, the fourth fallen angel, and the demon Baraqiel invented astrology and originally taught the science to humankind. For Tertullian, astrology was a demonic subset of magic. "Magic is punishable, of which astrology is a species, and assuredly the species is condemned in the genus." He grouped astrologers with "Chaldeans, enchanters, diviners, or magicians." He deplored zodiacal magic but did not deny that even Christians practiced it or that it could work.[25]

Though apologists dealt clumsily with the story of the star of Bethlehem, the governing patristic position on astrology was that to assert that a human being could discover the future in the stars impinged on free will and the prerogative of God to control destiny (granted that these two seem contradictory) and was therefore fraudulent. Whereas in pagan thought astrology was calibrated on a predetermined date of birth, for Christians baptism constituted a new birth that delivered individuals into the care of the Almighty and obviated stellar divination. Baptism, according to Peter Brown, "cancelled the influence of the stars."[26] The baptismal rite was not unique to the church. It was based on a Jewish penitential ritual, and other cults of the

---

24. John Chrysostom, Homily VI, in *Homilies of S. John Chrysostom*, 1:77–92. See also Thorndike, *History of Magic*, 1:472–75; Flint, *Rise of Magic*, 368–69.

25. Tertullian, *De idololatria* 9, 2:1108: "Attamen cum magia punitur, cuius est species astrologia. Utique et species in genere damnatur"; "Chaldaeos aut incantatores aut coniectores aut magos." Tertullian's understanding was inspired by *1 Enoch* 8, in *Complete Books of Enoch*, 30.

26. Brown, *Cult of the Saints*, 58. See also Ferguson, *Baptism*, 257.

period practiced a similar ceremony.[27] But the notion that the simple rite of baptism trumped the erudition of pre-Christian sages was a unique claim and confounded traditional pagan thought about the human personality. A new ethos of self-determination and personal liberation replaced the magic of the constellations.

Augustine forcefully refuted the assertions of *mathematici* and denied the possibility that the position of the stars at a person's birth could determine her or his future. These beliefs, he maintained, were demonic superstitions. He supported his argument by positing the experience of twins. "Now it can happen that some twins follow one another so closely out of the womb that no interval of time can be perceived between them and recorded in terms of constellations. It follows that some twins have the same constellations, and yet their actions and experiences turn out to be not the same but often quite different."[28] These dissimilar destinies, says Augustine, are "inexplicable if you believe in fate directed by the stars, but not surprising if you consider human free will and God's gift of grace."[29] He argued that although it is possible to chart the stars and deduce their future courses, information from the zodiac was not pertinent to an understanding of scripture and was associated with demonic disinformation, and so for that reason Christians should eschew it.

In regard to civil law, the approach to astrology was indexed less on theological discussions and more on long-held fears that stellar prognostication could upset the balance of political power. The *Theodosian Code* paints astrologers, diviners, augurs, magi, malefici, "invoker[s] of demons," and "all the rest whom the common people call magicians" with the same brush. They all warrant capital punishment. The code stipulates that the teaching of astrology must cease in public and in private. The penalty for infringement of the law, both for one who teaches astrology and for one who studies

---

27. See Ferguson (*Baptism*, 25–96) on pagan antecedents to baptism in classical and Hellenistic cultures.

28. Augustine, *De doctrina Christiana* 2.22.82–83, 94–97: "Fieri autem potest ut aliqui gemini tam sequaciter fundantur ex utero ut intervallum temporis iter eos nullum possit apprehendi et constellationum numeris adnotari. Unde necesse est nonnullos geminos easdem habere constellationes, cum paria rerum vel quas agunt vel quas patiuntur eventa non habeant."

29. Augustine, *De civitate Dei* 5.1–6, 1:128–34 (quotation 5.6, 1:133): "Quod est incredibilius, si astralia fata credantur; non autem mirum, is uoluntates hominum et Dei munera cogitentur." Augustine (*Confessionum* 4.3, 41–43) was, for a period, himself attracted to the claims of astrology. Augustine's position on the freedom of the will and its relationship to the stars was prevalent in his own period, and it became normative thereafter; see for example Basil of Caesarea (*Saint Basil Exegetic Homilies* 6.5–7, 90–95) and Pseudo-Clement (*Recognitions* 9.12, 17, 19, pp. 185–87; 10.12, pp. 195–96).

it, is torture and death.³⁰ The severity of this law was due to the fact that magicians had historically posed a threat by meddling in dynastic politics, but more interestingly, the text is witness to the law maker's belief in the efficacy of astrology. As was the case with other aspects of Christian thought in its early phases, the guidelines around divinatory astrology fluctuated from source type to source type and from writer to writer. One constant, however, was that astrology involved the participation of demons at some level and was forbidden to humans.

Divination by *Sortes*

A method of divination called *sortilegium*, practiced in ancient Hebrew, classical, and German societies, involved a simple ritual of drawing lots (*sortes*) or selecting at random a passage from a text and interpreting its meaning as a prognostication. The Hebrew scriptures depict Jewish high priests using the Urim and Thummim, a type of mantic lot, at the request of civic authorities in matters of public importance (1 Sam. 14:41–42). Romans practiced sortilegium by referring to a Homeromanteion or by turning at random to the works of the Roman poet Virgil (d. 19 BCE) and considering as an oracle the first verse that presented itself.³¹ From *Germania* (ca. 98 CE), an ethnography that the Roman aristocrat Tacitus (d. ca. 120) wrote describing the inhabitants of the province of Magna Germania, we learn that some German communities took auspices and made decisions by lots using branches of fruit trees that had been cut into small wands and inscribed. The tribal priest scattered the wands at random over a white cloth, and as he prayed, he picked up the wands three times each and interpreted them according to their markings, or runes (*notis*).³²

Although sortilegium came to be seen as flagrantly magical in Europe by around 500 and was by then the object of condemnation by virtually every kind of source or canon that addressed magic, it was not associated with demons in the antique church. Lots were involved in the choice of Matthias (d. ca. 80), who replaced Judas Iscariot (d. ca. 33) as the twelfth apostle

---

30. *Theodosian Code* 9.16, 237–39.
31. From Meerson ("Secondhand Homer"), a Homeromanteion was an oracle composed of lines from the works of the eighth-century poet Homer, which were usually interpreted by professional diviners. See also Klingshirn, "Defining the *Sortes Sanctorum*," 124–25.
32. Tacitus, *De origine* 10, 42: "Auspicia sortesque ut qui maxime observant. Sortium consuetudo simplex. Virgam frugiferae arbori decisam in surculos amputant eosque notis quibusdam discretos super candidam vestem temere ac fortuito spargunt. Mox, si publice consultetur, sacredos civitatis, sin privatim, ipse pater familiae precatus deos caelumque suspiciens ter singulos tollit, sublatos secundum impressam ante notam interpretatur."

(Acts 1:23–26), and there is no hint in the text that the process was sorcerous. Further, according to the *Apostolic Tradition*, the bishop assigned various responsibilities to the members of his community by the selection of sortes, which was simply a means of appointment to a position with no magical overtones.[33]

Augustine himself, who was among the most skeptical in regard to the efficacy of magical practices and very rigorous in interpreting pagan usages as superstitious, was inspired by the example of Saint Antony of the Desert to open his Bible and read the first passage that caught his eye.[34] This resulted in Augustine leaving the world of self-indulgence and petty rivalries to devote his life to God. A clear indication that the bishop did not think of sortes as demon driven can be found in his letter to a layman named Januarius. "Now, regarding those who draw lots from the pages of the Gospel, although it could be wished that they would do this rather than run around consulting demons, I do not like this custom of wishing to turn the divine oracles to worldly business and the vanity of this life, when their object is another life." Augustine differentiates demonic divination from a legitimate (though discouraged) method of seeking to know the future.[35]

Traditionally historians have identified incidents such as Augustine's consultation of the gospels as a Christian form of sorteligium that resembled the pagan practice of divining by way of random selections from pagan writings. The mechanism was that a person blindly selected a passage from a sacred text, such as the Bible or works of the church fathers, and decoded a message from the passage as a guide to the future. Historians have called such sortition *sortes sanctorum, sortes apostolorum* or *sortes bibliorum*. In 2002 William Klingshirn wrote an important article refuting the long-held notion that there was an unbroken tradition of biblical divination from late antiquity through the Middle Ages. He argues that the term "sortes sanctorum" did not denote fortune telling through random selections from holy writ. Rather, it is a reference to a specific prognosticatory text called *Sortes Sanctorum* (later known as *Sortes Apostolorum*) which was a collection of sayings. Be that as it may, rhapsodomancy and bibliomancy (*sortes biblicae*) were practiced in the early church. The procedure, however, was not thought

---

33. Hippolytus, *On the Apostolic Tradition* 3, 60–64.
34. Augustine, *Confessionum* 8.12.29–30, 131–32. Antony (Athanasius, *Life of Antony* 2, 31) was inspired to begin his ascetic career when he entered a church and "it happened that the Gospel was being read, and he heard the Lord saying to the rich man, 'If you would be perfect, go, sell what you possess and give to the poor, and you will have treasure in heaven'" (Matt. 19:21).
35. Augustine, *Letters* 55, 1:292.

Divinatory Dreams

Dream analysis was a method of divining the future on which Jews, pagans, and Christians shared common ground. There is a long tradition of prophetic dreaming in Jewish and pagan literature, and both played a formative role in Christian thinking about foreknowledge. God often communicates in dream visions with his chosen people in the Old Testament.[37] Roman deities also meted out information to their worshippers as they slept. For example, the goddess Isis of Tithorea came to devotees in dreams to invite them to her ceremonies, and Emperor Julian learned his fate when he dreamt that the *genus* of the Roman people departed his tent in sadness—its head and horn of plenty veiled. Shortly after, Julian died in battle.[38] Justin Martyr provides insight—though enigmatic—into pagan dream divination in his *Apology on Behalf of Christians* when he refers to "those whom magicians call dream-senders or attendants" who facilitate soothsaying by departed souls.[39]

For Christians, dream visions were potentially magical because, like other seemingly innocuous forms of divination, they opened a passageway that demons exploited for insinuating themselves into people's lives. The prophet Jeremiah, much revered in the early Middle Ages, warned of the danger in oneiromanic prophecies. "For thus says the Lord of hosts, the God of Israel: Do not let the prophets and the diviners who are among you deceive you, and do not listen to the dreams that they dream" (29:8). Dream clairvoyance was uncomplicated in terms of procedure; it was not ritualistic. In fact, the process of dreaming was by its nature submissive and receptive. Most likely one of the reasons the church could accept the

---

36. Klingshirn, "Defining the *Sortes Sanctorum*." There were numerous Christian divinatory texts in antiquity; see the articles in Luijendijk and Klingshirn, *My Lots Are in Thy Hands,* especially 19–59. From Luijendijk ("'Only Do Not Be of Two Minds,'" 309–29), rhapsodomancy typically involved a client and a facilitator, as was the case in the Gospel of the Lots of Mary.

37. For example, Gen. 37:40–41; Dan. 2:1–49, Dan. 4:1–37, Dan. 7:1–28. Enoch's "Book of Dreams," "Epistle of Enoch," and "Book of Giants" contain the teaching of dreams to Enoch's son Methuselah (*Books of Enoch*, 41–58). Dreams play a negligible rule in the New Testament, and they cluster in Matthew around the birth of Jesus (1:18–2:23; 27.19).

38. MacMullen, *Paganism*, 32; Ammianus Marcellinus, *History* 25.2.3, 2:486–7. Other examples in Ammianus Marcellinus's *History* at 21.2.1–2, 2:96–98; 23.3.3, 2:320–21; 25.10.16, 2:564–65; 26.1.7, 2:570–71.

39. Justin Martyr, *Apology on Behalf of Christians* 18.3, 123.

prognosticatory power of dreams was that it did not rely on elaborate rites, which Christians at the time eschewed.

Christian dream theory is anticipated in the Enochic *Book of Dreams* and evident in Lactantius's apologetic text, *Divine Institutions*.[40] Augustine and Gregory the Great accepted and glossed treatises of classical writers, particularly Calcidius's (fl. early fourth century CE) *Commentary on Plato's Timaeus* and Macrobius's (fl. 400 CE) *Commentary on the Dream of Scipio*.[41] Dreams could be angelic, demonic, or simply somatic—resulting from too much food or an agitated mind. The most rarefied dreams, the *visum* and the *revelatio*, took place in wakefulness and were truly revelatory. The challenge of every dreamer was to understand what meaning he or she should attach to an oneiromanic experience. Christian commentators urged caution in following advice delivered in dreams and visions, stressing that often seemingly angelic communications could be diabolical.[42] Even if a dream "came true," there was no assurance that it was benign. Lending dreams too much credence was a dangerous business, because Satan was thought to "transform himself to a seeming angel of light," in the words of Augustine. The apocryphal Gospel of Nicodemus (mid-fourth century) demonstrates the dangerous dimension of dreams when a group of men chide their friend, "Did we not tell you he is a magician? See, he has sent a bad dream to your wife."[43]

The conversations around dream theory establish that Christians and pagans shared a common storehouse of assumptions about the workings of the cosmos. Dreaming is also a case study in the young religion struggling to settle on which beliefs to endorse as its own. In this instance, the thinking on dreams as a form of communication with deities or devils passed essentially unbroken from the pagan to the Christian belief system. For example, both Christians and pagans characterized some dreams as demonically inspired, and both subscribed to the notion that healing was especially effective while the patient was in a dream trance.[44]

Many types of divination were virtually exclusive to men because they required formal learning and, in many cases, a public setting. Of all the

---

40. *1 Enoch* 13.1–10 to 14.1–25, pp. 33–34; *2 Enoch* 69–73, pp. 154–62 in *Complete Books of Enoch*; Lactantius, *Divine Institutes* 2.16, 163–64.

41. On Augustine and Gregory see Kruger, *Dreaming*, 35–55. On Augustine's treatment of Macrobius see Erickson, *Medieval Vision*, 35–38.

42. Augustine, *De civitate Dei* 22.22, 2:845; Kruger, *Dreaming*, 43–56; Fox, *Pagans and Christians*, 375–418.

43. Augustine, *De civitate Dei* 10.10, 1:283: "Quoniam satanas transfigurat se velut angelum lucis" (from 2 Cor. 11:14). In *De cura pro mortuis gerenda* (12–17, 643–58) Augustine discusses various aspects of dream visions. *Gospel of Nicodemus* 1.2, 431.

44. Klaniczay, *Dreams and Visions*, 147–57.

methods of knowing the future, prophecy and dreams were most open to women, and it is not a coincidence that neither required skill or initiative on the part of the medium, who was more a conduit through which information passed than an actor accessing the occult.[45]

Superstition

The attack on superstition began early in the Christian era but was not the primary focus of moralists in the first centuries. As explained above, the earliest battles of the church against magic involved overt idolatry and theurgia. Early Christians also were obliged to address maleficium, as allegations of trafficking in malicious sorcery were among the most potent accusations pagans pitched against the new religionists. But once the church had clarified its ideology about aspects of magic that played out in public settings and institutions (which included open charges of sorcery against apostles and saints) the task remained of sorting through the myriad everyday practices of the Christian flock to determine where demons were still lying in wait behind seemingly innocent observances. *Superstitio* was a predicament for the late antique and early medieval church because it was tightly woven into the everyday habits of the population up and down the social register, and it was therefore difficult both to isolate and to eradicate.

The classical, pagan term "superstition" had a narrow meaning of non-Roman religion—and more specifically, misplaced cultic forms of divination, but for early Christians, the definition was more ambiguous. It retained the connotation of false religion and excessive credulity. The meaning later broadened to encompass magic and paganism liberally, but patristic thinkers tended to reserve the term for customs of the ignorant or misguided (not necessarily the uneducated), whose behaviors theologians considered sinful because they involved sacrilege and were inherently idolatrous and implied a lack of confidence in the basic logic and ordered governance of the universe. Under this heading belonged informal folkways, habits, daily customs, and tricks that called on the aid of devils—implicitly or explicitly. Particular habits of the intellect such as undue curiosity about the workings of creation also led to "treacherous partnership" (*dolosae amicitiae*) with demons and facilitated vain and superstitious behaviors.[46]

---

45. See more on gender and divination in chapter 6.
46. Augustine (*De civitate Dei* 4.30, 1:124) called pagan temples "abodes of superstition" (*in aedibus superstitiosis*). Augustine, *De doctrina Christiana* 2.23.89, 98–99; Salzman, "'Superstitio' in the Codex Theodosianus."

People guilty of *superstitio* may or may not have supplicated demons knowingly or cared particularly what source of power their actions put into play. The object behind superstitious observances was to ensure a measure of stability and control over the vicissitudes of earthly existence. The sin in *superstitio* lay in the fact that those who indulged in superstitious behaviors or arrogant beliefs about their own abilities were, in effect, turning their backs on Christian aids and solutions to the vagaries of human life to rely instead on the assistance of devils. Seeking too ardently to protect oneself against misfortune, or even to do good works in the wrong state of mind, suggested both a wrongheaded, insolent hubris and a questioning of God's wisdom and grace. "Trickery" was a particular brand of superstition that fooled the practitioner and the gullible audience alike. Tricksters hoodwinked their viewers (or were accused of such by detractors) whether or not they were aware that their prowess with illusions was the work of demons to which they had unwittingly surrendered control.

Most superstitions were formulaic, required a precise ordering of procedures, and often relied on talismanic objects and substances. They involved what Augustine called "the thousand vacuous observances" (*milia inanissimarum observationum*) of the foolish, such as those listed at the opening of this chapter.[47] Superstitious behaviors were generally private, habitual, and prosaic—such as kicking a stone or hitting a dog or child when they ran between two people walking—not the grand and solemn communal affairs the word "ritual" often connotes.[48] Nonetheless, these personal conducts sprang from the same impulses as objectionable group rites in that they integrated dual worldviews, often soliciting the aid of God while at the same time reaching back into the pagan past for customs that were dependent on demons. The appeal of individual rites was that the actors assumed a sense of control over natural processes by participating in their outcome. The offense, then, was the recklessness in thinking that an un-Christian formula could affect the course of events.

Signs, Words, and Names

Romans had an entrenched belief in sympathetic magic,[49] which is the proposition that if two classes of events or objects share even superficial

---

47. Augustine, *On Christian Doctrine* 2.20.31, 54.
48. Muir, *Ritual*, 13–19.
49. Graf, *Magic*, 205–15; Noth, "Semiotics." Sympathetic magic is also called the "doctrine of signatures" (*similia similibus*), for which see Meaney, *Anglo-Saxon Amulets*, 6; Annequin, *Recherches sur l'action magique*, 28–29.

characteristics, such as a common shape, then a mystical connection exists between them and any impact on the event or object in one class will similarly affect the event or object in the other class. It is the principle behind the voodoo doll. In his history, Ammianus Marcellinus correlates two disparate occurrences illustrating his confidence in sympathetic magic. At the very moment that Emperor Constantius II fell dead, the soldier helping his successor, Julian, into a chariot slipped and fell.[50]

Augustine critiqued sympathetic magic in his discussion of signs, which is also the theological basis of his censure of *superstitio*. He distinguished "things" (*res*), which have meaning only in themselves, from "signs" (*signa*) which symbolize things beyond themselves. For example, a block of wood is a thing, while the word "wood" is a sign. "It is a carnal form of slavery to follow a sign divinely instituted for a useful purpose rather than the thing that it was instituted to represent."[51] This argument implicitly rejects superstitious magic. Augustine insisted that God created all parts of the universe and Divine Providence ordered it, including the movement of the stars and all seemingly odd occurrences such as "a mule giving birth or something being struck by lightning." He excoriated those who attributed special meanings or power to signs or "transitory things" (*rerum transeuntium*) Augustine wrote,

> What the apostle [Paul] said about idols and the sacrifices made in their honour must guide our attitude to all these fanciful signs which draw people to the worship of idols or to the worship of the created order or any parts of it as if they were God, or which relate to this obsession with remedies and other such practices. They are not publicly promulgated by God in order to foster the love of God and one's neighbour, but they consume the hearts of wretched mortals by fostering selfish desires for temporal things. So in all these teachings we must fear and avoid this alliance with demons, whose whole aim, in concert with their leader, the devil, is to cut off and obstruct our return to God.[52]

---

50. Ammianus Marcellinus, *History* 22.1.2, 2:186–187.

51. Augustine, *De doctrina Christiana* 1.2.4–6, 12–15; 3.7.28, 144–45: "Si ergo signum utiliter institutum pro ipsa re sequi cui significandae institutum est carnalis est servitus, quanto magis inutilium rerum signa instituta pro rebus accipere?" Augustine understood signs in a manner similar to modern semioticians; on this see Peirce, "Logic as Semiotic: The Theory of Signs" in *Philosophical Writings*, 98–119.

52. Augustine, *De doctrina Christiana* 2.23.91, 100–101: "si mula pariat aut fulmine aliquid percutiatur"; 2.7.18, 64–65: "rerum transeuntium"; 2.23.90, 98–99: "Quod autem de idolis et de immolationibus quae honori eorum exhibentur dixit apostolus, hoc de omnibus imaginariis signis sentiendum est quae vel ad cultum idolorum vel ad creaturam eiusque partes tamquam deum colendas trahunt vel ad remediorum aliarumque observationum curam pertinent. Quae non sunt divinitus ad dilectionem dei et proximi tamquam publice constituta, sed per privatas appetitiones

People who indulged their impulse for control by taking it upon themselves to read the natural world, whether motivated by curiosity or for the purpose of ordering their circumstances, were superstitious, ignorant, and worst of all, trafficking with "the society of . . . demons."[53] The manipulation of signs, though routine, was inherently ritualistic in that it employed formulaic and patterned sequences that sought both to align profane experience with the supernatural order and, by participation with that ordering, to direct the course of events. We have already seen this in the case of the child who was walloped for running between two people walking, which was a sign of misfortune meant to be obviated by the formal slap.

At the same time the clergy expressed ambivalence about ritualism because of its association with paganism, the church was developing its own vocabulary of pious rites. Christian leaders responded to parishioners' desire for external signs by developing new practices and symbols that all Christians could employ in place of those pagan customs that flirted with the demonic. In fact, three of the earliest rituals to emerge as signifiers of Christian truths—tracing the sign of the cross, baptism, and exorcism—incorporated the specific virtue of keeping demons at bay.

One of the symbols that was easiest to manipulate was the ritual signing of the cross. In keeping with the general prejudice of the early church against elaborate rites, signing with the cross was simple and employed casually. Crossing was a sign or symbol whose referent was the resurrection of Christ and the salvation of humankind, and it left no room for demonic infiltration like other signs might, in fact quite the opposite; the act of signing with the cross was meant to keep demons at a distance. Beginning with the earliest church literature, Christians were enjoined to ward off evil and ensure the protection of persons and property by signing with the symbol of the cross instead of employing other superstitious apotropaic procedures. In his *On the Military Garland* (*De corona*), Tertullian writes, "At every step and movement, at every entering and exiting, in dressing, in putting on shoes, at the bath, at the table, while lighting candles, when lying down or sitting, whatever we are doing, we mark our forehead by the sign [of the cross]."

He wrote approvingly of the Christian woman who "signed" her bed before lying down on it.[54]

---

rerum temporalium corda dissipant miserorum. In omnibus ergo istis doctrinis societas daemonum formidanda atque vitanda est, qui nihil cum principe suo diabolo nisi reditem nostrum claudere atque obserare conantur."

53. Augustine, *De doctrina Christiana* 2.23.89, 98–99: "societate hominum et daemonum."

54. Tertullian, *De corona* 3.4, 2:1043: "Ad omnem progressum atque promotum, ad omnem aditum et exitum, ad vestitum, ad calciatum, ad lauacra, ad mensas, ad lumina, ad cubilia, ad sedilia,

In his *Catecheses* (lectures for Lent), Bishop Cyril of Jerusalem (d. 386) says much the same, and adds, "Let the Cross, as our seal, be boldly made with our fingers upon our brow, and on all occasions; over the bread we eat, over the cups we drink; in our comings and in our goings; before sleep; on lying down and rising up; when we are on the way and when we are still. It is a powerful safeguard. . . . [The cross is] a terror to devils. . . . For when they see the Cross, they are reminded of the Crucified; they fear Him who has 'smashed the heads of the dragons.'"[55] Cyril uses the word "seal" in describing cruciform signing, which relates to the principle of binding. A simple Christian gestural ritual as a sign for salvation and God's potency here acts as a seal. Although sealing or binding did not have negative connotations in the early church, they could be accomplished by magical means for sinister reasons.

Athanasius promotes cruciform signing in the vita of Antony of the Desert, where the rite fortifies the saint against demons who are terrified by the gesture and vanish when it is performed.[56] The church father Bishop Epiphanius of Salamis, Cyprus (d. 403) told the story of a holy man who imparted to a jug of water the power "to set at naught all sorcery and enchantment" by mouthing a prayer and "tracing the sign of the cross on the vessel with his own finger."[57] Signing, then was one of the earliest, simplest, and most democratic Christian rituals for keeping demons subdued.

The basic initiatory rite of Christianity was baptism, which acted as a foil to demonic infiltration and was rich in evocative and introspective rituals. It is a good case study for seeing how the early struggle for identity was waged on the field of ritual. Although there was variation from locale to locale, generally speaking, the week leading up to baptism on Easter Sunday included fasting, prayer, and scriptural readings. The ceremony itself involved a ritual blessing of the baptismal waters, triple immersion, recitation of the creed, and anointing of the baptized.[58] By the mid-third century, the sacrament of

---

quacumque nos conversatio exercet, frontem signaculo terimus"; For Tertullian's *Ad uxorem* see Phillips, "Prayer in the First Four Centuries," 51. For further references on crossing in the early church see Dölger, "Beiträge zur Geschichte."

55. Cyril of Jerusalem, *Lenten Lectures* 13.36, in *Works of Saint Cyril*, 2:28.

56. Athanasius, *Life of Antony* 13, 41; 23, 48; 35, 57. On crossing that in-effectuates magic see ibid., 78, 88; Dölger, "Beiträge zur Geschichte," 23–34.

57. Epiphanius of Salamis, *Panarion* 2.30.12.5, 1:140.

58. See Acts 8:12–17 on the centrality of baptism; Hippolytus, *On the Apostolic Tradition* 21, 110–114; Cyril of Jerusalem, *First Lecture on the Mysteries* 1–4, in *Works of Saint Cyril*, 2:153–59; Gregory of Nyssa, *Catechetical Oration* 35, 101–6; Pseudo-Clement, *Recognitions* 7.34, 164. For controversy about the literal use of rituals in the *Apostolic Tradition* see Baldovin, "Hippolytus and the *Apostolic Tradition*." On the baptismal ceremony and its evolution in the post-apostolic era see Ferguson, *Baptism* 248–55, 314–15, 340–45, 351–55, 474–81, 506–8.

confirmation was added to the mix, followed by first communion and a ceremonial meal of milk and honey.

A central component of the "rebirth" inherent in baptism was renunciation of devils. Demons resided in water and frequented watery places, so the purifying power of the font challenged demons head-on. The baptismal sacrament incorporated an exorcism, an explicit renunciation of Satan, and a command that "all evil demons depart."[59] The repudiation amounted to an abandonment of wrongheaded ritual; the catechumen was to say, "I renounce you, Satan, and all your service [displays or rituals] and all your works."[60] The exorcism might be accompanied by the clerics' laying on of hands, signing with the cross, anointing with oil, and breathing or spitting on the initiate. Tertullian says of baptism, "When entering the water . . . we bear testimony with our mouth that we have renounced the devil, his pomp, and his angels." And Cyril of Jerusalem instructed the initiate to face west because that is where Satan, "crafty scoundrel of a serpent," reigns over his "empire of darkness."[61] Rather than drawing on demonic power, these Christian usages combated it. They were palliative and a counter to magic-ridden pagan rites. Ritual was not synonymous with magic, but exorbitant ceremony and complicated machinations with gaudy objects (all absent from baptism) were offensive to early Christians' sense of the proper approach to God.

A more vivid sort of exorcism was the casting out of demons, which was a defining aspect of Christ's ministry and an ability he passed on to his disciples.[62] The Gospels abound with stories of devils fleeing or cowering before the power of Christ and his apostles who seek to evict them from their domicile within the bodies and minds of innocent victims. The casting out of demons became a leitmotif in hagiography and a commonplace skill of any clergyman, and sometimes even laypeople. Exorcism of devils in the New Testament requires a modest word formula, and the rite retained its simple character throughout the early Middle Ages. For example, in the Gos-

---

59. Hippolytus, *On the Apostolic Tradition* 10, 111 (quotation);

60. John Chrysostom, *Baptismal Instructions* 2.20, 51. Brakke, *Demons*, 132. On "service" see ibid., 43.

61. For Tertullian see Ferguson, *Baptism*, 340. Cyril of Jerusalem, *First Lecture on the Mysteries* 4, in *Works of Saint Cyril*, 2:155–56. For holy breathing as a religious ritual see Janowitz, *Icons of Power*, 81–83; Benko, *Pagan Rome*, 79–84. From Ferguson (*Baptism*, 523), by the fourth century, during the exorcism candidates removed their outer garments, stood with feet on sackcloth and arms outstretched looking downward to demonstrate their state of servitude to the Devil and their need for divine mercy. In his *Baptismal Instructions*, John Chrysostom teaches that one must renounce "omens, charms, and incantations" (ibid., 637). See also ibid., 240, 253, 537–38, 259–63, 753–54.

62. For example see Matt. 10:1–8; Mark 3:15; Luke 9.1–2.

pel of Matthew, Jesus comes upon two men possessed of furious and defiant demons, and "the demons begged him, 'If you cast us out, send us into the herd of swine.' And he said to them, 'Go!' So they came out and entered the swine; and suddenly, the whole herd rushed down the steep bank into the sea and perished in the water" (8.31–32). The word "go" was all the ceremony necessary to send the demons to perdition.[63]

Superstitio involved more than a continued reliance on old pagan ways. Since the construct implied a misguided semiotic, it was very possible to use even Christian signs, symbols, and objects superstitiously or to commingle them with old pagan formulas. Augustine was sensitive to the wrongful use of the altar, Mass, relics, herbs, stones, numbers, prayers, holy water, and the like, which could themselves be manipulated in magical ways. In his *Treatise on Saint John's Gospel* he corrects those who think a demonic chant can be made Christian by substituting a prayer for an incantation.[64]

How, then, were well-meaning Christians to decipher the difference between a superstitious and a Christian use of symbols? The answer is that it was difficult; the average worshipper did well to listen to the bishop and follow his lead to avoid falling into error. Yet churchmen were left with a quandary as to how to clarify for their parishioners a question on which they themselves were foggy; that is, the subtle differences between practices condemned outright and those that were technically orthodox but depended too much on using signs with illegitimate referents (thereby inviting the intercession of demons) or exploiting sacraments in a transactional manner.[65]

One category of signs that was pervasive and potent in the ancient world was particular words or names. J. L. Austin argues that the very articulation of certain words, or "performative utterances," was instrumental. "To say is to act."[66] The notion of words and names as iconic was rooted in a long intellectual tradition from pagan philosophical discourse and Jewish exegesis. During their recitation, scribes of the ancient world committed

---

63. Although exorcism is central to Christian demonology, I devote little time to the topic because people who were possessed were not trafficking with demons; rather, they had been infiltrated by them against their will. On this see chapter 2.

64. Augustine, *In Iohannis evangelium tractatus* 7.6, 70. See *De doctrina Christiana* 2.14–41, 78–129, on Augustine's differentiation between learning that is useful and that which leads to superstitious misapplication.

65. Peters, *Magician*, xv.

66. J. Austin, *How to Do Things*, 133–47 (quotation 140). See also Kahlos, "Early Church," 151; Kropp, "How Does Magical Language Work?" In Hebrew scripture, God is "the Name" (*ha–Shem*), and the Temple is the "House of the Name." For an extensive treatment of sacred names in late antique Jewish texts see Janowitz, *Icons of Power*, chaps. 2, 4–5.

speech to writing, which sealed the spoken word.⁶⁷ In *Icons of Power*, Naomi Janowitz delivers a compelling analysis of the existential resonance between language and the cosmos in Neoplatonic writings. Vowels, for instance, were imitations of planet sounds.⁶⁸ "Speech acts" were a potent form of ritual and were more than metaphorical; they functioned literally to unite spheres of experience. Names were not arbitrary, rather they were stamped on people and things by celestial, universal forces. Actual energy inhered in names. Names of biblical personages such as Abraham, Isaac, and Jacob had great power if pronounced in Hebrew. This is evident in pagans' use of curse tablets that employed Hebraic names.⁶⁹ In the *Chaldean Oracles*, divine names leap into the world and are said to be a much more reliable window into the occult than, for example, the sneezings of birds, which was a commonplace method of fortune telling in late antique and early medieval sources.⁷⁰ The ceremonial use of verbalized words and names created a nexus by which pagan priests, pythonesses, and sybils participated in the workings of the cosmic structure.

This understanding of words did not diminish with the advent of Christianity, and many exegetes held that Adam came to exercise dominion over the birds and animals by naming them (Gen. 2:19–20). Origen and the Gallic bishop Hilary of Poitiers (d. ca. 367) followed Gnostic and Neoplatonic thought in the belief that names were immanent, so much so that when a name was translated into a different language it lost its relationship to the person it signified, who then could no longer be manipulated by the ritual use of that name.⁷¹ For Dionysius, names did not carry inherent power based on their sounds; however, they were anything but arbitrary. They had manifestations of the deity encoded in themselves.⁷² The numinous force of words properly uttered was capable of remolding the human soul in baptism and transforming bread and wine in the Mass.

---

67. Graf, *Magic*, 131.
68. Janowitz, *Icons of Power*, 33–43.
69. Weltin, "Concept of *Ex-Opere-Operato* Efficacy," 80–81; *Curse Tablets* 100–101, 112–13, 184–85, 206–207.
70. *Chaldean Oracles* 37, p. 63; 87, p. 83; 150, p. 107: "Names handed down by the gods to each race have ineffable power." From Jennings ("Divination and Popular Culture"), divination by the movements of birds was accessible to the average person, could be done "at home," and did not require the expense of a professional *mantis* for its interpretation. "Greek for 'bird' (*oiōnos*) means 'omen'" (195). Searle, *Speech Acts*, 16–19.
71. Origen, *Contra Celsum* 1.24, 23–24; 5.45, 299–300; Hilary of Poitiers, *Saint Hilary of Poitiers: The Trinity* 7.9–14, 231–39.
72. Janowitz, *Icons of Power*, 34.

The very name of Jesus vanquished demons and ensured healing. Tertullian affirmed that "all our mastery and power over [demons] comes from naming the Name of Christ." In his response to Celsus, Origen pits the potency of simple word formulas against the feebleness of magic and underlines the simplicity of Christian rites. "The name of Jesus is so powerful against the daemons that sometimes it is effective even when pronounced by bad men. . . . Christians make no use of spells, but only of the name of Jesus."[73] Nearly a hundred years later, Eusebius held that demons could be banished just by subjecting them to simple words or breath.[74] Calling on the names of angels and Old Testament patriarchs had the effect of commanding their attention. Although this obviously did not equate to demonism, there was tremendous danger in accessing any superhuman power unsupervised, and as Christian governance solidified, interaction with the supernatural became the job of the professional clergy.

Tertullian and Origen warned Christians against speaking the names of pagan deities because such utterances stimulated the demons the names referenced. At times demons aligned their own names with God's just so the unwary worshipper would inadvertently worship them instead of the Almighty.[75] Early church doctrine insisted on the proper use of the proper words in the proper situation.[76] Throughout Christian history, exact wording in rituals has remained important, but the early patristic notion that words in translation lose their potency tended to drop away, particularly after Augustine's rejection of the concept.

In addition to the threat of demonic interference, the jeopardy in signs, words, and names was heightened when their manipulation was highly ritualistic. This view was consistent across the early Christian period in the Eastern and Western churches. Justin Martyr extolled Christian worship in contrast to that of pagans or Jews, which he cast as magical because it was rigidly formal and relied on the use of cultic props. Early Christians leaders permitted the use of iconic words in place of pagan physical, totemic objects. Origen held that Moses's contest with Pharaoh's magi was not magic because it did not depend on a ritual crutch (the staff), but on the words Moses uttered. Eusebius agreed with the Neoplatonic philosopher Porphyry that rituals with

---

73. Tertullian, *Apologeticum* 23, 1:132: "Omnis haec nostra in illos dominatio et potestas de nominatione Christi." *Contra Celsum* 1.6, 10.

74. Eusebius, *History of the Church* 7.10, 293.

75. Tertullian, *De idololatria* 20–21, 2:1120–22; Origen, *Contra Celsum* 1.6, 9–10; 1.25, 24–26; 4.33–34, 209–10; Origen, *Exhortation to Martyrdom* 46, 189–90.

76. For example see Gregory of Nyssa, *Catechetical Oration* 37, 107–12; Sozomen, *Ecclesiastical History* 1.11, 26–27.

no theological basis were just magic and could never constrain God. Eusebius made the point that the Jewish symbols and rituals were not necessary to Christians, for whom the "truth" could not be contained in any symbols the Jews might concoct. Hilarion also boasted that Christian ritual relied on simple, properly spoken words, and John Chrysostom insisted that the use of words and the sign of the cross were all the ritual Christians needed.[77] Some Gnostic and Montanist Christians (both were charismatic, pentecostal mystery sects) even rejected corporeal baptism because of the water required in the ceremony—an earthly and corruptible substance.[78] Augustine bridled at the sober theurgic rites outlined in the *Chaldaean Oracles* because they implied that through ritual, humans could influence God by manipulating the elements of his creation.[79]

In short, signs had the power to tap into paranormal forces, and names or words themselves had essence. Their misuse (in the case of signs) and very pronunciation (in the case of names and words), especially in ritual contexts, called into play the source of power inhering in them, regardless of the speaker's intention, and that source could be demonic.

Suspensions and Ligatures

One of the most entrenched superstitious practices in the ancient world was the use of suspensions and ligatures. Suspensions are herbs, charms, bones, bits of materials containing writings (*characteres*), or other similar items hung from or attached to various parts of the body for the purpose of healing, warding off danger, or manipulating conception. Ligatures are magical knots or weavings. In *On Christian Doctrine*, Augustine denounces the magic arts and specifically condemns suspensions. "To this category belong all the amulets and remedies which the medical profession also condemns, whether these consist of incantations, or certain marks which their exponents call 'characters', or the business of hanging certain things up and tying things to other things, or even somehow making things dance."[80]

---

77. On Justin Martyr, Origen, Hilarion, and John Chrysostom see Janowitz, *Icons of Power*, 14–15; Eusebius, *Preparation for the Gospel* 5.10, pt. 2, 161–62; bk. 7, pt. 2, 320–76. Weltin, "Concept of Ex-Opere-Operato Efficacy," 83–89.

78. Irenaeus of Lyon, *Against the Heresies* 21.4, 1:79. See Tertullian (*De baptismo* 3–5, 1:278–82) on the centrality of water in the redemptive ritual of baptism.

79. Athanassiadi, "Chaldaean Oracles."

80. Augustine, *De doctrina Christiana* 2.20.75, 90–93: "Ad hoc genus pertinent omnes etiam ligaturae atque remedia quae medicorum quoque disciplina condemnat, sive in praecantationibus sive in quibusdam notis quos caracteres vocant, sive in quibusque rebus suspendendis atque illigandis vel

Some usages were demonic by their very nature, and suspending, tying, and binding-on were among them.

The bishop cites suspensions as an example when he cautions against the improper reverence for certain signs. According to him, animals, trees, plants, stones, or "other such things" are valid for disentangling enigmas of holy writ, but not as signs for remedies or for other "superstitious" uses.[81] He writes,

> For it is one thing to say, 'if you drink this plant in powdered form your stomach will stop hurting', and another to say, 'if you hang this plant around your neck your stomach will stop hurting'. In the one case the health-giving mixture is commendable, in the other the superstitious meaning is damnable. But in the absence of incantations or invocations or 'characters' it is often doubtful whether the thing tied on or attached in some way for healing the body works by nature—in which case it may be used freely—or succeeds by virtue of some meaningful association; in this case, the more effectively it appears to heal, the more a Christian should be on guard.[82]

Augustine mocks the mixtures and remedies that "they call these 'physical matters' using this bland name to give the impression that they do not involve a person in superstition but are by nature beneficial."[83] He also discriminates between valid medicines that operate through a force of nature and those that draw power through a signifying sign whose effectiveness is hidden. The problem with hidden efficacy (even when deceptively called

---

etiam saltandis quodam modo." For a survey of the medieval use of ligatures based on Augustine's work see Harmening, *Superstitio,* 235–47.

81. Augustine, *De doctrina Christiana* 2.29.110, 106–9: "De quo genere superius egimus eamque cognitionem ualere ad aenigmata scripturarum soluenda docuimus: non ut pro quibusdam signis adhibeantur, tamquam ad remedia vel machinamenta superstitionis alicuius." See also ibid., 2.39.141, 122–23, where Augustine says that the names of animals, herbs, trees, stones, numbers, and metals mentioned in scripture and written in Hebrew, Syrian, Egyptian, or any other foreign language should be investigated to uncover their deeper, possibly symbolic, meanings.

82. Ibid., 2.29.110–11, 106–9: "Aliud est enim dicere 'tritam istam herbam si biberis, uenter non dolebit' et aliud est dicere 'istam herbam collo si suspenderis, uenter non dolebit.' Ibi enim probatur contemperatio salubris, hic significatio superstitiosa damnatur. Quamquam ubi praecantationes et inuocationes et characteres non sunt, plerumque dubium est, utrum res, quae alligatur aut quoquo modo adiungitur sanando corpori, ui naturae ualeat, quod libere adhibendum est, an significatiua quadam obligatione proueniat, quod tanto prudentius oportet cauere christianum, quanto efficacius prodesse uidebitur." See also Noth, "Semiotics."

83. Augustine, *De doctrina Christiana* 2.20.75, 90–93: "non ad temperationem corporum, sed ad quasdam significationes aut occultas aut etiam manifestas; quae mitiore nomine physica vocant, ut quasi non superstitione implicare, sed natura prodesse videantur." Also see Augustine, *In Iohannis evangelium tractatus* 7.6, 70.

"natural") is that, first, it is most likely due to demons, and second, it depends on ritual usages that presuppose an atavistic and misguided understanding of the way God intended humans to function within the mundus. Augustine approved of the scientific and medical application of elements from the natural world, but not of their symbolic or ritual use outside the strictures of sacred texts. Because individualistic interpretation of signs and the resultant ritual patterns could lead to superstitious actions that beckoned devils, the high clergy of the church sought to structure habits of mind in order to align the worldview of worshippers with the ecclesiastical concept of causation, which eschewed demonic agency in favor of grand divine sovereignty. Discerning the wrongful use of suspensions was not an easy task for average Christians—all the more because clergymen themselves were not immune from engaging in magic practices, including the use of amulets. The councilors of the synod at Laodicea in Phrygia Pacatiana (ca. 363) recognized and condemned them in the harshest terms. "They who are of the priesthood, or of the clergy, shall not be magicians, enchanters, mathematicians, or astrologers; nor shall they make what are called amulets, which are chains for their own souls. And those who wear such, we command to be cast out of the Church."[84]

Binding and Loosing

Binding here includes a range of allied activities, such as knotting, sealing, and loosing, that were basic aspects of classical pagan religions, and their importance as occult aids continued unabated through the early Middle Ages. It is fitting to speak of binding as both metaphorical and literal in this period when the line between the two was permeable. Because reality was seen as a single actuality super infused throughout the cosmos, it was unbroken, and in that world metaphor itself made a real material impression. Binding was often accomplished by the use of words or the utterance of names, both of which were powerful in the ancient world, as discussed above. A name, for instance, constituted an inherent quality of a human being, and manipulation of that name in a ritual setting meant control over persons themselves. Late antique Judaism employed rites of binding, such as writing on the body and circumcision. Anointing with oil was an ancient form of Hebrew sealing

---

84. Council of Laodicea 36, in *Seven Ecumenical Councils,* 151. On the Council of Laodicea see Zeddies, *Religio et sacrilegium,* 80–83.

that Christians adopted in baptismal rituals. In the sermon called *2 Clement* (ca. mid-second century), "seal" is a synonym for baptism.[85]

Binding in late antiquity was so accepted an aspect of spiritual power that it was identified as magical only under certain circumstances, and it could be employed for good or ill. Whereas early Christian writers discarded many Jewish and pagan practices, they recognized binding's potency in the universe, which both saints and demons could manipulate. Binding was a decidedly legitimate spiritual tool, so much so that Jesus conferred on the apostle Peter (d. ca. 64) the special power to loosen and to bind. What Peter bound on earth would be bound in heaven; what Peter loosed would be loosed in heaven (Matt. 16:18). The ability to tie and untie was so central to the apostle's prerogative that, according to the fanciful *Recognitions* of Pseudo-Clement, Simon the Magician (or Magus) mimicked it, vaunting his knack of loosing bonds and barriers. Simon Magus envied Peter's power and tried to buy the secrets behind it, as though the laying on of hands amounted to a commodity and a contractual ritual (Acts 8:18–23).[86] When the Roman aristocrat Perpetua (d. 203) was incarcerated for identifying herself as Christian, the prison guards feared that through loosing charms, she would free herself and her coreligionists from custody. This ability to unbind (particularly to unbind prisoners) continued to be a hagiographical trope for both female and male saints throughout the early Middle Ages.[87]

Injurious binding was very common in the ancient world, and both pagans and Christians used it coercively. John Gager has edited a collection of curses tablets and binding spells (*defixiones*) from the ancient and late antique periods that demonstrate how routine magic was. These are ritual curses and spells inscribed on materials such as thin sheets of lead, papyrus, or wax tablets that were folded and fixed closed with nails. Individual clients purchased the curses from professional magi and placed them under thresholds, at the racecourse, near tombs, or wherever necessary to trigger the charm.[88]

The following is an example of a curse that depended on knotting and invoked demons to give an advantage to an athlete in a chariot race. "Most holy Lord Charakte^res [higher powers] tie up, bind the feet, the hands, the sinews, the eyes, the knees, the courage, the leaps, the whip (?), the victory and the crowning of Porphuras and Hapsicrate^s, who are in the middle left, as well as his co–drivers of the Blue colors in the stable of Eugenius. From

---

85. *2 Clement* 7, 97; Ferguson, *Baptism*, 207–9, 316.
86. Pseudo-Clement, *Recognitions* 2.9, 99. See Nock, "Paul and the Magus."
87. *Passion of S. Perpetua* 16, 84. See also Sozomen, *Ecclesiastical History* 14, 34–35. Audoin, *Vita Eligii* 1.18, 684; 2.15, 702–4; 2.80, 739–40.
88. *Curse Tablets*; Kropp, "How Does Magical Language Work?"

this very hour, from today, may they not eat or drink or sleep; instead, from the (starting) gates may they see daimones (of those) who have died prematurely, spirits (of those) who have died violently, and the fire of Hephaestus."[89] When linked to demons, magical ligatures such as ritual knots for worldly success, love magic, protection against misfortune, and counter charms fell under the same opprobrium as other forms of maleficium.

Trickery

Trickery (*ludus, ars, praestigia,* or *dolus*) was a kind of magic intended to demonstrate the virtuosity of the magician for the purpose of impressing an audience. Trickery constituted an abuse in both the pagan and the Christian view because it denoted a vulgarization of preternatural power in order to impress or manipulate viewers. People guilty of magical trickery were principally motivated by the desire for fame, wealth, or power, but the efficacy of the tricks required the support of demons. Illusionists played on public naïveté and susceptibility to superstitious belief. For example, in the eastern provinces, a man "from the lands called Gallic" gathered large crowds as he made the rounds of cities and market towns, peddling his clever spells and "magicians' tricks" and claiming powers over life and death. So great was his lure that throngs of men and women were drawn to him.[90]

Pagan intellectuals were scathing about the histrionics of personages in Christian sacred texts. Aaron's contests with the pharaoh's magi, for example, were viewed as competition in trickery (Ex. 7:8–8:19). Moses himself was, for pagans, an infamous master of prestidigitations. Many in the pagan intellectual community, such as Pliny and Celsus, considered Moses a sorcerer, and they took their lead from the Gospels themselves where Moses is drawn as a sort of shaman, having learned his craft in the ancient land of mystery ("So Moses was instructed in all the wisdom of the Egyptians and was powerful in his words and deeds" [Acts 7:22].) Apuleius grouped him with Zoroaster, Carmedas, and Damigeron.[91] The apocryphal *Eighth Book of Moses* circulated widely in the mid-fourth century CE and paints a picture of Moses as a magician and refers to a prayer he sings to the moon.[92]

---

89. *Curse Tablets,* 57–58. This curse was incised on a lead tablet in the late fifth century and found in Syria. From Shäfer ("Jewish Magic"), binding spells are also common in late antique Jewish texts.

90. MacMullen, *Christianizing the Roman Empire,* 38.

91. Pliny (*Natural History* 30.2, vol. 8 [418], 285–85) mentions Moses, Jannes, and Lotape among Jewish magicians. Origen, *Contra Celsum* 1.26, 26; 4.33, 209; 5.51, 226. Apuleius of Madaura, *Apulei apologia* 90. See Janowitz, *Magic in the Roman World,* 12.

92. Graf, *Magic,* 6–8.

Moses's persona as a wizard had currency as late as the seventh century, and an obscure passage in the epilogue of the *Penitential of Theodore* (although it is not clear when this passage accreted to the penitential) exculpates Moses from charges of sorcery, attesting to the tenacity of the tradition of Moses as magician.[93]

One of the earliest tasks of Christian propagandists was to counter slurs against Jesus and his apostles that they were nothing more than charlatans taking advantage of the superstitious disposition of the ignorant. Pagans slung insults at Christians for passing off tricks as miracles, and Christians retaliated in kind. The pagan philosopher and Origen's antagonist, Celsus, referred to Christian wonder working as a masquerade for scandalous "trickery," less impressive than the stunts of jugglers who performed in the marketplace. In turn, Origen slandered pagan priests by casting their wonders as scams.[94] Sometime between 217 and 238 CE, a Greek named Philostratus (d. ca. 250 CE) wrote a laudatory biography of the Neo-Pythagorean holy man Apollonius of Tyana (fl. 100 CE), whose career shared some superficial characteristics with Jesus's mature ministry. In the early fourth century, a provincial governor of Alexandria and Bithynia named Hierocles, seeking to defame the Christian movement and its eponym, brought the biography of Apollonius to light and wrote his own treatise contrasting Apollonius and Jesus, to Jesus's disadvantage. The eminent church historian Eusebius of Caesarea responded to Heirocles's barbs, and the two engaged in a combat of insults. Hierocles cast Jesus's miracles as conjuring and cheap stunts—the kind any street magician could pull off, and Eusebius responded by dismissing the marvels of Apollonius as "tricks of sorcery."[95] Accusations of rituals' misuse became a standard rhetoric of abuse with which one group sought to sully the other. This was a well-conceived strategy as virtually every educated man and woman in the ancient world disdained cons in the guise of religion and ostentatious tricks posing as sacred ritual. Miracles were an important factor that accounted for the mass appeal of various cults, including Christianity, and they often looked like tricks. But pagans and Christians shared the view that a miracle must be for the good, not self-serving trickery.[96]

The stunts of the infamous conjurer in the New Testament, Simon Magus, especially his flying contest with Peter and Paul, were held to be the result of pernicious trickery and, in the Christian tradition, became a metaphor

---

93. *Medieval Handbooks of Penance*, 213n185.
94. Origen, *Contra Celsum* 1.68, 62–63; 3.52, 164; 5.9, 270; Graf, "Augustine and Magic."
95. Eusebius, *Reply to Hierocles* 2.1, 156–57; Kollmann, *Jesus*, 101–6; M. Smith, *Jesus the Magician*, 84–93.
96. MacMullen, *Paganism*, 95–97.

for the usurpation of power. Pseudo-Clement's *Recognitions* elaborates on the misdeeds of this notorious illusionist. In addition to flying, Simon could become invisible, walk through fire, metamorphose into animals, animate statues, and, as his coup de grâce, create a living being from thin air. Along with Simon Magus, the Antichrist was another legendary manipulator of deceitful tricks mentioned in scripture and early Christian literature (1 John 2:18, 4:3, 2:22; 2 John 1:7). The chiliastic archvillain was to be surrounded by magicians and criminals, who, inspired by the Devil, would train him in the arts of trickery.[97]

In short, "tricks" were seemingly harmless enough, or they could be overtly perilous, as in the case of the deceptions of the Antichrist yet to come. But in every case, they drew on the power of demons, and for that reason fell under the umbrella of illicit magic.

Curiosity

Augustine equated theurgy with "the sin of sacrilegious curiosity" (*vitium sacrilegae curiositatis*). He held that all omens "are brimful of dangerous curiosity, agonizing worry, and deadly bondage."[98] Part of Augustine's condemnation of the superfluous and indulgent investigation of the world was a reaction to the secret, bizarre rituals that many mystery religious held as necessary to arrive at esoteric knowledge. Miracles, he said, "were brought about by simple faith and pious trust, not incantations and charms of execrable curiosity by a false art that they call either magic, or, by a more detestable name, *goetia*, or by the more honorable name of theurgy."[99] Here he pits the "simple faith and pious trust" of Christians against the "art" or ritualistic craft of magic.

Demons were thought capable of unlocking many of the secrets of the universe to which humans, unaided, were not privy. In fact, the plight of the first humans and the fall of humanity in the Garden of Eden stemmed from immoderate curiosity about realms of knowing that were not appropriate to

---

97. Pseudo-Clement, *Recognitions* 2.9, 99; 3.47, 126. On the competition between Peter and Simon, which mirrors that between paganism and Christianity, see Bremmer, "Pseudo-Clementines." From Nock ("Paul and the Magus," 309), Simon Magus was also thought able to call down the moon. On the "miracles" of the Antichrist see Peters, *Magician*, 6–7; McCready, *Signs of Sanctity*, 78–81.

98. For *"vitium sacrilegae curiositatis"* see Augustine, *De civitate Dei* 10.9, 1:282. Augustine, *De doctrina Christiana* 2.24.92, 100–101: "Quae tamen plena sunt omnia pestiferae curiositatis, cruciantis sollicitudinis, mortiferae servitutis." See also Augustine, *De civitate Dei* 10.9, 1:282; and 10.26, 1:301.

99. Augustine, *De civitate Dei* 10.9, 1:281: "Fiebant autem simplici fide atque fiducia pietatis, non incantationibus et carminibus nefariae curiositatis arte compositis, quam uel magian uel detestabiliore nomine goetian uel honorabiliore theurgian vocant."

mortals. In this case, curiosity was sated only with the help of the serpent-demon, Satan. Ill-placed curiosity led people to plumb realms of knowledge that were of no value to them. Or, even more grievous, it seduced them into meddling in affairs proper only to God. The scriptures and the authorities who interpreted them provided humans all they needed to know about the mysteries of existence.

Augustine's discussion of the misuse of signs is relevant to his suspicion of curiosity; however, he held that some aspects of the natural world were legitimate referents for higher truths. Herbs and stones, for instance, could sometimes admissibly be sought for their secrets. He established guidelines for arriving at the correct approach to the physical world through divinely instituted signs, which could be deciphered by a proper reading of the Bible. Human institutions "which involve an alliance with demons are, as I have said, to be completely rejected and abhorred, but those which men practise along with their fellow-men are to be adopted, in so far as they are not self-indulgent and superfluous."[100] Fundamentally, however, Augustine concluded that too much unrestricted erudition was ill-advised and iterated that gratuitous ritual was imprudent. Faith in Christ cleansed, healed, and protected infinitely more surely than the fruits of "pernicious curiosity" (*perniciosissimae curiositati*). Put another way by a wise old desert hermit, "Everything that is beyond the mean is the work of demons."[101]

The hypersensitivity concerning mirrors in late antiquity is rooted in a concern about excessive inquisitiveness. Apuleius stood trial in Sabratha near Tripoli in North Africa (ca. 158) when he was accused of winning the hand of his wife, Pudentilla, through the nefarious use of sorcery. One of the grounds of the prosecution's case was that Apuleius carried a mirror with him wherever he went.[102] The mirror was a powerful symbol of seeing, or peering beneath surfaces to esoteric and privileged truths. Jacques Le Goff observes that etymologically, *mir* is the root of "mirror," *mirari*, "which implies something visual," and of *mirabilia*. A marvel draws on "a whole series of visual images and metaphors," and the mirror was one of those metaphors that was sometimes literally thought to induce marvels. Doubtless for this reason, people with an immoderate attraction to mirrors

---

100. Augustine, *De doctrina Christiana* 2.26.102, 104–5. "Quorum ea quae ad societatem, ut dictum est, daemonum pertinent, penitus repudianda sunt et detestanda; ea vero, quae homines cum hominibus habent, assumenda, in quantum non sunt luxuriosa atque superflua."

101. Augustine, *De civitate Dei* 10.27, 1:302. The old man's advice is found in Martin of Braga's translation from Greek into Latin of *Sayings of the Egyptian Fathers* 79, in *Writings of Martin of Braga*, 30.

102. Apuleius of Madaura, *Apulei apologia* 13–16.

were often suspected of too ardent a desire to dabble in the arcane, which was a sure ticket to sorcery.[103]

In the *Recognitions*, Pseudo-Clement addresses the issue of those who would seek to understand the secrets of nature when he has Barnabas rebuke a heckler in the audience by telling him that it is not fitting to speak of creatures to those who are still ignorant of the creator.[104] Tertullian denounced magic because of its implicit mental attitude of *curiositas*, which propels a person to study nature without reference to God. Origen said that understanding the hidden and powerful properties of plants and stones was not difficult; it was just wrong. After all, he observed, even serpents and eagles recognize antidotes to poison and know how to use stones to preserve their young. Humans, however, ought not to pride themselves on discovering the secrets of the physical world. That sort of knowledge was unnecessary and fraught with peril.[105]

Healing

At times historians speak in terms of "black" and "white" magic, where the first is demonic and sinister and the second is beneficial, or even sublime. This characterization, however, is anachronistic for most of the Middle Ages.[106] In the late Middle Ages and early modern period, concepts of "natural magic" and "angelic magic" evolved, whereby some interactions with demons were desirable for the very few trained in the art of handling them.[107] In Christian thinking of late antiquity and the early Middle Ages, all traffic with demons was sinful, even if the results of that traffic ended up benefiting individuals. In a similar vein, a variety of medical cures fell under the umbrella of what might, in modern jargon, be called "victimless magic," because the intent of the therapy was to heal or give succor. However, regardless of the aim, healing that drew on devilish skills was sorcerous—even if practitioners were unaware that their procedures summoned demons.

The early church was particularly sensitive about pagan facility with medicine. Pastors felt it was critical for their flocks to understand that, although other gods (demons) could heal the body, only Christ, working through his

---

103. Le Goff, *Medieval Imagination*, 27–31.
104. Pseudo-Clement, *Recognitions* 1.8, 79.
105. Tertullian, *Ad nationes* 2.4–6, 1:46–52; Origen, *Contra Celsum* 4.86, 252. See Truitt, *Medieval Robots*, 2–10.
106. Zambelli, *White Magic, Black Magic*, 1–10.
107. For a useful summary of natural magic in the Middle Ages see Kieckhefer, *Magic in the Middle Ages*, 116–75.

designated vicars, could make the whole person sound—body and soul—and perpetuate that wellness into the next world.

The earliest Christian writings use the discourse of healing to describe the benefits of the new religion and cast Jesus or the church as "physician." In some contexts, this characterization was metaphorical, but it was just as often literal. Prayer, penance, supplication of saints, and pious living were thought to be genuinely curative.[108] On this point there was consistency across the late antique centuries. To list a few of countless examples, Ignatius of Antioch said of Jesus, "Our physician is the only true God," and the *Acts of Barnabas* indicates that the Gospel of Matthew was laid on bodies of the sick for the purpose of healing.[109] The conflation of physical and spiritual health is also evident in *2 Clement*, a first-century sermon, in which the anonymous author writes, "Let us give ourselves over to God who heals us, giving him our recompense." Origen spoke of God as the physician who "has cut open bodies and inflicted painful wounds in order to cut out of them the things which are harmful and hinder good health; he does not leave off with the pains and the incision, but by his cure he restores the body to the health that is intended for it."[110] The desert saint Hilarion told a blind woman, "If you had given to the poor what you have wasted on physicians, the true physician Jesus would have cured you." The heresiologic *Panarion* of Epiphanius is a "chest of remedies" containing cures for the poison of heresy.[111] Consecrated or exorcised oil was central to Christian rituals and salubrious in a variety of circumstances. Pope Innocent I (d. 417) held that not just the ordained, but any Christian, could use oil blessed by the bishops for healing.[112]

It is tempting to see Ignatius of Antioch's comments, *2 Clement*, the remarks of Eusebius, and the work of Epiphanius as metaphors and the *Acts of Barnabas* and Innocent's comments as literal, because the latter two are concretely somatic. But this assumption reflects presentist categories more than it does the thinking of early Christians. Where moderns tend to demarcate the body and mind, late antique thinking placed them on a continuum. Maintaining the wellness of the body and the soul was one endeavor.

Authors often employed the sanative figure of speech "contraries cure contraries" (*contraria contrariis sanantur*) to talk about the curative effect

---

108. Uhalde, "Juridical Administration," 107; Kollmann, *Jesus*, 61–118.
109. Ignatius of Antioch, *Epistle to the Ephesians* 7.2, 52; *Acts of Barnabas* 7, 332. *Acts of Barnabas* is a late fifth-century Cyprian collection of traditions.
110. *2 Clement* 9, 100–101. For background on Clement and 2 Clement see ibid., 14–26, 58–82. Origin, *Contra Celsum* 2.24, 89.
111. Jerome, *Life of Saint Hilarion* 15, 306; Epiphanius of Salamis, *Panarion*, Proem 1.1.1, 1:3.
112. Paxton, *Christianizing Death*, 29.

penance had on sin and illness of the soul. This phrase was borrowed from the Methodist school of medicine that developed in the late first and early second century CE.[113] John Cassian, the famous monk and theologian of Gaul, first employed the phrase to describe the operation of penance—penance cures transgression. Valerian, the bishop of Cimelium in Gaul (d. ca. 455), said in his homilies 6 and 9, "We should now set our hand to these subjects, and elaborate on them with the aid of the study of medicine. Thus, each vice will reveal the causes of its own infirmity" (6); "A doctor must employ continuous medication to prevent another man from groaning in pain, because a sickness which is daily developing requires medicine every day. If anything bloody or obnoxious happens to be in us, we, too, must take care to heal it by abundant alms" (9). In other words, vice is contrary to charity, which will counteract the infection of sin on the soul.[114]

The church's sought-after ownership of health provoked a rivalry with pagan cults, because certain of the deities had always been healers. The most renowned of the healing gods was the Greek Asclepius, offspring of Apollo from whom he learned his craft. By the fifth century BCE, the cult of Asclepius was firmly established in Greece. According to ancient tradition, the healing power of Apollo was introduced into Rome at the end of the second century to quell the fury of a plague, and when pestilence again racked the capital, the citizens erected a temple to his son who reached the city by ship in the form of a huge snake, the primeval symbol of regeneration. Asclepieia (temples/hospitals) operated in Epidaurus, Kos, and Pergamum through the end of the second century CE. In Pergamum, Asclepius was a favored god of the Roman aristocracy. His image was on coins; a hereditary priesthood honoring the god was established; and the enormous Asclepieion at Pergamum was a major medical school and a wonder of the ancient world. In the mid-second century, Asclepius came to be viewed as more than a physician; the Greek rhetorician Aeluis Aristides (d. ca. 181), a devotee and Asclepius's foremost publicist, called the god "Savior."[115]

Understanding the Asclepieia is important for grasping why Christians were threatened by this holy sanitarium. It was set in a grove of trees adorned

---

113. Lindberg, *Beginnings of Western Science*, 122–31; Drabkin, "Soranus and His System."

114. On John Cassian see Holze, *Erfahrung und Theologie*, 94, 165, 184–88, 209. Valerian, *Homilies* 6.1, 336; 9.2, 358 in *Saint Peter Chrysologus*. See also Augustine, *De doctrina Christiana* 1.14.27–30, 24–25.

115. Hart, *Asclepius*, 53–90; Kee, *Miracle*, 78–104, on Aristides see ibid., 93–104; Sigerist, *History of Medicine*, 2:45–60. See the first-century Latin writer Valerius Maximus (*Memorable Doings* 1.8, 100–105) on Asclepius's arrival in Rome. Asclepius is invoked in the Hippocratic oath and was worshipped at nearly seven hundred temples and shrines across the Mediterranean world.

by fountains in which ritual purity was imperative; no one was allowed to give birth or die in the temple precinct. The actual mechanism of healing in the Asclepieia was dream therapy. When the patients arrived, they bathed, purged their minds of impure thoughts, and donned white garments in preparation to enter the *incubatio*. When night fell and the patient slept, the god appeared, sometimes accompanied by his daughter Hygieia, his dog, or his snake. He cured the patient by touch, verbal command, the application of medicines, or, at times, surgery. The operations were sometimes fantastic, such as cutting off the head (which was later reattached) of a woman with dropsy in order to pour water from her body. The god could also recover lost objects or people by pointing out their whereabouts to the patient in a dream, and he could bring the dead back to life. Often to ensure continued health, supplicants left votive offerings at the shrine in the form of replicas of the body parts the god had doctored.[116]

The Asclepieia operated into late antiquity and incorporated many notions held in common with Christian ideas about healing. In the Asclepian cult, piety, faith, and spiritual purity were not divorced from physical health. The dreams that played a central role in Asclepius's therapy were not unlike the visions through which many saints bestowed posthumous cures. For example, in *The Account of the Miracles of Saints Cyrus and John* by the patriarch of Jerusalem, Sophronius (d. 638), one Theodoros becomes lame due to the machinations of magic, and the saints appear to him in a dream, revealing that "the wicked instrument of the sorcerer [a curse tablet]" is buried under the bedroom door. Once Theodoros finds and destroys the tablet, he is healed.[117]

Henry Sigerist rightly argues that of all the healing cults, the sect of Asclepius posed a particularly competitive challenge to Christians in the fierce rivalry over healing. Justin Martyr maintained that demons introduced the "myth" of Asclepius to challenge Jesus's prowess as a healer. Justin claimed that the Devil so feared Asclepius's popularity that the Evil One brought Asclepius forth to imitate the gospels and cheat men of their salvation.[118] In his biography of Saint Hilarion, Jerome smears Asclepius's name by associating him with love magic, though that was not a skill the ancients ascribed to

---

116. Sigerist, *History of Medicine*, 2:63–74. On votives of body parts see MacMullen, *Paganism*, 34.
117. Sophronius, *Account of the Miracles*, cited in *Curse Tablets*, 263. From Stanley ("Paul and Asklepios"), dream theory was common in the ancient world.
118. Sigerist, *History of Medicine*, 2:51–53. Justin Martyr, *Apology on Behalf of Christians* 54.10, 225; Justin Martyr, *Dialogue with Trypho* 69, 259. See also Tertullian, *Apologeticum* 23.4–6, 1:131; Kollmann, *Jesus*, 73–83, 95–98; Edelstein and Edelstein, *Asclepius* 2.75, 132–38; Kerényi, *Der göttliche Arzt*, 24–26.

the healing god. According to Jerome, Asclepius's priests instructed a young man on how to inscribe amatory spells on bronze plates to seduce a virgin. In fact, Asclepius did not rely on ritual magic at all, but on a vocabulary of gesture and simple word acts—methods Christian spiritual healers touted.[119] His application of herbs was without pomp; and his revivification was unostentatious. Jerome attempted to obscure the similarities between Christian and pagan healers by accusing Asclepius of common sorcery and vulgar rituals. As was emblematic of Christians' strategies, one way they hoped to distinguish their religion was by asserting that they did not rely on gaudy artifices which had the potential of inviting demons, and Jerome was playing this card when he cast Asclepius as a charlatan.

The competition over preeminence in medicine found voice in a variety of literary genres in antique Rome and became commonplace—even standard—in texts throughout the early Middle Ages. For instance, the sixth-century New Testament apocryphon titled the *Arabic Gospel of the Infancy of Jesus* tells the story of a girl who was cured of leprosy by perfumed water in which Mary had bathed the infant Jesus. She said of her disease, "We have consulted all the learned doctors, magicians, and sorcerers in the world, but none of them has benefited us." The *Recognitions* contains a homily in which Peter promises to cure any bodily ill through the simple ritual of prayer to God, even if "it is utterly incurable, and entirely beyond the range of the medical profession—a case, indeed, which not even the astrologers profess to cure." Augustine writes, "Physical medicines, applied by humans to other humans, only benefit those in whom the restoration of health is effected by God, who can heal even without them." He submits that both the mind and the body can be "cleansed" best by Christ, who is a better physician than doctors or sorcerers. He addresses his Neoplatonic readers: Christ became human "in order to cleanse humans, and all that goes to make them human, from the infection of their sins. If only you had learned to know him and trust him as the best healer . . . [rather than giving yourself over to] the completely pernicious practice of dealing with the occult."[120] In the examples

---

119. Jerome, *Life of Saint Hilarion* 21, 307. For an anthropological discussion of the concept of "word act" see Tambiah, "Magic Power of Words." Lalleman argues ("Healing by a Mere Touch," 356) that "the descriptions of healing by a mere touch in Christian texts have in common that the actual physical contact is so brief as to leave no room for any manipulations."

120. *Arabic Gospel of the Infancy of Jesus* 20–21, 190–92 (quotation, 191): "Nullum in mundo doctum aut magnum aut incantatorem omisimus quin illum accerseremus; sed nihil nobis profuit"; Pseudo-Clement, *Recognitions* 10.12, 306; Augustine, *De doctrina Christiana* 4.16.95, 238–39: "Sicut enim corporis medicamenta quae hominibus ab hominibus adhibentur nonnisi eis prosunt quibus deus operatur salutem, qui et sine illis mederi potest cum sine ipso illa non possint, et tamen

above, Christian curing trumps the work of those demons that empower the work of magicians, diviners, sorcerers, and astrologers.

It is strange, given their insistence on the benefits of Christian spiritual healing and their disdain for pagan medical sorcery, that Christian scribes, who copied from pagan medical texts, retained references to Asclepius and other pagan luminaries to magnify the prestige of the recipes. For instance, in the medical treatise on cures from animal substances, *Liber medicinae ex animalibus pecoribus, et bestiis vel avibus*, Sextus Placitus (fl. 370) says that his recipes were passed down from Asclepius through an Egyptian king, Idpartus, who gave them to Caesar Augustus. The *Herbarius Apulei Platonici Maudaurenses* (or *Pseudoapulei herbarius*) was a hugely influential herbal in late antiquity and the early Middle Ages. The text was named after Apuleius, author of *Metamorphoses* (though not written by him) because he was a famed physician.[121] The prologue of the *Herbarius* indicates that Apollo found and named the herb *Apollinaris* and gave it to Asclepius and that other remedies came from the centaur Chiron through Asclepius. The medieval treatise on the "marvelous herb betony" is introduced with a letter from the physician Antonius Musa (d. 14 BCE) to Augustus attesting to the value of the plant and assuring the emperor that Asclepius or Chiron the centaur first found it. The centaur found the herb *Centavria minor*, which was named after him, and the Homeric Greek hero Achilles discovered *Millefolium*.[122]

Antiquity also revered healing goddesses, such as Diana, who in one of her many avatars was a *medica*. Twin sister of the healing god Apollo, Diana was adept with medicines and a particular patroness of wildlife and vegetation—both used in the making of drugs. She instructed Asclepius on the applications of several herbs and empowered Hercules with the ability to ward off plague and cure disease.

---

adhibentur." Augustine, *De civitate Dei* 10.27, 1:302: Propterea quippe totum hominem sine peccato ille suscepit, ut totum, quo constat homo, a peccatorum peste sanaret. Quem tu quoque utinam cognouisses eique te potius quam uel tuae uirtuti, quae humana, fragilis et infirma est, uel perniciosissimae curiositati sanandum titius commisisses.

121. Harrison, *Apuleius: A Latin Sophist*, 69.

122. Pseudo-Apuleius, *Herbarius*, in *Corpus medicorum*, 21. The Cotton and the Caedmon (Winchester, ca. 1000) manuscripts of the *Herbarius* have a drawing of Plato giving a book of medicines to Chiron the centaur and Asclepius. *Apollinaris* 22, 61; *Peonia* 65, 121 (this was found in Crete and Sicily); *Moly* 48, 98; Antonii Musae, *De herba vettonica liber* (betony), prologue, 3; *Centavria minor* 35, 80; *Verbascum* 72, 129–30: "Hanc herbam dicitur Mercurius Ulixi dedisse, cum adveniset ad Circem, ut nulla mala facta eius timeret." *Millefolium* 89, 160: "Hanc herbam Achilles invenit . . . de hac sanasse Telephum dicitur"; all in *Corpus medicorum*. Odysseus, who had a reputation as a great healer, was said to have discovered the herb *Peonia*. He also tested the herb *Moly*, which Hermes gave him for defense against Circe's magic (Homer, *Odyssey*, bk. 10, 268–69).

It was common for Christians in antiquity to allegorize and assimilate things pagan, but in the case of the herbal *materia medica*, there was no effort to conceal or gloss over the origin of medicines that came from classical deities (who were, by Christian reckoning, demons). Pagan characters appear, without apology, in works that constituted a substantial portion of the corpus of herbal healing literature in late antiquity and the early Middle Ages. Many cures were accompanied by songs or chants that easily could be (and were) confused with magical incantations.[123]

Overall, *medici* and authors of medical texts were resistant to excise classical trappings and formulas that seemed efficacious, so in the field of therapeutics, the Christian struggle against magical superstitions was protracted. It was not easy for the new religion to suppress age-old remedies that were generally applied in intimate and quasi-private settings: the home and the monastery.[124] The time-honored feel of traditional cures and the texts that transmitted them added legitimacy to the rites that had kept people safe for generations, and gave comfort in the areas of human existence that Bronisław Malinowski identified as most vulnerable: "health and death."[125]

The first and greatest challenge for the early church in regard to magic was idolatry; a second and related concern was the divinatory methods that pagans used to interact with "false" gods and goddesses. In building a case against idolatry and divination, apologists set the groundwork for the early Christian and medieval understanding of many aspects of magic.

In the Roman world of the first centuries CE, virtually no pagan questioned the ability of humans to divine the future or ascertain the will of the gods, but long-established rites and the circumstances under which humans could lawfully and piously access the numinous power of deity were matters of dispute. The issues at stake were the form that divination and prophecy took and the source of the power that was tapped.[126] Classical augury was largely a male profession and was effected by formal and public rituals. Christians' understanding of divining was not dissimilar from that of

---

123. Sigerist, *History of Medicine*, 2:50–51.

124. Cato the Elder is an example of a gentleman farmer operating within the tradition of the Roman *paterfamilias* who practiced medicine on the farm for his family and his enslaved persons. Cato's *On Agriculture* (*De agri cultura* 115, 104–5; 156–60, 140–53) contains indigenous medical treatments (including one charm [160, 152–53]) that he recommends to the aristocratic householder. On Cato see Pliny, *Natural History* 29.8, vol. 8 (418), 192–93.

125. Malinowski, "Magic, Science and Religion," 31.

126. Caciola, *Discerning Spirits*, 1–9.

pagans, except that in their view haruspication was mediated by demons, as were private forms of foreseeing. Prophecy, on the other hand, involved direct communication initiated by God. It was not a human craft but a gift received with humility and effectuated guilelessly by both men and women. One had to be ever vigilant, however, to ensure that the interaction was deific and not demonic.

In the ecumenical councils of the fourth and fifth centuries, bishops tackled large questions of dogma and theology, and they reached a tenuous agreement on the general outlines of orthodoxy. Magic was not a central issue in any of the universal councils, but as missionary and pastoral work expanded in the fourth and fifth centuries, the mundane habits of the Christian flock came under the microscope, and in that process superstition was a central focus. Discussions of it were nowhere clearer than in the writings of Augustine. The challenge was to determine where demons were at work fostering idolatry behind ostensibly innocuous observances, some of which, such as healing, were benevolent. Identifying and then rooting out demonic superstitions was a tricky and delicate business, first, because they were integral to the ritual discourse of all segments of the population. Many of the acts that the Christian upper strata saw as devilish and superstitious were, in the view of new converts (both elite and common, both men and women) beneficial and pious. Second, appearances could be deceptive, and demonic agency might be at the core of a wide range of activities that looked innocent enough.

It seems clear that injunctions against what elites considered "superstition" were not very effective. But how could they be? How could average people examine their every move to determine the subtle differences between what was demonic and what was not? Even experts could not agree, and there was scant pastoral guidance for nonintellectuals and the illiterate—whether in villages or urban centers.

The problem deepened when ritual came into play, because it was more difficult to decode metaphor to get at underlying demonism than it was to observe straightforward daily behaviors. The church was wise to be nervous about ritual. Clifford Geertz explains, "The dispositions which religious rituals induce thus have their most important impact—from a human point of view—outside the boundaries of the ritual itself as they reflect back to color the individual's conception of the established world of bare fact."[127] Early Christian teachers intuited this and trod carefully in designing their own program of worship. They winnowed and culled the trove of inherited symbols

---

127. Geertz, *Interpretation of Cultures*, 119.

and signs in order to expunge rites governed by demons. So, where an explanation of the subtleties of dogma was not useful outside a narrow range of the population, rituals such as baptism, signing with the cross, and properly spoken words (for example the Lord's Prayer) helped instruct average people and kept them on a straight path to salvation. As church authority increased, superstitious habits were somewhat expunged from open or public view, but they nevertheless thrived in private and domestic settings.

Chapter 5

Maleficium and Traffic with the Dead

> [The Thessalian] witch buries in the grave the living whose souls still direct their bodies; while years are still due to them from destiny, death comes upon them unwillingly; or she brings back the funeral from the tomb with procession reversed and the dead escape from death.
>
> —Lucan, *The Civil War*

Maleficium referred to the misuse of occult powers, generally for personal advantage or gain, which required the employment of ominous beings or demons and was therefore always transgressive. For pagans, maleficium was, at best, shady, and for Christians it was unequivocally wicked. Virtually all its expressions required special skills and accoutrements, such as spells, potions, or curse tablets, and it often depended on inherent traits or predispositions of the type inhering in women. In its public ritual form, it could be controlled by religious or secular officials; however, most acts of maleficium were secretive and stealthy.

Malefici and *maleficae* were practitioners whose powers virtually nobody in classical Rome doubted, and they were the target of popular opprobrium. Maleficium, when used for justifiable ends, was legally neutral but socially suspect, offensive, and tawdry; when it harmed others, it was criminal and could result in capital punishment.[1] Pliny the Elder claimed, "There is indeed nobody who does not fear to be spell-bound by imprecations." Emperor Constantius ordered beheading for those who practiced malicious magic. In his history, Ammianus Marcellinus provides a glimpse of the dangers of maleficium in his description of the Roman prefect Apronian's (fl. mid-fourth

---

1. Harrison, *Apuleius: A Latin Sophist*, 41.

century) efforts to stem the tide of sorcery, which was becoming a public nuisance. Apronian himself lost an eye due to the insidious machinations of sorcery, and a plot to kill Emperor Valens (d. 378) by magic resulted in a purge of magicians. Concern about the incidents of maleficium was not in these cases on religious or moral grounds, but for public safety and political exigencies.[2]

The Romans would agree with Edmund Leach that ceremonial is beneficial when it "transmit[s] collective messages to ourselves" about the social order.[3] Public rituals that reinforced the status quo were an important tool for sustaining state solidarity, and pagan Rome abounded in them. Unlike primitive Christians, who tended to be chary of ceremony, Romans had no reservations about the importance of staged ritual theater. In fact, it provided a "reflexivity," giving the state an opportunity to craft communal values and the public an opportunity to lean in and experience its identity.[4] But maleficium's messages spoken in the language of ritual were not, by and large, communal; they were privileged, and they chipped away at the social order by virtue of their exclusivity and their attempt to control the course of events for private advantage. Secret rites unleashed their force in directions frightening to authorities because it was unknowable and uncontrollable. Bronisław Malinowski argues that concealment is one of the attributes distinguishing magic from religion in a vast number of cultures, and this captures the perspective in late antique Rome.[5]

Since the code of Roman law was first written around 450 BCE, secrecy was tantamount to conspiracy. The law reads, "No person shall hold meetings by night in the city."[6] In his trial for employing magic, Apuleius defended himself against charges of sorcery by insisting that his rites were sacred, not magical, because he performed them openly, and magic was carried out at night, cloaked in darkness. Magic, he claimed, presupposes "night-watches and concealing darkness, singular silence, and murmured incantations."[7] The Christian apologist Minucius Felix (d. ca. 250) penned a treatise called *Octavius* directed at educated non-Christians, which is a fictive conversation

---

2. Pliny, *Natural History* 28.4, vol. 8 (418), 14–15: "Defigi quidem diris deprecationibus nemo non metuit"; Ammianus Marcellinus, *History* 26.3–26.4.4, 2:580–87.
3. Leach, *Culture and Communication*, 45.
4. On "reflexivity" see Kapferer, "Ritual Process," 186–89.
5. Malinowski, "Magic, Science and Religion," 19, 54–60.
6. *Leges XII tabularum*, in *Fontes iuris Romani antiqui* 8.26, 32: "Ne qui in urbe coetus nocturnos agitaret." The Twelve Tables were Rome's first written law code; they were inscribed on twelve bronze tablets and displayed in the forum.
7. Apuleius of Madaura, *Apulei apologia* 47: "noctibus uigilata et tenebris abstrusa et arbitris solitaria et carminibus murmurata."

between Octavius Januarius and the pagan Caecilius Natalis. The text reveals Minicius's perception of Roman misgivings about secret rites, exclusive signs or symbols (*occultis se notis et insignibus noscunt*), and guilty secrets (*scelerta secreta*). Likewise, Celsus condemned Christians on the grounds that their "doctrine [was] secret."[8] In 364, Emperor Valens suppressed the ritual mysteries of Abydus in Egypt largely on the grounds that priests performed nocturnal sacrifices, and Ammianus Marcellinus inculpated three men who "by detestable arts of divination, had secretly learned the name of the man who was to succeed Valens."[9] For Ammianus, the addition of concealment to the appalling attempt to manipulate affairs of state through sorcerous rites made the charge all the more dire.

Women's magic was often clandestine—played out in the home or outdoors under the shroud of darkness. In his *History of Rome*, Livy (d. 17 CE) illustrates the long-standing classical distaste for the combination of ritual excess, unrestrained women, and secrecy. The Bacchanalia was an ancient female rite that was somber and diurnal at its inception, but in the second century BCE, innovation (a word almost as frightening as secrecy) crept into the ceremony which was heralded by "the noise and shrieking at night that resound[ed] throughout the city." Livy describes the depravity of the scene. "First of all, then, most are women, and they were the source of this plague; then there are males just like women, who submit to and in turn inflict sexual abuse, frenzied characters in a stupor from lack of sleep from drinking, and from the nightly hallaballoo and shouting. . . . What sort of meetings do you think are, first of all, held at night, and then attended by men and women together?"[10] In this text, Livy feminizes the men because they take part in the women's rituals, and he criminalizes the "conspiracy" because, first and foremost, it occurs in the silence of night.[11]

Christians interpreted maleficium in the same way their pagan contemporaries did in terms of its source of power, malevolence, ritual nature, secrecy, and gender identification. For both groups, it was magic accomplished through demons of the lower air whose aim was to exert dishonest domination over events or cause self-serving disruption and damage. Christian thinkers contrasted maleficium to theurgia. The latter sprang from understandable (even honorable) intentions, but still it was illicit because its practitioners drew on the wrong source of power and improperly used

---

8. Minucius Felix, *Octavius* 9–10, 12–15; Origen, *Contra Celsum* 1.7, 10.
9. Fowden, *Empire to Commonwealth*, 43; Ammianus Marcellinus, *History* 29.1.6, 3:190–91: "nomen imperaturi post Valentem detestandis praesagiis didicisse secretim."
10. Livy, *History of Rome* 39.15, 248–51.
11. Benko, *Pagan Rome*, 10–12.

demons to coax out of nature secrets that only God should reveal. *Malefici* and *maleficae* hoped to do more than comprehend the cosmos; they sought to control it through potions, magical written and oral formulas, ligatures, and covert rites. Even Augustine, always uncompromising in his insistence that all magic was demonic, evinced a deeper level of disgust at the vulgar, often criminal, practice of maleficium than he did with regard to the cosmological precepts of Porphyry's Neoplatonism.[12] In the end, however, it is important to remember that for Christians both maleficium and theurgia relied on demonic agency and were therefore condemnable.

Before it was legalized in 313, one of the most damning charges Roman pagans brought against primitive Christian groups was that they carried out their rites in concealment. Perhaps not surprisingly, once legalized, the church learned to abhor secret rites and embraced the fears and stereotypes about hidden rituals that pagan regimes once harbored against Christians.[13] Just as Romans had charged Christians with sinister secrecy, Christians in turn bludgeoned their enemies with the same accusation. There is little distinction between pre-Christian Roman law and the *Theodosian Code* (issued more than a hundred years after Constantine's conversion) in regard to the evils of clandestine maleficium. The code reflects the traditional Roman dread of secrecy and malicious magic when it designates capital punishment for those who attempt "during the nighttime to engage in wicked prayers or magic preparation or funeral sacrifices."[14] Augustine argued that before the birth of Jesus, worship of nature was permitted by the Almighty and carried out in the open. Since the Incarnation, rituals in honor of nature were odious to God, and the evidence of this was that they were carried on secretly "in the nighttime" (*nocturno*).[15]

Despite legal prohibitions and ecclesiastical sanctions, acts of malevolent sorcery of the type common in the pre-Christian empire continued unabated as Europe converted to the new religion. This is evidenced by extant *defixiones*

---

12. Augustine, *De civitate Dei* 10.11, 1:284–86, especially 286: "Certerum illos, quibus conuersatio cum diis ad hoc esset, ut ob inueniendum fugitiuum uel praedium comparandum, aut propter nuptias uel mercaturam uel quid huius modi mentem diuinam inquietarent, frustra eos uideri dicit coluisse sapientiam." See also ibid., 10.9, 1:281.

13. Minucius Felix, *Octavius* 10, 14–15. In Origen's *Contra Celsum* (preface 3, 8) Celsus's first charge against Christians is that they break the law by entering into secret associations. From Bowes (*Private Worship, Public Values*, 47–48), even murmured prayers were suspicious because they were secretive.

14. *Theodosian Code* 9.16.1–2, 7, pp. 237–38 (quotation 238).

15. Augustine, *De divinatione daemonum* 2.5, 602: "si quid autem nunc prohibitorum sacrificiorum fit occulte atque inlicite, non est illi pontificali sacrificiorum generi conparandum, sed in eodem deputandum, quod etiam nocturno fit tempore."

(the curse tablets mentioned in chapter 4). The use of these binding spells did not cease with the triumph of Christianity. We learn this from a variety of sources. The *Theodosian Code* requires capital punishment for chariot drivers who commission binding spells against rival drivers.[16] The eremitic Armenian monk Saint Euthymius (d. 473) cured a sick man by cutting "open the spot as if with a sword and withdrew from his stomach a tin strip which had certain *charaktêres* on it." In his *Account of the Miracles of Saints Cyrus and John* mentioned above, the patriarch of Jerusalem, Sophronius, relates the story of one Theophilos, whom doctors could not cure of his terrible affliction. The saints step in, and, following their instructions, Theophilos discovers a hidden "carved image in human form, made of bronze and resembling [him], with four nails driven into its hands and feet. . . . It became clear to all what abominable magic the charlatans had used against him in cooperation with those most evil demons."[17] These and numerous similar examples demonstrate the continued use of traditional curses and illustrate how Christian literature pits the power of the holy men against the machinations of *maleficos* in league with demons.

Although the identification of Christian women with maleficium was not a dimension of magic in the early church, it reemerged once the religion stood on firmer ground in the fourth century. In this way, gender and secrecy were comparable. In the apostolic and post-apostolic periods, the fledgling religion was under siege, and it relied on both secrecy and the support of rich and powerful women. Struggling new movements often ignore traditional social classifications such as gender, class, age, and race because the greater need is to get "all hands on deck" to ensure the group's survival. This was the case within the early Christian organization. That egalitarianism changed fairly early, however, as some church fathers were quick to reinstate stereotypes of females (even Christian women) as lascivious, vain, petty, and susceptible to demons' scheming.[18]

Although pagan and Christian concepts of maleficium were manifestly similar, there were a couple of differences. First, reliance on demons was an explicit and defining component of the church view of malevolent sorcery. Second, one type of maleficium that ecclesiastics did markedly reevaluate was necromancy.

---

16. *Theodosian Code* 9.16.11, 238.
17. *Curse Tablets*, 262–63.
18. On reversion to misogynist appraisals of women see famously Tertullian, *De cultu feminarum*, notably 1.2, 1:344–46; Epiphanius, *Panarion* 79, 3:637–45; Clark, "Early Christian Women"; Pagels, *Gnostic Gospels*, 61–69.

Necromancy

Necromancy in the ancient world generally pertained to the practice of calling the dead back to life for the purpose of learning the future, but the term also encompassed leaving magic tablets at tombs to compel corpses to perform particular spells, or using body parts and substances of cadavers in order to effect magical procedures.[19] Although many magical acts were tolerated and legal in the classical world, necromancy was always disreputable and usually criminal.

Roman literature portrays contact with the dead as ghoulish and repugnant, but if used gingerly and undertaken for a desirable ends, it could be justified. Revivification was a major feat that required concentrated syncopation with cosmic powers, and that collaboration was realized and made safe through carefully executed rituals. For example, in his novel *Metamorphoses*, Apuleius relates a story of the corpse of Telephron, whom the Egyptian prophet Zatchlas temporarily revivifies so that the deceased can solve a mystery regarding his sudden demise. Telephron had recently married, and he died shortly afterward. As his funeral procession winds through the streets of a city in Thessaly, the rumor goes out that his wife had killed him by the use of poison and the "evil arts" (*malis artibus*). She protests, and the crowd settles the matter by asking Zatchlas to recall the spirit from the grave for a brief time and reanimate the body as it was before his death. Zatchlas agrees. He begins the resurrection by mustering the mediating force of ritual. "He placed a bit of one herb on the cadaver's mouth and a bit of another on its chest. Then he turned to the east and prayed silently to the majestic Sun as it swelled over the horizon," asking that the corpse be granted a momentary reprieve. The dead man comes to life and says, "I'd drunk the waters of Lethe, I was already being ferried over the Stygian fen; Why, tell me, did you drag me back for this short stint among the living? Leave me alone—I'm begging you—and let me return to my rest." He then confirms his wife's murderous perfidy. In this case, the motive for interaction with the dead was worthy and was accomplished with a careful, simple rite and a silent prayer.[20]

The Thessalian crowd was comfortable beholding the restoration of Telephron because they were shielded by Zatchlas, the ritual specialist. It was a constant of ancient cultures that death was the realm of pollution, otherness, and unbeing. The dead were potent conveyors of knowledge about

---

19. The *Theodosian Code* stipulates that a woman can divorce her husband for being a "despoiler of tombs," which Grubbs ("Constantine and Imperial Legislation," 128n20) interpretates as pilfering body parts from cadavers for magical purposes.

20. Apuleius of Madaura, *Golden Ass* 2.28–29, 41–42.

the future because they were perpetually suspended in a liminal and timeless space. Magic also was most often loosed within liminal realms. Victor Turner observes that "liminal situations and roles are almost everywhere attributed with magico–religious properties . . . [and are] regarded as dangerous, inauspicious, or polluting."[21]

Liminal space-time was the domain of women—for good or ill. This connection is primordial due largely to the fact that women produce life and are at the threshold between non-being and being. In Greco-Roman cultures, Hekate, the goddess of ghosts and shades, was the very personification of liminality.[22] Although there are several examples of male necromancers in ancient and late antique sources, such as the prophet Zatchlas,[23] it was women who were adept at the truly gruesome traffic with the dead. In his *Metamorphoses*, Apuleius repeatedly demonstrates the association between women and the grave. In the story of the resurrected Telephron, after the dead man incriminates his wife for poisoning him, he amazes the crowd by revealing that this was not the first time he had risen from death's slumber. The previous night, a group of *sagae* (crafty women) had come to his wake and, calling his name, revived him from his resting place. "[His] sluggish joints and chilly limbs were struggling with slow effort to obey the commands of their magic art," Apuleius writes. These *sagae* were in the habit of gouging "at corpses' faces with their teeth: that's where they get the wherewithal for their practice of sorcery."[24] In the story, the male prophet Zatchlas performs the odious act of necromancy, but reluctantly, for a just cause, and at a safe distance from the corpse. The crafty women, on the other hand, traffic with polluted human carrion in order to trade in the black arts.

Classical antiquity gives us several other examples of women's ritual commerce with the dead. Clearly the most chilling tale of female necromancy comes from the Roman poet Lucan (d. 65 CE). In this history of the civil war of the first century BCE, Lucan describes the craft of Erictho, a medium who summons a spirit from the grave to reveal to the consul Pompey (d. 48 BCE) the outcome of his impending battle with Julius Caesar (d. 44 BC). Both Zatchlas and Erictho are necromancers, but Zatchlas sets about his

---

21. Turner, *Ritual Process*, 108–9.
22. See Farnell ("Hekate's Cult") for the goddess's place in the ancient pantheon. See Johnston ("Riders in the Sky") on Hekate's vital role in the *Chaldean Oracles*.
23. For an example of a necromancer decidedly less savory than Zatchlas, see Ammianus Marcellinus's, *History* (29.2.17, 3:224–25) where "Nemerius, a man of surpassing wickedness" (*malitia quendam exsuperantem*), cuts open the womb of a living woman in order to remove the embryo with the hope of raising the dead to question them on the future of the empire.
24. Apuleius of Madaura, *Golden Ass* 2.21, 36.

task with reluctance, while Erictho approaches her work with lustful zeal—comfortable in the land of shades. Unlike the work of Zatchlas, who awakes the dead gently, with prayerful words and untreated herbs, Erictho's craft is steeped in grisly, convoluted, and ghostly rituals necessitating spells and poison substances.

> At last she chose a corpse and drew it along with the neck noosed, and in the dead man's noose she inserted a hook. The hapless body was dragged over rocks and stones to live a second time. . . . Then she began by piercing the breast of the corpse with fresh wounds, which she filled with hot blood; she washed the inward parts clean of clotted gore; she poured in lavishly the poison that the moon supplies. . . . Next she put in leaves steeped with magic unutterable, and herbs which her own dread mouth had spat upon at their birth . . . and lastly her voice, more powerful than any drug to bewitch the power of Lethe, first uttered indistinct sounds untunable and far different from human speech. . . . "I never chant these spells when fasting from human flesh." . . . When she had spoken thus, she raised her head and foaming mouth, and saw beside her the ghost of the unburied corpse. It feared the lifeless frame and the hateful confinement of its former prison; it shrank from entering the gaping bosom. . . . She lashed the passive corpse with a live serpent. . . . Instantly the clotted blood grew warm; it warmed the livid wounds. . . . The vital organs thrilled within the cold breast; and a new life . . . wrestled with death. Next, the dead man quivered in every limb; the sinews were strained, and he rose, not slowly or limb by limb, but rebounding from the earth and standing erect at once. His mouth gaped wide and his eyes were open.[25]

The tale of Erictho captures, indeed with relish, the horror that pagans had of necromancy, especially when women carried it out. Female sorcery was attended by gruesome, nocturnal, chthonic, and tactile rituals performed in shadows. Pagans were not antagonistic to ritual, but acts such as piercing the breast of a corpse and feasting on carrion were worlds away from the lofty ceremonies of male priests who openly appealed to deities with time-honored verbal formulas and meaningful, circumscribed gestures.

Erictho, though a literary figure, epitomizes the repulsion that pagans felt toward, not just magic, but mortality itself. The scene is set up to conjure more than the image of a heinous old hag lashing a departed shade back to the world of the living; the whole backdrop bespeaks the ugliness of death,

---

25. Lucan, *Civil War* 6, 350–61.

which for Romans was anathematic and polluting. The liminality of the state of death was a no man's land where the living trod at their peril.

The dread of cadavers colored pagan attitudes toward Christians, who seemed to savor the dead. They frequented burial grounds, celebrated death days, held martyrs up as role models (cherishing their body parts), and circulated stories of Jesus as a heroic figure because he could bring the deceased from the grave. Christian practices seemed all too reminiscent of Erictho's secret rites of revivification and cannibalism. Initiates to the new religion were thought to engage in eating human flesh when, during the Eucharistic ritual, they consumed the body and blood of the dead Jesus. This was all the more serious because it was not the act of a lone miscreant, but the objective of a condoned, collective ritual. Worse than that, Minucius Felix's fictional, stereotypical pagan antagonist says of Christians, "They hungrily lap up [a murdered child's] blood and eagerly divide up his limbs. . . . Everything that is done by one of them is in accord with the wishes of them all." The view that Jesus and his followers were necromancers had a long run in late antiquity, and it necessitated a persistent denial from some of the best minds of the patristic era.[26]

Pagans were right in one respect: Christians did approach the dead differently than their polytheistic peers did, because Jesus had redefined death, and his adherents reinterpreted that liminal window—both temporal and physical—between life and death. Whereas most pagan and mystery cults dreaded, shunned, and burned the dead, Christians formed tender and mutually beneficial relationships with the spirits (and in some cases, the material remains) of those who ceased to exist on a mortal plane. Rather than ostracizing the dead beyond the city limits, by the second century, Christians sought out the remains of their loved ones and shared spaces in cemeteries made holy by their numinous presence.[27]

The idea that the dead could live again was a central tenet of Christian belief. Jesus was resurrected, and he assured humanity that the same was in store for them. The ability to bring the dead back from the grave was a distinguishing marker of sanctity. In Matthew (10:8), Jesus invests the disciples with the power to emulate his miracles, including resuscitating the dead. The earliest Christian biographies focus on saints imitating the miracles

---

26. Minucius Felix, *Octavius* 9, 12–14; Barb, "Survival," 101–25.

27. Lucian of Samosata, *Passing of Peregrinus* 13, 15; Lewis, "Popular Christianity"; *Soldiers of Christ*, xxii–xxiii; Paxton, *Christianizing Death*, 1–15; Pelikan, *The Shape of Death*, 11–123. See Peter Brown's pioneering work on the cults of the saints (*Cult of the Saints*, here 4–8, 38–42) as an entrée on the topic of Christian death, the historiography of which is extensive. For the polysemic possibilities of landscapes associated with death, see Andrews and Roberts, "Re-mapping Liminality," 6–7.

of their Lord, including revivification. However, it is significant that late antique vitae do not portray female saints in the role of *revivicatrices*. It may be that women, even holy women, bringing souls back from the grave conjured the chilling specter of female pythonesses of Roman literature, such as the dreaded Erictho and the *sagae* of the *Metamorphoses*. For men, there were positive role models of revivification (Jesus, of course, was the unassailable exemplar), but the same was not true of women. There were no inspirational stories from classical and early Christian narratives of virtuous women raising the dead.[28]

For Christians it was easy enough to distinguish between Jesus reviving a dead man, such as Lazarus, for purely charitable purposes, and the practice of fiends such as Erictho, dragging the dead back from Hades for mantic designs, revenge, and personal gain. "Jesus, again greatly disturbed, came to the tomb," reads the Gospel of John. "It was a cave, and a stone was lying against it. Jesus said, 'Take away the stone.' Martha, the sister of the dead man, said to him, 'Lord, already there is a stench because he has been dead four days.' . . . So they took away the stone. And Jesus looked upward and . . . cried with a loud voice, 'Lazarus come out.' The dead man came out, his hands and feet bound with strips of cloth, and his face wrapped in a cloth. Jesus said to them, 'Unbind him; let him go'" (11:17–44).

There are pointed differences between the revivification of Lazarus and the slain soldier in *The Civil War*. Erictho brings the soul back to the world against its will, not for its own benefit but to assuage the fears of those who engage her services. She is a female necromancer working in secrecy, under the cover of darkness. The work of Erictho is avaricious, bloody, and unnatural. The shade shrinks from its former body and enters it only when threatened, and then with great pain. The unfortunate soldier does not receive the gift of life, but an agonizing and bitter jolt back to an unwanted consciousness. The resurrection Jesus undertakes is unguarded, altruistic, loving, and selfless. Erictho uses elaborate rituals involving plants, poisons, cannibalism, and spells, while in John's gospel, the rite is more like that of the priest Zatchlas in Apuleius's novel; in both texts the actors employ simple controlled word formulations. However, a distinction can be drawn between Jesus's revivification and that by Zatchlas. The pagan priest brings the dead man to life for the purpose of uncloaking a mystery; the motive is just, but by Christian reckoning, the act would be a type of demonic second sight—imparting

---

28. Athanasius, *Life of Antony* 71, 83. Poulin, *L'idéal de sainteté*, 109–16. From Rampton ("Up from the Dead"), by the Merovingian era, female saints routinely emulated Jesus's spectacular miracles, such as revivification.

information beyond human ken. Jesus's favor to Lazarus, on the other hand, was a miracle done by the Lord—Jesus expected nothing in return. "Done by the Lord" is the important factor. Magic is antipodal to miracle because of the source of power that actualizes each. However, distinctions between miraculous resurrection and necromantic revivification were not always so clear-cut.[29]

An example of a pagan resurrection that closely resembles the rising of Lazarus comes from the pen of Philostratus, the Greek Sophist who wrote a biography of Apollonius of Tyana. As mentioned in chapter 4, Apollonius was a Pythagorean magus who lived in the first century and was well known for his knowledge of the occult, which he gained in Egypt, Greece, and India. This philosopher had miraculous powers to heal the sick, predict the future, and raise the dead. Apollonius's traffic with the underworld was somewhat unsavory for Roman tastes, but overall, he was held in awe for his facility with the preternatural.[30] Once, Apollonius conjured and spoke with the ghost of Achilles. On another occasion, he revived a maiden who was being borne to the grave, simply by touching her and speaking a few words,[31] very similar to the way in which Jesus raised the lifeless daughter of Jairus. "He took her by the hand and said to her, 'Talitha cum,' which means, 'Little girl, get up!'" [Mark 5:35–41]). Neither act required grandiose rites or ritual substances such as saliva, blood, or hairs, and in that way, they played to the sensibilities of the restrained Roman elect.

Jesus and his disciples were persistently compared to other magicians and holy men of the ancient world, such as Apollonius of Tyana and Asclepius, the mythical famed healer of the ancient world, who was also reputed to resuscitate those who died of illness.[32] Accounts of non-Christian resurrection and revivification plagued Christian religionists. Stupendous miracles constituted a vital component of Christianity's claim to authenticity, and pagan holy men who were able to bring people back from death posed as competition for the fledgling faith.[33] Justin Martyr, Tertullian, Origen, and Athanasius protested that Jews and pagans routinely represented Jesus as a

---

29. From Origen (*Contra Celsum* 2.48, 102–3), Celsus claims revivification is realized by "sorceries."

30. Bäbler and Nesselrath, *Philostrats Apollonios*, 1–17; Graf, *Magic*, 94–96. Annequin, *Recherches sur l'action magique*, 116–22.

31. Philostratus, *Apollonius of Tyana* 4.15–16, 1:346–55; 4.45, 1:418–23. Apollonius of Tyana was viewed as an ascetic and servant of God. From M. Smith (*Jesus the Magician*, 96–97), some magicians were thought to be able to conjure spirits, even without elaborate rites or spells.

32. Benko, *Pagan Rome*, 141.

33. Rampton, "Up from the Dead."

magician.³⁴ Lactantius, author and adviser to Emperor Constantine, attested that non-Christians commonly compared the marvels of Apollonius with those of Jesus. Lactantius went so far as to admit that it was not unreasonable to think Jesus was a necromancer, so closely did his miracles approximate magical tricks; however, he maintained that the difference was that Old Testament scripture anticipated Jesus's marvels.³⁵ As late as the fourth century, Augustine alluded to the fact that some praised the miracles of Apollonius along with those of Christ.³⁶ For pagans, there was no contumely per se in the comparison with Apollonius, because he was considered magnanimous. For Christians, the sting was in the charge that Jesus was a counterfeit. They considered Apollonius's powers demonic, as evidenced in Eusebius of Caesarea's work refuting pagan claims that Apollonius was the equal of Jesus of Nazareth.³⁷

In addition to the fact that the efficacy of the necromantic art rested on demons of the lower air, early Christians were anxious to clear themselves of the charge of necromancy in order to distinguish themselves from the many other religions and belief systems that formed a veritable montage in the ancient world. One of Origen's tasks in *Contra Celsum* was to defend Jesus specifically and Christians generally against accusations of maleficium. From the first century, Christian writers were insistent that the power of their holy men and women rested not on the demons that lurked between the moon and the earth, and not on elaborate rites, but on simple faith and God alone. Origen wrote, "Magic and sorcery [are] wrought by evil daemons who are enchanted by elaborate spells and obey men who are sorcerers. . . . We should know in this way who serves daemons and causes such effects by means of certain spells and enchantments, and who has been on pure and holy ground before God . . . and has received a certain divine spirit, and performs such wonders for the benefit of mankind."³⁸ It is significant that Origen conflates "elaborate" rituals with demonism. He also implies that one of the ways in which magic can be differentiated from miracle is by its dependence on sorcerous rites.

---

34. Justin Martyr, *Dialogue with Trypho* 69, 260; Tertullian, *Apologeticum* 21–23, 1:122–33; Origen, *Contra Celsum* 1.38, 37; 2.51, 105–6; Athanasius, *De incarnatione* 48, 256–7. On pagan views of Jesus see M. Smith, *Jesus the Magician*, 50–80.

35. Lactantius, *Divine Institutes* 5.3, 286–89.

36. Augustine, *Letters* 136, 3:15–17; 138, 3:50–52.

37. Eusebius, *Reply to Hierocles*. For more on the *Reply to Hierocles* see chapter 4. See Bäbler and Nesselrath (*Philostrats Apollonios* 123–38) on Philostratus as a deity.

38. Origen, *Contra Celsum* 2.51, 105–6. See also Athanasius, *De incarnatione* 48, 256–57.

In *Recognitions*, the apostles repeatedly find themselves in situations where they are forced to defend Jesus and themselves against charges of deceptive magic. According to one story in the text, James sends Peter to Caesarea to refute Simon Magus (Peter's challenger in miraculous feats), who is claiming to be Jesus Christ. In the same source, the character Niceta questions how it is possible to distinguish between Jesus's miracles and claims to divinity as put forth in the Gospels from those Simon Magus and false prophets generally proffered.[39]

The answer to Niceta's question emerged from an unexpected quarter that allowed Christians to back away from their early emphasis on miracle as the barometer of Jesus's validity. Through the first four centuries of the Christian era, a Mariology steadily developed in which the perpetual virginity of Mary became increasingly important, largely because of the implications it had for the uniqueness of Jesus.[40] In Matthew and Luke, the virgin birth demonstrates Jesus's preeminent and singular authority over other itinerant preachers and healers (Matt. 1:18–25, Luke 1:26–38). According to the patristic interpretation of these two gospel passages, the virginity of Mary was the criterial sign that Jesus was not just another prophet, but the Christ called Immanuel, "God is with us" (Matt. 1:23). For writers such as Justin Martyr, Origen, Lactantius, the preeminent Greek theologian Gregory of Nyssa (d. ca. 395), and Jerome, Jesus's miracles (including revivification), and even his own resurrection, were not the most significant indicators that he was the messiah. The fact that Jesus was born of a virgin, thus fulfilling Old Testament prophecy (Isa. 7:14), was the most demonstrable evidence of his divinity.[41] No doubt this argument rang true and was promoted, at least in part, because the ancient world was full of holy men, prophets, and magicians who could perform wonders, including raising people from the grave; this was in no way a unique claim. But the fulfillment of an ancient prophecy involving a virgin birth separated religion from common sorcery.

Questions surrounding necromancy created another doctrinal controversy within the Christian intellectual community. The new concept of the fluidity between the living and the dead confronted theologians as they sought to work out their own understanding of magic. That task

---

39. Pseudo-Clement, *Recognitions* 1.72, 96; 3.57–60, 129–30. See also ibid., 1.58, 92; 10.66, 209.

40. From Allen ("Augustine's Commentaries on the Old Testament"), veneration of Mary per se was slow to develop in North Africa; Mary was seldom a topic of sustained discussion outside expositions of her role in salvation history. Rampton, "Mary the Virgin"; Brown, *Body and Society*, 351–56.

41. Justin Martyr, *Apology on Behalf of Christians* 32–33, 163–175; Origen, *Contra Celsum* 1.33–37, 32–37; 1.49–51, 46–48; Shoemaker, "Epiphanius of Salamis"; Pelikan, *Mary through the Centuries*, 23–36, 55–65; Clayton, *Cult of the Virgin*, 1–24.

was compounded by the fact that their sacred texts contained stories of necromancy. The most dramatic case concerns a woman similar to the morbid Erictho. In Deuteronomy (18:9–14), God instructs Moses against heeding necromancers and other types of magicians (augurs, soothsayers, diviners, and sorcerers). King Saul of Israel (d. ca. 1000) reiterates that ban (1 Sam. 28:3), yet he himself, with the help of the so-called Witch of Endor (also known as the ventriloquist, belly-myther, or pythoness of Endor), successfully brings Samuel (d. ca. 1000), judge and prophet of the Israelites, from the grave. Note the familiar topos that necromancy takes place secretly, "by night."

> The Philistines assembled, and came and encamped at Shunem.... When Saul saw the army of the Philistines, he was afraid, and his heart trembled greatly.... Then Saul said to his servants, "Seek out for me a woman who is a medium, so that I may go to her and inquire of her." His servants said to him, "There is a medium at Endor."... They came to the woman by night. And [Saul] said, "Consult a spirit for me, and bring up for me the one whom I name to you."... Then the woman said, "Whom shall I bring up for you?" He answered, "Bring up Samuel for me." When the woman saw Samuel, she cried out with a loud voice; and the woman said to Saul, "Why have you deceived me? You are Saul!" The king said to her, "Have no fear; what do you see?" The woman said to Saul, "I see a divine being coming up out of the ground." He said to her, "What is his appearance?" She said, "An old man is coming up; he is wrapped in a robe."... Then Samuel said to Saul, "Why have you disturbed me by bringing me up?"

King Saul informs the dead Samuel that he is pressed hard by the Philistines and bids the ghost to look into the future and inform him of his fate. Samuel obliges and correctly predicts that Saul will fall in battle against the Philistines (1 Sam. 28:16–19).

The Witch of Endor's raising of Samuel not only proved disastrous for Saul, but also came to plague generations of Christian theologians who, throughout the first millennium, took a variety of positions on the incident.[42] Patristic writers held that magic, though often efficacious, was demonic and therefore taboo, but they differed on what kinds of magic actually worked. There are some uncomfortable moments in Matthew's account of the magi when the birth of the savior is announced to the Persian priests through astral signs and portents of the sort that Christians were forbidden to interpret. Even more bewildering, however, were the issues raised by the story

---

42. See Harmening (*Superstitio*, 207–16) on the pythoness. See also Schmitt, *Les revenants*, 25–42.

of the Witch of Endor. It created a quandary for church intellectuals, not because there is any sense in the story that necromancy was an innocent practice, but because there was no consensus on whether human beings actually could recall the dead for the purposes of divining. Did Saul really recall Samuel from the grave, or was it a demonic illusion? The episode also brought into question the nature of the afterlife. Did ordinary humans, aided by demons and armed with ritual trappings and verbal commands, have the power to compel souls to leave the spirit world?

Justin Martyr interpreted the incident from 1 Samuel literally and marshaled it to prove the immortality of the soul. He wrote, "The soul of Samuel was called up by the witch, as Saul demanded." In *Apology on Behalf of Christians*, he states, "For conjurings of the dead—both visions obtained through uncorrupted children and the summoning of human souls—and those whom magicians call 'dream-senders' or 'attendants'—and the things done by those who know these things—let these persuade you that even after death souls remain in consciousness."[43] Justin is unequivocal that the necromantic arts—even crafts of the most sordid kind, such as compelling unpolluted children to look into the future—were effective and could can raise the dead.

Origen took a similar position, claiming that Samuel's spirit actually appeared to the pythoness and spoke to Saul. He rejected the suggestion that a demon in the guise of Samuel deceived the woman and Saul, largely due to the fact that the specter correctly predicted Saul's defeat and death. In fact, in his effort to defend the general proposition that human souls survive the grave, Origen blurred the distinctions between Christian miracle and pagan marvels. In *Contra Celsum*, he defends the resurrection of Jesus on the grounds that others had come back from death before him. Origen brings to his defense Plato's assertion that Er, the son of Aremius, "rose again from the funeral pyre after twelve days and gave an account of his adventures in Hades." He also quotes the pagan philosopher and astronomer Heraclides of Pontus (d. ca. 325 BCE), who wrote about the pre-Socratic philosopher Empedocles's (d. ca. 430 BCE) revival of a woman who had not breathed for thirty days. Origen goes on to say, "Several people are recorded to have returned even from their tombs, not only on the same day, but even on the day after."[44] Belief in the actual revivification of the dead lived on in the popular *Recognitions*, where Simon Magus sacrifices a boy, pure of spirit, and

---

43. Justin Martyr, *Apology on Behalf of Christians* 18.3, 123.
44. Origen, "Homily"; Origen, *Contra Celsum* 2.16, 82.

summons the boy's soul by "unutterable adjurations." The conjuration of the dead boy's soul is clearly an evil act, but one that Simon is able to effect.[45]

Writing around the same time as Origen, Tertullian took an opposing view of the revivification of Samuel. He argued that the pythoness had not actually resurrected Samuel, but that the ghost was an illusion created by demons, that have the ability to conjure phantoms in the form of the dead. Two other churchmen of the fourth century also disputed Origen's position on the Witch of Endor. Gregory of Nyssa wrote a treatise in the form of a letter to Emperor Theodosius I arguing that Samuel's soul was already in paradise when Saul attempted to retrieve it, and he could not invoke a departed spirit. Rather, he said, a demon impersonated Samuel. In *On the Belly-Myther Against Origen*, Eustathius, the patriarch of Antioch (d. ca. 360), also denies that the pythoness recalled Samuel and denounces Origen's explanation because he feared it could have the calamitous effect of encouraging the simple to attempt the art of necromantic divination.[46]

Augustine followed the lead of his intellectual predecessors such as Tertullian in arguing that the raising of Samuel was the work of demons. Both men held that the security of the dead was threatened if mortals could force them from the bosom of Abraham (or in some cases the cauldron of hell). Tertullian claimed that even in his own day there were many followers of Simon Magus who were so puffed up by their art that they sought to retrieve the very souls of the prophets from Hades. "I believe," he said, "that they can do so by illusion," meaning that demons take on the guise of the living dead.[47]

In short, the earliest Christian theologians were conflicted about the efficacy of necromantic divination, but they were univocally in harmony with their pagan neighbors on the evils of using (or trying to use) the deceased either for fortune telling or to exploit the power of death's liminal state for nefarious purposes. Dealings with reanimated corpses involved the worst

---

45. Pseudo-Clement, *Recognitions* 2.13–15, 100–101; 3.44–49, 126–27. The notion that uncorrupted boys were psychic and could tell the future by gazing into basins of water was a common belief in the ancient world (and well beyond). Although in his trial for magic Apuleius denied having exploited a child in this way, he subscribed to the belief that it was possible to induce prophetic trances in fair and unblemished boys (Apuleius, *Apulei apologia* 42–43).

46. Tertullian, *De anima* 57, 2:866–67; Gregory of Nyssa, *Lettre sur la Pythonisse*; Eustathius of Antioch, *On the Belly-Myther*. On demons' ability "to change themselves into all forms and assume all appearances" see Athanasius, *Life of Antony* 25, 50. Also ibid., 23, 48–49.

47. Augustine, *De diversis quaestionibus* 2.3.1–3, 81–86; Augustine, *De cura pro mortuis gerenda* 15.18, 650–52; Tertullian, *De anima* 57, 2:866: "Et credo, quia mendacio possunt." On the "bosom of Abraham" (*in sinu Abrahae*) see Tertullian, *De idololatria* 13, 2:1113; Boase, *Death*, 19–37; Ariès, *Hour of Our Death*, 147–48.

sort of traffic with demons, and trying to broker death was abhorrent and wicked for Christians and pagans equally. Subscribers to all late antique spiritual systems, however, walked a tightrope on the issue of revivification. Jesus and his closest male followers resuscitated the deceased. All classes of Christians honored the spirits and bodily remains of male and female departed saints and fostered friendly relationships with these "special dead." Classical pagans revered heroes from the pages of Homeric epics, some of whom trafficked with the dead to learn the future. One example is Odysseus who entered the house of Hades to seek information about his fate from the prophet Tiresias.[48] In every case of heroic revivification, of course, the argument was that the ends were worthy.

It is notable that only men effected laudable revivification, and it was women who brought the dead to life through perverse necromancy. Although there are no cases of female necromancers in the early church, there was one such condemnable medium in the biblical record, that being the bellymyther of Endor. Issues of secrecy and ritual were central to necromancy, which relied on meticulous rites, whether simple or complex. It mattered a great deal whether necromancers skulked in the shadows and manipulated substances and objects to coerce the dead or whether they operated in the light of day using verbal formulas only. Both Christians and Neoplatonists parsed rituals based on the form they took. The more convoluted the rites, the more hideous the necromancy.

By about 400, the message on necromancy was clarified in a way that affirmed the Christian theology of the afterlife. Necromancy was unambiguously demonic because devils created the illusion of return from the grave. In fact, neither humans nor demons could gainsay God's power over life and death without his express involvement. In the early Middle Ages, the virtuous form of raising the dead, modeled after Jesus's revitalization of Lazarus, would continue in the hagiographical tradition and would be possible for both sexes. Meanwhile, the ghoulish female necromantic specter of the Erictho type lingered on in the form of the bloodsucking *lamiae* and screech owls called *striae*.

Maleficium emerged out of the classical paradigm into the Christian worldview almost unchanged. Whereas Christians fundamentally reframed and proscribed divination and theurgy, claiming that what, in the pagan past, had been venerable and pietistic was actually tawdry, fraudulent, and a sinful affront to God, the same is not true of maleficium. It was never fully

---

48. Homer, *Odyssey*, bk. 11, 279–84.

sanctioned or respected by pagans, who also understood it to be the sacrilegious work of demons of the lower air. Various Christian thinkers denied the efficacy of many forms of maleficium, but they did not doubt that people attempted it, and they held this manifestation of magic to be ghoulish, foolish, dangerous, presumptuous, and iniquitous. For pagans and Christians, the fact that demons were the agents of maleficium made it particularly pernicious.[49] That is because it relied heavily on coercion, such as spells and secret characters etched on lead tablets; even worse were the macabre rites practiced by Erictho, who used incantations, charms, and vicious machinations to raise her victims from the grave. That the rites were secret was a factor contributing to their villainy. So in addition to being idolatrous and hemmed in by ritual, maleficium was secretive and self-serving at best. At its worst, it was malicious, injurious, and tenaciously weed-like in its ability to break through the surface again and again despite the efforts of the church to pluck it out at the roots.

---

49. Brown, *World of Late Antiquity*, 53–56

CHAPTER 6

The Screech Owl, the Vampire, the Moon, and the Woman

> The attributes of liminality or of liminal *personae* ("threshold people") are necessarily ambiguous, since this condition and these persons elude or slip through the network of classifications that normally locate states and positions in cultural space. Liminal entities are neither here nor there; they are betwixt and between the positions assigned and arrayed by law, custom, convention, and ceremonial. As such, their ambiguous and indeterminate attributes are expressed by a rich variety of symbols.
>
> —Victor Turner, *The Ritual Process*

Through the first millennium, women were prominent in the practice of maleficium, but even more threatening than willful females working their sorcery through the agency of demons were she-creatures of an enigmatic nature called *striae* (also *strix, striga, stygio/a,* or *strigimaga*) and *lamiae* (also *lama*). *Stria* refers to an evil, ethereal creature, and a *lamia* was a crazed bloodsucker. The inscrutable striae and lamiae lurk doggedly in the shadows of the sources throughout the first millennium, but they are so furtive that it is difficult to get a clear sense of whether they were thought to be humans or demons. Although writers consistently condemn either the beings themselves or belief in them, there is no extended description of the striae or lamiae.

In the classical era, a stria, at its most basic, was a female being who shared characteristics with the screech owl. J. F. Niermeyer draws this definition from Merovingian-era law codes, which are themselves terse on the subject.[1] The lamia was basically a vampire. In the play *Vespae*, by the ancient Greek dramatist Aristophanes (d. ca. 385 BCE), the character Lamia is "a child-stealing nursery bogey." She becomes lover to Zeus, and as a result, the jealous Hera

---

1. Niermeyer, *Mediae latinitatis lexicon minus*, s.v. "Stria"; Forcellini et al., *Lexicon totius latinitatis*, s.v. "Lamia."

destroys her children. Lamia is savage with grief and takes to stealing and sucking the blood of other people's babies.[2] This Lamia was the eponym of a class of creatures who not only destroyed children, but also accreted to themselves a reputation for most every mode of maleficium characteristic of women. Lamiae worked love magic, flew, thrived in shadows, concocted potions and spells to work their will, and almost invariably pitted themselves against men.

The striae and lamiae were, to apply Derrida's concept, an "overabundant" (or stacked) signifier that both defined the "other" and dredged up fears and fantasies of female resistance to cultural norms.[3] Rituals and their symbols can be understood most effectively in their totality by looking at them in play, because for complex signifiers, meaning is always in play. Ritual can act as a "symbolic intercom" that facilitates the cohesion of a group and helps the actors define who they are not.[4] Ritual also provides an environment for resistance to power structures. These two aspects of ritual were nowhere more at work than in the case of the ever-mutating striae and lamiae, whose ineffability and otherness made them all the more terrifying. Of course, we would know nothing of the striae and lamiae if they had not been given flesh and bone by literate men whose dominance they imperiled.

In classical literature, the stria and lamia shape shift; drink blood; prey on cadavers; effect their magic with spells, herbs, rituals, and powders; call down the moon; and operate in an atmosphere of dark silence.[5] The inconsistent and diverse references to these creatures demonstrate that people of the late Roman world did not have a clear or univocal understanding of their makeup. For some writers, they were demons; for others, humans gone bad, mortals dominated by their animalistic natures; for others, they were no more than literary tropes. Certain intellectuals were incredulous about their ability to fly, shapeshift, transmogrify others, and sexually assault humans. But throughout the period, most did believe in a quasi-human or semi-demonic entity that exhibited the traits of the stria and lamia.

In his novel *Metamorphoses*, Apuleius summarizes the potency of a lamia called Meroe. She has "the power of a god. She can bring down the sky, hang the land in the air, turn springs to cement, wash away mountains, loft the dead, snuff out the stars, and light up the realm of Tartarus itself."[6] For this pagan writer, the lamia is a superhuman fusion of a goddess and a demon.

---

2. Hornblower et al., *Oxford Classical Dictionary*, s.v. "Lamia."
3. Derrida, "Structure, Sign, and Play," 367.
4. Munn, "Symbolism," 579.
5. Lucan, *Civil War* 6, 334–65; Apuleius of Madaura, *Golden Ass* 2.1–21, 21–36; 3.15–29, 55–86.
6. Apuleius of Madaura, *Golden Ass* 1.8, 6. Apuleius uses the term *"saga"* in this instance (*Metamorphoses* 1.8, 1:14), demonstrating the fact of overlapping nomenclature.

Meroe takes vengeance on her disdainful lover, Socrates, by means of exacting rituals. Incensed by Socrates's rejection, Meroe corners him at night, slits his body from gullet to groin, removes his heart, and replaces it with a sponge on which she has placed a hex that forbids it to touch fresh water. The next morning Socrates awakes, seemingly unchanged. But later in the day he drinks from a stream, and in so doing wets the sponge in his chest cavity and immediately dies.[7]

Another lamia appears in the biography of the holy man Apollonius of Tyana. His biographer, Philostratus, calls her a phantom and a vampire. She seduces a young, handsome philosopher by the name of Menippus, and the two would have married if, at the wedding breakfast, Apollonius had not revealed her true intent: to fatten Menippus up in order to devour this "beautiful young" boy, whose blood was "fresh." One of the notable aspects of Philostratus's story is that he analogizes the lamia to a snake. He tells the youth, "You are nursing a snake, and a snake is nursing you."[8] This hybridity demonstrates writers' conceptions of phantasmal female creatures in the late antique mind. They were protean—often indistinct, sharing and exchanging attributes.

The snake conjured various and contrasting images in late classical cultures—both positive and negative, both lethal and erotic—and they were usually female associated.[9] The snake was at times a symbol of life, such as the snake emblazing the rod of Asclepius, the healing god of the ancient world. The serpent also embodied death and was linked to the underworld and deceased ancestors, and so it often appears on funeral monuments. This reptile connoted the pythoness, that eerie female diviner and necromancer in pagan, Jewish, and Christian accounts, such as Erictho and the medium of Endor.

The Vulgate account of the primordial war in heaven casts the adversary of Saint Michael as the dragon, the serpent, the Devil, and Satan (Rev. 12:7–9). The snake (another avatar of Satan) was the villain in the garden responsible for Adam and Eve's expulsion from paradise (Gen. 3:1–6). Justyn

---

7. Apuleius of Madaura, *Golden Ass* 1.11–19, 8–14. Although *The Golden Ass* is fictional, it reflects a genuine dread of magic in the late antique period. Ammianus Marcellinus provides evidence of the horror and judicial cruelty that magic could arouse. For the trials instituted by Emperor Valentinian see *History* 28.1–57, 3:86–121; 29.1–2.28, 3:187–233.

8. Philostratus, *Apollonius of Tyana* 4.25, 1:370–77.

9. For example, Medusa, the famed Gorgon of classical mythology, when raped by Neptune in Minerva's temple, was punished by the goddess who turned Medusa's once magnificent hair into reptilian locks (Ovid, *Metamorphoses* 4.790–803, 170–71). From Horace (*Odes and Epodes,* Epode 5, 282–83), the sorceress Canidia's hair is "entwined with little snakes." See also Nussbaum, "Serpents in the Soul," 234–40.

Martyr first made the connection between the Edenic serpent and Satan, who was also perceived as a demon. The serpent's deception of Eve ushered death into the world. The woman and the snake were yoked, then, in the Christian tradition. Both were devious, and both signified death.[10] Gnostic sects often turned patristic doctrine on its head, and such was the case with the metaphor of the snake. Whereas the paradisiacal serpent was the very anagoge of evil for orthodox Christians, in the hands of many Gnostics, the snake became a feminine cosmogonic entity—a symbol, not of original sin, but of illumination and divine wisdom.[11] So although Gnostics challenged the traditional view of the two antagonists in the story of the fall, they were consistent with other Christian exegetes in pairing the snake and the woman.

This association of the female and the reptile in the Garden plays out in an interesting role reversal, where the Virgin Mary is Eve's antithesis. Because Eve (in collusion with the serpent) was held to have been responsible for the fall of the created order, she was a counterpoint to Mary, the woman through whom humankind and the whole *mundus* were saved. The author of the apocryphal *Acts of John in Ephesus* advances the parallel one step further when he compares the serpent spewing his poison whisperings into Eve's ear with the commonly held conception that Mary conceived Jesus through her ear. Justin Martyr, Irenaeus of Lyon, Augustine, and others developed the typological association of Mary as the anti-Eve, just as Jesus was the anti-Adam.[12] In Genesis 3:15, God chastises the serpent that tempted Eve to eat the disastrous apple, saying, "I will put enmity between you and the woman, and between your seed and her seed; she will bruise your head, and you will bruise her on the heel."[13] So, in the Vulgate, the Virgin Mary is depicted trampling the head of a serpent. This image conveys the message that the

---

10. Justin Martyr, *Apology on Behalf of Christians* 28.1, 158–59. For another example from a patristic author see Jerome, *Against Jovian* 1.27, 366–67.
11. Pagels, *Gnostic Gospels*, 28–31.
12. On Mary as the anti-Eve see Rubin, *Mother of God*, 37–40, 311–12; Pelikan, *Mary through the Centuries*, 39–52; Benko, *Virgin Goddess*, 233–45. On Eve's and Mary's ears see Rubin, *Mother of God*, 36–37; Benko, *Virgin Goddess*, 234
13. *Biblia sacra*: "Inimicitias ponam inter te et mulierem et semen tuum et semen illius ipsa conteret caput tuum et tu insidiaberis calcaneo eius." I specify the Vulgate here because a controversy surrounds the use of *"ipsa"* (she) in the verse, as in *"ipsa conteret"* (she will bruise). Martin Luther and subsequent Protestants exegetes held "ipsa" to be a copyist's error, and they claimed that the word should be "ipse" (he), meaning Jesus. The issue is the prominence of Mary in Catholic theology and her positioning in salvation history. This is a role Protestants sought to diminish. See Pelikan, *Mary Through the Centuries*, 26–27. Castelli ("'I will make Mary Male,'" 33–43) makes some insightful (at times reductionist) comments about the imagery of the woman and the head of the snake in Perpetua's diary.

Christian paragon of feminine excellence reversed the Edenic sin of Eve, who was symbolically conflated with the serpent.

Circe, Medea, Erictho, and Meroe (whom we saw switching out Socrates's heart for a sponge) are antique literary figures with occult powers who defy classification. They all sprang from the Greco-Roman psyche and were frequently brought to the service of early medieval literary narratives. Circe, from Homer's *Odyssey*, is not technically a stria or lamia but a goddess, yet she differs from other goddesses in that she engenders her power through ritual magic, which is sometimes fallible. One of her most noted talents is the ability to use spells to transmogrify men into beasts. Odysseus, however, is able to counter Circe's "long wand" with the aid of enchanted herbs.[14]

Medea (which means "the cunning one") from the Roman playwright Seneca's play of the same name, illustrates the blurring between types of powerful female literary characters. In many classical sources, Medea seems clearly to be human, but she also shares qualities with the striae and lamiae, and there are other traditions (both pagan and Christian) that make her a goddess. Medea is the niece of Circe, a deity, and the daughter of Aeetes, king of the Colchians, by his wife Eidyia (the knowing). In every iteration of the Medea story, the protagonist is a foreigner living on the boundaries of decent society; she is driven by her passions, adept at magic, and a murderess. Medea helps Jason recover the Golden Fleece through sorcery, and when she returns to Iolcus with Jason, she renews the youth of his father, Aeson, by preparing a boiling bath for him in which she places restorative herbs. Medea maliciously encourages the daughters of Pelias to rejuvenate their father, but she provides them with the wrong plant, and Pelias is fatally scalded. Medea murders Jason's bride with magic powders, and in a final spectacle, she kills her own children before she flies away to Athens. Amid a magnificent display of ritual theater she proclaims, "A path lies open to the heavens: twin serpents bend their scaly necks to fit the chariot yoke . . . I'll ride though the winds in my wing-borne chariot."[15] This grand and ghoulish figure calls on Hekate, goddess of liminality and death (itself liminal) to sanctify the sacrifice of her two sons. "You've resounded, O altars: I note that my tripods have shaken, showing the goddess' favor. I see Trivia's

---

14. Hornblower et al., *Oxford Classical Dictionary*, s.v. "Circe"; Homer, *Odyssey*, bk. 10, 265–78. See ibid., 74–77, on the reception of the Homerian opera in the classical world. From Meerson ("Secondhand Homer"), Homer's works were known in the Roman era, even outside the circles of the literati.

15. Seneca, *Medea*, Act 5, lines 1023–26, 49

[Hekate] hastening chariot."[16] Here the human sorceress and a goddess work in tandem and share features.

Medea was well known in late antiquity through Roman sources. She had a long pedigree as a female who embodied the elements of the femme fatale. Her sorcerous accoutrements were herbs and poison (often interchangeable). Ovid calls her *venefica* or *pharmaceutria*—both denoting magic and poison. This mythic "maiden-helper," becomes, by the end of the play, the quintessential female demon—killing children in lamia-like fashion.[17]

Erictho, one of the most blood-curdling monstrosities in all fiction, discussed in chapter 5 in her role as necromancer, concocts love potions and brews spells so powerful not even the god of hell can resist her—not even the Fates. Lucan uses the word *stygio* to describe Erictho—a reference to the River Styx at the entrance to hell. He also calls her Thessala (after Thessaly, her home and the hub of malevolent magic in classical lore) and *vates* or prophetess, and in doing so provides a partial catalogue of the terminology that adhered to women in the classical mind.[18]

Although Circe, Medea, Erictho, and Meroe each have their separate literary derivations, the importance of looking at them together is to illustrate the overlapping of the stria, the lamia, the goddess, and the human female sorceress in the classical tradition on which medieval authors drew. Circe is a goddess, of sorts, but uses spells and powders, more like the femme fatale Pamphile, the sorceress from Apuleius's *Metamorphoses* who transforms herself into a screech owl by means of charmed powders.[19] Medea and Erictho are bloodthirsty, scheming humans, and Meroe is a stria, but they all have traits that associate them with the preternatural.

Two other important female figures woven into the tapestry of the late Roman imagination are the goddesses Artemis/Diana and Hekate. Diana was generally not associated with magic in antiquity, and Hekate was so only at times. But they were both plucked out of ancient mythological traditions and emerged in the Middle Ages at the very center of beliefs about women and the black arts. The reasons for this metamorphosis have to do with the

---

16. Seneca, *Medea*, Act 4, lines 785–87, 40.
17. Nussbaum, "Serpents in the Soul"; Newlands, "Metamorphosis of Ovid's *Medea*." Apuleius of Madaura (*Golden Ass* 1.10, 7–8) compares Medea to Meroe.
18. Lucan, *Civil War* 6, 342 (*stygio*), 348 (*Thessala*), 352 (*vates*). On the classical motif of women "drawing down the moon" see *Magic, Witchcraft, and Ghosts*, 236–40.
19. Apuleius of Madaura, *Golden Ass* 3.15–29, 55–65.

extraordinary cosmogonic and soteriological power, respectively, that Diana and Hekate signified.[20]

Although her father, Zeus, evoked the day sky, Diana took her venue from her mother, Leto (hidden one). Diana and Apollo were born in Delos, the bright land in the East, place of the rising sun. An alternate legend places the twins' birth in Ortygia, land of the quail, the earliest bird of spring and an allegory for morning or rising light. Diana had many domains, among which was healing, but outside the herbal manuals, she entered medieval history most forcefully as goddess of the moon. Mistress of night, darkness, and shadows, Diana was a mentor for women and keeper of their secret rituals. She dropped magical dew on the earth's plants and responded to incantations that "called down the moon."[21]

Of all the pagan deities, Diana is most persistently associated with magic in medieval sources. Part of the reason for this infamy may be her role in the Acts of the Apostles, where Paul and his converts, preaching in Ephesus, meet overwhelming resistance in their attempt to unseat Artemis/Diana, the fertility goddess. Ephesus was the capital of the Roman province of Asia and one of the major cities in the empire. Its temple to Artemis, the largest the Greeks had ever built, was among the seven wonders of the ancient world. Ephesus itself became a metaphor for pagan power and demonic activity in competition with Christian evangelization in early church literature. In a passage from Acts, the population of Ephesus storms the Christian missionaries and "for about two hours all of them shouted in unison, 'Great is Artemis of the Ephesians!'" (19:34). The town clerk quiets the crowd by assuring them that "the city of the Ephesians is the temple keeper of the great Artemis and of the statue that fell from heaven" (Acts 19:35). Artemis and her cult, then, had a place in the Christian tradition that distinguished them from other pagan sects; they faced down and successfully thwarted the proselytizing efforts of the early evangelists.

Although Paul is routed in the contest with Artemis, the New Testament also records a Christian victory in the city—this epicenter of Dianic supremacy.

> Then some itinerant Jewish exorcists tried to use the name of the Lord Jesus over those who had evil spirits, saying, "I adjure you by the Jesus

---

20. Hekate and Diana were often fused in the ancient world. Vergil (*Aeneid*, bk. 4, 85) has Dido shouting out for succor to "Three-faced Diana, who is triple Hecate." Benko, *Virgin Goddess*, 191. On Hekate as a lunar deity see Johnston, *Hekate Soteira*, 29–38.

21. Fischer-Hansen and Poulsen, *From Artemis to Diana*, 11–17. On magical dew see Lucan, *Civil War* 6, 340–41.

whom Paul proclaims." Seven sons of a Jewish high priest named Sceva were doing this. But the evil spirit said to them in reply, "Jesus I know, and Paul I know; but who are you?" Then the man with the evil spirit leaped on them, mastered them all, and so overpowered them that they fled out of the house naked and wounded. When this became known to all resident of Ephesus, both Jews and Greeks, everyone was awestruck; and the name of the Lord Jesus was praised. Also many of those who became believers confessed and disclosed their practices. A number of those who practiced magic collected their books and burned them publicly. (Acts 19:13–19)

The missionaries are able to best the Jewish imitators in a ritual of exorcism and to demonstrate that "the word of the Lord grew mightily and prevailed" (Acts 19:20), but they fail to unseat Artemis. Ephesus was a hub of the magic arts, and persuading practitioners to give up their craft was a coup for Paul, but even given this success, the evangelist who wrote the Acts of the Apostles (presumably Luke) admits that Diana rivals the Christian god's supremacy in the hearts of the Ephesians.

Diana appears again in an early apocryphon in her enduring association with healing. The *Acts of Paul and Thecla* (ca. 160), which was widely known (especially in the East) recounts the story of the doctors of Seleucia, who lose all their patients to the miraculous cures of the newly converted Thecla. As a result, they accuse her of being a priestess of Artemis, who, they contend gave Thecla the power to cure. The anonymous author of the text aggrandizes his heroine by pitting her against Diana, the major pagan female challenger for preeminence as a healer.[22]

In another confrontation between Artemis and the apostle John, the goddess is less successful than she was in the biblical account. As recorded in the apocryphal *Acts of John* (150–200), the apostle converts pagans through public miracles of healing at the temple of Artemis. He prays, "God, who are God above all so-called gods, who to this day have been despised at Ephesus . . . In your name every idol, every demon, and every unclean spirit is banished. May the deity of this place, which has deceived so many, now also give way to your name." The altar of Artemis breaks into pieces and the temple falls down, whereupon the Ephesians cry out, "There is only one God, that of John, only one God who has compassion for us; for you alone are God; now we have become converted, since we saw your miraculous deeds." Undoubtedly this apocryphal incident is meant to reverse the "wrong outcome" of

---

22. *Acts of Paul and Thecla*, 491. Jenny-Kappers, *Muttergötten*, 83–90.

the biblical episode in Acts where Paul is outdone when the people chant, "Great is Artemis of the Ephesians." In the *Acts of John*, however, that mantra is reversed; the people cry, "There is but one God." Clearly that god is not Artemis.

The author of the *Acts of John* choose healing as the backdrop for the confrontation between John and the Ephesians, inasmuch as the apostle was providing healing miracles in the shadow of the temple of Artemis, herself a goddess of healing.[23] In this text John engages public ritual in what Victor Turner calls a "processional form" or "social drama" that follows the pattern of breach-crisis-redress-reintegration.[24] The breach is John's competition with the demon goddess in feats of healing; the crisis is the destruction of the temple by a simple word formula (so important to the early Christians); the redress is John's promise of redemption to the people, and the outcome is the conversion of the Ephesians. However, the good people of Ephesus may have rejoiced too soon as Diana and her prowess in magic were forces to be reckoned with for centuries to come.

Diana was one of the most awesome, imposing, and revered of the female deities; all her attributes were positive and her functions constructive. However, her intimacy with birth and death made her frightening. In order to mock what he deemed the outlandish superstitions of the ignorant, the pagan biographer and priest Plutarch penned an ironic portrayal of Diana in her role as benefactor of women.[25] "If hasting in fear from a hanging corpse, / If near to a woman in childbirth pain, / If come from a house where the dead are mourned, / Polluted you entered the holy shrine, / Or if from the triple cross-roads come / Drawn to the place by cleansing rites / For the part you bear to the guilty one."[26] As in ancient Greece, Plutarch has Diana associated with childbirth, but where she used to give succor, here, polluted by gore, she flees from the scene of the still-born child. He grossly perverts her traditional role as guardian of children, and ascribes to her acts of necromancy. The hideous rituals Diana oversees take place at crossroads, which symbolize liminality or the straddling of boundaries where cultural norms are suspended; the goddess is potent in that ambiguous realm that suits her best. Plutarch lists the features of Diana that will be picked up in the early Middle

---

23. *Acts of John* 37–42, 322–23 (quotation 323). MacMullen, *Christianizing the Roman Empire*, 26–27.

24. Turner, *Schism and Continuity*, 91–94; Turner, "Liminality," 20.

25. For most of his life Plutarch served as a priest at the Delphic Temple of Apollo where he interpreted the speech of the Pythian oracle. On Artemis as goddess of fertility and childbirth (represented as multi-breasted at her temple in Ephesus) see H. King, "Bound to Bleed."

26. Plutarch, *Superstition*, in *Moralia*, 484–87.

Ages, when she became the quintessential female demon. In the late Middle Ages and early modern era, she will become mistress of witches.

Another magnificent and fearsome goddess of the Roman pantheon was the enigmatic Hekate, whom we met helping Medea escape from Corinth in a blaze of hellish glory. Hekate's qualities were numerous and diverse. She was often confused with Diana because of her function as goddess of women and protector of children, but she was best known to the ancients as a chthonic deity, facilitator of sorcerers and sorceresses, and familiar of demons and shades of the dead.[27] The instructions to restrain a person in most binding spells were enjoined on chthonic powers, especially Mother Earth (also called Gaia) and Hekate,[28] who were able to strong-arm ghosts to do magicians' bidding. In late antique literature, Hekate is often the guide escorting disembodied souls or living people across the boundary between the realm of the living and the underworld at birth and at death, especially when the shades are having trouble making the crossing themselves. Hekate's medieval manifestation as a goddess of sorceresses is related to her classical association with thresholds, the *frontière*—crossroads, so to speak. John Dillon observes that she stood "on the border between the intelligible and the sensible worlds, acting both as a barrier and a link."[29]

By the second century, Neoplatonists conflated Hekate with other female deities as a sort of all-goddess who oversaw life, death, and the transition between the two. In the *Chaldean Oracles,* Hekate is a conduit for salvation: the Platonic Cosmic Soul. She could mediate the gulf between heaven and earth, and so was a pivotal figure in the theurgic effort to transcend the profane and approach deity, because for Neoplatonists, soul was the very substance through which the cosmic sympathy necessary to spiritual ascent worked. In short, Hekate's existence at boundaries and in liminal spaces gave her a splendid power that could be as threatening as it was sublime. She was linked with the moon because of its cosmological position between the upper and lower air, and she was a broker for demons because of their ontological placement between humans and gods.[30] Hekate

---

27. Hornblower et al., *Oxford Classical Dictionary*, s.v. "Hecate." From Annequin (*Recherches sur l'action magique*, 83–90), Hekate was Diana's cousin.

28. *Curse Tablets*, 6, 85–86, 90, 101–6, 126–27, 161–62, 164, 180–84, 207–9, 212, 216. For example, "I invoke you by the unconquerable god IAÔ BARBATHIAÔ BRIMIAÔ CHERMARI [epithet for Hekate]. Rouse yourselves, you *daimones* who lie here and seek out Euphemia. . . . Let her not be able to sleep for the entire night, but lead her until she comes to his feet loving him with a frenzied love, with affection and with sexual intercourse" (103).

29. Dillon, *Middle Platonists*, 394. See also Farnell, "Hekate's Cult."

30. Johnston, *Hekate Soteira*, 1–20, 149–52.

was the very essence of that "betwixt and between" that Victor Turner identifies as the crux of liminality.[31]

Jesus giving Peter the metaphorical keys to the kingdom of heaven might well have been seen in the early Christian world as a challenge to Hekate—if not directly, then implicitly. She was a favorite of Neoplatonists as a goddess who could open and shut the gates of Hades. Like Peter, she had the keys to the thresholds of the living and mastery over the powers of death (Matt. 16:18). As she was Peter's putative competitor, it was up to the ministers of the new church to persuade converts to forswear pagan personalities such as Hekate and accept Peter as the master gatekeeper between life and death.

The amalgamation and mixing of spiritually powerful female figures even extended to the Virgin Mary. The architects of the early church never envisioned Mary as anything but human, yet she was as close to a goddess as a human could get. As part of the project of understanding the nature of Jesus, the ecumenical councils of late antiquity had a lot at stake in sorting out just what kind of a human Mary was. She conceived without intercourse, she bore God, many held that she herself was free of sin, and in the fourth century the doctrine of Mary's dormition and apotheosis emerged, whereby she did not experience death the way most mortals must. Jerome and Gregory of Nyssa understood Mary to be the heavenly woman in Revelations (12:1). "A great portent appeared in heaven: a woman clothed with the sun, with the moon under her feet, and on her head a crown of twelve stars."[32] Here again, as in the personas of Diana and Hekate, the moon plays an anagogical role in the portrayal of a woman of great numinous presence. Even as Mary laundered the reputation of women by reversing Eve's sin in the Garden, the depiction of the Virgin standing on the moon conjures visions of Mary bringing Diana and Hekate to heel.

Given orthodox exegetes' *hyperdulia* of the Virgin,[33] it is not surprising that less theologically sophisticated converts from paganism would endow Mary with powers of the goddesses they were being asked to abandon. In fact, one of the reasons that Nestorius, the archbishop of Constantinople (d. ca. 451), opposed the concept of Mary as Theotokos (bearer of God) at the First Council of Ephesus (341) was that it smacked of goddess worship.[34]

---

31. Turner, *Dramas, Fields, and Metaphors*, 232; Turner, *Ritual Process*, 95. See the epigraph to this chapter.

32. Rubin, *Mother of God*, 53–57; Pelikan, *Mary through the Centuries*, 177–87; Rampton, "Mary the Virgin."

33. *Hyperdulia* is veneration offered to the Blessed Virgin Mary. From Augustine (*De civitate Dei* 10.3, 1:274–76), only God is worthy of supreme worship (*latria*).

34. Benko, *Virgin Goddess*, 45–62.

It is ironic that the Council of Ephesus, where the status of Mary was hotly debated, was held in the Church of Mary in Ephesus—the city formerly dedicated to the goddess Diana. In the late fourth century, a popular heresy arose whereby women called Kollyridians had seemingly transferred their veneration from pagan fertility and creation goddesses to the Virgin and called themselves priestesses of Mary. They honored the Virgin with cakes, as they had done to Demeter, a fertility goddess, and her daughter, Persephone, goddess of the underworld in the pagan Thesmophoria, a Greek festival.[35]

In short, echoes of the pagan past were distinct in the conflated attributes of Diana (fertility goddess of Ephesus), Hekate (world soul), Demeter and the Virgin (bringers of life). Three of these persons (the Virgin aside)—skilled in the use of rituals, plants, herbs, and poisons—would slip from classical lore into medieval thought. On the less savory end of the spectrum of female stereotypes were the striae and lamiae who represented an ill-defined notion of the enigmatic, alluring feminine—adept in the execution of maleficium. Central to the dread of the protean and illusive figures was the threat posed by the lethal stew of sorcery, secrecy, sexuality, and female virility.

Women and Prophecy

Christians eschewed divining per se, but they did sanction a type of fortune telling authorized by Yahweh in the form of prophecy. In both Hebraic and Greco-Roman cultures, divination was a craft or science of reading signs, whereas prophecy involved revelation, intuition, or clairvoyance; but the fine line between prophecy and divination is evident in repeated biblical warnings about false prophets who are nothing more than augurs.

In ancient Greece and Rome, the role of augur was a male occupation—professional, attended by time-honored rites, and played out in the public arena. Prophecy, on the other hand, was a spontaneous and seemingly artless communication from heaven to earth, and it was possible for women. The reason is undoubtedly because the prophetess was framed as an "empty vessel," a conduit between heaven and earth—perfect for the female, who was

---

35. Epiphanius, *Panarion* 3.79, 3:637–45; Rubin, *Mother of God*, 21–22, 43–49. On the cult of Diana see Shoemaker, "Epiphanius of Salamis"; Jenny-Kappers, *Muttergötten*, 141–59. Benko takes a controversial position in *Virgin Goddess* when he argues that "in its veneration of the Virgin Mary, not only did Roman Catholic Christianity absorb many elements of the cults of Greek and Roman goddesses, but Mary in effect replaced these deities and continued them in a Christian form" (2). He holds that Mary represented a feminine aspect of the divine "inherited from . . . pagan forerunners" (5). On the Kollyridians, see ibid., chap. 5.

generally perceived as passive and receptive.[36] Prophecy did not depend on craft but on submission of the self to higher powers, as is made clear in Deuteronomy when God tells the Israelites, "I will raise up for them a prophet; . . . I will put my words in the mouth of the prophet, who shall speak to them everything that I command" (Deut. 18:18).

In high Roman pagan culture, the sibyl, an oracle for the gods (particularly Apollo) and a specialist in the art of foreknowledge, was an important cultural anchor protecting the purity of the state.[37] Several centuries before Jesus, prophetic sayings of various sibyls were collected into the *Sibylline Books* and kept in Rome, where they were to be consulted only at the command of the Senate. A fire destroyed these *Sibylline Books* in 83 BCE, but they were later reconstructed. The last reference to the books is in Ammianus Marcellinus's history,[38] but snippets from them are contained in other texts. Even in Christian literary circles the prophecies commanded a position of respect. Justin Martyr, when talking about the prophets who knew the truth of the one God, lists the sibyls with Old Testament prophets.[39]

When Romans first interacted with the silvopastoral peoples of northern Europe, they recognized an authority the women wielded by virtue of their intuitive foresight. In his *Gallic Wars*, Julius Caesar comments on the German "matrons" who divine by lots, and the Roman Tacitus, in his first-century ethnography of Belgic peoples, also describes German women as prophetic. He mentions Velaeda and Albruna, who are prophetesses credited with remarkable prophetic capabilities.[40] Whether Caesar and Tacitus completely understood the Celtic and Germanic societies they described, their histories demonstrate that Romans were familiar with the principle of spiritually perspicacious women of the sibyl type and were able to identify them in other cultures.

---

36. Ludwikowska, "Uncovering the Secret," 83. See Kitzler (*"Passio Perpetuae,"* 15) for the woman as a "passive receptacle" of visions.

37. Cicero, *De divinatione* 2.54, in *De senectute*, 495; Pliny, *Natural History* 7.33–35, vol. 2 (352), 584–85. Gillmeister ("Cultural Paraphrase in Roman Religion") argues that by the early first century CE, the sibyl and the *Sibylline Books* were cultural artifacts and not vital elements of Roman religious rites. However (I add), both found their way into medieval discourse as credible mantic texts.

38. Ammianus Marcellinus, *History* 23.1.7, 2:314–15. On Augustus's reconstruction of the Sibylline books see Suetonius, *Deified Augustus* 31, 196–97. From Gallagher ("King Alfred and the Sibyl"), in England, verses were written in the sibylline tradition as late as the ninth century.

39. Justin Martyr, *Apology on Behalf of Christians* 44.12, 197.

40. Reference to Caesar is in Enright, *Lady with a Mead Cup*, 65, 210; Tacitus, *De origine* 8, 41: "Vidimus sub divo Vespasiano Veledam diu apud plerosque numinis loco habitam."

Prophetesses appear throughout the Hebrew Bible,[41] and the early church readily embraced female seers in the Christian movement.[42] The New Testament mentions Philip the Evangelist's four prophetic daughters (Acts 21:8–9) but says little about them; their prophetic capacity elicits no comment that conveys any sense that the women are out of the ordinary. The apostle Peter reminds the community at Jerusalem, "'In the last days it will be, God declares, that I will pour out my Spirit upon all flesh, and your sons and your daughters shall prophesy. . . . Even my slaves, both men and women, in those days I will pour out my Spirit; and they shall prophesy'" (Acts 2:17–18). The First Letter to the Corinthians, attributed to Bishop Clement of Rome (d. ca. 100), refers to the harlot Rahab of the Hebrew Bible, who hid Joshua and foreknew that the Israelites would be victorious in a coming battle (Josh. 2:1–24). The letter reads, "You see, beloved, that not only faith but also prophecy is found in this woman." Fringe groups such as Gnostics and the Montanists (which the church fathers considered heretical) also extolled and elevated women for their prophetic abilities.[43]

In addition to its respectable pedigree in the Bible and the earliest church writings, knowing the future was a stock motif of hagiography. The foreknowledge of the saints was not the result of traffic with demons, rather it was a gift from God for unusual sanctity. Women martyrs and saints did not lag behind men in using second sight. There was little discrimination in the role of oracle, except inasmuch as the perception of "the oracle" was itself gendered. Karen King observes that "prophecy is sometimes understood as the penetration of the body by a spirit, and thus was sometimes conceived and expressed in sexual terms. . . . [This is] a consequence of a system of heterosexual gender symbolization in which the penetrator is symbolically masculine and the penetrated is symbolically feminine."[44]

Among the most powerful stories of martyrdom in confessional literature is that of Perpetua (d. 203), an aristocratic woman of twenty-two years who, at the time of writing, had recently given birth and was subsequently put to death in the Carthaginian arena. In an eyewitness account of her martyrdom, the author invokes Acts 2:17–18 ("Your sons and your daughters

---

41. Deborah (Judg. 4:4), Miriam (Exod. 15:20), and Holda (2 Kings 22:14) were prophetesses, and Noadia was a false prophetess (Neh. 6:14). See also Num. 12; 2 Sam. 20:16–22; Joel 2:28–29; Deut. 13.1–5; Deut. 18:9–22; Isa. 8:19–20; Isa. 30.9–11; Mic. 3:11; Jer. 5:31; Jer. 14:14–16.

42. Eisen, *Women Officeholders*, 63–87.

43. Clement of Rome, *Letter* 12, 18–19. See also Irenaeus of Lyon, *Against the Heresies* 13.1–7, 1:55–59; Benko, *Virgin Goddess*, chap. 4; Trevett, *Montanism*, 151–97; Caciola, *Discerning Spirits*, 6–7. From Clark ("Early Christian Women," 23), the confidence in women's prophetic ability among so-called heretics contributed to orthodox Christians' opprobrium toward them.

44. K. King, "Prophetic Power and Women's Authority" (quotation 30).

shall prophesy") in his discussion of prophecy. This seems to be an allusion to Perpetua's gender and a reminder for Christians that the words of prophecy are God's language, not those of the woman or man through whom they are spoken. In the primitive phase of the religion, prophecy was a blessing. Although women's prophetic experience was almost without exception mediated by male reporters, King is correct that "women's prophetic speech was highly valued in early Christian movements and contributed to the construction of early Christian teaching and practice." The church needed its savants to counter the wise men and women of competitor cults and to observe God's Deuteronomic injunction to raise up true prophets in place of the soothsayers and augurs of other nations (Deu. 18:14–22).[45]

That is not to say that New Testament writers were unconcerned about false prophecy. Warnings against false prophets from the Old Testament echo in the New. Mark, Matthew, and John all warn against those puffed up with pride and an exaggerated sense of their own powers. In Matthew, Jesus warns his followers about charlatans claiming to have the gift of prophecy, saying, "Beware of false prophets, who come to you in sheep's clothing, but inwardly are ravenous wolves"(7:15). "On that day many will say to me, 'Lord, Lord, did we not prophesy in your name, and cast out demons in your name, and do many deeds of power in your name?' Then I will declare to them, 'I never knew you; go away from me, you evildoers'" (7:22–23). This caution is reflected in the early Christian text *Didache,* where the anonymous author alerts fellow worshippers about those who pose as prophets.[46] But in the early centuries of Christianity, the focus on false prophecy was minimal compared to other concerns about traffic with demons.

As time passed, orthodox Christianity tended to reserve the role of prophet for the holy ones, whether male or female; and most saints were prophetic at some point in their lives. As the church became more structured, prophesying became professionalized. Although lay prophecy continued, it was progressively suspect as a slippery slope to traffic with demons, and since women were always lay, confidence lessened in their ability to prophesy reliably. Catholic writers, who in the first century embraced female divines, came by the second century to criticize the Gnostics and the Montanists for

---

45. *Passion of S. Perpetua* 1, 60–62; See Kitzler, *From "Passio Perpetuae,"* 56–116 on the contemporary reception of Perpetua's revelations and prophecies. Harvey ("Women") notes that although women participated fully in the early Christian movement, they were often re-gendered as male to achieve acceptance. See Trevett (*Montanism,* 176–81) on Perpetua's visions of her own maleness. K. King, "Prophetic Power and Women's Authority" (quotation 32).

46. See also Matt. 24:11; Matt. 24:24; Mark 13:22; 2 Pet. 2:1–3; 1 John 4:1; *Didache* 11.5, 26–27. On false prophets see Aune, *Apocalypticism.*

the dominant role women played in their sects, singling out as particularly troubling their putative prophetic flair.[47] As indicated above, it is commonplace in new movements for traditional gender and class roles to be set aside in the interests of shared purpose and the necessity of protecting a precarious fledgling.[48] This was true within the early Christian movement as it pertained to female prophecy.

Poison

In the ancient and medieval worlds, poison was one of the most frequently employed resources that sorcerers and sorceresses used to ply their trade. Modern thinkers might see a logical fallacy in the claim that poison caused bodily injury magically, because we attribute agency to the natural deleterious effects of the substance itself. But unlike other provisions of the magic arts—such as wands, lead tablets, and wax figures—poison (*veneficium*) was a cover word for all *maleficium*, and so the very reference to poison in an antique or early medieval text might connote magic but not always.[49] Its normalcy complicates the task of the historian working to identify magic in the sources, particularly in regard to poison. A text might hint that a poison substance is magical without providing what would (to us) be helpful descriptive details. In most situations the importance of poison was that it killed; whether it was magically treated or simply a botanically deadly element was not an issue. In fact, the differentiation may not have been so clear to those administering or consuming it. As in many traditional cultures, fatality caused by illness or violence was comprehensible, but an unexplained and sudden death was suspicious. It was almost always ascribed to secretive *maleficium*, and poison was notorious in such cases.[50]

That poisoning was a form of magic is evident from Roman sources. In Homer's *Odyssey* (a text well-known in antique Rome), the messenger god, Hermes, appears to Odysseus as he is ascending the path to Circe's great house. Hermes warns Odysseus that Circe will assail him with "all her lethal spells and tricks. She will make you a potion mixed with poison. Its magic

---

47. Pagels, *Gnostic Gospels*, 59–61. From Hippolytus's *On the Apostolic Traditions* (97), by the third century, although revelation and dreams continued to be prized, prophecy in Christian communities had declined.
48. *Women in Early Christianity*, 7; Bitel, *Women*, 11–12; Salzman, *Making of a Christian Aristocracy*, 162; Brown, *Body and Society*, 259–84, 341–45; Archer, "Role of Jewish Women."
49. Jolly, Raudvere, and Peters, *Witchcraft and Magic*, 219. On *veneficium* as a technical term for *magia*, see Graf, *Magic*, 46–49, 66.
50. Graf, *Magic*, 47–48.

will not work on you because you have the herb I gave you (moly)." Here, spells, poison potion, herb, and magic are allied—even substitutable.[51]

The statesman Sulla (d. 78 BCE) sponsored the *Lex Cornelia de sicariis et veneficiis* (Cornelian Law of Assassins and Poisoners), which prohibits poisoning and makes the possession, sale, gifting, or production of poisons punishable by law.[52] The conflation of poison and sorcery is borne out by a prescript that Emperor Tiberius (d. 37 CE) passed which extended to all magicians certain prohibitions designed for poisoners. Because poison was one of the accoutrements of the black arts, the words "sorcerer" and "poisoner" were often used together or interchangeably.[53]

One of the reasons why poisoning was often linked with sorcery is that killing by poison was secretive and sly. Predictably, the complex of things clandestine, furtive, and injurious attached itself readily to women, who were infamous as poisoners. It is one of the few weapons women wielded to impose their will in a world where their access to direct political action and the use of violence was limited. According to a law Constantine enacted in 331, a man could repudiate his wife if she was an adulteress, a poisoner or procuress.[54]

The stereotype of women as poisoners was a tenacious caricature that propagated itself through prose and poetry. In *Medea*, the three evils of magical poison, secrecy, and a powerful woman come together when the sorceress treats a cloak with a magic toxin that kills her rival, Creusa.[55] In the Roman poet Ovid's (d. 17 CE) erotic elegy *Amores*, the protagonist speaks of the woman, Dipsas, who "knows Aeaean chants and magic's force / So well, she makes streams flow back to their source. / She knows her magic threads; what poisons to prepare / From herbs." Lucan's choice of the word "poison" (*virus*) in *the Civil War*, when he describes Erictho raising the dead to foretell Pompey's defeat, also captures the equivalence of magic and poison. The Thessalian *stygio* infuses a corpse with "the poison that the moon provides."[56]

The notion of poison as magical was unchanged in early Christian thinking. An interesting canon from the ecclesiastical Council of Ancyra (314) connects two kinds of magic by impressing a five-year penance on one who

---

51. Homer, *Odyssey*, bk. 10, 268.
52. *Lex Cornelia de sicariis et veneficis* (*Fontes iuris Romani antiqui*, 91); Janowitz, *Magic in the Roman World*, 12; Graf, *Magic*, 46; *Curse Tablets*, 258.
53. *Theodosian Code*, 9.38.1, 3, 4, 6, 7, 8, pp. 253–54; 9.40.1, p. 255; 11.36.1, p. 334; 11.36.7, p. 336.
54. Ibid., 3.16.1, 99.
55. Seneca, *Medea*, Act 3, lines 570–668, 33–36; Act 4, lines 670–844, 36–42.
56. Ovid, *Amores* 1.8 in *Ovid's Erotic Poems*, 35; Lucan, *Civil War* 6, 352–53.

"uses vatication" and "introduces anyone into his house for the sake of making a poison." Vatication is divination, and it is allied with the covert mixing of harmful poisons; are the poisons spell-infused potions? It is unclear.[57] Epiphanius of Salamis writes in his *Panarion* that the art of magic is antediluvian and was once called "pharmacy," meaning both sorcery and poisoning. This evil craft survived the flood and was cultivated and spread by Nimrod, the great-grandson of Noah.[58]

Most descriptions of poisoning are economical, and the application of magic poison was not particularly ritualistic. The accessibility of poisons and their ability to be administered furtively and without special learning is another reason magic poisoning was often gendered female. This is not to say that women were thought to be incapable of choreographing multifaceted rituals, such as those Erictho enacted; rather, magic procedures that required little skill tended to be female identified.

Love and Birth Magic

Among the most potent and dreaded skills of a sorcerer or sorceress was love magic, the goal of which was to excite or frustrate love and sexual desire. It was one of the most common magical practices in the ancient world and persisted unabated into the early Middle Ages and beyond. Pagan and Christian understandings of this sort of sorcery shared much in common, except that for the latter it was inextricably linked to the work of demons. Because there was virtually no skepticism about the efficacy of love magic, its actuality did not enter theological discussions in the early church. "Birth magic" (as I am using the term) refers to various methods of inducing conception or thwarting it, terminating a pregnancy, or infanticide, which contemporaries often considered a type of abortion. Some occurrences of love and birth magic could be classed with maleficium because they involved injurious rites, spells, and potions, but that was not always the case. Just as often, love and birth magic had the goal of inducing or preserving both amorous passion and new life. Regardless of the motives, however, both kinds of sorcery were triply alarming because they were demonic (by definition, for Christians), ritualistic, and, like other forms of maleficium, clandestine.

---

57. Council of Ancyra 24 (Ancient Epitome), in *Seven Ecumenical Councils*, 74
58. Epiphanius of Salamis, *Panarion* 1.1.3, 1:15; 1.3.3, 1:18. From Graf (*Magic*, 28), "*phámakon*" is a classical Greek word for medicine and magic used by Circe to transform Odysseus's men. See also Renehan, "Staunching of Odysseus' Blood." Grubbs ("Constantine and Imperial Legislation," 128) interprets poison as a form of magic.

Natal sorcery was, almost without exception, deeply symbolic, which is typical of rites surrounding liminal experiences—such as birth and death—that cross metaphorical thresholds from the mundane to the supercharged. There is some debate among scholars as to whether the liminal state is dominated by "antistructure" (an absence of rules) or "hyperstructure" (tightly articulated parameters), but it is most accurate to think in terms neither of antistructure nor of hyperstructure, but of new structures—different rules and re-enlivened perspectives laden with new possibilities.[59] The liminal state is by nature disorienting and indeterminate, and so structures form quickly within liminal time-space to provide a context for understanding and absorbing hyperreality. Because of the freedom from traditional patterns of constraint intrinsic to liminal situations, when constructing rituals around conception, pregnancy, birth, and postnatal infant mortality, people instinctively drew on archaic, pre-Christian rhythms.

Amatory magic was popularly perceived to be in the woman's wheelhouse and the most potent weapon in her arsenal against men. Greek and Roman writers delighted in portraying women in the role of the mystifying, enigmatic femme fatale. They indulged their nightmare that the female is a being—powerful, even lethal if uncontrolled—whose essence rests in her alluring, sexually seductive otherness. Golden Age Roman writers enthusiastically exploited this fantasy. In the *Aeneid*, Vergil (d. 19 BCE) portrays Queen Dido of Carthage bidding a priestess to work love magic against Aeneas when he deserts her. Horace (d. 8 BCE) casts Canidia as an adept at carrying out amatory rites. A love sick character in Ovid's *Amores* asks, "Had some witch cursed my name with voodoo dolls of wax / And stuck my liver's heart with prick attached? . . . So maybe it was magic verses made me nervous— / Or worse—and took my member out of service."[60] Apuleius's novel, *Metamorphoses,* captures the power of women's love sorcery. The premise of the story rests on the sorceress Pamphile's facility with love potions and ritual incantations to bring men under her spell, like the legendary characters Medea and Circe. These much-known female love magicians, at once tantalizing and terrifying, carry out their predatory sorcery through stealthy rites.

Julia Smith makes an important observation about the representation of women in classical and medieval texts that applies to the portrayal of pitiless women as consummate love magicians. "We must always remember that mastery of literacy was one of the ways in which hegemonic masculinity

---

59. Turner, *Ritual Process*, 166–203.
60. Vergil, *Aeneid*, bk. 4, 84–85; Horace, *Epode* 17, 312–19; Ovid, *Amores* 3.7 in *Ovid's Erotic Poems*, 94; See Frankfurter, "Social Context."

reproduced itself in the ancient and medieval worlds and that the texts in which gender ideology was embedded were, for the most part, generated by those centers which had the most at stake in the maintenance of hierarchies of power, whether sacred or secular."[61] Consistent with Smith's observation, it is mostly in literary sources produced by men that women are the masters of love and birth magic.

Outside of both pagan and Christian fiction, however, the picture is more gender balanced, as is evident in antique curse tablets and binding spells (*defixiones*), many of which have been exhumed from their hiding places. They attest to a lively trade in paraphernalia that all genders utilized to effect love magic.[62] For example, as discussed above, when Apuleius was taken to court for effecting amatory rites, he was accused of practicing love magic to persuade the wealthy widow, Pudentilla, to became his wife.[63] In Jerome's *Life of Saint Hilarion*, a man falls in love with "one of God's virgins" and turns to magic. He buries figurines sculpted of bronze under the threshold of her home. Unfortunately for the girl, the spell works all too well. "The maid began to show signs of insanity, to throw away the covering of her head, tear her hair, gnash her teeth, and loudly call the youth by name."[64] Also, the *Theodosian Code*, which harshly condemns amatory magic, does not specify women as the malefactors. The prohibition reads, "The science of those men who are equipped with magic arts and who are revealed to have worked against the safety men or to have turned virtuous minds to lust shall be punished and deservedly avenged by the most severe laws."[65] David Frankfurter observes that by recourse to love spells, women exercised their agency in order to ensure a measure of economic and connubial security in a repressive male environment. He goes on to say that whereas men's love spells were demanding, coercive, and pornographic, women's appeal to the deities who empowered spells and curses tended to be supplicative, suggestive, and appreciative.[66]

---

61. Brubaker and J. M. H. Smith, *Gender*, 17–18.
62. Rider, *Magic and Impotence*, 16–21; Dickie, "Who Practiced Love-Magic"; Graf, *Magic*, 176–90; *Curse Tablets*, chap. 2.
63. Apuleius of Madaura, *Apulei apologia*, vii–xx.
64. Jerome, *Life of Saint Hilarion* 21, 307–8.
65. *Theodosian Code* 9.16.3, 237.
66. Frankfurter ("Social Context"). A typical example of a male love charm: "Let her not be able to sleep for the entire night, but lead her until she comes to his feet, loving him with a frenzied love, with affection and with sexual intercourse. For I have bound her brain and hands and viscera and genitals and heart for the love of me, Theōn. . . . Grab Euphēmia and lead her to me, Theōn, loving me with a frenzied love" (*Curse Tablets*, 103–6).

CHAPTER 6

Even as *defixiones* did not disappear with the ascendance of Christianity, neither did the sure belief in love magic. Jerome accused the priest of the healing god Asclepius ("who does not heal souls but destroys them") of teaching a love-sick youth how to seduce a women by inscribing amatory spells and "revolting figures" on bronze plates, which were then to be placed under the threshold of her house.[67] Eusebius wrote about an early second-century itinerant male preacher whose appeal was partially based on his promise to make people attractive to the opposite sex. He "was a most clever deviser of spells and skillful at magicians' tricks." The huckster convinced men that he could compel women to yield to them, and he made the reverse promise to women.[68] Bishop Irenaeus of Lyon, at a loss to explain women's participation in the Gnostic cult of Valentinus (fl. second century), concluded that they were drawn to its charismatic leader, Marcus (fl. mid-second century), whom Irenaeus called a "sorcerer" (*goès*), and who used magic aphrodisiacs to seduce them.[69]

While it is true that woman as minx and specialist in love potions is a persistent motif in literature, we see from other evidence that men also practiced love/lust magic, and that females were frequently the hapless victims. However, even when sources cast men as love magicians, a reference to women was not far behind. Ammianus Marcellinus wrote that during Valens's purge of magicians, the emperor implicated many of his enemies by having his operatives plant "old wives' incantations and unbecoming love potions" among the men's possessions.[70] So in this case, men conjure, but women concoct the magical substances and are notorious for them. The lead tablets inscribed with amatory or sexual hexes were commonly secreted in cemeteries near the cadavers that carried out the macabre spells under the supervision of deities who were usually female. Hekate was a favorite in this context.[71] Although both men and women purchased and used love spells, it is interesting that most excavated figures dealing with love enchantment are in female form. Further, most spells themselves trace the genealogy of both the instigator and the victim of the invocation through the mother— unusual in late antique Rome, where descent was figured on the patriline.[72] A text found in Egypt dated to the third or fourth century CE is typical of hundreds of such spells. "Let Matrôna, to whom Tagenê gave birth, whose

---

67. Jerome, *The Life of Saint Hilarion* 21, 307.
68. MacMullen, *Christianizing the Roman Empire*, 38.
69. Irenaeus of Lyon, *Against the Heresies* 13.1–7, 1.55–59; Pagels, *Gnostic Gospels*, 59–61.
70. Ammianus Marcellinus, *History* 29.2.3, 3:213–17.
71. See note 29.
72. For an example of such a figurine see *Curse Tablets*, 98.

'stuff' you have, including the hairs of her head, love Theodôros, to whom Techôsis gave birth." This curse provides instructions to the departed spirit that will carry out the spell by identifying the target of the curse (Matrôna) by her mother's name (Tagenê).[73]

In the Roman world, both for pagans and for Christians, the ability of humans to tamper with the hearts and the fecundity of others through the manipulation of rituals and talismanic objects that engaged the agency of demons was a fact of life. Love and birth magic were ritualistic, dangerous, and commonplace, and although archeological evidence confirms that men did not hesitate to work love magic, the contemporary stereotype was that it fell chiefly within the woman's sphere. Although Christian male authors readily accepted pagan female figures as specialists in love and birth magic, Christian women are not portrayed practicing this sort of sorcery in early church texts. Femme fatales, such as Medea, Circe, and Pamphile, and sorcerous hags, such as Erictho, repeatedly appear both in late antique and early medieval literature, but there is no discourse of Christian women of the early church trafficking with demons to move the hearts of men or to regulate birth.

In the ancient world, magic was gendered. Women were thought to be prisoners of their physicality and sexual passions, and magic, particularly maleficium, played a role in this perception.[74] Female activities were largely domestic and private, and because gender identity and domestic space were co-constitutive, it made sense that women's use of magic would be guarded. Clandestine activities could be read as sly, and secrecy of all sorts was highly charged in Roman culture. Because women were thought to be libidinous, it followed that love magic was in their remit, and because they bore children, it followed that birth magic was their concern. The combination of gender, secrecy, and domesticity shaped the Roman vision of women's magic.

Female sorcery was not always sinister, but because it was usually framed in that way, it was a short leap to the stria and lamia, animalistic female beings who were the very embodiment of malice. In a vein similar to the stria and lamia were characters such as Circe, Medea, and the goddesses Diana and Hekate, who shared their dreadful, though vaguely defined, characteristics. In historical and literary sources, the stria and lamia regularly are confused, conflated, and interchanged with each other and with various female deities. Whether goddesses, humans, or demons, these mysterious beings have a

---

73. Ibid., 101.
74. Brown, *Body and Society*, chap. 1; Juvenal, "Against Women," in *Satires of Juvenal*, 63–90.

long history in European thought, and the magic of the stria and lamia was ritual at its worse: manipulative, harmful, and female.

Members of the primitive church did not initially emulate pagans in their assessment of women. On the contrary, in the earliest canonical Christian texts, women and men are idealized as spiritually on par; both are martyred, and both are saints. Although Eve came in for abuse as the human who broke paradise due to unbridled female inquisitiveness and disobedience, her transgression was eventually reversed by the Virgin—a non-sexual paragon of women. Jerome had a sanguine opinion of the abilities of Christian women and championed them for their contributions to the monastic movement.[75] This equivalence between men and women is reflected in Christian discussions of magic, where women are not singled out as particularly prone to idolatry, divination, superstition, or sorcery.

It is important to keep in mind that even as male authors extolled Christian women, they were not able to escape the magnetic drag of their cultures' misogynism. Early church fathers carried the same biases as their pagan peers. Even as they championed Christian heroines, they embedded their praise within the context of the exceptionality of their virtue and valor—astonishing given the inferiority of the female sex.[76]

---

75. The scholarship on patristic assessments of women (including Christian women) is vast and cannot be adequately dealt with here. That having been said, in the post-apostolic and patristic church, Kitzler (*From "Passio Perpetuae,"* 1) argues that although perhaps superficially and not for long or across the board, Christianity in its "early years of enthusiasm" improved the status of women. From Wilken (*First Thousand Years*, 105), "Monasticism allowed women to step free of inherited roles and expectations and opened up new vocations in the church and society.... Christian women were extolled in ways that would erode over time." See also Clark, "Early Christian Women."

76. Two good example are Tertullian, *De cultu feminarum*; Epiphanius of Salamis, *Panarion* 3.79, 3:637–45. From J. M. H. Smith ("Did Women Have," 557), "Christianity certainly offered women some scope for involvement in the life of their community," . . . (but) "how far was this on men's terms?"

PART 3

Traffic with Demons
Post-Roman Europe

Chapter 7

Sub Dio

> Augustine sent to Æthelberht to say that he had come from Rome bearing the best of news, namely the sure and certain promise of eternal joys in heaven.... Some days afterward the king came to the island [of Thanet] and, sitting in the open air, commanded Augustine and his comrades to come thither to talk with him. He took care that they should not meet in any building, for he held the traditional superstition that, if they practiced any magic art, they might deceive him and get the better of him as soon as he entered.
>
> —Bede, *Ecclesiastical History*

Late antiquity formed a bridge between the classical world and the early Middle Ages. Despite the vicissitudes of governments, armies, and imperial capitals, the life patterns and worldviews of those who lived under Roman governance were Roman—within the various permutations of the word. The peoples of the independent post-Roman kingdoms that grew up in the West during the fifth and sixth centuries were in most respects deeply imprinted with the seal of the classical vision of the world. The patterns of continuity manifest in the transition from ancient Rome to the early Middle Ages were as evident in magic as they were in virtually all other aspects of post-Roman civilization.[1]

Increasingly throughout the fourth century, imperial favoritism of Christianity and the efforts of missionaries and local elites chipped away at institutionalized paganism, yet the struggle to convert the peoples of the vast Roman Empire had barely begun. The project of proselytizing the diverse populations of nominal Christians across the Continent and the British Isles was one of the major undertakings of post-Roman ecclesiastical bodies and would continue for centuries.

---

1. J. M. H. Smith (*Europe After Rome*, 2) suggests that the term "post-imperial" is more apt than "post-Roman" because after about 500 most "aspects of Roman culture and practice persisted, little affected by changing political structures."

CHAPTER 7

The basic approach to magic in the Merovingian era resembled that of the early church in most respects. In both periods, the understanding of magic as traffic with demons continued unchanged, and patristic thinkers, such as Justin Martyr, Origen and Augustine, remained the bedrock authorities. Overt idolatry still troubled spiritual leaders, but less in the ancient cities of the Mediterranean and the Fertile Crescent and more in the forests and farms of northern and western Europe. Paganistic forms of worship flourished among the country dwellers (*pagani*),[2] and their stamping out is a persistent motif in the literature of this period, particularly in hagiography. But even trickier than eradicating organized cults was the menace of tenacious demonic superstitions that were thoroughly ingrained in the daily lives of the people, and this was true in the Levant, North Africa, and western Europe. Ironically, as ecclesiastics refined and more carefully sculpted the parameters of the religion, there were ever more superstitions to weed out, precisely because new practices were continually added to the catalogue of the forbidden. Many cultic behaviors, once thought of as sacred by the people who inherited them, were reframed and condemned as magical superstition.

In the late Roman Empire, magicians' ability to foretell (and thus manipulate) the course of political events meant that magic was most strenuously opposed in the civic realm. By the sixth century, magic still had a significant public dimension, for example fortune telling could affect the elevation of bishops, but the more immediate challenge was to bring ordinary people into conformity with what was a loosely conceived orthodoxy by weeding out routine superstition practiced in private settings, such as the villas, homes, fields, and forests of all classes—from the dominant to the unempowered.

Augustine framed much of the theology that would hold for centuries as to the true abilities of demons, but in the post-Roman period, there was still no consistent understanding as to which of the symbols, signs, and ritual objects inherited from classical paganism were acceptable for Christian devotions and which were so tainted by their pagan origins that they were, in fact, demonic. Added to that was the complicating fact that other paganisms—Germanic and Celtic—with their own symbologies and vocabularies of magic and ritual had to be scrutinized once they were encountered by those structuring the expanding Roman church. Many pagan rituals and ceremonies looked for all the world like orthodox Christian practice because pagan

---

2. See Filotas, *Pagan Survivals* (14–15), on the etiology of *"pagani."* The term had several derivations which coalesced in the post-Roman period.

and Christian religious systems drew from a common well of signs and symbols for their construction of meaning.

Although the substance of church doctrine was unique, pagan rites and Christian ritual forms were often homologous, and this may account for ecclesiastics' frustration with people using Christian symbols and rituals in a transactional fashion that was reminiscent of pagan approaches to deity. Those providing pastoral care saw their charges misaligning signifiers and the signified, but the efforts of the church to penetrate the Continent and the British Isles in order to bring people to a deep and full understanding of Christianity were bedeviled by the shortage of church personnel. There simply were not enough bishops, priests, nuns, and monks to do the job.[3] Without the resources to impart a sound and thorough grasp of dogma, ritual became an essential tool. Bishops sought to impart a program of ritual observances that would keep the *rustici* (not to mention the urbanites) on the path to salvation. So, while eradicating pagan, demonic, and superstitious practices, the early medieval church was tasked with the additional necessity of articulating a lingua franca of rites that employed recognizable signs, symbols, and objects, while separating them from their old pagan connotations. Whereas it might have been difficult to explain the doctrine of predestination, it seemed possible to convince all Christians that power inhered in the sign of the cross or the water of the baptismal font.

Bede, the famed monastic scholar of Northumbria, praised his colleague Aidan, the Irish bishop of Lindisfarne (d. 651), for his wise counsel to a Scottish priest regarding how to deal with the unconverted Anglo-Saxons. Aidan had advised, "It seems to me, brother, that you have been unreasonably harsh upon your ignorant hearers: you did not first offer them the milk of simpler teaching, as the apostle recommends, until little by little, as they grew strong on the food of God's word, they were capable of receiving more elaborate instruction and of carrying out the more transcendent commandments of God."[4] This forbearance was not unusual for those committed to the evangelization of Europe, who recognized the importance of handling gently the delicate fabric of human conviction and centuries-old traditions.

---

3. McKitterick, "England and the Continent," 73.

4. Bede, *Bede's Ecclesiastical History* 3.5, 228–29: "Videtur mihi, frater, quia durior iusto indoctis auditoribus fuisti, et non eis iuxta apostolicam disciplinam primo lac doctrinae mollioris porrexisti, donec paulatim enutriti uerbo Dei, ad capienda perfectiora et ad facienda sublimiora Dei praecepta sufficerent." On rural conversion see James, *Franks*, 121–29.

Theological treatises on sorcery are absent from this era, but we have an array of texts that bring into view (if not into sharp focus) all types of magic from sources such as penitentials, sermons, histories, law codes, church councils, and Bishop Isidore of Seville's *Etymologies*. Magic and magical ritual, especially in the form of maleficium and superstition, were a part of the everyday reality of women and men. Because of the control it gave demons over people's lives and the harm it caused those who were its victims, magic was a thorn in the side of clerics and secular authorities who labored ceaselessly to identify and eradicate it, often by introducing Christian rituals in place of those that summoned demons of the lower air.

Sacred Space and Nature Worship

One of the most unrelenting vestiges of idol worship centered on the veneration of nature or rituals enacted in natural settings. This had posed a threat to the town-based church of the apostolic and post-apostolic periods, but it was one thing for dwellers of cities and their immediate hinterlands, whose roots were firmly embedded in ancient urban culture, to embrace a new concept of indoor sacred space, and quite another to instill a radical reevaluation of the natural world in a people who had always been fundamentally rural. Getting Christians out of the woods and into the churches, both metaphorically and physically, was a major objective of churchmen and churchwomen for several centuries.[5]

Ecclesiastics were exceedingly distrustful of any activities that took place at trees, groves, stones, fountains, crossroads, turnings, or running water. Bans against worship in woods and fields were motivated in part by the uneasy awareness that the occupants of these wild, uncultivated areas were devils. But angst regarding worship at outdoor sites ran deeper than the dread of demons. Thomas Gieryn writes about "truth-spots" and argues that a combination of "location, materiality, and narration" inject a given space with a distinctive personality. The Christian "truth-spot" was the church house and the physical accoutrements of worship. The competitor was the natural world, and the "materiality" was trees, stones, and so forth.[6]

---

5. Although the consensus has long been that Christianity was initially urban-based and that it reached beyond the towns gradually, both MacMullen (*Second Church*, 101–2) and Robinson (*Who were the First Christians?*, 66–90, 223) challenge that view, arguing for a Christian presence in the countryside very early.

6. Gieryn, *Truth-Spots*, 3.

As Christianity spread north, trolls, elves, dwarfs, the living dead, and other indigenous spirits were assimilated into the classical concept of the demon. Such unholy creatures appear in *Beowulf*.[7] They are "misbegotten things" (l. 111) and "grim" (l. 102) specters. The ogre Beowulf ("bold devil" [l. 86], "demon foe" [l. 705], and "alien spirit" [l. 1349]) and his mother stalk "misty moors (l. 162), . . . marches (1.103), . . . and "fens" (l. 104) which Geoffrey Russom interprets as "hell." They are border-walkers who occupy wastelands and dwell in that liminal space between human and fiend "from hell" (l. 101). They exist between the sown and the wild where magical energies are most ignitable. The monster Beowulf is written into the biblical narrative of fallen angels raping human women (Gen. 6.1–4). He is a descendent of Cain (1. 107) and "lived for a time in the land of giants (l. 105) . . . who strove against God" (l. 113). Grendel and his mother assume the caricaturesque trappings of Mediterranean pagan worshippers. "At times they offered honor to idols / at pagan temples" (ll. 175–76).[8]

Numerous sources give a sense of how pervasive outdoor worship was in the post-Roman West and how ritualized a form it took, which made it all the more obstinate and pernicious. The prolific historian of sixth-century Gaul, Bishop Gregory of Tours (d. 594), lamented that the ancestors of the Franks "fashioned idols for themselves that took the form of the creatures of the forests and the waters, of the birds and the beasts, all of which they worshipped in place of God."[9] He also recounted the consternation of the bishop of Mende, who was troubled because his parishioners persisted in celebrating a three-day festival at a lake in nearby Mons Helarius. The people sacrificed animals and proffered offerings of many kinds, despite his

---

7. Liuzza (in *Beowulf*, 56n3) notes that the antagonists in *Beowulf* are a "collection of Germanic, classical, and biblical horrors." For a general discussion of the poem and its textual history see *Beowulf*, 11–48. Dating *Beowulf* has long been a subject of intense debate. See Neidorf and Pascual ("The Language of *Beowulf*"), Chase ("Opinions on the Date of *Beowulf*"), and R. Fulk ("Old English Meter") for those supporting a date of composition between 725 and 825. Owen-Crocker ("Beast Men," 277) and Kiernan ("Eleventh-Century Origin of *Beowulf* and the *Beowulf* Manuscript"), among others, favor a date of composition close to the production of the Nowell Codex at (roughly) 975–1025. At this point, the weight of scholarship rests with the earlier date.

8. *Beowulf*, 51, 52, 54, 70, 89. See Russom ("At the Center of *Beowulf*," 29–32) and Hall (*Elves in Anglo-Saxon England*, 69–70) on Grendel and his mother.

9. Gregory of Tours, *Decem libri historiarum* 2.10, 59: "Sibique silvarum atque aquarum, avium bestiarumque et aliorum quoque elementorum finxere formas, ipsasque ut Deum colere eisque sacrifitium delibare consueti." I draw liberally from Gregory of Tours's *Ten Books of Histories* when analyzing magic in Merovingian Gaul because his is our primary historical source for the period. Although Gregory's facts are sometimes undependable, his work vividly portrays contemporary life as seen through the eyes of a well-connected aristocrat. See Kitchen (*Saints' Lives*, 58–61), on historians' overemphasis on the *Histories*, which represent only a portion of Gregory's corpus and one aspect of his interests. See also I. Wood, "Gregory of Tours."

sermons against it. Fortuitously, the frustrated bishop was inspired to adopt a more subtle and thoughtful approach. He built a chapel a short distance from the sacred lake and invited the worshippers to bring their offerings to the life-giving church instead of throwing them into the lake in an empty ritual (*ritibus vanes*). Stories of this sort of accommodation of folk ways are common in missionary and pastoral literature in post-Roman Europe.[10] The bishop's intentions are clear from Gregory's account, but what about the *rustici*? How do we understand the motives of the celebrants? Gregory feared, and for good reason, that the ceremony acted to solidify an un-Christian group ethos. Given the bishop's assertion that he had warned the peasants, the rituals bespeak more than the allure of traditional patterns of worship, they also hint at a resistance—or at the least an indifference—to the ecclesiastical status of the bishop. In any case, Gregory and other clerics were trepidatious that because forests and waters were the setting for pagan veneration, outdoor celebrations of any sort could, by their very nature, engender a misconceived, pantheistic concept of deity. Groves, trees, fens, springs, rivers, and other natural sites were inextricably tethered to pagan, demonic cults.

In 572, the second Spanish Council of Braga decreed that each bishop call the people of his diocese together so they could be more thoroughly instructed in the basics of Christian dogma.[11] After the council, Archbishop Martin of Braga (d. 580) wrote a letter to Polemius of Astorga (fl. 570), an Iberian bishop, that lays out a model sermon meant for the rustics of Polemius's parish. Martin reviews the, by then, familiar genesis of demons who were cast from the heavenly kingdom with proud Lucifer, the archangel who would place himself on par with God, but ended up a "dark and horrible devil." Martin decries the behavior of peasants who "held captive in their former superstition of the pagans, pay more attention to demons than to God." The bishop rebukes those who adore "deep seas or springs of water" and explains that demons have dominion over these natural spaces and that "they began to show themselves to humans in various forms and to talk to them and ask them for sacrifices in the highest mountains and in the leafy forests." He urges Polemius to forbid worship at rocks, trees, streams, and crossroads. Martin added an element to the primitive church narrative of the fallen angels when he wrote that upon being expelled from heaven, the devils occupied "the sea, or rivers, or springs or woods" where people worshipped

---

10. Gregory of Tours, *Gloria confessorum* 2, 299–300.
11. *Concilia Bracanense II* 1, in *Concilios Visigóticos*, 81. Ferguson, *Backgrounds of Early Christianity*, 365.

them like gods. Whereas in Justin Martyr's telling fallen angels inhabited idols—the quintessential focus of Mediterranean pagan worship—the Spanish bishop instinctively saw natural settings as the locales where devils elicit adoration.[12]

Similarly, in several of his broadly distributed sermons, Bishop Caesarius of Arles chastises Christians who continue to fulfill vows at fountains or trees, and he equates such behavior to "diabolical divinations." "What is worse," he writes, "there are some unfortunate and miserable people who not only refuse to destroy the shrines of the pagans, but indeed are not afraid nor do they blush at rebuilding those that have been destroyed." Some, he continues, are enraged at those who would destroy the wood from felled sacred trees and exert violence on those who attempt to overturn these idols.[13] The imprecision in Caesarius's language is significant. When he speaks indiscriminately of "diabolical divinations," the bishop is not using the word "divination" in a technical or classical sense; making vows at natural sites is not mantic in any traditional sense of the word. What Caesarius seeks to condemn is traffic with demons, and any terminology for behavior with a whiff of paganism, magic, sacrilege, or superstition suits his purpose. In his vita of Bishop Eligius (d. 660) of Noyon (in modern Nord-Pas-de-Calais), Bishop Audoin of Rouen (d. 684) borrows liberally from the correspondence of Martin of Braga and the sermons of Caesarius. Eligius urges his readers, "Do not seek out enchanters, or diviners, or lot casters, or clairvoyants, nor place devilish charms at springs or trees or crossroads."[14]

---

12. Martin of Braga, *De correctione rusticorum* 1, 183: "Scribis ad me ut pro castigatione rusticorum, qui adhuc pristina paganorum superstitione detenti cultum venerationis plus daemoniis quam deo persolvunt"; 3, 184: "tenebrosus et horribilis diabolus"; 6, 186: "Alii adorabant solem, alii lunam vel stellas, alii ignem, alii aquam profundam vel fontes aquarum"; 7, 186–87: "Tunc diabolus vel ministri ipsius, daemones, qui de caelo deiecti sunt, videntes ignaros homines dimisso Deo creatore suo, per creaturas errare, coeperunt se illis in diversas formas ostendere et loqui cum eis et expetere ab eis, ut in excelsis montibus et in silvis frondosis sacrificia sibi offerrent ipsos colerent pro deo"; 8, 188: "Praeter haec autem multi daemones ex illis qui de caelo expulsi sunt aut in mare aut in fluminibus aut in fontibus aut in silvis president. Hen ("Martin of Braga's *De correctione rusticorum*") argues that Martin's *De correctione* was less for practical use in instructing the peasants and more a short treatise meant to define Christian orthodoxy against the "other," that is paganism. Hen writes that the text "should be regarded as evidence for norms, not facts" (46). He is accurate that *De correctione* acted as a template on paganisms for other writers, and it may not reflect contemporary behaviors. But Hen has not demonstrated that Martin's motives were polemical or that he was disinterested whether peasants were harboring the beliefs or carrying out the rituals the text describes.

13. Caesarius of Arles, *Sermones*, Sermons 13.5, 1:57–58; 14.4, 1:71–72; 19.4, 1:89–90; 53–54, 1:233–40. (Quotations, 54.1, 1:236: "diabolicas divinationes"; 53.1, 1:233: "Sunt enim, quod peius est, in felices et miseri, qui paganorum fana non solum destruere nolunt, sed etiam quae destructa fuerant aedificare nec metuunt nec erubescunt.")

14. Audoin, *Vita Eligii* 2.16, 707: "Non quaerantur praecantatores, non divini, non sortilogi, non caragi, nec per fontes aut arbores vel bivios diabolica filacteria exerceantur." Audoin and Eligius were

Hagiographical descriptions of the competition between conceptual Christianity and conceptual paganism often take on a boilerplate form. The motif of Christian evangelization and the fight against unrelenting idolatry and pagan ritual is captured in the vitae of numerous saints. Because of the vitality of a pagan worldview, holy men such as Bishop Martin of Tours (d. ca. 397) in Gaul, and the founder of Benedictine monasticism, Benedict of Nursia (d. 547), in Italy, though separated by 150 years, had it as a primary task to rid Christendom of demon worship, which was often a cipher for any undesirable behavior.[15]

A motif of religious transformation that became commonplace is established in the vita of Martin of Tours, who habitually destroyed outdoor pagan shrines, and "where Martin destroyed shrines, there he built churches or monasteries forthwith." Martin made room for Christian services, which took place within four walls. A sacred space purified of demons replaced an outdoor area polluted by them. Similarly, the first things Benedict of Nursia did when he arrived at the rocky Italian hill of Monte Cassino were to overturn the idol, level the sacred grove, and convert the temple of Apollo to a chapel dedicated to John the Baptist and Saint Martin (himself a "shrineoclast"). Similar stories occur in other vitae. For example, a blind woman regains her sight when she shows Saint Amand (d. ca. 675), the bishop of Tongeren-Maastricht, a tree she worshipped, which he then cuts down. Because hagiographical texts were copied and read aloud to monastic and lay audiences, the value of these epic battles for the holy had influence well beyond the moments of their occurrence (or literary construction).[16]

---

contemporaries and from a region of France long Christianized. The vita was well known in its time. See A. Murray ("Missionaries and Magic") on the role of missionaries countering pagan magic and appropriating pagan holy sites by converting shrines to altars.

15. Martin of Tours was among the most influential saints in the Christian West. He abandoned the Roman army to establish the monastery of Ligugé and was consecrated Bishop of Tours in 371. Although he lived in late antiquity, I have placed him in unit 3, because his career, vita, and impact were played out in a culture that was in all every practical sense post-Gallic. On Martin's life see *Vita Martini*, 1–25.

16. Sulpicius Severus, *Vita Martini* 13, 110–11: "nam ubi fana destruxerat, statim ibi aut ecclesias aut monasteria construebat"; Gregory the Great, *Dialogues* 2.8.11, 74. For Amand see I. Wood, *Missionary Life*, 39–42; Van Dam, *Saints and Their Miracles*, 128–35; Flint, *Rise of Magic*, 254–72; Wiśniewski ("Pagan Temples") makes the argument that expelling demons from temples in order to reallocate the space for Christian worship was more prevalent in the Christian East than in the West where, with a few exceptions, temples were destroyed to stop people from worshipping in them not to drive demons out. Couser ("Inventing Paganism") argues that the vitae of missionary figures were literary constructions written to outline mission agendas, and not a reflection of actual events. There is some truth to what Causer says, but his conclusion is reductionist given the rich complexity diversity of missionary hagiography.

In the letter Gregory the Great wrote to Abbot Mellitus (discussed in chapter 1), the bishop took a less confrontational tack in the competition for ritual space than Benedict, Martin, or Amand did, though no less resolute. Gregory displayed an intuitive anthropological understanding of ritual adaptation by reasoning that if some of the peasants' outward, tangible signifiers were left in place, they would more easily attach a new "signified" to familiar habits and cult objects. He advised the abbot not to destroy pagan shrines, but to turn them into churches by substituting Christian symbols for pagan ones. "The temples of the idols . . . must on no account be destroyed," he said. "The idols are to be destroyed, but the temples themselves are to be aspersed with holy water, altars set up in them, and relics deposited there. . . . And since they have a custom of sacrificing many oxen to demons, let some other solemnity be substituted in its place. . . . They are no longer to sacrifice beasts to the Devil but they may kill them for food to the praise of God." In this way, the peasants would "share in inward rejoicings" of the right kind.[17] Gregory recognized that religious rituals connect people to what Barbara Myerhoff identifies as "the forces of nature and purposes of the deities," and that that bond could not easily be severed.[18] But if the symbolic meaning behind rituals and objects (such as the flesh of oxen) were adjusted, a Christian sensibility would be gently implanted in the pagan thought-world.

In some special circumstances, it was possible to wrest natural settings from malignant forces and make them safe for Christian worship. Such was the case with Saint Cuthbert (d. 687), a Celtic monk of the Northumbrian church who, before he took up his eremitic habitation, rid the remote British island of demons by his holy presence.[19] But this type of phenomenal charisma was reserved for spiritual superstars and was the exception that proved the rule.

Rogationtide was another case where outdoor spaces were cleansed for Christian worship. Rogations were hallowed performative rituals that took place out of doors near Ascension and Pentecost, and Rogationtide was

---

17. Bede, *Bede's Ecclesiastical History* 1.30, 106–8. See Demacopoulos ("Gregory the Great") and Church ("Paganism in Conversion-Age") who put into context Gregory's seemingly contradictory instructions to Æthelbert of Kent regarding the destruction of the "buildings of shrines." They point out that Bede's letter to Æthelbert recommends a less yielding approach to conversion than the letter he wrote to Abbot Mellitus does. However, the fact that one letter regarding best practices is to a king and another to a cleric dictates the tone and approach befitting each. Gregory's letter to Mellitus functions within a particular rhetorical mode as it concerns pastoral role. For further historiography on this topic, see the notes in Demacopoulos's article throughout.

18. Myerhoff, "Death in Due Time," 152.

19. Bede, *Bede's Ecclesiastical History* 4.28, 434–37.

among the great holidays of the liturgical year. The observance lasted for three days and was devoted to penitential prayer and fasting. Clergymen led their congregations around the fields or from church to church chanting the Mass in supplication of a bountiful harvest, and in the process sanctified the borders of the parish against evil forces. This rite stemmed from either of two Roman celebrations which served much the same purpose: Robigalia or the May festival of Ambarvalia. Rogationtide was instituted in Rome by Gregory the Great, and Bishop Mamertus of Vienne (d. ca. 475) is credited with establishing the ritual procession in Gaul, although Nathan Ristuccia demonstrates that such an attribution is unfounded.[20] At the First Council of Orléans (511), the Merovingian king Clovis I endorsed Rogationtide as a time for the clergy and laity of every church to fast, pray, abstain from physical relations and gaming, and to process with their neighbors. Caesarius of Arles made explicit the stakes involved in the communal ceremony; it was to "stand, always armed, against many thousands of demons by day and by night . . . and guard ourselves against the ambush of the devil with spiritual weapons . . . So that with God's help we can finish our task and conquer that most inimitable enemy."[21]

By the early eighth century, the ritual had spread to England. The late tenth-century Vercelli Homily XII describes processions led by barefoot clergy. The parishioners were to process carrying crosses, books, and "holy relics (*reliquias*) that are the remains of holy men, of their hair or parts of their body or clothing, and with all these holy things we must go humbly around our land in those holy days. And our cattle (*ceap*) and our homeland (*eard*) and our woods and all our goods." Four of the tenth-century anonymous Blickling Homilies are sermons for rogation days Monday through Thursday, and the Anglo-Saxon reform cleric Aelfric, abbot of Eynsham

---

20. From Ristuccia (*Christianization and Commonwealth*, 26–62), the first authors to discuss Rogationtide in Gaul were Sidonius Apollinaris and Avitus of Vienne in the late fifth century. Each was interested in aggrandizing his city by promoting a competing version of the origins of the ceremony. The Gallican Rogationtide festival was not accepted into Roman usage until the papacy of Leo III (d. 816). On Roman pagan origins in England see *Eleven Old English Rogationtide Homilies*, xxi–xxii; Vecelli XII traces the observance back to pagans who enacted the ritual of paying homage to the gods of trees and stones and "other worthless materials."

21. Councilium Aurelianense 27–28, in *MGH Conc. aevi. Mer.*, 8. Caesarius of Arles, *Sermones*, Sermon 207, 2:828–29: "Quis enim contra tot milia daemonum die noctuque ita stare potuit semper armatus, ut numquam fuerit diaboli calliditate percussus? . . . Audiamus ergo consilium beati apostoli et contra diaboli insidias armis nos spiritalibus muniamus. . . . Ut ergo haec possimus deo auxiliante conplere et hostem callidissimum opitulante gratia divinare revincere, ieiuniorum vigiliarum vel orationum arma nobis debemus iugiter providere."

(d. ca. 1025) wrote eleven homilies on the ceremony.[22] The rites represented a metaphorical extension of the four walls of the church and were designed to embrace the fields of the parish under the direction of the bishop. Accoutrements such as crosses, relics, hand bells, holy water, and banners impressed the spiritual power of the church onto the natural environment for a limited period of time.[23]

It is noteworthy that women saints are never shown chasing demons from pagan sites and restructuring the setting for Christian worship. Although consecrated women are amply represented in the period as powerful actors in contests for the holy and makers of prodigious miracles, destroying pagan temples was not within their purview. Women, often cloistered in monasteries or operating in the private realm, would be unlikely ringleaders in large public spectacles of sacred virtuosity. Although vitae represent them performing stunning miraculous feats,[24] women are rarely portrayed organizing the community, and if they do, it is at their peril. For example, when the invading Huns approached the gates of Paris in 451, young Saint Genovefa (d. ca. 500) rallied the women to pray and fast. Because she foresaw that Paris would be saved, she implored the men not to remove their goods to a neighboring town. For this impudence of a mere girl, the people accused her of false prophecy, and she was only saved when an archdeacon from Auberry vouched for her.[25] Public bouts in the face of communal threats were appropriate only to men.

A corollary to the dread of ritual worship both in and of nature was the resolute insistence that Christianity be an indoor religion. The refrain, which began in late antiquity, reverberated through the post-Roman period and found voice in many genres. Sociologist Henri Lefebvre argues that an ideology can take root only if it produces a space, both physical and social, within which the ideology can crystallize. The constructed space, in turn, implies and conveys an intrinsic ideology that relies on the "produced" space for its actualization.[26] For centuries, the Christian establishment labored

---

22. *Blickling Homilies* 8–11, 68–91; *Eleven Old English Rogationtide Homilies*, xxi–xxii; Gittos (*Liturgy, Architecture*, 134–39) describes Anglo-Saxon outdoor processions, including rogations (quotation, 136).

23. *Concilium Aurelianense* 27–28, in *MGH Conc. aevi. Mer.*, 8; Casearius of Arles, *Sermones*, Sermons 207–209, 828–34; Sidonius Apollinaris 7.1.2–3, in *Liber Epistularum*, 103–4; Avitus of Vienne, Homilies 6–9, in *Ex Homiliarum Libro*, 108–20; Gregory of Tours, *Decem libri historiarum* 2.34, 81–84; 4.5, 138–39.

24. For miracles of Merovingian female saints see Rampton, "Frankish Holy Women."

25. *Vita Genovefae* 10–11, 218–19.

26. Lefebvre, *Production of Space*, 53–59.

persistently to fashion a environment appropriate to a unique vision of sacrality. That setting was the church. It was exclusionary, carefully controlled, and safe: no devils allowed.

A late fifth-century text from the Sanctuary of Monte Gargano tells of the archangel Michael's intervention in the pagan sect of Calchas in Apulia, Italy. The archangel demands that cultic prostration on the mountaintop be replaced by prayers in a consecrated church, and his request is heeded.[27] The *Second Synod of Saint Patrick* (sixth century) stipulates that Christianity be practiced indoors; canon 13 specifies that the Eucharist is not to be taken outside but is to be communicated under "one roof of faith" (*sub uno fidei*). As we saw at the beginning of this chapter, Bede writes in his *Ecclesiastical History* that when Bishop Augustine of Canterbury and his intrepid missionaries arrived in Kent, England, in 597, the Anglo-Saxon King Æthelbert insisted that he meet the Christians outdoors for fear that Augustine might enchant him if they gathered together in a building—under a roof. Ethelbert dreaded the competing spiritual power of Christianity and associated it with indoor rituals, so he sought safety within a space that was a metaphor of pagan power: the open air (*sub dio*).[28]

The celebration of the Kalends of January provides one of the most fruitful opportunities to observe authentically folkloric outdoor ritual at work.[29] The Kalends were the first days of the months in the Roman calendar. In the mid-second century, January first was set aside to mark the installation of the new consuls, and by the fourth century, the three-day Kalends festivals had become the largest empire-wide holiday in the Roman world. In addition to friends and families gathering to exchange gifts and make offerings to the domestic gods of the hearth, people of all classes decorated their homes, drank copious amounts of alcohol, joked, sang songs, danced, played dice, wore festive masks, and went from house to house asking for money in a sort of Trick-or-Treat fashion.[30]

Christian writers disparaged the revelry of the Kalends celebrations. John Chrysostom of Constantinople was among the first to complain of New Year's masqueraders. Preaching in Antioch, Chrysostom warned, "The

---

27. Flint, *Rise of Magic*, 169–70.
28. *Synodus II S. Patricii* 13, in *Irish Penitentials*, 188–89. On the synod see Meens, *Penance*, 40–45. Bede, *Bede's Ecclesiastical History* 1.25, 74–75.
29. My comments on the Kalends of January are indebted to Grig, "Interpreting the Kalends"; Max Harris, *Sacred Folly*, 237–256; Filotas, *Pagan Survivals*, 155–65; Künzel, "Paganisme"; Arbesmann, "'Cervuli'"; and Meslin, *La fête des kalendes*. See Markus (*End of Ancient Christianity*, 125–35) on the "Christianization of time."
30. Grig, "Interpreting the Kalends," 238–43; Max Harris, *Sacred Folly*, 11–13, Meslin, *La fête des kalendes*, 51–70.

days that mark the new year are coming, and the demons arrive with all their pomp; a fully-fledged workshop of idols is set up. And the new year is consecrated with age-old sacrilege." He bemoaned the "demons marching in procession in the marketplace, . . . the all-night devilish celebrations." Chrysostom's "devils" were people wearing seasonal masks—some in the guise of gods. In their turn, the Arian theologian Asterius of Amasea (d. ca. 400) and Bishop Peter Chrysologos of Ravenna (d. ca. 450) criticized the seasonal festivities during which mummers masqueraded as pagan gods and became thereby—according to Chrysologos's reckoning—a "sacrifice to the demons." The celebrants also enacted skits in which men dressed as women.[31] In late antiquity, this "cross-dressing" amounted to a form of role-playing for the sake of amusement, but in later sources Christian moralists described the practice as turpid grotesque, and unnatural, which (in Caesarius' of Arles words) made "the demons themselves wither" (*ipsi etiam daemones expavescunt*).[32]

In his longest extant sermon, Augustine wrote in tones of disgust of the folk play, dicing, intoxication, and frivolous songs that accompanied the holiday. He chided the participants, saying that the boisterous music beckoned demons. Augustine and Chrysologos paint traffic with demons with a broad brush when they suggest that celebrating an essentially secular traditional Roman holiday invited demons in. Augustine judged every aspect of the feast of the Kalends to be "pagan." The bishops' invective perpetuated the Christian prejudice against secular song and dancing that finds a strong voice in early medieval pastoral literature.[33]

Carnivals on the first of January persisted despite clerical censure, but the observances became more ritualistic and cult-like. By the late fourth century, a new element of the Kalends emerged in the sources, the precise origins of which we are ignorant.[34] Men and women impersonated animals (especially the stag, but also the heifer and she-goat) by wearing animal masks and pelts, attaching antlers to their heads, and mimicking the creatures' movements. The prohibitionary literature against the animal masquerade was concentrated in Gaul and northern Spain, and there are no records of it in North Africa or Ireland. The most distressing component of the Kalends of January

---

31. Grig, "Interpreting the Kalends," 242, 246; Filotas, *Pagan Survivals*, 162; Arbesmann, "'Cervuli,'" 114. On Chrysostom and Chrysologos see Max Harris, *Sacred Folly*, 14.

32. Caesarius Arles, *Sermones*, Sermon 193.1, 2:783.

33. Augustine, *Sermones*, 197, cols. 1021–24; 198, cols. 1024–69; Grig, "Interpreting the Kalends," 243.

34. Grig "Interpreting the Kalends," 253; Max Harris, *Sacred Folly*, 14; Arbesmann, "'Cervuli,'" 6, 91–95, 111.

for those who wrote about them was the animal mimicry. Bishop Pacian of Barcelona (d. ca. 390) wrote a now-lost treatise called *Cervulus* (*Stag*) to condemn the mask fetish. At this point the animalism was so central to the rituals that Pacian calls the feast simply, "playing the stag" (*cervulum facere*).[35]

There is no consensus regarding the historicity of the Kalends commemoration in medieval Europe. Lucy Grig cautiously concludes, "I would like to suggest that studying the Kalends of January provides an encouraging case study for the pursuit of late antique popular culture." Bernadette Filotas says that the Kalends mumming was actually practiced and continued to evolve throughout the early Middle Ages. On the other hand, Rudolph Arbesmann argues that the tradition of the Kalends rites in post-Roman Europe was "purely literary" and "represents a clear case of 'cutting and pasting' in the textual tradition, and refers to a moribund practice."[36] Elusive though the details of the January charades are, in my view there is no reason to doubt that the Kalends rituals were enacted along the lines laid out in the sermons, penitentials, and councils that forbid them. The descriptions of the Kalends include elements that had not been copied from classical sources, and details (such as specifics about the animal masks) differ from author to author who had not shared manuscripts. Arbesmann argues that accounts of the Kalends of January were written up in order to provide missionaries with an exhaustive list of all possible pagan superstitions and practices. This conclusion in unsatisfying because materials dealing with the Kalends celebration are well represented in writings other than missionary texts. Further, we are exceedingly well informed about the origins and nature of the pagan Kalends holiday in Rome, and many of the rites experienced remarkable continuity.

It would be nice to have more, but even if we could drill down deeper into better sources we would not arrive at a bedrock understanding of the Kalends of January events, because they were as impressionistic, amorphous, and shifting to those who described them as they are to us. Further, we can only guess at how well those who composed pastoral literature understood the Kalends or how faithfully they represented them. Whatever the case, once a depiction of the Kalends emerged in the sources, a template had been created that overlaid subsequent treatment of the new year's days. That treatment was not static; novel details accumulated over time.

---

35. Pacian of Barcelona, *Exhortatorius libellus*, col. 1081; Max Harris, *Sacred Folly*, 17; Filotas, *Pagan Survivals*, 162; Arbesmann, "'Cervuli,'" 95, 114, 116–18.

36. Grig, "Interpreting the Kalends," 256; Filotas, *Pagan Survivals*, 156; Arbesmann, "'Cervuli,'" 104–5.

Clerics perceived the Kalends ceremonial as an expression of idolatry among people who paid homage to brute beasts of the natural world. Chrysologos wrote of the revelers, "Man, made to the image and likeness of God must not transform himself into the image of a beast"—that is the likeness of a pagan god. One of the generic words for magician, in fact, is *masca* or *talamasca*, which is etymologically associated with the use of animal masks at festivals.[37]

Bishop Maximus of Turin (fl. 400) dedicated whole sermons to pointing out the errors of celebrating the Kalends of January. The Council of Auxerre (sometime between 578–603), the Second Council of Braga (572), Martin of Braga's *On the Correction of the Peasants* (after 572), the vita of Eligius (ca. 684), and the *Burgundian Penitential* (between 700–725), among other sources, contain condemnations of the Kalends of January. Each of the authors is scathing of participants masquerading as beasts and men cross-dressing, which the missionary monk Pirmin of Reichenau (d.753) called foul and disgusting (*turpe est*). He also evinced considerable consternation over people who exploited the Kalends of the month to predict future events. January 1 seems to have been especially conducive to divination. All the authors decried the ceremonies as demonic. In a section entitled "Auguries and Divinations" (*De auguriis vel divinationibus*), a Bedean penitential forbids celebrations on the Kalends of January, "like the pagans did" (*secundum paganicam*).[38]

The fullest description of the Kalends of January comes from Caesarius of Arles. He writes of the Kalends in terms similar to those of Chrysologos. "Demons are invited as if to their own sacrifices when the days of the calends or the vanity of other superstitions are observed. It is truly a delightful

---

37. Max Harris, *Sacred Folly,* 11–24; Filotas, *Pagan Survivals,* 155–72; Harmening, *Superstitio,* 135–36; J. B. Russell, *Witchcraft,* 15; Meslin, *La fête des kalendes.* On animism see Glosecki, *Shamanism,* 53–67. On Chrysologos see Arbesmann, "'Cervuli,'" 111.

38. Maximus of Turin, *Collectionem sermonum antiquam* 98, 390–92; *Synodus Autissiodorensis* 1, in *MGH Conc. aevi. Mer.*, 179; *Bracanense II* 73, in *Concilios Visigóticos,* 103; Martin of Braga, *De correctione rusticorum* 10, 189–90; Audoin, *Vita Eligii* 2.16, 705; *Poenitentiale Burgundense* 34, in *Die Bussbücher,* 2:322; Pirmin of Reichenau, *De singulis libris* 53, col. 1082. Pirmin's work is generally called *Scarapsus;* it is a collection of patristic quotations and scripture for use by missionaries or to be read at mealtime in monasteries. *Penitential of Pseudo-Bede* 30.3, in *Die Bussordnungen,* 272. From Meens (*Penance,* 113) and Frantzen ("Penitentials Attributed to Bede") there exists a collection of penitentials attributed to Bede the Venerable which are of uncertain authorship, provenance, and date. However, the various versions of the Bedean penitentials were certainly not written by Bede or produced in England. The Bedean texts were mixed with those attributed to Egbert, Archbishop of York (d. 766) in the mid-ninth century in the Rhineland. Both drew liberally from the *Penitential of Theodore.* The *Poenitentiale Bedae* (in *Die Bussbücher,* 1:556–64) and the *Excarpsus Pseudo-Bedae* (*Die Bussbücher,* 2:654–59) are essentially identical. See also Körntgen, *Studien zu den Quellen,* 237–44.

sacrifice for them.... What is so foolish as to disfigure one's face, to assume an appearance which even the demons themselves greatly fear?... What is so mad as... to be clothed in the manner of wild beasts and to become like a deer or a stag, so that a man who was made to the image and likeness of God becomes a sacrifice to the demons?"[39]

Grig, Klingshirn, and Arbesmann are largely focused on whether there was a continuous tradition of the Kalends of January from the Roman past.[40] I am less interested in whether the Kalends was a pagan survival than I am in the role it played in clerical thought. The observance of the Kalends of January was a type of social drama where participants, seemingly, entered a state of liminality. Or at the least they took a break from the structure of their everyday lives to the extent that the process that John MacAloon calls "ordering, disordering and reordering" took place. In the introduction to this book, I referred to Clifford Geertz's discussion of the man who became a parakeet in the ritual environment, but outside that space, although fully human, he retained his "parakeetness." If the *pagani* could become stags and calves in a mock metamorphosis, was it possible for them to return to the (to use Geertz's phrase) "world of bare fact" without retaining some of that fusion between themselves and the non-human world which, in the Christian scheme, was demonic?[41]

Caesarius asks this question in his own way. "For what wise man can believe that men are found to be of sound mind if they are willing to make themselves a small stag or to be changed into the conditions of wild beasts? Some are clothed in the skins of sheep, and others take the heads of wild beasts, rejoicing and exulting if they have transformed themselves into the appearance of animals in such a way that they do not seem to be men. From this they declare and show that they have not only the appearance of beasts but also their feelings. For although they want to express in themselves a likeness to different kinds of animals, still it is certain that the heart of sheep is

---

39. Caesarius of Arles, *Sermones*, Sermon 193.1, 2:783–84: "Sic enim fit, ut stultae laetitiae causa, cum observantur kalendarum dies aut aliarum superstitionum vanitas, per licentiam ebrietatis et ludorum turpem cantum, velut ad sacrificia sua daemones inviventur. Illorum enim est suave sacrificium.... Quid tam demens, quam deformare faciem, et vultus induere, quos ipsi etiam daemones expavescunt? Quid tam demens, quam inconpositis motibus et inpu dicis carminibus vitiorum laudes inverecunda delectatione cantare; indui ferino habitu, et capteae aut cervo similem fieri, ut homo ad imaginem dei et similitudnem factus sacrificium daemonum fiat." Translation: Caesarius of Arles, *Sermons* 193.1, 3:30–32.
40. Grig, "Interpreting the Kalends," 442; Klingshirn, *Caesarius of Arles*, 216–18, Arbesmann, "'Cervuli.'"
41. MacAloon, "Introduction: Cultural Performances," 3; Geertz, *Interpretation of Cultures*, 119.

within them rather than only their likeness."⁴² Humans, made in the image of God (Gen. 1:27), had no part of "stagness" to them, and to play act that they did was idolatrous, but even more serious, Caesarius feared that Christians might take on the "feelings" of a beast if they allowed themselves to be drawn into the Kalends rituals.

For Gregory of Tours, the calf brought forth the biblical image of the molten idol of Exodus whom the wayward Israelites worshipped in place of the true God (Exod. 32:4). And in the villages of Europe it was happening again; the mime show of the idolatrous stag dancers made a mockery of the worship of Christ.⁴³

Indicators suggest that a similar belief in the assimilation of beast and human was characteristic of Anglo-Saxon paganism. Steven Glosecki argues that prehistoric totemism and animal masquerade were entrenched in the rites of the Anglo-Saxons as demonstrated in Old English poetry, and they were slow to die. Certain animals, especially their horns, were symbols of might and domination, but more than that, they were an embodiment of the animal essence. Gale Owen-Crocker demonstrates that the use of animal names (wolf and boar) in *Beowulf* give the power of the beast to the men who adopt them. Paul Dutton notes that in the court of Charlemagne, members assumed animal pet names, thus "dressing [themselves] in the metaphorical skin of animals and animal powers."⁴⁴

It is possible to observe another ancient open-air ritual in rites related to the moon. The moon was at the center of a complex of beliefs about the natural operation of the physical universe. It was common wisdom in the early Middle Ages that all human enterprises and natural phenomena waxed and waned with the moon. Crops grew best if planted as the moon waxed, and timing activities to the phases of the moon was basic to medical treatment.⁴⁵ Augustine, Isidore of Seville, and Bede recognized the effect

---

42. Caesarius of Arles, *Sermones*, Sermon 192.2, 2:780: Quis enim sapiens credere poterit, inveniri aliquos sanae mentis, qui cervulum facientes in ferarum se velint habitus commutare? Alii vestiuntur pellibus pecudum; alii adsumunt capita bestiarum, gaudentes et exultantes, si taliter se in ferinas species transformaverintm ut homines non esse videantur. Ex quo indicant ac probant, non tam se habitum beluinum habere quam sensum: nam quamvis diversorum similitudinem animalium exprimere in se velint, certum est tamen, in his magis cor pecudum esse quam formam." Translation: Caesarius of Arles, *Sermons* 192.2, 3:27–28.

43. Gregory of Tours, *Decem libri historiarum* 2.10, 59.

44. Glosecki, *Shamanism*, 4, 26, 55, 192–204; Owen-Crocker, "Beast Men"; Dutton, "Charlemagne, King of Beasts," in *Charlemagne's Mustache*, 43–68 (quotation 47). On the "cultural prestige" of particular animals see Hall, *Elves in Anglo-Saxon England*, 61.

45. For example, Pseudo-Clement, *Recognitions* 8.45–46, 177–78; Melilotus, *Old English Herbarium*, in *Medieval Herbal Remedies*, 228–29; From M. L. Cameron (*Anglo-Saxon Medicine*, 159–161), understanding the zodiac and which sign of the zodiac controlled each part of the human physiology were

that the waxing and waning of the moon had in the natural ecosystem, but they all stressed that the moon operated within the boundaries of divine providence.[46] Appreciating the physical movements of the moon and the adoration of it were two very different issues. The church was insistent that clergy should regulate sacred ritual, but that proved difficult with respect to moon adulation, partly because the margins between legitimate sky-gazing and astrology were narrow, and partly because moon worship was securely embedded in very old pre-Christian traditions.

Christian theologians targeted moon magic in late antiquity. At several points, conciliar canons forbid attention to the moon, such as lunar divination and calling down the moon, a classical motif describing a lunar eclipse.[47] Because of the synonymy of the moon with the goddess Diana, reverence of the moon had in its background echoes of goddess worship. Martin of Braga rebuked those who adored the moon, and the Second Council of Braga, over which Martin presided, prohibited Christians from observing the moon or the course of the stars to determine whether it was lucky to build a house or to have conjugal relations. The counselors reasoned that in word and deed one should look only to "the lord Jesus Christ."[48]

The phases of the moon intensified other kinds of magic ritual. A penitential ascribed to Bede prohibits juggling, chanting, and divining, especially "when the moon is eclipsed, [and people] think that by their clamoring and unholy magic they can protect themselves."[49] Eventually, the moon became a metaphor for magic itself, specifically female magic.

The mind-set of those who honored the Kalends of January or called down the moon is unknown and unknowable, but we can know that the animal pantomimes persisted in some guise, despite censure, and that the

---

important to medical therapy. From Flint (*Rise of Magic*, 133–35), the connection between bloodletting and astrological charts appears as early as the *Carmen astrologicum* of Dorotheus of Dison in the first or second century, often represented in medieval texts as Zodiac Man. On bloodletting see ibid., 33–34, on crops ibid., 131–33; Meaney, "Aelfric and Idolatry," 126.

46. Augustine, *De civitate Dei* 5.6, 1:133–34. From Augustine (*De doctrina Christiana* 2.29.114, 110–11), the course of the moon is relevant only to establish the date of Easter. Isidore of Seville (*De natura rerum* 18–19, 36–40; 21, 42–43) stressed that the moon operates within the confines of divine providence. Bede, *De temporum ratione liber* 28, 2:365.

47. See Augustine (*De civitate Dei* 10.16, 1:290) who writes that most (marvels) are illusions, such as the trick of drawing down the moon. See also Harmening, *Superstitio*, 251.

48. According to the Enochic *Book of Watchers* (*Complete Books of Enoch*, 1 Enoch 8.1–4, 30), the demon Sareil first taught humans about the course of the moon. See my chapter 2 on women and the moon. Martin of Braga, *De correctione rusticorum* 6, 186; *Concilia Bracanense II* 72, in *Concilios Visigóticos*, 103: "Omnia quae facitis aut in verbo aut in opere omnia in nomine domini Iesu Christi facite, gratias agentes."

49. Penitential of Pseudo-Bede 30.3, 4, in *Die Bussordnungen*, 272: "Noli exercere, quando luna obscuratur, ut clamoribus suis ac maleficiis sacrilego usu de defendere posse confidunt."

rites were threatening to the clerical establishment. In the end the participants and their motives were likely mixed. The mummers may have been engaged in an exercise of resistance against the Christian attempt to eradicate time-honored ceremonies and symbols, or their rituals might have acted to integrate multiple realities: Christian and ancestral. Those calling down the moon were surely involved in a memetic pantomime for recognizing, venerating, and, by their engagement, facilitating natural processes. For Clifford Geertz, "rather than detachment, [religion's] watchword is commitment; rather than analysis, encounter . . . [It] seeks to create an aura of utter actuality."[50] Those who called down the moon participated in an awesome performative process that connected them to the power of the moon and integrated them into the cyclical pattern of the heavens. Within ritual, representations become truths. For the ecclesiastical establishment, that truth had to be of the proper sort, and any encounter, such as the celebration of the Kalends or cajoling the moon, that occurred outside the metaphorical or physical space that the clergy could monitor challenged their efforts to direct the psychic and spiritual life of the flock.

Animal guises and other celebrations on the Kalends of January were particularly insidious because of the importance Christians placed on the calendar, which was a liturgical atlas and the veritable road map for proper Christian worship, liberally signposted with sacred rites. The calendar became a battleground for theology, authority, and the management of ritual at several points, such as the celebration of Easter, the control of the workweek, the recognition of saints, and orthodoxy regarding the date of creation.[51] For Christians, time was as important as place for the grounding of the religion. Just as Christianity redefined sacred space, it also reframed time. Christian time was tied to theology in that God worked out his cosmic plan by subverting it to a timeline. Time began in the Garden, the Incarnation was time's most significant event, and at some point, time would end in a great chiliastic finale.

So tied was the notion of time to orthodoxy that a rejection of the sacral calendar in favor of folk, seasonal celebrations smacked of demonism. As indicated above, one of the characteristics of rituals, such as those on the Kalends of January, is that in liminal space, power relationships can become unstable, and even topsy-turvy. The actors themselves can quickly take to

---

50. Geertz, *Interpretation of Cultures*, 112.
51. One of the most important of these clashes, although it was not related to magic, involved the controversy over the date of Easter; see Bede, *Bede's Ecclesiastical History* 24, 294–309. See Wallis, "Medicine in Medieval Calendar," 106–118 on computus and substituting Christian holidays for pagan feasts.

dictating meaning. Such was the case in regard to dates, which were in and of themselves charged, shot through with innate sacramental power. Even "legitimate" expressions of worship on days the church had not designated as holy could quickly devolve into idolatrous or superstitious magic due to the dynamism between the ritual players and the inherited memory imprinted on the dates. Demons were accustomed to receiving veneration at particular times, so the church sought to neutralize the potential for slippage from Christian to magical worship and the confusion of form with substance by sanctifying a whole new array of calendric feasts.

A diversity of sources spanning the post-Roman era deliver the same message. Martin of Braga, in the letter he wrote to Bishop Polemius, recommended that Polemius warn the *rustici* against the error of celebrating January 1 as the beginning of the year. He draws on biblical authority and insists, "Just as holy scripture says, at the equinox of the Kalends of April [March 25] was made the beginning of the first year. For it is written, 'And God separated the light from the darkness.'" He cautions against placing wreaths about in observance of the Vulcanalia and the Kalends of the months.[52] Eligius of Noyon preached against the pagan celebration of February 22 and advocated substituting John the Baptist's feast day. Gregory the Great suggested that days marked out in honor of "devils" be changed to "the day of the dedication or the festivals of the holy martyrs."[53] Pagan forms, dates in these cases, were to be imbued with Christian meaning.

Singing, Dancing, Juggling

In the early church, singing, dancing, playing instruments, and other sorts of cavorting, such as acrobatics and juggling, were activities so associated with paganism that many felt they could not be separated from idolatry, regardless of the intentions of the worshipper. That consternation continued in the early Middle Ages, particularly when the frolicking came face to face with religious services. All the same, secular song persisted in Frankish culture and could not be curtailed by ecclesiastical prejudice against it.

In *Glory of the Confessors*, Gregory of Tours details scenes of riotous song and dance accompanying the rogations of the statue of the goddess

---

52. The Vulcanalia was a Roman celebration in honor of Vulcan, god of fire. Martin of Braga, *De correctione rusticorum* 10, 190: "Nam, sicut scriptura sancta dicit, VIII Kal. Aprilis in ipso aequinoctio initium primi anni est factum. Nam sic legitur: 'et divisit deus inter lucem et tenebras'" (Gen.1:4). See ibid., 16, 198 on the Kalends of January.

53. Audoin, *Vita Eligii* 2.16, 705–6; Bede, *Bede's Ecclesiastical History* 1.30, 108–9: "die dedicationis uel natalicii sanctorum martyrum."

Berecynthia around the fields in Autun, where, "according to the bleak custom of the pagans, the people carried this statue around in a wooden cart for the protection of their fields and vineyards."[54] In his history, the bishop stresses that the errant Hebrews who worshipped the molten calf did so among feasting, songs, and wanton dancing. Saint Eligius wrote with alarm of "diabolical games and dancing and forbidden heathen songs," and the Iberian bishop Leander of Seville (d. ca. 600) warned his sister, who was a nun, not to listen to the secular songs of married women because they concealed the snare of the devil. In his biography of Martin of Tours, Sulpicius Severus tells the story of demons' wild dancing as they assisted a monk named Anatolius in his attempt to hoodwink the brothers. "Around midnight the whole monastery seemed to be shaken from its foundations by the sound of feet beating on the ground." However, as a result of the monks' "hymns and psalms," Anatolius's deceit is exposed. For the author, the demonic is instinctively paired with devilish capering.[55]

Caesarius of Arles's suspicion of dancing was so profound that he wrote of "those unfortunate and miserable people who romp and dance in front of the churches of the saints themselves. . . . If they come to church as Christians, they leave the church as pagans, because the custom of such dancing still remains from pagan festivities." He accused some parishioners of wanting to come to the festivals of the martyrs just to drink, dance, sing shameful songs, and pantomime in "a diabolical fashion" (*diabolico more*). While they should have been doing the work of Christ, they were doing the work of the Devil.[56] For Caesarius, the very act of public celebration in a manner reminiscent of pagan rites, regardless of the intent of the celebrants, constituted idolatry. The dancing was in honor of the saints, but its ritual form betrayed it in Caesarius's eyes. Dancing, whirling, leaping, and singing off-color songs were more than excessive merriment unbecoming the sober, contemplative

---

54. Gregory of Tours, *Gloria confessorum* 76, 343–44: "Ferunt etiam in hac urbe simulachrum fuisse Berecinthiae, sicut sancti martyris Simphriani passionis declarat historia. Hanc cum in carpento pro salvatione agrorum ac vinearum suarum misero gentilitatis more deferrent." This ceremony resembles the processions at Rogationtide.

55. Gregory of Tours, *Decem libri historiarum* 2.10, 59; Audoin, *Vita Eligii* 2.16, 707: Ludos etiam diabolicos et vallationes vel cantia gentilium fieri vetate; Leander of Seville, *Training of Nuns* 1, 197. Leander was instrumental in the conversion of the Visigothic kings of Hispania, Hermengild and Reccared, from Arianism to Catholicism. Sulpicius Severus, *Vita Martini* 23, 122–23: "Itaque ad mediam fere noctem fremitu terram insultantium commoveri omne monasterium loco visum est." "Itaque reliquum noctis hymnis psalmisque consumitur."

56. Caesarius of Arles, *Sermones,* Sermons 13.4, 1:67: "Isti enim infelices et miseri, qui ballationes et saltationes ante ipsas basilicas sanctorum . . . et si christiani ad ecclesiam veniunt, pagani de ecclesia revertuntur; quia ista consuetudo ballandi de paganorum observatione remansit"; ibid., 6.3, 1:32; ibid., 16.3, 1:78; ibid., 55.1–2, 1:244–46.

posture that the church held up as ideal; they constituted trafficking with demons and were antithetical to the ideal of Christian worship, which was somber, directed by the clergy, and indoors.

The gender of dancing underwent a change in post-Roman Europe. In the late classical world, women or castrated men whirled and pranced at religious festivals in the service of goddesses. We still get a hint of this in Gregory's description of the peasants of Autun and Leander of Seville's advice to his sister. But by and large, sacramental dancing and song had ceased, and so too had the particular ascription of this custom to women. Part of this may have been the influence of Germanic practice, where dancing and the abandon concomitant with it never did have the "stain" of the effeminate that it did in the Roman world.

Weather Magic

Weather was unequivocally the prerogative of God. In his first sermon, Caesarius of Arles draws from the book of Amos to illustrate God's use of storms to chastise his people, and particularly his threat to send "upon one city rain, and upon another city none" (Amos 4.7). Gregory of Tours cites Jeremiah beseeching the Lord. "Can any idols of the nations bring rain? Or can the heavens give showers? Is it not you, O Lord our God? We set our hope on you, for it is you who do all this." (Jer. 14.22) God as rainmaker is pitted against the vain impotence of demonic idols. Chad (d. 672), the bishop of Mercia in Anglo-Saxon England, summarized God's control of storms when he described the deity as he who "moves the air, raises the winds, hurls the lightnings, and thunders forth from heaven so as to rouse the inhabitants of the world to fear Him and to remember the future judgment."[57]

Christian saints, both male and female, empowered through the virtue of their Lord to perform miracles, also caused or quelled storms.[58] The sixth-century Abbot Aredius (d. 591), who was a chancellor to the king of Austrasia and founded the monastery of Attanum, was adroit at manipulating

---

57. Caesarius of Arles, *Sermones,* Sermon 1.15, 1:12, quotation from Amos: "pluam super unam civitatem, et super aliam non pluam"; Gregory of Tours, *Decem libri historiarum* 2.10, 60. For Chad see Bede, *Bede's Ecclesiastical History* 4.3, 342–43: Mouet enim aera Dominus, uentos excitat, / iaculatur fulgora, de caelo intonat ut terrigenas ad timendum se suscitet, ut corda eorum in memoriam futuri iudicii reuocet."

58. For example see Gregory of Tours (*De beata Monegunde* prologue, in *Liber vitae patrum,* 286) who wrote that "even women" are expected to "enter the fight" and "win the prize for their valor." I do not take Gregory's remarks to imply an erasure of "gender" as understood by Kitchen (*Saints' Lives,* 3–22). On the contrary, Gregory only makes his point if it is understood that by virtue of their gender women are not normally valorous.

the weather, and Gregory of Tours provides unusually detailed information about the rituals the abbot used. He first prayed, then put the stick he was holding into the ground and twisted it in a circle two or three times, and from this a fountain gushed. Gregory is quick to remind his readers that miracles are accomplished at Aredius's hand but that God operates "through the strength of Saint Julian the martyr and Martin the holy confessor," not through Aredius's skill.[59] This is a lesson Gregory learned the hard way. At one point he impeded a storm through the agency of some obscure relics. "Then having taken the holy relics from my pocket, I raised my hand against the cloud, and it immediately divided into two parts." Gregory became vainglorious because of his feat, and shortly thereafter he was thrown from his horse. He attributed the accident to his pride and saw it as a heavenly reminder that power over the weather "is a favor from God bestowed through the great faith of the saints."[60] Gregory articulated the thinking of the time in separating miracles from magic based on the source of power that gave each its efficacy.

In Bede's history of the church, Bishop Germanus of Auxerre battles with demons over control of the elements. Germanus and his companion, Bishop Lupus of Troyes (d. ca. 478), are crossing the channel to England to preach against the Pelagian heresy, when demons "raised storms; they darkened the sky, turning day into night with clouds." Germanus reclaims God's rightful control over the weather when he stills the tempest by prayer and a few drops of holy oil. Predictably, Germanus triumphs over the disruption the demons cause, as holy men working rituals typically do. Bede relates how a drop of Aidan of Lindisfarne's (d. 651) holy oil calmed a storm at sea and stilled the winds.[61] In the cases of Aredius, Gregory, Germanus, and Aidan, the saints' behaviors are similar. Each controls the weather through rites, and the source of power at work is holy.

As discussed above, Rogationtide was an adaptation of a pagan ceremony designed to ensure a bountiful harvest, and it illustrates Pope Gregory's assertion from his letter to Abbott Mellitus, that a familiar ritual could be effectively reoriented. The rogation days affirmed both God's control of the

---

59. Gregory of Tours, *Decem libri historiarum* 10.29, 524: "per virtutem sancti Iuliani martyris Martinique confessoris beati in eius manibus Dominus operatus est." Moses also used his staff to control the waters of the Nile (Exod. 7:20).

60. Gregory of Tours, *Gloria martyrum* 83, 95: "Tunc extractas a sinu beatas reliquias, manu elevo contra nubem; quae protinus divisa in duabus partibus." "Dei illa munere per sanctorum fidem praestita praeconavi."

61. Bede, *Bede's Ecclesiastical History* 1.17, 54: "Concitant procellas, caelum diemque nubium nocte subducunt." For Saint Aidan, ibid., 3.15, 260.

weather and the entitlement of a priest to petition God on behalf of his congregation. We have details about the rogation rites, but little information on weather magicians, or *tempestarii*, from this early period, unless we interpret Aredius's ritual of twisting a stick thrust into the ground as a clue on how *tempestarii* worked. Still, we can assume that they were operating because of condemnations against them. For example, the First Council of Braga (561) contains language that forbids the very belief that devils have the power to make thunder, lightning storms, or drought, and holds the belief itself to be anathema.[62] An average person who tried to appropriate the power of the divine over the elements (however fatuously), or even held that such effrontery was possible, was guilty of traffic with demons.

A century and a half after the First Council of Braga, the *Burgundian Penitential* assigned seven years to "a magician, that is, a conjurer-up of storms," and a penitential ascribed to Bede prescribes seven years of penance for "those who conjure up storms."[63] These texts affirm that *tempestarii* are able to work weather magic. According to the *Theodosian Code* of the early fifth century, rain makers "innocently employed in rural districts" are exempted from "every kind of penalty" because by their "magic arts ... they bring it about that divine gifts [crops] and the labors of men are not destroyed."[64] In the law code and early medieval sources, the effectiveness of weather magic is not challenged.

In short, because of its potency, controlling the elements was an option open only to the most holy, but demons were also able to do it, and according to some sources, so could wayward human beings through collusion with demons. As the *Theodosian Code* indicates, the impulse in agricultural communities for some sort of control over rain and sun must have been instinctual and firmly rooted, and there was an array of ritual specialists from bishops to *tempestarii* competing to provide that service.

Life lived in post-Roman Europe was parochial, and, as Chris Wickham says, "micro-regional." The point of reference was local, homebound, resting in small-scale organizations such as monasteries and peripatetic courts. Ian Wood has established that although public paganism collapsed early in the conversion process east of the Rhine, rituals in the home for health, harvests, and the like persisted. Archeological evidence indicates that pagan shrine

---

62. *Concilia Bracanense I* 8–9, in *Concilios Visigóticos*, 68.
63. *Poenitentiale Burgundense* 20, in *Die Bussbücher*, 2:321: "Si quis vero maleficus, id est emissor tempesta"; *Penitential of Pseudo-Bede* 14, in *Medieval Handbooks of Penance*, 227.
64. *Theodosian Code* 9.16.3, 237.

temples were patronized in rural areas for a good century after they were largely abandoned in the cities, although we do not know in what capacity the shrines were used. In the immediate post-Roman period, authorities successfully suppressed cultic pagan religion, but not private, domestic magical practices or what Peter Brown calls "homegrown Christianity."[65] Idolatry was still an active problem, from the point of view of the church, made manifest in communal and ritual performances held outdoors, or, rather, out of the consecrated space of a church from which demons had been banished.

Proscriptive sources consistently denounce pagan celebrations, the rituals at the Kalends of January, calling down the moon, raising storms, and miscellaneous pagan rites *sub dio*. Authorities were not kibitzing about empty vestiges of old belief systems, but were engaged in a real-time struggle to supplant an ancient worldview in which unorthodox currents, sustained in communal rites, ran deep. It may well have been that the *pagani* who participated in the proscribed ceremonies did not see any incongruity between their old forms of worship and their new Christian rituals, but clerics did, and they did not hesitate to admonish parishioners through penitential tariffs and sermons preached from the pulpit.

---

65. I. Wood, "Pagan Religion and Superstitions"; I. Wood, *Missionary Life*, 253–56; Wickham, *Framing the Early Middle Ages*, 384–85; Brown, *Rise of Western Christendom*, 147. See also Goodman, "Temples in Late Antique Gaul," 171; See A. Murray ("Missionaries and Magic") on the extent to which paganism continued to pose a challenge for the church throughout the early Middle Ages.

Chapter 8

Victimless Magic and Execrable Remedies

> Once when the diocese was celebrating the birthday of the most blessed apostle Peter in a town not far from Noyon, Eligius went to the village to preach the word of God as he frequently did. He arduously denounced all the demonic games and impious dancing and all the vapid remnants of superstition which, by right, he abominated. Some of the local leaders bore his preaching most resentfully because he sought to upset their festivals and weaken what they thought were proper customs.... The townsmen agreed that if Eligius attacked their games like this again, they would kill him on the spot.... [They said to Eligius,] "Never, Roman, however much you try, will you uproot our customs, but we will continue our solemnities always and no man will prohibit us our ancient and most gratifying games."

Audoin of Rouen, *Life of Eligius* Patristic writers were of many minds over the efficacy of divination and conflicted about the legitimacy of Neoplatonic theurgy, which seemed for some to be a harmless—even sublime—technique for communing with deity. By around 500, however, the learned had virtually no questions about these practices. Utilizing rituals in order to divine the future or initiate a transcendental experience was injurious and futile. Such attempts provided fertile ground for the infiltration of demons, who, to make matters worse, were charlatans. So completely did the once mystical art of theurgy become associated with conjuring that it came to be regarded as vulgar soothsaying and just another form of trafficking with demons.

In early medieval Europe, Augustine's assessment was canonic that divination relied on devils, and that, although they could not actually discern God's plan, they did have particular talents that allowed them to understand the workings of the natural world better than mortals ever could. For instance, they soared high into the skies and observed impending rain before it was evident on earth, and they masqueraded as gods in response to theurgists' invocations or mediums' necromancy.[1] Demons, therefore, were able to proffer information that seemed prophetic, but all the time they were actually duping the unwary and endangering Christians' salvation. Just as in the early church, an authentic knowledge of future events was thought possible for humans through prophecy and dreams. The Greco-Roman understanding of oneiric revelation did not change significantly in the early medieval world view; dreams could be God-sent or demonic. The difference was difficult to assess, so more and more during the early Middle Ages, the clergy thought it safest to supervise prophetic activities and the interpretation of dreams.[2]

In the Merovingian period, the divide between public and private, which had been patent in late antiquity, degraded as administrative institutions were centered in monasteries and episcopal, royal, and comital households. In these settings, women's proximity to the workings of governance afforded them the influence that such access brought, or in the case of monasteries, women filled authoritative leadership roles. Women also made significant societal contributions by endowing churches, healing the sick, performing miracles, controlling property, and converting pagan husbands. The sociopolitical circumstances that positioned women to participate in decision-making had a positive impact on the perception of women's abilities. Concomitant with the respect they garnered for their general competence, women were also thought to be adept at manipulating the magic arts. The sources for this period portray women openly and publicly divining in their homes and villages and drawing large and credulous crowds that did not disparage their skill or charisma because of gender.

In his *Lady with a Mead Cup*, Michael Enright traces the development of the war band (*comitatus*) on the Continent and in England, from the late Roman period through the Viking age, and he argues that "prophecy and

---

1. Isidore of Seville, *Etymologiarum* 8.11.15–17, vol. 1. Isidore echoes Augustine's explanation of demons' clairvoyance.
2. Kruger, *Dreaming*, 11, 50–53; Keskiaho, "Paying Attention to Dreams."

provocation appear to have been typical behaviors of women amongst warrior groups in Germanic cultures." Enright observes that noble wives had formal roles as "peace-weavers" and clairvoyants who cemented relationships and buttressed the *comitatus*. Women could not only foresee the future, but they could determine outcomes by weaving and knotting magic. In fact, attaching a prophetess to his *comitatus* bolstered a warlord's prestige.[3] In northern Europe during the Migration Period (fifth and sixth centuries) women were depicted on amuletic bracteates with weaving implements that denote female diviners—an iconographic role for elite women in the period. There is evidence of similar imagery in southern Germany of the same period.

By the early sixth century, as missionaries proselytized non-Christian peoples in the North, the clergy viewed their soothsaying in the same way they had regarded Roman diviners and other pagan priestly classes in late antiquity. However, even when northern pagan religions were effectively suppressed, divining continued, and insular, Merovingian, and Visigothic didactic and penitential literature consistently censures fortune tellers and their clients. Prohibitions against divination from Ireland to Italy were picked up and incorporated into penitential literature and became a stock feature of the genre across time and geography. We wish we could pierce the memetic language of the canons to get a clearer view of life at street level. In lieu of that, reading between the lines will have to do, and that is facilitated by comparing various types of texts. Even then, it is important to remember that getting to know the non-literate is frustrated by the fact that virtually all our written sources emanate from a similar privileged, intellectual, Christian perspective.

In his exceedingly influential *Etymologies*, Isidore of Seville distinguishes between expressions of foreknowing. "There are two kinds of divination: art and folly," he writes. "There are those called spell-binders who accomplish their art through words. *Arioli* are so-called because they emit loathsome prayers around the altars of idols and offer fatal sacrifice, and through these rites they accept answers from demons."[4] Both were anathema, but foreseeing with words alone was less vile than when it was accompanied by

---

3. Enright, *Lady with a Mead Cup*, xii (quotation), 7, 68, 93; Enright, "Goddess who Weaves," especially 68–69. See also Hauck, "Motivanalyse eines Doppelbreakteaten"; Meaney, *Anglo-Saxon Amulets*, 122–23.

4. Isidore of Seville, *Etymologiarum* 8.9.14–17, vol. 1: "Duo sunt (autem) genera divinationis: ars et furor. Incantatores dicit sunt, qui artem verbis peragunt. Arioli vocati propter quod circa aras idolorum nefarias preces emittunt, et funesta sacrificia offerunt, iisque celebritatibus daemonum responsa accipiunt."

a sacrificial ceremony, in that case the fortune teller was a crass magician. Isidore's classicizing work echoes the early Christian distrust of ritual per se.

One of the earliest Irish penitentials, attributed to Saint Patrick (fifth century), imposes a penance of one year on anyone who consults a diviner "according to the customs of the pagans." The *Burgundian Penitential* recommends five years on bread and water for soothsayers who ply their trade, and if anyone commits sacrilege by auguries, whether he takes them by birds or through any other means, he must complete three years of penance, because both are accomplished with the assistance of demons.[5] At the hands of post-Roman writers, a congeries of terms and behaviors were frequently subsumed under a general classification of trafficking with demons. For example, in chapter 7 we saw that Caesarius of Arles idiosyncratically called outdoor vows "diabolical divinations." The word "vow" is not generally paired with divination. A Bedean penitential condemns auspices, auguries, and divination, the author basing his position on the authority of the church fathers. The text catalogues a variety of capital offenses, including "serving of things offered to idols, that is, for auspices and so forth."[6] Pseudo-Bede conflates two sorts of demonic trafficking that were distinct in patristic thinking: divining and "drink[ing] the cup of the Lord and the cup of demons" (1 Cor. 10:21); that is eating food sacrificed to demons. In post-Roman sources, terminology was slippery, and the exact categorization of types of magic was less important than the fact that magic was demonic.

Warnings about divination in the penitentials also resonate in other writings of the period. For example, in his sermon 79, Caesarius of Arles speaks of those who have recourse to "diviners, magicians, fortune tellers and those who read auspices" (*divinos, maleficos, caragios, et auruspices*) and stresses that even if seers tell the truth, even if magicians are able to cure, in the final analysis the Christians' lot will only become worse if they succumb to traffic with demons. Similarly, in his letter to Polemius of Astorga, Martin of Braga equates observation of divinations, auguries, the days of the idols, sneezings, and little birds with devil worship. Audoin of Rouen's vita of Bishop Eligius contains a strong condemnation of magic. Eligius is portrayed as saying that under no circumstances must a Christian approach seers,

---

5. *Synodus I S. Patricii* 14, in, *Irish Penitentials*, 56: "*More gentilium ad aruspicem iurauerit.*" *Poenitentiale Burgundense* 24–25, in *Die Bussbücher*, 2:321: (24) "Si quis sacrilegium fecerit id est aruspices uocant qui auguria collegent, Si per aues aut quocum que malo ingenio auguriauerit III ann cum pane et aqua peneteat." (25) "Se quis auriolus quos diuinos uocant aliquas diuinaciones fecerit quia et hoc demonum etc. V ann peneteat iii ex his in pane et aqua." See also ibid., 36, 2:322.

6. Caesarius of Arles, *Sermones,* Sermons 54.1, 1:236; Penitential ascribed by Albers to Bede 5.1, 6.13, in *Medieval Handbooks of Penance*, 226–27.

soothsayers, or enchanters, nor should a Christian analyze the sneezes or cries of birds when going on a journey. The saint recommends signing with the cross in the name of Christ instead, thus following the tradition of replacing pagan rituals with Christian ones.[7] Clearly, the elite held divination to be unequivocally magical.

As a general rule, Merovingian sources do not demonstrate the mistrust of ritual per se evident in early Christian materials. Part of the reason for this may be that Merovingian literature is less discursive. We do not get substantive treatises, such as those of the patristic period, that articulate at length the rationale behind forbidding or approving particular practices. Still, simple Christian rites, such as signing with the cross, were promoted as substitutes for the conjuring of the diviner, as we saw in Eligius's advocacy for a simple gesticular rite in place of pagan rituals.

False Prophecy

In the Merovingian period, legitimate foreknowledge was possible—not through divination, but by means of prophecy. Augury and its embellished rites were blatantly proscribed, but belief in prophecy was woven into the very fabric of the ancient and medieval understanding of cosmic correspondence. The creator's communication took various paths, often channeled through special individuals and without rites or ceremonies. Learned Christians, however, were sensitized to the danger of false prophecy, as warnings against it are frequent and terrifying in both the Old and the New Testaments. False prophets plagued Israel, and their proliferation was generally thought to be an indicator of troubled times—even of the apocalypse. In the Gospels, Jesus warns that not all who prophesy in his name are authentic (Matt. 24:5–7; 24:23–26; Mark 13:21–23) and that at the eschaton when the Son of Man comes again, there will be false prophets and signs. Sulpicius Severus incorporates the biblical warnings against false prophets into his vita of Saint Martin, who surmises "that the coming of

---

7. Caesarius of Arles, *Sermones*, Sermons 70.1, 2:296; 54, 1:235–40. From Filotas (*Pagan Survivals*, 233–34), "*Caragius*" (also *caragus, charagius, caraus, karagius, and ceraius*) is a term Caesarius used first and frequently, after which it appears approximately fifteen times between the mid-sixth and the mid-ninth centuries. The exact definition is unclear, but the best guess is some sort of fortune-teller. For a general study of Caesarius see Klingshirn, *Caesarius of Arles*. Martin of Braga, *De correctione rusticorum* 16, 198. For a discussion of the broad impact of Martin of Braga's work see Flint, *Rise of Magic*, 44. Audoin, *Vita Eligii* 2.16, 705.

the Antichrist is at hand" because of the multiplying number of fraudulent prophets in Gaul, Spain and the East [*Oriente*].[8]

In the early Christian period, prophecy and speaking in tongues were common to laywomen and laymen, and this pattern continued in pre-Carolingian Europe. In this period when Roman-style, state structures had given way to clan and family-based networks of influence, Gregory of Tours was deeply concerned about legitimate authority. He was determined to supervise "the holy" in his own diocese and was leery of anyone who sought power outside the management of the church and by doing so, endangered his reputation.[9] This tension is reflected in Gregory's discussions of valid prophecy. He held open the possibility that a person outside the organizational structure of the church could be divinely inspired to prophesy, but he was troubled by the likelihood of devilish fraud when laypersons took to predicting the future, because the workings of sacred and demonic inspiration could appear so similar.

For instance, in his history Gregory talks about the *rustici* being conned by deceptive impostors and healers, such as Desiderius who appeared in Tours and claimed he could work miracles of healing and had direct communication with the apostles Peter and Paul. Desiderius also had knowledge of people's conversations even when he was not in their presence, The country folk flocked to him, bringing their blind and infirm. Gregory began to suspect the holy man when he averred to be more powerful than Saint Martin, and the bishop accused him of working through necromancy (*nigromantiae artis*) rather than God's grace. Desiderius became so vainglorious as to claim divinity ("The things you have said about me are unworthy of my sanctity"), and Gregory finally determined that the man's familiarity with local affairs, which gave him the appearance of clairvoyance, actually came from familiar demons.[10]

Again from Gregory, a man attacked by a swarm of flies went insane by "some evil diabolic tricks." He wandered around dressed in animal skins (a totemic symbol, or perhaps an imitation of John the Baptist), boasting that he could prophesy the future. Becoming even bolder, he claimed to be Christ and had a woman with him called Mary, who he pretended was his sister. Great crowds flocked to see him and brought their sick, proffering gifts that he, in turn, gave to the poor. When the pretender sent naked

---

8. Sulpicius Severus, *Vita Martini* 24, 124–25: "Antichristi adventum imminere."

9. Zeddies, *Religio et sacrilegium*, 272–79; Moreira, *Dreams*, 77–107; Brown, *Society and the Holy*, 222–50.

10. Gregory of Tours, *Decem libri historiarum* 9.6, 417–19: "Hoc et illud de me effatus es, quae sanctitate meae erant indigna."

dancing messengers to harass Aurelius, bishop of Carthage (d. ca. 430), a servant killed this false prophet. Under torture, Mary revealed that the man was motivated by "hallucinations and magic tricks."[11] Both Desiderius and Mary had been manipulated by demons. So Gregory did not deny that laymen and laywomen could prophesy, but held they had to be watched closely, and all too often his fears were confirmed; lay prophecy readily concealed false prophecy facilitated by devils.

The presence of female prophets—both genuine and false—was not unusual in Merovingian Gaul.[12] In the Gospels, prophetesses are extolled, as in the case of Philip the Evangelist's four prophetic daughters (Acts 21:8–9) and in Peter's proclamation, "Your sons and daughters shall prophesy. . . . Both men and women . . . shall prophesy" (Acts 2:17–18). But in his history, Gregory decries psychic women as galling or deceptive. In one case the female imposter is modeled on an episode in the Acts of the Apostles (16:16–18). "A slave-girl who had a spirit of divination (*spiritum pythonem*) and brought her owners a great deal of money by fortune telling" irritates Paul and his companions as they travel through Greece, following them and calling out, "These men are slaves of the Most High God, who proclaim to you a way of salvation." Although the information the pythoness broadcasts is accurate, it is unwelcome because it comes from a demonic source.

In another incident, the very holy Abbot Aredius is about to die, and a woman assisted by a demon prophesies that he will soon pass to the other world, where she saw a group of saints' and martyrs' spirits that had come to welcome him.[13] Similar to the case of the pythoness in Acts, this female prophet correctly predicts the future, but only through the agency of a demon.

Gregory of Tours relates the story of the Merovingian duke Guntram Boso (d. ca. 600) who sent one of his servants to a woman (*phitonissa*) to ask her about the future; she supposedly had the power of prophecy. The medium reveals the day and hour of King Charibert's (d. 567) death, divines that Merovech (d. ca. 600) will become king, and predicts Guntram's (d. 593) elevation to the bishopric of a great city on the River Loire. When he hears this, Gregory laughs and says, "[Answers] should be bidden from God; we ought not give credence to the Devil's promises." He then has a dream in which an angel proclaims, "God has struck down Chilperic and all his sons."

---

11. Ibid., 10.25, 517–19: "unde intellegi datur, diabolici emissionis fuisse nequitiam," "Maria autem illa suppliciis dedita onmia fantasmata eius ac praestigias publicavit."
12. Examples of women who prophesy correctly without any taint of demonic inspiration are at ibid., 2.13, 63; 8.33, 401–3.
13. Gregory of Tours, *Decem libri historiarum*, 10.29, 524–25.

(Merovech was one of the sons of the Frankish king Chilperic I [d. 584]). Gregory's dream is true, and he realizes "how false are the things that fortune tellers promise."[14] It is significant that Gregory juxtaposes the two kinds of clairvoyance: demonic and angelic. Lay prophecy could be legitimate, but there was always a risk that the source of inspiration was malign, as in this case, where a purported prophetess proves to be a demonically inspired soothsayer.

In yet another incident of female clairvoyance, Gregory is not so skeptical about the veracity of female foresight. He suspects that a Parisian woman's divination is demonic but takes it in stride, so common were women fortune tellers. This Parisian sees that Paris will soon burn, and she is proved right. When she entreats the inhabitants to flee the city, they mock her saying she had her information from an augur, a "noontide demon," or a dream. Soon after, a great conflagration engulfed Paris. The reason Gregory relates the story is to explain how a man and his wife who took refuge in an oratory dedicated to Saint Martin were saved by their faith. Gregory makes no comment about the source of this women's foreknowledge that proved to be true; he does not deny that she was inspired by a demon, and he does not disparage her or her information. Women soothsayers seem to have been common place—not remarkable.[15]

For Gregory, women diviners, though common, were usually a threat, not just because they were lay, but because they could too easily trigger shadowy remembrances, just under the skin, of archetypal goddesses. For example, in one case a woman acquired a great quantity of gold and jewels for her divinatory work in helping victims of robbery by telling them where the thief had fled. "The people honored her as some sort of divinity." When news of this woman reaches the ears of the Bishop of Verdun, he arrests her, and, recalling Acts (16:16–18), determines that she is possessed of an unclean spirit. The bishop is unable to exorcise the demon, and the possessed woman then seeks sanctuary with Fredegund (d. 597), the queen consort of King Chilperic I—herself never loath to dally with demons. Like Gregory, the bishop turned to biblical models for his understanding of female clairvoyance. Instead of drawing on Philip's four prophetic daughters as an exemplar, he interprets the women's prophecy through the lens of the helpless slave girl with an

---

14. Ibid., 5.14, 210–11: "A Deo haec poscenda sunt, nam credi non debent quae diabolus repromittit"; "Heu heu! Percussit Deus Chilpericum et omnes filio eius"; "Tunc a liquidum cognovi, falsa esse quae promiserant arioli."

15. Ibid., 8.33, 401: "daemonii meridian," from Ps. 91:6.

oracular spirit (from Acts).[16] Gregory had at hand two biblical archetypes of female clairvoyance, but he focused on the negative portrayal of the slave girl rather than the positive models provided by Philip and Peter.

In the ancient church, lay prophecies of both men and women were embraced as a God-given aid (even necessity) to evangelization and a counter to the soothsayers of competing religions. By the sixth century, lay prophets were held in suspicion, because without the shield of the priesthood or the security of the cloister, demons could all too easily hoodwink even a well-meaning seer. Prophecy was a sacred means of communication from heaven to earth, but because of its nature, it was also a space that demons could easily penetrate. Prophecy was unbidden, and verbal formulas or manipulation of objects were not necessary to ignite the interaction between humans and the divine. This gave devils an opportunity to initiate contact with people rather than wait to be summoned. Demons were able to prey on the weak and unwary in order to feed them information that was sometimes felonious, as Gregory affirms in the story about Merovech's false soothsayer. Women were particular targets of demonic permeation because they were in that category of the "weak and unwary" who were so gullible and susceptible to deception.

Where there was weakness, however, there was also strength. The false prophetess lived in a social system where she could be derided, apprehended and tortured, but few doubted her ability to collude with devils to tell the future. However distasteful, fortune telling gave female mediums a public presence. Their ability to inspire awe and fear put them in a position to frustrate and compete with the clerical elite.[17]

Astrology

Astrology presents a case both of discontinuity and consistency from late antiquity to the early Middle Ages. In antiquity, astrology was a highly specialized science (or pseudoscience) based on complex calculations inspired by the wisdom of the "Orient." The synonymy of the East with the esoteric and the mysterious attested to in Roman sources continued in post-Roman Christian culture, but it no longer evoked reverence; rather, it provoked censure. "East" came to connote inappropriate curiosity about occult workings

---

16. Ibid., 7.44, 364–65: "ita ut putaretur esse aliquid divinum in populis." This is not a case of trafficking with demons because the woman was possessed; rather it demonstrates Gregory's distrust of prophetesses.
17. On prophecy and authority see Moreira, *Dreams*, 225–27.

of the universe. Gregory of Tours, no doubt informed by patristic writings, held magic to be an innovation from the East where Chus "showed humans the power of the stars" and went to live among the Persians, who called him Zoroaster, or "Living Star" (*viventem stelam*).[18] The magic of the East was indelibly identified with divination and exotic idolatrous religions. In the early Middle Ages, surveillance of the skies was less methodical and more impressionistic. Early medieval astrologers relied on observation of the zodiac and interpretation of portents and freakish happenings in the heavens.[19]

The pagans of northern Europe, like the pre-Christian peoples of the classical world, sought information from the stars. We do not have as much information about astrology in the Celtic and Germanic traditions as we do about Near Eastern and classical astrology because the northern pagans did not leave written records. There are few accounts of religious customs of "barbarians," and most of what we know of their sacred practices comes from Roman texts that disparage them or Christian sources that proscribe them. One of the pre-Christian descriptions is from the pen of Tacitus, who reports that the "Germans" held their business councils at the new or full moon because they were both auspicious.[20]

Christian authorities were chary about attention to the skies because of the possibility of demonic influence, but there were different opinions about what humans could safely glean from movement in the firmament. Caesarius of Arles complained that astrologers encouraged his parishioners to attribute their sins to destiny as determined by the planets. The first Council of Braga condemned magic of the heavens and any astrologer who "observes the twelve signs of the zodiac" (*duodecim signa de sideribus*), and a Bedean penitential expresses special concern about the activities of sorcerers when the moon is eclipsed.[21] Despite the caution, people recognized that knowledge of the heavenly bodies could be not only innocuous, but very useful to humans. Isidore of Seville, whose works are always redolent of early church

---

18. Gregory of Tours, *Decem libri historiarum* 1.5, 7: "Primogenitus vero Cham Chus. Hic fuit totius artis magicae, inbuente diabolo, et primus idolatriae ad inventor. Hic primus staticulum adorandum diabuli instigatione constituit, qui et stellas et ignem de caelo cadere falsa vertute hominibus ostendebat. Hic ad Persas transit. Hunc Persi vocitavere Zoroastren, id est viventem stelam." Pseudo-Clement (*Recognitions* 1.30, 85–86; 4.27, 140) attributed the origins of magic to Ham who then passed it to Mesraim, his son, who became Zoroaster.

19. For additional discussion on astrology in the Merovingian era, see "Superstition" below.

20. Tacitus, *De origine* 11, 43.

21. Caesarius of Arles, *Sermones*, Sermon 59.2, 1:259–60; *Concilia Bracanense I* 9, 10: "duodecim signa de sideribus, in *Concilios Visigóticos*, 68 (quotation 9); *Penitential of Pseudo-Bede* 30.3, 4, in *Die Bussordnungen*, 272.

writings, referred to scientific observation of the skies as natural astrology. He differentiated portents and prodigies, claiming that "portents show and reveal . . . [while] what are called prodigies predict the future." He also distinguished between astrology and astronomy. "Astronomy involves the revolution of the sky, the rising and setting and motion of the stars, and the reasons they are named as they are. Astrology is partially natural and partially superstitious. It is natural when it follows the course of the sun and the moon or the position of the stars at certain times. That which the astrologers follow when they practice divination by the stars is superstition." Bede made favorable mention of the fact that Archbishop Theodore of Canterbury (d. 690) taught astronomy to eager Anglo-Saxon students.[22] The error was in thinking that the stars determined human fate; that proposition was pagan and associated with demons.

Gregory of Tours, like many writers of the period, operated in a gray area in regard to his interpretation of astrological portents. He was an unapologetic believer that the movements of heavenly bodies—especially in unusual combinations—were prodigies of things to come. He repeatedly associated strange lights, fires, and columns of lightning in the skies with major political upheavals or the deaths of kings or bishops. He correlated comets, meteors, and blood raining from the sky with impending outbreaks of epidemics.[23] Stephen McCluskey demonstrates that in Gregory's *On the Course of the Stars* (*De cursu stellarum*) he is careful to stress that the movements of the heavens are under the dominion of God, but the bishop did specify that comets presage the future. There is nothing demonic per se in Gregory's interpretation

---

22. Isidore of Seville, *Etymologiarum* 11.3.2, vol. 2: "Portenta autem et ostenta, monstra . . . prodigia quod porro dicant, id est futura praedicant"; Ibid, 3.27.1–2, vol. 1: "Nam Astronomia caeli conversionem, ortus, obitus motusque siderum continet, vel qua ex causa ita vocentur. Astrologia vero partim naturalis, partim superstitiosa est. Naturalis, dum exequitur solis et lunae cursus, vel stellarum certas temporum stationes. Superstitiosa vero est illa quam mathematici sequuntur qui in stellis auguriantur"; Bede, *Bede's Ecclesiastical History* 4.2, 332–35.

23. Gregory of Tours, *Decem libri historiarum*: comet as prodigy, 4.31, 163–66; star in the sky means death of a king, 4.9, 141; death of Gundovald as *signa* in the sky, 7.1, 333; lightning as signs, 8.8, 376; earthquakes, 2.34, 83; rays of light in the sky, 5.18, 223–24; meteors indicate plagues, 5.23, 230; meteorological and geological disasters, 5.34, 239; ball of fire presages death of Theuderic, 6.34, 305; blood-red clouds, 8.17, 384; sky catches fire and rains blood, 6.14, 284; lunar eclipse, bread bleeds, earth trembles, a column of fire appears, 6.21, 289; luminous globe shines over Bishop Theodore's head, and suddenly the sky is illuminated by a ball of fire, 6.24, 292–93; flashes of light in the sky and snakes from the clouds, 9.5, 416. On Gregory and his approach to portents see Goffart, *Narrators*, 183–97. From Burgmann and Schlosses ("Gregor von Tours"), Bede was not as credulous as Gregory, but he did connect an eclipse of the sun in 664 with a subsequent plague (*Bede's Ecclesiastical History* 3.27, 310–13): "Eodem autem anno dominicae incarnationis DCLX quarto, facta erat eclipsis solis die tertio mensis Maii, hora circiter decima diei; quo etiam anno [erat] subita pesti/lentiae lues depopulatis prius australibus Brittaniae plagis." See Ahern, "Bede's Miracles Reconsidered," 286.

of astronomy, but his fascination with uncanny and extraordinary celestial portents demonstrates a mindset that came dangerously close to a magical interpretation of them as causal agents.[24]

Sortilegium

The belief that lots, or *sortes* (including opening the Bible or other sacred writings to a random verse) could forecast the future was ingrained in late Roman pagan and Christian thought, and descriptions of divination by lots in sacred and patristic texts assured its survival for many centuries. Keep in mind that the apostles of Jesus, Saint Antony, Augustine all turned to sortes to guide them in critical decisions.[25] Only gradually did Christian thinkers begin to appreciate the hidden danger in using holy objects and words in what they would come to consider a magical fashion. In the slow process of working through inherited traditions to bring them in line with the new religion (itself always dynamic), ecclesiastics turned their attention to sortition by the mid-fifth century, and church bodies began to condemn Christian sortilegium on the grounds that reading sortes was forcing God's hand.

In his meticulous study of *sortes sanctorum*, William Klingshirn argues that prohibitions against *sortes sanctorum* in Gallic councils do not refer to the general practice of divining from sacred texts; rather, they target a specific manual called *Sortes Sanctorum* which was first mentioned in the mid-fifth century.[26] Either professional diviners administered predictions from the handbook (sometimes they were clerics), or it could be self-managed. An individual wishing to know the future would throw dice three times, and the numbers that were rolled lined up with a passage in the book. For three sixes, for example, the questioner would go to this response: "After the sun the stars come out and the sun once more recovers its bright light. So too in a short while will your mind return to brightness from the point where you seem to be in doubt."[27]

---

24. McCluskey, "Gregory of Tours."
25. See chapter 4.
26. From Klingshirn ("Defining the *Sortes Sanctorum*" 81), "Between the fifth and eleventh centuries, *sortes sanctorum* referred neither to biblical lot divination nor to any *genre* of divination at all; rather, like *Sortes Apostolorum*, it served as the title of a specific text" (italics in original). I argue that even if *Sortes Sanctorum* refers to a specific manual, it is nonetheless a "genre of divination."
27. Klingshirn, "Defining the *Sortes Sanctorum*" (quotation 95). Ibid., 85, the Council of Vannes was largely concerned with sortilegium carried out by clerics: "(3) Some clergy are devoted to auguries, (4) and under the label of what pretends to be religion—(5) what they call saints' lots—(6) they profess a knowledge of divination, (7) or by looking into any kind of writings whatever (8) predict future events."

The blanket term for divination by random selections from sacred writings was called *sortes biblicae* not *sortes sanctorum*. That having been said, conciliar and prohibitionary literature roundly condemned divination by sortes of any kind, and although *sortes sanctorum* did not refer to a genre of lot divination, the use of the manual called *Sortes Sanctorum* was anathematized as illicit sortelegium.

The synod at Vannes, Brittany in 465 (the canons of which were published in a synodal letter to the bishops of Le Mans and Angers) equated sortilegium by sacred texts (*Sanctorum Sortes vocant*) with fortune telling and auguries. The Council of Agde (506), at which Caesarius of Arles presided, repeated the injunction. The first Synod of Orléans, which the Merovingian king Clovis convened in 511, prohibited divination and augury on pain of excommunication. If Klingshirn is correct, it is at this council that the booklet *Sortes Sanctorum* was first mentioned as a divinatory tool. The Council of Auxerre (sometime between 586–605) follows suit and introduces new information regarding sortelegium. The council condemns the making of lots with bread or wood (*vel quas de ligno aut de pane*).[28]

Isidore of Seville identified *sortes sanctorum* as one of the occult arts, akin to the maleficium the magi performed. He wrote, "Sortilegi are those who, under the name of false religion, claim to have knowledge of divination through what are called lots of the saints, or those who profess to know the future by examination of random scriptures." Isidore's view of lots is noteworthy because, whereas his opinions generally conform to patristic thinking, in the case of lots his stance diverges, and he labels as malicious magic a procedure that was an acceptable practice in the early church.[29]

The vita of Eligius contains unambiguous warnings against seeking answers of any kind by lot casting. In his *Commentary on the Acts of the Apostles*, Bede acknowledges that selection by lot (specifically the election of Matthias) was practiced in the primitive church but insists that the efficacy of sortes ended at Pentecost. He apologizes for the New Testament use of sortes and stresses the fact that prayer and nomination by his peers played as significant a role in Matthias's appointment as the fall of lots did. Bede

---

28. Council of Vannes 16.5, in *Concilia Galliae*, 156; Council of Adge 42, in *Concilia Galliae*, 210–11; Concilium Aurelianense 30, in *MGH Conc. aevi Mer.*, 9; Concilium Autissiodorensis 4, in *MGH Conc. aevi Mer.*, 180.

29. Isidore of Seville, *Etymologiarum* 8.9.28, vol. 1: "Sortilegi sunt qui sub nomine fictae religionis per quasdam, quas sanctorum sortes vocant, divinationis scietiam profitentur aut quarumcumque scripturarum inspectione futura promittunt." Klinshirn argues ("Defining the *Sortes Sanctorum*," 89) that Isidore's use of "sortes sanctorum" is not a reference to the manual called *Sortes Sanctorum*, rather that Isidore copied an ancient canon without being entirely clear what the term meant. This would explain why Isidore diverges from the classical understanding of sacred sorts.

recognizes that sometimes episcopal elections were still assisted by the use of lots, but insists that the practice is demonic.[30] A Bedean penitential and the *Burgundian Penitential* (both written around 700) condemn *Sortes Sanctorum* as just another form of divination, and assign it a penance of three years.[31]

Even after sortilegium was generally recognized as a forbidden practice, it did not disappear. In fact, the practice was surprisingly persistent considering the number of councils, sermons, and penitentials that condemned it. This tenacity may be because it had a place in the arsenal of some churchmen who used it unrepentantly, and two Christians of legendary status, Antony of the Desert and Augustine, relied on sortes to guide their life decisions.

Sulpicius Severus attributed the success of Martin of Tours's episcopal nomination to what amounts to sortilegium, although Sulpicius Severus does not use the term "sortes." A lector was inspired to read a certain passage in the Bible, which shamed and defeated Martin's opponent, Bishop Defender. "One of those present took up a psalter and seized upon the first verse he came across."[32] It is not surprising that a text written as early as the vita of Martin would continue to condone *sortes biblicae*, because the practice had early Christian and patristic precedence. But even later Merovingian hagiography and histories, such as Gregory of Tours's *Ten Books*, rely on sortes as a narrative device. According to Gregory of Tours, Saint Patroclus (d. ca. 576), an ascetic from the area of Berry in Francia, uncertain of his calling, places pieces of parchment inscribed with various options on the altar. After three days of prayerful vigil, he selects the parchment that directs him to pursue the life of a hermit.[33] And when Guntram Boso wishes to know the future of the dynasty, he consults a female soothsayer who assures him that Merovech will someday be king. This information is passed on to Merovech, but he had little faith in the *"phitonissa,"* so he turns to what he considers a more reliable method of fortune telling. He places the Psalter, the book of Kings, and the Gospels on Saint Martin's tomb and prays that these holy

---

30. Audoin, *Vita Eligii* 2.16, 705. On the *Vita Eligii* see Banniard, "Latin et communication"; Bede, *Expositio actum apostolorum* 1.26, 15.

31. Penitential ascribed by Albers to Bede 10.1, in *Medieval Handbooks of Penance*, 229: "He who observes auguries or the oracles which are falsely called *sortes sanctorum* . . . shall do penance for three years"; *Poenitentiale Burgundense* 28, in *Die Bussbücher*, 2.321: "Si quis sortes sanctorum, quas contra rationem vocant vel alias sortes habuerit vel quodcunque aliud ingenium sortitus fuerit vel veneraverit, III annos peniteat."

32. Sulpicius Severus, *Vita Martini* 9, 104–5: "Unus e circumstanibus sumpto psalterio, quem primum versum invenit, arripuit."

33. Gregory of Tours, *Liber vitae patrum* 9.2, 253. In describing Patroclus's sortes, Gregory uses the word "auspitio" (auspices)—an ambiguous term with connotations of the inappropriate approach to God.

books will reveal the future. After three days and nights he opens the books. All three correctly predict Merovech's doom.[34]

Gregory of Tours himself resorted to *sortes biblicae* in an incident that smacks of sympathetic magic. When his adversary Leudast was tormenting Gregory, the bishop reported, "I went into my oratory and picked up the book of the Psalms of David, feeling certain that when I opened it to any given verse it would give me comfort." He found succor in Psalm 78, which relates the story of the Red Sea consuming the enemies of the Hebrews. At that moment, the ferry carrying Leudast across the River Loire sank.[35] As was the case in the use of astrology, Gregory seems not to have completely absorbed the church's stance on the magical dimension of lots as explicated in various councils, or he interpreted it loosely. On one occasion Gregory refers to the biblical sortes-taking that predicted Childebert's birth, as *praesagitium*—essentially augury. Yet, in another case when Gregory practiced sortition by the chance opening of the "book of Solomon" (*Salomonis libro*), he concluded that God spoke through the lots "prepared by the Lord."[36]

An eighth-century collection of Irish canons describes a method of lot casting for determining who stole treasure from a church. Although generally penitentials forbid lots, as late as the seventh century some penitential materials were still endorsing them. The Old Irish *Law of Adamnán* (ca. 697) (also *Law of the Innocents*) was known in England and around Salzburg, and it advocates casting lots to ascertain the identity of the perpetrator in the case of death caused by charms. Each suspect's name is to be written on leaves and attached to a lot. The lots are put into a chalice on the altar, and the one drawn out reveals the culprit. This ritual procedure captures the ambiguity around the status of lots. Magic, the cause of death, is overcome by the competing power of the altar. A strict interpretation would reveal this technique as piling one form of magic onto another.[37]

Ordeal by lot is a mandated aspect of law in the Salian, Ripuarian, and Frisian codes. This rite was generally restricted to slaves when their culpability was uncertain. The suspect drew a straw with a marking on it from a bundle

---

34. Gregory of Tours, *Decem libri historiarum* 5.14, 212.
35. Ibid., 5.49, 259–60: "Haec ego audiens, dum in domo ecclesias resideram, mestus turbatusque ingressus oratorium, Davitici carminis sumo librum, ut scilicet apertus aliquem consolationis versiculum daret." On Childebert's birth see ibid., 8.4, 373. For another example of Gregory's use of sortes see ibid., 4.16, 149–50. See Zeddies (*Religio et sacrilegium*, 260–72), regarding Gregory and sortes, where she takes a short-cut for explaining the complexities of the history of sortes by referring to them erroneously as "Christian magic," in an argument similar to Flint's.
36. Ibid., 4.13, 209–210: "Consideravi hunc versiculum ad Dominum praeparatum."
37. *Die irische Kanonensammlung* 29.7, 101; *Law of Adamnán* 46, in *Medieval Handbooks of Penance*, 137; Meens *Penance*, 88.

of straws, and the result of this selection indicated his guilt or innocence. If the result of the ordeal conflicted with other evidence, the slave was tortured to obtain a confession.[38] The continuation of lots is not as surprising here as it is in Christian literature because early law codes reflect scant religious influence. Perhaps for the same reason, there is no hint in the texts that the procedure is magic. This is particularly evident in the Frisian code were lots are used to determine the perpetrators in a street riot. Twigs are laid out, and one of them is marked with the sign of the cross. The lots are then wrapped in pure wool and placed on the altar or on relics; the priest then selects one at random while calling on God.

Dreams

Like sortilegium, divination through dreams had a long and respectable history in the ancient and classical worlds. Jewish and pagan writings describe information, inspiration, confirmation, and warnings coming to human beings in dreams. The Hebrew Bible has God communicating his will through dream visions, and dream therapy at the temples of Asclepius was the most effective method of healing known to ancient medicine. But there was also a solid record of admonition about false and demonic dreams. Unlike sortilegium, dream divination was deemed illicit early in church history, and models of its condemnation were plentiful.

Gregory the Great's work on dreaming, informed by that of Macrobius and Augustine, was well known in the early Middle Ages. The standard position was that dreams could be revelatory. For example, Germanus of Auxerre established the cult of Saint Alban when the saint recounted the story of his martyrdom to Germanus in a dream vision, and both Gregory of Tours and King Guntram saw the death of Chilperic in a dream.[39] On another occasion, a man died and left his wife instructions for commemorative Masses. When those instructions were not followed, the husband appeared in his wife's dream and demanded to know why. Gregory comments that the woman was able to have this dream only because she was pure. His assessment accords

---

38. *Capitula legi Salicae addita 82*, in *Pactus legis Salicae*, 251. Kings Childebert I and Chlotar I added *Capitula legi Salicae* to *Pactus legis Salicae* in the sixth century. *Lex Ribuaria* 32, ed. Beyerle and Buchner 85; *Lex Frisionum* 14.1–2, MGH LL, 667–68. On *Pactus legis Salicae* and *Lex Ribuaria* see Faulkner, *Law and Authority*, 13–23; *Laws of the Salian Franks*, introd.

39. Gregory of Tours, *Decem libri historiarum* 8.5, 374. On the early medieval reception of late antique dream theory see Keskiaho, "Dreams and Visions, 7"; Kruger, *Dreaming*, 57–62; Schmitt, *Les revenants*, 51–62. Le Goff (*Medieval Imagination*, 193–231) gives an inventory of early medieval dreams and their Old Testament models.

with the position of the pagan Apuleius, as well as Augustine, Tertullian, and Gregory the Great; the purity of a dreamer's soul is crucial to her clarity of vision and the truthfulness of her dreams.[40]

Dreams could also be demonic, and reliance on them constituted traffic with demons. Martin of Braga advised his parishioners against trusting dreams. Quoting Solomon, Martin warned, "Divination and vane omens, ... do not give your heart to them, for [dreams] have tempted many." Note the use of "vana" (*vana*) here to indicate magic, which Martin of Braga also employed for magical weaving in his *Canons*.[41] The *Penitential of Theodore* (ca. 690) condemns oneiromancy along with celebrating auguries, omens from birds, or divination "according to the customs of the heathens." In the incident discussed above where a Parisian women warned her fellow townspeople that Paris would burn, they accused her of magic when they claimed she had received her vision in a dream.[42]

The early medieval clerical suspicion of those who claimed to know the future was rooted in alarm at that very possibility. Part of the muddle in determining whether a given dream was a vision or a demonic prediction was related to the fragmented and ill-defined notion of authority in both secular and ecclesiastical structures. Firm guidelines about access to "the sacred" were not yet fully articulated, and because of this, the laity had considerable license in foretelling. This state of affairs presented a potential clash. God had a pattern of communicating with the world, but demons could frustrate that pattern by insinuating themselves into dreams, the casting of lots, astrological charts, and prophesy. How was a layperson to discern the difference between godly and demonic occult communication? Women could be conduits for inspired dreams and prophecies, but their permeable bodies,[43] along with their feeble minds, increased the chance that demons and not angels imparted information to them. Eventually the church body would resolve this problem by following Gregory of Tours's instincts and setting its clergy up as the sole adjudicator of legitimate clairvoyance.

---

40. Gregory of Tours, *Gloria confessorum* 64, 335–36; Kruger, *Dreaming*, 42–45.

41. Martin of Braga, *De correctione rusticorum* 12, 191: "Divinationes et auguria vana sunt. . . . Ne dederis in illis cor tuum, quoniam multos scandalizaverunt [Eccles. 34:5–7]"; Martin of Braga, *Canones ex orientalium patrum synodi* 75, in *Martini episcopi Bracarensis opera omnia*, 141.

42. *Poenitentiale Theodori* 1.15.4, in *Councils and Ecclesiastical Documents*, 3:190: "secundum mores gentilium." Gregory of Tours, *Decem libri historiarum* 8.33, 401. From Keskiaho ("Dreams and Visions," 13–18), warnings about the dangers of heeding dreams appear first in pastoral texts. The *Penitential of Theodore* was the first of many penitentials that proscribed dreams as divinatory, and shortly thereafter the prohibition was widespread in Frankish handbooks of penance.

43. For the nature of the female body see Laqueur, *Making Sex*, chap. 2.

By the sixth century, for most Christian thinkers, learning the future and unveiling hidden knowledge was a special gift that God bestowed on particularly holy men and women. Pagan cultic divination, as such, was a thing of the past, but sorcerers and sorceresses persisted in attempts to read God's purpose and plans through ritualistic auguries that depended on the illusionary tricks of demons that did not actually have access to privileged information. God could and did reveal the future and his secret mysteries in dreams, visions, and portents, none of which relied on the intercession of human actors and ritual artifice. Reading sortes was somewhat different. It entered the game late, so to speak; it was a method of accessing undisclosed information that early Christians only lightly discouraged. Also, sortilegium did depend on rites for its efficacy, though rather simple ones. Regardless of the technique, the effort of magicians to force God's hand was a grave effrontery.

Superstition

If the post-Roman Church was making progress at suppressing formal pagan religions in northern Europe and east of the Rhine, it was less successful with those "thousand vacuous observances" that Augustine bemoaned in his own day.[44] Clerics unremittingly struggled to expunge some trivial rituals of daily life that had provided security and comfort to Europeans for centuries. At this point in time, the danger in folk play and homegrown customs was seldom one of self-conscious paganism but rather of ingrained, conventional superstitions, which were distinctly demonic from a theological and pastoral perspective—but not likely so from the viewpoint of the people who engaged them. At the beginning of this chapter, Saint Eligius has nearly come to blows with the locals because he denigrated their ludic games and "leaping" (*saltationes*). For the *rustici*, these were innocent frivolities, but Eligius saw only demonism.

Although those who provided spiritual guidance to the *rustici* were ever watchful against un-Christian observances, they understood that there was a difference between demonic worship and common habits. Even if those habits seemed puerile and unnecessary, they were generally tolerated as long as they did not cross that elusive line between orthodoxy and superstition. The clergy did not blindly and robotically condemn every practice that remotely resembled antique pagan religion; rather, they gave their flocks the benefit of the doubt. In general, bishops and priests recognized that the

---

44. Augustine, *De doctrina Christiana* 2.20.31, 54: "milia inanissimarum observationum."

ignorant might perpetuate customary and much-loved paganistic rites without understanding that their traditional rituals were actually demonic. Also, sometimes clergy were in the same position as their flocks and unclear about exactly what behaviors were demonic.[45] Still, there were instances when people blatantly and consciously persisted in worship of idols in the face of authoritative opposition.

Words, Binding, Loosing, Amulets

In the early Middle Ages, as in antiquity, written or spoken words—usually in an alien, mysterious language—could function as ritualistic talismans. The utterance of sounds was a simple kind of ritual that operated on the assumption that there was harmony in creation, and words were thought to be intrinsic to the thing named—not arbitrarily assigned by humans. Michel Foucault captures this concept in *The Order of Things* when he speaks of "resemblance," whereby words and things are one; in other words, the name of a thing is an existential aspect of it—that is to say its signature.[46] Jesus, after all, was "the Word" (John 1:1–2). Words, ritually spoken or written, had the potential to align a person with sources of power at odds with "right" religion. The church recognized that some words summoned demons and posed a threat to ecclesiastical regulation over how humans interacted ritually with the divine. All classes of Christians understood some words to be more than signifiers; they were the signified themselves, and so control over utterance was essential to the clergy.

The timeless dimension of words gave them the power of loosing and binding; in many cases a given ritual was ineffective without either the proper recitation of an oral formula or the accompaniment of a written charm. As was the case with many magical usages, there was a fine line between licit and illicit, between a prayer and a chant, between religious words legitimately uttered and magical words wrongfully spoken. The use of liturgical Latin (even specific prayers) frequently gave power to magical rites. This is particularly significant in Anglo-Saxon texts written in Old English, where Latin is sometimes inserted as an inscrutable language with occult power. In works produced on the Continent, Hebrew script played the same role.

Gregory of Tours was frightened when "unknown characters" (*signis, nescio quibus*) appeared suddenly on vases belonging to denizens of Chartres,

---

45. See Hauck ("Rituelle Speisegemeinschaft") for an analysis of such a case in Jonas of Bobbio's *Vita Comumbani*.
46. Foucault, *The Order of Things*, 25–30.

Orléans, and towns in the Bordeaux region. Gregory interpreted this as an omen of a king's death or some other catastrophe. This eerie occurrence was all the more ominous because the writing was in a strange and unknown language.[47] Martin of Braga condemned those who cast spells over herbs for evil purposes. The *Penitential of Theodore* outlines the procedure to be followed "if one is controlled by a demon," and although the penitential allows someone who is ill to "have stones and herbs," they must be used "without incantations." The verbal formula allows devils entrée.[48]

The power of binding words as a form of magic did not change significantly over the first millennium. Motifs of binding are common in late antiquity and the early Middle Ages. The market in binding curses incised on led or wax tablets continued unabated from antiquity, although in Christian *defixiones* different forces were called upon to activate the spell. Because it was recognized as a spiritual force, binding, both as symbol and as ritual, had importance in religion as well as in magic. One example of several comes from Bede's *Ecclesiastical History*. A nobleman named Imma was captured in battle and imprisoned, but his jailors were unable to keep him in fetters. They suspected he possessed written charms that were repelling the chains, but as it turned out, his brother had been saying Masses for him, and that accounted for the futility of the bonds.[49] In this case, prayers and the charms are set up as the positive and negative poles of the efficacy of words. The reader is to understand that the power of God would always outplay the workings of demons.

Binding as a magical procedure worried Caesarius of Arles, who forbade tying ligatures (also knots and phylacteries) because he classed them with other forms of sorcery. He counseled his flock against resorting to soothsayers, fortune tellers, diviners, herbalists, or those who use knots. Eligius (so frequently inspired by Caesarius's sermons) forbade a woman, while weaving or dyeing cloth, to solicit Minerva's aid in visiting a curse on a person named. Isidore of Seville described ligatures as "accursed" (*execrabilium*), especially when entwined with written enchantments and suspended from the neck.[50]

---

47. Gregory of Tours, *Decem libri historiarum* 9.5, 416.
48. Martin of Braga, *De correctione rusticorum* 16, 198; *Poenitentiale Theodori* 2.10.5, in *Councils and Ecclesiastical Documents*, 3:198: "Demonium sustinenti licet petras et holera habere sine incantatione."
49. Bede, *Bede's Ecclesiastical History* 4.22, 402–3.
50. Caesarius of Arles, *Sermones*, Sermon 52, 1:231; Audoin, *Vita Eligii* 2.16, 706–707: "Nec in tela vel in tincture sive quolibet opere. Minervam vel certas infaustas personas nominare, sed in omni opere Christi gratiam adesse optare, et in virtute nominis eius toto corde confidere"; Isidore of Seville, *Etymologiarum* 8.9.30–31, vol. 1. See Filotas (*Pagan Survivals*, 252) on the interchangeability of "knots," "phylacgteries," and "ligatures."

In Gregory of Tours's *Glory of the Confessors*, the bishop recounts with disapproval rituals that smacked of paganism at a sacred lake on Mons Helarius, as discussed in chapter 7. The items the locals threw into the water as offerings were unspun wool and woven cloth.[51] Audrey Meaney links these rites to binding spells. She also argues that scraps of cloth and threads that archeologists have found in amulets may well have been preserved because of the magic inherent in the woven material.[52] Sources of the period regularly evince concern about women weaving. For example, in his *Canones*, Martin of Braga warns Christian women about "observing vanities in their woolen works."[53] Because of the reputation for licentiousness of groups of "unsupervised" women weaving, "vanities" likely references love magic by which the women were binding their would-be lovers to themselves. Throughout the post-Roman kingdoms, cloth making was women's work, and always beneath its surface rippled the potential for innocuous weaving to slip into magical knotting.

Weaving and binding were far from malign in some early medieval cultures. Word craft and interactive charms were a woman's honored contribution in the warrior societies of northern Europe and England.[54] Michael Enright notes that Anglo-Saxon noblewomen performed binding rites that were not only their privilege, but their duty. Aristocratic women were the peace weavers who distributed gifts and offered the mead cup, which fortified bonds between leaders and their retainers. The women's ritual was accompanied by "wise words"—prophetic utterances that wove and fastened, like fate. The women of Anglo-Saxon heroic literature, such as *Beowulf*, also spun charms that "bespoke" victory in battle.[55] Contrary to the secretive nature of most women's magic in the Latin tradition, in Anglo-Saxon texts, the woman's craft was not merely beneficial; its results were celebrated in public settings and were an essential element of royal communal theater. The scenes in *Beowulf* of Wealhtheow as cupbearer distributing gifts of gold at Hrothgar's victory feasts in the royal mead hall illustrates the pride of place

---

51. Gregory of Tours, *Gloria confessorum* 2, 299–300.
52. Meaney, *Anglo-Saxon Amulets*, 8–9, 46–47, 185–86, 239–73.
53. Marten of Braga, *Canones ex orientalium patrum synodi* 75, in *Martini episcopi Bracarensis opera omnia*, 141: "Non licet mulieres Christianas vanitatem in suis lanificiis observare." Note that the use of "vanities" (*vanitatem*) here to indicate magic is also the term Martin of Braga (*De correctione rusticorum* 12, 191) employed to talk about magical omens in dreams.
54. Enright, *Lady with a Mead Cup*, 170–88.
55. Ibid., 22, 38, 117, 177–87, 286. See also Olesiejko, "Wealhtheow's Peace-Weaving" and Hauck, "Rituelle Speisegemeinschaft" on the role of the lady in the cup-bearing ritual. From Glosecki (*Shamanism*, 108), the word "spell" has its roots in the Old English *spellian*, which simply means "to speak."

reserved for women peace-weavers. Their authority was tied to an aptitude in magical binding. Although the *Beowulf* text does not mention magic in reference to Wealhtheow or literal binding or weaving.[56]

Demarcating legitimate from illegitimate uses of words and knots was far from simple. The difficulty of determining when they were demonic and when they were holy was steadily becoming a question of authority. But in pre-Carolingian Europe, sacral power and spontaneous ritual were widespread in lay culture, and in Saxon societies, women (never clerical) were traditionally associated with wisdom speech, which they spun out figuratively and literally.

The discursive treatises that marked the patristic era were missing from the first part of the early Middle Ages; therefore, historians must intuit principles of magic from the more economical texts. It is clear that the educated clergy were exposed to Augustine's explanation of signs and their misuse because the Hipponian bishop is explicitly referenced in a variety of sources. However, in the post-Roman era, the approach to Christianizing populations—both in the mission field and from the pulpit—was to eradicate wrong behaviors rather than lay out the extensive theology behind them. An example of this emphasis on aberrant practice comes from Martin of Braga's letter to Bishop Polemius, in which he urges that parishioners be warned against observing mice and days of the months in order to keep the vermin away from their bread. He explains that placing bread on water, placing fruit and water at the trunk of a tree, or paying attention to the right day to begin a journey all amount to devil worship.

Saint Eligius advised against taking note of one's day of birth or observing the moon to determine the best time to begin a journey.[57] Such behaviors relied for their efficacy on demons as intermediaries between humans and the planets and the ever-hazardous moon. The rites were meant to influence nature directly without deference to the creator of the natural world. These superstitions were in no way malicious, but they amounted to a misuse of signs and gave instrumentality to demons, which was a chronic hazard of activities transpiring outdoors. Martin, Eligius, and Bede may not have articulated the theology of signs so clearly as Augustine had, but the same fear of demonism was behind prohibitions against superstitions that misaligned

---

56. *Beowulf* lines 620–30, 68; lines 1160–1174, 84; lines 2015–21, 109; Enright, *Lady with a Mead Cup*, 189–95.

57. Martin of Braga, *De correctione rusticorum* 11, 190–91; 16, 198–200; Audoin, *Vita Eligii* 2.16, 705.

the signifier (such as months and mice) and the signified (safety and good fortune).

A common usage in popular magic (also, as we will learn, in medical materials) was the binding-on of amulets. As in the early church, Christians were admonished to redirect the impulse to ward off evil and ensure the protection of persons and property by signing themselves with the symbol of the Lord's passion instead of employing other apotropaic objects and rituals. In regard to amulets specifically, Isidore proscribed attaching them to any part of the body, explaining that the practice was superstitious and demonic, but it persisted nonetheless. For the bishop, cures that binding-on or hanging yielded were thoroughly demonic and inimical to humans[58] Likewise, in Merovingian Gaul, Caesarius of Arles warned his hearers (and readers) against hanging "diabolical phylacteries, signs, herbs, or amber either on themselves or their families" and associated these practices with sorcerers and magicians. He repeated the admonition on numerous occasions. His sermons 13, 19, and 50 are blueprints to some of the persistent problems the church had throughout the early Middle Ages in drawing those it served into its system of symbols and rituals. In sermon 13, Caesarius insists that the use of demonic palliatives will not heal the body as effectively as the Eucharist and prayer.[59]

Sermon 19 is a paraphrase of Augustine's teachings on using herbs as prophylactics. Caesarius warns his audience, "Nobody should presume to summon or consult magicians or fortune tellers, or sorcerers for irreverent pleasure or due to any sickness. Nobody should hang phylacteries or ligatures on himself or his things because if anyone does such an evil thing and will not submit to penance, he will lose the sacrament of baptism."[60] His sermon 50 continues in the same vein:

> What is deplorable is that there are some who seek soothsayers in every kind of infirmity. They consult seers and diviners, summon enchanters, and hang diabolical phylacteries and magic letters on themselves. Often enough they receive charms even from priests and religious,

---

58. Isidore of Seville, *Etymologiarum* 8.9.30–31, vol. 1.

59. Caesarius of Arles, *Sermones*, Sermons 13.5, 1:68: "fylacteria etiam diabolica, characteres aut herbas vel sucinos sibi aut suis adpendere." See also ibid, 14.4, 1:71–72; 19.4, 1:90. A phylactery was originally a prayer box filled with sacred script that was worn on the forehead and left arm of a Jewish man at prayer.

60. Caesarius of Arles, *Sermones*, Sermon 19.4, 1:90: "Nullus caraios aut divinos aut precantatores sacrilega voluptate de qualibet infirmitate aut adhibeat aut interrogare praesumat. Nullus filacteria aut ligaturas sibi aut suis adpendat: quia, quicumque fecerit hoc malum, si paenitentia non subvenerit, perdit baptismi sacramentum."

who, however, are not really religious or clerics but the Devil's helpers. See, brethren, how I plead with you not to consent to accept these wicked objects, even if they are offered by clerics. There is no remedy of Christ in them, but the poison of the Devil, which will not cure your body but will kill your soul with the sword of infidelity. Even if you are told that the phylacteries contain holy facts and divine lessons, let no one believe it or expect health to come to him from them. If some people have recovered their health by these charms, it was the Devil's cunning that did it.[61]

Caesarius's tone is one of urgency, and his frustration is palpable. He pleads with his flock and asks them how they dare persist in their errancy. The bishop rehearses the major themes of early medieval magic: divination, charming, and so forth are of the Devil; suspensions are a commonplace recourse for average Christians; all magic is deplorable, even for positive effects such as healing; the clergy is not exempt from sorcerous dealings; all forms of magic are dangerous and constitute traffic with demons.

Repeatedly in post-Roman sources, Christian symbols and ceremonies that were developed in the early church and designed to replace or redefine symbols and familiar rites are enjoined on newly converted Christians in Europe and the British Isles. In unambiguous terms, Caesarius pits Christian and demonic rituals against each other. It was necessary for clerics to do more than forbid behaviors that were second nature to the people of Europe; it was essential to help them feel equally safe with rituals that were consonant with the Christian message. As in the early church, the Christian rituals that were most frequently pressed into the battle against devils were making the sign of the cross, the Eucharist, baptism, and the veneration of saintly relics. In Caesarius's sermons 13, 19, and 50, he implores his parishioners to rely on the saving nature of baptism, not on demonic gadgets and tricks that strengthen the Devil's hand.

Some practices were considered so objectionable, so inextricably linked to demonic paganism and a wrongheaded understanding of signs, that they

---

61. Ibid., 50.1, 1:225: "Quod dolendum est, sunt aliqui, qui in qualibet infirmitate sortilegos quaerunt, aruspices et divinos interrogant, praecantatores adhibent, fylacteria sibi diabolica et caracteres adpendunt. Et aliquotiens ligaturas ipsas a clericis ac religiosis accipiunt; sed illi non sunt religiosi vel clerici, sed adiutores diaboli. Videte, fratres, quia contestor vos, ut ista mala, etiam si a clericis offerantur, non adquiescatis accipere: quia non est in illis remedium Christi, sed venenum diaboli, unde nec corpus sanatur, et infelix anima infidelitatis gladio iugulatur. Etiam si vobis dicatur, quod res sanctas et lectiones divinas filacteria ipsa contineant, nemo credat, nemo de illis sanitatem sibi venturam esse confidat: quia etiam si per ipsas ligaturas aliqui sanitatem receperint, diaboli hoc calliditas facit." Translation: Caesarius of Arles, *Sermons* 50.1, 1:253–54.

were forbidden in religious intercourse even when they involved sacred objects or referenced the Trinity or saints. Caesarius repeats three times that the sin of magic is a matter of particular behaviors and not intent. In other words, if Christians accept amulets thinking they are sanctified because they are offered by a priest or monk and told that they contain sacred writings, that does not save the parishioner from the "poison of the devil." The bishop demonstrates that not only the lay but also some priests have trouble understanding subtle the differences. Indeed, clerics themselves could be demons' assistants. Caesarius repeats this warning twice. The bishop then strikes a note that is a refrain in his writings—certainly a hard sell. Even though magic works ("people have recovered their health by these charms") it must not be used, because it is demonic and injurious to the soul.[62]

Caesarius's sermons were copied throughout the early Middle Ages for centuries, and full sections of them found their way into other genres such as penitentials and laws. So the bishop's injunction against suspensions (and thereby those of Augustine) would have been broadly known, and not just among the educated. The vita of Eligius and several of the Blickling homilies composed in England contain sizable sections adapted from the work of Caesarius. The Blickling homilies were written in Old English in the mid to late tenth century and were delivered to both clerical and lay audiences.[63]

Trickery

Magic trickery for the sake of gaining advantage was common in the sixth and seventh centuries, and it played on the people's credulity and predilection toward superstition. The stunts of Simon Magus (that archvillain of the Acts of the Apostles), especially his flying contest with Peter, were viewed as the result of pernicious trickery, and they were stock motifs in the writings on magic in the Middle Ages. By the chicanery that demonic forces made possible, magicians exploited the vulgar. In addition to the fact that tricksters used magic for personal gain, they claimed prerogatives over the sacred that

---

62. Caesarius contradicts himself in sermon 50 above. He says of amulets that "there is no remedy of Christ in them, but the poison of the Devil, which will not cure your body but will kill your soul," and in the next sentence claims that amulets can heal: "If anyone has recovered health by these charms, it was the Devil's shrewdness that did it."

63. Grig, "Caesarius of Arles"; R. Collins (*Early Medieval Spain*, 60) says that the sermons of Caesarius were known in Spain. Caesarius of Arles, *Saint Caesarius of Arles*, 1:v–xxiv; Harmening, *Superstitio*, 124–28. On the Blickling Homilies see *Blickling Homilies*, xv–li; Gatch, "Unknowable Audience."

the clergy would have liked to restrict to those holy men and women who had been authorized by elevation to a sacred office or memorialized in vitae.

The common villagers of the early Middle Ages were often at the mercy of itinerant charlatans. Given the expectation of believing Christians that purveyors of the miraculous lived and worked among them, following the Savior's imperative to perform miracles in his name, it is not surprising that traveling wonder-workers were able to sway provincial populations. One of the swiftest routes to local fame and fortune was marvelous virtuosity or, in the view of ecclesiastics, fraudulent tricks.

Gregory of Tours tells of a man who claimed to effect cures and predict the future. Great crowds flocked to him with their sick. By "illusions and tricks," he foretold that some of his supplicants would fall ill and that some would be healthy.[64] Gregory further writes that a number of men from various parts of Gaul gathered "foolish" women who treated them like saints. He uses the term "trickery" to explain these charlatans' influence over the common people. At another point, he writes of a fake holy man who came through Tours pretending to heal. He identifies the imposter's activities as tricks and describes them as magical.[65]

Increasingly the church tightened its custody of all that was holy. Mesmeric laypeople, independent prophets, and itinerant holy men and women came more and more under ecclesiastical opprobrium as tricksters and mountebanks in league with demons on whom their marvels and charisma depended. Those who held fast to the "wrong" use of signs, including suspensions, and those who puffed themselves up because of their facility with "tricks," came to be identified as average Christians practicing rogue rituals. They were rogue principally due to the fact that they involved trafficking with demons. But also baked into those performances was a skewed misconception that the relationship between humans and God was contractual. That means that if a procedure were properly performed, the ritual agent expected delivery on the agreement—from whom or what it may not have been clear to the trickster, but clerics had no doubt that the contract was with demons. As Caesarius warned his congregation, there is no remedy of Christ in signs, but "the poison of the Devil."

---

64. Gregory of Tours, *Decem libri historiarum* 10.25, 517–19: "phantasmata eius ac praestigias," "Sed haec omnia diabolicis artibus et praestigiis nescio quibus agebat."
65. Ibid., "mulierculas" for "foolish women," "praestigias" for "tricks"; ibid., 9.6, 417: "dolositas" for tricks.

Medical Treatments

Clerical rhetoric against demonic medical cures was relentless in the early Middle Ages, because traffic with demons was most eagerly sought in the effort to preserve wellness and avoid disease. It is not clear how thoroughly Christians understood which therapeutic remedies and home rituals were contemptible or why. We know what ecclesiastics wrote and have some idea of what preachers said from the pulpits about cures that relied on demonic intervention. All evidence would indicate, however, that even after centuries, admonitions, learned writings and sermons were not very effective at convincing ordinary Christians to discard ancient safeguards and cures that had always given comfort and relief. In was in the field of medicine that church rituals competed least favorably with un-Christian rites.

Chapter 4 lays out how tightly interwoven were health, illness, and religion, and why the church clung so fixedly to healing and fought to structure the discourse about it. Medieval authors embraced the early Christian use of the curative metaphor "contraries cure contraries" (*contraria contrariis sanantur*) when talking about spiritual health, particularly in penitential materials. The Irish monastic saint Finnian of Clonard (d. 549) applies the formula in his penitential. "Patience must arise for anger, kindliness and the love of God and neighbors for envy; for detraction, restraint of heart and tongue, for sorrow, spiritual joy, for greed, liberality." The Irish monk who composed the *Penitential of Cummean* (between 650–700) writes, "The eight principal vices contrary to human salvation shall be healed by these eight contrary remedies." In the prologue to the penitential, he demonstrates the belief in literal faith healing. "Here begins the prologue on the medicine for the salvation of souls." He quotes from James (5:14–16). "If anyone is sick, bring the priests of the church, and let them pray for him, and place their hands on him, and anoint him with oil in the name of the Lord, and the prayer of faith will save the sick person."[66]

Caesarius of Arles's rogation sermons are steeped in the language of sacred medicine, which is not surprising given that rogations were penitential in

---

66. *Penitential of Vinniai* 29, in *Die Bussbücher* 1:505–6: "Patientia pro ira, mansuetudo et dilectio Dei et proximorum pro invidia, pro detractione continentia cordis et ingue, pro tristitia gaudium spiritale, pro cupiditate largitas nasci debet"; *Paenitentiale Cummeani, prologus* 15, 110: "Statuunt itaque ut octo principalia uitia humanae saluti contraria his octo contrariis remediis sanantur. Uetus namque prouerbium est: Contraria contrariis sanantur." Ibid., *prologus* 1, 108–9 "Incipit prologus de medicinae salutarls animarum. De remediis uulnerum secundum priorum patrum diffinitiones dicturi sacri tibi eloqui, mi fidelissime frater." Ibid., *prologus* 9, 110: "Si quis infirmatur, inducat presbiteros ecclesiae et orent pro eo [et] inponent ei manus et unguentes eum oleo in nomine Domini, et oratio fidei saluauit infirmum." All in *Irish Penitentials*.

nature. The three-day ceremony is the "school of the heavenly physician" and "medicine for our souls. Whoever wants to heal the wounds of his sins must not overlook the beneficial medicine."[67] Caesarius asks penitents to avoid being bleed or taking medicines during Rogationtide. Presumably it is because the healing power of profane cures (which Caesarius does not disparage per se) ought not be on display in rivalry against penitential medicine.

Confessors were styled as moral physicians. Medicaments, remedies, and bandages were metaphors for penance. In the *Penitential of Columbanus* (ca. 600), the Irish missionary captures the conflation of physical and spiritual health. "So also should spiritual doctors treat with diverse kinds of cures the wounds of souls, their sicknesses [offenses], pains, ailments and infirmities ... to treat them, to restore what is weak to a complete state of health."[68] The preface to the *Bigotian Penitential* (between 700–800) is explicit about the role of the confessor as doctor. "Jerome, a man of blessed memory, carefully admonished the pastors and teachers of the church that they should take note of the qualities of the faults of sinners, saying, 'Let the power of the physician become greater as the degree in which the fever of the sick man increases.' Hence those who take care to heal the wounds of others are to observe carefully [the condition of the sinner]."[69] This insistence on healing as a spiritual therapy for maladies both of the body and the soul demonstrates how ardently church intellectuals sought to shape the substance and symbols of wellness.[70]

---

67. Meens, *Penance*, 14, 30; Caesarius of Arles, *Sermones*, Sermons 207–9, 828–34. (Quotation 207.1–2, 828–29: "Ecce, fratres dilectissimi, dies sancti ac spiritales adveniunt, et animae nostrae medicinales et ideo quicumque vult sanare peccatorum suorum vulnera, non dispiciat medicamenta salubria. . . . Nullus se a sancto conventu subducat; nullus ecclesiam quae est caelestis medici scola.")

68. *Poenitentiale Columbans* B.prologue, in *Die Bussbücher* 1:596: "Ita igitur etiam spiritales medici diversis curationum generibus animarum vulnera morbos [culpas] dolores aegritudines infirmitates sanare debent. Sed quia haec paucorum sunt, ad purum scilicet cuncta cognoscere, curare, ad integrum salutis statum debilia revocare." From Meens (*Penance*, 75–76), Columbanus's penitential was influenced by Irish models and was the base of eight other "simple Frankish penitentials" that circulated in northern France and Burgundy.

69. *Paenitentiale quod dicitur Bigotianum*, prologue, in *Irish Penitentials*, 198–99: "Hieronimus uir beatae memoriae eclesiae pastores et doctores ut qualitates uitiorum in peccantibus animaduertant diligenter amonuit dicens, 'Tanto maior potentia medici quanto magis creuit morbus egroti.' Hinc procurantibus aliorum sanare uulnera solerter intuendum est cuius aetatis ex sexus sit peccans. . . . Item de remediis uaris uulnerum, prout anitquorum auctorum approbatio tullit, conpendiosas carptim caraxamus eglotas." From Meens (*Penance*, 61–69), The *Bigotian Penitential* was purely insular and is one of a group of penitentials related to the Céli Dé monastic movement near Dublin in Ireland, which also includes the *Old Irish Penitential* and the *Penitential of Cummean*.

70. From *Sermones* (Sermon 54.1, 1:235–36), Caesarius also used the language of medicine to describe spiritual health.

Clerics' front line in the battle over the proper approach to healing was in the homes and fields of ordinary Christians. In his history, Bede has Cuthbert correcting the Northumbrian peasants' errors in turning to "incantations or amulets or any other mysteries of devilish art" during times of plague rather than putting their faith in the Christian sacraments.[71] Hagiographical texts illustrate the intractability of a population persisting in traditional, non-Christian healing rites, and they argue for the superiority of Christian over magical curative rituals. For example, in his *Miracles of Saint Martin*, Gregory of Tours records an anecdote in which the wife of a man named Serenatus is struck dumb, and her friends summon *harioli*, who treat the woman with herbs over which they have sung enchantments. The poultice proves to be ineffective, but Gregory's niece Eustemia is able to cure the patient by replacing the enchanted herbs with oil and wax from the tomb of Saint Martin.[72] The herbalists use ritual enchantments, Eustemia simple accoutrements of spiritual healing. Gregory's point is that the substance of the cure for dumbness is similar—both apply a poultice—but the source of the healing power is different.

A similar case is found in the seventh-century vita of a Frankish Benedictine nun named Austreberta (d. 704), which recounts the story of a woman who, plagued by pains in her feet, is healed at the shrine of the saint. This foolish woman, however, after having been cured, visits the home of a local wisewoman, who gives her an herb that, if bound to the feet, will keep them always free from pain. However, "immediately, when the woman who had received the heavenly healing put the deadly herbal juices on her healthy limbs, the pain she had experienced before returned worse than ever, by divine command. This miserable woman again repented . . . and returned to the saint's shrine. However, she did not deserve to receive the medicinal relief as quickly as the first time. She had to spend eight days in penance at the altar before she was again completely healthy."[73] The skeptic is punished because her misplaced acceptance of the local herbalist's remedy implies an incomplete faith in the gift of the affronted saint. Both the illegitimate healer and the saint are women competing for prowess as healers. Note that the wisewoman's therapy amounts to a ligature bound to the feet, a procedure that the clergy from Augustine on consistently singled out as demonic.

---

71. Bede, *Bede's Ecclesiastical History* 4.27, 432–33: "per incantationes uel fylacteria uel alia quaelibet daemonicae artis arcane."
72. Gregory of Tours, *De virtutibus S. Martini* 4.36, 208–9.
73. *Austreberta* 21, in *Sainted Women*, 324.

The saint's treatment relies on simple prayer and penance, while the wise-woman's cure depends on magic.

Gregory the Great's *Dialogues* contains a delightful comment on the dangers of putting faith in the curative power of demons. "One day," it begins, "as he was going to the Chapel of Saint John . . . [Benedict] met the ancient enemy of humankind disguised as a veterinarian carrying a horn and a mortar." Asked where he is going, the devil replies, "I'm going to the brothers to give them some medicine" (*potionem*). Benedict subsequently finds that one of his monks is possessed of an evil spirit and cures him by exorcism. The medicine the demon offers is deadly and easily trumped by the Benedict's sacrament. In another case in the same text, a demon seizes a woman, and her family—who is willing to destroy her soul in order to give her temporary bodily relief—attempts to cure her by recourse to local magicians. "She was taken to a river and submerged in the water while the magicians worked their serpentine incantations to try to expel the devil that had entered her." God punishes this presumption by sending a whole legion of devils that remain lodged in the possessed until she is delivered by the prayers of Bishop Fortunatus of Todi (d. 537).[74] The message could not be clearer: the most effective medicine is the healing ministrations God's vicars. In each of the examples above, a nun, a monk, and a bishop reverse the ill effects of healing accomplished through traffic with demons. Sacred biographies were written to inspire emulation, were read at public festivals, and were memorialized in wood and stone at local churches, so the saints' stories and struggles with the "wrong" kind of healing were cautionary tales to all who heard, read, or saw them.

The sermons of Caesarius of Arles are another fertile source for how zealously and persistently ecclesiastics importuned Christians to refrain from magical healing. He writes, "Mothers in grief and terror hasten when their children are troubled with various trials or infirmities . . . [saying,] 'Let us sacrifice a garment of the sick person, a girdle that can be seen and measured. Let us offer some magic letters, let us hang some charms on his neck.' . . . Sometimes women who are apparently wise Christians, when their children are sick, rely on nurses or other women through whom the Devil suggests

---

74. Gregory the Great, *Dialogues* 2.30.1, 220: "Quadam die, dum ad beati Iojannis oratorium . . . pergeret, ei antiquus hostis in mulomedici specie obuiam factus est, cornu et tripedicam ferens. . . 'Ecce ad fratres uado, potionem eis dare'"; ibid., 1.10.1–6, 42: "Ducta itaque est ad fluuium atque in aquam mersa, ibique diutinis incantationibus agere malefici moliebantur, ut is qui eam inuaserat diabolus exiret."

these practices."[75] This is a telling passage because it gives us a taste of the exact nature of the rituals women performed in the household. The sacrifice of a garment, measuring, magical writings, and suspensions are all employed by mothers, who also have access to what appears to be a professional class of women herbal healers (*harioli*). Caesarius counts as demonic the rituals carried out by the country "nurses" (*nutricibus*). It is important to stress that although Caesarius is clear that the females' medicine is devilish, he does not deny that the mothers and wisewomen have genuine (albeit illicit) aptitude. Their medicine works.

Healing accomplished by secular physicians was just a step above magical remedies. Note that in Gregory's story of the possessed monk, Satan disguises himself as a doctor complete with drugs and medicinal implements, and that arouses Benedict's suspicion. The church was not opposed to secular medicine per se, but no profane medicine was as worthy an option as the curative power of Christian rituals. What kind of well-being is it, Caesarius asks, that depends on medicines? "What doctors call healing, brothers," he says, "is not true health."[76] Gregory of Tours advised against earthly medicines (*terrena medicamenta*) in favor of celestial cures (*caelestis medicina*).[77] Physicians had a somewhat tainted reputation in late antiquity for charlatanry and price gouging, and vestiges of that prejudice, added to the fact that they represented a healing option outside the church, rendered their trade always inferior to spiritual medicine.

Along with histories and sermons, sacred biographies provide insight into the mentality of the period regarding healing. In the *Life of St. Cuthbert*, Bede tells the story of a young man who suffers from paralysis. When his "carnal physicians," after applying "all the medical skill they possessed," fail to heal him, he is made whole by Cuthbert's relics. Bede gives additional examples of the inferiority of secular medicine in the case of a young monk who develops a tumor on his eyelid, which physicians, despite their poultices, cannot correct. They fear the monk will lose his sight, but when he touches the relics of Cuthbert (hairs from the saint's head) to his eye, it quickly heals. In

---

75. Caesarius of Arles, *Sermones*, Sermon 52.5–6, 2:232: "quando aliquarum mulierum filii diversis temptationibus aut infirmitatibus fatigantur, lugentes et adtionitae currunt matres? . . . Sed dicunt sibi, 'Illum ariolum vel divinum, illum sortilegum, illam erbariam consulamus; vestimentum infirmi sacrificemus, cingulum qui inspici vel mensurari debeat, offeramus aliquos caracters, aliquas praecantationes adpendamus ad collum. . . . Interdum solent aliquae mulieres, quasi sapientes et christianae, aegrotantibus filiis suis, aut nutricibus aut aliis mulieribus, per quas diabolus ista suggerit." Translation: Caesarius of Arles, *Sermons* 52.5–6, 1:261–62.

76. Ibid., 21.7, 1:97: "Non enim vera salus est, fratres, quam dicunt medici."

77. Gregory of Tours, *Decem libri historiarum* 5.6, 203: "Hic tantum, quid neglegentibus evenerit, qui post virtutem caelestem terrena medicamenta quaeserunt."

another anecdote, a boy in the parish of Bishop John of Beverley (d. 721) suffers from dumbness and scabs on his scalp. The bishop miraculously restores the boy's speech, but leaves it to the physician to deal with the scabs, presumably a less demanding task. And when a physician "foolishly" (*insipienter*) bleeds a woman on the fourth day of the moon, Bishop John saves her life with a blessing.[78] According to various (stage-managed) texts, secular doctors were frequently retained by royal and comital courts, but they were often sidelined. For instance, the Frankish queen Balthildis (d. ca. 680) contracted a bowel disease, and though the doctors alleviated her suffering, she always took more comfort in "celestial medicine." Her real cure came through prayer.[79]

All of these accounts drive home the point that spiritual healing was superior to any cure a secular physician could accomplish. Still, the secular doctor was highly preferable to magical healing. Caesarius laments, "If only the sick would seek out health from the simple art of doctors. But they say to themselves, 'Let's consult that augur, that diviner, that fortune teller, that herbalist.'"[80]

In short, there were various approaches to curing: sacral healing, secular medicine, and magical remedies. By far the best of the three, according to the intellectual elite, was religious healing. Secular doctors operated in the period, but their efforts were second-rate compared to those of spiritual physicians. Recourse to demonic aid through magic was never acceptable. Even if it was successful in the short run, in the end it endangered the soul, so in effect it was not curative in the most important sense. Writers of sermons and hagiography implored their audiences to abjure magical rites, but asking parents to abandon healing rituals that had immediate results in favor of the rarefied benefits of spiritual wellness which could only be realized in another world was surely a hard pill to swallow. Both men and women were involved in the business of healing in the early Middle Ages, but polemicists directed their rhetoric particularly at women applying cures in the home. Barbara Myerhoff argues that rituals' "precise, authentic, and accurate forms" make them "authoritative and axiomatic."[81] Those listening to the church message

---

78. Bede, *Life of St. Cuthbert* 45, 298–301; Bede, *Bede's Ecclesiastical History* 4.32, 449; 5.2, 456–59; 5.3, 460–61.

79. *Vita Sanctae Balthildis* 12a, 497–98: "et nisi medicorum studia subvenissent, pene deficere. Sed magis ipsa ad caelestem medicum."

80. Caesarius of Arles, *Sermones*, Sermon 52.5, 1:232: "Et atque vitinam ipsam sanitatem vel de simplici medicorum arte conquirerent. Sed dicunt sibi, 'Illum ariolum vel divinum, illum sortilegum, illam erbariam consulamus.'"

81. Myerhoff, "Death in Due Time," 151–52.

often opted for "the authority" of restorative rites over the authority of the ecclesiastical organization, and in so doing exercised an independence of will that frustrated the hierarchical order.

Post-Roman societies were homogenizations of peoples with different traditions and historical memories, but their basic cultural grounding was indebted to classical Roman civilization—to a greater or lesser extent depending on location. Anglo-Saxon England, which never experienced the governance of the Roman imperial state, had its own distinctive social structures and ancestral traditions, but over the course of the early Middle Ages, England and the Continent came to resemble each other, largely due to the influence of the church.

Magic as practiced and perceived had shifted since the inception of the church in the first century. For example, communal celebrations of pagan deities and open public ritual had disappeared or metamorphosed into barely recognizable folk habits. The range of what spiritual specialists defined as magic had expanded. Pagan divination and superstitions aimed at navigating the personal and political vicissitudes of social life in late antiquity had been effectively vitiated and recast as demonic and aberrant. Some customs, unique to northern Europe, had come within the orbit of Roman clerical proscription.

By and large, however, the theological assessment of superstition (including sorcerous trickery) and divination remained consistent. In sermons, penitentials, and church councils, the mandarinate launched a wholesale assault on superstition—warning rustics that their homey rites were fruitless, dangerous, and less effective than faith and the simple rituals the church provided. The tone of the persuasion as captured in the sources is temperate but increasingly exasperated as clerics and pastors realized that their parishioners were either not getting or were ignoring the message, and that they continued old habits, such as dancing outside churches and running to local wisewomen for medical care.

Divination of all types was anathema because it was a means by which humans sought knowledge beyond their ken. Acquiring that insight too often involved trafficking with demons, even if diviners did not explicitly summon them. Trying to wheedle occult secrets out of the universe through divination or initiating a psychic encounter with the divine through theurgy implied an affront to God's majesty and was at odds with Christian doctrine. Astrology and augury challenged the principle of free will. If the stars, diseased livers, or fiendish dreams, for example, could predict the future, human choice became meaningless. The Lord provided humans all the information they needed through scripture, prayer, and his special vicars—saints and the clergy. Some thought divination, though demonic, was effectual, but increasingly in the post-Roman period, the prevailing opinion was that it was both demonic and fraudulent.

CHAPTER 9

The Awesome Power of the Woman's Craft

> If any woman works magic on another woman such that she is not able to have children, let her be judged liable for 2500 *denarii*, which make 62 and a half *solidi*.
>
> —Pactus legis Salicae

Maleficium was even more deplorable in the post-Roman world than it had been in late Rome where it was threatening, but not sinful. It was the most insidious form of dependence on demons of the lower air. Goetic activities grew in the early Middle Ages because more behaviors were ascribed to demons than in the early Christian era. There was not so large a gray area of things occult but relatively benign (like theurgy) as there had been in late antiquity.[1]

Post-Roman peoples recognized women in the spiritual realm as saints and honored them for their work as nuns, donors, and missionaries to their pagan husbands. In a mirror image, women commanded a grudging respect their for their skill with the magic arts. The sources depict women wielding clout as effective poisoners, false prophetesses, healers, and adepts with love and birth magic. Sorceresses were held in awe for their abilities both by the common people who had recourse to their services and by those who tried to rein them in through legal enactments, reprimands, and entreaties. Accusations of maleficium appear in a variety of texts were malicious magic and attendant rituals are used casually and frequently. As was true in the classical era, one criterial aspect of maleficium was that it was clandestine. Its

---

1. On theurgy see chapter 2.

secretive nature gave goetic practitioners anonymity; because of this and the fact that the paraphernalia of sorcery (often poison) was readily available, women could more easily practice maleficium than some other types of magic. Women's conjuring in post-Roman Europe was largely domestic, but in a period when public institutions were weak or ill defined, the home was the locus of the most meaningful societal activity, and so domestic power was power indeed. We see this most clearly in aristocratic households.

The church fathers struggled with the theological implications of magic and the ramifications of its use for practitioners' salvation. However, the consternation over sorcery in the post-Roman world had more in common with the pagan past than it did with the patristic era when the most significant fact about magic is that it challenged human progression and God's omnipotence. The era of the great Christian fathers and their theological tomes passed in the West with the death of Gregory the Great in 604, and the next generation of clerics and lawgivers concentrated on practical concerns. Penitentials, legal codes, conciliar records, and saints' lives address the ill results of maleficium as much as they do the sin of trafficking with demons.

The changed focus from magic-as-sin to magic-as-communal-disruption is evidenced in some of the penances for maleficium, where causing harm by sorcery is more serious than victimless magic. All maleficium was devious, secretive, cowardly, and made possible by underhanded demons, but when magic resulted in bodily injury, it was particularly pernicious. The *Penitential of Columbanus* establishes a three-year penalty for one who destroys another by magic, but adds, "If, however, someone is a magician for the sake of love and nobody is destroyed, he must complete a year's penance on bread and water." If nobody is injured, the sentence for using magic is lighter. The *Penitential of Theodore* confers various degrees of penance for manslaughter, depending on the conditions under which the killing takes place. A murder perpetrated in anger exacts three years' penance, an accidental murder one year, and one "by a potion (*poculum*) or any trick (*artem*), seven years or more." Both the words "potion" (*poculum*) and "trick" (*artem*) denote the involvement of magic. The issue here is manslaughter, but the use of sorcery makes the infraction worse because it demonstrates that the homicide is intentional. The *Burgundian Penitential* assigns a penance of three years for involvement with demonic auguries, but seven years for one who "destroys someone with magic." In other words, magic was iniquitous whatever the case, but when it resulted in harm to others, it was more serious.[2]

---

2. *Poenitentiale Columbans* B.6, in *Die Bussbücher*, 1:597: "Si autem pro amore quis maleficus sit et neminem perdiderit, annum integrum cum pane et aqua"; *Poenitentiale Theodori* 1.4.7, in *Councils and*

CHAPTER 9

The same phenomenon is evident in the laws. Like Roman law, vulgar legal codes prohibit maleficium, principally on the grounds of criminal assault and personal injury. The various redactions of Salic law touch on damage inflicted by means of potions, herbs, and spells. Nothing in these laws implies that magic in itself is illegal; rather, they take aim at homicide or attempted homicide.[3] The Burgundian law code (ca. 500), on the whole, neglects magic, although there is one reference to it in a section on divorce, which (like the Roman *Theodosian Code*), says that a man may divorce his wife for "maleficium." We do not learn very much about the nature of her malicious magic, but it is serious enough to dissolve a marriage. *Edictus Rothari* (643) of the Lombard code, includes a case where a man attempts to protect himself in a duel by carrying herbs or "other similar things" that have been prepared by sorceresses (*maleficiae*).[4] The criminality is not so much in using sorcery as it is in the unfair advantage the magical herbs give one party over the other.

The Visigothic law code (ca. 654) contains a general condemnation of magicians, and it is exact about their criminal activities. Any freeperson (man or woman) or slave who uses magic of any kind to strike dumb, maim, or kill humans or animals, to injure anything movable, or to destroy crops, vines, or trees will suffer in person or property the same damage he or she inflicted on the victim. Consistent with the law codes in general, the law of the Visigoths targets magic primarily when it is a threat to communal safety.[5]

The statute from Visigothic law attributes a broad range of magical powers to women, and the Lombard code speaks of sorceresses who prepare injurious herbs. Although the laws and penitentials indict men along with women, since the male is the normative default referent in virtually all medieval writings, when a text specifically includes women, we should assume that they were conspicuous in that given activity. In short, in the legal texts and penitentials of the pre-Carolingian era, maleficium had three strikes against it: a long tradition of illegality, the stain of demonism, and an association with women.

Ecclesiastical Documents, 3:180: "si per poculum vel artem aliquam IIII. annos aut plus"; *Poenitentiale Burgundense* 9, in *Die Bussbücher*, 2:320: "Si quis per veneficium aliquem perdiderit."

3. *Pactus legis Salicae* 19.1–4, 81–82. If death results the fine is 8,000 *denarii*, and if the victim survives, the fine is 2,000 *denarii*.

4. *Leges Burgundionum* 34.3, 68. There is another possible allusion to magic in the code (103.6, 115) which refers to a *veius*, or a person who is able to find lost animals. The medical text *Lacnunga* contains a charm for finding lost cattle (*Anglo-Saxon Remedies* 149, 103) involving a facilitated prayer that the cattle will return to their owner just like the "Cross of Christ was lost and is found." This is the kind of magic the *veii* may have used. See also Hollis, "Old English 'Cattle-Theft Charms.'" *Lex Longbardorum* 368, in *Die Gesetze*, 148: "nec alias tales similes res." On *Lacnunga*, see chapter 14.

5. *Leges Visigothorum* 6.2.1–5, 257–60.

Necromancy

Of all the forms of maleficium, necromancy was the darkest. Isidore of Seville defined a necromancer as one who resuscitates the dead for divining the future or receiving occult information, often by mixing water with gore to attract demons or the spirits of the deceased.[6] This narrow understanding of necromancy as a form of divination is classical. However, in other early medieval texts, the term assumes a broader connotation suggesting any type of maleficium, but particularly nefarious dealings with the dead or bodies of the dead.[7] Just as relics of saints' bodies were numinous, remains of corpses had power—magic power. Ritualized prophylactic use of relics was an appropriate method of tapping spiritual agency, whereas to enlist cadavers for whatever ends was quite a different thing. The external manifestations of the practices may have looked similar, but intellectuals, at least, were quite clear on the differences.[8]

Necromancy was universally deplored and illegal in post-Roman Christendom, but some of the ambivalence of early church writers about the efficacy of necromancy was still in play. For example, several church fathers had concluded that the pythoness in 1 Samuel did not actually retrieve Samuel from the grave; rather, they held that it was a devilish charade. However, Isidore of Seville was still unsure about the incident, and his comments as to whether the appearance of Samuel was a demon-induced illusion or a corporate return from the dead are ambiguous. He writes, "If it can be credited, there is the example of the pythoness when she summoned the spirit of the prophet Samuel from the shrouded region of the spirits and presented him to the view of the living." We must take into consideration the caveat that Isidore was devoted to his patristic authorities, and this may explain in part why he had not jettisoned the outdated notion that it was possible for average mortals to raise the dead.[9]

In Martin of Tours's vita, Sulpicius Severus shows the saint indulging in what seems to be the necromantic arts when he conjures the ghost of a dead

---

6. Isidore of Seville, *Etymologiarum* 8.9.11–12, vol. 1: "Necromantii sunt, quorum praecantationibus videntur resuscitati mortui divinare, et ad interrogata respondere.... Necromancers cruor aqua miscitur, ut cruore sanguinis facilius provocentur."

7. For example, Gregory of Tours (*Decem libri historiarum* 9.6, 417) uses the term *errore nigromantici* when talking about the activities of a false healer.

8. Geary, *Furta Sacra*, introd.

9. See Isidore of Seville (*Quaestiones in Vetus Testamentum* 20, cols. 407–410) where he quotes Augustine. Isidore is, however, ambivalent about the raising of Samuel: *Etymologiarum* 8.9.7, vol. 1: "Si credere fas est de Pythonissa, ut prophetae Samuelis animam de inferni abditis evocaret, et vivorum praesentaret conspectibus."

man, whom the people venerate as a martyr. Martin is suspicious of the unknown saint, so he goes to the village, and, standing on the tomb, "prayed the Lord to make know who was buried there." The "foul and menacing" (*sordidam trucem*) ghost appears and, on Martin's bidding, admits that he had led the very unholy life of a thief.[10] This incident resembles Zatchlas bringing the Thessalian youth to life in Apuleius's *Metamorphoses*, Erictho raising the young soldier in Lucan's *Civil War*, and the pythoness reviving the ghost of Samuel to speak to Saul. As in each of these cases, the revivification Sulpicius Severus describes is not a renewal of life, but a method of obtaining information from an unwilling phantom manipulated by ritual—in this instance, a prayer uttered in a graveyard. Vitae in the first half of the early Middle Ages frequently portray saints emulating Jesus in bringing the dead back from the grave,[11] but in the case of Martin, the dead man was not given new life, but exploited for information. Valerie Flint concludes from this story that the saints' ability to resuscitate the dead is the Christian equivalent of necromancy. I interpret the evidence differently. Clearly it was not Sulpicius's intent to frame the holy Martin as a magician trafficking with demons, and the vita does contain conventional stories of Martin effecting righteous resurrections. Rather, the incident indicates that in the early fifth century the exact contours of what constituted necromancy were still being negotiated.[12]

A condemnation of necromancy undergirds several law codes prohibiting the theft of dead bodies, although not all the codes are clear about the motives for plundering cadavers or robbing graves. *Pactus legis Salicae* (late fifth century) has several stipulations against despoiling corpses that are aimed both at men and women. Burgundian law follows Theodosian law (as noted above) when it indicates that there are only three reasons for which a man can seek divorce: adultery, maleficium, and "violation of graves."[13] The juxtaposition of maleficium and grave robbing suggests that necromancy is one of the grounds for the prohibition.[14]

---

10. Sulpicius Severus, *Vita Martini* 11, 106–7: "Oravit ad dominum, ut quis esset vel cuius meriti esset sepultus ostenderet."

11. For examples see Rampton, "Up From the Dead." See also Gregory the Great, *Dialogues* 2.11, 172–74.

12. Flint, *Rise of Magic*, 271–73. For other examples of revivification in Martin's vita see 7, 103; 8, 105.

13. *Pactus legis Salicae* 55, 205–9; *Leges Burgundionum* 34.3, 68: "sepulchrorum violatricem." See also *Lex Ribuaria* 5 (54), ed. Beyerle and Buchner, 103–4 (sixty *solidi* if not yet buried, two hundred *solidi* and twelve oathtakers if buried and exhumed).

14. De Salis (*Leges Burgundionum*, 68n4) interprets the grave robbery in the Burgundian code as a means of procuring the stuff of magic. The same is true of Zeumer (*Leges Visigothorum*, 403n2) in regard to the Visigothic code. On grave robbery see Filotas, *Pagan Survivals*, 335–37.

Pactus legis Alamannorum (ca. 615) legislates against grave robbery and desecrating corpses. If the criminal removes "something" (*quid*) from the grave, she or he forfeits forty *solidi*, eighty if the corpse is exhumed for the purpose of plundering the grave. In other words, the penalty for the theft of a cadaver is greater if the body is exhumed than if it is tampered with before burial. Although it is not certain that this title is discussing magic, the specific inclusion of women in the prohibition and the fact that the penalty is stiffer for exhumation of the intact cadaver suggests necromantic uses.[15] Visigothic law (although written forty years after *Pactus legis Alamannorum*) is explicit about the motives of those who loot graves and gives us a clue about the meaning of the Alamannic code. It attributes grave robbery to the act of obtaining riches or the stuff of necromancy (*remedium*).[16] Plundering graves is a crime often attributed to women, as in the Salic and Burgundian codes, and although laws regularly refer to women as victims of crimes or parties in property transactions, women are rarely active criminal agents the way they are with regard to maleficium and grave robbery.

Two insular penitentials of the eighth century indicate necromancy. In the penitential writings of Adamnan (ca. 700), death caused by charms, the concealment of the corpse, and "secret plunderings" are grouped together as part and parcel of the same transgression. The *Penitential of Pseudo-Egbert* (ca. 732–766) assigns a penance of seven years for asking about the future at burial places, which seems clearly to refer to seeking information about the future through the dead.[17]

The early medieval period inherited the Roman dread of traffic with the dead. Law codes and penitentials, which are terse and proscriptive, do not provide the exact rites used for necromancy, but some penitentials suggest the use of charms and magic words.

Poison and General Maleficium

Murder by poison often connoted maleficium because early medieval people viewed poison as a sort of potion. The link between magic and poison is implied in *Leges Visigothorum* (654), which classes poisoners with magicians

---

15. *Pactus legis Alamannorum* 16.1–3, 25. See also *Leges Visigothorum* 11.2.1–2, 403; *Pactus legis Salicae* 55.1–2, 205–6; 49.1–2, 108; *Leges Burgundionum* 34.1–3, 68.

16. The editor glosses this as *"medicamentum superstitiosum."*

17. Adamnan 46, in *Medieval Handbooks of Penance*, 137; *Penitential of Pseudo-Egbert* 4.16, cited in Meaney, "Aelfric and Idolatry," 131.

(*De maleficis et consulentibus eos adque veneficis*).[18] The Insular *Book of David* (sixth century) contains an injunction assigning a penance of three years to a man or a woman who "plans to kill a man with poisons."[19] The text does not impute the use of poison to women exclusively, but the fact that women are mentioned in the condemnation implies that the author viewed the crime as one likely to be committed by them. Otherwise he would have omitted specific mention of women, as he does in fourteen of the sixteen canons in the collection. The sixth-century collection of canons known as the penitential writings of Adamnan attributes killing by the administration of poison specifically to women.[20]

In his *Ten Books of Histories*, Gregory of Tours portrays women as authoritative in many realms—political, religious, and magical—and in the text, women's political power is instrumentalized through magic brews and poisons. The bishop relates the story of the rebellion at the convent of Poitiers (in west-central France), in which the perpetrators, Clotild and Basina, are asked if they wish to charge the abbess with any major crime, such as "promiscuity, murder, or sorcery" (*adulterii, homicidii vel maleficii*). Though they decline, this incident demonstrates how normal and unremarkable magic was in the period. It constituted a breach of secular and religious law (it was a *crimen capitale*), but sorcery was a form of wrongdoing possible for any woman—not a highly specialized quasi-science manipulated by the few experts who knew correct formulations. Magic must have been common enough that it quickly came to mind as feasible and credible that the abbess might have practiced it.[21]

Also from Gregory we learn of Septimima, nurse to the royal children, who, along with her lover Droctulf, had plans to effect the banishment of Queen Faileuba and the queen mother in order to control King Childebert II (d. ca. 595). If the king did not go along with the plot, Septimima was to kill him by magical means (*maleficiis*), and his sons were to replace him.[22]

---

18. *Leges Visigothrum* 4.2, 257. *Lex Longbardorum* (in *Die Gesetze* 142, 42) singles out slave women in the statute: "De venenum temperatum."

19. *Excerpta quaedam de libro Davidis* 11, in *Irish Penitentials*, 70–71: "uenenis hominem occidere uolentis." *Lex Longbardorum* 139, 41 classes the use of poison with other violent infractions such as arson, killing a slave, and so forth, but it does not mention magic. The fact that both men and women are called out as culprits in this canon while the other felonies in the law are clearly male behaviors may indicate that women are included because it is they who were generally poisoners.

20. Adamnan 45, in *Medieval Handbooks of Penance*, 137.

21. Gregory of Tours, *Decem libri historiarum* 10.16, 507. It is interesting that in the case of the abbess, sorcery is juxtaposed with promiscuity; this combination is often seen in denunciations of women, but rarely of men. For example, in the *Theodosian Code* (3.16.1, 76), a man can divorce his wife for *veneficium* and adultery, and a woman her husband for murder and magic, but there is no mention of sexual impropriety associated with the husband's sorcery.

22. Gregory of Tours, *Decem libri historiarum* 9.38, 458–59.

In this account the undisputed ringleader of the conspiracy is the woman, and her influence seems to rest largely on the fact that she works magic. She had already killed her husband through *maleficium*, and if the plot had succeeded, it is she who would have commanded the king and his sons. Gregory ascribes a potency to Septimima's sorcery that imperiled the royal succession.

Ten Books of Histories contains two further examples of the weight of women's magic. When Queen Fredegund's infant son, Theuderic, dies in 584, the queen receives information that the child had succumbed to "sorceries and incantations" (*maleficiis et incantationibus*) and that the prefect Mummolus was involved. Fredegund orders several Parisian housewives to be rounded up and tortured by the wheel, mutilation, and burning. Those who survive confess that they are sorceresses (*maleficae*) and had caused several deaths by means of magic. They admit to having sacrificed Fredegund's son for the benefit of Mummolus. When he is arrested and tortured, Mummolus confesses that the women in question had, from time to time, given him a miraculous herb which was meant to increase his prospects at the royal court. Comparably, a certain Count Eulalius had many mistresses, and when he abducted a nun and married her, his other lovers, motivated by jealousy, cast a spell over him "by sorceries" (*maleficiis*). As a result, the count took to homicide. These vignettes suggest that there were collections of women customarily mixing and peddling magical substances. The existence of these *maleficae* is disturbing to Gregory, but not implausible.[23]

In these stories, the very core of the Frankish political edifice is vulnerable to the threat of women using potions. They are a force to be feared, and in no small measure because their magic is unexceptional—practiced by ordinary village women. Not infrequently, female magic was troublesome on a local level, but it could also be a factor of kingdom-wide political consequence.

Gregory implicates Fredegund herself in magic plots and ties her to sorceresses. Often in an accusation of poisoning, the reference to magic is veiled. Because the word for poison, *venenum*, can also mean magic charm, an author such as Gregory can shrewdly use the term to insinuate without accusing.[24] However, in some cases he imputes the use of magical potions and poison to Fredegund directly. When the queen decides to eliminate King Childebert (d. ca. 595), who had accused her of being a *malefica*, she arranges for his murder (and, ironically, proves his point). She prepares potions to give the reluctant assassins courage and treats their knives with poison. It is

---

23. Ibid. 6.35, 305–6. Gregory does find it incredible that the women sacrificed Fredegund's son, but exactly what aspect of that detail he questions is not clear. Ibid.10.8, 490.
24. Ibid. 8.29, 392.

difficult from the text to be sure whether Gregory considered the courage-inducing potion and the poison magical, although that is the strong implication. This passage is typical of a number of references throughout the sources in which the text is ambiguous about the magical characteristics of herbs and poisons. As indicated earlier, writers often did not identify a clear dividing line between the natural and magical effects of substances. Whereas a modern writer would put enchanted materials in the second category, for the medieval writer, to whom magic was commonplace, the distinction was not so important. Gregory of Tours frequently classifies Fredegund with magicians and charlatans and incriminates her in mysterious poisonings. At one point he directly calls her a "malefica."[25]

As in late antiquity, poison was particularly insidious because of its position within the matrix of magic, murder, secrecy, and women. Geoffrey Scarre notes a phenomenon in early modern Europe, which applies equally to the early Middle Ages, whereby constraints imposed by patriarchal culture meant that women were more likely to resort to clandestine magic than men. "[Women's] social and economic position," he observes, "imposed greater constraints on their possibilities of action and self-defense."[26] Women in both early modern and early medieval Europe were obliged to achieve their aims furtively in ways that the aggressively masculine warrior culture found underhanded.

All genders used potions and poisons, but the practice was particularly adaptable to women's circumstances. It was lethal but not violent, and poison could be secured easily and applied with stealth in a private setting. The men of Poitiers readily suspected the abbess of sorcery, and the *maleficae* who killed Fredegund's son worked in "bands" and were adept at using potions. The ancient association of women and poison had not disappeared, and this stereotype was in the background of Gregory's attribution of its use to Fredegund.

Love Magic

In the Greco-Roman vocabulary of sorcery, women were consummate specialists in the art of love magic. The infamous heroines of classical plays, odes, and novels, such as Medea and Circe, formed for later periods an

---

25. Ibid. 7.14, 335. I. Wood (*Merovingian Kingdoms*, 31) writes that Gregory veils political comments that would have been dangerous to make openly. Associating Fredegund with magicians is an example of this.

26. Scarre, *Witchcraft and Magic*, 61.

image of the woman as an enchanting siren whose charms men could not resist.²⁷ The primitive church carved out a special conceptual zone for Christian women that gave them room to escape the classical characterization of females as intrinsically unstable due to their sexuality and weakness of mind. However, it did not take long for deep-rooted Roman stereotypes to creep back into Christian discourse on women's volatility. Every genre of early medieval literature indicates that women were the primary practitioners of love and birth magic. We saw by examining the archeological findings of *defixiones* that Roman men practiced love magic as readily as women did. Such material evidence against which the written sources can be checked is scarce in the early Middle Ages, so we must rely on aggregating texts from various genres to paint the picture of love magic in the Merovingian era.²⁸

The books of penance frequently mention women in conjunction with crimes of amatory magic, although it is not exclusively a female crime. Priests or monks, who were in many ways feminized in the period, were also reproached for love magic.²⁹ The *Penitential of Finnian* (sixth century) suggests that either "clerics" or "women" are likely to "give a potion for the sake of unrestrained love," which carries a penance of a year on bread and water. The same document singles out clerics and women for the sin of magical seduction and assigns it a stringent penalty of six years' penance—as much as for some forms of murder. The *Penitential of Columbanus* condemns those who are "magicians for the sake of love." It omits mention of women, but specifies penances for laymen, deacons, and priests. The language is borrowed and repeated in the Burgundian and Bobbio penitentials (between 700–725).³⁰ It is puzzling why priests and monks are envisioned as matchmakers. It is not uncommon for clerics to be associated with magic, but that is generally in regard to healing.

The *Penitential of Theodore*, an exemplar for manuals of penance throughout Europe, contains two canons connecting women with what appears to

---

27. Isidore of Seville (*Etymologiarum* 8.9.5, vol. 1) writes that Circe was "the most beautiful female magician . . . [who] changed the friends of Ulysses into beasts" (Fertur et quaedam maga famosissima Circe, quae socios Vlixis mutavit in bestias). Isidore had a tendency to accept (or at least record) classical perceptions of magic in a way that was not true of other thinkers of his era.

28. For archeological evidence of women's magic see Meaney, "*Anglo-Saxon Amulets*."

29. See Coon ("What If the Word") on priests and female imagery.

30. *Poenitentiale Vinniai* 18–19, in *Die Bussbücher*, 1:504: "Si quis clericus maleficus vel si qua mulier malefica," "pro inlecebroso amore dederat alicui"; *Poenitentiale Columbans* B.6, in *Die Bussbücher*, 1:597: "Si autem pro amore quis maleficus sit"; *Poenitentiale Burgundense* 10, in *Die Bussbücher*, 2:320; *Poenitentiale Bobiense* 10, in *Die Bussbücher*, 2:324. From Meens (*Penance*, 76–77), the Burgundian and Bobbio penitentials are two of a group of eight closely related texts called the "simple Frankish penitentials" that were produced in Burgundy and go back to a common source with connections to the foundation of Columbanus.

be sympathetic love magic.[31] Canon 1.14.15 prohibits women from mixing a man's semen in his food in order to stimulate his ardor. The recommended penance is three years. The following canon (1.14.16) forbids a wife from tasting her husband's blood as a remedy. The source is not explicit as to what the remedy is for, but likely, due to the juxtaposition of the two canons, the author means the reader to understand that he is still referring to a procedure for the improvement of sexual performance. Both of these canons are listed under the rubric "Penance Specific to Marriage" (*De penitentia nubentium specialiter*) and are not expressly magical or demonic. The penitential does contain a rubric for "worship of idols" (*De cultura idolorum*). We cannot be sure that the Disciple of Northumbria, who compiled the work, thought mixing semen in food or drinking blood was magical, although many medieval authors (such as Isidore of Seville and Raban Maur) coupled magic and various uses of blood. The Disciple mentions drinking blood or semen a second time in a section called "Of Many and Diverse Evils and What Necessary Things Are Harmless" (*De multis vel diversis maliis et quae non nocent necessaria*), but makes no mention of women or of magic.[32] In some penitentials, then, there is a correlation between love potions and women. The connection to traffic with demons is oblique but implied in the meaning of the word "potion" and the use of blood.

Secular law codes overall address love magic superficially, but the Visigothic *Breviarium Alaricianum* (ca. 506) patterns its condemnation of love magic on the Roman Theodosian codex, saying, "Magicians, enchanters, or conjurers of storms, or those who through the invocation of demons throw into confusion the minds of men, shall be punished with every kind of penalty." The code, like its Roman model, does not implicate women, but the Visigothic King Recceswinth's (d. 672) redaction of the laws (654) contains a twist condemning adulterous women who use magic to divert their husband's attentions from their own infidelities.[33] It makes sense that pre-Carolingian codes are taciturn about love magic because it is not the sort of thing the genre addresses unless love magic in some way causes bodily harm or damage to property.

---

31. *Poenitentiale Theodori* 1.14.15–16, in *Councils and Ecclesiastical Documents*, 3:188. As indicated earlier, Theodore's penitential was one of the most authoritative and imitated penitential texts on the Continent and in England and Ireland soon after it was compiled.

32. *Poenitentiale Theodori* 1.7.3, 3:182; 1.14.15–16, 3:188, both in *Councils and Ecclesiastical Documents*. Isidore of Seville associated magic with various uses of blood. Demons are enticed to reveal the future on the promise of blood as a reward offered by necromancers. Isidore of Seville, *Etymologiarum* 8.9.11–12, vol. 1; Raban Maur, *Poenitentiale ad Heribaldum* 30, col. 491.

33. *Theodosian Code* 9.16.3, 237. On *Breviarium Alaricianum* see Peters, *Magician*, 14.

Information from medical materials is particularly useful in shedding light on references to love magic that in other sources are jejune and lack detail. The herbals are full of remedies to correct sexual incompetence and manipulate birth, and when other texts refer to love potions or abortifacients, something like these recipes may be what they mean. The herbals never refer to the cures as demonic, but their very nature classifies them as such if we take as normative traditional learned views of traffic with demons.[34]

Some recipes refer specifically to male impotence brought on by magic spells that we can guess women cast, if we look back to the penitentials in which wives mix concoctions to control their husbands' passion. *De medicina de quadrupedipus* prescribes a brew to arouse sexual interest in men. The instructions say to grind the testicles of a deer, dry them, and administer the drug in a glass of wine. Another aid to male virility is to hang a foxtail on a man's arm. Similarly, pulverized bull testicles dried and imbibed will enable a man to overcome obstacles to coitus.[35] No words or enchantments are suggested for the procedures, but one of them requires a suspension, and the other two amount to sympathetic magic and what ecclesiastics would consider a misguided faith in false and demonic signs, because they rely on testicles to correct a default in the corresponding male sexual organs.

In the *Herbarius*, a man bewitched by love magic (*devotus defixusque in nuptiis suis*) brought about by knotting must find the herb *Pedeleonis* and prepare it during the waning of the moon (*coquito ex aqua luna descrescente*). The bewitched should cook the fruit of the plant, wash himself, and just as the moon rises in the night sky (*prima nocte*), he should go outside the threshold of the house, burn the *Pedeleonis* along with an herb called birthwort (*Aristolociam*), spread the ashes, and reenter the home without looking backward. This will "untie" him (*resoluisti eum*).[36] The goddess Diana is embodied in this ritual in that the impotence represented by the waning strength of the moon is reversed as the moon regains her energy. The requirement to walk backward is an ancient analogue for reversal that creates a liminal zone where magic is most potent. Symbols of reversal set aside ordinary time for the ritualized play frames that follow.[37]

---

34. See Jolly (*Popular Religion*, 71–95) on Augustine's influence on Aelfric and Wulfstan.
35. *De medicina* 2.13–14, 337 (deer testicles); 3.10, 341 (fox tail); 12.14, 369 (bull testicles), all in *Leechdoms*. Rubbing the udder of a boar on the male's genitals will cure sterility (*De medicina* 8.8, in *Leechdoms*, 359. Also see *Herbarius* 2.13–14, 337; 3.10, 341; 12.14, 369, all in *Corpus medicorum*. On remedies for impotence see Rider, *Magic and Impotence*, 21–26.
36. *Pedeleonis* 7.1, *Herbarius*, in *Corpus medicorum*, 37.
37. Turner, "Liminality," 27.

Sextus Placitus records a cure for a man who has been enchanted by knots and cannot enjoy "his lusts." A similar remedy against magical ligatures that reverses the deleterious effects of knotting on a person's sexual desire appears in the treatise on the uses of the badger (*Anonymi de taxone liber*). The testicles of the badger are to be cooked in honey and water from a running brook. The sufferer should then eat the testicles after a three-day fast. The symbol of virility becomes virility itself. Augustine (and generations of churchmen who echoed him) deprecated this kind of sympathetic magic as a misuse of signs that enabled demons to insinuate themselves into the healing process.[38]

In the above three cases, knotting would surely have been the result of rites practiced by women, who were given to weaving magical strands at their looms—or thought to be so. The communal workshops (*gynaecea*) where women made cloth and clothing were magnets for rumors of libidinous cliques, clandestine love affairs, and erotic plots—including magical knotting. In this deeply gendered space, where women were amassed (largely "unsupervised" by men), slurs based on stereotypes involving female sexuality and sorcery were predictable. Medical cures for impotence, which attribute the malady to magical knots, shed light on imprecise references to weaving magic from other sources, including penitentials, sermons, and council records.[39]

Medical texts also come to the service of those reading Gregory of Tours's *Ten Books of Histories*. The bishop talks about magic spells and machinations, but he does not describe their exact nature. The episodes involving Mummolus and Count Eulalius, recounted above, name sorcery and spells (*maleficiis et incantationibus*), which I take to mean two different things. Sorceries are physical substances, and incantations are word formulas. What was in the "sorceries" and how were the spells accomplished? The herbals hold clues to both questions.

Birth Magic

One of the charges most often lodged against women in early medieval laws, penitentials, and council records is that they kill children, either in the womb

---

38. *Anonymi de taxone liber*, in *Corpus medicorum*, 231. See also *De medicina* 4.1, in *Leechdoms*, 330–31.

39. Garver, *Women and Aristocratic Culture*, chap. 5; Rider, *Magic and Impotence*, 1–11; Herlihy, *Opera Muliebria*, 18–21, 29–40. Rezeanu ("Relationship between Domestic Space") defines gendered space as "particular locales that cultures invest with gender meanings, sites in which differentiated-practices occur or settings that are used strategically to inform identity and produce and reproduce asymmetrical gender relations of power and authority."

THE AWESOME POWER OF THE WOMAN'S CRAFT 261

or as infants, whether by magical means or otherwise. Infanticide accomplished through magic was one of the worst forms of maleficium. Using magic to bring about the opposite effect was almost as condemnable because any attempt to control conception by means of herbs or charms constituted traffic with demons. Caesarius of Arles says as much in his sermon 51.[40]

> When God wants women to have children, they should not take diabolical medicines or tie sorcerous knots to prevent their conception, and those whom God wishes to remain sterile should desire and seek this gift from God alone. . . . [Women] do wrong when they seek to have children by means of devilish drugs. They sin still more grievously when they kill the children who are already conceived or born, and, when by taking magical drugs to prevent conception, they condemn in themselves the nature that God wanted to be fruitful. Let them not doubt that they have committed as many murders as the number of children they might have begotten.[41]

Sterile women should accept their fate or seek fertility from God only and not appeal to the power of demons, who work through herbs, drugs, and knots. These things are "diabolical," whereas true succor is bestowed by the divine. Homemade substances that facilitate birth are demonic, even though bearing young is a worthy goal. More important than having children is abjuring demonic, magical aids and understanding the relationship between God and humans.[42]

In proscriptive sources such as penitentials and law codes, women are often censured for efforts to control conception and birth by the use of poisons or magical incantations.[43] The *Penitential of Finnian* imposes penance on men killing children, but there is no mention of magic. Yet the same document refers to the abortion of a fetus and attributes the sin specifically

---

40. It is important to remember the broad influence of Caesarius's sermons and how widespread his opinions on magic were, inasmuch as they found their way into sermon literature on the Continent and in England.

41. Caesarius of Arles, *Sermones*, Sermon 51.4, 1:229: "Et ideo, cui deus filios dare noluerit, non eos de aliquis erbis vel diabolicis characteribus aut sacrilegis ligaturis habere conentur. . . . Unde et illae male faciunt, si eos quibuscumque sacrilegis medicamentis habere voluerint; et illae gravius peccant, quae aut iam conceptos aut iam natos occidunt, vel certe unde non concipiant potiones sacrilegas accipiendo damnant in se naturam, quam deus voluit esse fecundam. Quantoscumque filios parere potuerant, tanta homicidia fecisse non dubitent." Translation: Caesarius of Arles. *Sermons* 51.4, 258–59.

42. Harmening, *Superstitio*, 318–19.

43. *Canones Hibernenses* (late seventh century) 1.6, 1.8, 1.11, in *Irish Penitentials*, 160; *Poenitentiale Bedae* 2.12, in *Councils and Ecclesiastical Documents*, 3:330; *Poenitentiale Burgundense* 35, in *Die Bussbücher*, 2:322; *Poenitentiale Bobiense* 31, in *Die Bussbücher*, 2:325.

to women using magic.[44] Penalties for abortion or infanticide could be harsh, and the severity of the punishment was consistent over the course of the early medieval centuries.

Two of the earliest law codes explicitly pinpoint women for terminating unwanted pregnancies by magical means, and others hint at it. Title 19 of *Pactus legis Salicae* singles out women who, by maleficium, prevent others from having children. The same section prohibits injurious magical uses of herbs and spells, but it specifies women only in connection with conception.[45] The *Pactus legis Alamannorum*, which was written a century after *Lex Salica*, contains a title that may refer to magically induced homicide. It stipulates that if, "through the act of another," a woman's child is born dead or does not live for nine nights, the accused must pay a fine or swear innocence. I interpret the word "act" (*facto*) as a reference to magic because the title is repeated verbatim in the early eighth-century *Lex Alamannorum* (which is based on the *Pactus legis Alamannorum*) with the heading, "If anyone bewitches [*instrigaverit*] a pregnant woman." Here the term "act of another" is more clearly defined; it refers to magic, specifically to the deeds of a *striga*. So both the seventh- and eighth-century codes view magic as a cause of abortion. The seventh-century law code does not specify the gender of the malefactor, but the eighth-century one implies that the offender is female.[46]

Visigothic law condemns a servile woman to flogging and a free woman to slavery who take potions to destroy a fetus. In this context the word *potio* strongly connotes a magically treated drink, although it is not completely certain whether King Recceswinth (or his scribes), who promulgated the laws, had magic in mind. The regulation goes on to censure any woman who "by a blow or any other means" induces a miscarriage in another woman. We can surmise (without certainty) that "other means" refers to a charmed drink because of the frequency of potions in charges of abortion.[47]

The *materia medica* contains curing rituals that facilitate women's participation in the natural process of birth, where they act as their own *medicae*. They do this in ways that are at odds with Caesarius's admonition that mothers, whether "fertile" or "sterile," must submit to God's will and not

---

44. *Poenitentiale Vinniai* 20, in *Die Bussbücher*, 1:504.
45. *Pactus legis Salicae* 19.4, 82; 24.6, 91. From Barré (*Les homéliaires carolingiens*, 157), in *Lex Ribuaria*, abortion is homicide and sacrilege; if done with potions, it is tantamount to magic.
46. *Pactus legis Alamannorum* 12, 24; *Lex Alamannorum* 76, 71: "Si quis muliere gravida instrigaverit."
47. *Leges Visigothorum* 6.3.1–2, 260–61; ibid., 6.3.3, 261: "Si mulier ingenua per aliquam violentiam aut occasionem ingenue partum excusserit au eam ex hoc debilitasse cognoscitur . . ." ibid., 6.3.1–7, 260–62 legislates on abortions caused by men as well as women.

challenge it by the use of herbs and magical procedures.[48] The Latin *Herbarius* records a procedure employing a ligature; it stipulates that during a delivery, "a boy or girl virgin hold against the left thigh near the groin eleven or thirteen grains of coriander seed in a clean cloth tied with a warp thread, and as soon as all the birth will have taken place remove the remedy quickly lest the intestines follow." The herb has to be picked in the morning and lifted from the ground without the patient naming the herb or carrying it with her. In another recipe, coriander is an aid in parturition when a ligature is used as a periapt. The soon-to-be mother is advised to keep the root of henbane or seeds of coriander strapped to her thigh during delivery to assure a successful birth.[49] *De Medicina de quadrupedius* has two recipes for handling women's menstrual flow pursuant to conception. The recipes are illuminating inasmuch as they show women themselves actively effecting a therapy without a medic. To stop the menstrual flow, a woman should comb her hair under a mulberry tree, gather the loose hair from the comb, and hang it on a mulberry twig turned upward "until it is clean." When she retrieves the hair, her blood will stop. To start the blood again she should go to the same mulberry tree and repeat the exact motions in reverse by hanging the hair on a mulberry twig turned downward. There is a third recipe with this set that could refer either to abortion or to the removal of the placenta after delivery. It says, "If you want a woman cleaned who might never be cleaned, work a salve for her from the hair and dry it, and put it on her body; then shall she be cleansed."[50]

Also in *De medicina de quadrupedipus*, female patients are advised to pluck the small bone from the ear or womb of a deer and suspend it from the arm in order to expedite conception. The continental version of the text (*Liber medicinae Sexti Placiti Papyriensis ex animalibus pecoribus et bestiis vel avibus*) gives essentially the same recipe, but indicates that this procedure should be followed to prevent rather than induce conception. The same source contains other medicinal aids to conception that require parts of the hare. For

---

48. Caesarius of Arles, *Sermones*, Sermon 51.4, 1:229: "quam deus voluit esse fecundam"; "quas deus stereles voluit permanere."

49. *Coriandrum* 103.2, *Herbarius*, in *Corpus medicorum*, 185: "Mulier ut cito pariat: Herbae coriandri semen grana XI aut XIII in linteolo mundo de tela adligato, puer aut puella virgo ad femur sinistrum prope inquinem teneat, et mox ut omnis partus fuerit peractus, remedium cito tollat, ne intestinae sequantur"; *Old English Herbarium* 104, 195, in *Medieval Herbal Remedies*. On this cure see M. L. Cameron (*Anglo-Saxon Medicine*, 126, 176), who notes that sometimes henbane is used with coriander, and the concoction blocks nerve fibers of the parasympathetic nervous system and contains hypnotic elements, which induce sleep. See chapter 12 (Burchard of Worms, *Decretum* 19.5.194, 2:452) for a virgin bringing a ritual to fruition.

50. *De medicina* 1.6–8 in *Leechdoms*, 333.

example, pregnancy will result if the belly of the hare is dried and ground into a liquid; both the man and the woman must drink the mixture or the child will be androgynous. A hare's rennet in liquid will also help a woman conceive if she drinks it from a female hare and her husband from a male.[51]

By the criteria of elite clerical culture, these procedures were sorcerous. Even though they did not call on demons directly. The byzantine rituals and arcane symbols are not drawn from the portfolio of Christian aids such as prayer, penance, or the sign of the cross. The exploitation of the warp of the thread, the mulberry tree, the deer bone, and the rabbit's stomach is antithetical to a Christian theology of causation. The same is true of the rituals such as tying ligatures that are not analgesic but talismanic, the application of substances to the thigh, the instructions for obtaining coriander, and the rites set in the woods at the mulberry tree. Reversal, inversion, and sympathetic magic (woman drinks from female hare, man from the male hare, a virgin completes the therapy of a mother) are at the core of the rites. Karen Jolly and Ciaran Arthur (among others) suggest that the people who followed these recipes did so without pause because they were produced in a Christian milieu.[52] But we do not know how the women applying these cures (or the clerics who recorded them) conceived of their source of power—natural, magical, or holy. They may have understood perfectly well that their curative rites were at odds with those endorsed in sermons and the stories of the saints but chose to ignore that fact, either because the cures "worked" or because the lay persons were committed to their rituals even when they flew in the face of Christian power networks. One thing is clear; the cures bear out that women were credited with the ability to work birth magic and to cure through the use of rituals that were at best a-Christian and at worst superstitious.

Throughout the early Middle Ages, clerical sanctions against amatory and natal magic were firm but largely ineffective. Unlike some other forms of magic that the ecclesiastical elite considered vain and fatuous, the efficacy of love and birth magic went largely unchallenged. Although men and women practiced love and birth magic, both were preponderantly attributed to women. The sources demonstrate a belief that women were active, effective manipulators of the magic arts and that they orchestrated the kind of rituals that the religious apparatus ardently disapproved. Women wielded a

---

51. *De medicina* 1.17, in *Leechdoms*, 339; *Liber medicinae* 1.14, in *Corpus medicorum*, 238; *De medicina* 4.12, 345; 4.14, 347, both in *Leechdoms*.

52. Jolly, *Popular Religion*, 96–116. Arthur, "Charms."

terrifying and awesome power and used it to control male sexuality as well as to regulate their own reproduction.

Striae and Lamiae

In the first centuries of the common era, the most troubling magic was dominated by men, because the primary concern of the church was public official worship of demons. Perhaps as a result, no systematic position on the stria and lamia was formulated. Early Christian writers brought from their classical legacy, a nebulous and vaguely conceptualized concept of an enigmatic female who was at the same time fiendish and alluring, enchanting and ruinous.[53] In these creatures the attraction and menace of female sexuality joined forces with the electricity of magic. Mythopoeic classical characters such as Circe, Medea, Erictho, Diana, and Hekate raised questions that early medieval clerical culture inherited.[54] Intellectuals were interested in the theological questions their activities provoked. What was the exact nature of these female beings? Were they human women who used magic or were they demons?

In order to assess the theological implications of human shape-shifting, Isidore brought two classical examples to bear. First, he discussed Circe's putative ability to metamorphose Ulysses and his companions. Second, he considered reports about the Arcadians who claimed that if someone ingested the burnt offerings prepared for their god, that person could be changed into a beast. Isidore concluded that transmogrification was not entirely doubtful.[55] Although there was not a clear or univocal understanding of their nature, the educated generally viewed Erictho, Circe, and Medea as human women practicing run-of-the-mill sorcery. Diana and Hekate, however, were still perceived as goddesses—that is to say, demons, and Isidore of Seville tapped into an ancient tradition in discussing Diana in the context of her role as a healer.[56]

The sixth-century penitential canons ascribed to Saint Patrick declare anathema any Christian who believes in or accuses any woman of being

---

53. Isidore of Seville (*Etymologiarum* 8.9.102, vol. 1) defines a lamia as a woman who snatches children and tears them apart.
54. In the Jewish tradition there is a lamia called Lilith (Isa. 34:14), but I have not discussed her because she does not figure in late antique or Christian sources. On Liliths (male and female) see Pintel-Ginsberg, "Lilith"; Schäfer, "Jewish Magic"; 84; Patai, *Hebrew Goddess*, 221–54.
55. Isidore of Seville, *Etymologiarum* 8.9.5, vol. 1.
56. Ibid. 17.9.45, vol. 2.

a lamia or stria.[57] In this early penitential decree, the very belief that these creatures exist is forbidden, but in *Pactus legis Salicae,* striae are very real and dangerous, though not themselves demons. They eat humans, and as in the Patrick text, to falsely accuse another of being a stria is criminal. The penalty for wrongfully maligning someone as a stria (and in some codices the word "whore" [*meretrix*] is added) is a fine of sixty-two *solidi,* roughly equivalent to the payment for other kinds of false accusation or assault. But "if a stria eats a person and it can be proven," she is liable to a two-hundred-*solidi* fine. In a similar vein, title 64 forbids labeling a man a *"hereburgium"* without proof; this is a reference to one who carries a cauldron (*aeneum* or *inium*) to the place where striae cook. The penalty for that is sixty-two *solidi*.[58] The framers of the Salic Law credited the existence of striae and believed that they were able to carry out their maleficium. However, the prescripts do not attribute any fantastic feats to the striae. They traffic with demons by causing death through potions and herbs, which they apparently cook at communal gatherings, and they kill and eat people, but as far as we can tell from the regulations, they do not fly, cause people to change shape, or revivify the dead. In the two Salic *tituli,* striae are human beings, not demons, who meet at a particular spot for some kind of cannibalistic cooking ritual. The women are central to this gruesome rite, and the men who carry the pots are accomplices.

Pactus legis Alamannorum exacts a penalty of twelve *solidi* from a woman who calls another woman a "stria" or an *"[h]erbaria."* Theodore John Rivers translates *"herbaria"* as poisoner. The term denotes one who deals with magically treated herbs, which, in a sense, describes poison and is in keeping with the common association of women and poison. If "anyone" accuses a woman of "the crime of being a stria or herbaria," seizes her, and puts her in a hurdle or tortures her, he must compensate the relatives. The rate of reparation differs with the social standing of the inculpated woman. If the charge is true, the accuser must still pay the woman's *wergeld* (amount of compensation due to injured parties). Behind these stipulations is an effort to protect women and their families from a very serious charge, but there is no denial of or even skepticism about the reality of striae or their use of poison herbs.[59]

---

57. *Synodus I S. Patricii* 16, in *Irish Penitentials,* 56: "Christianus qui crediderit esse *lamiam* in saeculo, quae interpraetatur *striga,* anathemazandus quicumque super animam famam istam inposuerit, nec ante in ecclesiam recipiendus quam ut idem creminis quod fecit sua iterum uoce reuocat et sic poenitentiam cum omni diligentia agat."

58. *Pactus legis Salicae* 64.1–3, 230–31: "Si stria hominem comederit et conuicta fuerit."

59. *Pactus legis Alamannorum* 13.1, 24: "Si femina aliam stria aut erbaria clamauerit"; 14.1–5, 24: "Si quis alterius ingenuam de crimina seu stria aut herbaria." *Laws of the Alamans,* 50; most people

Edictus Rothari of *Lex Longobardorum* (ca. 643) is similar to *Lex Salica* in that to accuse a woman of being a stria or a sorceress (*masca*) is very grave. A man who makes such an allegation against a woman over whom he has guardianship stands to lose her *mundium* (legal guardianship of a person, either oneself [*selpmundia*] or another). There is no implication in the ordinance that striae or *mascae* are illusionary; they are human women trafficking with in the magic arts. If a man indicts a woman who is not under his guardianship of being a *striga* (stria) or a harlot *(fornicariam)*, he must pay twenty *solidi* (not a particularly stringent fine) if he is willing to recant. If the accuser persists in his claim and cannot prove the charge in combat, he must pay the woman's *wergeld*. If the accuser is successful in combat, the woman is to be punished "as written in this code."[60] These laws demonstrate that Lombard legalists believed in the ability of women to perform sorcery and that the craft went hand in hand with sexual promiscuity, as it does in some redactions of *Lex Salica*. The charge is severe, as it incurs the loss of the full *wergeld* of a free person. We learn at a later point in the text about one ability of the *strigae* that the authors of Rothari's code discredit. In title 376, the idea that any Christian would believe that a woman can eat a living man from within is ridiculed. This accusation is presented as both illegal and impious. Therefore, if anyone kills another man's female slave on the pretext that she is a cannibalistic *striga* or a *masca*, he must pay the slave woman's *wergeld* and a fine of one hundred *solidi*.[61]

The Lombard legislators, then, vaguely understood the *striga* to be a dangerous, predatory female. In title 198 she is like a harlot; in statute 365 she is reputed to eat men's innards (although the king does not accept this as possible). Rothari's laws display a no more articulate understanding of the exact nature of the *striga* than do the authors of the penitentials, but she appears in *Leges Longobardorum* to be an ordinary sorceress working through demons, not a demonic harpy herself.

The discussion of the striae and lamiae in the codes, taken as a whole, provides hints about the form their rituals took. They disclose information about women gathering together to carry out rites of cooking herbs and mixing magical poisons in pots provided by men, and they kill and eat humans. We also know something about the communal reaction to these nefarious women. Because the stria and lamia were feared as sorceresses, they were

---

would have trouble raising the payment for a freeman's *wergeld* of 160 *solidi*; as a result, a large *wergeld* often resulted in debt slavery.

60. *Lex Longbardorum* 197–98, in *Die Gesetze*, 76.
61. *Lex Longbardorum* 376, in *Die Gesetze*, 153.

liable to being tortured and put on the hurdle. The reaction of the populace was based on the belief that the women were necromancers with the ability to carry out dreadful, cannibalistic rituals. The laws seek to prevent people taking justice into their own hands, and they also reflect disquietude over the credence that people give the "bogus" rites, such as ingesting a person from the inside.

Similarly, in post-Roman England, feminized chthonic beings from the Anglo-Saxon tradition were brought under the Christian umbrella as she-demons. English literature attests to the concept of an unnatural female entity, which in *Beowulf* is called a *merewif*, an appellation that describes Grendel's mother. Jane Chance notes that Grendel's mother blurs sexual and social roles. "For example she arrogates to herself the masculine role of the warrior or lord."[62] Like her historic counterparts, this *merewif* dwells with shades and is a terror to men. She symbolizes descent below the abode of male warriors and is slain only by a ritual killing that involves "dreamtime" weapons. The *merewif* feasts on flesh and rules over a coven of man-eating monsters.[63] The "mighty women" and "witches" in the Anglo-Saxon healing charms discussed in chapter 14 also share some characteristics with the stria. They are malevolent female spirits who fly like darts and send "screaming spears."[64]

Diana is clearly a goddess demon, not a stria or a lamia, but she belongs in a discussion of the other female creatures due to her association with the magical power of women.[65] Her role as healer and midwife essentially disappeared in the early Middle Ages, and her attribute as mistress of the moon became normative. Clerics feared and forbade popular beliefs about commerce with Diana in the form of calling down the moon, lunar divination, and believing that women rode across the moonlit sky in company with Diana. Moon veneration clearly suggests traffic with demons. According to the Book of Enoch, the demon Sasiel taught humans to divine from the course of the moon, and the moon was itself sometimes viewed as the demon Diana. Caesarius of Arles wrote, "Stupid people think that they should help the moon in its eclipse." He held that an eclipse was natural, but some people, by incantations, trumpets, shouting, tinkling of bells, and paganistic "profane shouting," think they can beguile the moon. A Bedean penitential expresses special concern about the activities of sorcerers when

---

62. Chance, *Woman as Hero*, 95–108 (quotation 97).
63. Glosecki, *Shamanism*, 165–72.
64. Ibid., 116–18.
65. Filotas, *Pagan Survivals*, 357.

the moon is eclipsed. Implicit moon veneration is persistent in the popular, but forbidden, magical moonlunars, where momentous events or quotidian affairs are predictable by the phases of the moon.[66]

In his sermon 107, Bishop Maximus of Turin refers to a crazed, beastly *"auruspex"* called a *"dianaticus,"* a priest of the goddess Diana. In an intoxicated state he careens through the forests, striking and beating himself. The *dianaticii* were reputed to be prophetic. Although Maximus refutes this claim, it is indicative of the evolving linkage between Diana, clairvoyance, and demonism. There is also a brief mention of Diana in Gregory of Tours's sixth-century histories, where he relates the story of Saint Vulfolaic's destruction of her statue in Trier, which the people "worshipped like a god." The story has obvious echoes of Paul's encounter with the cult of Artemis in Ephesus, which no doubt acted as an archetype.[67]

In sum, there was a change in the early Middle Ages in the beliefs about the stria and lamia. In Roman antiquity these she-creatures were difficult to categorize; they were somewhere in the complex of human, divine, and demonic. The fluidity of pagan thought about the spectrum of beings meant that an understanding of the exact nature of these creatures was not particularly determinable or important. Circe, for example, shared characteristics of a goddess and a human temptress; a lamia was a cross between a succubus (a demon in the shape of women who seduces men and then dematerializes) and a goddess. However, for Christians a specific taxonomy was critical; good and evil were demarcated, and the lines between them were imperative. In the Christian paradigm, the stria and lamia lose their imprecision; they are humans trafficking with demons, pure and simple. They are not beings with preternatural abilities, but they do have sinister powers that come from demonic, malign rituals performed covertly at night.

In the post-Roman Western world, women's expertise with particular kinds of magic was taken for granted. Their sorcery was terrifying—indexed on ancient rituals drawn from rhythms of the natural world. Women wove their textiles with magic incantations, met at graveyards in the depth of night, mixed deadly potions, and consumed humans from the outside inward

---

66. Caesarius of Arles, *Sermones*, Sermon 52.3, 1:231: "Et illud quale est, quando stulti homines quasi lunae laboranti putant se debere succurrere . . . Vana paganorum persuasione sacrilegis clamoribus propitiam faciant"; Bedean Penitential 30.3, 4, in *Die Bussordnungen*, 272. On moonlunars see Flint, *Rise of Magic*, 128–46.

67. Maximus of Turin, *Collectionem sermonum antiquam* 107.2, 420–21; Gregory of Tours, *Decem libri historiarum* 8.15, 381–82: "Hic Dianae simulacrum, quod populus hic incredulus quasi deum adorabat.

(some believed) or vice versa. Just as impressive as the woman's facility with the black arts was her skill with love magic, by which the control over men and the world of men was formidable and chilling. The male sex was weak in "affairs of the heart," and sexuality was a point of particular vulnerability. Keeping control of carnal urges was one of the reasons the celibate clergy were set apart as extraordinary and heroic. Women, who were themselves defined by their corporeality, had an intuitive affinity for magic of the body. Both healing and birth magic were domains in which competition between the church, wives, and mothers was rife. As Caesarius of Arles made clear, God was directly involved in a clash with women over control of their bodies.

Perceptions of women's magic in late antiquity and post-Roman Europe had much in common; they drew on familiar themes developed around specific larger-than-life biblical and literary characters. The stereotype of women avariciously wielding magic to ensnare men and upset the body politic through secretive sorcery are absent in patristic writings about Christian women, but that archetype resurfaced in early medieval sources. Yet, however fearful, sinful, and illegal women's magic was, their sorcery was taken seriously and acted to empower them.

PART 4

Skepticism
The Carolingian Era

CHAPTER 10

Placemaking and the Natural World

> Dearest brothers . . . just a few days ago I was at home . . . [and] at the beginning of night there arose such great shouting from people that that irreverent (noise) pierced the heavens. When I asked what this clamor meant, they told me that their shouting would come to the assistance of the suffering moon and help it by their passions (to overwhelm) its failure (eclipse). But I laughed and was amazed at your vanity, that you, as supposedly devoted Christians, were bringing help to God as if he were weak and feeble and could not protect the stars he created unless helped by our voices.
>
> —Raban Maur, Homily 142

It is difficult to generalize about magic between 750 and 1025 because there was such disparity between Europe's core lands and its margins. Here, "core" is a reference to the regions that had been Romanized, proselytized in the early phase of conversion, and introduced to the concept of centralized regnal government by post-Roman kings. The "margins" are areas of the Continent that were folded into the dominant Christian culture as a result of Merovingian expansion.[1]

In the latter half of the early Middle Ages, Europe and England underwent an accelerated program of Christian renewal. Manifestations of worship that cultural elites deemed to be residual paganisms or unsanctioned innovations continued to be interpreted as traffic with demons. However, intellectuals talked about the problem of magic differently than their predecessors had. The majority were skeptical about most of the putative abilities of magicians and tended to focus on errors of belief more than on the commission of magic acts they considered futile. Where magical activities were discussed, the emphasis was largely on the disruption to the Christian community caused by sins of intention rather than on the immediate harm

---

1. My notion of "core" and "margins" is informed by Costambeys, Innes, and MacLean, *Carolingian World*, 9–16; Innes, *State and Society*, 1–10; Althoff, *Spielregeln der Politik*, 126–53; Airlie, "Aristocracy," 99–104.

those acts inflicted. Authorities were interested in stamping out persisting un-Christian ritual and superstitious practices (along with the beliefs that generated them) and bringing irregular behaviors in line with the increasingly centralized church and state ideology and ritual strategies. The efficacy of female sorcery in particular came under attack with the result that women's prestige was undermined.

In the margins, clergy were engaged in evangelization and putting in place a basic ecclesiastical structure, much as they had been in the core lands during the late antique and the post-Roman periods. The types of magic their predecessors perceived had not changed.[2] Even specific practices were similar to those of the past, except we know more about them because those who kept records did so with more precision and specificity. Their thoroughness makes thick description possible and enhances our ability to determine whether the behaviors laid out in the sources were taking place in real time.[3] What did change, however, was the governing response to the magical and superstitious customs both of the peoples newly incorporated into the empire and of populations that had long been Christianized. Although nobody questioned demons' existence or their ability to trick and deceive, hierarchs were dubious that humans in league with devils were able to impose their will in the world with any real effect. Most magic was illusionary and not harmful except to the deluded individuals who attempted it and to the body politic that tolerated it. Efforts to impose uniformity and expunge illicit activity intensified and became ever more strident under the Carolingian partnership of bishops, missionaries, kings, and queens.

Idolatry, Sacred Space, and Nature Worship

As Slavic, Celtic, and Norse paganisms were folded into Christian cultural hegemony in post-Roman Europe and the British Isles, new, nominally, or differently Christianized peoples vacillated between the state religion and the pagan cults of their ancestors. Overt paganism and outdoor rites persisted

---

2. From McKitterick (*New Cambridge Medieval History*, 93), the continuation of paganism in the eighth century demonstrates that there was a cultural boundary between the margins and core lands along the old Roman border, although Carolingian governance straddled it.

3. From Hen (*Early Medieval West*, 192), Carolingians were more "systematic and extravagant" in collecting "recycled old prohibitions," and so they produced "larger, fuller, and more elaborate canonical compilations." From Geertz (*Interpretation of Cultures*, 3–30), thick description is a method of explaining human actions with as much detail as possible. "The essential task of theory building here is not to codify abstract regularities, but to make thick description possible; not to generalize across cases, but to generalize within them" (quotation 26).

throughout the later part of the early Middle Ages. Certainly this was true on the margins, but even in the core lands, familiarity with nature deities was often enacted quite openly (if not in self-identified cults), and continued to pose a challenge for the royal/ecclesiastical establishment. In *Truth-Spots*, Thomas Gieryn asks the question, "What are places distinctively good at doing?" In the early Middle Ages, particular outdoor spots were good at triggering the cultural memory of a populist sacrality not promoted in the enclosed space of the Christian church. For the establishment, the outdoors was the playground of devils and good at enabling idolatrous pantheism and traffic with demons.[4]

A text called the *Indiculus superstitionum et paganiarum*, which was promulgated 744 or 745, contains several interdictions against veneration of nature or worship in natural settings. It is an adumbration of superstitions and pagan customs that appears to be an index of practices that may have been appended to a now-lost manuscript that explained the behaviors in more detail, but the genesis, author and purpose of the list are uncertain. The *Indiculus* is preserved in a codex following the canons of the German Council of 742. Boniface or one of his companions may be the author.[5] In the inventory of forbidden rituals and the beliefs underlying them, the *Indiculus* lists as suspect rites in the woods, "those things that they do on stones," activities at fountains, or sacrifices at "indeterminant places that they celebrate as holy."[6] The catalogue reveals alarm about worship that has any reference to the sun, moon, and stars, such as the forbidden "feasts of swine in February" or sun festivals.[7] Several entries in the *Indiculus* refer to practices that are not evident in earlier materials, making it likely that the rites (or reports of the rites) were local and contemporaneous.

---

4. Gieryn, *Truth-Spots*, 171–77 (quotation 172). On outdoor cults see Filotas, *Pagan Survivals*, chap. 3; I. Wood, *Missionary Life*, 253–61. From Bowes (*Private Worship, Public Values*, 162), Christianization of the countryside was not a contest between "pagans" and "Christians," but between "different kinds of Christian communities." For a similar view see Fifshitz (*Norman Conquest*, 4) who notes that conversion was often a matter of convincing rustic folk to "abandon their definition of Christianity in favor of a new one."

5. The title of the *Indiculus* (meaning "short list of superstitions and pagan practices") is a modern one. Hen ("Early Medieval West," 183) writes that the *Indiculous* "stands at the core of any discussion of magic in the early medieval West." Dierkens, "Superstitions, christianisme."

6. *Indiculus superstitionum* 6 (*De sacris silvarum quae nimidas vocant*); 7 (*De hiis quae faciunt super petras*); 11 (*De fontibus sacrificiorum*); 18 (*De incertis locis que colunt pro sanctis*), all at 223.

7. Ibid., 3 (*De spurcalibus in Februario*); 21 (*De lunae defectione quod dicunt 'vince luna'*); 30 (*De eo quod credunt quia femine lunam comendet, quod possint corda hominum tollere iuxta paganos*), all at 223. See also *Homilia de sacrilegiis* 3.10, 3.12, both p. 8. On the moon see Filotas, *Pagan Survivals*, 120–32.

As Carolingian culture expanded into Saxony, intellectuals blithely applied the term *superstitio* to Saxons' "foreign" customs.[8] Geoffrey Koziol rightly notes that Carolingian thinkers did not develop a concept of "myth" as a prism for appreciating different cultures; rather, they defined the mythologies of the "other" as misguided, superstitious, and sacrilegious.[9]

The Carolingians' "Saxon problem"—that being their repeated apostasy—was a thorn festering in Charlemagne's side during his early reign, and the First Saxon Capitulary (issued at an assembly in Paderborn in 782 or 785) was a response to that perceived perfidy.[10] The capitulary stipulates that the Saxons adhere to Christian rituals and attend Christian churches instead of practicing pagan rites at the shrines of idols. For example, if anyone sacrifices a man to demons "according to the custom of the pagans, he will be put to death." Anyone who wished to conceal himself, scorn baptism, and remain a pagan was also to be put to death. The capitulary imposes a fine on anyone who offers prayers at springs, trees, or groves, or who makes an offering in the manner of the Gentiles and consumes it in honor of demons.[11] The text exudes frustration with the vitality of demonic paganism and infuriation at the rejection of Christian rites. Sometime between 817 and 830, Einhard composed a biography of Charlemagne that characterizes the prevailing view of the Saxons during their conflicts with the Carolingians. "The Saxons, like most of the German peoples, were fierce by nature and given to the worship of demons. [They were] opposed to our religion, and did not consider it dishonorable to transgress and violate human or divine law."[12]

---

8. From Rembold (*Conquest and Christianization*, 4–11), early medieval Saxony extended over the greater part of what is modern northwest Germany. The Carolingian polity under Charlemagne essentially imposed an ethnogenesis on a range of peoples who lived in the same region but had no internally coherent sense of ethnicity, culture, or governmental authority. "Saxony" first came into being in the imagination of Frankish conquerors and from there took on a reality.

9. Koziol, "Truth and Its Consequences."

10. From Rembold (*Conquest and Christianization*, 85–140), the *Stellinga* revolt (841–842/3) occurred about sixty years after the first Saxon wars. The Saxons did not self-identify as pagans; rather, the tag "pagan" was employed to discredit Emperor Lothar who supported the *Stellinga*. From Goldberg ("Popular Revolt"), during the *Stellinga* uprising, pagan symbols and rites became a banner of resistance for lower status groups as a part of their protest against the nobles' collaboration with the Carolingian warring factions. From Couser ("Inventing Paganism"), a similar situation obtained in the case of "pagan" uprisings in Carantania from 769–772. See Wickham, *Framing the Middle Ages*, 585–88; Karras, "Pagan Survivals."

11. Capitulatio de partibus Saxoniae 6, 8–9, 21, in *MGH Cap.* 1.26, 68–69 (quotation 9: "more paganorum daemonibus obtulerit, morte moriatur"). See Effros, "De partibus Saxoniae" on burial and human sacrifice.

12. Einhard, *Vita Karoli Magni* 7, 9: "Que nullum neque prolixius neque atrocius Francorumque populo laboriosius susceptum est; quia Saxones, sicut omnes fere Germaniam incolentes nationes, et natura feroces et cultui daemonum dediti nostraeque religioni contrarii neque divina neque humana iura vel polluere vel transgredi inhonestum arbitrabantur." It is well to keep in mind that *The Life of*

There was more at stake in the Saxon wars than an effort to impose ideological and behavioral standardization. Conversion went hand in hand with political assimilation, and baptism was a tool of the state to bring the conquered to heel. In other words, religion was brought to the service of the royal government, and law was brought to the service of the church. The penalizing nature of the mandates makes it difficult for a modern reader to imagine that one of the goals of the capitulary was edification and redemption of souls, but in a tough-love sort of way, this was the case. The draconian treatment of the Saxons was not simply a policy of raw domination. For Charlemagne and his reform party, an enlightened and safe society was a Christian society.[13]

The language of the Saxon Capitulary regarding prayers at springs, trees, or groves and feasting on sacrificial meat is reminiscent of Merovingian councils, vitae, sermons, penitentials, and letters. For example, it echoes Martin of Braga's warning to his congregation about lighting candles at "rocks and at trees and at streams and at crossroads."[14] It is tempting to dismiss the charges against the Saxon pagans as devitalized indictments inspired by authoritative literature from an earlier period and not reflective of Saxon pantheistic nature cults. It is true that the language of the capitularies is imitative and likely—given clerics' knowledge of Merovingian legal, pastoral, and canonical writings—that earlier texts were used as a template. However, there are aspects of the First Saxon Capitulary that are distinctive. For example, sacrificing a man to demons or hiding to avoid baptism are not elements copied from earlier materials. In any case, the point is that the Carolingian author associated traffic with demons and the natural world.

The emblematic act of destroying a pagan place of worship and replacing it with the Christian counterpart, captured in Merovingian-era heroic texts, continued into the Carolingian period on the margins of the core lands. Like Saint Martin before him, Boniface, the famed missionary who proselytized in Frisia and was martyred there in 754, felled a sacred tree, Jupiter's

---

Charlemagne presents a romanticized version of the emperor which was written many years after his death when he had become a legend—larger than life—and it is modelled after Suetonius's *Lives of the Caesars*. However, that does not diminish the value of this text as evidence for the view of the Saxons in the late eighth- and early ninth-centuries. See McKitterick, *Charlemagne*, 7–25, 103–6; 251–71.

13. See Alberi ("Evolution of Alcuin's Concept") for a discussion of Alcuin's conception of "the Carolingian *imperium* that united many Christian *populi* under a lord dedicated to the conversion of the nations before the Last Judgement" (8) and how the struggle against pagan idolatry was necessary in order to maintain that *imperium*. See de Jong ("Empire as *Ecclesia*," 226), "No preaching of the faith was possible without rulers dominating those to be converted."

14. Martin of Braga, *De correctione rusticorum* 16, 198: "ad petras et ad arbores et ad fontes et per trivia."

Oak, near Fritzlar in northern Hesse. According to his biographer, Willibald (d. ca. 787), this dramatic (and staged) spectacle was necessary because the people were offering sacrifices to trees and springs and inspecting entrails for auguries while chanting incantations. Boniface was in the process of chopping the oak down when a wind arose and blew the ancient tree over. In the tradition of textual depictions of post-Roman missionaries, the saint used the wood to build a church dedicated to Saint Peter.[15]

Charlemagne followed suit in 772 when the Franks and Saxons were in all-out war; he destroyed the holy tree-shrine called an Irminsul in an effort to eradicate non-Christian sites, which were invariably open-air. When Charlemagne came upon the Irminsul, it stood in a place barren of water, but owing to the king's piety and by "divine grace" (*divina gratia*), water began to flow so that Charlemagne could keep his men there several days while they destroyed the shrine completely.[16] The miraculous spring denotes a contrast between the fecundity of life-sustaining Christianity and the sterility of the pagan Irminsul. It was a ritual baptism of space. Charlemagne's highly symbolic actions had an important political dimension in that they magnified the imperative of compliance to the Carolingian regime's religion. The felling of the Irminsul was evocative because its message was multivariate and written in ritual code. The synergetic bond between nature and paganism was robust in the margins, and Charlemagne ceremoniously broke it asunder. Together, king and church worked to eradicate the sanctification of nature.

A few years after Charlemagne obliterated Irminsul, in his vita of Saint Sturm (d. 779), Eigil (d. 882), first abbot of Fulda, has Sturm preaching to the people of Flanders and drawing on a standard formula. "Forsake idols and images, take up the faith of Christ, destroy the temples of [the pagans] gods, mow down their groves, and build holy churches [in their place]."[17] The author of the anonymous late-eighth-century *Homilia de sacrilegiis* (*Homilia*) disallows a Christian worshipping at trees, mountains, rivers, rocks, or "other places he goes," (*alia loca uadet*) and forbids him from offering animals to idols and feasting on them in such places. Pastorals echo this refrain: Mass should not be celebrated out of doors;[18] it is the domain of devils. Across

---

15. Willibald, *Vita Bonifati* 6, 30–36. On the vita of Boniface see *Soldiers of Christ*, xxxi–xl, 107–8.
16. Annales regni Francorum 772, 34–35.
17. Eigil, *Vita S. Strumi* 22, 376: "Ut idola et simulacra derelinquerent, Christi fidem susciperent, deorum suorum templa destruerent, lucos succiderent, sanctas quoque bisilicas aedificarent."
18. *Homilia de sacrilegiis* 2.2, 6 (quotation); 3.10, 3.12, 8. Carl Paul Caspari, a Norwegian professor of Old Testament theology, first discovered and edited the *Homilia* in 1881. Theodulf of Orléans, First Capitulary 11, 110: "Missarum solemnia nequaquam alibi nisi in ecclesia celebranda sunt, non in quibuslibet domibus et in vilibus locis, sed in loco quem elegerit dominus."

the channel in Anglo-Saxon England, Aelfric of Eynsham condemned worship in and adoration of the outdoors in traditional language. Some are "so blinded, that they bring their offerings to an earth-fast stone, and eke to trees, and to well-springs . . . and will not understand how foolishly they act, or how the dead stone or the dumb tree can help them, or give them health. . . . The Christian man must cry to his Lord with mind and with mouth, and beseech his protection." Audrey Meaney notes that Aelfric spoke with particular urgency in response to the influx of a vigorous paganism entering England with the Viking invasions from Scandinavia.[19]

Church promotional literature always offered worshippers who were deprived of their outdoor sacred sites the traditional alternative—the safe space of the consecrated church. When Boniface was bishop of Mainz and proselytizing in the forests of largely unconverted Frisia, he wrote to Pope Zacharias criticizing priests who carried on their ministry, not in churches, but "in the open country in the huts of the country folk."[20] One of the problems with unhallowed spaces was that devils may be lurking. When the bishops attending a ninth-century synod held in Cologne dedicated a church to Saint Peter, the voices of several devils were heard complaining that now they would have to find a new abode. Demons could not tolerate consecrated walled spaces.[21] This motif was an inheritance from the early church clearly memorialized in the pages of Eusebius's history; Constantine and his mother Helena crisscrossed the Holy Land annihilating the dwelling places of demons and replacing them with houses of God.

The concern with improper ritual and religious behavior are topics in Charlemagne's sweeping, programmatic reform capitularies, which are heavily dependent on scripture and ecclesiastical decrees. Personal habits at odds with sanctioned forms of observance were thought to be disruptive to the societal peace, harmony, and unity on which the security of the state depended. Among these habits was outdoor worship. The most

---

19. Aelfric of Eynsham, *On Auguries*, in *Aelfric's Lives of Saints*, 1:364–83 (quotation 372–75). Meaney, "Aethelweard, Aelfric, and the Norse Gods." On the church reform movement in England see Jurasinski (*Old English Penitentials*, 209) who notes: "The clerical reform of Anglo-Saxon legal institutions over the course of the tenth century is commonly and rightly regarded as an attempt to model English legislation after Carolingian example."

20. Boniface, *Die Briefe* 80, 172–80: "non in aecclesia catholica, sed per agrestia loca, per cellas rusticorum." On pagan outdoor worship, see I. Wood, "Pagan Religion and Superstitions," 255–57, 268–78; Flint, *Rise of Magic*, 172.

21. *Annales Fuldenses* 870, 72. On the Carolingian artistic and architectural construction of sacred space see S. Collins, *Carolingian Debate*. On outdoor space see Treffort, "Consécration de cimetière."

significant of the reform documents was the General Admonition (789).[22] It states, "Regarding trees and stones and springs where foolish people place candles or carry out other such observances, we categorically command that these most offensive practices, execrable to God, be uprooted and destroyed wherever they are found." The reference to placing candles is reminiscent Martin of Braga's letter to Bishop Polemius about using candles as markings in the woods. Another principal reform capitulary issued from Frankfurt (794), asserts the authority of the king to destroy trees and groves, which Charlemagne had done in 772 at Heresburg in Saxony.[23]

Although the language of the councils is staunchly traditional, it is reasonable to assume that ritualistic nature veneration of some sort was taking place. This is the case particularly in what I have called the margins (such as Saxony and east of the Rhine). A hint of this is the fact that the Frankfurt Council was called in response to setbacks in Saxony in 792, and the sanctions against sacred trees and groves may have needed to be reinforced. However, more important than whether or not councils realistically represented contemporary behaviors is the fact that restrictions against what canonists considered residual pagan practices, that were once the business of missionaries and priests, found voice in Carolingian secular legislation. The substance of capitular prohibitions was similar to proscriptive church literature of an earlier era, but the language had hardened. Outdoor activities became the concern of the crown because they were "execrable to God" (*Deo execrabilis*) and inimical to a rightly ordered society. Magic behaviors and the rituals that supported those behaviors, which had at one time been of pastoral concern for the sake of the individual soul or matters of personal injury to others, became relevant to public policy. This shift is attributable to the shared goals of Carolingian ecclesiastical and secular reformers.[24]

As Christian writings had done from the first century, Carolingian-era texts proscribe lunar rites. The *Indiculus* prohibits moon worship, the goal

---

22. The General Admonition is more than just a legal document; it is Charlemagne's manifesto for a new social order and the political blueprint for a city of God that lays out the proper relationship of the parts to the whole: bishops dealing with priests, men with women, laypeople with clerics, and the king with his subjects. Eastwood, *Ordering the Heavens*, 6–8; McKitterick, *Frankish Church*, 1–19.

23. *Die Admonitio generalis*. 64, 216: "Item de arboribus vel petris vel fontibus, ubi aliqui stulti luminaria vel alias observationes faciunt, omnino mandamus, ut iste pessimus usus et deo execrabilis, ubicumque inveniatur, tollatur et distruatur." Martin of Braga, *De correctione rusticorum* 16, 198; *Synodus Franconofurtensis* 43, in *MGH Cap.* 1.28, 77.

24. See McKitterick (*New Cambridge Medieval History*, 103) on the Frankfort Council. From S. Collins (*Carolingian Debate*, 121–29), the Carolingian period witnessed fraught debates on the nature of religious space and whether or not a building could be a sanctuary of absolute purity, different than and separate from the mundane world.

of which was to override eclipses by calling out the name of the moon. It reads, "Of the eclipse of the moon, what they call: 'Triumphant Moon.'"[25] The supportive—even nurturing—relationship between the moon and those who revered her is familiar from classical pagan and Christian literature. The injunction against coming to the rescue of the moon in the *Indiculus* is economical,[26] but other sources describe moon veneration in more colorful detail. The *Homilia* forbids Christians from call[ing] out the new moon against the old or "striking wood bowls with straps when the moon is in '*defeccionem*" (eclipse)." The inclusion of wooden bowls and straps are details new to the lexicon of prohibitions against lunar magic. The archbishop of Mainz Raban Maur (d. 856), known as the Teacher of Germany, was one of the keenest minds and prolific writers of the Carolingian era. His homily 142 demonstrates that moon magic was practiced in ninth-century northern Francia. This chapter opens with Raban Maur's gentle chiding of his parishioners because they believe that human beings have the ability to participate in natural processes by encouraging the moon in her efforts to fight against an eclipse. The bishop goes on to describe other novel popular rites related to the moon, such as shooting burning arrows toward it.[27]

The church was insistent that it manage sacred ritual with unconditional veto power, but that proved difficult with respect to moon worship. Despite attempts to stop the practices, people continued to carry out highly ritualized lunar rites, and according to Raban Maur's homily, the rituals assumed a performative dimension as participants gathered as a community to aid the moon in her fight against obliteration. Barbara Myerhoff notes that "no primitive society is so unempirical as to expect to cause rain by dancing a rain dance. . . . A rain dance is, in Burke's felicitous phrase, a dance with the rain, the dancing of an attitude, . . . collectively attending, dramatizing, making palpable unseen forces." The same is true of calling out the moon, which engaged peasants in a universal phenomenon, vast and awesome.[28] The people banged pans and shot arrows into the sky in homey rituals that gave them a share in a natural process that was both cosmic and

---

25. *Indiculus superstitionum* 21, 223: "De lunae defectione quod dicunt, 'vince luna!'"
26. Chazelle (*Crucified God*, 2–3) argues that inherited texts often adapt traditional imagery to express the values of their redactors.
27. *Homilia de sacrilegiis* 5.16, 10: "Quicumque [in] defeccionem lunae, quando scuriscere solet, per clamorem populi uasa lignea et erea amentea battent, ahb strias depositam ipsa luna reuocare in caelum credent[les], uel qui grandinem per laminas plubeas scriptas et per cornus incantatos auertere potant, isti non christiani sed pagani sunt." Raban Maur, *Homilia* 142, cols. 78–80 (quotation 78): "laboranti lunae vestra vociferatio subvenisset, et defectum eius suis studiis adjuvaret." The epigraph to this chapter is from Raban Maur's homily translated by Dutton in *Carolingian Civilization*, 365.
28. Myerhoff, "Death in Due Time," 170.

personal.²⁹ Rituals such as calling down the moon were participatory as much as instrumental, but in such rites the potential was prodigious for the attitudes fostered in moon ceremonies to take hold, and those sensibilities were un-Christian. They implied symmetry between humans and the movement of the celestial bodies and cooperative causation.

Ample evidence attests that other "aberrant" religious rituals were endemic throughout the Carolingian era. However, the sources—never written by the participants—cannot tell us whether the Christianized *rustici* who gathered outdoors and honored the elements were consciously honoring alternative numinous forces—other deities—or simply continuing time-honored ceremonies without attention to their orthodoxy. Jean-Claude Schmitt rightly warns of the danger of too deftly making assumptions about belief from behavior in just such a case as this where the actors cannot explain their motives.³⁰

It would appear that authorities of the era were often as unsure as we are of the peasants' aims, and they gave the *rustici* the benefit of the doubt. Those who set policy did not blindly and automatically condemn every practice that remotely resembled paganistic folk customs or seemed superstitious. Rather, they recognized that the ill-informed parishioners might, at times, perpetuate traditional and much-loved rites without understanding that their outdoor rituals were demonic. This is because in the Carolingian era, intention is what mattered. The magic in itself was vain, but the ill-placed faith people put in it was dangerous. This approach resembles early Christian sensitivities to the motives of well-intentioned Christians who lived in a pagan society where it was difficult to distinguish between customs that were innocuous from those that smacked of demonism. Two documents that acknowledge the nuances of act and intention are a letter from Boniface and a ninth-century penitential. The first is from the margins of the Carolingian polity, and the second comes from a region long Christianized

Boniface disparaged nominally Christian (or badly socialized) rural clergy who indulged in numerous pagan practices, including sacrificing bulls and goats to heathen gods and eating the flesh or offering it to the dead. He put this seeming paganism down to stupidity and not genuine idolatry, or trafficking with demons.³¹

---

29. Geertz (*Interpretation of Cultures*, 113–18) says that at some point rituals cross spontaneously into communal theater, and the ceremonies for calling down the moon are examples.
30. Schmitt, *Les revenants*, 19.
31. Boniface, *Die Briefe* 80, 172–77. On the correspondence of Boniface see *Letters of Saint Boniface*, preface.

In the early-ninth century, Bishop Halitgar of Cambrai (d. ca. 831) wrote the *Pseudo-Roman Penitential* (late 820s) on the instructions of Ebbo (d. 851), the archbishop of Reims. In it Halitgar seeks to untangle the mixed motives of the peasants who perform outdoor rites.[32] The penitential is divided into chapters, each treating a particular type of offense. Regulations against magic and sacrilege are separated. Under magic, the author lists malicious homicide, love magic, abortions, and conjuring storms. He views sacrilege somewhat differently; it is demonic, but not in the same way as maleficium. For Halitgar, sacrilege includes various types of divination and a person making or releasing another from a vow beside a tree, spring, lattice, "or anywhere except in a church." Haltigar avows that the enclosed Christian space is a bastion against demonic incursion. Anyone who eats or drinks at natural sites must do a year's penance. It is forbidden to eat food from a sacrifice even when it is not consumed at the natural site but carried home. The reason for these prohibitions is clear: "This is a sacrilege or a demonic thing."[33] "Sacrilege" is synonymous with traffic with demons. The canon is a hybrid of Paul's injunction, "You cannot partake of the table of the Lord and the table of demons" (I Cor. 10:20–21), and a vow taken at a natural site.

Halitgar is concerned because the sacrilege may imply intentional idolatry and even active cult organization, or it may be, in the spirit of Boniface's assessment of errant Frisian priests, the result of ignorance or gluttony. The author carefully seeks to unravel the motives of the peasants who perform the rites to order to ascertain their state of mind.

> If anyone eats or drinks next to a [pagan] shrine, if he does this through ignorance, he must promise never to repeat it, and he must do penance on bread and water for forty days. If, however, out of contempt, he does it, that is after a priest has told him this it is sacrilege, then he has communicated at the table of demons. If he did this filthy thing only from gluttony, he will do penance for three forty-day periods on bread and water. But if he did this truly for the worship of demons and in honor of an idol, he must do three years penance. . . . If anyone has sacrificed under compulsion a second and third, he will be subjugated

---

32. Significantly, Ebbo of Reims (d. ca. 860), who ordered the work to be written, was himself born a peasant.

33. *Poenitentiale Romanum* 38, in *Die Bussbücher* 1:479: "Si quis ad arbores vel ad fontes vel ad cancellum vel ubicumque excepto in ecclesia, votum voverit aut exsolverit, III annos cum pane et aqua poeniteat, quia hoc sacrilegium est vel daemoniacum." From Frantzen (*Literature of Penance*, 7–9), the intention and inner state of a penitent were present in penitential discipline from its earliest development in the sixth century, but motive for such considerations were of a different nature by the ninth century. For example see *Poenitentiale Columbans* B.24, in *Die Bussbücher*, 1:600.

to a three-year penance. . . . If anyone consumes blood or carrion or whatever has been sacrificed to idols and it is not necessary to do so, he, will fast for twelve weeks.[34]

The *Pseudo-Roman Penitential* shows sensitivity to intent and isolates the sin of consent. Ignorance gets a slap on the wrist, gluttony receives a sharper sanction, but genuine idolatry is a grave offense. Both Boniface and Halitgar recognized the complex interplay of magic, ritual, and the social pressure inherent in communal collective behavior, and they understood how all three were knotted together within long-established patterns of conduct. Neither man responded to rude traditionalism in the same way they did to persisting idolatry. Their modulated response to demonism demonstrates that for Carolingian thinkers the peril of magic was not in the immediate danger it posed. Nor was the question as to what demons could or could not do of great interest. If that were the case, the intention of the actor would be less irrelevant. The state of mind of the offender was most at issue because magic was a byproduct of the wrong-headed beliefs of those who tried to carry it out. Whereas post-Roman legislation against magic turned on the harm it caused to others, the *Pseudo-Roman Penitential* is intently focused on volition.

The rituals on the Kalends of January that so bedeviled the Merovingians continued into the next dynasty, or at least descriptions of them continued. However, the Carolingians chronicled Kalends rituals less frequently and with decreased fervor, immediacy and detail. It seems improbable that public celebrations at which people donned the masks of animals and roamed the village byways persisted from the late fifth century into the ninth century. Because historians are so well informed about the specifics of the original January first events, we can more easily evaluate whether Carolingian descriptions of them are based on real-time observation, which I judge they

---

34. Poenitentiale Romanum 42–44, in *Die Bussbücher*, 1:480: "Si quis manducaverit aut biberit juxta fanum, si per ignorantiam, promittat deinceps, quod numquam reiteret, et quadraginta diebus in pane et aqua poeniteat, si vero per contemptum hoc fecerit, id est, postquam sacerdos ei praedicavit, quod sacrilegium hoc erat, mensae daemoniorum communicaverit, si gulae tantum vitio hoc fecerit, tres quadragesima in pane et aqua poeniteat. Si vero pro cultu daemonum et honore simulacri hoc fecerit, tres annos poeniteat. . . . Si quis secundo et tertio immolatus per vim, tres annos subjaceat, et duobus sine oblatione communicet, tertio ad perfectum suscipiatur. Si quis manducaverit sanguinem aut morticinum aut idolis immolatum, et non fuit ei necessitas, jejunet hebdomadas duodecim." The reference to sacrificing *"per vim"* in Halitgar's penitential is noteworthy. That phrase implies the existence of people forceful and committed enough to the rituals surrounding the sacrificial meal that they are able to coerce the unwilling to participate in a ceremony that includes an idol. However, this reading begs the question as to why, if a person is compelled to sacrifice, the sentence is so severe, particularly in a chapter where the canonist is sensitive to intention.

are not. For one thing, a brazen display of such a patently extra-ecclesiastical nature would certainly have been taken up in reform legislation.

There is little doubt that anxiety over the notion of popular Kalends-type celebrations persisted over several centuries. New elements of the New Year's observations surface in Carolingian prohibitionary writings, where they merge with traditional Kalends activities. The *Homilia* forbids celebrations at the Kalends of January and discourages people from leaving their hearths and homes on the first night of any month. The homilist outlines specific customs that attend the celebration of January first. They include ornamenting the table with bread, dressing in the skins of deer and cattle, and men cross-dressing. The Iberian *Penitential of Silos* (ca. 1050), from the monastery of San Millán in northern Spain, forbids woolen work in connection with the numinous Kalends of January, when girls desiring husbands offer pieces of woven wool to spirits. The *Saint Hubert Penitential* (ca. 850) reproves those who cross-dress or disguise themselves as beasts.[35] As in the Merovingian period, totemism was the major factor motivating censure of the Kalends ceremonies. The celebration of January One had become the demon's smorgasbord, aflame with idolatry and a threat to Christian cultural hegemony. Ritual is a method of "making meaning,"[36] and the Kalends of January did just that by providing an environment where peasants staged performances of their own design. The actors drew on a-Christian myths and engaged in un-Christian—the is demonic—rites, or so the clergy imagined.

Weather Magic

The Christian position throughout the first millennium was that the weather fell under God's purview. Atypically, Carolingian elites, who were generally skeptical about the grandiose claims of magicians, were of several minds as to whether humans, aided by demons, could actually control the elements. Weather making is a frequent motif in early hagiography, where it is acceptable only for especially holy men and women, but even saints shy away from weather marvels in Carolingian texts. This is due partially to the fact that some Carolingian thinkers attempted to provide a corrective to what they

---

35. *Homilia de sacrilegiis* 5.17, 10; 7.23–26, 12–15; 7.26, 15: "Non potestis mense domini partitipare et mense demoniorum"; *Paenitentiale Silense* 7.106, 27; *Medieval Handbooks of Penance*, 288n8; *Poenitentiale Hubertense* 42, in *Die Bussbücher*, 2:311–12. The woven cloth the girls offer to spirits as recorded in the Silos penitential ties back to the perception that women wove love spells in the *gynaecea*. From Meens (*Penance*, 169, 221), the Silos penitential was composed under royal initiative based on Carolingian exemplars.

36. MacAloon, "Introduction: Cultural Performances," 1–3.

considered an overemphasis on miracles by reinforcing a theme, nascent in patristic writing, that devotion and Christian virtue were the most meaningful and criterial attributes of sanctity.[37] As Carolingian hagiographers moved away from ascribing stupendous and histrionic marvels to their protagonists, the discomfort about those who would imitate God's meteorological wonders rose concomitantly.

Although all Carolingian sources are clear that weather manipulation is an attempt to traffic with demons, authors are inconsistent about its efficacy. As pernicious an affront to God's majesty as conjuring by storms was, it was not universally discredited the way other stupendous feats of magic, such as necromancy, were. The notion that meddling with the climate was a possibility, and not an illusion, shows up in numerous sources. Several councils condemned weather makers, the *Indiculus* warns against those who manipulate the elements by use of horns and shells, and the *Homilia* does the same in regard to horns and writings on lead plates. A 789 Carolingian capitulary forbids baptizing bells and hanging charms on poles to ward off hail, and an anonymous eighth-century sermon urges peasants to protect themselves from storms by seeking out a church rather than resorting to "diabolical observances."[38]

In the capitular General Admonition, *tempestarii* control the skies by use of cow horns and spoons. Around 775 an insular scholar named Cathwulf wrote to Charlemagne warning the king to be on the lookout for *tempestarii* and other *malefici*.[39] The *Pseudo-Roman Penitential* forbids conjuring up storms and assigns a penance of seven years on bread and water.[40] The record of the reform Council of Paris (829) reads, "By their magic they are able to stir up the air and bring down hail."[41] This reveals an unambiguous posture on the reality of *tempestarii*. These *malefici* are "able" (*posse*) to cause storms. All of these texts (three of them produced within the orbit of Carolingian courts) censure weather magic but do not deny its actuality. Archbishop Agobard of

---

37. Rampton, "Frankish Holy Women." In Rogations rituals, Christians, under the direction of a pastor, sought to influence the weather and propitiate the divine for favorable growing conditions. This, however, was a far cry from weather magic. See Dutton, *Charlemagne's Mustache*, 182–83. For England see *Eleven Old English Rogationtide Homilies*, xv–xvii.

38. *Indiculus superstitionum* 22, 223; *Homilia de sacrilegiis* 4.16, 10. It is tempting to correlate the spell tablets to the lead plates used in late antiquity for binding spells; see chap. 4. *Duplex legationis edictum* 34, in *MGH Cap.* 1.23, 64. See Filotas (*Pagan Survivals*, 274) for the sermon.

39. *Admonitio generalis* 64, 216; Cathwulf, *Letter to Charlemagne*, 504; Story, "Cathwulf." Garrison notes ("Letters") that Cathuulf [sic] "gave legitimacy to the notion that the Old Testament was a source of legislation applicable to contemporary conditions."

40. *Poenitentiale Romanum* 33, in *Die Bussbücher*, 1:479.

41. Council of Paris 69, 669: "Ferunt enim suis maleficiis aera posse conturbare et grandines inmittere."

Lyon's (d. 840) tract *On Hail and Thunder* further documents the prevalence of belief in weather magic when he observes that "almost everyone—nobles and common people, city folk and country folk, the old and young—believe that hail and thunder can be caused by the will of humans."[42]

Agobard's position on the effectiveness of weather magic differed from that of other Carolingian elites, and it was absolute: no mortal can control the elements, tout court. His *On Hail and Thunder* attests to a widespread opinion among the Lyonnais that mortals are able to manage the weather and that specialists exist who exercise that control. Bishop Agobard came upon a crowd (sometime in 815 or 816) about to stone four captives, three men and one woman, whom they had bound in chains. The villagers said they apprehended sailors from skyborne boats coming from the mystical land of Magonia (magic land) "from which ships travel in the clouds." For a price, local *tempestarii* produced ruinous storms through incantations; then the Magonians collected the flattened crops from the fields that had been thrashed by the storms. Weather magicians could also prevent storms if they were sufficiently recompensed. In this treatise against *tempestarii*, Agobard of Lyon relies on Old Testament evidence from Exodus, Job, the Psalms, Joshua, and Ecclesiastes, among others, to demonstrate that none but God controls the weather. He asks how great is the crime of those who attribute to humans the work of God? Not only does Agobard emphatically deny that *tempestarii* actually affect the elements, he also faults those who subscribe to the proposition that anyone but God can raise or quell storms.[43]

How should we view Agobard's stance on the effectiveness of weather sorcery given the evidence from other contemporary sources? The Spanish *Penitential of Silos* (Agobard, was himself a Spaniard) contains language that resembles Agobard's viewpoint; it forbids the belief that devils have the power to make thunder, lightning, storms, or drought. Valerie Flint suggests that the unusual ruling in this Iberian penitential is likely a reaction against the Priscillianist heresy, which maintained that rain occurs when the "Light-Virgin" and the Prince of Darkness have amorous relations.[44] Both Agobard

---

42. Agobard of Lyon, *De grandine et tonitruis* 1, 3: "In his regionibus pene omnes homines, nobiles et ignobiles, urbani et rustici, senes et iuuenes, putant grandines et tonitrua hominum libitu posse fieri."

43. Ibid., 3, 4–5; 7, 7–9; (2, 4: "ex qua naues ueniant in nubibus"). One of the reasons Agobard wrote his tract was to discourage the credulous from paying for weather-making services that could only be ineffective (15, 14). See Dutton, "Thunder and Hail over the Carolingian Countryside," in *Charlemagne's Moustache*, 169–88; Boshof, *Erzbischof Agobard von Lyon*, 170–76.

44. *Paenitentiale Silense* 11.207, 37; Flint, *Rise of Magic*, 111. Priscillianism is a Christian heresy that developed in Roman Spain in the fourth century under the leadership of Priscillian. It incorporated Gnostic and Manichean theologies.

and the *Penitential of Silos* anathematize the very belief that weather magic is possible, although that skepticism is not characteristic of most Carolingian judgments on the subject.[45]

In his essay on Agobard's short treatise, Paul Dutton notes that rainmaking was a male endeavor, and this is true of open and public spectacles of weather making and magic in general throughout the first millennium. Burchard of Worms, however, writes of female weather magicians who work in private, out of the public sphere, as is typical of female sorceresses in the period. Burchard condemns those who believe or participate in the perfidy that a *"tempestatum"* is able to raise storms through incantations to devils.[46] According to Burchard, the would-be sorceresses assemble a number of virgin girls, designating one as the leader. They strip this girl naked and bring her outside the village to find and dig up the herb henbane with her little finger. When the women have obtained the plant, the maiden drags it, tied to the toe of her right foot, to a stream, where the matrons sprinkle the young girl with water; "and in this way they hope to have rain by their incantations." The virgin then returns to the village, walking backward.[47] The female weather-makers adopt an un-Christian conception of the world where humans are instrumental in natural processes through the proper manipulation of ritual. That Burchard saw the rite as vain is not surprising. This rain magic relies on ordinary peasant women, and, were it effective, it would put mighty forces in the hands of women working in secret to unleash the fearsome power of the heavens. Burchard can only see the ceremony as absurd and the women who perform it as ridiculous, not threatening except in their stupidity. He refutes the effectiveness of weather magic by male *tempestarii*, but he does not belabor their fatuous activities, which he would have known about from earlier tracts on the subject. However, he goes into great detail in relating and denouncing the bizarre superstitious rites of what amount to *tempestariae*. In this and other canons, the bishop is fixed on women's credulity and foolishness.

---

45. Medical texts are exempted from most of my generalizations about magic in Europe and England because they were not systematically examined and "corrected" as a result of the reform movements. On a recipe recommending the herb *Ricinus* to avert storms see chap. 14.

46. Burchard of Worms, *Decretum* 19.5.68, 2.425; 19.194, 2:452; Dutton, "Thunder and Hail over the Carolingian Countryside," in *Charlemagne's Mustache*, 176.

47. Burchard of Worms, *Decretum* 19.5.194, 2.452: "Et sic suis incantationibus pluviam se habere sperant." The prescription that the ritual be enacted by a virgin recalls a feature common to magical procedures before, and long after, the composition of the *Decretum*. For example, *Lex Frisionum* (14.1, 56) stipulates that the person who draws the lots to determine the identity of a malefactor must be an innocent boy (*puer quilibet innocens*), and in Pseudo-Apuleius's herbal (*Coriandrum* 103.2, *Herbarius*, in *Corpus medicorum*, 185), a girl or boy virgin is required to effectuate a cure.

Burchard's rain ritual is new to the lexicon of European magical practices. It is always a challenge to penetrate a text for the realities behind it, but innovation is often a signal that the behaviors described are more than stock recitations of earlier prohibitions. This suggests that either rainmaking was (or was reported to be) active in his period. But regardless of the veracity of the elaborate rituals of the women rainmakers, Burchard believed the women carried them out in the woods (though without effect). The same is true of Agobard's treatise; it provides particulars unknown from earlier sources, details that Agobard himself learned from the villagers firsthand. The text reveals that for the peasants, weather-making was a reality.

In regard to weather magic, two things are clear: there was some ambiguity regarding the efficacy of *tempestarii*, and all writers condemned storm magic whether or not they subscribed to the notion that it worked. Behind the discussion of *tempestarii* lies a question of control. Dutton observes that in the Carolingian countryside, people had a variety of beliefs from which to choose—some paganistic, some Christian. Dutton argues that *tempestarii* presented a threat to Carolingian sovereignty because paganism was a decentralizing force, and counts, at times, sided with wise men and women to create their own power bases. Bernadette Filotas makes a similar point in her suggestion that, quite apart from a fear of magic, Carolingian authorities sought to protect the country folk from montebanks, tramps, and self-proclaimed holy people who would take advantage of their credulity.[48] Dutton's and Filotas's observations lend weight to the argument that authorities were not principally concerned with magic per se, but sorcery often attended other kinds of problems.

In the end, manipulating the weather, or trying to, was a form of magic counter to the program of Carolingian regularization. The church incorporated its own means of propitiating God for rain or sun within the ritual calendar through the rogation days and other processional ceremonies, so the impulse to ensure favorable climatic conditions could be met without resort to demons or to rogue charismatic wonder-workers.

Singing, Dancing, Juggling

As in the Merovingian past, singing, dancing, and riotous cavorting continued to alarm church personnel because of the pagan connotations of such comportment. The condemnations against revelry were not fueled

---

48. Dutton, "Thunder and Hail over the Carolingian Countryside," in *Charlemagne's Mustache*, 170–75. Filotas, *Pagan Survivals*, 273–74.

by the fear that the people were worshipping other gods, but rather by the belief that these vestiges of pre-Christian veneration were inappropriate and pleasing to demons. Rebukes against intemperate behavior, which appear mostly in manuals of penance, show that it constituted an offensive public display, and it was important that communal conduct be molded to meet a Christian ideal of worship. The penitential *Judgment of Clement* (ca. 750) stipulates that if during any festival a parishioner comes into church singing or dancing, he will be excommunicated until he does penance.[49] This is a strong sanction, and it was motivated by more than an objection to unseemly conduct. The basis of the ruling is that idolatry is implicit in celebrating a Christian festival in a manner resonant with the pagan past. In the sixth century, Caesarius of Arles had implored worshippers to refrain from singing and dancing because it was diabolical (*diabolico more*), but by the mid-eighth century the stance was toughened, and the penalty of expulsion demonstrates that.[50]

The Iberian *Penitential of Silos* states that "it is not fitting for Christians to dance and leap about when going to a wedding." "Those, who in the dance wear women's clothes and strangely devise them and employ jawbones and a bow and a spade . . . shall do penance for one year."[51] This text introduces elements of dancing not encountered in earlier penitentials. The significance of the jawbones, bow, and spade is not entirely obvious, but they suggests an elaboration on earlier penitential rulings that may have been local to Silos. The penitential also picks up the element of cross-dressing encountered in Merovingian pastoral texts and the *Homilia*, where it is performed at the festivals on January 1. This strengthens the probability that the penitential's author objected to the dancing not because it was indecorous, but because it was oddly un-Christian. The paraphernalia that accompanied the dancing hint at an involved ritual, one that encompassed more than simple frolicking. They were fetish implements that had nothing to do with the trappings of Christian worship, such as bells and censers. Whatever the jawbones, bows, and spades may have meant to the peasants wielding them, they were clearly

---

49. *Judicium Clementis* 20, in *Councils and Ecclesiastical Documents*, 3:227: "Si quis in quacunque festivitate ad ecclesiam veniens pallat foris, aut saltat, aut cantat orationes amatorias, ab Episcopo aut presbytero aut clerico excommunicetur et, dum poenitentiam non agit, excommunicetur."

50. Caesarius of Arles, *Sermones*, Sermons 13.4, 1:67: "Et si christiani ad ecclesiam veniunt, pagani de ecclesia revertuntur; quia ista consuetudo ballandi de paganorum observatione remansit"; ibid., 6.3, 1:3; ibid., 16.3, 1:78; ibid., 55.1–2, 1:244–46.

51. *Paenitentiale Silense* 11.188, 35; 11.194, 36: "Non oportet christianos ad nubtias euntes ballare uel saltare (188); "Qui in saltatione femineum (h)abitum gestiunt et monstruose fingunt, et maias, et arcum, et palam, et his similia exercent 1 annum peniteant (194, translated by McNeill and Gamer, in *Medieval Handbooks*, 289).

not authorized ritual accoutrements. The aversion to cross-dressing winds through Christian literature throughout the first millennium, and it is associated with behavior labelled "demonic."

In the *Saint Hubert Penitential* (ca. 850), the connection between dancing and magic is implied. Dancing in front of churches is associated specifically with those who sing enchantments for charming or bewitching (*praecantaverit ad fascium*). The persons singing and those listening are subject to penance for 120 days—draconian indeed.[52] The canon implies the sin of idolatry and links the singing and dancing to malicious magic (*maleficium*). It reiterates the position, which had taken shape in the early church, that the only permissible music is the singing of the creed, psalms, or the Lord's Prayer.

Riotous singing, dancing, and capering were viewed as dangerous because of their heathen origins. But this was especially the case because the ritual dimension of song and dance spoke to the participants at a visceral level—a level, in this case, not divorced from pagan associations, or so their pastors feared. We know that dancing and singing were significant to detractors and to the participants because it continued even in the face of repeated warnings and stiff tariffs. It is worth noting that the correlation of women and sensual dancing was, at this point, long relegated to the classical past; the sources no longer exhibit fascination with this sort of female lack of inhibition.

Idolatry manifested itself during the Carolingian period in many ways, and all of them had in common the natural world: all idolatrous activities took place outside the four walls of the church. Christian sacred spaces were emplaced, to use Thomas Gieryn's term, meaning they were encoded.[53] Churches were enclosed, creating a zone where behaviors were sculpted by the long traditions of hallowed ritual and supervised by the clergy. On the margins of the Carolingian and Anglo-Saxon polities in areas such as Saxony, Frisia, and Northumbria, overtly pagan communities flourished in the early Carolingian period. Methods for evangelizing pagan peoples from these regions were much as they had been for centuries. In the core lands of Christian England and Europe, polytheistic cults, as such, no longer existed, but certain behaviors and rituals were so like those that defined the worship of demon deities that, for the ministers, they amounted to latent idolatry.

---

52. *Poenitentiale Hubertense* 42, 54 in *Die Bussbücher*, 2:337–38.
53. Gieryn, "Space for Place."

CHAPTER 10

Dancing, rituals in the woods, and raising storms—all outside the church house—smacked of paganism.

The sources at our disposal for understanding magic in the later part of the early Middle Ages are tricky because they reflect many generations of thought. Law codes, penitentials, council records, and treatises all draw from traditional and authoritative works that Carolingian and Anglo-Saxon clerics were loath to discard; and therefore, we must read against the grain of the texts. Some behaviors were atavistic and no longer live by the eighth century. Some admonitions are stilted and use language from past documents that authors reframed slightly to describe contemporary usages. In many cases, deliciously specific detail has been added to stock material, and when this occurs, we are tempted to conclude that the events were taking place at or near the time they were chronicled—or at the least, that people thought they were taking place. That temptation should be curbed to some extent because writers were likely to have been recording information they heard second or third hand, but there are exceptions. Agobard's treatise on weather magic and Raban Maur's homily document events the bishops learned about personally, and so we have high confidence that weather and moon magic were practiced in the eighth-century core lands of the Carolingian empire.[54]

Magic was a disruptive force within early medieval reform movements, where conformity to church and state programs of renovation was a priority. In an effort to establish and sustain orthodox thinking and proper Christian conduct, church and state officials found themselves face to face with atavistic pagan survivals, superstition, and magic. By and large, elites were incredulous about the efficacy of trafficking with demons, but they were concerned with the state of mind of those who attempted to tap demons to do their bidding. Authorities were solicitous of people unwittingly swept up in the rituals of idolaters, who created situations that put innocent people at risk, such as serving meat dedicated to demons. Clerical and secular denunciations of paganism or pagan survivals were firm, but those in authority did understand that there were degrees of culpability in expressions of idolatry, and they paid attention to actors' intentions.

Because the Carolingian-era elite were dubious about the efficacy of magical rituals, they were less concerned than their predecessors had been with the actual damage those using the magic arts could effect. The church

---

54. According to Agobard of Lyon (*De grandine et tonitruis* 7, 9), none of the peasants in his tale of weather magic admitted to ever seeing the Magonians personally, but they had heard about them on good authority.

was, of course, interested in the threat to the salvation of individuals who practiced the magic arts, but new to the Carolingian era was the pressing motivation to bring behaviors, and the worldview driving those behaviors, in line with the guiding principles that councils and reform legislation carefully laid out in order to ensure the purity and longevity of the new Zion.

CHAPTER 11

Superstition and Divination Questioned

> [Jesus] indeed is a prophet and the lord of all prophets, who is the way, the truth, and the life, the creator in both testaments, not just in the old but also in the new, who rejects and condemns all errors and divinations and the noxious arts. Not from anyone other than from [God] should you want to look for truth or health which comes from the father and the holy spirit, who is the one true and omnipotent God, who alone accomplishes great miracles.
>
> —Raban Maur, *De magicis artibus*

Standardization was the watchword of Carolingian rulership, and that was as true of mundane behaviors as it was of state and ecclesiastical affairs. The church endeavored to set the contours of the proper Christian life as it had done from its inception, but in the Carolingian era, government aided in that endeavor and assumed stewardship of all aspects of religious life from theological debates to quotidian habits.[1] Prohibitions against superstition and magic, which were traditional in religious literature, found a place in profane texts as the effort to bring diverse behaviors into conformity intensified. When reformers, both in England and on the Continent, wrote about magic, they did so within the larger context of comprehensive programs of *renovatio*. Numerically there are more mentions of magic in Carolingian texts than in post-Roman works, but that is not because of an increased focus on sorcery; rather, it is a function of the fact that the Carolingians were more prolific writers and better record keepers than their Merovingian era peers had been.

---

1. Depreux notes ("Ambitions et limites") that despite the effort to impose uniformity throughout the Carolingian empire, there was diversity in implementation of the reform agenda from local to locale.

Divination

The understanding of divination and prophecy was essentially unchanged from the Merovingian period. Divination was traffic with demons, but of a specific kind. It was magical because any effort to see into the future without the miraculous intercession of God was an implicit call to demonic aid. However, consternation over divining and false prophecy died down in the later centuries of the early Middle Ages. Proscriptions against foretelling are repeated in didactic, legal, and pastoral texts, but they are comparatively sparse and are more formulaic they had been in the past. Admonitions against prophecy feel perfunctory and imitative in that there are few embellishment or novel details. A second difference is that, consistent with their general perception of women's sorcery, Carolingian elites did not credit average women with the capacity for divinatory magic. Access to prophecy became privileged and was the domain of specialists—that is, holy people and clergy, rather than the laity. Because all women were lay, this development had more impact on them than it did on laymen. In an environment where state and church governments were able to monitor the population more effectively than they had in earlier centuries, false prophecy was more easily detected, and the kinds of rogue roaming prophets we meet in Gregory of Tour's history are rare in the Carolingian record, particularly in the core lands.

Censure of divination appears in a range of religious texts from across Europe in the mid-eighth, ninth and tenth centuries. None of them are original in general outline or detail, and they often appear in familiar laundry lists of magical errors. Reference to augury is common, and its methods are familiar from post-Roman sources. Boniface's notes of the Frankish council of 747 stress predicting the future. Bishops must take annual stock of their dioceses and "search out and forbid pagan rites, divinations or sorceries, fortune telling, herbal charms, incantations and all the filth of the heathen."[2] This general council was important because it was the only one held in decades in the West and the first that could rightly be called Carolingian. In it, the concerns about magical practices echo patristic and Merovingian texts.[3]

Wrongful recourse to astrology persisted as one of the stock magical transgressions in the Carolingian period. However, as was true of divination in general, references to demonic stellar prognostication were relatively few.

---

2. Boniface, *Die Briefe* 78, 164: "investigare et prohibere paganas observationes, divinos vel sortilogos, auguria, filacteria, incantationes vel omnes spurcitias gentilium."

3. Schieffer, "Neue Bonifatius-Literatur."

Yet, according to Bruce Eastwood, "the desire to predict the future from the heavens was neither absent nor severely restrained at the literate level. Only the practices of the unlettered, common people were seen as dangerous and to be prohibited." Charlemagne was inquisitive about astrology, and he called upon Alcuin and the Irish monk Dungal of Bobbio (d. ca. 828) to explain unusual celestial occurrences, such as the solar eclipse in 810.[4]

Around 840 when Louis the Pious saw a comet in the night sky, his anonymous counselor, whom we call the Astronomer, was compelled to tell the emperor that a comet should not be trusted as a predictor of the future because God, not the stars, controls fate. Citing Jeremiah (10:2) the courtier gently admonished Louis, "Do not fear the signs from the sky that the nations fear."[5] This was by no means a new concept. It had been fastidiously developed by Augustine, and Isidore of Seville had written that "portents show and demonstrate, and what I call prodigies are thought to show, demonstrate, and somehow to predict the future."[6] Although the difference between portents and prodigies was sometimes misconstrued, even by clerics, intellectual reformers such as the Astronomer were steadfastly sensitive to the arguments of the church fathers.

The author of the anonymous eighth-century *Homilia de sacrilegiis* labels "pagan" anyone who believes in the good or bad predictions of a fortune teller. The same text warns against taking auguries through sparrows and other birds, the barking of dogs, and general hissings and sneezings. In his treatise *On the Magic Arts*, the archbishop Raban Maur of Mainz relies heavily, even slavishly, on patristic works and brings orthodox arguments to the service of his condemnation of incantations and divinations. The *Penitential of Silos* legislates against "diviners, enchanters or fortune tellers who follow auguries, omens or elements." These malefactors are required to perform penance for five years; for consulting demons, the penance is eight years. The *Pseudo-Roman Penitential* follows suit, condemning to a five-year

---

4. Eastwood, *Ordering the Heavens*, 17; Alcuin, *Ep.* 145, 231–35; Dungal, *Ep.* 1, 570–78.

5. Astronomer, *Vita Hludowici imperatoris* 58, 518–24 (quotation 522: "A signis caeli ne timueritis, quo pavent gentes"). Many hypotheses have been advanced as to the identity of the Astronomer. Most recently Booker (*Past Convictions*, 293n129) suggests that the Astronomer was Walafrid Strabo. On the Astronomer see *Charlemagne and Louis the Pious*, 219–26. Computus was a scientific discipline devoted to the study of astrology (also called astronomy) for the sake of establishing dates for Christian feasts far into the future. The study of computus expanded in the ninth century, and Charlemagne mandated that computus be studied in schools. See Eastwood, *Ordering the Heavens*, 1–29; Stevens, "Alternatives to Ptolemy"; Wallis, "Medicine in Medieval Calendar"; Contreni, "Carolingian Renaissance," 740–42; McCluskey, "Astronomies in the Latin West."

6. Isidore of Seville, *Etymologiarum* 11.3.1–3, vol. 2: "Portenta autem et ostenta, monstra atque prodigia ideo nuncupantur, quod portendere atque ostendere, monstrare ac praedicare aliqua futura videntur."

penance anyone committing sacrilege by attending to augurs or omens, as well as "those whom they call diviners . . . for this is demonic." The *Saint Hubert Penitential* (ca. 850) imposes three years of penance on those who pay heed to fortune tellers, criers, or those peddling cures. The error of divination in these Carolingian sources follows traditional models, and the texts provide few new details about the practices. This conventionality need not be read as clerical indifference to divination or a denial that it was "a demonic thing," but it does means we cannot get significant insight as to how divination was playing out in real time.[7]

Some of the discussion of astrology revolved around the question of the star of Bethlehem, as it had done for exegetes of the early church. Edward Peters makes the point that the revival of interest in patristic texts within the Carolingian reform movement influenced how the erudite treated magic.[8] Raban Maur's *On the Magic Arts* is a good example of this, as it is highly derivative of learned treatises of the church fathers. Regarding astrology, he follows the thinking of Isidore of Seville (who himself was dependent on the patristic authors) in his stance that the astrological skills of the magi were magical, but on the unique occasion of Christ's birth, divination was indulged for a lofty and holy purpose. God ignored stellar sorcery so that the birth of the Christ child could be announced. The effectiveness of astrological divination ended when the magi arrived in Bethlehem, and the birth of Jesus invalidated all pagan divination.[9] The ninth-century commentary on Matthew by Pseudo-Bede also repeats the stance of some of the church fathers to the effect that the magi were simply acknowledging the prophecy of Balaam, who predicted, "A star shall come out of Jacob, and a scepter shall rise out of Israel," which would rule the nations of the world (Num. 24:17).[10] This reasoning is undergird by the argument that the magi were operating in their capacity as philosophers, not magicians. All in all, most Carolingian writings about astrology were strictly conventional.[11]

Though divination by sortes had long been recognized as a forbidden practice, it did not completely disappear, and even clergy continued to engage in it. The Silos and Roman penitentials, the *Homilia de sacrilegiis*, the General Admonition that Charlemagne issued from Aachen in 789, a 842/843

---

7. *Homilia de sacrilegiis* 3.4, 6–7; 9–10, 7–8; Raban Maur, *De magicis artibus*, col. 1095; *Paenitentiale Silense*, 7.105, 27; 11.197, 36; *Poenitentiale Romanum* 35, in *Die Bussbücher*, 1:479: "Quos divinos vocant... quia hoc daemoniacum est"; ibid., 34, 1:479; *Poenitentiale Hubertense* 25, in *Die Bussbücher* 2:335.

8. Peters, *Magician*, 15–18.

9. Raban Maur, *De magicis artibus*, col. 1098.

10. Pseudo-Bede, *Expositio in Evangelium S. Matthaei* 1.2, cols. 12–13.

11. See Dutton, *Charlemagne's Mustache*, 116–20.

penitential of Raban Maur, Regino of Prüm and Burchard of Worms all make mention of the practice, and the prohibition became standard in the later canon law collections. However, over all, references to sortilegium waned, and by all accounts, sortition was no longer a source of grave distress.[12]

False Prophecy

Gregory of Tours's *Ten Books of Histories* is full of warnings against false prophecy, which, if we accept the bishop's account, was rife in Merovingian Gaul. Gregory's assessment of the problem, however, was informed by the fact that popular prophets posed a challenge to the hierarchical organization of the church and his own authority. In the Carolingian period, false holy men and women were less common—or written about less commonly, but either way, they were not threating to ecclesiastical control. The exception that proves the rule is evident in lightly-Christianized areas on the margins of the empire that resembled Gregory's Gaul. In two letters Boniface expresses consternation over false prophets. One was Adelbert (d. ca. 750) who set up crosses in the fields, received bogus letters from heaven, and distributed his hair and nails as relics. He was particularly patronized by "silly little women laden with sins, driven by various desires."[13]

In his *History of the Lombards*, Paul the Deacon (d. 799) demonstrates no particular interest in magic, but there are chance references to magicians in the work. For instance, the Lombard king Agiluf's soothsayer, "who by diabolical art understood what future happenings strokes of lightning portended," informs him that because lightning had just struck, Theudelinda (d. 628), queen of the Lombards, would someday be his bride.[14] The augury relied on traffic with demons, yet is was accurate. Note that Paul's assessment of spectacular celestial occurrences resembles that of his contemporary Louis the Pious who wondered if the comet he saw in the night sky

---

12. *Poententiale Silense* 7.106, 27; *Poenitentiale Romanum* 37, in *Die Bussbücher*, 1:479; *Homilia de sacrilegiis* 3.8, 7; *Die Admonitio generalis* 64, 216; Raban Maur, *Poenitentium liber ad Otgarium* 31, col. 492. On Raban Maur's penitential see Kottje, *Die Bussbücher Halitgars*. Regino of Prüm, *De synodalibus causis* 2.365, 352; Burchard of Worms, *Decretum* 10.9, PL 140, cols. 834–37. In *Annales Xantenses* (845, 14–15) pagan prisoners cast lots to determine the relative strength of their deities against the Christian God; there is no hint of magic in the text concerning this event.

13. Boniface, *Die Briefe* 57, 102–5; 59, 111: "Duxit post se mulierculas oneratas peccatis, quae ducebantur variis desideriis." Boniface quotes from Paul's letter 2 Timothy 3:6. See Innes ("'Immune from Heresy'") on Adelbert's heresy. Filotas, *Pagan Survivals*, 202. Raban Maur warns of false prophets (*De magicis artibus* col. 1095), insisting that only God can call a prophet.

14. Paul the Deacon, *History of the Lombards* 3.30, 141. For a discussion of Paul's work see Goffart, *Narrators of Barbarian History*, 329–431.

portended "a change in the kingdom and the death of its prince."[15] Paul is dismissive of suggestions from his own sources that women can exercise magical powers. In *The History of the Lombards*, the text Paul likely used for much of his history, the sibyl Gambara accurately prophesies the migration of the Winnili (ancestral tribe of the Lombards), but Paul does not include this information in his own work.[16] He did not find the information about this female diviner noteworthy or, perhaps, credible.

The motif of the ersatz prophetess appears once in the *Annals of Fulda*. In 847 a "false prophetess" (*pseudoprophetissa*) named Thiota came from Alemannia to Mainz, claiming she knew the sure date for the end of the world; it would end that very year. "By her predictions, she upset the diocese of Bishop Salomon more than a little," the annalist reports. The people have confidence in her prophetic abilities and bring her gifts and offer her prayers. Some men in holy orders follow her "as a teacher come from heaven." She is brought before bishops at Saint Alban's in Mainz, and when questioned admits that a priest had coached her for gain. Thiota is flogged and "stripped of the ministry of preaching that she had irrationally seized and presumed to claim for herself against the custom of the church."[17] In this story, the explicit objection to the woman's behavior is that she was teaching outside the authorization of the church establishment, a function long forbidden to Christian women when exercised anywhere but the home or monastery. The indictment makes no mention of magic. The priest invented the false and troubling information for this woman; she was not speaking with the aid of a demon. This incident forms a stark contrast to Gregory of Tours's stories of prophetic women whose demonic source of power is ultimately exposed, but who are nonetheless genuine actors, not simply imposters. The people of Mainz believe in Thiota's abilities, but the annalist does not. Although she is a nuisance and disturbs the peace, her powers are facile, and she herself is foolish.

---

15. Astronomer, *Vita Hludowici imperatoris* 58, 518–24. (Quotation 522: "mutationem enim regni mortemque principis.")

16. *Chronicon Gothanum* 3, 5; 7, 8; 8, 10. Gambara mothered the mythical twin tribal chiefs, Ibor and Agio. See Goffart, *Narrators of Barbarian History*, 382n163. The *Historia* was written in the court of King Pippin of Italy 806 to 810.

17. *Annales Fuldenses* 847, 36–37: "Salomonis episcopi parroechiam suis vaticiniis non minime turbaverat," "quasi magistram caelitus," "Quapropter synodali iudicio publicis caesa falgellis ministerium praedicationis, quod inrationabiliter arripuit et sibi contra morem ecclesiasticum vindicare praesumpsit." See Gillis, *Heresy and Dissent*, 112–113. From Dutton (*Politics of Dreaming*, 126–68), Thiota's role in this context is less about the woman's prowess in the magic arts and more a comment on ninth-century apocalyptic thought.

Dreams

Raban Maur commented upon and expanded Augustine's and Gregory the Great's discussion of dreams.[18] Like his predecessors, Raban recognized several levels of dreaming, from the revelatory to the demonic. Taking advice from dreams was dangerous because of demons' ability to infiltrate the unwary mind at rest. As Paul Dutton demonstrates, dreaming could be a tremendously powerful political tool.[19] For example, Louis the German saw his father, Emperor Louis the Pious, in a dream, and Louis the Pious addressed his son, saying that he was in "dire straits" (*angustiis constitutum*) and needed help if he were to be saved. The emperor's punishment was due to his failure to oppose the heresy of the Nicolaitans (married clergy) as urged by the Archangel Gabriel and the courtier Abbot Einhard. The dutiful son sent letters to various monasteries asking the monks to pray for his father's soul, and this gave his political agenda a significant boost.[20]

The capitular General Admonition includes giving credence to dreams in a list of pagan and magical practices it condemns, and canon law consistently opposed the use of dreambooks. The dream manuals worked like the *Sortes Sanctorum*. Dreamers opened any texts of their choosing and noted the first letter on which the eyes fell. That letter was then keyed to a specific prediction in the dreambook. For instance, "A" signified a fortunate journey. Similar vatic manuals that facilitated interpretation of dreams were called a dreamlunars. These books predicted future events based on the position the moon assumed while the dream was taking place. A similar handbook called the *Somniale Danielis* was also useful in deciphering dreams. Carolingian clerics denounced such dreambooks as vile and fruitless divination.[21]

Superstition

Superstition is an amorphous, lumpy concept—both for ourselves and for people living in the early Middle Ages. The basic contours, as understood by the elite, did not change over the first Christian millennium. Augustine continued to be an undisputed guide: superstition consisted of vacuous observances,

---

18. From Kruger (*Dreaming*, 57–62), the works on dreaming by Macrobius, Calcidius, Augustine, and particularly Gregory the Great were well known in the early Middle Ages. See Eastwood (*Ordering the Heavens*, chaps. 2, 5) on the Carolingian usage of Macrobius and Calcidius.

19. Dutton, *Politics of Dreaming*, 195–224, 252–59. See de Jong (*Penitential State*, 136–37) on the moralistic dimensions of dreams.

20. *Annales Fuldenses* 874, 82; Dutton, *Politics of Dreaming*, 219–24.

21. *Die Admonitio generalis* 65, 216; Kruger, *Dreaming*, 7–11.

the perversity of which lay in the fact that they gave devils entrée into Christians' day-to-day experience.[22] Reliance on apotropaic props and rituals that beckoned demons in order to improve personal circumstances, and reading meaning into chance happenings were insulting to God. He had given humans all they needed to know through the scriptures, and his church had constructed the ritual architecture necessary to keep believers safe and on their way to salvation. However, even in the early church, even in Augustine's sermons, the term "superstition" was to some extent a catch-all for a collection of disparate behaviors that courted devils.

Capitulum 17 of the *Indiculus superstitionum* forbids "the observances of pagans on the hearth or in the inception of any business."[23] The *Homilia de sacrilegiis* contains descriptions of several similar incantations, which involve the superstitious use songs and chants (*carmina vel incantationes*) for curing an array of human and animal maladies, putting weapons in the field to make the day begin, and attempting to expel winter in the month of February. For Raban Maur magic consisted of "perverse observances" (*observationibus perversis*) and "various superstitions" (*superstitionibus diversis*).[24] Burchard of Worms censured those who followed pagan habits such as waiting for the new moon in order to build a house or to arrange a marriage, and listening for the direction of the cock's crow before starting a journey.[25] All of these homey rituals were held to be tenacious atavisms of the pagan past and therefore pernicious and an invitation to demons. The sin in these behaviors was that putatively protective customs, such as leaving a room with the wrong foot, putting weapons in the field, and watching for the new moon were not, as the superstitious believed, guarantees of safety. Health and security rested with God, not footfalls, weapons, or the moon.

Rituals involving "reversal" (such as walking backward or carrying out an act in a contrary direction or position) many of which we learn about from Burchard of Worm's writings on the customs of Rhenish peasants, were disallowed, perhaps because their very inversion signaled a liminal interval where ordinary strictures were loosened and odd behaviors were given free rein. The mysterious, deleterious effect of looking backward features in

---

22. From Timmerman ("An Authority"), a considerable amount of "textual media," which was produced by the educated class and digested by local clergy, reached ordinary Christians—largely through sermons, baptismal instructions, and handbooks. Augustinian percepts were often filtered through early medieval pedagogical writings such as those by Caesarius of Arles.

23. *Indiculus superstitionum* 17, 223: "De observatione paganorum in foco vel in incoatione rei alicuius."

24. *Homilia de sacrilegiis* 3.12, 8; 5.17, 10; 8.27; 10, 16; Raban Maur, *De magicis artibus* col. 1095.

25. Burchard of Worms, *Decretum* 19.5.60, 2:422; 19.5.61, 2:423; 19.5.66, 2:424; 19.5.68, 2:425; 19.5.91, 2:429. See chap. 12 for more detail on the *Decretum* and superstition.

classical and biblical literature. In the classical myth, Orpheus, when leading his lover Eurydice from hell, was warned that if he looked back he would lose her forever. Looking rearward also features in the case of Lot's wife, who turned into a pillar of salt because she looked back at the burning cities of Sodom and Gomorrah (Gen. 19:26). Many European folk rituals (often those associated with healing) contain specifications against looking around or backward.[26] The *Penitential of Silos* forbids a person to "bathe himself in a reverse position," but if he does it with incantations, his penance is almost ten times more severe.[27] This and stylized silence during the performance of certain procedures are in that category of "unusual phenomena," or superstitious observances condemned in church literature. In the Silos penitential, such practices are made worse when explicit magical incantations enter the mix.

The church had developed its own rites for the security and safety of its followers, and they were exacting like the superstitious rituals were. Boniface was distressed because an ignorant priest in his mission field used an incorrect trinitarian baptismal formula; Boniface feared the sacrament would not be binding if the proper words were not spoken.[28] Pope Leo IV (d. 855) enjoined precision with respect to making the sign of the cross. "Sign the chalice and the host with a right cross and not with circles or with a varying of the fingers, but with two fingers stretched out and the thumb hidden within them, by which the Trinity is symbolized. Take heed to make this sign rightly, for otherwise you can bless nothing."[29] The English Abbot Aelfric of Enysham emphasized the exactitude necessary for the ritual of crossing. "A man may wave about wonderfully with his hands without creating any blessing unless he make the sign of the cross. But if he does, the fiend will soon be frightened on account of the victorious token. With three fingers one must bless himself for the Holy Trinity."[30]

Superstitious rituals often took place in the home and for the protection of the family, which suggests the involvement of women. Burchard of Worms's *Corrector* expounds with great precision, superstitious activities,

---

26. Hornblower et al., *Oxford Classical Dictionary*, s.v. "Orpheus."
27. *Paenentiale Silense* 11.192, 36: "Qui per aliquam incantationem pro qualiuet re inuersum se balneaberit, I annum peniteat; sine incantatione autem XL dies peniteat."
28. Boniface, *Die Briefe* 80, 173–74. From Innes ("Immune from Heresy," 118–25), Zacharias did not concur entirely with Boniface and cautioned him to be less rigid. On Carolingians' development of ritual see Nelson, "Carolingian Royal Funerals"; MacLean, "Ritual Misunderstanding."
29. Thurston, *Catholic Encyclopedia*, s.v. "Sign of the Cross"; Beresford-Cooke, *Sign of the Cross*, 23.
30. Aelfric of Eynsham, *Homilies of the Anglo-Saxon Church*, in Thurston, *Catholic Encyclopedia*, s.v. "Sign of the Cross."

particularly those of women. The text contains detailed accounts of female magic, many of which are original to Burchard's collection and were not handed down from earlier penitential documents. The bishop contends that the rites he describes are fatuous and that the women who carry them out are deluded. He denies women's magical prowess, and attests that they are gullible and disposed to accept foolish superstitions. He censures women who set the table with food, drink, and silverware so that the "three sisters," or the Fates, can enter and take refreshment at the house.[31] The Fates have a classical pedigree, but the notion that they enter homes to sup does not. Burchard's "sisters" may have been a holdover from the Germanic belief in cunning women who served food or mead and manipulated threads to see and set the future.[32] Burchard did not accept the reality of the Fates, but he was concerned that ignorant Christians continued to believe in these mythical creatures and thought they could engage them through impious rites.

In another canon of the *Corrector*, the bishop bemoans women going to the grave to transfix with a stake the bodies of children who died without baptism or the bodies of women who passed away in childbirth, so that the dead could not return and harm the living. "If you have done or consented to or believed this," he says, "you should do penance for two years on the proper days."[33] These rituals integrated multiple realities: the host and baptism with women's ancestral preeminence over birth and death. For Burchard, there was ensconced in rites, not only an attempt to call on demonic power, but a belief system that was in sharp contrast with the Christian perception of the very narrow circumstances under which the dead return to life.

In canons such as these, Burchard is not asking the penitent to disbelieve that women actually carry out rituals; rather, he is forbidding anyone to be a party to them or to subscribe to their efficacy. In other words, the bishop does not acquit women of the common perception that they are given to infantile superstitions—in fact, he promotes the view by his extended, almost belabored, descriptions. Nor is he, as Valerie Flint says, fostering a "protection of women's rights."[34] Rather, his work has the double effect of disempowering women without dignifying them. (They cannot work magic, but they think they can.) There is more than fear of superstition at the base of the *Corrector*'s canons that deal with women's magic. There is alarm at what, in Burchard's view, is an ill-defined female power operating on the

---

31. Burchard of Worms, *Decretum* 19.5.145, 2:441; 19.5.153 2:443.
32. P. Shaw, *Pagan Goddesses*, 41–43; Enright, *Lady with a Mead Cup*, 125–27, 139.
33. Burchard of Worms, *Decretum* 19.5.180, 2:448: "Si fecisti, aut consensisti, aut credidisti, duos annos per legitimas ferias debes ponitere."
34. Flint, *Rise of Magic*, 125.

village level. Rites engaged by laywomen that were not in conformity with the official program of church ritual were a threat to it.

Binding, Loosing, and Suspensions

Binding and loosing were recognized as cosmic forces that could be manipulated by saints or demons. This particular form of magic did not change materially over the first millennium. Motifs of binding and loosing were common in late antiquity and throughout the Merovingian and Carolingian periods, and, as in the past, when holy men and women engaged in binding and loosing, it was meritorious. Jonas of Orléans (ca. 843) makes this clear in *De institutione regia*; it was a power bishops were expected to wield.[35] When the efficacy of binding and knotting relied on traffic with demons it was magic. Proscriptive sources consistently contain warnings against the magical use of bonds. The *Indiculus superstitionum* condemns people who make magical ligatures,[36] and Burchard of Worms attributes magical knotting to swineherds, plowmen, and hunters.[37]

Knotting at the loom constituted a special category of ligatures whose manipulation women monopolized.[38] As indicated in chapter 9, in the early Middle Ages weaving and cloth making were women's work and so was the binding magic that weaving facilitated.[39] The *gynaecea* (cloth manufacturing shops) were the domain of women—women working together beyond the male gaze. Gendered spaces such as the *gynaecea* sparked male authors' anxiety over the possibility of resistance to masculine hegemony. As such, this female space was vulnerable to slander in texts written by men. Slurs against the women weaving cloth—namely, that they were wanton and inclined to love magic—were indexed on long-held stereotypes about quintessential female proclivities that were especially common when their dealings were cloaked. The *Penitential of Silos* contains a reference to sorcery associated with woolen works performed on the Kalends. "No Christian may [magically] manipulate wool." The inclusion of the Kalends in the canon highlights the gravity of both women at their looms and activities on the first

---

35. Jonas of Orléans, *De institutione regia* 2, 136–37.
36. *Indiculus superstitionum* 10, 223: "De filacteriis et ligaturis."
37. Burchard of Worms, *Decretum* 19.5.63, 2:423–24.
38. *Die Admonitio generalis* 79, 232.
39. For a discussion of the close affiliation of women with weaving and cloth making see Garver, *Women and Aristocratic Culture*, chap. 5; Enright, "Goddess Who Weaves"; Herlihy, *Opera Muliebria*, 18–21, 29–40. Löw's observations ("Social Construction of Space") about the ways in which gender and space are produced in interactions influencing and being influenced by larger social structures are applicable here.

of January—that perilous day onto which demons had latched. Saying that a given activity took place on the Kalends of January was a signal that whatever was being discussed was particularly noxious.[40] Archbishop Rudolph of Bourges (d. 866) compiled a book of canons around 850, and it includes a ruling about women weaving in language that is recognizable from standard texts on magical behaviors. "Christian women are not allowed to observe vanities in their wool making, but they should call on the aid of God who gives them the knowledge of weaving."[41] "Vanities" is a reference to magical knotting, and Rudolph sets it up as the hostile antithesis of prayer. Hincmar of Reims elevated the insidiousness of bonding magic by going so far as to equate weaving women (*feminae genichiales*) with lamiae.[42]

A document of particular importance to the discussion of women and magic is *On Synodal Cases and Ecclesiastical Discipline* by Regino, a Frankish noble and the abbot of Prüm in western Germany. He edited a work on church governance for which he collected canons from a variety of sources, including decisions of late antique, Merovingian, and Carolingian councils. *On Synodal Cases* is not a penitential per se, but penitential materials are abundant in the collection.[43] Regino forbade Christian women from observing "vanities" (*vanitatem*) in their woolen works, an activity he lists with *"incantationibus, maleficis, et sortilegis."*[44]

Burchard of Worms, who borrowed liberally from Regino's *On Synodal Cases*, twice mentions magical knots women produce while sewing and weaving. His canon 64 reads, "Have you assisted or consented to the vanities which women practice in their woolen work, who, in their webs, when they begin their webs, hope to be able to do with incantations and with the manipulation of the threads of the warp and the woof, which become so tangled that unless they add other incantations of the Devil, the whole thing

---

40. *Paenitentiale Silense* 7.105, 27: "Si quis christianus obseruaberit diuinos, incantatores, sortilegos, auguria, aruspicia uel elementa obseruauerit, uel inspe(c)tiones scribturarum, somnia aut laneficia uel maleficia exercent adque exquirunt, V annos peniteant."

41. Rudolph of Bourges, *Capitula Rodulfi* 38, MGH *Cap. ep.* 1, 262–63: "Nec christianas mulieres licet vanitatem in suis lanisiciis observare, sed deum invocent adiutorem, qui eis sapientiam texendi donavit."

42. Hincmar of Reims, *De divortio de Lotharii regis*, Reponsio 15, 206.

43. For background on Regino see MacLean, *History and Politics*, introd.; Körntgen, "Canon Law and the Practice of Penance." For a discussion of sources see Fournier and Le Bras, *Histoire des collections*, 248–56; Regino of Prüm, *De synodalibus causis*, preface.

44. Regino of Prüm, *De synodalibus causis* 2.375, 358. Notice the use of the term *"sortilegis,"* which does not indicate the use of sortes in this case. Sortilegium had become a general terms for magic, meaning much the same as maleficium.

will perish?"⁴⁵ The phrase "hope to be able to do" (*sperant se utrumque posse facere*) is telling in that it implicitly discredits the capability of women to actually weave magical incantations. In canon 104, Burchard condemns those who, on the first of January, "that holy night, wind magic skeins, spin, sew; every work everywhere they are able to begin by diabolical prompting."⁴⁶ Neither the author of the Silos penitential nor Burchard specify women when they speak of magical spinning, but it is a given that they had them in mind because of the gendered subtext of cloth work.

The canons that censure magic knotting open a small window into the nature of the canonists' assessment of women's penchant for working magic. We know that knotting was associated with the Kalends of January and the acquisition of food (through swineherds, plowmen, and hunters). The Silo penitential speaks of women's "customs," which may be the rapid movements of warp and woof interspersed with the incantations that Burchard describes. The word used to denote the women's magic is "vanities," connoting "silly," "frivolous," and "worthless." Silly though they were thought to have been, and however insipid women's mysterious rituals within the female space of the *gynaeceum* were, they still worried canonists because they were out of line with Christian rituals of supplication.

The use of suspensions—that is, hanging or binding amulets onto the body—which was a concern for Augustine and prominent in the sermons of Caesarius of Arles, is not mentioned often in Carolingian sources outside medical materials.⁴⁷ The infrequency of the prohibition may indicate that this practice had subsided, although that is somewhat unlikely because of its prominence in healing manuals. However, there are a few exceptions. The use of prophylactic amulets is condemned in two texts that were composed by Boniface or his circle: the records of the Frankish synod called by Karlomann in 742 and the *Indiculus superstitionum*.⁴⁸ The *Pseudo-Roman Penitential* assigns a penance of three years for making amulets.⁴⁹ This is a standard

---

45. Burchard of Worms, *Decretum* 19.5.64, 2:424: "Interfuisti, aut consensisti vanitatibus quas mulieres exercent in suis lanificiis, in suis telis, quae cumordiuntur telas suas, sperant se utrumque posse facere, cum incantationibus et cum aggressu filarum, ut et fila staminis, et subtegminis in invicem ita commisceantur [ut], nisi his iterum aliis diaboli incantationibus econtra subveniant, totum pereat?"

46. Burchard of Worms, *Decretum* 19.5.104, 2:432: "Qui ea sancta nocte filant, nent, consuunt, omnes opus quodcunque incipere possunt diabolo instigante." See *Medieval Handbooks of Penance* (335n49) on the translation of "filant" as "magic skein." On weaving and fate see Enright, *Lady with a Mead Cup*, 111–12.

47. Trahern, "Caesarius of Arles," 114–19.

48. Boniface, *Die Briefe* 56, 100; *Indiculus superstitionum* 10, 223.

49. *Penitentiale Romanum* 40, in *Die Bussbücher*, 1:480.

prohibition. The mid-eighth-century *Homilia de sacrilegiis* lists objects that, contrary to proper Christian observance, can be suspended (or placed about) for protection against demons or *maleficia*. The text forbids hanging or placing in the house incantations, roots, herbs, and iron, or putting iron nails under the bed or colored sticks into the ground. The anonymous author concludes, "This is not Christian, but sacrilege."[50] The *Homilia* is particularly notable because it is not exclusively a catalogue of old prohibitions from earlier sources, but it includes details such as the manipulation of iron and colored sticks, which do not exist in the writings of Augustine or Caesarius of Arles, or in standard penitentials and sermons.

Superstitious practices were suppressed not just because they were foolish and sacrilegious, but because they relied on ritual elements that inferred a concept of causation and human control of natural forces that the clergy held to be the purview of the divine. The church vision was also the imperial vision. Although churchmen, churchwomen, and secular authorities considered them demonic, people found personal rituals effective. They provided comfort and a sense of control, and had for centuries countered dangers, illness, and general bad luck.

Veneration of Saints and Angels

Although interest in many kinds of magic cooled in the Carolingian era, heretical thinking or unsanctioned forms of worship drew the attention of policy makers. The foolishness of amulets, for example, was a picadillo compared to veneration of unauthorized saints and angels and the form such adoration took. Misdirected *dulia* stood to jeopardize the right order on which the security of Christian rulership depended.[51] This can be seen in regulations regarding uncanonical spirits, which were infrequent before the Carolingian era when standardization of the sacred became a priority. Authorities were categorical that some modes of reverence smacked of idolatry even when Christian personages or the Trinity were substituted for pagan deities.

The *Indiculus superstitionum* has two headings that indicate this concern. "Of the sacrifice which is made to any of the saints" and "Of this, that they fasten onto the idea that dead persons of whatever sort are saints."[52] In a

---

50. *Homilia de sacrilegiis* 6.22, 12: "Isti non christiani, sed sagrilici sunt." Eckert ("Volksglauben zur Zeit," 139–40) detects elements of Jewish practice in the use of amulets in some legal collections, notably, Burchard of Worms.

51. *Die Admonitio generalis* 63, 215–15; 80, 234–38.

52. *Indiculus superstitionum* 9 ("De sacrificio quod fit alicui sanctorum"), 25 ("De eo quod sibi sanctos figunt quoslibet mortuos"), 222–23.

council of 745 that Pope Zacharias convened, he denounced Adelbert, "the heretic," for summoning unknown angels, and under the guise of angels, "he summons demons in his prayers to help him." The German Council of 742 denounced "foolish folk" who performed incantations in the churches "in the name of the holy martyrs or confessors."[53] The alarm over nonconformist veneration of would-be holy persons evident in the *Indiculus* was taken up nearly fifty years later in Charlemagne's General Admonition. The capitulary prohibits invoking names of angles other than those known on good authority: Michael, Gabriel, and Raphael. There was a political dimension to the General Admonition's prohibition against novel saints and angels. Paul Fouracre writes persuasively about the importance to Frankish rulers of regulating saints' cults in order to establish a level of social control. He notes that in the seventh and early eighth centuries, "sanctity really came to terms with political power." One hundred years later, Bishop Herard of Tours (d. 871) was still forbidding his priests to allow the invocation of "the names of any unknown angels or saints."[54]

The desire for control over sacred vocabulary that struck at the issue of authority was one factor driving these proscriptions. Another was preventing the infiltration of pagan names into Christian worship. Unknown angels could be demons, and that would change the virtue of prayer to the vice of idolatry. Even though the object of reverence was ostensibly a saint or angel, the conjuring of unknown "holy" powers raised the specter traffic with demons.

Demons were wily; they insinuated themselves into the fabric of everyday life, and this prospect necessitated constant vigilance against inadvertent traffic with them. Customary observances such as avoiding cracks and leaving the house backward were to be avoided because the supposed good luck these superstitions claimed to ensure was, in fact, an appeal to demons. If people wished to guarantee a measure of security from ill fortune and evil forces, they should protect themselves with the sign of the cross, which, along with other Christian rites such as baptism, were to replace observances that were not explicitly Christian. For churchmen and churchwomen,

---

53. Boniface, *Die Briefe* 59, 117: Quia octo nomina angelorum, que in sua oratione Aldebertus invocavit, non angelorum praeterquam Michaelis, sed magis demones in sua oratione sibi ad prestandum auxilium invocavit. Ibid., 56, 100: "sub nomine sanctorum martyrum vel confessorum."

54. *Die Admonitio generalis* 16, 192: "Ut ignota angelorum nomina nec fingantur nec nominentur nisi illos, quos habemus in auctoritate, id sunt Michahel, Gabrihel, Raphahel"; Herard of Tours, *Capitula Herardi archiepiscopi Turonensis* 3, 764: "De ignotis angelorum, aliorumque sanctorum nominibus ut non recitentur." Fouracre, "Origins" (quotation 165).

superstitio denoted a misuse of signs and substituted atavistic rites that were vacuous and ineffective because they failed to achieve the desired result, and they nourished un-Christian beliefs about the workings of creation. Superstitions intimated a faith in forces other than God, and whether the superstitious knew it or not, those forces were demonic.

A confounding factor in ferreting out superstition was that even the clergy sometimes had trouble, not just in weaning their congregations from the comfort of customary traditions, but in recognizing which behaviors were innocent and which amounted to traffic with demons. Both Augustine and Caesarius made it clear that at times the clergy recommended suspensions. And just as with mundane superstitions, it could be difficult to distinguish between nefarious magicians, who played on the credulity of their audiences, and bone fide holy people. For example, Gregory of Tours was uncertain as to whether the wandering magician Desiderius was genuine until he claimed to be superior to Martin of Tours.[55] Carolingians were less troubled by fraudulent tricksters because the church had taken a firmer stance on keeping idiosyncratic religiosity under its supervision.[56] The most impenetrable problem of all was states of mind, such as curiosity, pride, and covetousness, which predisposed a person to reliance on demons. Monks and nuns were particularly vulnerable to thinking that by virtue of their austerity they were inoculated from infection by demons. That was a mistake; after all, vainglory was the cause of Satan's fall that brought magic into the world.[57]

Over time, there were changes in the assessment of *superstitio*. In late antiquity and the first medieval centuries, the sources tremble with a sense of frustration that superstitious behaviors thrive despite continued efforts to curb them. The sweeping, summative Carolingian capitularies and some conciliar records take up many of the same issues, but the canons that address magic read as sterile inventories of various superstitions that had accumulated over the centuries. Condemnations appear less frequently than they did in texts from earlier centuries, and space devoted to petty superstitions pale in comparison to more pressing problems and abuses that were taken up by the literati. For example, penitentials rarely mention suspensions, and roaming tricksters are virtually absent from the sources. An exception is the letters Boniface wrote to Pope Zacharius about fraudulent abuses in Germania, but

---

55. Gregory of Tours, *Decem libri historiarum* 9.6, 417.
56. See Gillis (*Heresy and Dissent*, introd.) on the intolerance of the ecclesiastical elite to religious individualism.
57. On pride and the seven deadly sins see McDaniel, "Pride Goes before a Fall."

Boniface was writing from the margins of the Carolingian realm, where the conditions on the ground resembled those of post-Roman Francia.

This is not to say that the Carolingians had solved the problem of fatuous superstitious rites; we know this from Burchard's *Decretum* in which the bishop describes peasant superstitions in vivid detail, particularly those of women who emerge very clearly as given to superstitious beliefs and rituals. It is safe to assume that village-level customs persisted, despite the fact that official records of the Carolingian era are largely deaf to them. But it is significant that when an author turned to the demonic practices of the peasants, he focused on women's rites carried out in secluded spaces and the privacy of the home. If Carolingian legislation brought public superstitious behaviors to heel, it did not control the domestic sphere. This may be due to the fact that in the later part of the early Middle Ages, women's homey rites were considered innocuous because women had no real power to manipulate demons, and their futile efforts to do so were not a serious threat to the social order.

Divination assumed that the universe operated in harmony—one part to the other. The material world was infused (or participated in) the divine. For polytheists, clairvoyance was possible because of this sympathy among things and between spirit and matter. For pagans as well as Christians, divination depended on demons.[58] Christian thinkers subscribed to the vision of a synchronized created order, but held that learning the future and unveiling hidden knowledge was a special gift God bestowed on particularly holy men and women. Although some thought that genuine divination through demons was possible—albeit iniquitous and dangerous—most held that attempts on the part of sorcerers and sorceresses to read God's purpose and plans in his creation were illusory tricks of demons, who did not really have access to privileged information. God could and did reveal the future and his secret mysteries in dreams, visions, and portents. But the efforts of magicians to force God's hand was futile and constituted grave impudence.

There was change over the first millennium in the Christian approach to foreknowledge. In the early church, divination was an urgent issue because communication between humans and heaven was taken for granted, and the question as to what kinds of interactions were acceptable had to be resolved. However, Christian foreknowledge was distinctive because it did not rely on gaudy rituals. Christians insisted that their clairvoyance came from the Almighty unbidden, uncoerced, and uncontaminated by human intention or ritualistic performance. Of course, Christians did employ symbols, but

---

58. Graf, *Magic*, 23–24.

they were minimal—the sign of the cross, spoken words, or simple song. Men's and women's prophecy and dreams, neither of which required elaborate rites, were God's methods of providing humans occult understanding. As paganism began to give way, Christian concern with divination waned. So did the suspicion of ritual per se.

Merovingians, Visigoths, and Anglo-Saxons continued to denounce divination and false prophecy. Lay prophecy was an ancient Christian tradition, but clerics such as Gregory of Tours worried that clairvoyance outside the confines of the church was too susceptible to the infiltration of demons. Carolingians mentioned divination or false prophecy less frequently because both had been successfully managed and the words no longer carried the same sting they did in earlier eras.

As the contours of "the holy" emerged and came under the purview of the institutional church, laypeople were rarely perceived to be recipients of foreknowledge. When authors mention visions of "simple folk," "little women," or "babes," they are quick to segue to the interpretation of those visions by clerical specialists, who shape their meaning and give them authority.[59] In this process, women lost influence because they were absent from the priesthood, and over the first millennium, female monasteries declined. In the early Christian period, female perspicacity and false prophecy were taken seriously, for good or ill, respectively. As elite society came to see laypeople as unlikely to receive prophetic communication from God, women lost the social status of "prophet" and indeed of "false prophet." In earlier eras, even when prophetesses exercised their powers as a result of traffic with demons, they had access to power nevertheless, and this was an avenue of influence no longer available to women within the Carolingian worldview.

---

59. Enright, *Lady with the Mead Cup*, 94; de Jong, *Penitential State*, 136.

CHAPTER 12

Women's Magic Challenged

> Have you done or consented to those vanities which foolish women are accustomed to enact [who] while the corpse of a dead person still lies in the house, run to the water and silently bring a jar of water, and when the dead body is raised up, pour this water under the bier, and as the body is being carried from the house, watch that it is not raised higher than the knees, and do this as a means of healing?
>
> —Burchard of Worms, *Decretum*

There was a significant change in the Carolingian era in terms of the way women's magic was perceived and proscribed that was related to women's exercise of sacred power generally.[1] In the Merovingian period, the monastic movement gave women an opportunity to exercise leadership and exert influence within their societies. By the beginning of the eighth century, the number of new communities, both male and female, was in decline, which was due in part to saturation. The decrease in female houses, however, was dramatic in contrast to the drop in male communities, and as a result, access to religious careers for women diminished. Female monasticism did not regain the appeal it enjoyed in the first surge of missionary activity from 500 to 700 until the twelfth century.[2]

The ninth and tenth centuries also saw changes in the nature of monastic establishments. The establishment of double monasteries (religious

---

1. Much of chapter 12 is taken from Rampton, "Burchard of Worms and Female Magical Ritual" published in *Medieval and Early Modern Ritual: Formalized Behavior in Europe, China and Japan*, edited by Joelle Rollo-Koster.
2. On the dwindling of women's religious impact in the Carolingian period see Gibson, "Carolingian World"; Muschio, "Men, Women," 209–10; Pestell, *Landscapes of Monastic Foundation*, 101–7; Venarde, *Women's Monasticism*, 1–12; McNamara, *Sisters In Arms*, 148–75; Contreni, "Carolingian Renaissance," 719–20; Schulenburg, "Women's Monastic Communities."

houses of monks and nuns governed by an abbess) was forbidden by the second ecumenical Council of Nicaea in 787, although it took time for the enactment to take hold. Regulations regarding female claustration were more frequently promulgated, consequently, convents were hampered by reduced resources, numbers, autonomy, and prestige as nuns' ability to promote their houses, obtain relics, participate in the education of children, solicit revenues, and entertain prospective donors was hampered.[3] Female monasticism became a less effective means of exercising leadership and controlling wealth, and so it lost its attractiveness to many, especially royal and noble women. As legitimate miracle working was generally perceived to be the prerogative of the secular or regular clergy, one result of the changes in ninth-century monastic patterns was that fewer women than men were in a position to perform miracles under the auspices of the church.[4] Miracle making in general declined in late Merovingian and Carolingian hagiography, but the decrease is more marked in the vitae of female saints. After 800, women were less likely to be publicly acknowledged as saints and miracle makers.[5]

Women were involved in Carolingian power structures and governance in many ways. They were active in sponsoring and distributing books; they aggressively furthered political and military objectives; they played a central role in the courts of Europe as patrons of the arts and advisers to kings.[6] But the essence of ninth-century reforms, renovations, and revitalizations is grounded in a rethinking, revamping, and reconfiguration of religious institutions and Christian worship, and although involved and supportive, women were not primary figures in these endeavors. In regard to both lay spirituality and ecclesiastical affairs, Carolingian women were increasingly marginalized or defined out. The idealized models of normative, meritorious female behavior that emerges from the literature of the Carolingian period portray women as submissive or in supporting roles. Mothers were

---

3. Auty, *Lexikon des Mittelalters*, s.v. "Doppelkloster"; Giorda and Cozma, "Beyond Gender"; J. M. H. Smith, "Problem of Female Sanctity"; McNamara, *Sisters in Arms*, chap. 6; Parisse, *Les nonnes*, 19–28; Parisse, "Noblesse et monastères," 187–89.

4. Schulenburg, *Forgetful of Their Sex*, 4–8.

5. Hen, "Paganism and Superstitions," 234–40; Rampton, "Frankish Holy Women." For a similar decline in women's roles vis-à-vis the liturgy see Muschiol, "Men, Women." From Poulin (*L'idéal sainteté*, introd.), Carolingians tended to rework the lives of Merovingian saints rather than beatify new saints or write new lives. For an overview of the "multiplication of saints" in Merovingian Gaul see Bouchard, *Rewriting Saints and Ancestors*, 214–18.

6. Lifshitz, "Demonstrating Gun(t)za"; Nelson, "Women at the Court of Charlemagne"; Nelson, "Les femmes et l'évangelisation."

expected to provide ballast in the home as teachers and to personify the pious Christian lifestyle, but those roles were relegated to the domestic sphere.[7]

In Merovingian Europe, government was intensely local, and familial networks formed the basis of societal structures. Under these circumstances, women's influence expanded because they were integral to family strategies. So in both Merovingian and Carolingian cultures, women's place was in the home, but what made all the difference in their ability to impact their societies was the extent to which the home was the locus of power structures. When governing apparatuses were located outside the home, aristocratic women's sway was weakened. In Carolingian politics, the household remained the fulcrum of royal and imperial authority, but power became increasingly diffused and embedded in extra-domestic organizations, particularly monasteries. To get a sense of women's dominance in aristocratic households, compare the court of Merovingian King Clovis where his wife Fredegund, under her own auspices, killed competitors and had bands of sorceresses tried, tortured, and executed, to Louis the Pious's court, which scandalized his detractors because the king did not keep his wife in check.[8]

The same impulse that relegated women to auxiliary or informal roles at court and in most offices of the church structure affected the assessment of their magical effectiveness. The decline in the perception that women's magic was potent and powerful—capable of causing serious harm—is related to a broader understanding of the ideal place for the woman in spiritual matters. In miracle she was diminished, and in magic she was tamed. This, at least, was the perception of the literate. Before 750, proscriptions against male and female divination, false prophecy, magical healing, and sorcery are routine in a variety of sources, but those prohibitions began to change in the mideighth century. Although there was no significant reevaluation as to what constituted magic (in general) and women's magic (specifically) there was a shift in the way writers targeted for censure activities specific to women. Carolingian authors acknowledged that women practiced sorcery, but dismissed it as bootless and trivial.

Necromancy

Early medieval intellectuals held conjuring the dead to be irreligious, illegal, and blatantly impossible, but people (especially women) continued to attempt

---

7. This model of the ideal Christian woman is not out of alignment with that constructed in the first century. But in the specific context of the Carolingian era of reform, the archetype had more force. See J. M. H. Smith ("Gender and Ideology") on how biblical and patristic notions of gender shaped Carolingian thinking. See Garver (*Women and Aristocratic Culture*, 1–20) on the maternal role.

8. For Fredegund see chap. 9; for the court of Louis the Pious see chap. 13.

it. Well before Roman antiquity, women were experts in traffic with the dead, which gave them a formidable stature. Raban Maur repeated Isidore of Seville's claim that necromancy was a type of fortune telling, but he did not accept its efficacy. When it appeared to happen, it was nothing more than a demonic illusion. In his letter of 775, Cathwulf sought Charlemagne's aid against the multiplying number of *"phitionissae"* (and other magicians), and the *Homilia de sacrilegiis* contains a ruling against consulting pythonesses (*diuinos vuel diuinas, id est pitonissas*) through whom demons—not the dead—respond if they are questioned at the sepulcher.[9] Neither source gives particulars about the necromancy they condemn. Cathwulf is worried about the increase in female mediums, but provides little detail and does not indicate whether he credits their abilities. The *Homilia* perceives of *phitionissae* as garden-variety soothsayers. There are hints about other necromantic activities Carolingian writers thought men and women attempted by using the stuff of the grave, for example, Hincmar of Reims refers to men and women fatuously divining with the bones of the dead.[10]

The disavowal of necromancy's efficacy and injunctions against trying it applied to men as well as women, but women dominated necromantic rites in the early Middle Ages, so the impact of clerical opprobrium fell more heavily on women than men. Even in reference to legitimate revivification, that is saints raising the dead in imitation of Jesus, Carolingian hagiographic sources ascribe this miracle to women much less commonly than they do men. This is in contrast to post-Roman sacred biographies where female saints are regularly responsible for prodigious miracles.[11]

In his treatise on the divorce of a King Lothar II (d. 869), Hincmar of Reims discusses the Old Testament pythoness of Endor (who putatively raised Samuel from the dead to tell King Saul the future [1 Sam. 28:7–20]) and maintained that she could not actually resuscitate the dead; Saul saw the specter of Samuel by the permission of God.[12] This is a novel take on the

---

9. Raban Maur, *De magicis artibus*, col. 1095: "Necromantici sunt, quorum praecantationibus videntur resuscitari mortui... ad quos suscitandos, cadaveri sanguis adjicitur. Nam amare daemones sanguinem dicuntur: ideoque quoties necromantia fit, cruor aquae miscetur, et colore sanguinis facilius provocantur." On Raban Maur's knowledge of Isidore see Holtkemper, "Kompilation und Originalität"; Cathwulf, "Letter to Charlemagne," 504; *Homilia de sacrilegiis* 3.5, 6–7. On the provenance of Cathwulf's letter see Story, "Cathwulf." The homilists refers to both men and women as pythons, and uses the feminine plural to describe them. This is most likely an scribal error.

10. Hincmar of Reims, *De divortio Lotharii regis*, Responsio 15, 206. It is worth a reminder that when women are stipulated in early medieval sources, the writer has them specifically in mind. See chapter 1 under "Gendered Language."

11. Rampton, "Frankish Holy Women."

12. Hincmar of Reims, *De divortio Lotharii regis*, Interrogatio 9, Responsio 9, 166.

biblical story; most patristic writers held that a demon masqueraded as Samuel and that the medium and Saul were completely fooled. In either interpretation, the woman is inept. The English cleric Aelfric took a more typical approach to the authenticity of women's necromancy. "Witches still go to cross-roads and to heathen burials with their delusive magic; and call to the devil; and he comes to them in the likeness of the man who is buried there, as if he arise from death; but she cannot bring it about that the dead arise through her magic."[13] Hincmar and Aelfric portray the pythoness and those sorceresses who labor in trade with the dead as gullible, not commanding.

Burchard of Worms's *Corrector* contains a series of exhaustive descriptions of "erring" women meddling with the dead. He did not credit any of it and held as misguided those who believed in the superstitions. Many of the ritualistic procedures that Burchard recorded appear for the first time in his writings, and this give us some confidence that peasants carried them out—or thought that their neighbors did—in the bishop's own region. This chapter opens with canon 96 that describes a resurrection ritual, and canon 97 prohibits a woman putting an ointment into the hand of a dead man so that he will survive the grave. Neither canon 96 nor 97 address necromancy per se, but they both attest to women's interactions with the dead. The epigraph that begins this book is canon 170 of the *Corrector*. It describes a type of revivification that is reminiscent of the handiwork of Lucan's Erictho. Wives leave their husbands' beds at night, slay Christians, devour their bodies (like Erictho who never conjures until she has feasted on human flesh), then revivify them for a short time. The difference between Lucan's and Burchard's descriptions of women necromancers is that the former trusts in their power, while the latter mocks it.[14]

Further, Burchard writes, "It is appropriate to prohibit women the thing they do while they keep watch through the night in cemeteries, where, always under the guise of prayer and religious activity, they secretly commit sins."[15] Burchard is almost certainly referring to some form of necromancy, but he does not elaborate on the cryptic "thing they do." His goal is to prevent women from nefarious meetings and to expose "sins" cloaked as piety. Although the bishop does not give details about the women's activities, we may assume they have a ritual dimension that mimics prayer and Christian

---

13. Aelfric of Eynsham, *On Auguries*, in *Lives of Saints*, 1:364–83.

14. Burchard of Worms, *Decretum* 19.5.96, 2:430; 19.5.97, 2:431; 19.5.170, 2:446 in *Die Bussbücher*. For Erictho see Lucan, *Civil War* 6, 350–61.

15. Burchard of Worms, *Decretum* 10.35, *PL* 140, col. 838: "Placuit prohiberi re feminae in coemeterio pervigilent, eo quod saepe sub obtentu orationis et religionis, latenter scelera committant."

ceremonies. The transgression at issue for Burchard is misguided rituals that compete with the formulas of prayer.

Although Carolingian and Anglo-Saxon writers did not believe that magicians could do any significant damage in the physical sense, they sought to control rogue ritual that could construct its own inner logic. As Barbara Myerhoff argues, "By its repetitive character [ritual] provides a message of pattern and predictability. . . . It bids us to participate in its messages, even enacting meanings we cannot conceive or believe; our actions lull our critical faculties, persuading us with evidence from our own physiological experience until we are convinced."[16] At the graveyard, women mixed prayer with what Burchard saw as un-Christian rites. They performed their Christianity in a way that had the potential to subvert meaning as constructed by the cultural elite.

Poison

The linkages between poison, magic, and women were unaltered in the Carolingian era. Just as in the classical past, giving poison was a secretive act, and because it was stealthy and sly, the administration of a magic potion was a form of hostility accessible to women, for whom overt acts of violence were not an option.

Women worked magic with poison across Carolingian society. For instance, in the amendments to *Lex Ribuaria*, the title "Concerning Magic" (*De maleficio*) reads, "If a man or Ripuarian woman kills anyone through a poison, that person must compensate with his wergeld."[17] The *Penitential of Egbert* (ca. 750) charges killing by the administration of poison to women. It is interesting that the author adapted canon 7.7 from canon 1.4.7 of Theodore's penitential, in which the poisoner is male, not female. In other words, for the author of Egbert's penitential, that the female would apply poisons rang truer.[18] According to the 899 entry of the *Annals of Fulda*, paralysis besets the Carolingian king of East Francia, Arnulf (d. 899), and he falls ill because certain "men and women" had administered a poison to him. Among them is a woman called Ruodpurc, who is found by strict investigation

---

16. Myerhoff, "Death in Due Time," 151–52.
17. *Lex Ribuaria* 86.5, ed. Brunner, 265: "Si quis vir seu qua mulier Ribvaria per venenum, seu per aliquod maleficium aliquem perdiderit, weregildum conponat." Brunner's edition of *Lex Ribuaria* uses *"venenum,"* and Beyerle uses *"maleficium."* As indicated earlier, the two terms overlapped and it is difficult to know exactly what kind of magic the author had in mind, but generally "venenum" refers to something administered. On background for *Lex Ribuaria* see Faulkner *Law and Authority*, 16–22.
18. *Poenitentiale Egberti* 7.7, in *Die Bussbücher*, 1:580.

to have been the instigator of the crime; she "was hanged on a gibbet at Aibling." Although the text seems equivocal as to whether or not the poison was a magical potion, the translator, Timothy Reuter, calls Ruodpurc's actions "witchcraft."[19] In Regino of Prüm's canonical collection, compiled around the same time as the entry in the *Annals of Fulda*, killing by a poison drink is explicitly a female act. He writes, "If a woman kills anyone by magic, that is by a [poison] drink or through another magical act, she must be penitent for seven years."[20]

The emphasis in the above examples is traditional in that maleficium is presented primarily as a crime of aggression. But in Charles the Bald's 873 capitulary issued from Quierzy-sur-Oise, an additional dimension of maleficium's effect is perceptible in the condemnation of sorcerers and *"sortiariae,"* who, in several parts of the empire, were said to cause illness and death through philters and poisons. The decree reads, "We therefore expressly recommend the lord of the realm to seek out and apprehend with the greatest possible diligence those who are guilty of these crimes in their respective counties. If they are convicted, whether they are men or women, they must perish, for justice and the law demand it. . . . The associates and accomplices of those who are really guilty, both men and women, shall be put to death so that all knowledge of such a heinous crime may vanish from our realms."[21] The canon stresses that both men and women are culprits, which indicates that women were very much at the forefront of the canonist's mind or he would not have been specified them.

The capitulary elucidates the way in which Carolingian law approached magic broadly as a political concern (the offense must "vanish from our realms") rather than simply as a civil case of one party causing bodily harm

---

19. *Annales Fuldenses* 899, 132–33: "a viris ac feminis." "Ruodpurc quae eiusdem sceleris auctrix deprehensa certa examinatione inveniebatur Eipilinga in patibulo suspensa interiit"; *Annals of Fulda*, 139n2.

20. Regino of Prüm, *De synodalibus causis* 2.81, 246: "Mulier, si aliquos interimit arte malefica, id est, per poculum aut per aliquam artem, VII annis poeniteat." Poison is implied.

21. *Capitulare Carisiacense* 7, in *MGH Cap.* 2.278, 345: "Et quia audivimus, quod malefici homines et sortiariae per plura loca in nostro regno insurgunt, quorum maleficiis iam multi homines infirmati et plures mortui sunt, quoniam, sicut sancti Dei homines scripserunt, regis ministerium est impios de terra perdere, maleficos et veneficos non sinere vivere, expresse praecipimus, ut unusquisque comes in suo comitatu magnum studium adhibeat, ut tales perquirantur, et comprehendantur. Et si iam inde comprobati masculi vel comprobatae feminae sunt, sicut lex et iustitia docet, disperdantur. Si vero nominati vel suspecti et necdum inde comprobati sunt vel per testes veracos inde comprobari non possunt, Dei iudicio examinentur; et sic per illud Dei iundicium aut liberentur aut condemnentur. Et non solum tales istius mali auctores, sed et conscii ac complices illorum, sive masculorum, sive feminarum, disperdantur, ut una cum eis scientia tanti mali de terra nostra pereat." The root of *"sortiariae"* is *sortes*, which historically referred to divination by lots, but it had become a generic term for "magician." On this capitulary see also Nelson, *Charles the Bald*, 231; Harmening, *Superstitio*, 269–70.

to another. There is a discernible shift in this capitulary to an emphasis on the grave effect the practice of magic had on the body politic. It is also noteworthy that this text introduces a biblical injunction from Exodus (22:18) that was virtually absent from Merovingian condemnations of magic. "You shall not permit a female sorcerer to live." In other words, in the capitulary of Quierzy the focus is on larger issues than just maleficium. Magic put the society in jeopardy and the reasons were rooted in scripture.

Stria, Lamia, Diana

Carolingian-era sources expand on descriptions of female figures associated with the most insidious of magical deeds—in other words, the striae, lamiae, succubi, and Diana (that mysterious, multifarious wild runner who lurks in the shadows of texts written over hundreds of years). For some writers they were no more than literary tropes, and for others they were very human, unmanageable, and wayward women. In the Merovingian period, intellectuals were incredulous about their ability to fly, change shape, revivify, and sexually assault men, but they did not question the existence of these females or that they sought to traffic with demons. The Carolingians, however, attacked the very belief in these powerful women beings. The message in most of the sources is that the striae and lamiae are imaginary; the worry is the superstitious foolishness of the population that holds them to be real.

Although Carolingian writers condemned those who nourished the belief that female harpies existed and anathematized anyone who accused a woman of being a lamia or stria, it seems clear from the continual elaboration and the emphatic tone of the prohibitions that "the ignorant" continued to believe in some form of quintessentially dominating and fearsome female entities. Condemnations of lamiae and striae persisted over hundreds of years, unmasking a popular belief that would not die, despite ecclesiastical opprobrium. Thanks to Burchard of Worms, we are well informed about the Rhineland, where either the belief in the striae and lamiae was on the rise, or churchmen were more intent than ever on ending the myth of powerful and predatory women, or possibly both. Europeans had absorbed the Christian message to the point that most "demonic" rituals and "wrong-headed" values had been subverted or reoriented, but among the peasantry there still existed a deeply cherished and carefully guarded un-Christian mythos of an awesome cosmic she-ness that orthodox Christian theology had never reached or replaced.

In the era of the primitive church, several break-away groups emerged in which a female principle of deity was central; I am not referring to goddesses, but rather to a gendering of the principles of wisdom and generation as female.[22] All these sects were condemned as heretical and successfully suppressed. As the orthodox religion developed, it did find a place for women luminaries as martyrs, saints, and—pride of place—the mother of God, but all these roles were stripped bare of any fundamental, existential femaleness. Heroines of martyrial accounts and saints' lives are re-gendered. The young Roman mother Perpetua was able to face her passion only when she entered into a vision that she was transformed into a male gladiator. Gregory of Tours lionized Monegund only after he explained that God recognizes the valor of women in fighting the good fight. And Mary, mother of God, did not bring forth her child in pain as the Lord said all women must (cf. Gen. 3:16). She was ever virgin. All holy men and holy women gave up their sexuality at some point in their lives as a pre-condition for consummate asceticism, but undoing gender was more fateful for women because in Roman and medieval cultures, women were defined by their physicality. To give up gender signifiers was not to become an extraordinary women; it was to become a man.[23] The people whom Carolingian elites entreated to abandon their attachment to the fantasy of she-creatures may not have been holding on to the principle of evil as much as they were to the magnificence inhering in the cosmic feminine.

Medieval writers who referenced striae and lamiae had in mind a stew of concepts similar to those of their classical predecessors, including all the confusion in definitions. In that confusion or ambiguity lay their menace—not because the elite believed in these beings, but because the "ignorant" did. They were porous symbols with multiple intentionalities. This was so much the case that it is fair to speak of a composite of these female entities as a complex of symbols, in the sense that Victor Turner and Paul Ricoeur use the term "symbols." More than signs, which denote the thing signified, they were ambiguous, and thereby supported multivocal and nonfalsifiable interpretations. They were polysemic windows into cultural meaning with manifold connotations that simultaneously defined and transmuted meaning.[24] In other words, references to the stria and lamia and others like them opened up a labyrinth of images, concepts, and emotions centering on female autonomy,

---

22. Benko (*Virgin Goddess* 5–15) holds that Mary was particularly assimilated to the goddess Cybele (the Great Mother) through the Montanist and Gnostic movements.

23. *Passion of S. Perpetua* 10, 76; Gregory of Tours, *De beata Monegunde* preface, in *Liber vitae partum*, MGH SRM 1.2, 286. See J. M. H. Smith ("Gender and Ideology," 55–58) on Gregory of Tours. See Castelli, "'I will Make Mary Male'" on Mary Magdalene, Perpetua, and Thecla.

24. Turner, *Dramas, Fields, and Metaphors*, 50–57; Turner, *Forest of Symbols*, chaps. 1 and 4; Ricoeur, "Symbol Gives Rise." See also Bell, *Ritual Theory, Ritual Practice*, 109.

the threat uncontrolled females posed to men, and the personification of the dangerous and potent powers of ritualized circumstances. This, and not because they were thought to be real, is the reason why the power base feared them.

This dread is patent from the repeated and increasingly insistent prohibitions against those who claimed the stria and lamia were real. One of the titles of the *Indiculus superstitionum* says, "About this: those who believe that women command (swallow?) the moon so that they are able to remove the hearts of men just like the pagans." The *Homilia de sacrilegiis* has striae themselves bringing down the moon.[25] Cathwulf's letter to Charlemagne, a ninth-century treatise by Hincmar of Reims, the early tenth-century *Canon episcopi*, and the *Corrector* of Burchard of Worms of the early eleventh century all contain proscriptions either against women of the stria/lamia type or against those who believed in their existence.[26]

Lamiae and striae are subjects of legislation in the First Saxon Capitulary of 782. It is not surprising that they would surface in this edict, which was written and issued under Charlemagne's direct supervision in order to combat the paganism of the rebellious Saxons. This Germanic people did have a tradition of goddesses and female clairvoyants, but were they actually like the striae and lamiae? It is more plausible that Carolingians measured Saxon religious beliefs against an archetype of "the pagan," which had formed over the Christian centuries. Further, in the redacted Merovingian codes, lawmakers had at hand a neat model of the evil female harpy on which to draw. Capitulum 6 of the Saxon capitulary reads, "If anyone, deceived by the devil, will believe (according to the customs of pagans) that a given man or women is a stria and is able to eat people, and because of this will burn her and give her flesh to be eaten or will eat it himself, he is to suffer the capital sentence."[27] Unlike the earlier "barbarian" laws on the subject, this ordinance maintains a definitive disbelief in the reality of the striae. In *Lex Salica*

---

25. *Indiculus superstitionum* 30, 223: "De eo quod credunt quia femine lunam comendet, quod possint corda hominum tollere iuxta paganos"; *Homilia de sacrilegiis* 5.15, 10: "strias depositam ipsa luna."

26. Eckert, "Volksglauben zur Zeit"; Cathwulf ("Letter to Charlemagne," 504) complains of striae and appears to believe in their powers. Hincmar of Reims, *De divortio Lotharii regis, Responsio* 15, 206; Regino of Prüm, *De synodalibus causis* 2.371, 355; Burchard of Worms, *Decretum* 19.5.70, 2:425.

27. *Capitulatio de partibus Saxoniae* 6, MGH Cap. 1.26, 68–69: "Si quis a diabulo deceptus crediderit secundus morem paganorum, virum aliquem aut feminam strigam esse et hominess commedere, et propter hoc ipsam incenderit vel carnem eius ad commendendum dederit vel ipsam commederit, capitali sententiae punietur."

(ca. 507), a stria incurs a fine for eating human flesh,[28] but in the Carolingian capitulary, a person incurs capital punishment for acting on the very belief in the diabolical deception that striae exist or that they consume corpses. Capitulum 6 indicates that either a man or a woman can be accused of being a stria, but this is most likely an error on the part of the scribe. It is the only instance in any source where a man is called a stria. Also, all the pronouns in the capitulum referring back to the striae are feminine, which would be unusual if the reference were to both men and women.

References to lamiae and striae are absent from the most important capitularies, such as the General Admonition. The same is true of the Programmatic Capitulary (802). In the General Admonition, of eighty-two *tituli* only four touch on magic; one mentions women specifically.[29] The Programmatic Capitulary contains forty titles, only one of which concerns magic; it requires counts to rid their territories of "thieves and bandits, killers, adulterers, magicians, enchanters or fortune tellers, and all sacrilegious people."[30] Carolingian law, then, like all other types of written sources in the period (except medical materials), deemphasizes, denies, or ignores the ability of women to work magic. The striae and lamiae were so inconsequential, or so incredible, that they did not merit mentioning.

The pagan goddess Diana was a female personality that the Carolingians found difficult to eradicate. She is a persisting focal point for an embodiment of the superhuman feminine found in an astounding variety of early medieval texts. All the members of the ancient pantheon were thought to be demons or fallen angels, but it was Diana whom bishops Regino Prüm and Burchard of Worms single out in their penitentials as a particularly pernicious devil.[31]

In *On Synodal Cases*, Regino penned the *Canon episcopi*, a prohibition against placing credence in powerful airborne females. The regulation carried considerable authority beyond the Middle Ages and into the early modern era, as it was mistakenly believed to have been issued at the prestigious fourth-century Council of Ancyra.[32] "Some wicked women," Regino writes, "turning back to Satan, seduced by illusions and phantasms of demons, believe and claim—in the hours of night, with Diana, goddess of the pagans, and an innumerable multitude of women—to ride on certain beasts, and, in the

---

28. *Pactus legis Salicae* 64.1–3, 230–31.
29. *Die Admonitio generalis* 16, 18, p. 192; 64, p. 216.
30. *Capitulare missorum generale* 25, in *MGH Cap.* 1.33, 96: "fures latronesque et homicidas, adulteros, malificos adque incantatores vel auguriatrices omnesque sacrilegos."
31. Ginzburg, *Ecstasies*, 89–130, 157; Ando, "*Interpretatio Romana.*"
32. J. B. Russell, *Witchcraft*, 75–80.

dismal silence of night, to traverse great spaces of earth and to obey her commands as mistress and go to her service."[33]

Regino does not use the terms "stria" or "lamia," and he seems genuinely to allude to different phenomena. He refers to women who imagine they possess special powers, beastly and frightful. They fly like nocturnal birds, but Regino does not associate them with the consumption of human flesh or any other nefarious deeds. The important figure in the *Canon episcopi* is the goddess Diana, who is not a stria or lamia but one of the most powerful deities of the Roman pagan pantheon. She is, then, by Christian reckoning, a major demon. Centuries after the formal worship of Diana was suppressed, this assiduous goddess continued to appear in a plethora of contexts and in several guises. In Regino's *On Synodal Cases*, Diana seems to be functioning in her classical role as goddess of the moon.[34] Her retinue of women flying on beasts, however, is an important accretion. The *Canon episcopi* denies the reality of the flying female horde and proscribes the very belief that women, even when possessed, can fly; still, these wayward women believe themselves to be trafficking with demons and are doing it willingly, and therein lies the problem. The fantasy persisted, however, despite recurring reproofs. Burchard of Worms repeated the *Canon episcopi* in his eleventh-century penitential.

In the *Corrector*, Burchard included the most extensive compilation of regulations regarding female magical practices of all the canonists in the early Middle Ages. Although the *Corrector* is a collection of various canons from different authors, there is ample evidence to assume that specific chapters genuinely reflect Burchard's thinking. This is due to the fact that he interpreted sources freely—modifying nearly six hundred inscriptions and altering the substance of some of the documents he copied in order to bring them into line with his own ideas about church legal reform.[35] Furthermore, some of the canons do not appear in other sources but originated with the *Corrector*.[36]

---

33. Regino of Prüm, *De synodalibus causis* 2.371, 355: "Illud etiam non omittendum, quod quaedam sceleratae mulieres retro post satanam conversae daemonum illusionibus et phantasmatibus seductae, credunt se et profitentur nocturnis horis cum Diana paganorum dea et innumera multitudine mulierum equitare super quasdam bestias, et multa terrarum spatia intempestae noctis silentio pertransire, eiusque iussionibus velut dominae obedire, et certis noctibus ad eius servitium evocari."

34. Hornblower et al., *Oxford Classical Dictionary*, s.v. "Diana."

35. G. Austin, *Shaping Church Law*, 199–221.

36. An important example is the substitution of the goddess Hulda in place of Diana in the *Canon episcopi*. On this see Künzel, "Paganisme," 158.

Although Burchard focused on female magic more than any other penitential writer, his work is not an exception to the trend of Carolingian writers perceiving women as magically impotent—quite the contrary. This collection of canons outlines activities that the author himself thinks are impossible, but which he says are credited by the uninformed. Many of the canons begin, "Have you believed that there is any woman who can . . ." and then go on to describe fantastic skills that women, "deceived by the devil," think they have mastered. Like Regino of Prüm, Burchard does not describe and condemn women's magical practices because he accepts them; rather, he is determined to debunk myths of female power. It is unclear whether Burchard thought women were meeting together and actually engaging in bizarre rituals or, perhaps mimicking transvection. But he seemed to fear the effect of rituals that could withstand and subvert the ecclesiastical power structure by nurturing a worldview in which women reassumed an illegitimate spiritual potency that Carolingian literate culture had systematically eroded.[37]

Diana and the moon that signifies her are axial symbols of female autonomy and role reversal in both Burchard's work and the sources from which he drew. To use Derrida's concept, this symbol's meaning is "forever deferred," unfixed, and polymorphous.[38] In any given instance, Diana represents birth, death, healing, and the endless mutations of meanings stored in these words, so she competed with Christian symbols that covered the same terrain. Popular rituals kept Diana as a polysemic metaphor of female power associated with magic. These associations account for Burchard's particular anxiety about the goddess and his female parishioners who thought they followed her at night. For Burchard, the virile, unmarried Diana and the moon were codes for female strength operating outside ecclesiastical controls and within liminal space where role reversal occurs. Even though Burchard did not believe women flew, there was a danger if they themselves believed it, because that conviction had the potential to empower them.

For instance, in canon 70, Burchard repeats the essence of Regino of Prüm's *Canon episcopi* and denies that women can fly through the air at night on beasts in the company of demons, led by *Hulda*, who have transformed themselves into the likeness of women. In one of the seven surviving manu-

---

37. Glosecki (*Myth in Early Northwest Europe*, xiv–xxvi) affirms that "myth and rite seem elementally interfused" (xv), but he rejects some of the essentialist views of the myth-ritualist school whereby all myth "arises to validate inherited routines" (xix). Rather, Glosecki argues that ritual is not the sole source of myth and that "contemporary theory has moved away from universal templates" (xxvi).

38. McCance, *Derrida on Religion*, 26–30.

scripts of the text, the word "stria" appears as a descriptor for Hulda.[39] However, Burchard makes some very important changes to Regino's canon. First, he indicates that some of the women riding at night are actually demons. Second, he names Hulda (also Holda, Holt, or Holle) as the leader of the group instead of Diana. Hulda was a northern German goddess of fertility and leader of the wild chase (*wilde Jagd*), a motif whose roots go back to the earliest recorded history.[40] The wild chase is a procession of beings who roam through the countryside reveling, killing, despoiling, and consuming anything in their path. It is usually associated with the Norse god Odin, but Burchard and Regino change the gender of the leader.[41] Although Burchard, like Regino, identifies a goddess at the head of the frenzied army, he conceives of Hulda more as a lamia than a deity. Canon 90 of the *Corrector* echoes the warning contained in canon 70 about the ability of women to fly through the night, but this time Burchard follows Regino's lead and identifies the leader of the pack, not as Hulda, but as "Diana, a goddess of the pagans," and in so doing he perpetuates a fusion, implied by Regino, between the personae of Diana, the goddess of the moon and protector of women, and the wild and dangerous Hulda, leader of the roving, airborne pack.[42] Note that both are involved in childbirth—Holda safeguarding fertility, and Diana as a midwife. Canons 70 and 90 are both listed under sins *"de arte magica,"* and there was no surer way to traffic with demons that to sail in their space between the earth and the moon.

Stria-like women make another brief appearance in the *Decretum*. Burchard starts the relevant canon by exhorting bishops to expunge their dioceses of both male and female practitioners of sorcery. He then focuses on what is clearly for him a different subject: "sceleratae mulieres" who, deceived by Satan, think they fly through the night sky with the goddess Diana or with "Herodiade." This is a restatement of Regino of Prüm's proscription. Burchard continues to explain that Satan transforms himself into an angel of light and seizes the minds of little women (*mulierculae*) or harlots (often associated with sorceresses), subjects them to himself, and causes them to hallucinate that they leave their bedrooms and fly through the night. Not

---

39. Burchard of Worms, *Decretum* 19.5.70, 2:425.
40. In the Hebrew Bible (2 Kings 22:14), Huldah is a prophetess who warns Israel of imminent destruction. It seems unlikely, however, that this is the person Burchard is referencing, because of Hulda's negative connotations in the canon.
41. Ginzburg, *Ecstasies*, pt. 2, chap. 1; Ginzburg, *Night Battles*, 42–50.
42. Burchard of Worms, *Decretum* 19.5.90, 2:429.

only should the stria-like women who claim this fantastic ability be chastised by the bishop, but so should anyone who believes these tales.[43]

In this version of the *Canon episcopi*, Burchard implicates Herodias along with Diana as the leader of the flying horde. There has been no satisfactory explanation of why the name Herodias appears in this canon beside Diana. Herodias was the infamous wife of Herod Antipas (d. 39 CE), Roman ruler of Galilee who was responsible for having John the Baptist (d. between 28–36) arrested and beheaded.[44] Jeffrey Russell suggests that Herodias was evoked because she is a villainess and her name is similar to Hekate, pagan goddess of birth, death, and the underworld, who was often conflated with Diana.[45] Burchard does not mention Hekate as the leader of the flying cavalcade of women in his penitential. For whatever reason Burchard used the name Herodias in the canon—whether as a substitution for Hekate or because Herodias was a widely known model of the iniquitous and seductive woman—this is another example of Burchard's tendency to blur distinctions when discussing charismatic females, human or not. In fact, Burchard is often unclear as to whether particular female characters are humans or demons. This is the case with Herodias, this very human wife of Herod, who becomes a flying devil.

In canons 70, 90, and 171, Burchard is not actually affirming that women have fantastic magical powers; in fact, his intent is to dissuade his audience from any misconception that woman can fly. In canon 90, he suggests that some women may think they go through the night air with Diana, but says it is an mirage instigated by Satan. With canon 171, Burchard returns to flying women, but in this case they are not led by a demonic goddess; rather, the women are reputed to fly with demons through openings in the clouds to a place where they fight with others (*aliis*).[46] Burchard tackles the idea of women flying through the air at night a fourth time in canon 170, under the titulus "*De incredulis*," where he describes what seems to be the *wilde Jagd* of Hulda.

> Have you believed what many women, turned back to Satan, believe and affirm to be true, [that is] you believe that in the silence of the quiet night when you have gone to bed, your husband lying at your

---

43. Burchard of Worms, *Decretum* 10.1, *PL* 140, col. 831.
44. Matt. 14:3–12; Mark 6:17–25; Luke 3:19.
45. J. B. Russell, *Witchcraft*, 310n25.
46. Burchard of Worms's *Decretum* (19.5.70, 2:425; 19.5.90, 2:429; 19.5.171, 2:447) brings to mind the late medieval tradition of the *benandanti*, who rode through the night sky and battled with the witches. See Ginzburg, *Night Battles*.

side, you are able bodily to go out through closed doors and, with others deceived by similar error, can traverse spaces of the earth and, without visible arms, can kill people baptized and redeemed by the blood of Christ, and eat their cooked flesh, and in place of their heart put straw or wood or any such thing, and when they are eaten make them alive again to give them intervals of life? If you believed this, you must do penance for forty days, that is, a "carina," on bread and water and in the seven succeeding years a similar penance.[47]

There are abundant misdeeds described in these canons to make any cleric shudder, but again, the offense Burchard describes is a belief, not an act. Here the bishop omits any reference to a goddess who leads demons and human beings. Those who believe in these nocturnal exploits think they are acted out strictly by human women—women who fly with demons and behave amazingly like Meroe, the lamia in Apuleius's *Metamorphoses*, who claws out Socrates's heart and replaces it with a sponge.

The *Corrector* demonstrates an effort to secure church control over a variety of behaviors in a sort of competition for ritual expression. This is true of magic rituals in general, but Burchard treats the types of magic women performed (or were thought to perform) differently than he does magic that men dominated. Burchard denies that men can perform certain feats of magic; for instance, he follows canonical tradition in refuting the power of *tempestarii* in league with demons, as discussed in chapter 10.[48] But the bishop concentrates his philippic on female magic and beliefs about women and she creatures (real or imagined). We hear virtually nothing about male phantoms, such as elves, brownies, Green Men, or Kobolds, or about pagan male deities. We know that gods and male apparitions participated in the wild chase, for instance, but Burchard does not mention them. Delusions of female magic were more dangerous than those commonly attributed to men because loosed women operated more frequently in the realm of the liminal (in the space between the upper and lower air), and they activated a complex

---

47. Canon 170 is the epigraph for the introduction to this book, but it bears repeating here. Burchard of Worms, *Decretum* 19.5.170, 2:446: "Credidisti quod multae mulieres retro Satanam conversae credunt et affirmant verum esse, ut credas inquietae noctis silentio cum te collocaveris in lecto tuo, et marito tuo in sinu tuo jacente, te dum corporea sis januis clausis exire posse, et terrarum spacia cum aliis simili errore deceptis pertransire valere, et homines baptizatos, et Christi sanguine redemptos, sine armis visibilibus et interficere, et decoctis carnibus eorum vos comedere, et in loco cordis eorum stramen aut lignum, aut aliquod hujusmodi ponere, et commestis, iterum vivos facere, et inducias vivendi dare? Si credidisti, quadraginta dies, id est carinam in pane et aqua cum septem sequentibus annis poeniteas."

48. Burchard of Worms, *Decretum* 19.5.68, 2:425.

of powerful, multidimensional symbols fostering what, for Burchard, was a perverse "communitas" beyond the control of the structures of organizational religion and classificatory boundaries. Victor Turner observes that "from the perspectival viewpoint of those concerned with the maintenance of 'structure,' all sustained manifestations of communitas must appear as dangerous, and anarchical and have to be hedged around with prescriptions, prohibitions, and conditions."[49]

Turner's insight is useful in understanding Burchard's proscriptions of female ritual magic in which wives leave their husbands' beds, prepare brews to impede their spouses' potency, and exercise control over the very forces of night and death.[50] Surely part of the reason Burchard was so insistent that female magical rituals and symbols be discredited was that they posed a challenge to masculine dominance. This brings to mind other texts from roughly the same period in Anglo-Saxon England, where flying female-identified elves, or *maeres*, overpower men when they are ill and most vulnerable—a symbol of sexual supremacy. The *maere* is a sort of succubus: a rider that "mounts" her victim and transgresses gender boundaries.[51]

Another type of menacing female persons called the Fates (*Parcae*) appears in Burchard's canons where he writes, "Have you believed what certain people are accustomed to believe, that those whom the common people call the Fates either exist or are able to do that which many believe? That is, when a person is born they can designate [his life] as they like. Regardless of what the person wants, they can turn him into a wolf, which the deluded common people call a werewolf, or into any other shape. If you believe this, which never happened nor ever could happen, that the divine image can be changed into any shape or likeness by any but the omnipotent God, you should do penance for ten days on bread and water" (canon 151). Burchard comes back to the Fates again in canon 153 where they are less intimidating, but, for Burchard, no less ridiculous. The wife is to set out a meal for the three sisters, who will then leave the family in peace.[52]

---

49. Turner, *Dramas, Fields, and Metaphors*, 231–71; Turner, *Ritual Process*, 109.

50. Caroline Walker Bynum ("Women's Stories, Women's Symbols") has criticized Victor Turner's theory of ritualization on the basis that the experience of liminal role reversal, as Turner describes it, is generally a male phenomenon. Catherine Bell (*Ritual Theory, Ritual Practice*, 101–4) questions whether liminality necessarily involves a sharp dialectic of opposites.

51. On *maeres* see Hall, *Elves in Anglo-Saxon England*, 124–26, 140–43. On steeds see Meaney, *Anglo-Saxon Amulets*, 15–17.

52. Burchard of Worms, *Decretum* 19.5.151, 2:442: "Credidisti quod quidam credere solent, ut illae quae a vulgo parcae vocantur, ipsae, vel sint, vel possint hoc facere quod creduntur; id est, dum aliquis homo nascitur, et tunc valeant illum designare ad hoc quod velint ut quandocumque ille homo voluerit, in lupum transformari possit, quod vulgaris stultitia weruvoff vocat, aut in aliam aliquam

In these "Fates" Burchard combines two classical stereotypes: the Roman deities Nona, Decuma, and Morta—the *Parcae*—and the lamia and stria. The *Parcae*, according to one Roman tradition, determined the fate of newborns. The word *Parcae* comes from *parere* (to give birth). The three goddesses are named after a nine-month birth, a ten-month birth, and a stillbirth, respectively, and they often assisted deliveries as midwives.[53] However, in canon 151, the Fates are identified with harsh images of coercion and bestiality rather than birth. Burchard has abandoned the traditional domestic imagery of the *Parcae* spinning or preparing food with mortar and pestle, has refashioned them as lamiae, and has given them the ability to change men into various animals—not a capability traditionally associated with the Roman *Parcae*. This portrait resonates with Burchard's fear that people might believe that the Fates can rival the power of God. The bishop clearly does not believe in the existence of the "three sisters" or interpret them as minor demons. Rather, he attributes credence in the Fates to "past generations and old-fashioned stupidity."[54] He is alarmed that anyone might accept that the "divine image [meaning the human being] can be changed into any shape or likeness by any but the omnipotent God."

In canon 152, Burchard introduces yet another kind of preternatural female creature called "the sylvan ones" (*sylvaticae*), female beings (whether human or demon is unclear) who seduce men in the woods. "Have you believed what some are inclined to believe," he says, "that there are wild women whom they call *sylvaticas* who they say are able to assume bodies, and when they want, they can show themselves to their lovers, and they say when [these sylvan ones] have amused themselves with their lovers, they withdraw themselves and vanish?"[55] The sylvan ones are reminiscent of

---

figuram? Si credidisti, quod nunquam fieret aut esse possit, ut divina imago in aliam formam aut in speciem transmutari possit ab aliquo, nisi ab omnipotente Deo, decem dies in pane et aqua debes poenitere." Ibid., 19.5.153, 2:443.

53. Hornblower et al., *Oxford Classical Dictionary*, s.v. "Fate"; Isidore of Seville, *Etymologiarum* 8.11.93, vol. 1. On the Frank's Casket there is a representation of the *Norns* or *Parcae*, who are placed opposite the three magi. From Flint (*Rise of Magic*, 372–73), one interpretation has it that this iconography suggests that the reign of magic was toppled by Christ's birth. Here the three magi have a positive connotation as erstwhile magicians who recognized the superior power of Jesus.

54. Burchard of Worms, *Decretum* 19.5.153, 2:443: "tres illae sorores, quas antiqua posteritas et antiqua stultitia parcas nominavit." Ibid., 19.5.151, 2:442: "[Credidisti] quam illa divina mens quae est in homine sua fide et crucis signaculo?" For the *bonae mulieres* as minor demons see J. B. Russell, *Witchcraft*, 53.

55. Burchard of Worms, *Decretum* 19.5.152, 2:442: "Credidisti quod quidam credere solent, quod sint agrestes feminae, quas sylvaticas vocant, quas dicunt esse corporeas, et quando voluerint ostendant se suis amatoribus, et cum eis dicunt se oblectasse, et item quando voluerint, abscondant se et evanescant? Si credidisti, decem dies in pane et aqua poeniteas."

Philostratus's classical lamia, who appears, takes her pleasure with young Menippus, and disappears.[56] They also resemble succubi. Burchard stands in a long tradition of canonists when he maintains that it is not possible for human beings to bring about paranormal effects with the aid of demons, such as flight and transmogrification.[57] Demons can engender weird phantasmagorias in human minds that make them think they are performing marvels, which are, in fact, possible only through God. This much is clear in Burchard's chapter 5.

Less clear is Burchard's thinking about the nature of the creatures he discusses—that is, which of them is a human woman and which a demon. The bishop's penitential contains an amazing array of female beings with fantastic powers. His primary interest in chapter 5 of the penitential is to debunk certain mythologies about those powers and not to define or understand the beings themselves, most of whom he holds to be fictive, or worse, diabolical chimeras. In canons 70 and 90, he denies that human women fly at night, but he does not doubt that demons do so. Given early medieval cosmology, in which demons of the lower air were the very real and powerful agents of magic, he does not deny the reality of Diana, but he is appalled that anyone would attribute divine powers to her. She cannot really change the shape of God's creatures or make humans fly. He castigates "the error of the pagans when it is thought there is any divinity or spiritual authority except the one God."[58]

At first glance, Burchard's skepticism regarding the sylvan ones seems peculiar. The sylvan ones might easily be construed as the demonic succubi, whose reality is attested in other sources. But if we look more closely at canon 152, it seems that the *"vulgi"* (and Burchard) interpret the sylvan ones not as demons but as human women. In other words, Burchard denies that human women have the power to appear, ravish men, and disappear.[59]

---

56. See chapter 6.

57. Isidore of Seville (*Etymologiarum* 8.9.6, vol. 1) did not necessarily doubt that women changed men into beasts: "Hinc apparet non esse in toto dubium." Augustine (*De civitate Dei* 18.18, 2:420–29) speaks of women performing spells to transform people, but he does not believe it is possible; rather, he thinks it is the result of a delusional trance. Raban Maur (*De magicis artibus*, col. 1097) follows Augustine.

58. Burchard of Worms, *Decretum* 19.5.90, 2:429: "in errore paganorum volvitur cum aliquid divinitatis aut numinis extra unam Deum esse arbitratur."

59. Vogel, "Pratiques superstitieuses." Augustine left the door open for incubi (*De civitate Dei* 15.23, 2:488–89). He said that scripture attests to angels taking bodily form, and he was not willing to discount firsthand accounts of incubi, or devils that the Gauls call *dusii* (*daemones, quos Dusios Glli nuncupant*). Raban Maur (*Commentaria in Genesim* 2.5, col. 512). Hincmar of Reims (*De divortio Lotharii regis, Responsio* 15, 206) takes a position similar to Augustine's. Hincmar credits the existence of the *dusii*: "Some women have endured forced sexual encounters with demons in the shape of men

In all the canons discussed, Burchard debunks the extraordinary abilities of women, both human and demonic. He is not denying their power because they are female, but he perceives female power—or putative power—as incredible. Because he blurs definitions (for instance, between the goddesses and striae) and is imprecise in his language, Burchard gives the sense that he is quick to lump together and dismiss all strong female beings without giving much thought to their different natures. Given Christian demonology, he goes as far as is doctrinally feasible in denying the existence of superhuman females. He does not disallow the force of the demon Diana, but Burchard was not interested in Diana. His concern was with common women parishioners and their fallacious superstitious. Although it is understandable why the bishop of Worms was alarmed by claims that humans exercise powers that he believed were unique to God, it is interesting that he was incredulous about the efficacy of some kinds of magic but not others. Burchard was willing enough to believe in magic generally, yet when it came to procedures that were within the purview of women, he was prone to insist their powers were not real and that it was the belief that women so readily trafficked with demons that was dangerous. An element of Burchard's alarm about women and female beings, such as the sylvan ones and the predatory wives who left the marital beds, is that, empowered by belief in their own magical skills, they posed a threat to male hegemony.

Alaric Hall makes a similar argument in regard to tenth-century Anglo-Saxon medical materials that portray female-identified beings as the martial, weapon-wielding, frightening, and commanding *maeres* (discussed above in their role as succubae). He argues that during the eleventh century, authors increasingly aligned sex and gender so that these nightmarish warriors devolved into beautiful, sprite-like elves that had more in common with the nymphs of classical mythologies than with the female warriors of northern lore. These elves were seductive, but not dangerous. He correlates this transformation to a decline in nuns' autonomy and leadership roles in Christian culture.[60]

Love Magic

Love magic and birth magic continued to be condemned as both crime and sin on the Continent and by monastic reformers in England. Although, as in

---

for whom they burn with love [due to spells]." (Feminae a dusiis in specie virorum, quorum amore ardebant, concubitum pertulisse inventae sunt.)

60. Hall, *Elves in Anglo-Saxon England*, 75–95, 164–65.

the classical and Merovingian worldviews, virtually no one denied the very real ability of humans to collude with demons or other mysterious forces in order to tamper with the heart and the womb, in many sources (such as laws, canonical records, histories, and so forth) proscriptions against love and birth magic are anemic or absent altogether. Love and birth magic emerged as relevant issues when they had an impact on court politics, social order, matrimonial fidelity, and canon law, but even then, charges of sorcery were only truly pertinent when they bolstered other, more serious accusations. Carolingian texts follow an earlier pattern in representing love and birth magic as dominated by women.

The sources for the period can be deceptive about the relevance of love and birth magic because writers were more discursive about the nature of the sins they described, and the penitentials and learned treatises elucidate magical rituals in more detail than their counterparts in the Merovingian period did. Also, penitential proscriptions against love and birth magic are more numerous than they were in the past, but this is largely due to the fact that canonists such as Regino of Prüm and Burchard of Worms produced comprehensive compendia of penitential literature that recapitulated regulations beginning with the fourth century on. So we cannot conclude that there was an alarming uptick in the practice of or consternation over love and birth magic. The section that follows captures scattered, representative references to love and birth magic from disparate Carolingian-era sources from the ninth to the eleventh century. They reflect a running ledger from the post-Roman period, and what is notable is that they are relatively few. Love and birth magic that had empowered women in the past failed to draw much attention by the ninth century.

Authors of Carolingian penitential and hortatory material were incredulous about many of the magical superstitions they condemned, but they all believed in the actuality of demonic love magic and saw it as primarily a sin of women. The ninth-century pastoral guide of Bishop Ghaerbald of Liège (f. 809) says that the priests under his care must discourage women from administering potions intended to increase a man's love. The *Pseudo-Roman Penitential* portrays women as the primary practitioners of love magic, but it also mentions deacons and priests. The penitential Raban Maur wrote (ca. 841) prohibits a woman from mixing menstrual blood in her husband's food, and he cites the late seventh-century *Penitential of Theodore* as his source. He clearly sees this procedure as demonic because it is included in his section on magic. Although Raban generally follows the *Penitential of Theodore* punctiliously, he deviates from it in his specification of women feeding men their blood as magic; in Theodore's penitential, the magical dimension of this practice is implied but not explicit.⁶¹ This practice resonates with many recipes in the healing manuals, such as one in the Anglo-Saxon *Bald's Leechbook* (ca. 950–1000) for a man who is suffering from a strong love potion. Raban also adds elements of love magic that do not come from the *Penitential of Theodore* when he forbids women using dead men's testicles, ground to powder, as a magical aphrodisiac, or dousing men with tonics made from burn human skulls. The *Saint Hubert Penitential* (ca. 850) condemns love enchantments but is not specific about the gender of those who use them. The penitential says, "If anyone sings magical enchantments for a love spell . . . that person shall do penance for three forty-day periods on bread and water."⁶²

Regino of Prüm, in *On Synodal Causes*, writes, "It ought to be determined if there is any woman who, it is said, through certain magic and incantations, is able to alter the minds of men, that is turn hatred to love or love to hatred, or [by her magic] is able to destroy or pilfer men's goods."⁶³ He lists mixing semen in food as a female magical practice. But this canon is not grouped with sins of magic; instead it is classed under misdeeds involving unclean food (*De carnibus immundis*), although the penitential does have a section for magical transgressions (*De maleficio*). Nevertheless, the formula seems clearly to refer to sympathetic love magic.

There is a recipe for love magic in *Bald's Leechbook* by which women protect themselves against the "elfin race and nocturnal goblin visitors and for the women with whom a devil has carnal commerce." These devils sound like the incubus that Isidore of Seville described as a demon in male form who seduced females.⁶⁴ The afflicted woman is to carry out a ritual using an herbal mixture; she sings nine Masses over the brew, sets it under the altar, and throws it into running water after boiling the herbs in butter. If a goblin approaches her at night, she should smear the butter on his forehead and eyes.⁶⁵ The use of butter probably reflects the fact that it was often used in place of chrism in religious ceremonies in England. This recipe will also work on a human aggressor if the female victim adds the sign of the cross.

---

61. See Devailly ("La pastorale en Gaule," 49) for Ghaerbald of Liège; *Poenitentiale Romanum* 32, in *Die Bussbücher*, 1:479; Raban Maur, *Poenitentiale ad Heribaldum* 30, 491.

62. *Leechbook*, 3.42, in *Leechdooms*, 337; Raban Maur, *Poenitentiale ad Heribaldum* 30, 491; *Poenitentiale Hubertense* 54, in *Die Bussbücher*, 2:338: "Si quis praecantaverit ad fascinum . . . III quadragesimas in pane et aqua poeniteat." *Saint Hubert Penitential* is one of the "simple Frankish penitentials" that circulated in northern France and Burgundy; see *Paenitentialia minora Franciae*, 105–15.

63. Regino of Prüm, *De synodalibus causis* 2.5.45, 212: "Perquirendum, si aliqua femina sit, quae per quaedam maleficia et incantationes mentes hominum se immutare posse dicat, id est, ut de odio in amorem, aut de amore in odium convertat, aut bona hominum aut damnet aut subripiat ?"

64. Isidore of Seville, *Etymologiarum* 8.11.103–4, vol. 1.

65. *Leechbook* 3.61, in *Leechdoms*, 345.

Like other magical recipes in the medical texts, this cure is steeped in Christian symbolism, although some of the rituals, such as the procedures that activate the herbal blend, draw on un-Christian signifiers.

The *Vallicellian Penitential* (between 1000–1100) draws from the *Penitential of Theodore* in forbidding a woman to drink her husband's blood *"pro remedio"* or, as in Raban's penitential, to mix his semen into her food for the sake of love (*ut majorem amorem inde accipiat*).[66] Burchard of Worms repeated a canon attributed to the Council of Ancyra (314), forbidding the belief that women can, by magic and incantations, change the minds of men from hate to love or from love to hate. A female ritual that Burchard described in painstaking detail involves women's magical control over men; it may simply refer to domination, but love magic is also a reasonable possibility. The ceremony stipulates that women strip naked, smear their bodies with honey, and roll around in wheat. They then collect the wheat that has adhered to their skin, grind it into flour in a mill, which they cause to turn backward "against the sun," and make bread from the flour. When wives give this bread to their husbands, the men "wither and weaken."[67] Common motifs emerge from this canon, such as the reversal (backward) that is so common in both magical formulas and ritual play frames where the topsy-turvy creates a liminal space. The concoction that gives women mastery over their husbands is prepared "against the sun"—the reverse of the moon, symbol of womanhood. The perverse ritual is a tool in the hands of females who are therefore able to corrupt the proper order of things and defer the reversal acted out in the ritual into ordinary experience.

Burchard repeats Regino's canon almost verbatim in books 1 and 10 of his *Decretum*. In the *Corrector*, Burchard impugns women (specifically adulteresses), writing that "by some magical trick they extinguish the desire of men so that they are not able to perform with their legitimate [wives] and cannot have intercourse with them." Burchard assigns a forty-day penance for those who "have done or taught others to do this."[68] Neither Regino nor Burchard questions that women can work love magic against men—manipulating their affections and causing impotence (and stealing their goods while they

---

66. *Poenitentiale Valicellanum* 2.69, in *Die Bussbücher*, 1:382. From Meens (*Penance*, 176–77), the *Vallicellian Penitential* is one of a group of texts produced in central and southern Italy from the late tenth to the early twelfth centuries. The penitentials were compiled in the context of a canon law project promulgated through Italian monasteries.

67. Burchard of Worms, *Decretum* 19.5.193, 2:451: "retrorsum contra solam molam circuire faciunt," "marcescant et deficiant."

68. Ibid., 19.5.186, 2:450: "Fecisti quod quaedam mulieres adulterae facere solent . . . quadam arte malefica libidinem virorum extingunnt, ut legitimis prodesse non possint neque cum eis coire? Si fecisti aut alios docuisti XL dies in pane et aqua poenitere debes."

are at it). Also, unlike other continental penitential authors, Burchard mentions only women, never men, in connection with love magic. Both Regino and Burchard railed against the very belief that women could, among other fantastic feats, leave their husbands' beds and ride through the night air with Diana. But neither man denounced others for harboring a belief in love magic, nor did they themselves question its veracity—just the practice itself. Throughout the first millennium, then, love magic was real, and on this the elite and uneducated could agree.

Birth Magic

Burchard of Worms was concerned about women who spent their time in graveyards carrying out nocturnal ceremonies under the guise of religion, but the bishop was not specific about the nature of the rituals.[69] Something like the charm for sterile women recorded in the Anglo-Saxon medical text *Lacnunga* (ca. 1000) may have been similar to the rituals Burchard had in mind.

> The woman who cannot rear her child: let her go to a dead man's grave and then step thrice over the grave, and then say these words thrice: / "This (is) my remedy for the loathsome (?) slow birth; / this (is) my remedy for the grievous black birth; / this (is) my remedy for the loathsome misformed birth," / And when the woman is with child and goes to her husband in his rest [or bed]. Then let her say: / "Up I go, over you I step; / With a living child, not a dying one, / With a child brought to full-term, not with a doomed [i.e., premature] one." / And when the mother feels that the child is alive, then let her go to church, and when she comes before the altar then let her say: / "(?) to Christ, I have said, this is made manifest."[70]

Lacnunga also outlines a ritual whereby an aggrieved mother who has lost a child due to an inability to nourish it is to go to her dead one's burial spot, take some of the "child's grave" (presumably some of the earth), wrap it in

---

69. Burchard of Worms, *Decretum* 10.35, PL 140, col. 838.
70. *Lacnunga* 161, in *Anglo-Saxon Remedies*, 112–13. *Lacnunga* (*Remedies*) is a collection of miscellaneous Anglo-Saxon and Irish medical texts and prayers written principally in Old English and Latin. The text contains numerous unique charms and prayers. From Harris-Stoertz ("Midwives in the Middle Ages," 58–61, 63–69"), she and Monica Green, the eminent historian of women's medicine in the Middle Ages, indicate that there is no clear evidence of midwifery in the early Middle Ages. In the *Infancy Gospel of Matthew* and the *Life of Saint Wilfrid* there are brief mentions of midwives at the birth of Jesus and "mulieres" at Wilfrid's birth.

black wool, and sell it to traders, saying, "I sell it, you sell it! / This black wool and grains [*or* seed, *or* source] of this sorrow."⁷¹

Despite the altar as a Christian prop in the recipe for barrenness, these profoundly symbolic rituals draw on enigmatic sources of healing and generative power. The women do not supplicate God or his saints, but they attempt to harness and manipulate the power of death. It may seem ironic to a modern reader that a birth ritual would enter the psychic realm of death, but very ancient European patterns of belief are reflected in the symmetry between the two. In the same way that the goddess Diana embodied the seemingly polar opposites of birth and death in her guise as midwife (I say "seemingly" because if life is cyclical, birth and death are not opposites), these remedies draw on macabre images to foster life. In stepping over, first a grave (symbol of death), and then the husband (generative source of fruitfulness), the woman crosses the threshold between life and death, harnessing the former and subduing the latter.

Lacnunga has another magical charm for the cure of women's ills. A woman who cannot nourish her child is told to sip milk from a cow of one color, spit it out in running water, and drink water from the stream, saying, "Everywhere I have carried the glorious, strong son. / By means of this glorious, strong food / I will keep him ((?)for myself) and go home." She must then leave the brook without looking backward, return to a different home from the one she came from, and there eat food.⁷² The injunction to refrain from looking backward and the instructions to enter a neighbor's home are playing on the connotations of reversal, and in so doing draw on common ritual motifs not found in the repertoire of Christian ceremonial.

In monotheistic religions, life giving is an awesome force reserved for God, but women usurp it in these birth rituals. Despite some references to Christian features, the criterial energy in the rites emanates from powers outside the church—both the church building and church doctrine. As is typical of cures, the recipes say nothing about demons, but the referents in the remedies are by no means those set out in Christian dogma as supplications for fecundity—no prayers, no crossing, no entreaty at holy shrines.⁷³

---

71. *Lacnunga* 162, in *Anglo-Saxon Remedies*, 112–13. Emphasis in original; Weston, "Women's Medicine, Women's Magic."

72. *Lacnunga* 163, *Anglo-Saxon Remedies*, 114–15. See Buck, "Woman's Milk." In this ritual the reference to a cow of one color resonates with Old Testament symbology of ritual purity. Meens ("Pollution") notes that Old Testament notions of ritual purity are evident in the penitentials.

73. Following is a sampling of penitentials that prohibit abortion or infanticide. *Poenitentiale Valicellanum* 6–7, 1:259–60 (infanticide); 10, 1:262–63 (smothering); 24, 1:280–81 (abortion); 29, 1:282 (abortion); *Poenitentiale Romanum* 21, 1:477 (abortion); *Poenitentiale Hubertense* 50, 2:338 (smothering); Burchard of Worms, *Decretum* 19.5.182–83, 2:449 (smothering); all in *Die Bussbücher*. *Poenitentiale*

Women are often active participants in the rites; in many cases they carry out the entire procedure without the aid of a specialist. Such is the case in the *Lacnunga* charm where the mother is the sole actor in staving off a miscarriage. Churchmen such as Caesarius of Arles were right to be frustrated with women who sought to have children "by means of impious drugs."[74] It was clearly a stubborn problem for those who sought to promote a Christian mental universe.

Clerics who composed the penitentials were troubled by abortion, but whether the parents employed magic as a means was less an issue than the infanticide itself. The *Penitential of Vigilanus* (between ca. 800–900) holds a woman responsible for murder if she takes a potion that works as an abortifacient. Ghaerbald of Liège's pastoral insists that the priests under his care stop women from administering abortifacients. The *Pseudo-Roman Penitential* refers to a male and female *"herbarius"* who slays children, and the *Vallicellian Penitential* calls a woman who takes herbs that interfere with conception or delivery a murderer. It is clear that the Vallicellian author views the herbs as a magical substance because the canon falls under the title *"De maleficio"* and is listed with consultation of *ariolos, divinos, aruspices,* and so forth. Burchard of Worms indicts a woman who prevents conception or aborts a fetus by means of "her magic and her herbs."[75]

In cases of abortion and infanticide, the penitential writers specifically either single out or include women in their condemnations, but clerics also constitute a category of persons who are likely to bring about the death of the young. As for the method of killing, whether by men or women, magic does not emerge as a significant issue; rather, it is just one of the means employed for eliminating children. Furthermore, as stated above, the actual number of references to female birth magic does not significantly change over the early medieval centuries. But because Carolingian penitentials are, on the whole, much longer and more exhaustive than earlier penitentials, the references in them to women and birth magic are proportionately fewer.

Vigilanum 45, in *Die Bussordnungen*, 530 (abortion); *Old Irish Penitential* 5.6, in *Irish Penitentials*, 272 (abortion). From Meens (*Penance*, 165–79), the *Penitential of Vigilanus* was written in Spain by a monk called Vigilanus, produced in the interests of canon law, not pastoral care.

74. Caesarius of Arles, *Sermones,* Sermon 51.4, 1:229: "Unde et illae male faciunt, si eos quibuscumque sacrilegis medicamentis."

75. *Poenitentiale Vigilanum* 45, in *Die Bussordnungen*, 530. On Ghaerbald see Devailly, "La pastorale en Gaule," 24; *Poenitentiale Romanum* 97, in *Die Bussbücher*, 1:487. See Niermeyer (*Mediae latinitatis lexicon minus*, s.v. "Herbarius") on the word *"herbarius."* Franck, "Geschichte des Wortes Hexe"; *Poenitentiale Vallicellanum* 2.57, in *Die Bussbücher*, 1:378; Burchard of Worms, *Decretum* 19.5.159, 2:444: "suis maleficiis et suis herbis."

WOMEN'S MAGIC CHALLENGED 339

Law codes also address the issues of abortion and infanticide, but the drafters of the laws are less explicit than the penitential authors in their views of magic as a tool in the hands of women to terminate pregnancy. In the mid-eighth-century *Lex Baiwariorum* (which is based on the Alammanic code and is very similar to it in most ways), the accusation of magically induced abortions is foggy. The Bavarian code, title 8.18, fines any woman who gives a *"potio"* to another woman to induce an abortion. Title 8.19 punishes anyone (*quis*) who causes an abortion or the death of the mother through a blow. T. J. Rivers indicates that 8.19 is patterned after title 70 of *Lex Alamannorum* (717), where bewitching, not a blow, is the agent of the abortion.[76]

One of the Carolingian revisions of *Lex Salica* reflects a different view of abortion than the sixth-century *Pactus legis Salicae*, which accuses women of causing miscarriages by *maleficium*. *Lex Salica emendata* (798) starts its prohibition of abortion with, "If anyone gives herbs to a woman . . ." It does not impute the crime of abortion specifically to women, nor, unlike some versions of the *Pactus legis Salicae*, does it imply that the deadly herbs are to be mixed in a *potus* or magically treated.[77] The capitularies tend to neglect abortion, and they virtually never attribute it to magic. For example, the recently discovered capitulary text from the reign of Louis the Pious refers to destroying a child in utero, but does not indicate the gender of the perpetrator or the means used.[78]

In short, although Carolingian lawmakers and clerics forbade abortion, it was a minor issue for them in the larger constellation that made up their social agenda. They did not question that women were able to manipulate conception or terminate the lives of the young, but magic was downplayed. In the arena where women had traditionally wielded a fearsome power, the Carolingian clergy were skeptical.

The view of dangerous, preternatural females of the stria/lamia type underwent significant evolution over the first millennium. In classical antiquity and the first centuries of the early Middle Ages, they and the goddess Diana were forces to be reckoned with. The stria and lamia magically killed and cannibalized humans; worked in secret; shape-shifted; consumed blood;

---

76. *Lex Baiwariorum* 8.18–19, 361–63 (statutes 20–23 [363–65] deal with abortion caused by men); *Lex Alamannorum* 12, 24; Rivers, *Laws of the Alamans*, 141.

77. *Lex Salica emendata* 21.4, in *Lex Salica: The Ten Texts*, col. 116: "Si quis mulieri herbas dederit, ut infantes habere non possit" (compared to *Pactus legis Salicae* 19.4, 82). On the composition, redactions, and transmission of *Lex Salica* see *Laws of the Salian Franks*, 52–55.

78. *Capitula adhuc conferenda* 8, in Mordek, "Recently Discovered Capitulary Texts," 452; Mistry, *Abortion*, 211–12.

frequented tombs; plied their craft with spells, herbs, rituals, and powders; called down the moon; and intimidated defenseless men. In law codes the mere suggestion that a woman is a stria is a serious charge, one that incurs costly penalties if the accusation is false. Diana, herself unmarried, inspired women to throw off all constraints, leave their husbands' beds, and fly free through the night. By the mid-eighth century, legal documents call into question the very existence of the stria and lamia, and Charlemagne's sweeping programmatic capitularies do not refer to them at all. Tenth-century penitentials strip Diana of the power that "misguided" women had ascribed to her. In the worldview of the elite, the insidious, malevolent, and dominating females had become silly but troublesome fictions.

Although the educated were thoroughly convinced of the chimerical nature of the female beings discussed here, it was still necessary to expunge them from the vocabulary of all Christians, and that is what writers such as Regino and Burchard sought to do. Neither man intended to question the existence of demons in female form (they credited the reality of Diana and Hulda) or that those demons could fly; rather, they both insistently denied that human females could achieve paranormal effects. Their aim reached further than prohibiting deluded women from trafficking with demons; it was to debunk myths enshrouding symbols of female magical power.

Over the first millennium, Christians observed a pattern with very deep roots in human culture by seeking to traffic with deities and mysterious forces to control passions and reproduction. In the Christian era those deities became demons, but the basic contour of the belief that with herbs, potions, spells, and rites, people could affect the course of events through ritual participation with the workings of nature did not change. In regard to many other aspects of magic (revivification, night flight, raising storms, astrology, and so forth), there was modification over time, and the standard educated evaluation by the Carolingian period was that humans did not have the power to accomplish such marvels. Magicians' would-be wonders were demonic figments designed to lead the foolish away from God. But in the case of magic related to love, abortion, and infanticide, such a change in perception did not occur. No source intimates incredulity about the real efficacy demons had to aid humans in the craft of love and birth magic.

Amatory and natal magic were virtually always secretive and private. Either this is the reason they were female identified, or their being female identified is the reason they were secretive. It is hard to say which one was the case, because women and covert magic were so closely linked. In the late antique period, female love magic was the subject of titillating tales men told each other of beautiful, wanton women, who, despite their spell-induced sway over men, were bested in the end. The archeological evidence evens out the picture a bit, but even with regard to curse tablets that men avidly employed, women are still at the heart of love spells. If they themselves are not perpetrators, the cosmic feminine is inherent in the symbols and rituals on which the spells rely. In the early Middle Ages, the perception of women as the agents of love and birth magic did not change. What did change in the Carolingian world was the weight of female sorcery. It is identified as a transgression in the penitentials, but rarely comes up in laws, conciliar records, or histories.[79]

Ironically, given the clandestine nature of love and birth sorcery, Carolingian-era penitential authors have left remarkable specifics about potions and spells, such as those involving grinding men's testicles to powder, women drinking semen or rolling themselves in flour, and maidens walking backward from a stream. Medical materials in particular give shape to the rites and accoutrements of love and birth magic and fill in gaps where references to them in other sources are more cryptic. All extended descriptions of love and birth sorcery involve multilayered rituals that were out of sync with rites prescribed by the church. Caesarius of Arles's appraisal of the proper approach to procreation sums up the guiding principle of Christian belief: whether a woman is fruitful or sterile, she should "desire this from God alone."[80] Magical love and birth rituals were dangerous because they incapsulated a refusal to accept the subversion of human initiative to the will and grace of God. They gave people the means to manipulate humans' deepest passions and the process of birth itself.

---

79. Although women were most closely associated with the manipulation of love and death magic from late antiquity through the Carolingian era, the affinity was not an absolute. Both pagan and Christian men were active in the trade of binding spells in late antiquity. Throughout the early Middle Ages there are references to the manipulation of love and reproduction by priests, and often cures and canons are vague and condemn "anyone" who raises or squelches ardor in another or interferes with birth.

80. Caesarius of Arles, *Sermones*, Sermon 51.4, 1:229: "De solo deo hoc debent desiderare."

CHAPTER 13

Magic, Women, and the Carolingian Court

> King Lothar was ensnared in a blind passion by the
> devilish wiles of his concubine.
>
> —Regino of Prüm, *Chronicon*

Female magic rarely features in histories or similar documents about public affairs, this chapter examines two exceptions from two Carolingian courts where love and birth magic featured in high-stakes politics.

The Case of Empress Judith

In the charged atmosphere of civil strife in the 830s, Empress Judith (d. ca. 843), the most powerful woman in the empire of Louis the Pious, was brought to trial for adultery, and underlying that charge was a suspicion that she employed the magic arts, most likely love magic. In this period, women's sorcery does not often appear in the sources as a major concern. Amatory magic was an exception, especially when it had the potential to impact political events.[1]

Judith's position in Emperor Louis's court is best understood by considering the household of his father, Charlemagne. The emperor's daughters

---

1. On the political events surrounding the charges against Judith see Paschasius Radbert, *Confronting Crisis*, 1–46; de Jong, *Penitential State*, 185–213; Booker, *Past Convictions*; Koch, *Kaiserin Judith*; E. Ward, "Caesar's Wife"; Nelson, *Charles the Bald*, 87–104; McKitterick, *Frankish Kingdoms*, 169–72; Cabaniss, *Judith Augusta*, 7–50.

occupied unofficial, carefully nuanced roles in regnal (then imperial) politics that were instrumental in keeping the royal household running smoothly. Janet Nelson has written about women's informal influence in the court of Charlemagne. Based largely on evidence from poetry, Nelson demonstrates that the daughters, who lived in the inner chambers with the emperor, controlled access to Charlemagne; maintained networks of communication and patronage through letters and the exchange of gifts (often books); participated in hunting, feasting, and sacred court rituals; and were in a position to dispense favors (sometimes sexual) to courtiers.[2]

Along with women's very active and positive functions,[3] there is also evidence of discomfort with women wielding political clout. Alcuin, a preeminent scholar and one of the architects of the Carolingian reform program, warned of the power of the "crowned doves" flitting lightly through the palace chambers—who, in fact, carried considerable weight.[4] The courtier Einhard was critical of his patron's wife, Fastrada (d. 794), and of her influence, which he claimed clouded the emperor's judgment. Einhard said of her, "The cruelty of Queen Fastrada is thought to have been the cause and origin of plots, as it was under her influence that the king was believed to have carried out actions that were innately contrary to his good nature and gentleness."[5] This unease with women in irregular positions of power was explicit in regard to the Eastern Roman *basilissa*, Irene (d. 803). Under the year 801 in the *Lorsch Annals*, the annalist justifies the crowning of Charlemagne on the grounds that there was currently no rightful leadership among the Greeks because Irene's *femineum imperium* was not legitimate.[6]

When Louis took over the governance of the palace at Aachen upon his father's death in 814, one of his first acts was to rid the court of his aunts and other female relatives (*coetus femineus*). Abbott Paschasius Radbert of Corbie (d. ca. 860) suggested that the reason for this was their immorality, but it is more plausible that Louis was eager to replace his father's power base with his own. Louis brought advisers from Aquitaine, which he had been ruling as subking for many years. He also sent away his half-brothers and banished

---

2. Nelson, "Women at the Court"; Nelson, "Gendering Courts," 190–97. See letters from Alcuin, *Ep.* 50, 93–94; *Ep.* 96, 140; *Ep.* 102, 148–49; *Ep.* 190, 317; *Ep.* 196, 323–25.

3. Stafford, *Queens, Concubines, and Dowagers*, 99–114; Nelson, *Frankish World*, 183–97.

4. Alcuin, *Ep.* 244, 392.

5. Einhard, *Vita Karoli Magni* 20, 26: "Harum tamen coniurationum Fastradae reginae crudelitas causa et origo extitisse creditur. Et idcirco in ambabus contra regem conspiratum est, quia uxoris crudelitati consentiens a suae naturae benignitate ac solita mansuetudine inmaniter exorbitasse videbatur."

6. *Annales Laureshamenses* 34 (801), 38. From Nelson ("Women at the Court," 48), in the *Libri Carolini*, Theodulf of Orléans objects to Irene's role in organizing the Seventh Ecumenical Council.

his male cousins, Adalard (d. 827), Charlemagne's political adviser, and Wala (d. 836), abbot of the monastery of Corbie in the valley of the River Somme, to the monasteries of Noirmoutier and Corbie, respectively.[7] Louis himself was not uneasy with women in key, informal, advisory positions. He was under the tutelage of his stepmother, Fastrada, during the winter of 791 and profited from the counsel and active support of both his first and second wives.[8] Although in the courts of Charlemagne's successors, women were removed from the political center, they were still involved in sustaining the good order of the palace.[9]

Judith entered a family that had experienced exceptional stability as a unit; Louis had been married to Ermengard (d. 818) for twenty-four years. The couple produced three sons, among whom they divided responsibility for the governance of the empire in 817—an enactment formalized by the *Ordinatio imperii*. Louis's eldest son, Lothar, was to inherit the title of emperor from his father. Less than a year after his first wife's death, Louis married the young and beautiful Judith, and in 823 she bore a male child, Charles, whose interests she sought to protect. In 829, plans for a new distribution of the empire were drawn up, according to which Charles would inherit Alemannia.

There is a long-lived historiography that puts Judith at the center of the rebellion of the emperor's sons when the *Ordinatio imperii* was redrawn. The narrative asserts that by manipulating her aging husband, Judith destabilized the status quo to her stepsons' disadvantage in order to ensure a patrimony for Charles. However, that portrait of events has now dimmed. Janet Nelson rejects the argument that contemporaries judged Judith's influence in the court of Louis to be excessive or untoward. She argues that the emperor and empress worked together to accomplish mutual aims, and Louis was not dominated by a calculating, overbearing wife. Nelson notes that neither the *Royal Frankish Annals* nor the Astronomer give any indication that Judith was the broker behind the reallocation of lands in 829, although Nelson recognizes that Nithard and the *Prior Metz Annals* accuse the empress of inappropriate influence at court.[10] Also, a not-so-carefully-veiled inference

---

7. On the court of Louis the Pious see Paschasius Radbert, *Confronting Crisis*, 15–29; Booker, *Past Convictions*; Airlie, "Bonds of Power"; Schieffer, *Die Karolinger*, 112–38; Nelson, *Charles the Bald*, 41–74. On Paschasius Radbert and Wala see de Jong, *Epitaph for an Era*, 44–68; *Charlemagne's Cousins*, introd.

8. See Airlie ("World," 65–67) on women in Nithard's *Histories*.

9. Nelson, *Charles the Bald*, 43–44.

10. Ibid., 87. On the same question see Staubach, "Des grossen." The following (now dated) studies portray Judith as domineering: Riché, *Carolingians*, 149–53; Fichtenau, *Carolingian Empire*, 40; Halphen, *Études critiques*, 101.

that Judith unduly controlled imperial patronage comes through Einhard's assertion that even Angel Gabriel had to go through proper channels (meaning Judith) if he wanted to communicate with Louis. Paschasius Radbert's funeral oration for Abbot Wala of Corbie, was anything but subtle. "[Louis] took no one into confidence unless [Judith] approved, nor was he willing to listen to anyone or show them affection or agree with them . . . unless she commended them to him in faith, and—what is more ominous—he had no other will (as they say) than what she herself willed."[11] Nelson's analysis is certainly correct in that, upon her marriage, Judith was quickly integrated into the royal family and Louis's sons' resentment over the property allocation of 829 was centered on Louis himself, not on Judith or Charles. But by 830, some writers clearly came to see Judith's authority as overweening and threatening. However, it was not in the realm of land allocation that the queen's position was begrudged, but in the domain of the imperial family—the realm in miniature.

Bernard of Septimania (d. 844), the count of Barcelona and an adviser to Louis, was implicated along with Judith for adultery and sorcery. He was Louis's godson and distant cousin, whom Louis appointed chamberlain. This infuriated other magnates. Bernard had been charged with the defense of southern Aquitaine against Arab attacks. In 826 to 827 he proved his ability while Count Hugh of Tours (d. 837) and Count Matfrid of Orléans (d. 836), two long-standing notables of the Carolingian court (Hugh was Lothar's father-in-law), bungled military defenses in the same area. They were stripped of office and, but for the intercession of Wala of Corbie, might have been executed for their incompetence. Meanwhile, Bernard received accolades. In his history of the conflicts of Louis's sons, Nithard (d. 844) said the emperor entrusted young Charles to Bernard "and made [the duke] second only to himself in the empire." For the Astronomer, Bernard had become a bulwark against Louis's enemies.[12]

Important players in the allegations against Bernard and Judith were Archbishop Agobard of Lyon; Counts Matfrid of Orléans and Hugh of Tours (whom Bernard had outshone in the field); Abbot Paschasius Radbert and

---

11. Nelson, "Women at the Court" and "Gendering Courts," 190–97. Paschasius Radbert, *Epitaphium Arsenii* 2.9, 172.

12. Nithard, *Historiarum* 1.3, 3: "Ad quod Bernardum quendam, ducem Septimaniae, pater in supplementum sibi sumens camerarium constituit Karolumque eidem commendavit ac secundum a se in imperio praefecit." Nithard's history of the sons of Louis the Pious was written for an aristocratic audience by a man involved in the events he narrates. Nelson ("Public *Histories*") demonstrates that this history is both a public record and a private exposé of conflicting values and loyalties. McKitterick (*Carolingians and the Written Word*, 236–37) doubts whether Nithard's history ever reached the noble audience for which it was intended. Astronomer, *Vita Hludowici imperatoris* 43, 434.

Wala of Corbie, an intimate of Lothar. All these men were unsettled in one way or another by Louis's reallocation of his patrimony in 829.

In 830, Hugh, Matfrid, and Wala rallied Lothar's partisans and launched a campaign of intra-palace slander against Bernard and the empress. They accused the two of adultery, Bernard of perfidious disloyalty and ambition, and Judith of exerting an overweening and altogether inappropriate feminine influence over Louis. The emperor himself was not spared in the calumny. Although his detractors held him innocent of overt crimes, he was said to have failed as a king because he did not keep his wife in check.[13] Sorcery was among this complex of denunciations.

Two treatises comprise the principle texts for the defamation of Judith in the 830s: the *Liber apologeticus* of Agobard of Lyon and the *Epitaphium Arsenii* of Paschasius Radbert. Elizabeth Ward notes that both authors understood Judith through the hermeneutic of powerful and malign Old Testament queens.[14] I add that in addition to the charges of adultery and unnatural feminine regimen, another important similarity between the works is that in both, Judith is compared to Jezebel, who, according to the biblical books of Kings, oversees the introduction of foreign cults and idol worship into the household of Ahab, the Hebrew king. In both the Old and New Testaments, the infamous Queen Jezebel is conniving and manipulative; she dominates her husband and leads him to make disastrous decisions that imperil Israel.

During the 820s, Agobard had run afoul of royal power, so when the dynastic crisis erupted in 830 he was already predisposed to oppose the emperor. His two treatises, the first against Judith and the second in defense of Louis's sons, are contemporary with the events of the second filial revolt in 833, having been written when the sons held their father in captivity. Agobard expresses the expectation that the home (even the very politicized royal household) be loyal and harmonious, and he is vexed that this is not the case in Louis's extended family. He blames Judith in the harshest terms and lays at her feet the responsibility for the discord in the palace. He charges that she is frivolous in the extreme, expecting to rule an empire when she cannot run a palace.[15] Agobard is circumspect in accusing the empress of magic. He describes her actions as *facini*, a word that means crimes or villainies but also connotes magic, and he writes that she got her way with Louis through

---

13. de Jong, *Epitaph for an Era*, 138–39, 142. Agobard of Lyon (*Liber apologeticus* 1.1–2, 309–10) said that Louis's downfall was precipitated by his failure to satisfy Judith in bed.

14. E. Ward, "Agobard of Lyons."

15. Agobard of Lyon, *Liber apologeticus* 1.5, 311–12; Boshof, *Erzbischof Agobard von Lyon*, 195–208.

granting carnal favors and indecent flatteries (*per carnalium blandimenta et cupidorum scelestos favores atque indecoras adolationes*).[16]

Furthermore, he compares her reign to periods of backsliding in the Old Testament when the people worshipped idols (*idola et simulacra*). In his second book, Agobard continues the analogy linking Judith to the villainous biblical queen Jezebel, who introduced false gods and "whoredoms and sorceries" into the palace (2 Kings 9:22).[17] Jezebel "killed off the prophets of the Lord,"[18] instituted the worship of Baal, and led her husband to pay this god obeisance (1 Kings 16:31–33). In Revelations, the angel of the lord castigates the church in Thyatira saying "But I have this against you: You tolerate that woman Jezebel, who calls herself a prophet and is teaching and beguiling my servants to practice fornication and to eat food sacrificed to idols"(Rev. 2:20). By equating Judith and Jezebel, Agobard elevates the evils of magic to the cuckolding an aging king. Even beyond the offense of destabilizing a precarious political situation, for Agobard, the fact that the empress had trafficked with demons constituted a strike at the very heart of the peace and concord, the honor and glory of the unified Christian empire. It was polluting.

Although Agobard stops short of accusing Judith of *maleficium*, he implies it. His insinuation that both she and Jezebel are whores and sorceresses is not subtle. Agobard calls Judith "the author of evils" (*auctrice vero malorum*).[19] The juxtaposition of Judith's *facini* with her salacious seductions points to love magic. Sex and concealment, the traditional elements of women's magic, come together in Agobard's condemnations.

In *Epitaphium Arseni*, the second text regarding the events of 830, a charge of magic is unambiguous. However, Radbert makes it against Bernard directly, but against Judith only obliquely.

> From all quarters [Arsenius] began to hear about things infamous and obscene, immoral and dishonourable—not just of any sort, but such as have never been heard of in this age of ours. . . . The palace, which had once been a seat of honour, had become a theatre in which so many

---

16. Agobard of Lyon, *Liber apologeticus* 1–2, 309–10.
17. Ibid., 2.9–11, 316–18. For a comparison of similar treatments of earlier queens see Nelson, "Queens as Jezebels." Keller ("Zum Sturz Karls III") compares conflicts involving Judith and Bernard of Septimania to issues surrounding Bertilla, the wife of Berengar I (d. 924).
18. 1 Kings 18:4; 1 Kings 18.13; 1 Kings 18.19; 1 Kings 19.1.
19. Agobard of Lyon, *Liber apologeticus* 1.2, 310. According to the Carolingian espousal of public penance, sinners sent to monasteries to perform penance were expected to stay throughout their lives. From de Jong (*Penitential State*, 228–34), Agobard was furious that this was not the case with Judith in 830.

recurring impostures of soothsayers were bubbling up as one would never believe to have existed in the entire world.

Then, when [Arsenius's messengers] understood what was going on, they reported to Arsenius evils in this world that had scarcely ever been heard of, that in such a glorious empire everything had suddenly been transformed. The palace had become a brothel where fornication held sway and an adulterer ruled, where crimes piled upon one another, where every type of evil deed and sorcery of magicians could be found, so much as I never could have believed still existed in the world.

There is neither mind, tongue nor voice that can relate the schemes that this madman [Naso] undertook, enveloped as he was in the filth of every sort of crime. For he intended to take control of everything through diabolical sorcery and prevail not through counsel, but to usurp power through omens and divination, because he had so deluded the most sacred emperor through his impostures. . . . The emperor was going like an innocent lamb to the slaughter. The great and merciful emperor, deceived by the one (*qua*) whom Solomon had warned him about.[20]

By Radbert's account, it was only out of dire necessity that Wala ("mourning and grieving") agreed to join the revolt against his king, but he was driven by desperation to rid the realm of the tyrant, Bernard, along with the sorcerers, "diviners, soothsayers and the mute, the dream-interpreters and those who inspect entrails, and many others who had been trained in the dark arts." By this "devilish craft," he goes on to say, Louis was actually unaware of what was going on and that the tricks and dark arts were being practiced against him—the very king. This section of text is followed directly with the author's judgment that Judith so tightly controlled access to Louis that not even his bishops and loyal counselors were able to reach him. This claim implicates Judith in the plot to bewitch and incapacitate Louis with spells. She isolated the king and kept him spellbound by magic, or she facilitated the other sorcerers in the palace.[21]

After the revolt of 830, Louis exiled Wala for a fourth time to Corbie, and Radbert painted his political eclipse as a moral triumph, framing it in the context of the banishment of the prophet Elijah, banished by a powerful

---

20. Paschasius Radbert, *Epitaphium Arsenii* 2.8, 164; 2.8, 167; 9.2, 169. Arsenius is a pseudonym for Wala, and Naso is an alias for Bernard. On the theatrical elements of the *Epitaphium* see Booker, "Hypocrisy."

21. Paschasius Radbert, *Epitaphium Arsenii* 2.9, 171–72.

queen whose religious proclivities tended to the demonic. Or Wala is like the prophet Jeremiah in the court of Nebuchadrezzar (d. ca. 561 BCE), who warned Israel against false prophets, diviners, idolaters, and those who dream (Jer. 27:9; Jer. 29:8).[22]

Paschasius saw magic as a palpable and menacing factor in the events of the realm; his accusations are more than slurs.[23] However, whereas he blatantly accuses Bernard of magic, he dances around Judith, clearly implicating her by drawing parallels between her and pagan biblical queens, but he never directly charges her. What sort of magic is Judith putatively practicing? Because the reference is oblique, it is hard to tell. Amatory magic frequently is paired with lasciviousness in sources from late antiquity throughout the Middle Ages, and given that Judith's offenses involved emasculating a king and—Jezebel-like—seducing a courtier, love magic is most likely.

It seems logical that the reason Radbert was careful only to hint at Judith's involvement in magic was because the *Epitaphium Arsenii* was written in the mid- to late 850s,[24] when Judith's son, Charles, was securely on the throne. A direct accusation against Judith may have been too risky (even though Radbert was at that time estranged from Charles). Bernard, on the other hand, was dead and his family had lost all power. However, I suggest that this is not the reason that Radbert failed to portray Judith as the instigator in the coven of maleficii at the palace. For one thing, there is no evidence that the *Epitaphium Arsenii* was intended for or reached an audience outside of Corbie.[25] Second, Radbert's defamation of Judith's character and morals is so unabashed that it is doubtful that a more direct charge of sorcery would have made the author's position any less politically secure. Judith is not the ringleader because Radbert, like other Carolingian writers, was disinclined to view women as particularly commanding in the manipulation of sorcery. Radbert can clearly depict her as a seductress and adulteress, but not as a ringleader in the use of black arts; that role is reserved for Bernard. Unlike the masterful Merovingian queen consort, Fredegund, another queen accused of magic in a very different era, Judith is complicit in the maleficium but is not the master of it.

---

22. Ibid., 13–15, 162–34; de Jong, *Epitaph for an Era*, 138–39, 162–66; Booker, *Past Convictions*, 43–47.

23. Ganz ("*Epitaphium Arsenii*," 548–50) argues that Radbert's disappointment with Louis was due to the king's disregard of the imperial ideal in favor of vulgar partisan politics.

24. Ibid., 538–41.

25. Paschasius Radbert, *Confronting Crisis*, 12–15; Ganz, "*Epitaphium Arsenii*," 538.

An assembly was held at Nijmegen in 831 at which Judith was to answer "anyone who would charge her or a crime," but nobody came forth.[26] In Agobard's treatise, the allegations of magic were muted and served more to bolster and intensify other charges—specifically, infidelity (the king's marriage bed had been infiltrated)—and he describes no rituals or accoutrements of magic. For Radbert, the most compelling and damaging indictment was that she had made Bernard her lover. The male conspirator was fashioned as the master magician; Judith was more the harlot who could only ply her sorcery in the bedroom.[27]

Another aristocratic woman was executed for magic shortly after Judith's exoneration: Gerberga, the sister of Bernard of Septimania. Little is known of the circumstances surrounding her death. In 834, Lothar seized Gerberga from her convent, condemned her for magic (*mores maleficorum*), and had her thrown into the Saône River. This incident is recorded in Nithard's history, the West Frankish *Annals of Saint Bertin*, Thegan's (d. ca. 850) *Life of the Emperor Louis*, and the Astronomer's biography of Louis the Pious.[28] All entries are cryptic regarding the event, but it is clear that his sister's execution was related to Bernard of Septimania's disgrace in 830 and his subsequent political misfortunes. What is less clear is why the recrimination against Gerberga took the form it did. Why was she accused of sorcery? Was it love magic employed to further the interests of her brother? The killing of Gerberga was consequential as demonstrated by the fact that it is recorded in four histories. Even though each source mentions the offense of employing the magic arts, it is unlikely that Gerberga was hunted down for trafficking with demons. If magic were the actual issue, the annalists would have been more explicit about the nature of the crime and what damage it had caused. It seems more likely that Gerberga was killed because she was Bernard's sister, and the charge of sorcery provided a tidy link with her brother's criminality. In this era, a woman's magic was not, in and of itself, worth a manhunt.[29]

The historical texts written about the rebellion of 830 mention magic because it relates to imperial politics and the conflicting interests of Louis and his sons, and they provide an important example of the way that accusations

---

26. *Annales Bertiniani* 831, 3: Percunctatusque est populus, si quislibet in eam aliquod crimen obicere vellet. Cumque nullus inventus esset, qui quodlibet illi malum inferret, purificavit se secundum iudicium Francorum de omnibus quibus accusata fuerat.

27. From Nelson ("Women at the Court," 58), charges of lasciviousness in Carolingian courts were "code for political opposition."

28. Nithard, *Historiarum* 1.5, 7–8. Nithard's history belongs to a genre that McKitterick (*Carolingians and the Written Word*, 238–39) calls "aristocratic or royal house histories." *Annales Bertiniani* 834, 9; Thegan, *Gesta Hludovici Imperatoris* 52, 244; Astronomer, *Vita Hludowici imperatoris* 52, 496.

29. Booker, *Past Convictions*, 153–54.

of magic could become a tool used against the publicly powerful or well connected, both men and women.[30] Carolingian histories (like Merovingian ones) include matters that had an impact on affairs of state, but for Carolingian historians, the magical machinations of women were rarely significant in and of themselves. In the case of Judith, her love magic created disorder in the royal household and threatened family unity, but it was Bernard who had the real capacity to destabilize the empire through the magic arts. Even the Benedictine monk and poet, Notker the Stammerer (d. 912), was very willing to interpret events in terms of the supernatural or demonic, did not talk about female sorcery in his history.[31] In the latter half of the early medieval period, women's magic, even love magic, was not represented as a commanding force. This pattern plays out again in the next generation of Carolingian queens.

The Case of Theutberga and Waldrada

Upon his father's death in 855, Lothar II inherited the northern portion of Middle Francia as his share of the emperor's patrimony.[32] That same year, out of purely political motives, he married the noblewoman Theutberga. The problem arose from the fact that the new king was devoted to a woman other than his wife. His real desire was to be with Waldrada (d. after 869), his mistress of several years and the mother of his offspring. After two years of a childless marriage with Theutberga, Lothar sought to rid himself of this barren wife and to make Waldrada his queen, but he soon found that this was not going to be easy. Lothar's efforts created a political maelstrom that set in motion a complex chain of events lasting from 855 to 869, one in which the principal noble, royal, and episcopal rulers of Europe had a stake.[33] In the domestic affairs of Lothar II, the question of marriage came to the fore,[34] and

---

30. McNamara, *Sisters in Arms*, 170–71.
31. Notker the Stammerer, *The Deeds of Emperor Charles the Great*, in *Charlemagne and Louis the Pious*, 59–118; Goetz, *Strukturen der spätkarolingischen Epoche*, 59–69.
32. By the early tenth century this area was called Lotharingia, after Lothar II. It stretched from west of the Rhine River to the Scheldt River and from the North Sea south to the Jura Mountains. The division was ratified on Lothar's deathbed at a monastery in Prüm. See *Annales Bertiniani* 855, 45; Regino of Prüm, *Chronicon* 855, 77.
33. The following discussion of the events surrounding the divorce is indebted to Noble, "Pope Nicholas I and the Franks"; *Divorce of King Lothar*, introd.; Heidecker, *Divorce of Lothar II*; Esmyol, *Geliebte oder Ehefrau*, 159–81; Airlie, "Private Bodies"; Hincmar of Reims, *De divortio Lotharii regis*, introd.; Nelson, *Charles the Bald*, 190–220; McKitterick, *Frankish Kingdoms*, 176–79; Devisse, *Hincmar, archévêque de Reims*, 1:354–60, 1:386–429; Brühl, "Hincmariana II."
34. Heidecker, *Divorce of Lothar II*, 1–8, 77–86, 105–28, 152–57, 176–79; Kottje, "Kirchliches Recht"; Hincmar of Reims, *De divortio de Lotharii regis, Responsio*, 65–74.

the matrimonial conflict gave rise to a lengthy treatise by Hincmar of Reims (d. 882), which provides insight into this powerful bishop's understanding of amatory sorcery and his perception of women's magical abilities.

Even before his father's death, Lothar had entered a liaison with Waldrada, daughter of a noble family of Alsace, but political exigencies dictated that he marry Theutberga. She was a daughter of the house of Count Boso (d. 855), and, fearing the aggressive ambitions of his brother, Louis, king of Italy (d. 875), Lothar created a large duchy just north of the Alps and granted it to Boso's son, Hubert (d. 864), lay abbot of Saint Maurice d'Agaune. In 855, to further cement the relationship, Lothar reluctantly put away his mistress and accepted Hubert's sister, Theutberga, in marriage. The union, however, was unhappy from the start. Lothar and Waldrada chafed under their separation, and when in 857 Theutberga had not produced a son, the king sought to divorce her so that he could resume and formalize his relationship with Waldrada. Lothar was in need of an heir to bolster his territorial position against the aggression of his uncles, and Waldrada had already borne him a son, Hugh (d. 895).[35]

In the effort to extricate himself from his lawful marriage, Lothar and his bishops requested an annulment on the grounds that Theutberga and her brother, Hubert, had practiced sodomy before her marriage and that she had conceived and then aborted a child.[36] The method of termination remains unclear. Bishop Hincmar of Reims, who produced an extensive treatise on the divorce, writes that Theutberga purportedly drank a potion (*potus*) to end pregnancy. He does not identify the potion as magic, nor do any of the other sources that discuss the divorce. However, sorcery is implied. The overlapping dimensions of "potion," "poison," and a magical drink were intrinsic to the classical and early medieval understanding of the terms. As discussed in chapter 6, the important fact about poison is that it was toxic; what accounted for that toxicity—simple poison, herbal mixtures, magic, or a combination of all three—was, for the most part, of secondary importance.[37]

---

35. Konecny, *Die Frauen*, 108, puts Hugh's birth later, around 860. On Lothar's and Waldrada's emotional attachment see *Annales Xantenses* 861, 19: "The king truly loved his concubine, and because of that love he abandoned his wife" (Rex vero concubina, cuius amore uxorem reliquit publice usus est). On Lothar's and Theutberga's mutual hatred see *Annales Bertiniani* 860, 52: "Lothar hated his queen, Theutberga, irrevocably"(Lotharius reginam suam Teutbergam irrevocabili odio habitam). The queen returned the sentiment saying that "she would rather flee among the pagans than see again the face of the glorious king Lothar" (cited in Bishop, "Bishops as Marital Advisors," 63). See also Rampton, "Love and the Divorce of Lothar II."

36. *Annales Bertiniani* 860, 53; Hincmar of Reims, *De divortio Lotharii regis*, Interrogatio 1, 114.

37. From Filotas (*Pagan Survivals*, 277), common terms for magically treated drinks are *potiones*, *potatones*, *potus* or "that which is given in cups (*in pocula*)."

The equivalence of "potus" to a magically treated drink is consistent over the early medieval centuries. In Gregory of Tours's discussion of Mummolus, whom Fredegund arrested for killing her son, his female acolytes—self-identified *maleficae*—provide him with a miraculous herb that was to be concocted into a drink. Caesarius of Arles denounced women who took "poisonous draughts" to cause "premature death to their children." Caesarius does not specify magic, but the proscription in included in a sermon on magical practices. In the section on murder in the *Penitential of Theodore*, there are various tariffs for killing. A murder "by a potion or some trick" occasioned a stiff penance of "seven years or more." Both the words "potion" (*poculum*) and "trick" (*artem*) denote magic in this context. The Bavarian code, title 8.18, fines any woman who gives a *"potio"* to another woman to induce an abortion. Three ninth-century pastoral texts list preparing or imbibing *potiones* in and among other patently magic practices. In his *On Synodal Causes*, Regino of Prüm establishes a line of questioning to determine whether a woman has induced abortion, prevented conception, or killed her husband, and he uses "herbs," "potions," and "poison" interchangeably. In the same source the author assigns a seven-year penance "if a woman kills anyone by magic, that is, by a drink."[38] In short, the allegation that Theutberga terminated her pregnancy by a *potio*, is tantamount to an allegation of magic.

To counter the scandalous claims regarding incest and abortion, in 858 Queen Theutberga appeared before a crowd of nobles at the palace of Aachen to clear herself of all charges through the judicial ordeal by water. Theutberga's proxy thrust his hand into a boiling pot and drew out a scalding stone.[39] After three days, the wound had healed; it was "uncooked" (incoctus),[40] and the queen was reinstated to her throne, but not, by his design, to the king's bed.

Zubin Mistry makes the observation that although abortion was among the charges Lothar's partisans brought against Theutberga in the early stages of the divorce proceedings, the issue was soon backgrounded, and by 863 abortion had long since "evaporated from the sources."[41] Other offenses, such as incest, had become more pressing both for Lothar's case and for his

---

38. Gregory of Tours, *Decem libri historiarum* 6.35, 305–6; Caesarius of Arles, *Sermones*, Sermon 52, 1:231; *Poenitentiale Theodori* 1.4.7: "si per poculum vel artem aliquam IIII. annos aut plus," in *Councils and Ecclesiastical Documents*, 3:180; Filotas, *Pagan Survivals*, 278; Regino of Prüm, *De synodalibus causis* 1.5.8, 209; ibid., 2.81, 246: "Mulier, si aliquos interimit arte malefica."

39. On Theutberga's confession and trial by ordeal see Heidecker, *Divorce of Lothar II*, 63–67; Hartmann, *Die Synoden der Karolingerzeit*, 377; Hyams, "Trial by Ordeal." On ordeal by boiling water see *Pactus legis Salicae* 56, 210–14; *Lex Ribuaria* 32, 85.

40. Hincmar of Reims, *De divortio Lotharii regis*, Interrogatio 1, 114.

41. Mistry, *Abortion*, 244–61 (quotation 244).

detractors. In his treatise on the divorce, Hincmar dismisses the whole idea of a magically induced abortion.

Over the next several years, Lothar lived with Waldrada and lobbied his uncles and bishops for support of a divorce.[42] A series of ecclesiastical tribunals at Aachen between 860 and 862 heard the case. The decision was far from unanimous, but in 862 the majority of Lothar's bishops supported his wishes and accepted the king's union with Waldrada as legitimate.[43] Pope Nicholas I (d. 867), on hearing the decision, categorically rejected it. Over the next seven years, Lothar, his "wives," his bishops, his uncles, and two popes maneuvered, jockeyed, schemed, formed and broke alliances, and debated over this critical domestic affair that had become anything but private.[44]

Unfortunately for Lothar, his timing was inopportune. He sought a divorce at just the point in the development of canon law when the subject of marriage was undergoing scrutiny and revision by reforming theologians.[45] Among the principals in the dispute was Bishop Hincmar of Reims, who, at the behest of dissident Lotharingian bishops and magnates who opposed their sovereign's divorce, took up the question of matrimony in an extensive treatise called *On the Divorce of King Lothar and Queen Theutberga*.

Repudiating noble women was not as easy as it had been in Charlemagne's day. More and more churchmen were frowning on divorce and remarriage if both members of the couple were still living, especially if the marriage had been consummated. But it could be done. Count Stephen of Auvergne was a supporter of Charles the Bald, and in exchange for his *honores* he was required to marry the daughter of Count Raymond. He did so, but sought to rescind the betrothal after only a few months. Hincmar puts this case in the context of magically induced impotence, writing that if, "by the workings of the devil" (*operante diablo*), a couple's ability to have intercourse is impeded, and after satisfactory effort the problem is not solved, the two can separate and marry elsewhere. Here Hincmar takes the position that magically induced impotence is legitimate grounds for separation. This decision may have been motivated to some extent (Hincmar wished to please his

---

42. Konecny, *Die Frauen*, 104–5. *Annales Bertiniani* 858, 50. Lothar was forced to take the queen back, but he locked her up.
43. *De divortio Lotharii regis, Responsio* 1, January 860, 119–21; February 860, 121–22; *Annales Bertiniani* 862, 60; Airlie, "Private Bodies."
44. *Annales Bertiniani* 865–69, 74–101; *Annales Fuldenses* 865–69, 63–70; Regino of Prüm, *Chronicon* 866, 86–87; Nicholas I, *Ep.* 42, 315–16; *Ep.* 46, 319–22; *Ep.* 48, 322; *Ep.* 48, 329–32.
45. Joye, "Family Order"; Heideker, *Divorce of Lothar II*, 11–35; Bitel, *Women*, 164–89; Olsen, "Marriage in Barbarian Kingdom," 162–79; Chélini, *L'Aube*, 171–98; Wemple, *Women in Frankish Society*, chaps. 4 and 5; See McNamara and Wemple ("Marriage and Divorce") on changes in marriage and the move to monogamy.

patron Charles the Bald), or his views shifted later in the year. When it came to the divorce of Lothar and Theutberga, the bishop did not leave room for divorce due to the effects of the magic arts.[46]

During the conflict over Lothar's divorce, the accusations of magic lodged against the women involved followed a pattern familiar in the early medieval world. Waldrada, although officially powerless, had an informal bond to the king that put her in a position to shape the kingdoms of Europe.[47] She was accused of using love magic to ensnare Lothar. Theutberga, whose authority was in every way legitimate, was nonetheless assailed by slurs of abhorrent lasciviousness when Lothar's bishops suggested she used sorcery to effect the abortion of the child she had supposedly conceived with her brother, Hubert.[48] This charge brought against Theutberga was indexed on the hot-button issue of incest, which was the strongest in Lothar's arsenal because it had long been an undisputed impediment to marriage. Virtually no one questioned the tenet that incest rendered the offender unfit for marriage.[49] The accusation that the queen had "known" her brother was sweetened by charges of sodomy, abortion, and sorcery.[50] None of these was as damning as incest, but they made the case stronger.[51]

Valerie Flint has suggested that "Hincmar truly believed that witches were very widely to be found, that they could exercise a real and preternatural power and that they were usually female."[52] I interpret Hincmar's work differently. There is no reason to doubt that the bishop believed in the efficacy of magic, but it is questionable whether he thought "witches were very widely to be found." Hincmar evinced relatively scant interest in sorcery throughout his writings, but he brought up magic in *The Divorce of King Lothar* because it presented an argument for countering the divorce. When in 857 Lothar's

---

46. Hincmar of Reims, *Ep.* 136, 87–107; Ubl, *Inzestverbot*, 352–56; Rider, *Magic and Impotence*, 39–42; Bishop, "Bishops as Marital Advisors."
47. Heidecker, *Divorce of Lothar II*, 154. For a discussion of "articulate" and "inarticulate power" see Douglas, *Witchcraft Confessions and Accusations*, xiii–xxxviii; and Brown, "Sorcery."
48. Regino of Prüm, *Chronicon* 864, 81: "Thietbirga confessa fuisset, semetipsam fratris germani incestudo concubitu esse pollutam." See also see Hincmar, *De divortio Lotharii regis*, Interrogatio 1, 114.
49. Hincmar (*De divortio Lotharii regis*, Responsio 12, 195–96) accepted that incest before marriage was grounds for divorce. From Airlie ("Private Bodies," 19), incest was the key accusation against Theutberga, and although it did not appear in the texts until 860, it was likely part of the initial accusation in 857. See also McNamara and Wemple, "Marriage and Divorce," 99–102.
50. On sorcery see Regino of Prüm, *Chronicon* 864, 80; *Annales Bertiniani* 862, 60; and the discussion of Hincmar's *De divortio Lotharii regis* later in this chapter.
51. On the incest taboo and Lothar's divorce see Ubl, *Inzestverbot*, 340–59. On conciliar marriage legislation, see Fransen, "La rupture du marriage."
52. Flint, *Rise of Magic*, 293.

circle accused Theutberga of polluting herself through incest and aborting a child with the aid of a magic potion, they asserted that she did all this while maintaining physical virginity.[53] Hincmar did not credit the allegation that Theutberga conceived and aborted a birth by magical means, but he also did not offer in Theutberga's defense the proposition that the magic arts are incapable of inducing a miscarriage. Rather, it was other details of the accusation that he found unconvincing. In *The Divorce of King Lothar,* the bishop points out that Theutberga could not have conceived a child with Hubert because they were reputed to have had intercourse between her thighs "the way men are accustomed to do these foul deeds with other men," and that she would not have been physically intact if she had experienced coitus and/ or abortion.[54] In any case, because Theutberga had cleared herself through the ordeal, Hincmar considered moot her culpability in the charges of incest, pregnancy, and sorcerous abortion.[55] But the king's mistress was another story.

It was rumored that Waldrada, like Theutberga, used sorcery, but to "ensnare" and "dement" Lothar by driving him into a "blind passion" through love magic.[56] In his discussion of the subject, Hincmar does not question the premise that women can and do manipulate demons to achieve certain ends.[57] Although Hincmar relies on authorities, at times verbatim, and employs traditional topoi, some of his descriptions of magical practices draw in customs that are not copied from other sources.[58] He shames women who "debilitate" men by weaving spells into their woolen works,

---

53. Council of Aachen 862 in MGH Conc. aevi Kar. 4.9, 68–89. This argument was important for Lothar's party, which had asserted that the queen was sterile due to the abortion she had induced. *De divortio Lotharii regis, Interregatio* 1, 114–16, and *Interregatio* 12, 177. Rider, *Magic and Impotence,* 35. See Flint ("Susanna and the Lothar Crystal") on the magical dimensions of the crystal and its relationship to the accusations against Theutberga. Flint's analysis has been rightly belied by Kornbluth's "Susanna Crystal."

54. *De divortio Lotharii regis, Interrogatio* 1, 114: "Uxor domni regis Hlotharii primo quidem reputata est de stupro, quasi frater suus cum ea masculino concubitu inter/femora, sicut solent *masculi in masculos turpitudinem operari* [Rom. 1:27]." Hincmar (*De divortio Lotharii regis, Responsio* 12, 182) protested that the only woman to conceive without heterosexual intercourse was the Virgin Mary. See Mistry, *Abortion,* 238–61; Heidecker, *Divorce of Lothar II,* 68.

55. Hincmar of Reims, *De divortio de Lotharii regis, Interrogatio* and *Responsio* 6, 146–60.

56. *Annales Bertiniani* 862, 60: "Hlotharius Waldradam concubinam, maleficis ut ferebatur artibus dementatus, et ipsius pellicis, pro qua uxorem suam Theotbergam abiecerat, caeco amore inlectus." See also Regino of Prüm, *Chronicon* 864, 80; and Karras, *Unmarriages,* 38–45.

57. Hincmar of Reims, *De divortio de Lotharii regis, Responsio* 15, 207–8.

58. Ibid., 205–13, examples of magic acts and substances that Hincmar did not take from other sources include measuring a person with thread, conjuring by juggling, coals, herbs, bits of snail, shells, snakes, livers, hair, ashes, and shoulder blades of animals. On shells and women's spells see Enright, *Lady with a Mead Cup,* 116. See also Rider, *Magic and Impotence,* 34, 52.

and he accepts the reality of the striae and lamiae, who, while their male victims are intoxicated with certain foods and drinks, hypnotize and seduce them and, with the help of demons, create a phantasm to convince their victims that they have been transformed.[59] Hincmar asserts that women make love philters with "bones of the dead, ashes, coals, and pubic hairs of men and women, which they tie together with many colored threads and various herbs, snails and serpent parts while singing incantations." Continuing, he writes that while men are "dressed and covered with enchanted clothing, demented by the food and drink of the sorceresses, and spell bound by the songs of witches," women enthrall their prey.[60]

In *The Divorce of King Lothar*, Hincmar poses the basic question as to whether "it is possible, as many people say, that there are women who by their magic are able to send irreconcilable hatred between man and wife and to join the man and woman again by indescribable love?"[61] He had already addressed this question in his treatise on Stephen. In both cases his answer to the question is, yes, this is possible. Magic can induce ungovernable passion between a couple, and it can also make two people repugnant to each other. He demonstrates the first type of magic by reference to Old Testament figures and a story about a woman of a neighboring parish who had bewitched her son-in-law, rendering him impotent. To illustrate the opposite effect of love magic, Hincmar relates the tale of a senator named Proterius, who hoped to dedicate his daughter to a monastery. A young man of the village, however, desires the girl, and he seeks out a *maleficus* whose charms, as it turned out, are not strong enough to move the girl's heart. So the magician refers his client directly to demons. The devils lift the lad to Satan's court, where the two enter into a contract: the girl's love for the boy's soul.[62]

The point of each story is that although love magic can be effective, its effects can also be reversed. In the case of Proterius's daughter, the young

---

59. Hincmar of Reims, *De divortio de Lotharii regis*, *Responsio* 15, 208: "Vel quibuscumque mensuris mensurandis et quas superventas feminae in suis laneficiis vel textilibus operibus nominant." alii vero tantum carminibus a strigis fascinati et quasi enerves effecti reperti sunt. Ibid., 206: "Quidam autem a lamiis sive genichialibus feminis debilitati."

60. Ibid., 206: "Turpe est fabulas nobis notas referre et longum est sacrilegia computare, quae ex huiusmodi de ossibus mortuorum atque cineribus carbonibusque extinctis et de capillis atque pilis locorum genitalium virorum ac feminarum cum filulis colorum multiplicicum et herbis variis ac clocleolis et serpentium particulis composita cum carminibus incantata," and "Quidam etiam vestibus carminatis induebantur vel cooperiebantur, alii potu, alii autem cibo a sorciariis dementati."

61. Ibid., 205: "De hoc, quod interrogatum est, si hoc verum esse possit, quod plures homines dicunt, quia sunt feminae, quae maleficio suo inter virum et uxorem odium inreconciliabile possint mittere et inenarrabilem amorem iterum inter virum et feminam serere."

62. Ibid., 205-6, 210.

man who seduced her comes to regret his diabolical bargain and is able to extricate himself from it with the help of his bishop, Basil of Caesarea. The bishop saves the marriage by the application of "sacred medicine" (*medicinam ecclesiasticam*), which includes prayers, blessings, holy water, salt, and exorcisms.[63]

The application of Hincmar's story to Lothar and Theutberga was clear. Lothar's abhorrence of his wife and her inability to conceive should not be barriers to their continued marriage because they were caused by Waldrada's magic and so were remediable.[64] Consistent with the prevailing ecclesiastical opinion of his time, the bishop's prime interest was to preserve legally constituted marriage. He felt divorce was justifiable in cases of prohibited degrees (marrying close kin) and irreversible impotence, but not because one party or the other had been enchanted.[65] He concluded that magic could be undone and should therefore not be an impediment to marriage, nor should it constitute the grounds for divorce. For Hincmar, women's facility with love magic, although real and exasperating, was not in the final analysis particularly effective. It could be managed.

In two Carolingian courts, three queens found themselves at the epicenter of highly consequential and intense imperial politics. All were accused of untoward sexual license, and those accusations were accompanied by allegations of magic. However, in each case, the charge of sorcery was not really about magic per se; it was motivated by the women's political position. The notion that Judith, Waldrada, and Theutberga could have employed the magic arts was credible to all the men who addressed the subject, but it was equally true that in each case the women's magic was marginally effective and easily undone. This was the worst of both worlds. It stripped women of power accessible through the use of magic, but it did not exonerate them from the crime of trying it. Hincmar's text on the divorce of Lothar and Theutberga typifies ninth-century perceptions of female love magic. It was not crushingly potent and could not irrevocably interfere with the holy institution of matrimony. The binding power of Christian marriage was more durable than the machinations of love magicians.

---

63. Ibid., 206.
64. Added to this is the fact that in canon law, as it was developing, neither barrenness nor disaffectedness were reasons for divorce. See Olsen, "Marriage in Barbarian Kingdom," 177–79.
65. Hincmar of Reims, *De nuptiis Stephani*, 132–53; d'Avray, *Medieval Marriage*, 74–88; Olsen, "Marriage in Barbarian Kingdom," 175–79; Le Jan, *Famille et pouvoir*, 277–84; Gaudemet, *Le mariage en Occident*, 109–32; Brundage, *Law*, 144–45; Gaudemet, "Indissolubilité et consummation."

How great a contrast there is between Gregory of Tours's perceptions of female magical power and those of his Carolingian counterparts. How unlike the masterful Fredegund is Judith, who, according to her detractors, was complicit in the sorcery taking place in Louis's court but not the meaningful agent of it. How stark is the difference between Lothar's "wives" and the bands of Merovingian women who asserted themselves in their world with unguents, spells, and sorceries.

CHAPTER 14

Magic and *Materia Medica*

> Remember Mugwort, what you declared, / What you brought about at the Great [or Divine] proclamation. / You are called *Una* [one] the oldest of herbs; / You have power against three and against thirty, / You have power against poison and against flying disease.
>
> —Nine Herbs Charm, *Lacnunga*

The medical tradition as a whole experienced exceptional continuity through the first millennium. That stability does not, however, infer stagnation, nor does it indicate that no original matter entered the medical corpus. Novel texts were produced in Anglo-Saxon England, and ancient herbals were tweaked, amended, enlarged, summarized, reorganized, translated, and adjusted to local circumstances.[1] A fundamental goal of the ninth-century program of reform in Carolingian Europe was to scrutinize every aspect of social and intellectual life and to emendate virtually all genres of the written word.[2] In that pursuit the Carolingians demonstrated remarkable energy and creativity; however, there is a category of literature that was not swept up in this *renovatio*, and that is the herbal *materia medica*. As far-reaching and comprehensive as the Carolingian renaissance was, there was no deliberate, thoroughgoing revision of healing manuals.

---

1. Leja, "Sacred Art"; Nokes, "Several Compilers"; Wallis, "Medicine in Medieval Calendar Manuscripts"; Riddle, "Theory and Practice in Medieval Medicine"; Voigts, "Anglo–Saxon Plant Remedies."

2. On revision and production of texts see Nelson, *Frankish World*, 1–36; Contreni, "Carolingian Renaissance"; McKitterick, *Carolingians and the Written Word*. From McKitterick (*Charlemagne*, 307), "Enormous stress was placed on correct texts. . . . Charlemagne's bishops and abbots were to play a key role in implementing these reforms."

Meg Leja provides a corrective to a perception that few advancements were made in the science of medicine in the early Middle Ages and that virtually all healing in the period was centered around *Mönchsmedizin*. Leja argues that at the turn of the ninth century, Carolingian intellectuals pursued an agenda of establishing medicine as "a sacred art." She demonstrates that scribes manipulated images and text in classical manuscripts in order to "establish medicine's orthodoxy within a reformed Christian society" and within networks that encompassed court, monastery, and the laity.[3] Carolingian intellectuals did classify medicine among the liberal arts and elevated it as a field of inquiry that a well-educated man should master, at least on the theoretical level.[4] For example, Raban Maur and Walafrid Strabo (d. 849), a renowned poet and abbot of Reichenau Abbey, wrote manuals about the healing properties of domesticated plants. Further, a pharmaceutical text produced at Lorsch Abbey was most likely commissioned by Charlemagne.[5] However, herbal manuals experienced a different historical trajectory than learned medical literature, in as much as intellectuals largely ignored them.

As was true in the earliest church writings, in the ninth century, Carolingian and Anglo-Saxon theologians staked a claim on healing. The word "health" (*salus*) can also mean salvation, and since soundness of the body and the soul were interwoven, spiritual and physical wellness continued to be expressed in the language of healing. The clergy and the saints were thought to administer the most effective medicine in the form of prayers, blessings, and miraculous cures. Secular physicians were a suitable second choice, but magic was never an acceptable option for healing. To receive bodily cures from magic imperiled the soul and was ultimately self-defeating, even if it worked in the short run.

The equivalence of physical and spiritual health in the Carolingian era is reflected in the following prayer from the Saint Gall sacramentary (ca. 800). It was designed to accompany the anointing of the sick. "I anoint you with sanctified oil so that in the manner of a warrior prepared through anointing for battle you will be able to prevail over the aery hordes. Do your work, creature of oil, in the name of the Father, and the Son and the Holy Spirit,

---

3. Leja, "Sacred Art." Wallis ("Medicine") points out that no comprehensive history of early medieval medicine has been written since Loren MacKinney's *Early Medieval Medicine* was published in 1937.

4. *Epistola de litteris colendis*, a document John Contreni calls "the manifesto of the Carolingian Renaissance" ("John Scottus, Martin Hiberniensis," 24), encouraged study of the liberal arts.

5. Walafrid Strabo, *Hortulus*; Raban Maur, *De universo* 18.5, 2:209–12. Everett, "Manuscript Evidence"; Butzer, "Classical Tradition," 575–77; Riddle, *Contraception and Abortion*, 106–7.

so that no unclean spirit will remain either in the limbs, marrow, or joints of this [person]." This prayer demonstrates the role of Christian symbology in sustaining health and is particularly clear in tying disease to demons (unclean spirits).[6]

The early ninth-century councils of Riesbach, Salzburg, and Freising used the language of healing to recommend that magicians and soothsayers be locked up, "not to lose life, but to be healed/saved in imprisonment." The 813 Council of Tours upbraided the faithful who sought cures by trafficking with demons—using incantations, herbs, or bones. Priests were enjoined to advise their parishioners that ritual charms and spells would not help sick and dying humans or animals.[7] The ninth-century vita of Saint Anstrude (d. ca. 700), abbess of Saint John at Laon, tells of a nun who is afflicted by a "flow of blood" (*fluxum sanguinis*). She has a vision in which a sister nun admonishes her to take no other medicine but dust scraped from the sepulcher of the holy virgin Anstrude.[8] In Burchard of Worms's *Decretum*, infirmity, disease, and fractures are best cured by adherence to the "true" religion, not to false prophets. To obviate deadly disease, humans should seek God through prayers, fasts, and almsgiving. Carrying a candle or performing any ceremony for the sake of health, except under the spiritual guidance of the clergy, was idolatry. Like many canonists before him Burchard, approved of collecting medicinal herbs as long as the harvesting was attended by the creed or the paternoster and not charms. The bishop even recommended the use of herbs, without incantations, to cure devil sickness.[9]

The admonition in Aelfric of Eynsham's eleventh-century *Passion of St. Bartholomew* is explicit about the competing virtues of spiritual and magical healing. "The Christian man who is afflicted with any illness and who

---

6. Paxton, *Christianizing Death*, 8–30, 111–13: "Ungo te de oleo sanctificato, ut more militis uncti praeparatus ad luctam possis ereas superare catervas. Operare, creatura olei, in nomine Patris et Filii et Spiritus sancti, ut not lateat spiritus immundus nec in membris nec in medullis nec in ulla conpage membrorum huius hominis" (quotation 111). See also the 813 *Concilium Cabillonense* (33–34, in *MGH Conc. aevi Kar.* 2.1, 280) which refers to ecclesiastics as moral physicians who must be as severe in using the knife or cautery to cure a sick soul as doctors are in curing diseased bodies. *Annales Fuldenses* (869, 69), compares the skill of doctors to "caelesti medico." See also Skinner, "Cure for a Sinner."

7. *Concilia Rispacense, Frisingense, Salisburgense* 15, in *MGH Conc. aevi Kar.* 2.1, 209: "ne vitam perdant, set ut salventur in carcere"; *Concilium Turonense* 42, in *MGH Conc. aevi Kar.* 2.1, 292.

8. *Vita Anstrudis abbatissae Laudunensis* 29, in *MGH SRM* 6, edited by Bruno Krusch and Wilhelm Levison (Hanover: Hahn, 1993), 76.

9. Burchard of Worms, *Decretum* 10.10, *PL* 140, col. 834; ibid., 10.50, *PL* 140, col. 851: "Daemonium sustinenti licet peras vel herbas habere sine incantatione." Burchard of Worms, *Decretum* 19.5.65, in Schmitz, *Die Bussbücher*, 2:424: "Collegisit herbas medicinales, cum aliis incantationibus cum symbolo et Dominica oratione, id est cum Credeo in Deum et pater Noster cantando?'"

then seeks health by forbidden practices, or in accursed incantations, or by any sorceries is like heathen men who made offerings to devils for bodily health and so destroyed their souls.... It is not allowed to any Christian man to get his health from any stone, nor from any tree, unless it be the holy sign of the cross, nor from any place, unless it be the holy house of God. He who does otherwise undoubtedly commits idolatry." This quotation not only demonstrates the competition between magical and sacred healing, but it also echoes the fundamental distrust of nature discussed in chapter 10. Trees, stones, and spaces other than the enclosed church intensified the sin of sorcerous healing. Only those symbols and rites (such as crossing) that were indisputably Christian were safe. In the same vein, Aelfric writes, "No one shall enchant an herb with magic, but with God's words shall bless it, and so eat it."[10] If the clergy could convince the population that the church had more powerful medicine than the devils working through magical cures, it could more easily wrench from the ignorant the symbols and rituals of healing that kept them rooted in ways of thinking that challenged Christian spiritual hegemony.

Magic and Ritual in the *Materia Medica*

There is an active scholarship on magic in the early medieval herbal texts—especially robust among Anglo-Saxonists. I am interested in this body of research because it holds clues about how magic was viewed and practiced in the early Middle Ages and puts meat on the bones of references to magic and demons from a variety of other sources. Gerhard Baader uses the term *Herbariencorpus* to describe herbals copied in or around Ravenna in the sixth and seventh centuries, which form the body of most early medieval herbal literature.[11] The *Herbariencorpus* includes *Ex herbis femininis* by Pseudo-Dioscorides; the immensely popular *Herbarius Apulei Platonici Maudaurenses*; *De herba vettonica* by Pseudo-Antonius Musa; *Liber medicinae ex animalibus, pecoribus bestiis vel avibus* by Sextus Placitus; and the anonymous *De taxone liber*.

The Anglo-Saxon medical tradition shared much in common with that of the Continent. Several texts known in England were edited translations of antique Latin works. *Herbarium Apuleis*, for example, formed a part of the

---

10. Aelfric of Eynsham, *Passion of St. Bartholomew the Apostle*, in *Homilies of the Anglo-Saxon Church*, 1:476–77.
11. Baader, "Die Anfänge," 669–718; Baader, "Zur Überlieferung," 139–41. See also Everett, "Manuscript Evidence." In the seventh and eighth centuries, Latin manuscripts of Greek medical texts entered France through Italy.

English corpus of vernacular medical texts, and it contains portions of *Ex herbis femininis*, *De herba vettonica*, *De taxone*, and *De medicina de quadrupedibus*. This collection is generally thought to have been compiled in the tenth century, but Hubert De Vriend suggests that it may have come together as early as the seventh or eighth century in Northumbria.[12] In addition, there are two works written around 900 to 1050 in Old English that draw on continental sources and exist in unique manuscripts: *Lacnunga* and *Bald's Leechbook*.[13]

In the early and medieval Christian worldview, ultimately all sickness was thought to be punishment for sin and inflicted by disease-infesting demons. However, the herbals, on a practical day-to-day basis, leave the theology and etiology of illness in the background and concentrate on treating symptoms.[14] Healing recipes are purely descriptive, not polemical or didactic, and their purpose is completely pragmatic: to cure disorders. But in the case of certain diseases, those where the causes do not seem clearly somatic, the demonic theory of disease comes to the foreground. In these instances, the texts hold demons directly and overtly responsible for given maladies.

The nomenclature for illness and wellness in the herbals is revelatory of the basal concept of disease. For example, although in the ancient world the snake signified health and regeneration, not illness (Asclepius cured with the aid of a snake, and the therapeutic role of the snake is commemorated in his symbol of medicine), in the Judeo-Christian tradition the snake or serpent is viewed differently—as the tempter. This may account for the fact that in herbals (especially Anglo-Saxon texts), a favorite allusion to sickness is the

---

12. As the title suggests, *Liber medicinae ex animalibus, pecoribus bestiis vel avibus* (in Old English, *De medicina de quadrupedibus*) is not an herbal; it is a healing manual on the use of products obtained from animals to cure human diseases. When I refer to herbals, I am including zootherapeutical texts. Note the variant spelling of Pseudo-Apuleius's work; the Latin is "Herbarius," and the Old English is "Herbarium." See Lev, "Traditional Healing"; *"Old English Herbarium" and "Medicina de Quadrupedibus,"* v–vi, xlii.

13. Bald's *Leechbook* consists of three books combined, which were compiled in or around the court of King Alfred in the furtherance of his intellectual and educational reforms. For the *Leechbook* see Kesling, *Medical Texts*, 23–56; Nokes, "Several Compilers"; Meaney, "Variant Versions"; *The Anglo-Saxon Leechbook III*, xxxvii–xli; *Bald's Leechbook*, introd. *Lacnunga*, meaning "remedies," is a collection of miscellaneous Anglo-Saxon healing texts. It is written in Old English with some Latin and was compiled around 1000. See Kesling, *Medical Texts*, 95–129.

14. Medieval ideas on physiology were grounded in Hippocratic theory, which describes human physiology in terms of a balance of three humors: phlegm, blood, and bile, but this is not the guiding theoretical or organizational principle in the herbal manuals. See also Wallis, "Medicine," 110." The cures generally are listed from head to toe; meaning that cures for ailments of the head, face, and so forth are first.

snake or the worm, which is sometimes metaphorical and sometimes literal.[15] Other variations are the serpent, adder, dragon, viper, scorpion, toad, and, sometimes, the pest.[16] Medical writers often employed the words "venom" and "poison" when speaking of pain or affliction, and this relates to *veneficium* as one of the words for demonic maleficium. So there is a correspondence in the texts between Satan, snakes, sickness, and magic.[17]

The following recipe from *Lacnunga* is a vivid example of herbalists' use of reptilian imagery. "My God ... when we call for your help; upon hearing whose name the *serpens* [serpent] is still and the *draco* [dragon] flees, the *vipera* [viper] is silent, and the *rubita* [venomous toad] which is called *rana* [frog] becomes quietly torpid, the *scorpius* [scorpion] is destroyed and the *regulus* [venomous serpent] conquered, and the *spalangius* [poisonous spider or fly] works no harm at all, and all venomous and hitherto most ferocious reptiles and noxious animals are covered with darkness and all roots adverse to health of man dry up. You, Lord, destroy this venomous poison."[18] These creeping creatures and poison roots are in this case not in themselves disease, but bearers of it. The leech and/or the patient hope that by the simple ritual of naming the enemies, the Lord will bring all under control.

Other terminology for illness was dart, arrow, *maere*, dwarf, and elf. As was the case with the snake, Anglo-Saxons more commonly used these descriptors than continental writers did, but they can be found throughout the *materia medica*. Because elves were bringers of disease, they easily could be (and most often were) assimilated to demons in the Christian idiom in the ninth through eleventh centuries.[19] The longest prayer in *Lacnunga* is the *Lorica*, a redaction of a seventh-century Irish poem in which the speaker asks the protection of Christ and the angels against the assaults of demons.

---

15. For one of many examples, in *Anglo-Saxon Remedies* (77, 68–69), the term "worm" is used for an anal fistula. See Glosecki, *Shamanism*, 121; Meaney, "Anglo-Saxon View."

16. On illnesses as serpents, demons, etc., see *Anglo-Saxon Remedies*, xxxii–xxxiv. For tarantulas, scorpions, and frogs see *Leechbook* 1.4, in *Leechdoms*, 27–29. On Cockayne's translations of Bald's *Leechbook* see *Medieval Herbal Remedies*, 1–67; "The Anglo-Saxon Leechbook III," 1–11.

17. For Satan as a dragon, see *Penitentialis Vinniani* 34, in *Irish Penitentials*, 86: "Non cessandum est eripere predam ex ore leonis uel draconis, id est de ore diabuli." From the earliest church literature, the serpent was viewed as the seducer of Adam and Eve, for example see *De doctrina Christiana* 3.80, 166–67.

18. *Lacnunga* 64 in *Anglo-Saxon Remedies*, 39. Pliny (*Natural History* 8.48, vol. 3 [353], 78–79) mentions the *rubita*, and the fine line between salubrious medicine and harmful poison is implied in the belief that the *rubita* is full of medicinal substances that it discharges daily, leaving only the poison. A portion of this recipe, including the catalogue of poisonous creatures, is included almost verbatim in "Contra venenum," *Book of Nunnaminster*, 90.

19. Kesling, *Medical Texts*, 57–94 (on *dweorh*, 73); Hall, *Elves in Anglo-Saxon England*, 71–74, 130, 155–56, 174; Griffith, *Aspects of Anglo-Saxon Magic*, 47–58; Jolly, *Popular Religion*, 134; Glosecki, *Shamanism*, 123.

The patient is to recite, "O God, with your impenetrable protection, / defend me everywhere . . . so that the foul demons cannot into my sides / Hurl shafts, as they are accustomed." In *Lacnunga*'s "For a Sudden Stitch" and "Against Dwarf," an assailing army on horseback delivers the "spear" (*spere*) and "darts" (*garas*) of disease.[20] As seen in the recipes above, medical writers often envisioned diseases as airborne, and because demons, the agents of ailments, fly through the vapor, and in fact infiltrate the lower air, the notion that sickness comes at people like darts through the atmosphere is fitting.[21]

There is no ambiguity in herbal medicine that demons are the background cause of illness. However, the use of magic as a cure is not as transparent. Herbal texts represent a mélange of what moderns would call scientific medicine and magical remedies, but to determine how cures might have been read by contemporaries we must look outside the herbals themselves and examine the larger cultural and literary context into which they fit. Although a diversity of sources outside the *materia medica* contain ample references to magic herbal concoctions, such as magical love formulas and potions, those nonmedical texts reveal little as to the ingredients of the preparations.

For instance, the Council of Ancyra (314) stipulates a punishment of ten years for mothers who cause abortions by magic remedies that they or other women prepare. In the *Edictum Rothari* of the Lombard law code, a combatant seeks to protect himself in a duel by carrying herbs or "other like things" that sorceresses (*maleficiae*) have prepared.[22] What was in those herbal mixtures? Perhaps we are seeing an answer to that question in the medical texts, where there are several recipes for conception, abortion, and protection against assault and danger. Gregory of Tours criticized the messengers whom King Gundovald (d. ca. 585) sent to King Guntram (d. ca. 593), because they maintained the old Roman diplomatic tradition of carrying "consecrated wands . . . so they would not be seized." How had those wands been treated? Herbals contain many recipes for preparing objects carried on a journey to evade molestation. Gregory also wrote of a man suspected of sorcery because in his bag he had "roots of various plants, moles' teeth, the

---

20. Glosecki, *Shamanism*, 65, 44–47. For *Lorica* see *Anglo-Saxon Remedies* 65, 41–55; *Anglo-Saxon Minor Poems*, 121–23.

21. Glosecki, *Shamanism*, 110–19.

22. Council of Ancyra 21, in *Seven Ecumenical Councils*, 73. *Lex Longbardorum* 368, in *Die Gesetze*, 148: "necalias tales similes res." See further references to potions in chapter 13.

bones of mice, and the claws and fat of bears."²³ The council nor the Lombard law nor Gregory give us details of the magical preparations, but the herbals may well be doing that—even in recipes that seem banal and inoffensive, even though the medical authors themselves do not identify their recipes as magical.

Karen Jolly rightly warns against identifying cures as magical just because they seem irrational to the modern, scientific sensibility. She argues that magic charms existed "in a neutral sense," and cures associated with "Christian names, rituals, and prayers" were, by definition Christian. What seems to be demonic, she argues, is actually a "folkloric" synthesis of different cultural expressions, which are fundamentally orthodox. "All things," she concludes, "were interconnected." Ciaran Arthur builds on Jolly's conclusions, and in his book, *"Charms," Liturgies, and Secret Rites,* he takes the position that the Old English word for charm, *galdor* (pl. *galdru*) has been misunderstood. He invites the reader to abandon altogether the classification of "charms" and argues that *galdru* were not vestiges of Teutonic paganism or the result of clumsy scribal miscopying, but they were learned, orthodox, liturgical Christian rituals. Arthur's argument rests on the position that if what appears to be a magical charm ritual is included in the writings of orthodox churchmen, then by that very inclusion, the charm cannot be magic.²⁴

I suggest, however, that it is possible to separate out magic in the *materia medica* and to define particular cures as magical (that is demonic), not because they seem "irrational" or unscientific, but because they fit the description of magic from other contemporary sources and standard texts that were common fixtures in monastic libraries across Europe and England. Many of the herbal cures I call magical are activated by chants, spells, and rituals. Many, however, are rather prosaic—not at all what moderns would identify as magical or irrational. But going back to the words of Augustine, it was not necessary for an herb to be attended by chants for the use of that herb to be sorcerous, and sometimes even herbs over which prayers had been said or Christian gestures made were demonic if they were put to superstitious uses. The determining factor for Augustine as to whether a concoction was magical was the agency by which it was assumed to work. Augustine's views

---

23. Gregory of Tours, *Decem libri historiarum* 7.32, 352: "Post haec misit iterum Gundovaldus duos legatos ad regem cum virgis consecratis, iuxta ritum Francorum, ut scilicet non contingerentur"; ibid., 9.6, 419: "de radicibus diversarum herbarum, ibique et dentes talpae et ossa murium et ungues atque adipes ursinos."

24. Jolly, *Popular Religion*, specifically 101–3. Arthur, *"Charms,"* 2, 24, 134, 217–18. See Rampton, review of *"Charms."* See Grattan's and Singer's once normative (now dated) appraisal of the irrationality of Anglo-Saxon medicine (*Anglo-Saxon Magic and Medicine*, 92).

dominated theological discourse in the early Middle Ages. His writings were ubiquitous in Christendom throughout the first millennium, and they were incorporated into myriad other works. In England and Europe, there was a resurgence of attention to patristic works within the reform movements of the ninth century.[25]

The use of suspensions or ligatures was one of the superstitions most often and ardently condemned from the pulpit and the page in early medieval Europe, and yet the herbal authors frequently specify that in order to properly exploit the healing power of a given herb, it must be suspended, carried, or attached in the very manner that Augustine and subsequent generations of ecclesiastics condemned as superstitious, magical, and devilish. Aelfric of Eynsham is exemplary on this issue, and he uses Augustine as his point of reference. "The wise Augustine said, that it is not perilous though anyone eat a medicinal herb; but he reprehends it as an unallowed charm, if any one bind those herbs on himself."[26]

Nevertheless, amulets suspended or bound-on are commonplace in the *materia medica*. In the *Old English Herbarium*, there are several recipes similar to the cure for madness that stipulates using the herb *Ranunculus*, which, if draped around the neck, remediates lunacy. From the *Herbarius*, *Carduus leucographus* sets snakes to flight if hung on the neck, and *Melilotus*, if attached to a length of yarn and hung from the neck, corrects dimness of the eyes. *Botracion statice* must be draped around the neck in order to treat lunacy. *Orbicularis*, if suspended from the neck and positioned against the spleen, cures internal distress. *Usterion* remedies falling sickness "if the herb is suspended around the sufferer's neck." This herb has peculiar qualities: "It shines in the night sky like a star . . . found by shepherds."[27] The Roman physician Sextus Placitus's (fl. 370) colorful manual on medicinal uses of animal parts recommends suspending the tail of a fox from the arm for exciting sexual desire, and the author assures the patient that the heart of a newly killed rabbit, if suspended from the neck or the arm, will relieve those suffering from quatrain fever. *Bald's Leechbook* outlines a practice that falls under the rubric of sympathetic magic and the misuse of signs, as these

---

25. Jolly, *Popular Religion*, 72–81. Peters, *Magician*, 15–18.

26. Aelfric of Eynsham, *Passion of St. Bartholomew the Apostle*, in *Homilies of the Anglo-Saxon Church*, 1:476–77. Jolly, *Popular Religion*, 92–93.

27. *Ranunculus* 10, *Old English Herbarium*, in *Medieval Herbal Remedies*, 152; *Botracion statice* 9.1, *Herbarius*, 41; *Orbicularis* 17.3, *Herbarius*, 52; *Usterion* 60.1, *Herbarius*, 114: "et ipsam herbam in collo habeat suspensam, remediabitur." "Haec herba nocte tamquam stella in caelo lucet . . . maxime autem a pastoribus pecorum invenitur." All in *Corpus medicorum*. The application of Usterion is classic contagious magic; see chapter 1.

concepts were articulated by churchmen from Augustine to Aelfric. For swollen eyes, the leech is to take a live crab, put out its eyes, and return it alive to the water. The sufferer is then to hang the disembodied eyes around his neck.[28]

Bald's Leechbook recommends unusual practices, similar in principle to suspensions. For erysipelas, the Leechbook directs the sufferer to catch a fox and, while it is alive, strike off the canine tooth. The fox should be allowed to escape, and the extracted tooth must be bound in a fawn's skin and kept on the patient's body. For the treatment of stomachache, the herbal says, "It is helpful to [the sufferer] that a fat child should sleep by him, and that he should put it always near his stomach." In the same vein, a rabbit's foot carried against the abdomen will relieve stomach pain. Sextus Placitus's text contains a recipe for correcting swollen glands and keeping snakes at bay. This cure requires going about with the knee bone of a deer.[29] *Teucrium polium* corrects lunacy if the juice of the plant is mixed with vinegar and smeared on the madman and the leaves and root of the plant are bound around his neck. *Peonia* prevents madness if carried, and if the plant is placed upon the lunatic, he will soon be whole.[30] Coriander is curative if gathered in the morning and carried for a full day, then discarded in the evening without looking backward. This "backwardness" resonates with other rituals of reversal, such as those condemned in the *Penitential of Silos* and Burchard of Worms's *Decretum*.[31] In short, suspensions are utterly forbidden in canonical and pastoral Christian texts that circulated widely throughout the first millennium, yet herbals continue to recommend them. The same is true of other remedies, including procedures regulated by astrological signs, chants, charms, carrying magically treated talismans to ward off evils, and superstitious ritualistic procedures that misuse signs (as understood by Augustine). The herbals escaped the examination and systemization of the Carolingian (and to a lesser extent, Anglo-Saxon) reformers, who, had they applied the same rigorous scrutiny to the *materia medica* that they did to so many other texts, may have reconciled inconsistencies and excised or reframed cures that depended on demonic aid. Emendation of the herbal texts also may have

---

28. Sextus Placitus, *Liber medicinae* 2.10, 240 (fox tail); 3.4, 241 (rabbit), both in *Corpus medicorum*; Leechbook 3.2, Leechdoms 306.

29. Leechbook 1.39, Leechdoms, 105 (fox tooth); Leechbook 2.27, in Leechdoms, 225 (fat child); Sextus Placitus, *Liber medicinae ex animalibus* 3.17, in *Corpus medicorum*, 245 (rabbit's foot); ibid., 1.1, and 1.6, in *Corpus medicorum*, 236 (deer's knee).

30. *Teucrium polium* 58, Old English Herbarium, in Medieval Herbal Remedies, 175; *Peonia* 65, Herbarius, in *Corpus medicorum*, 120.

31. *Coriandrum* 103.2, Herbarius, in *Corpus medicorum*, 185; Paenitentiale Silense 11.192, 36. One example from Burchard of Worms: *Decretum* 19.5.194, 2:452.

exposed the profusion of rites that were at best byzantine and indecipherable, and at worst antagonistic to the Christian economy of ritual.

Returning to nonmedical sources that reference magic, such as Gregory of Tours's censure of Gundovald and his protective "consecrated wands." Might those wands have been treated with the herb *Verbascum*? The *Old English Herbarium* reads, "If anyone carries with him even one twig of this plant [*Verbascum*], no terror will frighten him, no wild beast will scare him, nor will any evil approach him." Other such talismans are *Heraclea*, which should be carried by a person wishing to travel on a long journey in order to put robbers to flight, and *Peonia* staves off storms if the patient carries it onto a boat. *Ricinus* will "turn away hail and storms" if it is kept on one's person, hung on the bow of a ship, or placed in the house. An herbalist should be clean when gathering *Ricinus* and "must pick this plant while saying this . . . 'Ricinum plant, I ask that you be present at my songs (*incantationibus*) and that you turn away the hail and lightning flashes and every storm, through the name of almighty God, who caused you to be made.'"[32]

Scholars have queried how best to interpret the incorporation of a Christian symbol or utterance in a cure that otherwise draws on formulas and mental frames that the body of Christian theologians across the centuries identified as superstitious, pagan, magical, and demonic (keeping in mind that those words were imprecise and used indiscriminately to tag suspicious and seemingly un-Christian behavior). This is a question which, again, cannot be answered from the herbal texts alone. The intent of clerics who copied the herbal recipes may have been to put religion to a perfectly legitimate use, not to cure by magical means. For example, several ecclesiastical authorities had instructed Christians, in words similar to those of the *Penitential of Theodore*. "One who is possessed of a demon is allowed to have stones and herbs without using an incantation."[33] The line between "orthodox" and "magical" was often thin—easy for a well-meaning healer to blur.

Clerics were frequently censured for engaging in magical practices,[34] so the involvement of a clergyman could not sanitize an otherwise magical

---

32. Gregory of Tours, *Decem libri historiarum* 7.32, 352; *Verbascum* 73, *Old English Herbarium*, in *Medieval Herbal Remedies*, 180; *Heraclea* 74, *Old English Herbarium*, in *Medieval Herbal Remedies*, 180; *Ricinus* 176, *Old English Herbarium*, in *Medieval Herbal Remedies*, 225; *Poenia* 65, *Herbarius*, in *Corpus medicorum*, 120.

33. *Poenitentiale Theodori* 2.10.5, in *Councils and Ecclesiastical Documents*, 3:198: "Demonium sustinenti licet petras et holera habere sine incantatione."

34. Warnings against sorcerous clerics and injunctions against accepting magical substances from clergy became a refrain throughout the early Middle Ages. Two among myriad examples: Caesarius of Arles (*Sermones*, Sermon 50.1, 1:225: do not "consent to accept these ligatures, even if they are offered by clerics" (Et aliquotiens ligaturas ipsas a clericis ac religiosis accipiunt; sed illi non

activity, at least according to ecclesiastical principles. Even so, many recipes that incorporate rites and charms outside the traditional Christian lexicon of ritual require the involvement of a bishop, priest, or monk to either sing Masses over herbs or to officiate at particular healing ceremonies. Sometimes to exploit the properties of a given plant, elaborate rituals employing Christian symbology, or what Karen Jolly calls "liturgical elements," were required.[35] For example, a recipe from *De taxone liber* stipulates that the large teeth of a badger be extracted from the living animal while the practitioner says, "In the name of the omnipotent I behead you."[36] The extracted teeth are to be suspended from the arm by a gold or silver thread in such a way that they do not touch the body. No harm will come to the wearer, whether from a heavenly body, hail, illness, or his enemies. The recipe makes a nod to orthodox religion by asking the practitioner to call on the omnipotent God, but there is no escaping the fact that the cure relies on magical suspensions and blasphemous claims that the badger's teeth can disarm astrological determinants and bad weather. The anathema of those who would control the weather is enshrined in penitentials, sermons, hagiography, councils, laws, and even histories, and yet what amounts to weather magic is prescribed in medical texts.

The use of magical elements generally occurs in remedies for what I will call "arcane" illnesses such as elf disease, theft (not by modern standards a disease), or madness.[37] Gary Ferngren describes these disorders as "abnormal psychic or mental states" manifested in "bizarre behavior." Jolly uses the term "mind-altering maladies" with "invisible causes," and M. L. Cameron, groping for a way to classify these disorders, identifies them as "intractable . . . to rational procedures."[38] "Irrational" may not be the correct characterization, but the medieval *medicus* appears to have conceived of preternatural afflictions as a distinct type or category of illness. Herbals often refer to these arcane

---

sunt religiosi vel clerici, sed adiutores diaboli); *Concilium Aurelianense* (511) 30, in *MGH Conc. aevi Mer.*, 9: "If a secular cleric or a monk believes in divination or fortune telling . . ." (Si quis clericus, monachus, saecularis divinationem vel auguria credederit . . .).

35. *Anglo-Saxon Leechbook III* 62.1–4, 143–49; Jolly, *Popular Religion*, 96–131.
36. *De taxone liber*, in *Corpus medicorum*, 229: "In nomine omnipotentis decollo te."
37. For example, *Anglo-Saxon Leechbook III* 64.1, 153: Against a devil and insanity a gentle drink: put in ale sedge, roots of lupine, fennel, radish, betony, hindheal, celery, rue, wormwood, catnip, helenium, enchanter's nightshade, wolf's comb. Sing twelve masses over the drink and drink it. He will soon be better." For theft curable by a charm see *Anglo-Saxon Remedies* 149, 103. Some of the diseases that are attributed to demons would be considered somatic today, such as yellowing eyes and a scarlet complexion. See *Anglo-Saxon Leechbook III* 62.1–4, 143–49.
38. Ferngren, *Medicine and Health Care*, 57; Jolly, *Popular Religion*, 132–68 (quotations 133, 113); M. L. Cameron, "Anglo–Saxon Medicine and Magic," 210. Hall (*Elves in Anglo–Saxon England*, 123) uses the term "mind–altering ailments" to explain some of the ills resulting from elves.

illnesses as "devil sickness." In Anglo-Saxon texts, the term "elf disease" is more common, and sometimes "disease" is simply expressed by the noun "evil" (*yfel*). Although the cures for such maladies are not sectioned off together in any of the herbals or animal-anatomical texts, and recipes for them are interspersed with those for strictly physiological illnesses (such as stomachache, nosebleed, or treatment of wounds), herbalists obviously thought they required a different therapeutic approach than did infirmities such as broken bones and suppurating wounds. Those curative measure were often—by learned Christian thinking—demonic

There is a tendency on the part of some modern scholars to identify as "magical" those cures that require extensive and seemingly otiose ritualistic procedures (such as drinking warm blood and gouging out creatures' eyes), as if ritual—in and of itself—constituted a type of magic. In other words, some conclude that recipes requiring byzantine rites are magical, while they view as natural those cures achieved by processes with which we are more familiar and comfortable. But not all medieval magic was ritualistic, and certainly not all medieval ritual was magical.[39] The correlation between magical cures and ritual is no stronger than that between ritual and remedies that are (by modern standards) clearly physiological. For example, hanging an herb around the neck is magic, but it is not ritualistic; it is a simple application of a treatment.[40] Some cures are both magic and ritualistic. For instance, the herb *Proserpinaca* will alleviate sore eyes if the sufferer circumscribes the plant with a gold ring before the rising of the sun and places the herb around the neck.[41] This cure is magical—not because it requires the ritual procedures with the gold ring—but because of the suspension, because it seeks to control the natural process of illness, and because it draws on an unspecified source of power. It is unclear what force gives the herbal remedy potency, but the use of the ligature points to demons.

As indicated above, it is puzzling that generations of clergy from across Europe and the British Isles recorded and dispensed healing cures that seem clearly to be magical according to the ecclesiastical literate culture of which they were, to a greater or lesser extent, a part. Given that the herbals contain magical recipes for suspensions, talismans, and prophylactics that involve a misuse of signs, it is baffling that these therapies are included in healing

---

39. Jolly, *Popular Religion*, 102–3. Flint, for example (*Rise of Magic*, 283–86) conflates magic and ritual by labelling judicial ordeal as magical.

40. Jolly, *Popular Religion*, 159–65. Brennessel, Drout, and Gravel ("Reassessment of the Efficacy") have determined that most of the Anglo-Saxon recipes were not physiologically effective, but they almost certainly worked on a psychoactive level.

41. *Proserpinaca* 18.4, *Herbarius*, in *Corpus medicorum*, 54.

literature, which was transcribed by generations of monastic scribes who, at the same time, copied proscriptive texts that forbade the use of many of the cures in the herbals. It is a fair assumption that is was obvious to copyists that they were passing on forbidden practices, because either these same monks copied the theological and pastoral literature condemning magical cures, or, at the least, clerical scribes were sensitive to the delicate competition between Christian and lay or paganistic remedies. Discourse on the synonymy of spiritual and physical health was too pervasive to have been missed by one schooled, even minimally, in church doctrine.

This raises a question about those who copied, used, and transmitted medical texts, and permitted (or turned a blind eye to) the supplication of demons for medical cures.[42] This is a compelling issue that confronts every scholar exploring the cultural and theological dimensions of the *materia medica*. J. H. G. Grattan and Charles Singer seek to solve this mystery when they say, "It was the business of the leech to treat his patients, not to search out the nature of his remedies."[43] Karen Jolly writes, "What appears to the modern eye to be a confusion of sources was actually a coherent synthesis," and she asserts that the orthodoxy of suspensions, chants, and charms is implied by their mere appearance in texts that Christian religious produced. She argues that seemingly magical charms would not have been viewed as such by the Anglo-Saxon clerics who copied and employed them. Those with a "Germanic" worldview were able to interpret pagan practices within a Christian framework. Like Jolly, Ciaran Arthur perceives no dissonance resulting from charms incorporated into religious literature, because, he argues, their placement within Christian texts means that they are not charms—in other words, they are not magic.[44]

Richard Sowerby observes that it is dangerous "to suppose that exegesis provided early medieval ecclesiastics with a uniform set of symbols whose meanings were fixed and universally understood." He is writing about angelology, but his remarks are germane to exploring why clerics tolerated and transmitted seemingly magical elements in herbal texts. John Blair's approach uncomfortably implies that Anglo-Saxon clerics, being more susceptible to "popular superstitions" than churchmen on the Continent,

---

42. An exception to this is discussed in Horden, "Sickness and Healing," 424–25, where Alexander of Tralles (d. ca. 605) admits to using magical amulets if necessary.

43. Grattan and Singer, *Anglo–Saxon Magic and Medicine*, 58; Glosecki, *Shamanism*, 113.

44. Jolly, Raudvere, and Peters, *Witchcraft and Magic*, 30–42; see also Horden, "What's Wrong"; Arthur, "Charms," 2, 24, 134, 217–18. Kesling (*Medical Texts*, 171–84) understands *galdor* in much the same way Arthur does: charms have variant meaning depending on the context in which they were used.

did not entirely grasp the theology of signs and healing, "leaving clergy enmeshed within structures of thought rather different from those manifest in Latin canons."[45]

Having raised the question, I do not have a better solution to the riddle of magic in the herbals than so many others who have written about it. I am tempted to suggest that monastic scribes may have bowed to the hoary history of herbal texts and were disinclined to change, or even question, the source manuscripts from which they were copying. But that hypothesis is marred by the fact that herbals were constantly amended, not just from copy to copy, but within a given text by interstitial notes and corrections. The doses of a given drug have been crossed out and replaced by an adjusted amount. Perhaps monastic healers, hesitant to abandon remedies that had proven efficacious, shrugged off troubling contradictions in the materials that appeared to be unorthodox—or even demonic.

Women and Medical Magic

In the ancient world, the goddess Diana played an important role in healing, especially of women's diseases and arcane maladies.[46] This personage had an enduring presence in late antique and early medieval healing materials, which was particularly evident in the pivotal role the moon occupies in magical cures. The *materia medica* seldom mentions the goddess Diana explicitly, but she is figuratively present through her nocturnal symbol. I do not claim that every time the moon is referenced in a cure the author is making an implicit reference to Diana.[47] Rather, I argue that the ancient association of Diana with healing and the moon, the explicit role of Diana (Artemis) in medieval herbals, and the regular association of the moon with demonic diseases whose cures were timed to the moon kept Diana alive as a powerful agent of magic in early medieval culture and had an impact on the perception of human women as agents of magic. Diana is apparent in the herbals in two ways: first, by direct references to the goddess and the plant that was named after her, and second, by oblique allusions to this female healer when the role of the moon is required in magical healing recipes.

---

45. Sowerby, *Angels in Early Medieval England*, 50; Blair, *Church in Anglo-Saxon Society*, 210–14 (quotation 214). See also Liuzza ("Spere of Life and Death") and Lea ("Inscription of Charms") on religious syncretism in Anglo-Saxon medical texts.

46. Fischer-Hansen and Poulsen, *From Artemis to Diana*, 11–17; H. King, "Bound to Bleed"; Calame, *Les choeurs de jeunes filles*, 330–33, 411–20; Van Straten, "Gifts for the Gods."

47. However, Isidore of Seville (*Etymologiarum* 8.9.56–58, vol. 1) makes this correlation explicit.

Myriad influential classical texts link the moon with the power of herbs. For example, Lucan claimed that when the moon was called down to earth she dropped foam on the plants below, and Horace's Canidia calls on the power of Night and Diana (the moon) as witnesses of her enterprises and to enhance the power of her plants.[48] The affiliation between Diana and medicinal plants is reflected in the herb called *Artemisia* as it appears in the *Herbarius* (and *Herbarium*) of Pseudo-Apuleius. This herb was named for the goddess Diana; Cotton Vitellius C III reads, "Indeed, about the three plants that we call *artemisia* (mugwort), it is said that Diana found them and gave knowledge their power and medicinal value to the centaur Chiron, who was the first to prescribe a medicine using this plant and who named the plant *artemisia* after Diana."[49] M. L. Cameron observes that mugwort (the Anglo–Saxon name for *Artemisia*) "was the female herb par excellence, and that it was used for all problems of the womb including suppression of menses."[50] This is in keeping with Diana's role in classic mythology as a guardian of women in childbirth and a specialist in women's disorders. The herb was also efficacious for a variety of ailments such as sore feet, sore bladder, gout, fevers, and "the sore of sinews and swelling." But of most interest here is its association with arcane or demonic illnesses. *Artemisia* was recommended for one going on a trip. According to the author of the *Herbarius*, if a person takes the herb along, "he will not feel the labor of the journey." It also "puts devil sickness to flight and deters evil medicines." One who keeps *Artemisia* in his home protects it from enchantment and "the [evil] eyes of evil men." One particular species of the herb, if kept in the house, protects the home from any kind of damage.[51]

Mugwort is also associated with arcane diseases in the insular sources, such as *Lacnunga* and *Bald's Leechbook*, where to put it in travelers' shoes

---

48. Lucan, *Civil War* 6, 340–41: "Phoebeque serena non aliter diris verborum obsessa venenis . . . et patitur tantos cantu depressa labores donec suppositas propior despumet in herbas." Horace, *Odes and Epodes*, Epode 5, 376–79: "O rebus meis / non infidelis arbitra, / Nox, et Diana, quae silentium regis / arcana cum fiunt sacra, / nunc, nunc, adeste, nunc in hostilis domos / iram atque numen vertite."

49. *Artemisia* 10, *Herbarius*, in *Corpus medicorum*, 42–43; *Mugwort* 13, *Old English Herbarium*, in *Medieval Herbal Remedies*, 153 (quotation). For images of Chiron giving *Artemisia* to Diana see Grape-Albers, *Spätantike Bilder*, 44–46.

50. M. L. Cameron, *Anglo-Saxon Medicine*, 177.

51. *Artemisia* 10.1, *Herbarius*, in *Corpus medicorum*, 42: "Si quis iter faciens eam secum in manu portaverit, non sentiet itineris laborem. Fugat et daemonia et in domo posita prohibet mala medicamenta. Auertit oculos malorum hominum"; *Mugwort* 11, *Old English Herbarium*, in *Medieval Herbal Remedies*, 152. Pliny (*Natural History* 26.89, vol. 7 [393], 374–75) also mentions that *Artemisia* obviates fatigue on a journey: "Artemisiam et elelisphacum alligatas qui habeat viator negatur lassitudinem sentire."

prevents them from tiring. *Artemisia* must be plucked before the sun rises, and this is undoubtedly because of Diana's identification with the moon. Before harvesting, the herbalist must recite, "I will take you, *Artemisia*, lest I am weary on the way."[52] To complete the remedy, one must sign with the cross. *Lacnunga*'s prayer-charm that begins this chapter, The Nine Herbs Charm, petitions several potent plants to protect the patient against onflight,[53] venom, "bewitchment of evil creatures," "nine poisons," and "nine flying diseases," and four of those herbs are characterized as female. The first is mugwort: "Remember Mugwort, what you declared, / What you brought about at the Great [or Divine] proclamation. / You are called *Una* [One], the oldest of herbs; / You have power against three and against thirty, / You have power against poison and against flying disease, / You have power against the loathsome one that travels throughout the land."[54] This plant named for Diana is clearly very powerful, even achieving primacy over all other herbs. The second herb, *Waybroad*, is called "mother of herbs" (*wyrta mōdor*).[55] Mugwort, then, although the oldest of the herbs, is primordial but not generative, not described by maternal imagery. This is consistent with the nature of the virgin goddess after whom the plant is named. These recipes demonstrate that the female, nocturnal, magical healing qualities of the goddess Diana were preserved in medical materials. Diana's role in early medieval healing, that activity the Christian religion so jealously guarded, may be one explanation for why it was she, of all the pagan goddesses, who came in for the contumely of canonists in the *Canon episcopi*—more than Minerva, who oversaw women's magic at the loom, and more than Venus, goddess of erotic love.

In addition to the goddess Diana, the herbals introduce other female forces or entities that act as vehicles of healing, one of which is the earth. *Bald's Leechbook* has a short prayer for water-elf disease, which petitions Mother Earth. It is in Old English, not Latin, the language typically used for Christian prayers: "May the earth diminish you [referring to the disease] with all its might and main." A Latin manuscript of English provenance contains a

---

52. *Leechbook* 1.86, in *Leechdoms*, 154: "t[o]llam te artemesia / ne lassus sum in via."
53. Onflight is a reference to infectious disease conceived as flying through the air like a dart.
54. *Anglo-Saxon Remedies* 76, 61. *Anglo-Saxon Minor Poems*, 119–21. On the Nine Herbs Charm see Glosecki, "Stranded Narrative."
55. *Waybroad* grows in open fields. Not only is it a feminine name, but the gender identification à la mother earth is further emphasized by the description: "Over you carts creaked, over you women rode, / Over you brides (?) trampled." *Anglo-Saxon Remedies* 76, 60–61.

drawing of a haloed figure giving mana to the herbs in the name of the earth goddess. "Dea sancta Tellus, rerum naturae parens."[56]

An extraordinary extended supplication made to the deified mother earth was found bound with herbal recipes compiled in the late tenth or early eleventh century; it is currently held at the University of Leiden. J. H. G Grattan and Charles Singer argue that the compiler of this document mistook the Divine Mother for the Virgin Mary. Although this would explain the inclusion of this patently pagan prayer in a Christian healing manual, there is nothing in the text itself that supports this conclusion.[57]

> Holy Goddess Earth, mother of nature, who generates all things and brings forth anew the sun which you alone show to the folk on earth.... You are the force of the nations and the mother of the gods without whom nothing can be born or come to maturity.... Grant freely to all nations upon earth all herbs that your majesty brings to life and allow me to gather your medicines [herbs]. Come to me with your healing powers; grant success to whatsoever I shall make from these herbs, and may those to whom I administer them thrive. May all your gifts to us prosper. To you all things return. Let men take these herbs from my hand, I beseech you now, O Goddess, and may your gift make the sick whole. I beseech you as a suppliant that by your majesty you grant me this boon.[58]

Little is known about the document, but the medieval compiler identifies the prayer as one that pagans spoke when gathering herbs. The narrator in the charm is clearly a medical practitioner.

For the disease called dwarf (*dweorh*), a synonym for devil sickness,[59] there are two female agents of healing. To effect a cure, the leech takes wafers inscribed with the names of the Seven Sleepers of Ephesus,[60] sings a charm into the patient's ear, and commissions a virgin to hang the wrapped wafers around her neck. The second female healer, "sister Ear," appears in a charm

---

56. *Leechbook*, 3.63, in *Leechdoms*, 353.
57. Grattan and Singer, *Anglo–Saxon Magic*, 46.
58. The prayer to Mother Earth is from Voss. Lat. Q., Rijksuniversiteit, Leiden, Holland. For a translation see "Prayer to Mother Earth," 41–42. For an old but still useful discussion of Tellus in Roman religion see Dieterich, *Mutter Erde*.
59. M. L. Cameron (*Anglo–Saxon Medicine*, 152) observes that *dweorh* sometimes means "fever"; however, Edward Pettit (in *Anglo–Saxon Remedies*, xxxiii) questions this conclusion.
60. The Seven Sleepers of Ephesus is a legend of seven youths who hid inside a cave near Ephesus (in modern Turkey) to avoid the Decian persecution in 250. They slept for three hundred years and awoke when Christianity was legal. See Gregory of Tours, *Gloria Martyrum* 94, 100–102; van der Horst, "Pious Long-Sleepers."

in which the leech sings into the ears of the sick man. Elliott Van Kirk Dobbie reads "sister Ear" as *deores* or *dweores*, meaning dwarfs. This feminine entity, sister Ear, who "came stalking in, . . . made an end, and oaths she swore that never this one the sick should harm,"[61] is terrifying in the face of disease. As is often the case with the herb *Artemisia*, a pagan goddess is called on to cure the mysterious malady of dwarf. A virgin appears twice more in *Lacnunga* wielding healing magic. If a man has pains in his heart (which have nothing to do with love), a virgin must go to a running spring, draw water in the direction of the current, and sing the creed and paternoster over it for nine days in a row. And again, for a fever, a virgin hangs inscribed and sanctified sacramental wafers around the neck of the patient for three days, in the fashion of a suspension.[62]

The compiler of *Lacnunga* perceives disease as brought on by demons in both male and female shapes: the Aesir (the pantheon of northern "high gods"), the elf, martial women, and evil sorceresses. Here the female element acts not as a source of succor for the afflicted, but as a metaphor of illness. One such image is of the "mighty women." "I stood under the limewood shield [or linden tree], under a light shield. / Where [or when] the mighty women deliberated upon their power, / And they sent yelling spears. / I will send another back to them."[63] The "mighty women" are bringers of disease, or a synonym for disease, such as the term "elf" or "dwarf." The image of "mighty women" with "whizzing darts" fashions females as carriers of infection—in other words, perhaps, as demons.[64] The healing charm called "For a Sudden Stitch" reads, "If it were shot of gods [or spirits], or if it were shot of elves, / Or if it were shot of witch [or witches], now I will help you."[65]

In The Nine Herbs Charm, discussed above, there are several potent herbs (mugwort among them) that are particularly useful against onflight, venom, "bewitchment by little beings," and "nine spirits of evil." The text reads: "You have power against thee and against thirty, / You have power against poison and against flying disease, / You have power against the loathsome one that travels throughout the land.[66] It is worth noting that

---

61. *Anglo-Saxon Minor Poems*, 121.
62. *Anglo-Saxon Remedies* 174, 120–21; 86, 72–73.
63. Ibid., 127a, 90–91.
64. Glosecki (*Shamanism*, 115–16) describes these women as "valkyrie–like."
65. *Anglo-Saxon Remedies* 127, 94–95. See Hall, *Elves in Anglo-Saxon England*, on "elf-shot" (96–118) and on the suggestion that "elf" could be positive and useful at times (156).
66. *Anglo-Saxon Remedies* 66, 61; *Anglo-Saxon Minor Poems*, 119–21. For an extended discussion of the scholarship on the Nine Herbs Charm see *Anglo-Saxon Remedies*, 99–162. Elves and elf-shot are mainly restricted to the medical materials; see Hall, *Elves in Anglo–Saxon England*, 3, 7.

in the Nine Herbs Charm, iron is identified as sorceresses' work (*haegtessan geweorc*). This is a reference to the spear, which is another analogue of disease, and it is wielded by a commanding female entity. Iron has a long history as a vicious, polluting, menacing, magical substance. Iron appears often in the herbals, and to use it in procuring a root or preparing a medicine invalidates the potency of an herb. This iron taboo often shows up in cures for the arcane diseases.[67]

A creature called the *maere* appears as an elusive but clearly malign character in the *Leechbook*. *Maere* is essentially another word for possession, fear, or disorientation, and Oswald Cockayne and Alaric Hall correlate the word "mare" to nightmare. *Maere* is a female noun with a connotation of riding, and a *maere* afflicts a man by riding him. For Hall, as discussed in chapter 12, the *maere* is a type of succubus, "riding" and "mounting" the victim. For protection against the *maere*, the would-be target is to make a bouquet of lupins, garlic, betony, and frankincense, bind them in a fawn's skin, and keep this charm with him "as he goes into his home."[68]

As demonstrated, female metaphors for healing or illness are pervasive throughout the herbal *materia medica*, but what of women as healers and authors of medical texts? M. L. Cameron writes that although he suspects women practiced some form of medicine, "there is not a shred of evidence."[69] I would say the situation is not that dreary. Scholars are not aware of any direct female involvement in the actual writing or preservation of the herbals. All the books were housed in monasteries, although one copy of the apotropaic prayer *Lorica* was kept at Nunnaminster, an abbey in Winchester, England. In her review of Andrew Kadel's *Matrology*, Catherine Peyroux observes "how complex is the task of adjudicating female authorial identity and how precariously the assumptions modern print culture generates about authorial voice and self perch atop the medieval production and redaction of texts."[70] This insight is germane to the early medieval *materia medica*. There

---

67. From Glosecki (*Shamanism*, 106 and 138), "Iron was inherently magical all over medieval Europe." On herbs collected without iron see *Ebulum* 92.5, *Herbarius*, in *Corpus medicorum*, 167: "For spleen problems drink a mixture of *ebulum* standing on a threshold; pick without iron. It is also useful against all evils"; *Anglo-Saxon Remedies* 127, 92–93. Collecting mandrake requires iron. That plant will attempt to flee from the herbalist, and so she must circumscribe it with iron, especially if the person gathering the herb is impure. See *Mandragora*, in *Herbarius*, in *Corpus medicorum*, 222.

68. *Anglo-Saxon Leechbook III* 1.64, 99; Hall, *Elves in Anglo-Saxon England*, 124–26. On steeds see Meaney, *Anglo-Saxon Amulets*, 15–17.

69. M. L. Cameron, *Anglo-Saxon Medicine*, 22. See also *Book of Nunnaminster*, 3–34; S. Crawford, "Nadir of Western Medicine?"

70. Peyroux, review of *Matrology*, 845.

are faint whispers of the female authorial voice in the healing material, but they must be culled from disparate texts and chance references.

If women did not author therapeutic texts, they likely collaborated with those who did. There are numerous cures for women's diseases that show evidence of having been tweaked from one redaction of a given herbal to the next, so although surviving evidence indicates that it was monks and male physicians who recorded healing recipes, these *medici* certainly received information from their female patients. In some cases, direct female participation in medicinal preparations is clear from internal evidence. For instance, in *Lacnunga*, "woman's milk" (*wifes meoluc*) is one of the required ingredients.[71]

It is proverbial wisdom that medieval women had a central role in maintaining the health of their families, and this is borne out by virtually every source that treats the topic of healing.[72] Juxtaposing canons from handbooks of penance, sermons, and vitae with abstruse medicinal recipes begins to bring into focus the fuzzy picture of women as healers. In his homily entitled *On Auguries* (between 990–1002), Abbot Aelfric of Eynsham reviles "witless women [who] go to cross-roads, and draw their children through the earth, and thus commit themselves and their children to the devil." Around 1008, Wulfstan (d. 1023), the bishop of London, wrote the so-called "Canons of Edgar" for the secular clergy of his parish. Among the approximately seventy canons, three condemn magical practices. The most extensive of the three forbids a variety of offenses from necromancy to worship at stones, and among them is the same description of the puzzling practice of dragging children through the earth. Because the homily and canon are terse, it is hard to get a full sense of the rationale behind the procedure, but it is a one that both authors clearly consider demonic. Wulfstan's text reads, "It is right that every priest extinguish every heathen practice [like] that devil's craft which is performed when children are drawn through the earth."[73] The

---

71. Buck, "Women's Milk"; Buck, "Women and Language." *Puleium* 93.7, 9–10, *Herbarius, Corpus medicorum*, 169. *Solata* 75.3, *Herbarius, Corpus medicorum*, 135; *Pastinaca silvatica* 81.1–2, *Herbarius, Corpus medicorum*, 147 are all recipes for helping postpartum women, including one for removing the placenta after a stillbirth. *Simfoniaca* 4.7, *Herbarius, Corpus medicorum*, 33, is for a pain in a woman's breast. *Mercurialis* 83.2, *Herbarius, Corpus medicorum*, 149 and *Rubus* 88.3, *Herbarium, Corpus medicorum*, 157 are recommended for bringing on menstruation (it is unclear whether these are abortifacients). See also Deegan, "Pregnancy and Childbirth." The section of Bald's *Leechbook* that deals with women's medicine is lost. We have the a list of its contents, however; see M. L. Cameron, *Anglo-Saxon Medicine*, 174–84. Bullough and Campbell, "Female Longevity and Diet."

72. M. H. Green, "Women's Medical Practice"; Achterberg, *Woman as Healer*, 41–59.

73. Aelfric of Eynsham, *On Auguries*, in *Aelfric's Lives of Saints*, 1:375. Wulfstan, so-called "Canons of Edgar" 16, in *Councils and Synods*, 1:320. On Aelfric's cure see Meaney, "Aelfric and Idolatry," 130.

fact that it involves mothers and children suggests that it might have been a prophylactic or healing rite.

A remedy found in *De medicina* for epilepsy and demonic dreams requires that a mountain goat's brain be drawn through a gold ring and given to a sick child to swallow. There is a plausible equivalency between goats' brains being "drawn through" a ring, and children being "drawn through" the earth. The notion of "drawing through" is comparable to a child coming through a disease. In this case, information from the herbal sheds light on the ill-understood procedure of drawing children through the earth. Wulfstan and Aelfric considered the "drawing through" to be devilish, but in the cure from *De medicina* it is used to ward off demonic dreams.[74]

Another cure first mentioned in the *Penitential of Theodore* that is subsequently condemned in various other sources over several centuries, attests to the magical nature of women's remedies applied in the home. The penitential forbids a woman putting her daughter on the roof or in an oven for the purpose of curing a fever. The reason for the prohibition is not clear from the wording of the canon: "If a woman puts her daughter on the roof or in the oven to cure a fever, she must do penance for seven years."[75] There is some sort of pagan significance to the act because the proscribed behavior is classed with sins that involve worship of idols (*De cultura idolorum*). The penalty of seven years is very severe; it is the same as for homicide. The penitential ascribed by some to Bede (early eighth century) enjoins the practice but assigns a penance of only five years. This penitential categorizes the practice under the heading "On Auguries and Divinations."[76] This women's domestic healing rite is repeated in Carolingian-era writings. The tenth-century work of Regino of Prüm also proscribes women putting their children on the roof or in an oven to cure a fever, under the heading "Of Incantations, Sorcery and Divining by Lots" (*De incantatoribus, maleficis et sortilegis*). Similarly, book 10 of Burchard of Worms's *Decretum*, entitled "On Incantations and Auguries" (*De incantatoribus et auguribus*), includes the injunction against women putting their daughters on roofs or in ovens to cure a fever, which he identifies as having come from the *Penitential of Theodore*.[77] A penitential of Raban Maur

---

74. *De medicina* 5.12, in *Leechdom*, 353. Dieterich (*Mutter Erde*, ch. 7) describes a (perhaps unrelated) late antique curative ritual whereby sick children were taken from their beds and placed on the earth.

75. *Poenitentiale Theodori* 1.15.2, in *Councils and Ecclesiastical Documents* 3:190: "Mulier si qua ponit filiam suam supra tectum vel in fornacem pro sanitate febris VII. annos peniteat."

76. Penitential ascribed by Albers to Bede 2, in *Medieval Handbooks of Penance*, 229.

77. Regino of Prüm, *De synodalibus causis* 2.368, 353; Burchard of Worms, *Decretum* 10.14, *PL* 140, col. 835.

repeats the canon and attributes it to the *Penitential of Theodore*, and the Old English *Confessional of* (pseudo) *Egbert*, which was compiled in the late tenth century, also describes the sin and assigns a penance of seven years. In all of these cases, the authors view the offense as both magical and exclusive to women.[78] Some light might be shed on this practice by looking at Michael Enright's discussion of the Gundestrup Cauldron, where he draws a parallel between the "rite of passage" scene on the cauldron and the ancient sacrament of placing children in fire to make them immortal. The cauldron's symbolism and the "pagan" practice may have similar origins.[79]

The *Penitential of Theodore* introduces yet another abstruse ritual, which involves burning grains at the place a person has died in order to ensure the health of the living. This offense comes under the heading "Of the Veneration of Idols" (*De cultura idolorum*). The author does not ascribe it particularly to women, but the domestic nature of the procedure and the fact that the canon is included with other proscriptions of women's charms suggest that the text refers to them.[80] The same sanction is included in the *Penitential of Silos* in a canon that lists several magical misdemeanors. Most of the thirty-eight sins listed begin, "If anyone," and so the sins are not gendered, but in making reference to burning grain, the author targets women specifically, saying, "If a woman burns grain where a man has died, for the health of the living, she shall do penance for one year" (not five years, as in the other penitentials that mention this practice). In his penitential composed for Heribald, bishop of Auxerre (d. ca. 875), Raban Maur repeats the judgment of Theodore on burning grain; he forbids it but does not ascribe the practice to women. He also includes an enigmatic healing ritual in which he describes a wife seeking to cure her husband by throwing his dish into the fire and feeding him the ashes. In a series of canons on pagan observances, Regino of Prüm includes burning grains where a man has died, and he does indicate that women carry out the activity. The *Confessional of (pseudo) Egbert* repeats Theodore's injunction almost verbatim: burning grain where a man has died for the sake of the living is condemned, nongendered, and expiated by a penance of five years.[81]

---

78. Raban Maur, *Poenitentiale ad Heribaldum* 30, col. 491; *Confessional of Egbert* 33, in *Bussordnungen*, 313.

79. Enright, "Ritual and Technology," 108, 112. Nielsen et al., "Gundestrup Cauldron." The cauldron is a silver bowl found in Jutland in 1891; it was most likely forged in the lower Danube in the late first century BCE.

80. *Poenitentiale Theodori* 1.15.3, in *Councils and Ecclesiastical Documents* 3:189–90.

81. *Paenitentiale Silense* 11.198, 36: Mulier si grana arserit ubi mortuus est homo pro sanitate uibentium, 1 annum peniteat. Raban Maur, *Poenitentiale ad Heribaldum* 30, 491; Regino of Prüm, *De synodalibus causis* 2.368, 353; *Confessional of Egbert* 34, in *Die Bussordnungen*, 409.

There are two noteworthy aspects to the above set of women's cures. First, the act of drawing through is both curative and divinatory. Second, fire is used to fight fire, or fever in these cases. A basic premise of classical and medieval thinking in regard to healing is that opposites cure opposites. Why were the acts of placing children in odd places and burning grain so distained? They were demonic magic, as specified by the various authors, but also, they drew on rituals that were well outside the church's vision of appropriate healing. This fact may be as responsible for clerics' injunctions against the procedures as the actual substance of the cures.

Among the most profound of human needs is the maintenance of physical health, and the desire to stay well has always made for great vulnerability, so it is not surprising that preservation of wellness has been a central occupation of spiritual systems in virtually all cultures. In the first millennium, despite the church's desire for a monopoly over health, Christianity was obliged to compete in an open marketplace of healing options. In late antiquity, pagan cults offered methods for avoiding or curing illness that shared similarities with Christian approaches. Both recognized a relationship between mind, body, and soul, but for Christians, by far the most significant of the three was the soul. Writers' insistence that the most potent medicine was spiritual did not impede secular therapeutics nor did it oust traditional herbal remedies that generations of Christian ecclesiastics had insisted drew on demons for their efficacy.

In this chapter I have looked at several aspects of healing, women, magic and ritual. The herbal *materia medica* enshrines images of female strength, both positive and negative. On the one hand, female entities are bellicose bringers of disease, piercing human bodies like spears. On the other hand, personified female herbs such as *Artemisia* effectively combat disease and bring comfort to those who are sick, or weary, or fearful. Female imagery is particularly evident in arcane cures. The powerful "feminine" portrayed in the herbals is not evident in other Carolingian writings, and that is doubtless because herbal literature was never subjected to the Carolingians' comprehensive emendation of texts that might have brought the herbals in line with orthodox thinking both on the nature of medicine and the power of the cosmic feminine.

Conclusion

> In a ritual, the world as lived and the world as imagined, fused under the agency of a single set of symbolic forms, turns out to be the same world.
>
> —Clifford Geertz, *Interpretation of Cultures*

Several features of magic were consistent across the first millennium. For pagans and Christians, demons were natural—not supernatural. These airy creatures of the sublunar region had their place in the great chain of being, below the angels but above humans. By virtue of their incorporeal form, they had powers people lacked, which allowed them to fly, transmogrify, and permeate material substances. In the pagan worldview, demons could act for good or evil, but by late antiquity they were generally cast as agents of malicious magic. Christian intellectuals were heir to the view that demons were malevolent, but they introduced a new element to classical demonology by claiming that pagan deities were themselves demons. They were the fallen angels described in Genesis—cast from heaven with Satan—whose goal was to tempt humans to sin. Traffic with these demons was the very definition of magic, and through this traffic, people were ensnared in a web of wrongdoing. This perspective on demons did not change over the centuries from Christian late antiquity through the early Middle Ages. What did change was the understanding of what precisely constituted traffic with demons.

For Roman pagans, magic was an innate and harmonizing component of the cosmic order and by no means irrational. Through the arrangement of various substances, words, stances, and rituals, it was possible for human beings to manipulate the natural world and to compel demons, personalities

CONCLUSION 385

higher than themselves on the chain of being, to do their bidding. Magic spanned the spectrum from the sublime and transcendental to the tawdry and vicious. When magic was the mechanism through which people committed crimes, it was punishable by law. Demons were often the intermediaries between sorcerers and the object of their sorcery, but by no means was that always the case. At times deities, minor spirits, and the shades of the dead were responsible for bringing magic formulas to fruition. Or, in some ritual magic and spells, efficacy was not attributable to animate beings at all, but rather to the proper exploitation of a force in the universe, such as "sympathy" between two classes of objects. Christians agreed with their pagan neighbors that people assisted by demons did have the power to exert an influence over natural forces (to a greater or lesser extent), but for them magic was essentially "wrong religion." It was wicked whether it worked or not because it depended on the agency of demons.

Early Christian thinkers, notably Augustine, scrutinized most aspects of pagan thought and practice and in that process developed a theology about magic, which formed the framework for the remainder of the early Middle Ages. The chief principle was that conjuring any preternatural power without direct reliance on God or his saints constituted traffic with demons. Many practices that pagans had thought of as benign or even commendable (such as theurgy) were folded into the definition of the demonic.

By the sixth century, awesome abilities attributed to demons in the early phase of Christianity were debunked. Much of their putative power was now thought to be fraudulent: they could not predict the future, raise the dead, or metamorphose the shapes God assigned to his creatures. Still, demons had skills and access that humans did not. They could, for example, effect cures, find lost objects, raise storms, and interfere with love and sexual passion. Ultimately, however, regardless of any advantages that might be gained through magic, Christians were to have no traffic with demons on any terms, and tapping (or trying to tap) superhuman power with demonic aid was a sinful affront to God, who provided human beings all the knowledge, power, and contact they needed through the scriptures, saints, and the church. All superstitious behaviors that resembled the rites or implied the mental attitudes of paganism were demonic. Given this stand, the realm of ritual became very significant, because it was in ritual that old customs and beliefs were most stubbornly embedded.

In antique Christian sources, the gendered dimension of magic is not as prominent as it becomes in later texts, because the aspects of magic that alarmed leaders of the early church were theological, political, and quintessentially public. Tikva Frymer-Kensky writes that in the Old Testament, "there is no real 'woman question.'"[1] Perhaps the same could be said about magic and women in the primitive church. What is most striking about female magic in the earliest Christian period, as presented in texts, is its egalitarian nature. Christian women's idolatry, divination, superstition, and amatory sorcery were perceived to be no more or less pervasive or pernicious than men's idolatry, divination, superstition, and amatory sorcery. Women's prophecy—holy or false—was credited or discredited on the same basis as that of men. Christian writings, which were dominated by works of the church fathers and hagiographers, painted an idealized picture of the early movement, including the piety and moderation of its women.

The Christian assessment of pagan women was different. They were portrayed both by pagans and by Christians as given over to unrestrained sensual behavior and frenzied ritual theater, and they were thought more likely than men to traffic with demons stealthily for malicious ends. Their maleficium was usually domestic and private, drawing its potency from ancient chthonic ceremonial. Late antique pagans were fascinated by stories of the witchlike striae and lamiae, and they projected the characteristics of these creatures onto goddesses and mortal women. They also held the goddess Diana in high esteem as mistress of the moon and an expert in obstetrics. However, although these female personages would reemerge in early medieval texts, they do not play a significant role in foundational church writings, which are more focused on developing theology, promulgating dogma, and defending Christians against an array of charges for anti-social behavior, including working the magic arts.

Despite the efforts of theologians such as Justin Martyr and Origen to explain logically the dissimilarity between the work of demonic pagan deities and the miraculous power of God,[2] in the first several centuries of the church's existence much of Christianity's appeal to the pagan lay in the belief that the Christian God's "magic" was stronger than that of ancestral gods and goddesses. Cries similar to those heard in fourth-century Gaza, "Great is the God of the Christians," echo through the literature as pagan communities watch their deities lose to Christian missionaries in contests for control of the numinous.[3] Such enthusiasm may have led people to conversion, but it lacked the deeper message the clergy hoped to convey. Because of the difficulty of communicating sophisticated theological concepts to the masses, architects of the early church invested in a program of carefully

---

1. Frymer-Kensky, *In the Wake*, 121.
2. Justin Martyr, *Second Apology* 5–7, 285–99; Origen, *Contra Celsum* 1.6, 9–10; 1.68, 62–63.
3. MacMullen, *Christianizing the Roman Empire*, 87 (quotation), 107–13.

crafted, simple rituals whereby "truths" could be communicated at a visceral, emotional, symbolic level. Christians slowly broke down traditional power structures and customary social interactions by working within the domain of ritual. As Peter Brown writes, "The Christian teachers offered a view of man and the world that cut many of the Gordian knots of social living in a manner that was all the more convincing for being safely symbolic."[4] But ritual may not have been as safe as it seemed.

First, articulate Christian ritual practices were slow to develop and often irregular from location to location. Further, patristic writers were conflicted about ritual per se, and were especially suspicious of exaggeratedly rigorous or exorbitant rites because of their similarity to Jewish and pagan religious expression. But most tricky of all was that Christian leaders had the challenge of sorting out which traditional pagan practices were clearly demonic and had to be completely expunged from Christian observance, and which habits were innocuous and could be incorporated into church ritual if coded with new meaning. For ritual to be useful it has to provide a level of security and comfort, and this can only happen if the components of the ritual are recognizable. That meant that the church had to start with familiar actions or talismanic props and pry them from the symbolic subtext with which pagan communities had imbued them, so that Christian significance could take the place of long-established meaning. The ritual form itself is inherently combustible, so depending on it, especially when many of the symbols, formulas, and objects were traditional, was risky, but the church had no choice. It was imperative that it be nimble with ritual if it were to convert humanity to a new view of the universe. Gregory the Great appreciated this when he urged his colleague to substitute the hallowed rite of animal sacrifice with a Christian "solemnity." Robert Nisbet writes, "[Metaphor] is, at its simplest, a way of proceeding from the known to the unknown. . . . What we think of as revolutions in thought are quite often no more than the mutational replacement, at certain critical points in history, of one foundation-metaphor for another." The Christian challenge was to promulgate that mutation.[5]

Magic from about 450 to 750 shared characteristics with sorcery in the centuries before and after it. In late antique pagan thought, even though many aspects of magic (as pagans defined it) were not technically criminal, magic was deplorable and base because of its often secretive nature. It was not quite honorable to gain advantage through the occult. Early medieval

---

4. Brown, *Making of Late Antiquity*, 73.
5. Bede, *Bede's Ecclesiastical History* 1.30, 106–8. Nisbet, *Social Change and History*, 4–6.

Christians shared this distaste for magic and went one step further; in addition to being criminal and distasteful, it was sinful and aberrant. As in Roman antiquity, Merovingian-era magic was a civic and legal matter; it caused disruption of the peace, personal injury, and domestic conflict. As would be expected, this is evident in the period's judicial documents. Church writings also frame magic as a public nuisance and a transgression that put personal salvation at risk. But in a much more profound sense, magic interfered with efforts to proselytize pagan peoples and to expand Christendom.

In the multicultural and socially diverse world of the Merovingian era, there were strata after strata of symbols, meanings, fears, and emotional triggers that responded to very ancient stimuli and found solace and strength in a worldview that thrived beneath the conscious level of dogma and rules. The sixth- and seventh-century church recognized this and readily developed distinctive rites; gone was the primitive religion's prejudice against ceremony per se. But crafting a thoroughgoing program of Christian ritual was a slow process, especially in this era of multiple princes and kings when the hegemony of both church and secular governments was fractured, and influence rested in small-scale organizations such as monasteries and peripatetic courts. The competition with age-old, beloved, and "workable" traditions was fierce—made more so by the nature of ritual itself. Symbols, the building blocks of ritual, are flexible and can carry multiple levels of meaning. Because the Christian and lingering pagan populations worked with the same storehouse of cultural objects, words, and gestures, and because they both sacralized the same liminal experiences and numinous impulses, it was often difficult for the church to be sure that demons were not lurking beneath the surface of seemingly Christian practices and ceremonies. Some of the rites promoted by the church, such as signing with the cross, which was clearly Christian, were zealously promoted as replacements for a myriad of pre-Christian demonic usages. The same was true of the insistence on worshipping in an enclosed and consecrated space—the house of God—as opposed to out of doors. Rogation ceremonies competed with weather magic, sacred cultic altars were destroyed and replaced with sanctified churches, and saints' graves took the place of pagan shrines as locales for votive offerings.

The suppression of paganism and the evangelization of European communities was an intensely local process—proceeding at different rates, in different ways, and driven by different forces from locale to locale. By the eighth century, institutional Christianization had been somewhat realized in regard to public life, though still, in that realm, maintaining consistent orthodox observance required constant vigilance and regular reprimands of kings, queens, priests, monks, and nuns. Not only rank-and-file Christians, but also members of the clergy, could come dangerously near (or cross the line into) magical thinking and verboten practices by the misuse of signs, sacred objects, places, and rituals, that is, according to the way the church understood misuse. But in the private domain of hearth and field, the progress of standardizing religious practice was less remarkable. Old superstitions endured; feasting and ceremonies at the hearth and in the woods persisted. Spells, sorcery, fortune telling, and potions continued to be used to gain an advantage in battle or love or to ensure the health of the body. One of the attributes of magic was that it was individualistic; it amounted to a privatization of agency and charisma and was therefore a threat to the clergy, which fostered an hierarchical orientation.

In Merovingian-era and Anglo-Saxon cultures from roughly 450 to 750, the home was the locus of power, prestige, livelihood, and security, and political authority was more personal than institutional. It was in the domestic sphere that women's particular forms of magic were most in evidence. Women have a manifest presence in some sources for particular types of magic, but this was not because they were more inclined than men to resort to traffic with demons. Rather, it was because they dominated aspects of home life where efforts to eradicate magic and un-Christian patterns of behavior were less effective. Women concocted healing charms for their families, wove spells at their looms, manipulated husbands and lovers, dallied with corpses, indulged in dark maleficium, imposed their will with poison potions and ligatures, encroached on Christian death with pagan mourning rituals, and continued their ancient role as soothsayers or prophetesses. Tales of Diana, the striae, and the lamiae kept alive the specter of female figures with awesome powers over reproduction and death.

Sometimes sorcerous women made their way into public records such as histories and annals when their actions affected political events, but it is outside the political narrative genres in hortatory and pastoral literature that females loom large as practitioners of certain kinds of magic. Just as women in the sixth through the mid-eighth centuries were influential in virtually all aspects of religious life—from endowing churches, to the administration of prominent religious houses, to advising kings and princes, to prophesying—they were also a force to be reckoned with in "anti-religion," or trafficking with demons. Their magic gave them power throughout society.

The latter half of the early Middle Ages in Europe and the British Isles was characterized by increasing examination and regulation of political systems, the written word, private life, and religious expression. Whereas in the early Christian and Merovingian eras the views of the literate and nonliterate can be assumed to have been essentially similar on the question of magic, that was less true as a result of the reform movements of the ninth and tenth centuries. The thought and discourse of Carolingian and Anglo-Saxon intellectuals became more linear, systematized, and ideological, so that the "common tradition" of which Richard Kieckhefer speaks began to break down, if by "common tradition" we mean common interpretations of some basic assumptions about magic.[6] The threat of pesky demons and elves no longer fit into the cognitive calculus of the elites. For them, demons existed, to be sure, but the perception of their competence changed; most of the wonders that devils credited to themselves were fraudulent. Whereas in the Merovingian period both the educated and the masses shared a belief that commerce with demons could work for petty ends, Carolingian thought was more nuanced. The elite and the common still shared a mutual vocabulary of magic, but they had moved apart as to what aspects of magic they accepted as real.

As the Carolingian and Anglo-Saxon aristocracies of church and kingdom strengthened institutions and enhanced their ritual programs, they confronted traffic with demons head-on. Magic was a problem because of its effect on law, social morality, and individual salvation, and, more seriously, because individuals' reliance on demonic forces had the power to disrupt the Christian ecumene—the new Zion. This was an impediment to creating a profound Christian worldview, a project that depended on the "proper" orientation of the whole organism (meaning both the individual and the state), and one that was threatened by magic—especially when it took a ritual form. As I have said many times throughout this book, ritual was powerful because it operated at several levels (psychic, physical, emotional, communal), because it played out in symbolic language that evoked time-honored rhythms and patterns of thought, and because it harbored what seemed to be innocuous behaviors that masked the work of devils. Magic persisted in the later portion of the early Middle Ages because it was integrated within daily habits, and because for so many who engaged it, traffic with demons worked.

The kinds of sources that discuss contemporary concerns in the core lands of the Carolingian era do not stress trafficking with demons the way those same genres do in the Merovingian period. Censure of magic in Carolingian and Anglo-Saxon literature exists, but, by and large, the attention of the reformers in Francia and Anglo-Saxon England was focused elsewhere. Monastic and ecclesiastical restructuring, expansion of Christian hegemony, political stability, and the elucidation of theological orthodoxy absorbed the

---

6. Kieckhefer, *Magic in the Middle Ages*, 56–94.

time and attention of writers of the period. There are exceptions, of course, as when Agobard of Lyon encountered the *tempestarii* and the visitors from Magonia and Raban Maur learned of the moon magic taking place just outside his door. But both were curiosities. Magic surfaced in the texts when it had an impact on larger matters. For example, when sorcery threatened the royal succession in the courts of Louis the Pious and Lothar II, it drew attention, but it was not a determinative issue in either crisis.

The situation was different in the margins of the Carolingian and Anglo-Saxon kingdoms. There, where missionaries were still proselytizing and pagan people were struggling with the challenges of conversion to the culturally privileged form of Christianity, injunctions against magic have a more immediate feel to them. Standard long-standing proscriptions still appear in penitentials, council records, and so forth, but many new elements emerge from the texts, notably from the compendia of Regino of Prüm and Burchard of Worms.

As centralizing governments developed mechanisms for structuring social and domestic life, women's perceived power over occult forces waned concomitantly. The Carolingians eroded the perception of women as effective magical practitioners. Church and secular leaders were determined to nullify myths of female power and to destroy a matrix of symbols that had the potential to mold concepts of reality outside the liminal space in which they were incubated. Female rituals, which made sense of birth, death, and women's participation in cosmic mysteries, threatened a competing symbolic/ritual system promoted by an invigorated and increasingly regulated Christianity that understood birth, death, and the role of women in quite a different way. A wide variety of sources suggest that the literature the Carolingians produced is less likely to represent women in strong roles as wielders of magic than the same types of literature written before the Carolingian reform. This is true even in sources in which the overall concern with magic increases, such as the penitentials.

The only genre of texts in which this pattern is not evident is the herbal medical material, because practical healing was a field in which Carolingian and reform Anglo-Saxon intellectuals did not take great interest or make significant strides. Although scribes copied herbals and medical treatises, there was no systematic attempt to scrutinize, revamp, or standardize them, the way there was for laws, council records, and penitentials.[7] It is

---

7. The Anglo-Saxon *materia medica*, such as *Lacnunga* and *Bald's Leechbook*, was not used on the Continent, so it would not have undergone Carolingian revision in any case; however, Anglo-Saxon reformers likewise did not engage in a systematic review of medical texts.

no coincidence that it is in medical literature that the association between strong women (or awesome female-identified forces) and effectual magic is most enduring.

Two important Carolingian documents, the General Admonition and the records of the Council of Paris, summarize the state of affairs in the late eighth and early ninth centuries. As discussed earlier, the General Admonition is a sweeping reform capitulary written in 789 by Alcuin and promulgated during Charlemagne's reign for the structuring of church and kingdom. Capitulum 18 states, "People are not allowed to be *cauclearii*, magicians, enchanters, or enchantresses." Only one of these practitioners is specifically female. Capitulum 65 in the same document summarizes the magic practices that had accumulated over time, such as taking auguries, heeding dreams, general soothsaying, weather prophecy, tying ligatures, communicating with familiar spirits, and performing outdoor rites. The text reads, "Therefore we order that sorcerers, enchanters, weather magicians, and *obligatores* are forbidden." In this case, none of the practitioners specified are female.[8]

The churchmen responsible for the document were relatively unconcerned with what had traditionally been female forms of magic, or with sorceresses. Women are targeted only once in the proscriptions against magic, although it is arguable that they were perceived to have participated in some of the other demonic activities described in the text, especially "tying ligatures" and "communicating with familiar spirits" (which is reminiscent of the biblical pythoness of Endor). In the early Middle Ages, women's magic generally involved maleficium in the form of love magic, dangerous potions, or killing children, but the General Admonition is more concerned with idolatry than with maleficium. Both were demonic, but whereas maleficium was harmful to the victim and to the soul of the practitioner, idolatry put a whole people at risk. Women's magic was pernicious but not as significant as communal idolatry, which could be disastrous. Their magical abilities might cause difficulties, but they were ultimately trivial and futile.

The records of the Council of Paris (829), drawn up by Jonas of Orléans in Louis the Pious's reign, are similar to his father's General Admonition. The assembly was a wide-ranging reform congress, and the record of it lists

---

8. *Die Admonitio generalis* 18, 192: "Item in eodem concilio, ut cauclearii, malefici, incantatores, vel incantatrices fieri non sinantur"; ibid., 64, 216: "Ideo praecipimus ut cauculatores nec incantatores nec tempestarii vel obligatores no fiant." The words "cauclearii," "cauculatores," and "obligatores" were used throughout the early Middle Ages, and although it is clear that they refer to magical practitioners, there is no evidence as to the nature of the magic they performed; on this see Filotas, *Pagan Survivals*, 219.

a full range of magical activities that the framers of the document held to be most deleterious:

> There exist other most insidious evils, which, no doubt, remain with us from heathen rites, such as sorcery, soothsaying, drawing lots, poisonings, divination, incantations, and interpreting dreams. . . . Doubtless, as many have noted, there are those who, by the same deceptions and diabolical illusions, infect the minds of others by love potions, drugged food, or charms, so that they become insane and are not aware of the abuses they suffer. It is said that they can, by their sorcery, disturb the air, send hailstorms, predict the future, move fruit and milk from one person to another, and innumerable other such things. If someone of this sort should be found, whether men or women, they should be very sternly corrected because in their crimes and temerity, they do not fear to serve the Devil nor do they renounce him publicly.[9]

In this canon, as in the General Admonition, women's magic is, for the most part, lacking. It is true that both men and women are named as perpetrators, and some of the types of magic that were particularly female are listed, such as poisoning and love potions. However, this canon largely overlooks female magic. There is no mention of weaving, birth magic, or the activities of the striae, the lamiae, or Diana. The canon lists magic that is seen as threatening to the well-being of the realm—that threatens wholesale pollution from a "heathen" era before the victory of Christianity. And in this litany of truly dangerous illusions and deceptions, women's magic is underrepresented.

In 860 Hincmar of Reims exposed love magic, arguably women's most potent magical skill, as negligible. By 1000, Burchard of Worms painted a vivid image of a peasantry alarmingly deluded about the ability of women to execute astounding acts of sorcery, and his legislation against belief in the pernicious arts of women is extensive. But this scrutiny did not represent a reversal of the attitudes evident in earlier Carolingian texts. Rather, Burchard described in graphic detail the absurdity of the sorts of beliefs with

---

9. Council of Paris 69, 669: "Et alia pernitiosissima mala, quae ex ritu gentilium remansisse non dubium est, ut sunt magi, arioli, sortilegi, venefici, divini, incantatores, somniatorum coniectores. . . . Dubium etenim non est, sicut multis est notum, quod a quibusdam praestigiis atque diabolicis inlusionibus ita mentes quorundam inficiantur poculis amatoriis, cibis vel filacteriis, ut in insaniam versi a plerisque iudicentur, dum proprias non sentitunt contumelias. Ferunt enim suis maleficiis aera posse conturbare et grandines inmittere, futura praedicere, fructus et lac auferre aliisque dare et innumera a talibus fieri dicuntur. Qui ut fuerint huiusmodi conperti, viri seu femine, in tantum disciplina et vigore principis acrius corrigendi sunt, in quantum manifestius ausu nefando et temerario servire diabolo non metuunt."

which this book began—that women can leave the home to fly through the night sky with other loosed women, imperil their husbands, raise storms, and take on martial roles—and he did this in order to debunk the popular myths of female competence in the magic arts and commerce with demons. Burchard and other authors worked vigilantly to disarm the most threatening symbols of female autonomous power—the striae and the lamiae—and denied these specters' very existence. Diana, more and more over the centuries, had become the quintessential female embodiment of magic. She was the mystical, magical, nocturnal, feminized moon, protectress of magical herbs, and finally, at the hands Burchard of Worms, an airborne demon, queen of a ghoulish horde of wild demons and crazed women, freed from their domestic restraints, orgiastically pursuing the wild hunt. Yet as titillating as tales of Diana were, she was, in the end, a garden-variety demon, and her aerial horde a phantom. But phantom or not, and even if women were ineffectual in marshaling demons to do their bidding, they could and did manipulate rituals, myth, and symbols, and for that reason, the ruling elite went to some length to neutralize the powerful images of autonomous women encoded in them. That is to say, women designed and acted in rituals that called on malevolent forces, and although the church considered these women deceived if they thought that through their rites they could actually direct demons, that did not decrease the threat of the rituals themselves.

The models of normative female behavior as portrayed in literature do not tell the whole story. It is very likely that in real-life existence, beyond most texts, women's acumen in magic continued to be respected and feared, and sometimes we get hazy glimpses of this. But what we are able to see clearly is that the elite thought women were ineffectual at working magic with any real consequences because they were generally inept in sacral endeavors, including trafficking with demons. Where concepts of female power and autonomy were kept most alive in symbolic systems and ritual, the Christian assault on rites that bolstered that power was thoroughgoing.

🕮 Bibliography

Abbreviations

CCCM	*Corpus Christianorum continuatio mediaevalis*
CCSL	*Corpus Christianorum, series Latina*
CSEL	*Corpus scriptorum ecclesiasticorum Latinorum*
EME	*Early Medieval Europe*
LCL	Loeb Classical Library
MGH	*Monumenta Germaniae Historica*
AA	*Auctores Antiquissimi*
Cap. 1	*Capitularia regum Francorum 1*. Edited by Alfred Boretius. Hanover, Hahn, 1883.
Cap. 2	*Capitularia regum Francorum 2*. Edited by Alfred Boretius and Victor Krause. Hanover: Hahn, 1897.
Cap. ep. 1	*Capitulia episcoporum 1*. Edited by Peter Brommer. Hanover: Hahn, 1984.
Conc. aevi Kar. 2.1	*Concilia aevi Karolini 2.1*. Edited by Wilfried Hartmann. Hanover: Hahn, 1993.
Conc. aevi Kar. 4	*Concilia aevi Karolini 4*. Edited by Wilfried Hartmann. Hanover: Hahn, 1998.
Conc. aevi Mer.	*Concilia aevi Merovingici*. Edited by Friedrich Maasen. Hanover: Hahn, 1893.
Epp. sel.	*Epistolae selectae*
Epp. Kar. aevi	*Epistolae Karolini aevi*
LL	*Leges in folio 3*. Edited by Heinrich Pertz. Hanover: Hahn, 1862. *Leges in folio 5*. Edited by Heinrich Brunner. Hanover: Hahn, 1875–89.
LL nat. Germ.	*Leges nationum Germanicarum*
SRG	*Scriptores rerum Germanicarum in usum scholarum separatim editi*. 81 vols. Hanover: Hahn, 1871–2016.
SRM	*Scriptores rerum Merovingicarum*
SS	*Scriptores*
PG	*Patrologiae cursus completus series Graeca*. Edited by J.–P. Migne, 161 vols. Paris: Garnier, 1857–66.
PL	*Patrologiae cursus completus series Latina*. Edited by J.–P. Migne. 221 vols. Paris: Garnier, 1844–65.

Biblical references are from the New Revised Standard Version.

Primary Sources—Single Text or Author

2 Clement: Introduction, Text, and Commentary. Translated by Christopher Tuckett. Apostolic Fathers. Oxford: Oxford University Press, 2012.

Acts of Barnabas. Translated by Glenn E. Snyder. In *New Testament Apocrypha: More Noncanonical Scriptures*, edited by Tony Burke and Brent Landau, 317–26. Vol. 2. Grand Rapids, MI: Eerdmans, 2016.

Acts of John the Apostle. In *The Apocryphal New Testament: A Collection of Apocryphal Christian Literature in an English Translation*, translated by J. K. Elliott, 303–47. Oxford: Oxford University Press, 1993.

Acts of Paul and Thecla. In *Fathers of the Third and Fourth Centuries*, edited by A. Cleveland Coxe, 487–96. Ante-Nicene Fathers 7, 8. Grand Rapids, MI: Erdmans 1989.

Aelfric of Eynsham. *Aelfric's Lives of Saints: Being a Set of Sermons on Saints' Days Formerly Observed by the English Church.* Translated by Miss Gunning and Miss Wilkinson, edited by Walter W. Skeat. 2 vols. Early English Text Society 76, 82 (vol. 1), 94, 114 (vol. 2). London: N. Trübner, 1835–1912. Reprint, Oxford: Boydell & Brewer, 2014.

———. *Homilies of Aelfric: A Supplementary Collection.* Edited by John C. Pope. 2 vols. Early English Text Society 259 and 260. London: Oxford University Press, 1967–68.

———. *The Homilies of the Anglo-Saxon Church: The First Part, Containing the Sermones Catholici or Homilies of Aelfric.* Edited and translated by B. Thorpe. 2 vols. London: Richard and John E. Taylor, 1844–46. Vol. 1 reprint, New York: Johnson Reprint, 1971.

Agobard of Lyon. *De grandine et tonitruis.* In *Agobardi Lugdunensis opera omnia*, edited by L. van Acker, 1–15. CCCM 52. Turnhout, Belgium: Brepols, 1981.

———. *Liber apologeticus.* In *Agobardi Lugdunensis opera omnia*, edited by L. van Acker, 307–19. CCCM 52. Turnhout, Belgium: Brepols, 1981.

Alcinous. *The Handbook of Platonism.* Translated by John Dillion. Clarendon Later Ancient Philosophers. Clarendon Press: Oxford, 1993. Reprint, 2002.

Alcuin. *De virtutibus et vitiis liber ad Widonem Comitem.* PL 101, cols. 613–39.

———. *Epistolae.* Edited by Ernst Dümmler, 1–493. MGH Epp. Kar. aevi 4.2. Berlin: Weidmann, 1895.

———. *Vita Willibrordi.* Edited by Wilhelm Levison, 81–141. MGH SRM 7. Hanover: Hahn, 1920.

Ammianus Marcellinus. *History.* Translated by John C. Rolfe. 3 vols. LCL 300, 315, 331. Cambridge, MA: Harvard University Press, 1935–40.

"The Anglo-Saxon Leechbook III: A Critical Edition and Translation." Edited and translated by Barbara M. Olds. PhD diss., University of Denver, 1984.

Annales Bertiniani. Edited by Geoge Waitz. MGH SRG in usum scholarum separatim editi 5. Hanover: Hahn, 1883.

Annales Fuldenses sive annales regni Francorum orientalis. Edited by Friedrich Kurze. MGH SRG in usum scholarum separatim editi 7. Hanover: Hahn, 1891. Reprint, 1978.

Annales Laureshamenses. Edited by G. H. Pertz, 19–39. MGH SS 1. Hanover: Hahn, 1826.

BIBLIOGRAPHY

Annales regni Francorum. Edited by Friedrich Kurze. *MGH SRG in usum scholarum separatim editi* 6. Hanover: Hahn, 1895.

Annales Xantenses qui dicuntur. In *Annales Xantenses et Annales Vedastini,* edited by B. de Simon, 1–33. *MGH SRG in usum scholarum separatim editi* 12. Hanover: Hahn, 1909.

The Annals of Fulda. Translated by Timothy Reuter. Ninth-Century Histories 2. Manchester Medieval Sources Series. Manchester: Manchester University Press, 1992.

Apuleius of Madaura. *Apulei apologia sive pro se de magia liber.* Edited by H. E. Butler and A. S. Owen. Oxford: Clarendon, 1914. Reprint, Hildesheim: Georg Olms, 1967.

———. *The Golden Ass.* Translated by Sarah Ruden. New Haven, CT: Yale University Press, 2011.

———. *Metamorphoses.* Edited and translated by John Arthur Hanson. 2 vols. LCL 44, 453. Cambridge, MA: Harvard University Press, 1989.

The Arabic Gospel of the Infancy of Jesus (Evangelium infantiae Salvatoris Arabicum). In *Evangelia Apocrypha,* edited by Constantin von Tischendorf, 181–209. Hildesheim: Olms, 1966.

Aristotle. *The Politics of Aristotle: A Treatise on Government.* Translated by William Ellis. Auckland, NZ: Floating Press, 2009. First published in 1912.

Asser. *The Medieval Life of King Alfred the Great: A Translation and Commentary on the Text Attributed to Asser.* Translated by Alfred P. Smyth. Basingstoke, UK: Palgrave, 2002.

Astronomer. *Vita Hludowici imperatoris.* In *Theganus* Gesta Hludowici Imperatoris. *Astronomus* Vita Hludowici Imperatoris, edited by Ernst Tremp, 279–555. *MGH SRG in usum scholarum separatim editi* 64. Hanover: Hahn, 1995.

Athanasius. *De Incarnatione.* In *Athanasius: "Contra Gentes" and "De Incarnatione,"* edited and translated by Robert W. Thomson, 134–277. Oxford Early Christian Texts. Oxford: Clarendon, 1971.

———. *The Life of Antony* ["The Life and Affairs of Our Holy Father Antony"]. In *The Life of Antony and the Letter to Marcellinus,* translated by Robert C. Gregg, 29–99. Classics of Western Spirituality. New York: Paulist, 1980.

Audoin. *Vita Eligii episcopi Noviomagensis.* Edited by Bruno Krusch, 634–741. *MGH SRM* 4, Hanover: Hahn, 1902.

Augustine. *Confessionum Libri XIII.* Edited by Lucas Verheijen. *Sancti Augustini opera.* CCSL 27. Turnholt, BE: Brepols, 1990.

———. *Contra Julianum Pelagianum.* PL 44, cols. 641–874.

———. *De civitate Dei.* Edited by Bernard Dombart and Alphonso Kalb. 2 vols. In *Aurelii Augustini opera.* CCSL 47, 48. Turnhout, BE: Brepols, 1954–55.

———. *De cura pro mortuis gerenda.* Edited by Joseph Zycha, 619–60. In *Sancti Aureli Augustini opera.* CSEL 41. Vienna: Tempsky, 1900.

———. *De diversis quaestionibus ad simplicianum.* Edited by Almut Mutzenbecher. *Aurelii Augustini opera,* 5–91. CCSL 44. Turnhout, BE: Brepols, 1970.

———. *De divinatione daemonum.* Edited by Joseph Zycha, 597–618. In *Sancti Aureli Augustini opera.* CSEL 41. Vienna: Tempsky, 1900.

———. *De doctrina Christiana.* Edited and Translated by R. P. H. Green. Oxford: Clarendon, 1995.

———. *De utilitate credendi*. Edited by Joseph Zycha. In *Sancti Aurelii Augustini opera*, 1–48. CSEL 25. Vienna: Tempsky, 1891.

———. *Enarrationes in Psalmos LI–C*. Edited by E. Dekkers and J. Fraipont. In *Aurelli Augustini opera*. CCSL 39. Turnhout, BE: Brepols, 1956.

———. *In Iohannis evangelium tractatus CXXIV*. Edited by Augustine Mayer. In *Aurelli Augustini opera*. CCSL 36. Turnhout, BE: Brepols, 1954.

———. *Letters: Volume I (1–82)*. Translated by Wilfrid Parsons. Fathers of the Church 12. Washington, DC: Catholic University of America Press, 1951.

———. *Letters: Volume III (131–164)*. Translated by Wilfrid Parsons. Fathers of the Church 20. Washington, DC: Catholic University of American Press, 1953.

———. *On Christian Doctrine*. Translated by D. W. Robertson Jr. The Library of Liberal Arts. Indianapolis: Bobbs-Merrill, 1981. First published in 1958.

———. *Quaestionum in Heptateuchum libri VII*. Edited by J. Fraipont. In *Aurelii Augustini opera*, 1–377. CCSL 33. Turnhout, BE: Brepols, 1958.

———. *Sermones*. PL 38.

Avitus of Vienne. *Ex Homiliarum Libro*. In *Opera quae supersunt*, edited by Rudolf Peiper, 103–57. MGH AA 6.2. Berlin: Weidmann, 1883.

Bald's Leechbook: British Museum Royal Manuscript 12D. xvii. Edited by Cyril Ernest Wright. Early English Manuscripts in Facsimile 5. Copenhagen: Rosenkilde & Bagger, 1955.

Barnabas. *The Letter of Barnabas*. Translated by Francis X. Glimm. In Dressler, *Apostolic Fathers*, 187–222.

Basil of Caesarea. *Saint Basil Exegetic Homilies*. Translated by Agnes Clare Way. Fathers of the Church 46. Washington, DC: Catholic University of America Press, 1963.

Bede. *Bede's Ecclesiastical History of the English People*. Edited by Bertram Colgrave and R. A. B. Mynors. Oxford Medieval Texts. Oxford: Clarendon, 1969.

———. *De temporum ratione liber*. In *Bedae venerabilis opera*, edited by C. W. Jones and F. Lipp, 263–460. Vol. 2. CCSL 123b. Turnhout, BE: Brepols, 1977.

———. *Expositio actum apostolorum*. In *Bedae venerabilis opera*, edited by M. L. W. Laistner and David Hurst. CCSL 121. Turnhout, BE: Brepols, 1983.

———. *Life of St. Cuthbert*. In *Two Lives of Saint Cuthbert: A Life by an Anonymous Monk of Lindisfarne and Bede's Prose Life*, edited and translated by Bertram Colgrave, 141–307. Cambridge, MA: Cambridge University Press, 1985. First published in 1940.

Beowulf. Translated by R. M. Liuzza. Ontario, Canada: Broadview, 2000.

Biblia sacra: iuxta Vulgatam versionem. Edited by Robert Weber, Roger Gryson, and Bonifatius Fischer. Editionem quintam emendatam retractatam. Stuttgart: Deutsche Bibelgesellschaft, 2007.

The Blickling Homilies: Edition and Translation. Edited and translated by Richard J. Kelly. London: Continuum, 2003.

Boniface. *Die Briefe des Heiligen Bonifatius und Lullus*. Edited by Michael Tangl. MGH Epp. sel. 1. Berlin: Weidmann, 1916. Reprint, Munich: MGH, 1978.

———. *The Letters of Saint Boniface*. Translated by Ephraim Emerton. Records of Western Civilization. New York: Columbia University Press, 2000.

The Book of Nunnaminster. (An Ancient Manuscript Belonging to St. Mary's Abbey, or Nunnaminster, Winchester). Edited by Walter De Gray Birch. Hampshire Record Society. London: Simpkin and Marshall, 1889. Reprint, Instrumenta Liturgica Quarreriensia 5. Rome: C.L.V.–Edizioni Liturgiche, 2001.

The Books of Enoch: Aramaic Fragments of Qumrân Cave 4. Edited by J. T. Milik and Matthew Black. Oxford: Clarendon, 1976.

Burchard of Worms. *Decretum*. In Schmitz, *Die Bussbücher und die Bussdiscipline*, 403–67. Vol. 2.

———. *Decretum*. PL 140, cols. 537–1058.

Caesarius of Arles. *Saint Caesarius of Arles, Sermons*. Translated by Mary Magdeleine Mueller. 3 vols. Fathers of the Church 31, 47, 66. Washington, DC: Catholic University of America Press, 1956–73.

———. *Sermones. Sancti Caesarii Arelatensis*, edited by Germain Morin. 2 vols. CCSL 103, 104. Turnhout, Belgium: Brepols, 1953.

Cassian, John (Jean Cassien). *Conférences: I–VII*. Edited by E. Pichéry. Sources chrétiennes 42. Paris: Cerf, 1955.

Cathwulf. *Letter to Charlemagne*. Edited by E. Dümmler, 501–5. MGH Ep. Kar. aevi 4.2. Berlin: Weidmann, 1939.

Cato. *On Agriculture. Cato and Varro*. Translated by William Davis Hooper. Revised by Harrison Boyd Ash, 1–157. LCL 283. Cambridge, MA: Harvard University Press, 1935.

The Chaldean Oracles: Text, Translation and Commentary. Edited and translated by Ruth Majercik. 2nd ed. Platonic Texts and Translations 8. Westbury, UK: The Prometheus Trust, 2013.

Chronicon Gothanum – Spicilegium e veteris Langobardorum edicti codicibus. Centre Traditio Littearum Occidentalium. Turnhout: Brepols, 2015.

Chrysostom, John. *Baptismal Instructions*. In *Practice*, vol. 2 of *The Cambridge Edition of Early Christian Writings*, edited by Ellen Muehlberger, 244–72. Cambridge: Cambridge University Press, 2017.

———. "Exposition of Psalm 41." Translated by Oliver Strunk, revised by James McKinnon. In *Source Readings in Music History*. 2nd ed. Edited by Oliver Strunk, revised by Leo Treitler, 123–26. New York: W. W. Norton, 1998.

———. *The Homilies of S. John Chrysostom, Archbishop of Constantinople, On the Gospel of St. Matthew*. Library of Fathers of the Holy Catholic Church 11. Oxford: J. H. Parker, 1843–51.

Cicero. *De Legibus*. In *De Re Publica. De Legibus*, translated by Clinton Walker Keyes, 296–519. Vol. 16 of Cicero. LCL 213. Cambridge, MA: Harvard University Press, 1928.

———. *De natura deorum*. In *De natura deorum. Academica*, translated by H. Rackham, 2–387. Vol. 19. LCL 268. Cambridge, MA: Harvard University Press, 1951. First published in 1933.

———. *De Senectute. De Amicitia. De Divinatione*. Translated by William Armistead Falconer. Vol 20 Cicero. LCL 154. Cambridge, MA: Harvard University Press, 1923.

Clement of Alexandria. *The Writings of Clement of Alexandria*. Translated by William Wilson. Ante-Nicene Christian Library 4.1. Edinburgh: T. and T. Clark, 1884.

Clement of Rome. *The Letter of St. Clement of Rome to the Corinthians.* Translated by Francis X. Glimm. In Dressler, *The Apostolic Fathers*, 9–58.

Complete Books of Enoch. 1 Enoch (First Book of Enoch), 2 Enoch (Secrets of Enoch), 3 Enoch (Hebrew Book of Enoch). Translated by A. Nyland. Mermaid Beach, AU: Smith and Stirling, 2010.

Con. Gal. A. 314–A. 506. Edited by C. Munier. CCSL 148. Turnholt, Belgium: Brepols.

Confessional of Pseudo-Egbert. PL 89, cols. 402–32.

Council of Paris (*Concilium Parisiense*). Edited by Albert Werminghoff, 605–80. MGH Con. aevi Kar. 2.2. Hanover: Hahn, 1979.

Cyril of Jerusalem. *The Works of Saint Cyril of Jerusalem.* 2 vols. Translated by Leo P. McCauley and Anthony A. Stephenson. Fathers of the Church 61, 64. Washington, DC: Catholic University of America Press, 1969–70.

The Didache: Text, Translation, Analysis, and Commentary. Translated by Aaron Milavec. Collegeville, MN: Liturgical Press, 2004.

Die Admonitio generalis Karls des Grossen. Edited by Michael Glatthaar, Hubert Mordek, and Klaus Zechiel-Eckes. MGH Fontes iuris Germanici antiqui in usum scholarum separatim editi 16. Wiesbaden: Otto Harrassowitz, 2013.

Die Gesetze der Langobarden. Edited by Franz Beyerle. Germanenrecht. Weimar: H. Böhlaus Nachf, 1947.

Dungal. *Epistolae.* Edited by Ernst Dümmler, 568–85. MGH Epp. Kar. aevi 4.2. Berlin: Weidmann, 1895.

Ebbo. *Epistolae.* Edited by Ernst Dümmler. MGH Epp. Kar. aevi 5.3. Hanover: Weidmann, 1899.

Eigil. *Vita S. Strum.* Edited by Georg Heinrich Pertz, 365–77. MGH SS 2. Hanover: Hahn, 1829.

Einhard. *Vita Karoli Magni.* Edited by O. Halder-Egger. MGH SRG 25. Hanover: Hahn, 1911.

Epiphanius of Salamis. *The "Panarion" of Epiphanius of Salamis: Book I (Sects 1–46).* Translated by Frank Williams. 2nd ed. Nag Hammadi and Manichaean Studies 63. Leiden: Brill, 2009.

———. *The "Panarion" of Epiphanius of Salamis Books II and III. De Fide.* Translated by Frank Williams. 2nd ed. Nag Hammadi and Manichaean Studies 79. Leiden: Brill, 2013.

Eusebius. *The History of the Church from Christ to Constantine.* Edited and translated by G. A. Williamson. New York: Barnes and Noble, 1965.

———. *The Life of Constantine.* Translated by Averil Cameron and Stuart G. Hall. Clarendon Ancient History Series. Oxford: Clarendon Press, 1999.

———. *Preparation for the Gospel.* Translated by Edwin Hamilton Gifford. 2 vols. Grand Rapids, MI: Baker Book House, 1981. First published in 1903.

———. *Reply to Hierocles.* In *Apollonius of Tyana*, edited and translated by Christopher P. Jones, 154–257. LCL 458. Cambridge, MA: Harvard University Press, 2012. First published in 2006.

Eustathius of Antioch. *On the Belly-Myther, Against Origen.* In *The "Belly-Myther" of Endor, Interpretations of 1 Kingdoms 28 in the Early Church,* edited by Rowan A. Greer and Margaret M. Mitchell, 62–157. Writings from the Greco-Roman World 16. Atlanta: Society of Biblical Literature, 2007.

Fontes iuris Romani antiqui. Edited by Carolus George Bruns and Theodore Mommsen. 5th ed. Freiburg: Mohr Siebeck, 1887.

Fredegar. *The Fourth Book of the Chronicle of Fredegar, with Its Continuations*. Translated by J. M. Wallace-Hadrill. Medieval Classics. London: Thomas Nelson and Sons, 1960.

Gospel of Nicodemus. In *Fathers of the Third and Fourth Centuries*, translated by A. Cleveland Coxe, 416–58. Ante-Nicene Fathers 8. Edinburgh: T. and T. Clark, 1989.

Gregory of Nyssa. *The Catechetical Oration of St. Gregory of Nyssa*. Translated by J. H. Srawley.

Early Church Classics. London: Society for Promoting Christian Knowledge, 1917.

———. *Lettre sur la Pythonisse*. In *Lettre canonique, Lettre sur la Pythonisse, et Six homélies pastorales*, translated by Pierre Maraval, 95–113. Sources chrétiennes 588. Paris: Cerf, 2017.

Gregory of Tours. *Decem libri historiarum*. In Krusch, *Gregorii episcopi Turonensis opera*, edited by Bruno Krusch and Wilhelm Levison. MGH SRM 1.1. Hanover: Hahn, 1951.

———. *De virtutibus S. Martini*. In Krusch, *Gregorii episcopi Turonensis miracula et opera minora*, 134–211.

———. *Gloria confessorum*. In Krusch, *Gregorii episcopi Turonensis miracula et opera minora*, 294–370.

———. *Gloria martyrum*. In *Gregorii episcopi Turonensis miracula et opera minora*, 34–111.

———. *Gregorii episcopi Turonensis miracula et opera minora*. Edited by Bruno Krusch. MGH SRM 1.2. Hanover: Hahn, 1885. Reprint, 1969.

———. *Liber vitae patrum*. In Krusch, *Gregorii episcopi Turonensis miracula et opera minora*, 211–94.

Gregory the Great. *Dialogues*. Edited by Paul Antin and Adalbert de Vogüé. Sources chrétiennes 265. Paris: Editions du Cerf, 2013.

———. *Saint Gregory the Great Dialogues*. Translated by Odo John Zimmermann. Fathers of the Church 39. Washington, DC: Catholic University of America Press, 2002. First published in 1959.

Herard of Tours, *Capitula Herardi archiepiscopi Turonensis*. PL 121, cols. 763–76.

Hilary of Poitiers. *Saint Hilary of Poitiers: The Trinity*. Translated by Stephen McKenna. Fathers of the Church 25. Washington, DC: Catholic University of America Press, 1954.

Hincmar of Reims. *De divortio Lotharii regis et Theutbergae reginae*. Edited by Letha Böhringer. MGH Conc. 4, supplementum 1. Hanover: Hahn, 1992.

———. *De nuptiis Stephani et filiae Regimundi comitis*. PL 126, cols. 132–53.

———. *The Divorce of King Lothar and Queen Theutberga: Hincmar of Rheims's "De Divortio."* Translated by Rachel Stone and Charles West. Manchester Medieval Sources Series. Manchester: Manchester University Press, 2016.

———. *Epistolae*. Edited by Ernst Perels. MGH Epp. Kar. aevi 8.1. Berlin: Weidmann, 1939.

Hippolytus. *On the Apostolic Tradition: An English Version with Introduction and Commentary*. Translated by Alistair Stewart-Sykes. Popular Patristics Series. Crestwood, NY: St. Vladimir's Seminary, 2001.

Homer. *The Odyssey*. Translated by Emily Wilson. New York: W. W. Norton, 2018.

Homilia de sacrilegiis: Aus einer Einsiedler Handschrift des achten Jahrhunderts herausgegeben und mit kritischen und sachlichen Anmerkungen, sowie mit einer Abhandlung begleitet. Edited by C. P. Caspari. Christiania: A. W. Brögger, 1886.

Horace. *Odes and Epodes*. Edited and translated by Niall Rudd. LCL 33. Cambridge, MA: Harvard University Press, 2004.

Raban Maur. *Commentaria in Genesim*. PL 107, cols. 439–670.

———. *De magicis artibus*. PL 110, cols. 1095–110.

———. *De universo: The Peculiar Properties of Words and Their Mystical Significance*. Translated by Priscilla Throop. 2 vols. Charlotte, VT: MedievalMS, 2009.

———. *Epistolae*. Edited by Ernst Dümmler, 379–533. MGH Epp. Kar. aevi 5.3. Berlin: Weidmann, 1899.

———. *Homilia 142*. PL 110, cols. 78–80.

———. *Poenitentiale ad Heribaldum Antissiodorensem*. PL 110, cols. 467–96. (481).

———. *Poenitentium liber ad Otgarium*. PL 112, cols. 1397–1424 (ca. 853).

Iamblichus. *Les mystères d'Égypte*. Edited and translated by Édouard Des Places. Collection des universités de France. Série grecque 174. Paris: Les Belles Lettres, 2012.

Ignatius of Antioch. *Epistle to the Ephesians*. In Roberts and Donaldson, *Apostolic Fathers*, 45–58.

———. "Epistle to the Smyrnaeans." In Roberts and Donaldson, *Apostolic Fathers*, 86–92.

Indiculus superstitionum et paganiarum. Edited by Alfred Boretius, 222–23. MGH Cap. 1. Hanover: Hahn, 1883.

Irenaeus of Lyon. *St. Irenaeus of Lyon's "Against the Heresies."* Translated by Dominic J. Unger, revised by John J. Dillion. Vol. 2. Ancient Christian Writers 64. New York: Paulist, 1992.

Isidore of Seville. *De natura rerum Liber*. Edited by Gustavus Becker. Amsterdam: Hakkert, 1967.

———. *Etymologiarum sive originum libri XX*. Edited by W. M. Lindsay. 2 vols. Scriptorum Classicorum Biblioteca Oxoniensis. Oxford: Clarendon, 1911. Reprint, Oxford: Oxford University Press, 1957. [This book has no page numbers.]

———. *Liber differentiarum [II]*. Edited by María Adelaida Andrés Sanz. CCSL 111a. Turnhout, Belgium: Brepols, 2006.

———. *Quaestiones in Vetus Testamentum*. In Regum II. PL 83, cols. 207–424.

Jerome. *Against Jovian*. In Fremantle, Lewis, and Martley, *Jerome: Letters and Select Works*, 346–416.

———. *Jerome: Letters and Select Works*. Translated by H. Fremantle, G. Lewis, and W. G. Martley. Nicene and Post-Nicene Fathers 6. 2nd ser. New York: Christian Literature, 1893. Reprint, Peabody, MA: Hendrickson, 1999.

———. *The Life of Saint Hilarion*. In Fremantle, Lewis, and Martley, *Jerome: Letters and Select Works*, 303–15.

Jonas of Orléans. (*De institutione regia*). *Jonas d'Orléans et son "De institutione regia."* Edited by Jean Reviron. Les idées politico-religieuses d'un évêque du IXe siècle. l'église et l'état au Moyen Âge 1. Paris: J. Vrin, 1930.

Justin Martyr. *Apology on Behalf of Christians*. In Minns and Parvis, *Justin, Philosopher and Martyr*, 80–269.

———. *Dialogue with Trypho*. In *Writings of Saint Justin Martyr*, translated by Thomas B. Falls, 139–366. Fathers of the Church 6. Washington, DC: Catholic University of America Press, 1977. First published in 1948.

———. *Justin, Philosopher and Martyr: Apologies*. Edited and translated by Denis Minns and Paul Parvis. Oxford Early Christian Texts. Oxford: Oxford University Press, 2009.

———. *Second Apology*. In Minns and Parvis, *Justin, Philosopher and Martyr*, 270–323.

Juvenal. *The Satires of Juvenal*. Translated by Rolfe Humphries. Midland Book MB 20. Bloomington: Indiana University Press, 1958.

Lactantius. *The Divine Institutes*. Translated by Anthony Bowen and Peter Garnsey. Texts for Historians 40. Liverpool: Liverpool University Press, 2003.

The Laws of the Salian Franks. Translated by Katherine Fischer Drew. The Middle Ages. Philadelphia: University of Pennsylvania Press, 1991.

Leander of Seville. *The Training of Nuns and the Contempt of the World*. In Barlow, *Writings of Martin of Braga, Paschasius of Dumium, and Leander of Seville*, 183–228.

Leges Alamannorum. Edited by Karl Lehmann and Karl A. Eckhardt. MGH LL nat. Germ. 5.1. Hanover: Hahn, 1966.

Leges Burgundionum. Edited by L. R. De Salis. MGH LL nat. Germ. 2.1. Hanover: Hahn, 1892.

Lex Alamannorum. MGH Legum 3. Edited by George Heinrich Pertz. Hanover: Hahn, 1863.

Leges Visigothorum. Edited by Karl Zeumer. MGH LL nat. Germ. 1. Hanover: Hahn, 1902.

The Letter of Barnabas. Translated by Francis X. Glimm. In *Apostolic Fathers*, 187–222. Fathers of the Church 1. Washington, DC: Catholic University of America Press, 1947. Reprint, 2008.

Lex Alamannorum. In Karl Lehmann and Karl A. Eckhardt, 35–157.

Lex Baiwariorum. Edited by Ernst von Schwind. MGH LL nat. Germ. 5.2. Hanover: Hahn, 1926.

Lex Frisionum. Edited by Karl A. Eckhardt and Albrecht Eckhardt. MGH Leges. Fontes iuris Germanici antiqui in usum scholarum separatism editi 12. Hanover: Hahn, 1982.

Lex Ribuaria. Edited by Franz Beyerle and Rudolf Buchner. MGH LL nat. Germ. 3.2. Hanover: Hahn, 1954.

Lex Ribuaria. Edited by Heinrich Brunner. MGH Legum 5. Hanover: Hahn, 1875–89.

Lex Salica. Edited by Karl A. Eckhardt. MGH LL nat. Germ. 4.2. Hanover: Hahn 1969.

Lex Salica: The Ten Texts with the Glosses, and the Lex Emendata. Edited by Jan Hendrik Hessels and Hendrik Kern. London: J. Murray, 1880.

Livy. *History of Rome*. Edited and translated by J. C. Yardley. Vol. 11. LCL 313. Cambridge, MA: Harvard University Press, 2018.

The Lombard Laws. Translated by Katherine Fischer Drew. Sources of Medieval History. Philadelphia: University of Pennsylvania Press, 1973.

Lucan. *The Civil War*. Translated by J. D. Duff. LCL 220. Cambridge, MA: Harvard University Press, 1977. First published in 1928.

Lucian of Samosata. *On the Syrian Goddess*. Edited and translated by J. L. Lightfoot. Oxford: Oxford University Press, 2003.

———. *The Passing of Peregrinus*. Translated by A. M. Harmon, 1–52. In *Lucian*. Vol. 5. LCL 302. Cambridge, MA: Harvard University Press, 1936.
Macrobius. *Commentary on the Dream of Scipio*. Translated by William Harris Stahl. Records of Western Civilization. New York: Columbia University Press, 1990. First published in 1952.
Manilius. *Astronomica*. Translated by G. P. Goold. LCL 469. Cambridge, MA: Harvard University Press, 1977.
Martin of Braga. *De correctione rusticorum*. In *Martini episcopi Bracarensis opera omnia*, edited by Claude W. Barlow, 183–203. New Haven, CT: Yale University Press, 1950.
———. *Martini episcopi Bracarensis opera omnia*. Edited by Claude. W. Barlow. American Academy in Rome. New Haven, CT: Yale University Press, 1950.
———. *Pride*. In Barlow, *Writings of Martin of Braga, Paschasius of Dumium, and Leander of Seville*, 43–49.
Maximus of Turin. *Collectionem sermonum antiquam*. Edited by A. Mutzenbecher. CCSL 23. Turnhout, Belgium: Brepols, 1962.
Medieval Herbal Remedies: "The Old English Herbarium" and Anglo-Saxon Medicine. Translated by Anne Van Arsdall. New York: Routledge, 2002.
Minucius Felix. *Octavius*. Edited and translated by Jean Beaujeu. Collection des Universités de France. Paris: Société d'édition "Les Belles Lettres," 1964.
Nicolas I. *Papae epistolae*. Edited by Ernst Perels, 257–690. MGH Epp. Kar. aevi 6.4. Berlin: Weidmann, 1925.
Nithard. *Historiarum libri IV*. Edited by Ernst Müller. MGH SRG in usum scholarum separatim editi 44. 3rd ed. Hanover: Hahn, 1907.
Origen. *Contra Celsum*. Translated by Henry Chadwick. Cambridge, MA: Cambridge University Press, 1953.
———. *Exhortation to Martyrdom*. In *Prayer: Exhortation to Martyrdom*, translated by John J. O'Meara, 141–96. Ancient Christian Writers 19. New York: Newman, 1954.
———. "Homily on 1 Kings 28." In *Origen: Homiles on Jeremiah. Homily on 1 Kings 28*, translated by John Clark Smith, 319–33. Fathers of the Church 97. Washington, DC: Catholic University of America. 1998.
Ottonian Germany: The "Chronicon" of Thietmar of Merseburg. Translated by David A. Warner. Manchester Medieval Sources Series. Manchester: Manchester University Press, 2001.
Ovid. *Ovid: "Metamorphoses." A New Verse Translation*. Translated by David Raeburn. Penguin Classics. London: Penguin, 2004.
———. *Ovid's Erotic Poems "Amores" and "Ars Amatoria."* Translated by Len Krisak. Philadelphia: University of Pennsylvania Press, 2014.
Pacian of Barcelona. *Exhortatorius libellus, ad poenitentiam*. PL 13, cols. 1081–90.
Pactus legis Alamannorum. In Lehmann and Eckhardt, *Leges Alamannorum*, 21–34.
Pactus legis Salicae. Edited by Karl A. Eckhardt. MGH. LL nat. Germ. 4.1. Hanover: Hahn, 1962.
Paenitentiale Silense. In *Paenitantialia Hispaniae*, edited by Francis Bezler, 15–42. Vol 2 of *Paenitentialia Franciae, Italiae et Hispaniae saeculi VIII–XI*. CCSL 156a. Turnholt, Belgium: Brepols, 1998.
Paschasius of Dumium. *Questions and Answers of the Greek Fathers*. In Barlow, *Writings of Martin of Braga, Paschasius of Dumium, and Leander of Seville*, 117–71.

Paschasius Radbert. *Epitaphium Arseni. Confronting Crisis in the Carolingian Empire: Paschasius Radbertus' Funeral Oration for Wala of Corbie.* Translated by Mayke de Jong and Justin Lake, 47–223. Manchester: Manchester University Press, 2020.

The Passion of S. Perpetua. Edited by J. Armitage Robinson. Texts and Studies 1.2. Piscataway, NJ: Gorgias, 2004.

Paul the Deacon. *History of the Lombards.* Translated by William Dudley Foulke, edited by Edward Peters. Middle Ages Series. Philadelphia: University of Pennsylvania Press, 2003.

———. *Pauli historia Langobardorum.* Edited by Ludowici Bethmann and George Waitz, 12–197. *MGH Scriptores rerum Longobardicarum et Italicarum, saecula VI–IX.* Hanover: Hahn, 1878.

Philostratus. *Apollonius of Tyana.* Edited and translated by Christopher P. Jones. 2 vols. LCL 16, 17. Cambridge, MA: Harvard University Press, 2012. First published in 2005.

Pirmin of Reichenau. *De singulis libris canonicis Scarapsus.* PL 89, cols. 1029–50.

Pliny. *Natural History.* Edited and translated by D. E. Eichholz, W. H. S. Jones, and H. Rackham. 10 vols. LCL. Cambridge, MA: Harvard University Press, 1938–63.

Plutarch. *Moralia.* Translated by Frank Cole Babbitt. Vol. 2. LCL 222. Cambridge, MA: Harvard University Press, 1928.

"Prayer to Mother Earth." In *Life in the Middle Ages,* translated by George Gordon Coulton. Vol. 1. Cambridge Anthologies. New York: Macmillian, 1928.

Prudentius. *The Origin of Sin.* In *Prudentius,* translated by H. J. Thomson, 200–273. Vol. 1. LCL 387. Cambridge, MA: Harvard University Press, 1949.

Pseudo-Bede. *Expositio in Evangelium S. Matthaei.* PL 92, cols. 9–132.

Pseudo-Boniface. *Sermones.* PL 89, cols. 843–72.

Pseudo-Clement. *Recognitions.* In *The Writings of the Fathers Down to A.D. 325,* edited by A. Cleveland Coxe, 75–211. Fathers of the Third and Fourth Centuries. American Edition. The Ante-Nicene Fathers 8. Buffalo: Christian Literature Company, 1886.

Regino of Prüm. *Chronicon cum continuatione Treverensi.* Edited by Friedrich Kurze. *MGH SRG in usum scholarum separatim editi* 50. Hanover: Hahn, 1890.

———. *De synodalibus causis et disciplinis ecclesiasticis.* Edited by F. G. A. Wasserschleben. Leipzig: Engelmann, 1840. Reprint, Graz: Akademische Druck- u. Verlagsanstalt, 1964.

Rudolf of Bourges. *Radulf capitula.* Edited by Peter Brommer, 233–35. *MGH Cap. ep.* 1. Hanover: Hahn, 1984.

Seneca. *Epistles.* Translated by Richard M. Gummere. 3 vols. LCL 75, 76, 77. Cambridge, MA: Harvard University Press, 1953.

———. *Medea.* Translated by Shadi Bartsch. In *Seneca: The Complete Tragedies,* edited by Shadi Bartsch, 5–39. Vol. 1. Chicago: University of Chicago Press, 2017.

———. *Natural Questions.* Translated by Harry M. Hine. The Complete Works of Lucius Annaeus Seneca. Chicago: University of Chicago Press, 2010.

Sidonius Apollinaris. *Liber Epistularum* 1. In *Epistulae et Carmina,* edited by Christian Lüetjohann, 1–172. MGH AA 8. Berlin: Weidmann, 1887.

Sozomen. *The Ecclesiastical History of Sozomen: Comprising a History of the Church from A.D. 324 to A.D. 440.* Translated by Edward Walford. Bohn's Ecclesiastical Library. London: Bohn, 1855.

Suetonius. *The Deified Augustus*. Translated by J. C. Rolfe, 150–309. Vol. 1 of *Lives of the Caesars*. LCL 31. Cambridge, MA: Harvard University Press, 1998. First published in 1913.
Sulpicius Severus. (*Vita Martini*) *Sulpicius Severus' "Vita Martini."* Edited by Philip Burton. Oxford: Oxford University Press, 2017.
Tacitus. *De origine et situ Germanorum*. Edited by M. Winterbottom, 35–62. In *Cornelii Taciti: Opera Minora*. Scriptorum Classicorum Biblioteca Oxoniensis. Oxford: Clarendon, 1975.
Tertullian. *Ad nationes*. Edited by J. G. Ph. Borleffs, 9–75. In *Tertulliani opera*. Vol. 1.
——. *Ad uxorem*. Edited by A. Kroymann, 371–94. In *Tertulliani opera*. Vol. 1.
——. *Apologeticum*. Edited by E. Dekkers, 85–171. In *Tertulliani opera*. Vol. 1.
——. *De anima*. Edited by J. G. Ph. Borleffs, 779–869. In *Tertulliani opera*. Vol. 2.
——. *De baptismo*. Edited by J. G. Ph. Borleffs, 275–95. In *Tertulliani opera*. Vol. 1.
——. *De corona*. Edited by A. Kroymann, 1037–65. In *Tertulliani opera*. Vol. 2.
——. *De cultu feminarum*. Edited by A. Kroymann, 341–70. In *Tertulliani opera*. Vol. 1,.
——. *De idololatria*. Edited by A. Reifferscheid and G. Wissowa, 1099–124. In *Tertulliani opera*. Vol. 2.
——. *Tertulliani opera*. 2 vols. CCSL 1, 2. Turnhout, Belgium: Brepols, 1954.
Thegan. *Gesta Hludowici Imperatoris*. In *Theganus Gesta Hludowici Imperatoris. Astronomus Vita Hludowici Imperatoris*, edited by Ernst Tremp, 167–280. MGH SRG in usum scholarum separatim editi 64. Hanover: Hahn, 1995.
Theodulf of Orléans. First Capitulary. MGH Cap. ep. 1, 73–142.
Theodulf of Orléans. Second Capitulary. MGH Cap. ep. 1, 142–84.
Valerius Maximus. *Memorable Doings and Sayings*. Edited and translated by D. R. Shackleton Bailey. Vol. 1. LCL 492. Cambridge, MA: Harvard University Press, 2000.
Vergil. *The Aeneid*. Translated by Sarah Ruden. New Haven, CT: Yale University Press, 2008.
Visio Baronti monachi Longoretensis. In *Passiones vitaeque sanctorum*, edited by Wilhelm Levison, 368–94. MGH SRM 5. Hanover: Hahn, 1910.
Vita Genovefae Virginis Parisiensis. In *Passiones vitaeque sanctorum aevi Merovingici*, edited by Bruno Krusch, 204–38. MGH SRM 3. Hanover: Hahn, 1896.
Vita Sanctae Balthildis. Edited by Bruno Krusch, 475–508. MGH SRM 2. Hanover: Hahn, 1888.
Walafrid Strabo. *Hortulus*. Translated by Raef Payne. Pittsburgh: Hunt Botanical Library, 1966.
Willibald. *Vita Bonifatii*. In *Vitae Sancti Bonifatii archiepiscopi Moguntini*, edited by Wilhelm Levison, 1–58. MGH SRG in usum scholarum separatim editi 57. Hanover: Hahn, 1905.

Primary Sources—Collections (by Title)

Acta primorum martyrum sincera et selecta. Edited by Thierry Ruinart. Paris: F. Muguet, 1689. Reprint. Amsterdam: Officina Wetsteniana, 1713.
The Anglo-Saxon Minor Poems. Edited by Elliott van Kirk Dobbie. The Anglo-Saxon Poetic Records 6. New York: Columbia University Press, 1942.

Anglo-Saxon Remedies, Charms, and Prayers from British Library MS Harley 585: The Lacnunga. Vol. 1, *Introduction, Text, Translation, and Appendices.* Edited and translated by Edward Pettit. Mellen Critical Editions and Translations 6a. Lewiston, NY: Edwin Mellen, 2001.

The Apocryphal Gospels: Texts and Translations. Translated by Bart D. Ehrman and Zlatko Pleše. Oxford: Oxford University Press, 2011.

The Apostolic Fathers. Edited by Hermigild Dressler. Fathers of the Church 1. Washington, DC: Catholic University of America Press, 1947. Reprint, 2008.

The Apostolic Fathers, Justin Martyr, Irenaeus. Edited by Alexander Roberts and James Donaldson. Ante-Nicene Fathers 1. Buffalo, NY: Christian Literature, 1885. Reprint, Peabody, MA: Hendrickson, 1999.

Carolingian Civilization: A Reader. Edited by Paul Edward Dutton. 2nd ed. Readings in Medieval Civilizations and Cultures 1. Toronto: University of Toronto Press, 2004.

Charlemagne and Louis the Pious. The Lives by Einhard, Notker, Ermoldus, Thegan and the Astronomer. Translated by Thomas F. X. Noble. University Park, PA: Pennsylvania State University Press, 2009.

Charlemagne's Cousins: Contemporary Lives of Adalard and Wala. Translated by Allen Cabaniss. Syracuse, NY: Syracuse University Press, 1967.

Concilia Galliae 511–695. Edited by Karl de Clercq. *CCSL* 147a. Turnholt, Belgium: Brepols, 1963.

Concilios Visigóticos e Hispano-Romanos. Edited by José Vives, Tomás Marín Martínez, and Gonzalo Martinez Díez. 2 vols. Consejo Superior de Investigaciones Científicas. Barcelona: Instituto Enrique Florez, 1963.

(Corpus medicorum Latinorum). Antonii Musae de herba Vettonica liber. Pseudoapulei Herbarius. Anonymi de taxone liber. Sexti Placiti liber medicinae ex animalibus pecoribus, et bestiis vel avibus. Edited by Ernst Howald and Henry E. Sigerist. Corpus medicorum Latinorum 4. Leipzig: Teubner, 1927.

Councils and Ecclesiastical Documents Relating to Great Britain and Ireland. Edited by Arthur West Haddan and William Stubbs. Vol. 3. Oxford: Clarendon, 1871. Reprint, 1964.

Councils and Synods with other Documents Relating to the English Church. Edited and translated by Dorothy Whitelock, M. Brett, and Christopher N. L. Brooke. 2 vols. Oxford: Clarendon, 1981.

Curse Tablets and Binding Spells from the Ancient World. Edited by John G. Gager. New York: Oxford University Press, 1992.

Die Bussbücher und die Bussdiscipline der Kirche: Nach handschriftlichen Quellen dargestellt. Edited by Herman J. Schmitz. 2 vols. Düsseldorf: Von L. Schwann, 1898. Reprint, Graz: Akademische Druck-u. Verlagsanstalt, 1958.

Die Bussordnungen der abendländischen Kirche nebst einer rechtsgeschichtichen Einleitung. Edited by F. W. H. Wasserschleben. Halle: Graeger, 1851. Reprint, Graz: Akademische Druck-u. Verlagsanstalt, 1958.

Die irische Kanonensammlung. Edited by W. H. Wasserschleben. 2nd ed. Leipzig: Tauchnitz, 1885. Reprint, Aalen: Scientia, 1966.

Eleven Old English Rogationtide Homilies. Edited by Joyce Bazire and James E. Cross. King's College London Medieval Studies 4. Toronto: Toronto University Press, 1989. First published in 1982.

Fathers of the Second Century: Hermas, Tatian, Theophilus, Athenagoras, and Clement of Alexandria. Edited by Alexander Roberts, James Donaldson, and Arthur Cleveland Coxe. Ante-Nicene Fathers 2. Peabody, MA: Hendrickson. First published in 1885.

Fontes iuris Romani antique. Edited by Carolus George Bruns and Theodore Mommsen. 5th ed. Freiburg: Mohr Siebeck, 1887.

Hermetica: The Greek "Corpus Hermeticum" and the Latin "Asclepius." Edited and translated by Brian P. Copenhaver. Cambridge, MA: Cambridge University Press, 1992.

The Irish Penitentials. Edited by Ludwig Bieler and Daniel A. Binchy. Scriptores Latini Hiberniae 5. Dublin: Dublin Institute for Advanced Studies, 1963.

Laws of the Alamans and Bavarians. Translated by Theodore John Rivers. Philadelphia: University of Pennsylvania Press, 1977.

Leechdoms, Wortcunning and Starcraft of Early England. Edited and translated by Oswald Cockayne. 3 vols. (Vol. 1, *De medicina de quadrupedibus.* Vol. 2, *Bald's Leechbook*). Rerum Britannicarum medii aevi scriptores, or Chronicles and Memorials of Great Britain and Ireland During the Middle Ages. Rolls Series 35. London: Holland Press, 1961. First published in 1864–66.

Les canons des conciles mérovingiens (VIe–VIIe siècles). Texte Latin de l'édition C. de Clercq. Translated by Jean Gaudemet and Brigitte Basdevant-Gaudemet. 2 vols. Sources chrétiennes 353, 354. Paris: Cerf, 1989.

Magic, Witchcraft, and Ghosts in the Greek and Roman Worlds: A Sourcebook. Edited by Daniel Ogden. Oxford: Oxford University Press, 2002.

Medieval Handbooks of Penance: A Translation of the Principal "Libri Poenitentiales." Translated by John T. McNeill and Helena M. Gamer. Records of Western Civilization. New York: Columbia University Press, 1990. First published in 1938.

The "Old English Herbarium" and "Medicina de Quadrupedibus." Edited by Hubert Jan de Vriend. Early English Text Society 286. London: Oxford University Press, 1984.

Paenitentialia minora Franciae et Italiae saeculi VIII–IX. Edited by Raymund J. Kottje. CCCM 156. Turnhout, Belgium: Brepols, 1997.

Sainted Women of the Dark Ages. Edited and translated by Jo Ann McNamara and John E. Halborg, with E. Gordon Whatley. Durham, NC: Duke University Press, 1992.

Saint Peter Chrysologus: Selected Sermons and Saint Valerian Homilies. Translated by George E. Ganss. Fathers of the Church 17. Washington, DC: Catholic University of America Press, 2004. First published in 1953.

The Seven Ecumenical Councils of the Undivided Church. Edited by Henry R. Percival. Nicene and Post-Nicene Fathers 14. 2nd ser. Peabody, NY: Hendrickson, 2004. First published in 1900.

Soldiers of Christ: Saints and Saints' Lives from Late Antiquity and the Early Middle Ages. Edited Noble, Thomas F. X., and Thomas Head. University Park, PA: Pennsylvania State University Press, 1995.

Theodosian Code and Novels and the Sirmondian Constitutions. Translated by Clyde Pharr, with Theresa Sherrer Davidson and Mary Brown Pharr. The Corpus of Roman Law (*Corpus Juris Romani*) 1. Princeton, NJ: Princeton University Press, 1952.

Witchcraft in Europe, 400–1700: A Documentary History. Edited by Alan Charles Kors and Edward Peters. 2nd ed. Philadelphia: University of Pennsylvania Press, 2001.
Women in Early Christianity. Edited by Patricia Cox Miller. Washington, DC: Catholic University of American Press, 2005.
Writings of Martin of Braga, Paschasius of Dumium, and Leander of Seville. Vol. 1 of *Iberian Fathers.* Translated by Claude W. Barlow. Fathers of the Church 62. Washington, DC: Catholic University of America Press, 1969.

Secondary Sources

Abou-El-Haj, Barbara. *The Medieval Cult of Saints: Formations and Transformations.* Cambridge, MA: Cambridge University Press, 1997. First published in 1994.
Abt, Adam. *Die Apologie des Apuleius von Madaura und die antike Zauberei: Beiträge zur Erläuterung der Schrift De magia.* Religionsgeschichtliche Versuche und Vorarbeiten 4.2. Giessen: Töpelmann, 1908. Reprint 1967.
Achterberg, Jeanne. *Woman as Healer.* Boston: Shambhala, 1990.
Ahern, Eoghan. "Bede's Miracles Reconsidered." *EME* 26, no. 3 (2018): 282–303.
Airlie, Stuart. "The Aristocracy in the Service of the State in the Carolingian Period." In Airlie, Pohl, and Reimitz, *Staat im frühen Mittelalter,* 93–111.
——. "Bonds of Power and Bonds of Association in the Court Circle of Louis the Pious." In Godman and Collins, *Charlemagne's Heir,* 191–204.
——. "Private Bodies and the Body Politic in the Divorce Case of Lothar II." *Past and Present* 161, no. 1 (1998): 3–38.
——. "The World, the Text and the Carolingian: Royal, Aristocratic and Masculine Identities in Nithard's *Histories.*" In Wormald and Nelson, *Lay Intellectuals in the Carolingian World,* 51–76.
Airlie, Stuart, Walter Pohl, and Helmut Reimitz, eds. *Staat im frühen Mittelalter.* Forschungen zur Geschichte des Mittelalters 2. Vienna: Österreichischen Akademie der Wissenschaften, 2006.
Alberi, Mary. "The Evolution of Alcuin's Concept of the *Imperium christianum.*" In Hill and Swan, *Community, the Family and the Saint,* 3–17.
Allen, Pauline. "Augustine's Commentaries on the Old Testament: A Mariological Perspective." In *From Rome to Constantinople: Studies in Honor of Averil Cameron,* edited by Hagit Amirav and Bas ter Haar Romeny, 137–52. Late Antique History and Religion 1. Leuven, Belgium: Peeters, 2007.
Almond, Philip C. *The Devil: A New Biography.* Ithaca, NY: Cornell University Press, 2014.
Althoff, Gerd. *Die Macht der Rituale: Symbolik und Herrschaft im Mittelalter.* Darmstadt: Primus, 2003.
——. *Spielregeln der Politik im Mittelalter: Kommunikation in Frieden und Fehde.* Darmstadt: Wissenschaftliche Buchgesellschaft, 1997.
Amos, Thomas L. "Preaching and the Sermon in the Carolingian World." In Amos, Green, and Kienzle, *De ore domini,* 41–60.
Amos, Thomas L., Eugene A. Green, and Beverly Mayne Kienzle, eds. *De ore domini: Preacher and Word in the Middle Ages.* Medieval Institute Publications SMC 27. Kalamazoo: Western Michigan University Press, 1989.

Anderson, Thomas, Jr. "Roman Military Colonies in Gaul, Salian Ethnogenesis and the Forgotten Meaning of Pactus Legis Salicae 59.5." *EME* 4, no. 2 (1995): 129–44.
Ando, Clifford. "Interpretatio Romana." *Classical Philology* 100, no. 1 (2005): 41–51.
Andrews, Hazel, and Les Roberts. "Re-mapping Liminality." In *Liminal Landscapes: Travel, Experience and Spaces In–Between*, edited by Hazel Andrews and Les Roberts, 1–13. Contemporary Geographies of Leisure, Tourism and Mobility 30. London: Routledge, 2012.
Angenendt, Arnold. *Monachi Peregrini: Studien zu Pirmin und den monastischen Vorstellungen des frühen Mittelalters*. Münstersche Mittelalter-Schriften 6. Munich: W. Fink, 1972.
Annequin, Jaques. *Recherches sur l'action magique et ses représentations (Ier et IIème siècles après J. C.)*. Centre de recherches d'histoire ancienne 8. Annales littéraires de l'Université de Besançon 146. Les Belles Lettres: Paris, 1973.
Arbesmann, Rudolph. "The 'Cervuli' and 'Anniculae' in Caesarius of Arles." *Traditio* 35 (1979): 89–119.
Archer, Léonie J. "The Role of Jewish Women in the Religion, Ritual and Cult of Graeco–Roman Palestine." In Cameron and Kuhrt, *Images of Women in Antiquity*, 273–87.
Ariès, Philippe. *The Hour of Our Death*. Translated by Helen Weaver. New York: Vintage Books, 1981.
Arjava, Antti. *Women and Law in Late Antiquity*. Oxford: Clarendon, 1996.
Arthur, Ciaran. *"Charms," Liturgies, and Secret Rites in Early Medieval England*. Anglo-Saxon Studies 32. Woodbridge, UK: Boydell, 2018.
Athanassiadi, Polymnia. "*The Chaldaean Oracles*: Theology and Theurgy." In *Pagan Monotheism in Late Antiquity*, edited by Polymnia Athanassiadi and Michael Frede, 149–83. Oxford: Clarendon, 1999.
Aune, David E. *Apocalypticism, Prophecy, and Magic in Early Christianity: Collected Essays*. Grand Rapids, MI: Baker, 2008. First published in 2006.
Austin, Greta. "Jurisprudence in the Service of Pastoral Care: The *Decretum* of Burchard of Worms." *Speculum* 79, no. 4 (2004): 929–59.
———. *Shaping Church Law Around the Year 1000: The "Decretum" of Burchard of Worms*. Church, Faith and Culture in the Medieval West. Farnham, UK: Ashgate, 2009.
Austin, J. L. *How to Do Things with Words: The William James Lectures Delivered at Harvard University in 1955*. 2nd ed. Oxford: Clarendon Press, 1975. First published in 1962.
Auty, Robert, ed. *Lexikon des Mittelalters*. 10 vols. Munich and Zurich: Artemis-Verlag, 1977–99.
Baader, Gerhard. "Die Anfänge der medizinischen Ausbildung in Abendland bis 1100." In *La scuola nell' Occidente latino dell' alto Medioevo: 15–21 april 1971*, edited by Ernesto Sestan, 669–718. Vol.2. Settimane di studio del centro Italiano di studi sull' alto Medioevo 19. Spoleto: Presso la Sede del Centro, 1972.
———. "Zur Überlieferung der lateinschen medizinischen Literatur des frühen Mittelalters." *Forschung, Praxis, Fortbildung* 17 (1966): 139–41.
Bäbler, Balbina, and Heinz-Günther Nesselrath. *Philostrats Apollonios und sein Welt: Griechische und nichtgriechische Kunst und Religion in der "Vita Apollonii."* Beiträge zur Altertumskunde 354. Berlin: De Gruyter, 2016.

Bailey, Michael D. "From Sorcery to Witchcraft: Clerical Conceptions of Magic in the Later Middle Ages." *Speculum* 76, no. 4 (2001): 960–90.
———. "The Meanings of Magic." *Magic, Ritual and Witchcraft* 1, no. 1 (2006): 1–23.
Bailey, Michael D., and Brian P. Copenhaver. "From the Editors." *Magic, Ritual and Witchcraft* 1, no. 1 (2006): v–viii.
Baker, L. G. D. "The Shadow of the Christian Symbol." In Cuming, *Mission of the Church*, 17–28.
Baldovin, John F. "Hippolytus and the *Apostolic Tradition*: Recent Research and Commentary." *Theological Studies* 64, no. 3 (2003): 520–42.
Banniard, Michel. "Latin et communication orale en Gaule franque. Le témoignage de la *'Vita Eligii.'*" In *Le septième siècle: Changements et continuités: actes du Colloque bilatéral franco–britannique tenu au Warburg Institut les 8–9 juillet 1988 / The Seventh Century: Changes and Continuity: Proceedings of a Joint French and British Colloquium held at the Warburg Institute 8–9 July 1988*, edited by Jacques Fontaine and J. N. Hillgarth, 58–86. Studies of the Warburg Institute 42. London: Warburg Institute, 1992.
Barb, A. A. "The Survival of the Magic Arts." In Momigliano, *Conflict between Paganism and Christianity*, 100–125.
Barnes, Timothy David. *Tertullian: A Historical and Literary Study*. Oxford: Clarendon, 1971.
Barré, Henri. *Les homéliaires carolingiens de l'école d'Auxerre: authenticité, inventaire, tableaux comparatifs, initia*. Studi e Testi (Biblioteca Apostolica Vaticana) 225. Città del Vaticano: Biblioteca Apostolica Vaticana, 1962.
Barthélemy, Dominique. "Devils in the Sanctuary: Violence in the *Miracles of Saint Benedict*." In *Feud, Violence and Practice: Essays in Medieval Studies in Honor of Stephen D. White*, edited by Belle S. Tuten and Tracey L. Billado, 71–94. Farnham, UK: Ashgate, 2010.
Bartlett, Robert. "Rewriting Saints' Lives: The Case of Gerald of Wales." *Speculum* 58, no. 3 (1983): 598–613.
Bates, Donald G. *Knowledge and the Scholarly Medical Traditions*. Cambridge, MA: Cambridge University Press, 1995.
Bell, Catherine. *Ritual: Perspectives and Dimensions*. New York: Oxford University Press, 1997.
———. *Ritual Theory, Ritual Practice*. New York: Oxford University Press, 1992.
Benko, Stephen. *Pagan Rome and the Early Christians*. Bloomington: Indiana University Press, 1984.
———. *The Virgin Goddess: Studies in the Pagan and Christian Roots of Mariology*. Numen Book Series: Studies in the History of Religions 59. Leiden: Brill 2004.
Bennett, Judith M., Elizabeth A. Clark, Jean F. O'Barr, B. Anne Vilen, and Sarah Westphal-Wihl, eds. *Sisters and Workers in the Middle Ages*. Chicago: University of Chicago Press, 1989.
Beresford-Cooke, Ernest. *The Sign of the Cross in the Western Liturgies*. Classic Reprint. London: Forgotten Books, 2016.
Berrens, Stephan. *Sonnenkult und Kaisertum von den Severern bis zu Constantin I. (193–337 n. Chr.)*. Historia 185. Stuttgart: Franz Steiner, 2004.
Betz, Hans Dieter. *Gottesbegegnung und Menschwerdung: Zur religionsgeschichtlichen und theologischen Bedeutung der "Mithrasliturgie" (PGM IV.475–820)*.

Akademieunternehmen "Griechische Christliche Schriftsteller" der Berlin-Brandenburgischen Akademie der Wissenschaften 6. Berlin: De Gruyter, 2001.
Betz, Hans Dieter, Don S. Browning, Bernd Janowski, and Eberhard Jüngel, eds. *Religion Past and Present: Encyclopedia of Theology and Religion*. Vol. 7. Leiden: Brill, 2010.
Bishop, Jane. "Bishops as Marital Advisors in the Ninth Century." In *Women of the Medieval World: Essays in Honor of John H. Mundy*, edited by Julius Kirshner and Suzanne F. Wemple, 53–84. Oxford: Blackwell, 1985.
Bitel, Lisa M. *Women in Early Medieval Europe, 400–1100*. Cambridge Medieval Textbooks. Cambridge, MA: Cambridge University Press, 2002.
Blair, John. *The Church in Anglo-Saxon Society*. London: Oxford University Press, 2005.
Bloch, Maurice. "Symbols, Song, Dance and Features of Articulation: Is Religion an Extreme Form of Traditional Authority?" In *Ritual, History and Power: Selected Papers in Anthropology*, 19–45. London School of Economics Monographs on Social Anthropology 58. London: Athlone, 1989.
Boase, T. S. R. *Death in the Middle Ages: Mortality, Judgment, and Remembrance*. Library of Medieval Civilization. New York: McGraw-Hill, 1972.
Booker, Courtney M. "Hypocrisy, Performativity, and the Carolingian Pursuit of Truth." *EME* 26, no. 2 (2018): 174–202.
———. *Past Convictions: The Penance of Louis the Pious and the Decline of the Carolingians*. The Middle Ages. Philadelphia: University of Pennsylvania Press, 2009.
Boshof, Egon. *Erzbischof Agobard von Lyon: Leben und Werk*. Kölner historische Abhandlungen 17. Cologne: Böhlau, 1969.
Bouchard, Constance Brittain. *Rewriting Saints and Ancestors: Memory and Forgetting in France, 500–1200*. The Middle Ages. Pennsylvania: University of Pennsylvania Press, 2015.
Boudet, Jean-Patrice. *Entre science et nigromance: Astrologie, divination et magie dans l'Occident médiévale (XIIe–XVe siècle)*. Histoire ancienne et médiévale 83. Paris: Publications de la Sorbonne, 2006.
Bougard, Francois. "En marge du divorce de Lothaire II: Boson de Vienne, le cocu qui fut fait roi?" Francia. Forschungen zur westeuropäischen Geschichte 27, no. 1 (2000): 33–51.
Bourdieu, Pierre. *Outline of a Theory of Practice*. Translated by Richard Nice. Cambridge Studies in Social and Cultural Anthropology 16. Cambridge: Cambridge University Press, 1993. First published in 1977.
———. "Symbolic Power." Translated by Colin Wringe. In *Identity and Structure: Issues in the Sociology of Education*, edited by Denis Gleeson, 112–19. Issues in Sociology, Politics and Education. Driffield: Nafferton Books, 1977.
Boureau, Alain. *Satan the Heretic: The Birth of Demonology in the Medieval West*. Translated by Teresa Lavender Fagan. Chicago: University of Chicago Press, 2006.
Bowes, Kim. *Private Worship, Public Values, and Religious Change in Late Antiquity*. Cambridge, MA: Cambridge University Press, 2008.
Bradshaw, Paul F., Maxwell E. Johnson, and L. Edward Phillips. *Apostolic Tradition: A Commentary*. Edited by Harold W. Attridge. Minneapolis: Fortress, 2002.

Brakke, David. *Demons and the Making of the Monk: Spiritual Combat in Early Christianity*. Cambridge, MA: Harvard University Press, 2006.
Bremmer, Jan N. "The Birth of the Term 'Magic.'" In Bremmer and Veenstra, *Metamorphosis of Magic*, 1–11.
——. "*Magic and Religon*." In Bremmer and Veenstra, *Metamorphosis of Magic*, 267–71. (Italics in original).
——. "Pseudo-Clementines: Texts, Dates, Places, Authors and Magic." In *The Pseudo-Clementines*, edited by Jan N. Bremmer, 1–23. Leuven, Belgium: Peeters, 2010.
Bremmer, Jan N., and Jan R. Veenstra, eds. *The Metamorphosis of Magic from Late Antiquity to the Early Modern Period*. Groningen Studies in Cultural Change 1. Leuven: Peeters, 2002.
Brennessel, Barbara, Michael D. C. Drout, and Robyn Gravel. "A Reassessment of the Efficacy of Anglo-Saxon Medicine." *Anglo-Saxon England* 34 (2005): 183–95.
Brown, Peter. *The Body and Society: Men, Women and Sexual Renunciation in Early Christianity*. Lectures on the History of Religions, n.s., 13. New York: Columbia University Press, 1988.
——. *The Cult of the Saints: Its Rise and Function in Latin Christianity*. The Haskell Lectures on History of Religions, n.s., 2. Chicago: University of Chicago Press, 1981.
——. *The Making of Late Antiquity*. Carl Newell Jackson Lectures. Cambridge, MA: Harvard University Press, 1978.
——. *The Rise of Western Christendom: Triumph and Diversity, AD 200–1000*. 10th anniversary rev. ed. Chichester: John Wiley and Sons, 2013. First published in 1997.
——. *Society and the Holy in Late Antiquity*. Berekely: University of California Press, 1982.
——. "Sorcery, Demons, and the Rise of Christianity: From Late Antiquity into the Middle Ages." In *Religion and Society in the Age of Saint Augustine*, 119–46. New York: Harper & Row, 1972.
——. *The World of Late Antiquity AD 150–750*. History of European Civilization Library. New York: Harcourt Brace Jovanovich, 1971.
Brubaker, Leslie, and Julia M. H. Smith, eds. *Gender in the Early Medieval World: East and West, 300–900*. Cambridge, MA: Cambridge University Press, 2004.
Brühl, Carlrichard. "Hincmariana II, Hinkmar im Widerstreit von kanonischem Recht und Politik in Ehefragen." *Deutsches Archiv für Erforschung des Mittelalters* 20, no. 1 (1964): 55–77.
Brundage, James A. *Law, Sex, and Christian Society in Medieval Europe*. Chicago: University of Chicago Press, 1987.
Brunner, Karl. "Publikumskonstruktionen in den Predigten des Caesarius von Arles." In Diesenberger, Hen, and Pollheimer, eds. *Sermo Doctorum*, 99–126.
Buck, R. A. "Woman's Milk in Anglo-Saxon and Later Medieval Medical Texts." *Neophilologus* 96 (2012): 467–85.
——. "Women and Language in the Anglo-Saxon Leechbooks." *Women and Language* 23, no. 2 (2000): 41–50.
Buc, Philippe. *The Dangers of Ritual: Between Early Medieval Texts and Social Scientific Theory*. Princeton, NJ: Princeton University Press, 2001.

——. "The Monster and the Critics: A Ritual Reply." *EME* 15, no. 4 (2007): 441–52.
Bullough, Vern. *Carolingian Renewal: Sources and Heritage*. Manchester: Manchester University Press, 1991.
Bullough, Vern, and Cameron Campbell. "Female Longevity and Diet in the Middle Ages." *Speculum* 55, no. 2 (1980): 317–25.
Burgmann, W., and W. Schlosses. "Gregor von Tours und der rote Sirim." *Francia* 15 (1987): 42–74.
Burke, Kenneth. *A Grammar of Motives* and *A Rhetoric of Motives*. Cleveland, OH: World Publishing, 1962.
Burton, Dan, and David Grandy. *Magic, Mystery, and Science: The Occult in Western Civilization*. Bloomington: Indiana University Press, 2004.
Butzer, Karl W. "The Classical Tradition of Agronomic Science: Perspectives on Carolingian Agriculture and Agronomy." In Butzer and Lohrmann, *Science in Western and Eastern Civilization*, 539–96.
Butzer, Paul Leo, and Dietrich Lohrmann, eds. *Science in Western and Eastern Civilization in Carolingian Times*. Basel: Birkhäuser, 1993.
Bynum, Caroline Walker. "Women's Stories, Women's Symbols: A Critique of Victor Turner's Theory of Liminality." In *Anthropology and the Study of Religion*, edited by Robert L. Moore and Frank E. Reynolds, 105–24. Studies in Religion and Society. Chicago: Center for the Scientific Study of Religion, 1984.
Cabaniss, Allen, *Judith Augusta: A Daughter-in-Law of Charlemagne, and Other Essays*. New York: Vantage, 1974.
Caciola, Nancy. *Discerning Spirits: Divine and Demonic Possession in the Middle Ages*. Conjunctions of Religion and Power in the Medieval Past. Ithaca, NY: Cornell University Press, 2003.
Cadotte, Alain. *La romanisation des dieux: L'interpretatio romana en Afrique du Nord sous le Haut-Empire*. Religions in the Greco-Roman World 158. Leiden: Brill, 2007.
Calame, Claude. *Les choeurs de jeunes filles en Grèce archaïque*. Filologia e critica 20–21. Rome: Edizioni dell'Ateneo, 1977.
Camargo, Martin. *Ars dictaminis, ars dictandi*. Typologie des sources du Moyen Âge occidental 60. Turnhout, Belgium: Brepols, 1991.
Cameron, Alan. *The Last Pagans of Rome*. Oxford: Oxford University Press, 2011.
Cameron, Averil, and Amélie Kuhrt. *Images of Women in Antiquity*. Detroit: Wayne State University Press, 1983.
Cameron, M. L. *Anglo-Saxon Medicine*. Cambridge, MA: Cambridge University Press, 1993.
——. "Anglo-Saxon Medicine and Magic." *Anglo-Saxon England* 17 (1988): 191–215.
——. "Bald's *Leechbook*: Its Sources and Their Use in Its Compilation." *Anglo-Saxon England* 12 (1983): 153–82.
Carozzi, Claude. *Le voyage de l'âme dans l'au-delà, d'après la littérature latine (Ve-XIIIe siècle)*. Collection de l'Ecole française de Rome 189. Rome: Diffusion de Boccard, 1994.
Castelli, Elizabeth. "'I Will Make Mary Male': Pieties of the Body and Gender Transformation of Christian Women in Late Antiquity." In *Body Guards: The Cultural Politics of Gender Ambiguity*, edited by Julia Epstein and Kristina Straub. New York: Routledge, 1991.

Chance, Jane. *Woman as Hero in Old English Literature*. Syracuse: Syracuse University Press, 1986.
Charles-Edwards, Thomas. "The Penitential of Theodore and *Iudicia Theodori*." In *Archbishop Theodore: Commemorative Studies on His Life and Influence*, edited by Michael Lapidge, 141–74. Cambridge Studies in Anglo-Saxon England 11. Cambridge, MA: Cambridge University Press, 1995.
Chase, Colin ed. *The Dating of "Beowulf"*. Toronto Old English Series 6. Toronto: University of Toronto Press, 1997.
———. "Opinions on the Date of *Beowulf*, 1815–1980." In Chase, *Dating of "Beowulf"*, 3–8.
Chazelle, Celia. *The Crucified God in the Carolingian Era: Theology and Art of Christ's Passion*. Cambridge, MA: Cambridge University Press, 2001.
Chélini, Jean. *L'Aube du Moyen Âge: Naissance de la chrétienté occidentale. La vie religieuse des laïcs dans l'Europe carolingienne (750–900)*. 2nd ed. Paris: Picard, 1997.
Church, S. D. "Paganism in Conversion-Age Anglo-Saxon England: The Evidence of Bede's *Ecclesiastical History* Reconsidered." *History* 93, no. 310 (2008): 162–80.
Clark, Elizabeth A. "Early Christian Women: Sources and Interpretation." In Coon, Haldane, and Sommer, *That Gentle Strength*, 2–35.
Clauss, James J., and Sarah Iles Johnston, eds. *Medea: Essays on Medea in Myth, Literature, Philosophy, and Art*. Princeton, NJ: Princeton University Press, 1997.
Clayton, Mary. *The Cult of the Virgin Mary in Anglo-Saxon England*. Cambridge Studies in Anglo-Saxon England 2. Cambridge, MA: Cambridge University Press, 1990.
Cochrane, Charles Norris. *Christianity and Classical Culture: A Study of Thought and Action from Augustus to Augustine*. Oxford: Oxford University Press, 1957. First published in 1940.
Cohn, Norman. *Europe's Inner Demons: The Demonization of Christians in Medieval Christendom*. Rev. ed. Chicago: Chicago University Press, 2000. First published in 1975.
Collins, David J., ed. *Cambridge History of Magic and Witchcraft in the West: From Antiquity to the Present*. New York: Cambridge University Press, 2015.
Collins, Roger. *Early Medieval Spain: Unity in Diversity, 400–1000*. 2nd ed. New York: St. Martin's, 1995.
Collins, Samuel W. *The Carolingian Debate over Sacred Space*. The Middle Ages. New York: Palgrave Macmillan, 2012.
Congourdeau, Marie-Hélène. "Jérusalem et Constantinople dans la littérature apocalyptique." In Kaplan, *Le sacré et son inscription*, 125–36.
Contreni, John J. "The Carolingian Renaissance: Education and Literary Culture." McKitterick, *New Cambridge Medieval History*, 709–57.
———. "John Scottus, Martin Hiberniensis, the Liberal Arts, and Teaching." In *Insular Latin Studies: Papers on Latin Texts and Manuscripts of the British Isles: 550–1066*, edited by Michael W. Herren, 23–44. Papers in Medieval Studies 1. Toronto: Pontifical Institute of Mediaeval Studies, 1981.
———. "Masters and Medicine in Northern France during the Reign of Charles the Bald." In *Charles the Bald: Court and Kingdom*, edited by Margaret T. Gibson and Janet L. Nelson, 267–82. 2nd rev. ed. Variorum Collected Studies Series. Aldershot, UK: Variorum, 1990.

Coon, Lynda. "'What If the Word Is Not Semen?' Priestly Bodies in Carolingian Exegesis." In Brubaker and Smith, *Gender in the Early Medieval World*, 278–300.

Coon, Lynda, Katherine J. Haldane, and Elisabeth W. Sommer eds. *That Gentle Strength: Historical Perspectives on Women in Christianity*. Charlottesville: University Press of Virginia, 1990.

Cooper, Kate. *The Virgin and the Bride: Idealized Womanhood in Late Antiquity*. Cambridge, MA: Harvard University Press, 1996.

Costambeys, Marios, Matthew Innes, and Simon MacLean. *The Carolingian World*. Cambridge Medieval Textbooks. Cambridge, MA: Cambridge University Press, 2011.

Couser, Jonathan. "Inventing Paganism in Eighth-Century Bavaria." *EME* 18, no. 1 (2010): 26–42.

Cramer, Peter. *Baptism and Change in the Early Middle Ages, c. 200–1150*. Cambridge Studies in Medieval Life and Thought 20. 4th ser. Cambridge, MA: Cambridge University Press, 1993.

Cramer, Thomas. "Defending the Double Monastery: Gender and Society in Early Medieval Europe." PhD diss., University of Washington, 2011.

Crawford, Jane. "Evidences for Witchcraft in Anglo-Saxon England." *Medium Aevum* 32, no. 2 (1963): 99–116.

Crawford, Sally. "The Nadir of Western Medicine? Texts, Contexts and Practice in Anglo-Saxon England." In Crawford and Lee, *Bodies of Knowledge*, 41–51.

Crawford, Sally, and Christina Lee. *Bodies of Knowledge: Cultural Interpretations of Illness and Medicine in Medieval Europe*. BAR S2170 Studies in Early Medicine 1. Oxford: Archaeopress, 2010.

Cross, Frank Leslie, and Elizabeth A. Livingstone, eds. *The Oxford Dictionary of the Christian Church*. 3rd ed. New York: Oxford University Press, 1997.

Cubitt, Catherine. *Anglo-Saxon Church Councils, c. 650–c. 850*. Studies in the Early History of Britain. London: Leicester University Press, 1995.

Cuming, G. J., ed. *The Mission of the Church and the Propagation of the Faith: Papers Read at the Seventh Summer Meeting and the Eighth Winter Meeting of the Ecclesiastical History Society*. Cambridge, MA: Cambridge University Press, 1970.

Cushing, Kathleen G. "Law and Reform: The Transmission of Burchard of Worms' *Liber decretorum*." *New Discourses in Medieval Canon Law Research: Challenging the Master Narrative,* edited by Christof Rolker, 33–43. Leiden: Brill, 2019.

Davies, Wendy, and Paul Fouracre, eds. *The Settlement of Disputes in Early Medieval Europe*. Cambridge, MA: Cambridge University Press, 1986.

Davis, Craig R. "Theories of History in Traditional Plots," in Glosecki, *Myth In Early Northwest Europe*, 31–45.

d'Avray, David. *Medieval Marriage: Symbolism and Society*. Oxford: Oxford University Press, 2005.

Deegan, Marilyn. "Pregnancy and Childbirth in the Anglo-Saxon Medical Texts: A Preliminary Survey." In *Medicine in Early Medieval England: Four Papers*, edited by Marilyn Deegan and D. G. Scragg, 17–26. Manchester: University of Manchester Centre for Anglo-Saxon Studies, 1989.

de Jong, Mayke. "*Ecclesia* and the Early Medieval Polity." In Airlie, Pohl, and Reimitz, *Staat im frühen Mittelalter*, 113–32.

———. "The Empire as *Ecclesia*: Hrabanus Maurus and Biblical *Historia* for Rulers." In *The Uses of the Past in the Early Middle Ages*, edited by Yitzhak Hen and Matthew Innes, 191–226. Cambridge, MA: Cambridge University Press, 2000.

———. *Epitaph for an Era: Politics and Rhetoric in the Carolingian World*. Cambridge: Cambridge University Press, 2019.

———. *The Penitential State: Authority and Atonement in the Age of Louis the Pious, 814–840*. Cambridge, MA: Cambridge University Press, 2009.

———. "Power and Humility in Carolingian Society: The Public Penance of Louis the Pious." *EME* 1, no. 1 (1992): 29–52.

———. "What Was Public about Public Penance? *Paenitentia publica* and Justice in the Carolingian World." In *La Giustizia nell'alto medioevo (secoli IX–XI)*, 863–902. Vol. 2. Settimane di studio del centro Italiano di studi sull'alto medioevo 44. Spoleto: Sede del Centro, 1997.

Delen, K. M., A. H. Gaastra, M. D. Saan, and B. Schaap. "The *Paenitentiale Cantabrigiense*: A Witness of the Carolingian Contribution to the Tenth-Century Reforms in England." *Sacris eruditi* 41 (2002): 341–73.

Demacopoulos, George. "Gregory the Great and the Pagan Shrines of Kent." *Journal of Late Antiquity* 1, no. 2 (2008): 353–69.

Dendle, Peter, and Alain Touwaide. *Health and Healing from the Medieval Garden*. Woodbridge, UK: Boydell, 2008.

de Nie, Giselle. "Caesarius of Arles and Gregory of Tours: Two Sixth-Century Gallic Bishops and 'Christian Magic.'" In *Cultural Identity and Cultural Integration: Ireland and Europe in the Early Middle Ages*, edited by Doris Edel, 170–96. Medieval Studies. Dublin: Four Courts Press, 1995.

———. *Views from a Many-Windowed Tower: Studies of Imagination in the works of Gregory of Tours*. Studies in Classical Antiquity 7. Amsterdam: Rodopi, 1987.

Depreux, Philippe. "Ambitions et limites des réformes culturelles à l'époque carolingienne." *Revue historique* 307, no. 3 (2002): 721–53.

Derrida, Jacques. "Structure, Sign and Play in the Discourse of the Human Sciences." In *Writing and Difference*, translated by Alan Bass, 351–70. Routledge Classics. London: Routledge, 2001. First published in 1978.

De Ste. Croix, G. E. M. "Why Were Christians Persecuted?" In *Christian Persecution, Martyrdom, and Orthodoxy*, edited by Michael Whitby and Joseph Streeter, 105–51. New York: Oxford University Press, 2006.

Devailly, Guy. "La pastorale en Gaule au IXe siècle." *Revue d'histoire de l'Église de France* 59, no. 162 (1973): 23–54.

Devisse, Jean. *Hincmar, archevêque de Reims, 845–882*. 3 vols. Travaux d'histoire ethico-politique 29. Geneva: Droz, 1975–76.

Dickie, Michael W. "The Fathers of the Church and the Evil Eye." In Maguire, *Byzantine Magic*, 9–34.

———. "Who Practiced Love-Magic in Classical Antiquity and in the Late Roman World?" *The Classical Quarterly* 50, no. 2 (2000): 563–83.

Dickinson, Tania M. "An Anglo-Saxon 'cunning woman' from Bidford-on-Avon." In *In Search of Cult: Archaeological Investigations in Honour of Philip Rahtz*, edited by Martin Carver, 45–54. University of York Archaeological Papers. Woodbridge, UK: Boydell, 1993.

Dienst, H. R. "Zur Rolle von Frauen in magischen Vorstellungen und Praktiken–nach ausgewählen Quellen." In *Frauen in Spätantike und Frühmittelalter. Lebensbedingungen- Lebensnormen- Lebensformen*, edited by Werner Affeldt, 173–94. Sigmaringen: J. Thorbecke, 1990.

Dierkens, Alain. "Superstitions, christianisme et paganisme à la fin de l'époque mérovingienne: À propos de l'*Indiculus superstitionem et paganiarum*." In *Magie, sorcellerie, parapsychologie*, edited by Hervé Hasquin, 9–26. Brussels: Éditions de l'Université de Bruxelles, 1984.

Diesenberger, Maximilian, Yitzhak Hen, and Marianne Pollheimer, eds. *Sermo Doctorum: Compilers, Preachers, and their Audiences in the Early Middle Ages*. Sermo: Studies on Patristic, Medieval, and Reformation Sermons and Preaching 9. Turnhout, Belgium: Brepols, 2013.

Dieterich, Albrecht. *Mutter Erde: Ein Versuch über Volksreligion*. 3rd ed. Leipzig: Teubner, 1925. First published in 1905.

Dillon, John M. *The Middle Platonists: A Study of Platonism, 80 B.C. to A.D. 220*. London: Duckworth, 1977.

Dölger, Franz Joseph. "Beiträge zur Geschichte des Kreuzzeichens VI." *Jahrbuch für Antike und Christentum* 6 (1963): 7–34.

Douglas, Mary. *Natural Symbols: Explorations in Cosmology*. 2nd ed. London: Routledge, 2003. First published in 1996.

———, ed. *Witchcraft Confessions and Accusations*. ASA Monographs 9. London: Tavistock, 1970.

Dozier, Edward P. "The Concepts of 'Primitive' and 'Native' in Anthropology." *Yearbook of Anthropology* (1955): 187–202.

Drabkin, I. E. "Soranus and His System of Medicine." *Bulletin of the History of Medicine* 25, no. 6 (1951): 503–18.

Durkheim, Émile. *The Division of Labor in Society*. Translated by George Simpson. 2nd ed. Glencoe, IL: Free Press, 1960. First printed in 1933.

———. *The Elementary Forms of Religious Life*. Translated by Karen E. Fields. New York: Free Press, 1995. First published in 1915.

Dutton, Paul Edward. *Charlemagne's Mustache and Other Cultural Clusters of a Dark Age*. The New Middle Ages. New York: Palgrave Macmillan, 2004.

———. *The Politics of Dreaming in the Carolingian Empire*. Regents Studies in Medieval Culture. Lincoln: University of Nebraska, 1994.

Eastwood, Bruce Stansfield. "The Astronomy of Macrobius in Carolingian Europe: Dungal's Letter of 811 to Charles the Great." *EME* 3, no. 2 (1994): 117–34.

———. *Ordering the Heavens: Roman Astronomy and Cosmology in the Carolingian Renaissance*. History of Science and Medicine Library 4. Medieval and Early Modern Science 8. Leiden: Brill, 2007.

Eckert, Willehad Paul. "Volksglauben zur Zeit Bischof Burchards I." In Müller, Pinkert, and Seeboth, *Bischof Burchard I*, 134–40.

Edelstein, Emma J., and Ludwig Edelstein. *Asclepius: A Collection and Interpretation of the Testimonies*. 2 vols. Ancient Religion and Mythology. Salem, NH: Ayer, 1988. First published in 1945.

Edwards, Cyril. "German Vernacular Literature. A Survey." In McKitterick, *Carolingian Culture: Emulation and Innovation*, 141–70.

Edwards, Mark, Martin Goodman, Simon Price, and Christopher Rowland, eds. *Apologetics in the Roman Empire: Pagans, Jews and Christians*. Oxford: Oxford University Press, 1999.

Effros, Bonnie. "*De partibus Saxoniae* and the Regulation of Mortuary Custom: A Carolingian Campaign of Christianization or the Suppression of Saxon Identity?" *Revue belge de philologie et d'historie* 75, no. 2 (1997): 267–86.

Ehrman, Bart. *Lost Christianities: The Battle for Scripture and the Faiths We Never Knew*. Oxford: Oxford University Press, 2003.

Eisen, Ute E. *Women Officeholders in Early Christianity: Epigraphical and Literary Studies*. Translated by Linda M. Maloney. Collegeville, MN: Liturgical Press, 2000.

Elliott, Dyan. "Tertullian, the Angelic Life, and the Bride of Christ." In *Gender and Christianity in Medieval Europe: New Perspectives*, edited by Lisa M. Bitel and Felice Lifshitz, 16–33. The Middle Ages. Philadelphia: University of Pennsylvania Press, 2008.

Elm von der Osten, Dorothee. "'Perpetua felicitas': Die Predigten des Augustinus zur *Passio Perpetuae et Felicitatis* (S. 280–282)." In *Die christlich-philosophischen Diskurse der Spätantike: Texte, Personen, Institutionen: Akten der Tagung vom 22.–25. Februar 2006 am Zentrum für Antike und Moderne der Albert-Ludwigs-Universität Freiburg*, edited by Therese Fuhrer, 275–98. Stuttgart: Franz Steiner, 2008.

Enright, Michael J. "The Goddess Who Weaves: Some Iconographic Aspects of Bracteates of the Fürstenberg Type." *Frühmittelalterliche Studien* 24 (1990): 54–70.

———. *Lady with a Mead Cup: Ritual, Prophecy and Lordship in the European Warband from La Tène to the Viking Age*. Dublin: Four Courts, 1996.

———. "Ritual and Technology in the Iron Age: An Initiation Scene on the Gundestrup Cauldron." In Glosecki, *Myth in Early Northwest Europe*, 105–20.

———. *Shamanism and Old English Poetry*. Albert Bates Lord Studies in Oral Tradition 2. Garland Reference Library of the Humanities 905. New York: Garland, 1989.

Erickson, Carolly. *The Medieval Vision: Essays in History and Perception*. New York: Oxford University Press, 1976.

Errington, R. Malcolm. *Roman Imperial Policy from Julian to Theodosius*. Studies in the History of Greece and Rome. Chapel Hill: University of North Carolina Press, 2006.

Esmyol, Andrea. *Geliebte oder Ehefrau? Konkubinen in frühen Mittelalter*. Beihefte zum Archiv für Kulturgeschichte 52. Cologne: Böhlau, 2002.

Evans-Pritchard, E. E. "Sorcery and Native Opinion." *Africa: Journal of the International African Institute* 4, no. 1 (1931): 22–55.

———. "Witchcraft (*Mangu*) amongst the A-zande." *Sudan Notes and Records* 12, no. 2 (1929): 163–249.

———. *Witchcraft, Oracles, and Magic among the Azande*. Abridged by Eva Gillies. Oxford: Clarendon, 1976. First published in 1937.

Everett, Nicholas. "The Manuscript Evidence for Pharmacy in the Early Middle Ages." In *Writing the Early Medieval West: Studies in Honour of Rosamond McKitterick*, edited by Elina Screen and Charles West, 115–30. Cambridge, MA: Cambridge University Press, 2018.

Fanger, Claire. "Christian Ritual Magic in the Middle Ages." *History Compass* 11, no. 8 (2013): 610–18.
Farnell, L. R. "Hekate's Cult." In *The Goddess Hekate*, edited by Stephen Ronan, 17–35. Studies in Ancient Pagan and Christian Religion and Philosophy 1, Hastings, UK: Chthonios Books, 1992.
Faulkner, Thomas. *Law and Authority in the Early Middle Ages: The Frankish* Leges *in the Carolingian Period*. Cambridge Studies in Medieval Life and Thought. 4th ser. Cambridge: Cambridge University Press, 2016.
Ferguson, Everett. *Backgrounds of Early Christianity*. 2nd ed. Grand Rapids, MI: Eerdmans, 1993.
———. *Baptism in the Early Church: History, Theology, and Liturgy in the First Five Centuries*. Grand Rapids, MI: Eerdmans, 2009.
Ferngren, Gary B. *Medicine and Health Care in Early Christianity*. Baltimore: Johns Hopkins University Press, 2009.
Fichtenau, Heinrich. *The Carolingian Empire*. Translated by Peter Munz. Studies in Mediaeval History 9. Toronto: University of Toronto Press, 1978. First published in 1957.
Filotas, Bernadette. *Pagan Survivals, Superstitions and Popular Culture in Early Medieval Pastoral Literature*. Studies and Texts 151. Toronto: Pontifical Institute of Mediaeval Studies, 2005.
Firey, Abigail, ed. *A New History of Penance*. Brill's Companions to the Christian Tradition 14. Leiden: Brill, 2008.
Fischer-Hansen, Tobias, and Birte Poulsen, eds. *From Artemis to Diana: The Goddess of Man and Beast*. Danish Studies in Classical Archaeology. Acta Hyperborea 12. Copenhagen: Museum Tusculanum Press, 2009.
Fleischer, Jens. "Living Rocks and *locus amoenus*: Architectural Representations of Paradise in Early Christianity." In Petersen et al., *Appearances of Medieval Rituals*, 149–71.
Fleischman, Suzanne. "On the Representation of History and Fiction in the Middle Ages." *History and Theory: Studies in the Philosophy of History* 22, no. 3 (1983): 278–310.
Flierman, Robert. "Religious Saxons: Paganism, Infidelity and Biblical Punishment in the *Capitulatio de partibus Saxoniae*." In Meens et al., *Religious Franks*, 181–201.
Flint, Valerie I. J. *The Rise of Magic in Early Medieval Europe*. Princeton, NJ: Princeton University Press, 1991.
———. "Susanna and the Lothar Crystal: A Liturgical Perspective." *EME* 4, no. 1 (1995): 61–86.
Forcellini, Egidio, Giuseppe Furlanetto, Francesco Corradini, and Josephus Perin. *Lexicon totius latinitatis*. 6 vols. Bonn: A. Forni, 1965.
Foucault, Michel. *The Order of Things: An Archaeology of the Human Sciences*. New York: Vintage Books, 1994. First published in 1970.
———. *Power and Knowledge: Selected Interviews and Other Writings, 1972–1977*. Edited by Colin Gordon. Translated by Colin Gordon, Leo Marshall, John Mepham, and Kate Soper. New York: Pantheon, 1980.
———. "The Subject and Power." In *Michel Foucault: Beyond Structuralism and Hermeneutics*. 2nd ed., edited by Hubert L. Dreyfus and Paul Rabinow, 208–26. Chicago: University of Chicago Press, 1983.

Fouracre, Paul. "The Origins of the Carolingian Attempt to Regulate the Cult of Saints." *The Cult of Saints in Late Antiquity and the Early Middle Ages: Essays on the Contribution of Peter Brown*, edited by James Howard-Johnston and Paul Antony Hayward, 143–65. Oxford: Oxford University Press, 2002. Originally published in 1999.

———. "'Placita' and the Settlement of Disputes in Later Merovingian Francia." In Davies and Fouracre, *Settlement of Disputes*, 23–43.

———. "The Work of Audoenus of Rouen and Eligius of Noyon in Extending Episcopal Influence from the Town to the Country in Seventh-Century Neustria." *Studies in Church History* 16 (1979): 77–91.

Fouracre, Paul, and Richard A. Gerberding, eds. *Late Merovingian France: History and Hagiography, 640–720*. Manchester Medieval Sources Series. Manchester: Manchester University Press, 1996.

Fournier, Paul. "Le Décret de Burchard de Worms." *Revue d'histoire ecclésiastique* 12 (1911): 451–73, 670–701.

Fournier, Paul, and Gabriel Le Bras. *Histoire des collections canoniques en occident depuis les fausses décrétales jusqu'au Décret de Gratien*. Vol. 1. Paris: Recueil Sirey, 1931.

Fowden, Garth. *Empire to Commonwealth: Consequences of Monotheism in the Ancient World*. Princeton, NJ: Princeton University Press, 1993.

Fox, Robin Lane. *Pagans and Christians*. New York: Knopf, 1987.

Franck, Johannes. "Geschichte des Wortes Hexe." In *Quellen und Untersuchungen zur Geschichte des Hexenwahns und der Hexenverfolgung im Mittelalter*, edited by Joseph Hansen, 614–60. Bonn: Carl Georgi, 1901.

Frangoulidis, Stavros. *Witches, Isis and Narrative: Approaches to Magic in Apuleius' Metamorphoses*. Trends in Classics – Supplementary Volumes 2. Berlin: De Gruyter, 2008.

Frankfurter, David. *Evil Incarnate: Rumors of Demonic Conspiracy and Ritual Abuse in History*. Princeton, NJ: Princeton University Press, 2006.

———. "The Social Context of Women's Erotic Magic in Antiquity." In *Daughters of Hecate: Women and Magic in the Ancient World*, edited by Kimberly B. Stratton and Dayna S. Kalleres, 319–39. Oxford: Oxford University Press, 2014.

Fransen, Gérard. "La rupture du marriage." *Canones et quaestiones: Évolution des doctrines et système du droit canonique* 2 (2002): 343–70.

———. "Le *Décret* de Burchard de Worms: Valeur du texte de l'éditon; Essai du classement des manuscrits." *Zeitschrift der Savigny-Stifung für Rechtsgeschichte: Kanonistische Abteilung* 42, no. 1 (1977): 1–19.

Frantzen, Allen J. *The Literature of Penance in Anglo-Saxon England*. New Brunswick, NJ: Rutgers University Press, 1983.

———. "The Penitentials Attributed to Bede." *Speculum* 58, no. 3 (1983): 573–97.

———. "The Significance of the Frankish Penitentials." *Journal of Ecclesiastical History* 30 (1979): 409–21.

Frazer, James G. *The Magic Art and the Evolution of Kings*. Part 1, vol. 1 of *The Golden Bough: A Study in Magic and Religion*. 3rd ed. London: Macmillan and Company, 1955. First published in 1907–13.

Frede, Michael. "Origen's Treatise *Against Celsus*." In Edwards et al., *Apologetics in the Roman Empire*, 131–55.

French, Marilyn. *Beyond Power: On Men, Women, and Morals*. New York: Summit Books, 1985.
Frymer-Kensky, Tikva. *In the Wake of the Goddesses: Women, Culture, and the Biblical Transformation of Pagan Myth*. New York: Fawcett Columbine, 1993.
Fulk, Angela. "Patriarchal Rituals: Anglo-Saxon Readings of Genesis and the Shift from Pagan to Christian Religious Practice." *The Heroic Age: A Journal of Early Medieval Northwestern Europe* 19 (2009): 1–29.
Fulk, R. D. "Old English Meter and Oral Tradition: Three Issues Bearing on Poetic Chronology." *Journal of English and Germanic Philology* 106, no. 3 (2007): 304–24.
Gaastra, A. H. "Penance and the Law: The Penitential Canons of the *Collection in Nine Books*." *EME* 14, no. 1 (2006): 85–102.
Gager, John G. *Kingdom and Community: The Social World of Early Christianity*. Prentice-Hall Studies in Religion Series. Englewood Cliffs, NJ: Prentice-Hall, 1975.
Gallagher, Robert. "King Alfred and the Sibyl: Sources of Praise in the Latin Acrostic Verses of Bern, Burgerbibliothek." *EME* 27, no. 2 (2019): 279–98.
Gameson, Richard, and Henrietta Leyser, ed. *Belief and Culture in the Middle Ages: Studies Presented to Henry Mayr-Harting*. Oxford: Oxford University Press, 2001.
Ganz, David. "The *Epitaphium Arsenii* and Opposition to Louis the Pious." In Godman and Collins, *Charlemagne's Heir*, 537–50.
Garipzanov, Ildar H. *Graphic Signs of Authority in Late Antiquity and the Early Middle Ages, 300–900*. Oxford Studies in Medieval European History. Oxford: Oxford University Press, 2018.
———. *The Symbolic Language of Authority in the Carolingian World (c. 751–877)*. Brill's Series on the Early Middle Ages 16. Leiden: Brill, 2008.
Garrison, Mary. "The Emergence of Carolingian Latin Literature and the Court of Charlemagne (780–814)." In McKitterick, *Carolingian Culture: Emulation and Innovation*, 111–40.
———. "Letters to a King and Biblical Exempla: The Examples of Cathuulf and Clemens Peregrinus." *EME* 7, no. 3 (1998): 305–28.
———. "The Franks as the New Israel? Education for an Identity from Pippin to Charlemagne." In Hen and Innes, *Uses of the Past in the Early Middle Ages*, 114–61.
Garver, Valerie L. *Women and Aristocratic Culture in the Carolingian World*. Ithaca, NY: Cornell University Press, 2009.
Gasparri, Stefano. "Columbanus, Bobbio and the Lombards." *Columbanus and the Peoples of Post-Roman Europe*, edited by Alexander O'Hara, 255–58. Oxford Studies in Late Antiquity. Oxford: Oxford University Press, 2018.
Gatch, Milton McC. "The Unknowable Audience of the Blickling Homilies." *Anglo-Saxon England* 18 (1989): 99–115.
Gaudemet, Jean. "Indissolubilité et consommation du mariage, l'apport d'Hincmar de Reims." *Revue de droit canonique* 30, no. 1 (1980): 28–40.
———. *Le mariage en Occident: Les moeurs et le droit*. Histoire. Paris: Cerf, 1987.
Geary, Patrick J. *Before France and Germany: The Creation and Transformation of the Merovingian World*. New York: Oxford University Press, 1988.
———. *Furta Sacra: Thefts of Relics in the Central Middle Ages*. Princeton, NJ: Princeton University Press, 1978.

———. "Oblivion Between Orality and Textuality in the Tenth Century." In *Medieval Concepts of the Past: Ritual, Memory, Historiography*, edited by Johannes Fried and Patrick J. Geary, 111–22. Publications of the German Historical Institute. Cambridge, MA: Cambridge University Press, 2002.

Geertz, Clifford. *The Interpretation of Cultures: Selected Essays by Clifford Geertz*. New York: Basic Books, 2000. First published in 1973.

———. "Religion as a Cultural System." *Anthropological Approaches to the Study of Religion*. Vol. 1 of Religion, Rites, and Ceremonies. Edited by Michael Banton, 1–46. Routledge Library Editions. Anthropology and Ethnography. London: Tavistock Publications, 1966. Reprint, London: Routledge, 2004.

Gehrke, Pamela. *Saints and Scribes: Medieval Hagiography in Its Manuscript Context*. University of California Publications in Modern Philology 126. Berkeley: University of California Press, 1993.

Getz, Faye. *Medicine in the English Middle Ages*. Princeton: Princeton University Press, 1998.

Gibson, Kelly. "The Carolingian World through Hagiography." *History Campass* 13, no. 12 (2015): 630–45.

Gieryn, Thomas F. "A Space for Place in Sociology." *Annual Review of Sociology* 26, no. 1 (2000): 463–96.

———. *Truth-Spots: How Places Make People Believe*. Chicago: University of Chicago Press, 2018.

Gillis, Matthew. *Heresy and Dissent in the Carolingian Empire: The Case of Gottschalk of Orbais*. Oxford: Oxford University Press, 2017.

Gillmeister, Andrzej. "Cultural Paraphrase in Roman Religion in the Age of Augustus: The Case of the Sibyl and the Sibylline Books." *Acta Antiqua Academiae Scientiarum Hungaricae* 55, no. 1 (2015): 211–22.

Ginzburg, Carlo. *Ecstasies: Deciphering the Witches' Sabbath*. Translated by Raymond Rosenthal. New York: Penguin, 1991.

———. *The Night Battles: Witchcraft and Agrarian Cults in the Sixteenth and Seventeenth Centuries*. Translated by Anne Tedeschi and John Tedeschi. Routledge Library Editions: Witchcraft 4. London: Routledge, 2011. First published in 1983.

Giorda, Maria Chiara, and Ioan Cozma. "Beyond Gender: Reflections on a Contemporary Case of Double Monastery in Orthodox Monasticism—St. John the Baptist Monastery of Essex in England." *Religions* 10, no. 8 (2019): 453–72.

Gittos, Helen. *Liturgy, Architecture, and Sacred Places in Anglo-Saxon England*. Medieval History and Archaeology. Oxford: Oxford University Press, 2013.

Glosecki, Stephen O., ed. *Myth in Early Northwest Europe*. Medieval and Renaissance Texts and Studies 320. Arizona Studies in the Middle Ages and the Renaissance 21. Tempe, AZ: ACMRS, 2007.

———. *Shamanism and Old English Poetry*. Albert Bates Lord Studies in Oral Tradition 2. Garland Reference Library of the Humanities 905. New York: Garland, 1989.

———. "Stranded Narrative: Myth, Metaphor, and the Metrical Charm." In Glosecki, *Myth in Early Northwest Europe*, 47–70.

Godman, Peter, and Roger Collins, eds. *Charlemagne's Heir: New Perspectives on the Reign of Louis the Pious (814–840)*. Oxford: Clarendon, 1990.

Goetz, Hans-Werner. *Strukturen der spätkarolingischen Epoche im Spiegel der Vorstellungen eines zeitgenössischen Mönchs: Eine Interpretation der "Gesta Karoli" Notkers von Sankt Gallen*. Bonn: Habelt, 1981.

Goffart, Walter. *The Narrators of Barbarian History (AD 550–800): Jordanes, Gregory of Tours, Bede, and Paul the Deacon.* Princeton, NJ: Princeton University Press, 1988.

Goldberg, Eric J. "Popular Revolt, Dynastic Politics, and Aristocratic Factionalism in the Early Middle Ages: The Saxon Stellinga Reconsidered." *Speculum* 70, no. 3 (1995): 467–501.

———. *Struggle for Empire: Kingship and Conflict under Louis the German, 817–876.* Conjunctions of Religion and Power in the Medieval Past. Ithaca, NY: Cornell University Press, 2006.

Goodman, Penelope J. "Temples in Late Antique Gaul." In *The Archaeology of Late Antique "Paganism,"* edited by L. Lavan and M. Mulryan, 165–93. Late Antique Archaeology 7. Leiden: Brill, 2011.

Goody, Jack. "Against 'Ritual': Loosely Structured Thoughts on a Loosely Defined Topic." In *Secular Ritual*, edited by Sally F. Moore and Barbara G. Myerhoff, 25–35. Assen, NL: Van Gorcum, 1977.

Graf, Fritz. "Augustine and Magic." In Bremmer and Veenstra, *Metamorphosis of Magic*, 87–103.

———. *Magic in the Ancient World.* Translated by Franklin Philip. Revealing Antiquity 10. Cambridge, MA: Harvard University Press, 1997.

Grape-Albers, Heide. *Spätantike Bilder aus der Welt des Arztes: medizinische Bilderhandschriften der Spätantike und ihre mittelalterliche Überlieferung.* Wiesbaden: Guido Pressler, 1977.

Grattan, J. H. G., and Charles Singer. *Anglo-Saxon Magic and Medicine: Illustrated Specially from the Semi-Pagan Text "Lacnunga."* 2 pts. Wellcome Historical Medical Museum. London: Oxford University Press, 1952.

Graus, F. "Hagiographie und Dämonenglauben: Zu ihren Funktionen in der Merowingerzeit." *Settimane de Studie* 36 (April 1989): 93–120.

Green, Eugene A. "Aelfric the Catechist." In Amos, Green, and Kienzle, *De ore domini*, 61–74.

———. "Enoch, Lent, and the Ascension of Christ." In Amos, Green, and Kienzle, *De ore domini*, 13–25.

Green, Monica H. "Women's Medical Practice and Health Care in Medieval Europe." In Bennett et al., *Sisters and Workers in the Middle Ages*, 39–78.

Griffiths, Bill. *Aspects of Anglo-Saxon Magic.* Rev. ed. Hockwold-cum-Wilton, UK: Anglo-Saxon Books, 2003.

Grig, Lucy. "Approaching Popular Culture in Late Antiquity: Singing in the Sermons of Caesarius of Arles." *Studia Patristica* 69, no. 17 (2013): 197–204.

———. "Caesarius of Arles and the Campaign against Popular Culture in Late Antiquity." *EME* 26, no. 1 (2018): 61–81.

———. "Interpreting the Kalends of January: A Case Study for Late Antique Popular Culture." In Grig, *Popular Culture in the Ancient World*, 237–56.

———, ed. *Popular Culture in the Ancient World.* Cambridge, MA: Cambridge University Press, 2017.

Grubbs, Judith Evans. "Constantine and Imperial Legislation on the Family." In Harries and Wood, *Theodosian Code*, 120–42.

Guillot, Oliver. "Une *ordinatio* méconnue: Le Capitulaire de 823–825." In Godman and Collins, *Charlemagne's Heir*, 455–86.

Gurevich, Aron. *Medieval Popular Culture: Problems of Belief and Perception*. Cambridge Studies in Oral and Literate Culture 14. Cambridge: Cambridge University Press, 1988.

Halfond, Gregory I. *Archaeology of Frankish Church Councils, AD 511–768*. Medieval Law and Its Practice 6. Leiden: Brill, 2010.

Hall, Alaric. *Elves in Anglo-Saxon England: Matters of Belief, Health, Gender and Identity*. Anglo-Saxon Studies 8. Woodbridge, UK: Boydell, 2007.

Halphen, Louis. *Études critiques sur l'histoire de Charlemagne, les sources de l'histoire de Charlemagne, la conquête de la Saxe, le couronnement impérial, l'agriculture et la propriété rurale, l'industrie et la commerce*. Paris: F. Alcan, 1921.

Halsall, Guy. "Gender and the End of Empire." *Journal of Medieval and Early Modern Studies*. 34, no. 1 (2004): 17–39.

Hamilton, Sarah. *The Practice of Penance, 900–1050*. Royal Historical Society Studies in History, n.s. Woodbridge, UK: Boydell, 2001.

Harley, David. "Rhetoric and the Social Construction of Sickness and Healing." *The Society for the Social History of Medicine* 12, no. 3 (1999): 407–35.

Harmening, Dieter. *Superstitio: Überlieferungs- und theoriegeschichtliche Untersuchungen zur Kirchlich-theologischen Aberglaubensliteratur des Mittelalters*. Berlin: Erich Schmidt, 1979.

Harries, Jill, and Ian Wood, eds. *The Theodosian Code*. Ithaca, NY: Cornell University Press, 1993.

Harris, Marvin. "Emics and Etics Revisited." In *Emics and Etics: The Insider/Outsider Debate*, edited by Thomas N. Headland, Kenneth L. Pike, and Marvin Harris, 48–61. Frontiers of Anthropology 7. Newbury Park, CA: Sage, 1990.

Harris, Max. *Sacred Folly: A New History of the Feast of Fools*. Ithaca, NY: Cornell University Press, 2011.

Harrison, S. J. *Apuleius: A Latin Sophist*. Oxford: Oxford University Press, 2000.

Harris-Stoertz, Fiona. "Midwives in the Middle Ages? Birth Attendants, 600–1300." In *Medicine and Law in the Middle Ages*, edited by Wendy J. Turner and Sara M. Butler, 58–87. Medieval Law and Its Practice 17. Leiden: Brill, 2014.

Hart, Gerald D. *Asclepius, The God of Medicine*. London: Royal Society of Medicine, 2000.

Hartmann, Wilfried. "Burchards Dekret: Stand der Forschung und offene Fragen." In *Bischof Burchard von Worms 1000–1025*, edited by Wilfried Hartmann, 161–66. Quellen und Abhandlungen zur mittelrheinischen Kirchengeschicte 100. Mainz: Gesellschaft für mittelrheinische Kirchengeschichte, 2000.

——. *Die Synoden der Karolingerzeit im Frankenreich und in Italien*. Konziliengeschichte. Reihe A: Darstellungen. Paderborn: Schöningh, 1989.

——. *Kirche und Kirchenrecht um 900: Die Bedeutung der spätkarolingischen Zeit für Tradition und Innovation im kirchlichen Recht*. MGH Schriften 58. Hanover: Hahn, 2008.

——. "Laien auf Synoden der Karolingerzeit." *Annuarium historiae conciliorum* 10, no. 2 (1978): 249–69.

Harvey, Susan Ashbrook. "Women in Early Byzantine Hagiography: Reversing the Story." In Coon, Haldane, and Sommer, *That Gentle Strength*, 19–35.

Hauck, Karl. "Motivanalyse eines Doppelbrakteaten: Die Trager der goldenen Götterbildamulette und die Traditionsinstanz der fünischen Brakteatenproduktion." *Frühmittelalterliche Studien* 19 (1985): 139–94.

———. "Rituelle Speisegemeinschaft im 10. und 11. Jahrhundert." *Studium generale* 3, no. 1 (1950): 611–21.

Hausmann, Chris, Amy Jonason, and Erika Summers–Effler. "Interaction Ritual Theory and Structural Symbolic Interactionism." *Symbolic Interaction* 34, no. 3 (2011): 319–29.

Head, Thomas. *Hagiography and the Cult of Saints: The Diocese of Orléans, 800–1200*. Cambridge Studies in Medieval Life and Thought 14. 4th ser. Cambridge, MA: Cambridge University Press, 1990.

Heidecker, Karl. *The Divorce of Lothar II: Christian Marriage and Political Power in the Carolingian World*. Translated by Tanis M. Guest. Conjunctions of Religion and Power in the Medieval Past. Ithaca, NY: Cornell University Press, 2010.

Heinzelmann, Martin. *Gregor von Tours (538–594): "zehn Bücher Geschichte," Historiographie und Gesellschaftskonzept im 6. Jahrhundert*. Darmstadt: Wissenschaftliche Buchgesellschaft, 1994.

Helvétius, Anne-Marie. "L'organisation des monastères féminins à l'époque mérovingienne." In *Female vita religiosa Between Late Antiquity and the High Middle Ages: Structures, Devlopments and Spatial Contexts*, edited by Gert Melville and Anne Müller, 151–69. Vita regularis: Ordnungen und Deutungen religiosen Lebens im Mittelalter 47. Zurich: Lit, 2011.

Hen, Yitzhak. *Culture and Religion in Merovingian Gaul, A.D. 481–751*. Cultures, Beliefs and Traditions: Medieval and Early Modern Peoples 1. Leiden: Brill, 1995.

———. "The Early Medieval West." In D. Collins, *Cambridge History of Magic and Witchcraft*, 148–82.

———. "Martin of Braga's *De Correctione rusticorum* and Its Use in Frankish Gaul." In *Medieval Transformation: Texts, Power, and Gifts in Context*, edited by Esther Cohen and Mayke de Jong, 35–49. Cultures, Beliefs, and Traditions 11. Leiden: Brill, 2001.

———. "Paganism and Superstitions in the Time of Gregory of Tours: *Une Question Mal Posée!*" In *The World of Gregory of Tours*, edited by Kathleen Mitchell and Ian Wood, 229–40. Cultures, Beliefs and Traditions 8. Leiden: Brill, 2002.

———. "The Structure and Aims of the *Visio Baronti*." *Journal of Theological Studies* 47, no. 2 (1996): 477–97.

Hen, Yitzhak, and Matthew Innes, eds. *The Uses of the Past in the Early Middle Ages*. Cambridge: Cambridge University Press, 2000.

Herlihy, David. *Opera Muliebria: Women and Work in Medieval Europe*. New Perspectives on European History. New York: McGraw-Hill, 1990.

Higham, Nicholas J., and Martin J. Ryan. *The Anglo-Saxon World*. New Haven, CT: Yale University Press, 2013.

Hill, Joyce, and Mary Swan, eds. *The Community, the Family and the Saint: Patterns of Power in Early Medieval Europe; Selected Proceedings of the International Medieval Congress, University of Leeds, 4–7 July 1994, 10–13 July 1995*. International Medieval Research 4. Turnhout, Belgium: Brepols, 1998.

Hillgarth, J. N. *Christianity and Paganism, 350–750: The Conversion of Western Europe*. The Middle Ages. Philadelphia: University of Pennsylvania Press, 1986. First published in 1969.

Himmelfarb, Martha. *Ascent to Heaven in Jewish and Christian Apocalypses*. New York: Oxford University Press, 1993.

Hlawitschka, Eduard. "Die Herrscher der Ottonenzeit (911–1024)." In *Die Kaiser: 1200 Jahre europäische Geschichte*, edited by Gerhard Hartmann and Karl Rudolf Schnith, 99–177. Graz: Verlag Styria, 1996.

Hoffmann, Hartmut, and Rudolf Pokorny. *Das Dekret des Bischofs Burchard von Worms: Textstufen, frühe Verbreitung, Vorlagen*. Hilfsmittel 12. Munich: Monumenta Germaniae Historica, 1991.

Hollis, Stephanie. "Old English 'Cattle-Theft Charms': Manuscript Contexts and Social Uses." *Anglia* 115, no. 1 (1997): 139–64.

Holtkemper, Franz-Josef. "Kompilation und Originalität bei Hrabanus Maurus." In *Pädagogische Blätter. Heinrich Döpp-Vorwald zum 65. Geburtstag*, edited by Franz-Josef Holtkemper, 58–75. Düsseldorf: A. Henn, 1967.

Holze, Heinrich. *Erfahrung und Theologie im frühen Mönchtum: Untersuchungen zu einer Theologie des monastischen Lebens bei den ägyptischen Mönchsvätern, Johannes Cassian und Benedikt von Nursia*. Forschungen zur Kirchen- und Dogmengeschichte 48. Göttingen: Vandenhoeck & Ruprecht, 1992.

Honoré, Tony. *Law in the Crisis of Empire 379–455 AD: The Theodosian Dynasty and its Quaestors*. Oxford: Oxford University Press, 2011. First published in 1998.

Horbury, William. "Jewish-Christian Relations in Barnabas and Justin Martyr." In *Jews and Christians: The Parting of the Ways A.D. 70 to 135*, edited by James D. G. Dunn, 315–45. Grand Rapids, MI: Eerdmans, 1999. First published in 1992.

Horden, Peregrine. "Sickness and Healing." In Noble and Smith, *Early Medieval Christianities*, 416–32.

———. "What's Wrong with Early Medieval Medicine?" *Social History of Medicine* 24, no. 1 (2011): 5–25.

Hornblower, Simon, Antony Spawforth, and Esther Eidinow, eds. *The Oxford Classical Dictionary*. 4th ed. Oxford: Oxford University Press, 2012.

Hummer, Hans J. *Politics and Power in Early Medieval Europe: Alsace and the Frankish Realm, 600–1000*. Cambridge Studies in Medieval Life and Thought 65. 4th ser. Cambridge, MA: Cambridge University Press, 2005.

Humphries, Mark. "Chronicle and Chronology: Prosper of Aquitaine, His Methods and the Development of Early Medieval Chronography." *EME* 5, no. 2, (1996): 155–75.

Hunt, E. D. *Holy Land Pilgrimage in the Later Roman Empire, AD 312–460*. Oxford: Clarendon, 1982.

Hyams, Paul R. "Trial by Ordeal: The Key of Proof in the Early Common Law." In *On the Laws and Customs of England: Essays in Honor of Samuel E. Thorne*, ed. Samuel E. Thorne. Studies in Legal History, 90–126. Chapel Hill: University of North Carolina Press, 1981.

Innes, Matthew. "'Immune 'from Heresy': Defining the Boundaries of Carolingian Christianity." In *Frankland: The Franks and the World of the Early Middle Ages*, edited by Paul Fouracre and David Ganz, 101–25. Manchester: Manchester University Press, 2008.

———. *Introduction to Early Medieval Western Europe, 300–900: The Sword, the Plough and the Book*. London: Routledge, 2007.

———. *State and Society in the Early Middle Ages: The Middle Rhine Valley, 400–1000*. Cambridge Studies in Medieval Life and Thought 47. 4th ser. Cambridge, MA: Cambridge University Press, 2000.

Innes, Matthew, and Rosamond McKitterick. "The Writing of History." In McKitterick, *Carolingian Culture: Emulation and Innovation*, 193–220.

Iogna-Prat, Dominique. *La maison Dieu: Une histoire monumentale de l'Église au Moyen Âge (v. 800–v. 1200)*. L'Univers Historique. Paris: Seuil, 2006.

James, Edward. *The Franks*. The Peoples of Europe. Oxford: Blackwell, 1988.

Janowitz, Naomi. *Icons of Power: Ritual Practices in Late Antiquity*. Magic in History. University Park: Pennsylvania State University Press, 2002.

———. *Magic in the Roman World*. Religion in the First Christian Centuries. London: Routledge, 2001.

Jarvie, I. C., and Joseph Agassi. "The Problem of the Rationality of Magic." *The British Journal of Sociology* 18 (1967): 55–74.

Jefford, Clayton N. "Introduction: Dynamics, Methodologies, and Progress in Didache Studies." In *The Didache: A Missing Piece of the Puzzle in Early Christianity*, edited by Jonathan A. Draper and Clayton N. Jefford, 1–13. Early Christianity and Its Literature 14. Atlanta GA: Society for Biblical Literature Press, 2015.

Jennings, Victoria. "Divination and Popular Culture." In Grigg, *Popular Culture in the Ancient World*, 189–207.

Jenny-Kappers, Theodora. *Muttergöttin und Gottesmutter in Ephesos: Von Artemis zu Maria*. Zurich: Daimon, 1986.

Johanek, Peter. "Herrscherdiplom und Empfängerkries: Die Kanzlei Ludwigs des Frommen in der Schriftlichkeit der Karolingerzeit." In *Schriftkultur und Reichsverwaltung unter den Karolingern: Referate des Kolloquiums der Nordrhein–Westfälischen Akademie der Wissenschaften am 17.–18. Februar 1994 in Bonn*, edited by Rudolf Schieffer, 167–88. Abhandlungen der Nordrhein–Westfälischen Akademie der Wissenschaften 97. Opladen: Westdeutscher Verlag, 1996.

Johannessen, Hazel. *The Demonic in the Political Thought of Eusebius of Caesarea*. Oxford Early Christian Series. Oxford: Oxford University Press, 2016.

Johnston, Sarah Iles. *Hekate Soteira: A Study of Hekate's Roles in the Chaldean Oracles and Related Literature*. American Classical Studies 21. Atlanta: Scholars, 1990.

———. "Riders in the Sky: Cavalier Gods and Theurgic Salvation in the Second Century A.D." *Classical Philology* 87, no. 4 (1992): 303–21.

Jolly, Karen L. *Popular Religion in Late Saxon England: Elf Charms in Context*. Chapel Hill: University of North Carolina Press, 1996.

Jolly, Karen L., Catharina Raudvere, and Edward Peters. *Witchcraft and Magic in Europe: The Middle Ages*. Athlone History of Witchcraft and Magic in Europe 3. London: Athlone, 2001.

Jones, G. I. "A Boundary to Accusations." In Douglas, *Witchcraft Confessions and Accusations*, 321–32.

Joye, Sylvie. "Family Order and Kingship According to Hincmar." In *Hincmar of Rheims: Life and Work*, edited by Rachel Stone and Charles West, 190–211. Manchester: Manchester University Press, 2015.

Jurasinski, Stefan. *The Old English Penitentials and Anglo-Saxon Law*. Studies in Legal History. Cambridge, MA: Cambridge University Press, 2015.

Kahlos, Maijastina. "The Early Church." In D. Collins, *Cambridge History of Magic and Witchcraft*, 183–206.

Kaiser, Reinhold. "Königtum und Bischofsherrschaft im frühmittelalterlichen Neustrien." In *Herrschaft und Kirche: Beiträge zur Entstehung und Wirkungsweise episkopaler und monastischer Organisationsformen*, edited by Friedrich Prinz, 83–108. Monographien zur Geschichte des Mittelalters 33. Stuttgart: Hiersemann, 1988.

Kapferer, Bruce. "The Ritual Process and the Problem of Reflexivity in Sinhalese Demon Exorcisms." In MacAloon, *Rite, Drama, Festival, Spectacle*, 179–207.

Kaplan, Michel, ed. *Le sacré et son inscription dans l'espace à Byzance et en Occident: Études compareés*. Byzantina Sorbonensia 18. Paris: Éditions de la Sorbonne, 2001.

Karras, Ruth Mazo. "Pagan Survivals and Syncretism in the Conversion of Saxony." *Catholic Historical Review* 72, no. 4 (1986): 553–72.

———. *Unmarriages: Women, Men, and Sexual Unions in the Middle Ages*. The Middle Ages. Philadelphia: University of Pennsylvania Press, 2012.

Kee, Howard Clark. *Miracle in the Early Christian World: A Study in Sociohistorical Method*. New Haven, CT: Yale University Press, 1983.

Keller, Hagen. "Zum Sturz Karls III." *Deutsches Archiv für Erforschung des Mittelalters* 34 (1966): 333–84.

Kerényi, Karl. *Der göttliche Arzt: Studien über Asklepios und seine Kultstätten*. Basel: CIBA, 1978. First published in 1956.

Kerff, F. "*Libri paenitentiales*" und kirchliche Strafgerichtsbarkeit bis zum "*Decretum Gratiani*": Ein Diskussionsvorschlag." *Zeitschrift der Savigny-Stiftung für Rechtsgeschichte Kanonistische Abteilung* 75, no. 1 (1989): 23–57.

Kern-Ulmer, Brigitte. "The Depiction of Magic in Rabbinic Texts: The Rabbinic and Greek Concept of Magic." *Journal for the Study of Judaism in the Persian, Hellenistic, and Roman Period* 27, no. 3 (1996): 289–303.

Kertzer, David I. *Ritual, Politics, and Power*. New Haven, CT: Yale University Press, 1988.

Kéry, Lotte. *Canonical Collections of the Early Middle Ages (ca. 400–1140): A Bibliographical Guide to the Manuscripts and Literature*. History of Medieval Canon Law. Washington, DC: Catholic University of America Press, 1999.

Keskiaho, Jesse. *Dreams and Visions in the Early Middle Ages: The Reception and Use of Patristic Ideas, 400–900*. Cambridge Studies in Medieval Life and Thought 99. 4th ser. Cambridge: Cambridge University Press, 2015.

———. "Paying Attention to Dreams in Early Medieval Normative Sources (400–900): Countering Non-Christian Practices or Negotiating Christian Dreaming?" *EME* 28, no. 1 (2020): 3–25.

Kesling, Emily. *Medical Texts and Anglo-Saxon Literary Culture*. Anglo-Saxon Studies 38. Cambridge: D. S. Brewer, 2020.

Kieckhefer, Richard. *Forbidden Rites: A Necromancer's Manual of the Fifteenth Century*. Magic in History. University Park: Pennsylvania State University Press, 1997.

———. *Magic in the Middle Ages*. 2nd ed. Cambridge, MA: Cambridge University Press, 2014.

———. "The Specific Rationality of Medieval Magic." *American Historical Review* 99, no. 3 (1994): 813–36.

Kiernan, Kevin S. "The Eleventh-Century Origin of *Beowulf* and the *Beowulf* Manuscript." In Chase, *Dating of "Beowulf,"* 9–22.

Kilde, Jeanne Halgren. *Sacred Power, Sacred Space: An Introduction to Christian Architecture and Worship.* Oxford: Oxford University Press, 2008.

King, Helen. "Bound to Bleed: Artemis and Greek Women." In Cameron and Kuhrt, *Images of Women in Antiquity*, 109–27.

King, Karen L. "Prophetic Power and Women's Authority. The Case of the Gospel of Mary (Magdalene)." In *Women Preachers and Prophets Through Two Millennia of Christianity*, edited by Beverly Mayne Kienzle and Pamela J. Walker, 21–41. Berkeley: University of California Press, 1998.

———. *What Is Gnosticism?* Cambridge, MA: Harvard University Press, 2003.

King, P. D. *Law and Society in the Visigothic Kingdom.* Cambridge Studies in Medieval Life and Thought 5. 3rd ser. Cambridge, MA: Cambridge University Press, 1972.

Kitchen, John. *Saints' Lives and the Rhetoric of Gender: Male and Female in Merovingian Hagiography.* New York: Oxford University Press, 1998.

Kitzler, Petr. *From "Passio Perpetuae" to "Acta Perpetuae": Recontextualizing a Martyr Story in the Literature of the Early Church.* Translated by Josef Srejber and Rachel Thompson. Arbeiten zur Kirchengeschichte 127. Berlin: De Gruyter, 2015.

———. "*Passio Perpetuae* and *Acta Perpetuae*: Between Tradition and Innovation." *Folia philogica* 130, no. 1 / 2 (2007): 1–19.

Klaniczay, Gábor. "Dreams and Visions in Medieval Miracle Accounts." *Ritual Healing: Magic, Ritual and Medical Therapy from Antiquity until the Early Modern Period*, edited by Ildikó Csepregi and Charles Burnett, 147–70. Micrologus' Library. Florence: SISMEL, 2012.

Klingshirn, William E. *Caesarius of Arles: The Making of a Christian Community in Late Antique Gaul.* Cambridge Studies in Medieval Life and Thought 22. 4th ser. Cambridge, MA: Cambridge University Press, 1994.

———. "Defining the *Sortes Sanctorum*: Gibbon, Du Cange, and Early Christian Lot Divination." *Journal of Early Christian Studies* 10, no. 1 (2001): 77–130.

Koch, Armin. *Kaiserin Judith: Eine politische Biographie.* Historische Studien 486. Matthiesen: Husum, 2005.

Kollmann, Bernd. *Jesus und die Christen als Wundertäter: Studien zu Magie, Medizin und Schamanismus in Antike und Christentum.* Forschungen zur Religion und Literatur des Alten und Neuen Testaments. Göttingen: Vanderhoeck & Ruprecht, 1996.

Konecny, Sylvia. *Die Frauen des karolingischen Königshauses: Die politische Bedeutung der Ehe und die Stellung der Frau in der fränkischen Herrscherfamilie vom 7. bis zum 10. Jahrhundert.* Vienna: VWGÖ, 1976.

Kornbluth, Genevra. "The Susanna Crystal of Lothar II: Chastity, the Church, and Royal Justice." *Gesta* 31, no. 1 (1992): 25–39.

Körntgen, Ludger. "Canon Law and the Practice of Penance: Burchard of Worms's Penitential." *EME* 14, no. 1 (2006): 103–17.

———. *Studien zu den Quellen der frühmittelalterlichen Bussbücher.* Quellen und Forschungen zum Recht im Mittelalter 7. Sigmaringen: J. Thorbecke, 1993.

Kottje, Raymund J. *Die Bussbücher Halitgars von Cambrai und des Hrabanus Maurus: Ihre Überlieferung und ihre Quellen.* Beiträge zur Geschichte und Quellenkunde des Mittelalters 8. Berlin: De Gruyter, 1980.

———. "Kirchliches Recht und päpstlicher Autoritätsanspruch: Zu den Auseinandersetzungen über die Ehe Lothars II." In *Aus Kirche und Reich: Studien zu Theologie, Politik, und Recht im Mittelalter*, edited by Hubert Mordek, 97–103. Sigmaringen: J. Thorbecke, 1983.

———. "Überlieferung und Rezeption der irischen Bussbücher auf dem Kontinent." In *Die Iren und Europa im früheren Mittelalter*," edited by Heinz Löwe, 511–23. Vol. 1, *Veröffentlichungen des Europa Zentrums Tübingen Kulturwissenschaftliche Reihe*, 1. Stuttgart: Klett-Cotta, 1982.

Kottje, Raymund, and Helmut Maurer, eds. *Monastische Reformen im 9. und 10. Jahrhundert*. Vorträge und Forschungen 38. Sigmaringen: J. Thorbecke, 1989.

Koziol, Geoffrey. *Begging Pardon and Favor: Ritual and Political Order in Early Medieval France*. Ithaca, NY: Cornell University Press, 1992.

———. "Review Article: The Dangers of Polemic: Is Ritual Still an Interesting Topic of Historical Study?" *EME* 11, no. 4 (2002): 367–88.

———. "Truth and Its Consequences: Why Carolingianists Don't Speak of Myth." In Glosecki, *Myth in Early Northwest Europe*, 71–103.

Krige, J. D. "The Social Function of Witchcraft." *Theoria* 1, no. 4 (1947): 8–21.

Kritzinger, Peter. "Cult of Saints and Religious Processions of Late Antiquity and the Early Middle Ages." In *An Age of Saints? Power, Conflict and Dissent in Early Medieval Christianity*, edited by Peter Sarris, Phil Booth, and Matthew Dal Santo, 36–48. Brill's Series on the Early Middle Ages 20. Leiden: Brill, 2011.

Kropp, Amina. "How Does Magical Language Work? The Spells and *Formulae* of the Latin *Defixionum Tabellae*." In *Magical Practice in the Latin West. Proceedings of the International Conference on Magical Practice in the Latin West (2005: Zaragoza: Spain)*, edited by Richard L. Gordon and Francisco Marco Simon, 357–80. Leiden: Brill, 2010.

Kruger, Steven F. *Dreaming in the Middle Ages*. Cambridge Studies in Medieval Literature 14. Cambridge, MA: Cambridge University Press, 1992.

Künzel, Rudi. "Paganisme, syncrétisme et culture religieuse populaire au haut Moyen Âge: Réflexions de méthode." *Annales, économies, sociétés, civilisations* 47, no. 4/5 (1992): 1055–69.

Lalleman, Pieter J. "Healing by a Mere Touch as a Christian Concept." *Tyndale Bulletin* 48, no. 2 (1988): 355–61.

Lambert, Tom. *Law and Order in Anglo-Saxon England*. Oxford: Oxford University Press, 2017.

Laqueur, Thomas. *Making Sex: Body and Gender from the Greeks to Freud*. Cambridge, MA: Harvard University Press, 1990.

Larner, Christina. *Witchcraft and Religion: The Politics of Popular Belief*. Edited by Alan Macfarlane. New York: Blackwell, 1984.

Lawrence-Mathers, Anne. "The Problem of Magic in Early Anglo-Saxon England." *Reading Medieval Studies* 33 (2007): 87–104.

Leach, Edmund R. *Culture and Communication: The Logic by Which Symbols Are Connected*. Themes in the Social Sciences. Cambridge, MA: Cambridge University Press, 1976.

———. "Magical Hair." *Journal of the Anthropological Institute of Great Britain and Ireland* 88, no. 2 (1958): 147–64.

Lefebvre, Henri. *The Production of Space*. Translated by Donald Nicholson-Smith. Oxford: Blackwell, 1991.
Le Goff, Jacques. "Culture cléricale et traditions folkloriques dans la civilisation mérovingienne." In *Pour un autre Moyen Âge: Temps, travail et culture en Occident: 18 essais*, 223–35. Paris: Gallimard, 1977.
———. *The Medieval Imagination*. Translated by Arthur Goldhammer. Chicago: University of Chicago Press, 1988.
Leja, Meg. "The Sacred Art: Medicine in the Carolingian Renaissance." *Viator* 47, no. 2 (2016): 1–34.
Le Jan, Régine. *Famille et pouvoir dans le monde franc (VIIe–Xe siècle): essai d'anthropologie sociale*. Histoire Ancienne et Médiévale 33. Paris: Publications de la Sorbonne, 1995.
Levack, Brian P. *The Witch-Hunt in Early Modern Europe*. 4th edition. London: Routledge, 2016.
Lev, Efraim. "Traditional Healing with Animals (Zootherapy): Medieval to Present-Day Levantine Practice." *Journal Of Ethnopharmacology* 85, no. 1 (2003): 107–18.
Lévy-Bruhl, Lucien. *How Natives Think*. Translated by Lilian Ada Clare. London: Routledge, 2018. First published in 1926.
———. *On Primitive Mentality*. Translated by Lilian Ada Clare. New York: AMS Press, 1978. First published in 1923.
Levy, Ernst. "Vulgarization of Roman Law in the Early Middle Ages as Illustrated by Successive Versions of *Pauli Sententiae*." *Medievalia et Humanistica* 1 (1943): 14–40.
Lewis, Nicola Denzey. "Popular Christianity and Lived Religion in Late Antique Rome: Seeing Magic in the Catacombs." In Grig, *Popular Culture in Ancient Rome*, 257–76.
Lewy, Yochanan, and Michel Tardieu. *Chaldaean Oracles and Theurgy: Mysticism, Magic and Platonism in the Later Roman Empire*. 2nd ed. Paris: Études Augustiniennes, 1978.
Leyser, Conrad. "Angels, Monks, and Demons in the Early Medieval West." In Gameson and Leyser, *Belief and Culture*, 9–22.
———. "Review Article: Church Reform-Full of Sound and Fury, Signifying Nothing?" *EME* 24, no. 4 (2016): 478–99.
Lifshitz, Felice. "Beyond Positivism and Genre: 'Hagiographical' Texts as Historical Narrative." *Viator*, 25 (1994): 95–113.
———. "Demonstrating Gun(t)za: Women, Manuscripts, and the Question of Historical 'Proof.'" In *Vom Nutzen des Schreibens: Soziales Gedächtnis, Herrschaft und Besitz im Mittelalter*, edited by Walter Pohl and Paul Herold, 67–96. Forschungen zur Geschichte des Mittelalters 5. Vienna: Österreichischen Akademie der Wissenschaften, 2002.
———. *The Norman Conquest of Pious Neustria: Historiographic Discourse and Saintly Relics 684–1090*. Studies and Texts 122. Toronto: Pontifical Institute of Mediaeval Studies, 1995.
———. *Religious Women in Early Carolingian Francia: A Study of Manuscript Transmission and Monastic Culture*. Fordham Series in Medieval Studies. New York: Fordham University Press, 2014.

Lindberg, David C. *The Beginnings of Western Science: The European Scientific Tradition in Philosophical, Religious, and Institutional Context, Prehistory to A.D. 1450*. 2nd ed. Chicago: University of Chicago Press, 2007. First published in 1992.

Liuzza, Roy Michael. "The Sphere of Life and Death: Time, Medicine, and the Visual Imagination." In *Latin Learning and English Lore*. Vol. 1. Studies in Anglo-Saxon Literature for Michael Lapidge, edited by Katherine O'Brien O'Keeffe and Andy Orchard, 28–52 Toronto Old English Series 14. Toronto: University of Toronto Press, 2005.

Lovejoy, Arthur O. *The Great Chain of Being: A Study of the History of an Idea: The William James Lectures Delivered at Harvard University, 1933*. Cambridge, MA: Harvard University Press, 1964. First published in 1936.

Löw, Martina. "The Social Construction of Space and Gender." Translated by Paul Knowlton. *European Journal of Women's Studies* 13, no. 2 (2006): 119–33.

Ludwikowska, Joanna. "Uncovering the Secret: Medieval Women, Magic and the Other." *Studia Anglica Posnaniensia* 49, no. 2 (2014): 83–103.

Luijendijk, AnneMarie. "'Only Do Not Be of Two Minds.'" In Luijendijk and Klingshirn, *My Lots are in Thy Hands*, 309–29.

Luijendijk, AnneMarie, and William E. Klingshirn, eds. *My Lots Are in Thy Hands: Sortilege and Its Practitioners in Late Antiquity*. Religions in the Graeco-Roman World 188. Leiden: Brill, 2019.

Lukes, Steven. "Power and Structure." In *Essays in Social Theory*, 3–29. New York: Columbia University Press, 1977.

MacAloon, John J., ed. *Rite, Drama, Festival, Spectacle: Rehearsals toward a Theory of Cultural Performance*. Philadelphia: Institute for the Study of Human Issues, 1984.

——. "Introduction: Cultural Performances, Culture Theory." In MacAloon, *Rite, Drama, Festival, Spectacle*, 1–15.

Macfarlane, A. D. J. "Definitions of Witchcraft." In *Witchcraft and Sorcery*, edited by Max Marwick, 41–44. 2nd ed. Harmondsworth, UK: Penguin, 1970.

MacKinney, Loren C. *Early Medieval Medicine with Special Reference to France and Chartres*. The Hideyo Noguchi Lectures. Publications of the Institute of the History of Medicine, The Johns Hopkins University 3. 3rd ser. Baltimore: Johns Hopkins Press, 1937.

MacLean, Simon, ed. *History and Politics in Late Carolingian and Ottonian Europe: The "Chronicle" of Regino of Prüm and Adalbert of Magdeburg*. Manchester Medieval Sources Series. Manchester: Manchester University Press, 2009.

——. "Ritual Misunderstanding, and the Contest of Meaning: Representations of the Disrupted Royal Assembly at Frankfurt (873)." In *Representations of Power in Medieval Germany 800–1500*, edited by Björn Weiler and Simon Maclean, 97–119. International Medieval Research 16. Turnhout, Belgium: Brepols, 2006.

MacMullen, Ramsay. *Christianity and Paganism in the Fourth to Eighth Centuries*. New Haven, CT: Yale University Press, 1997.

——. *Christianizing the Roman Empire (A.D. 100–400)*. New Haven, CT: Yale University Press, 1984.

——. *Paganism in the Roman Empire*. New Haven, CT: Yale University Press, 1981.

——. *The Second Church: Popular Christianity A.D. 200–400*. Writings from the Greco-Roman World Supplement Series 1. Atlanta: Society of Biblical Literature, 2009.

Macy, Gary. *The Hidden History of Women's Ordination: Female Clergy in the West.* Oxford: Oxford University Press, 2008.

Magennis, Hugh. "'Listen Now All and Understand': Adaptation of Hagiographical Material for Vernacular Audiences in the Old English Lives of St. Margaret." *Speculum* 71, no. 1 (1996): 27–42.

Maguire, Henry, ed. *Byzantine Magic.* Dumbarton Oaks Byzantine Studies. Washington, DC: Harvard University Press, 1995.

———. "Magic and Money in the Early Middle Ages." *Speculum* 72, no. 4 (1997): 1037–54.

Malinowski, Bronisław. "Magic, Science and Religion." In *Magic, Science and Religion and Other Essays,* 17–92. Prospect Heights, IL: Waveland, 1992. First published in 1948.

Markus, Robert A. "Augustine on Magic: A Neglected Semiotic Theory." *Revue des études Augustiniennes* 40 (1994): 375–88.

———. *The End of Ancient Christianity.* Cambridge, MA: Cambridge University Press, 1990.

———. "Gregory the Great and a Papal Missionary Strategy." In Cuming, *Mission of the Church,* 29–38.

———. *Gregory the Great and His World.* Cambridge: Cambridge University Press, 1997.

———. "Gregory the Great's Pagans." In Gameson and Leyser, *Belief and Culture,* 23–34.

Martin, Dale Basil. "When Did Angels Become Demons?" *Journal of Biblical Literature* 129, no. 4 (2010): 657–77.

Martin, Lawrence T. "The Two Worlds in Bede's Homilies: The Biblical Event and the Listeners' Experience." In Amos, Green, and Kienzle, *De ore domini,* 27–40.

Marwick, Max. "Some Problems in the Sociology of Sorcery and Witchcraft." In *African Systems of Thought: Studies Presented and Discussed at the Third International African Seminar in Salisbury, December, 1960,* edited by M. Fortes and G. Dieterlen, 171–91. London: Oxford University Press, 1965.

Mathisen, Ralph W. "Epistolography, Literary Circles and Family Ties in Late Roman Gaul." *Transactions of the American Philological Association* 111 (1981): 95–109.

Matthews, John. "The Making of the Text." In Harries and Wood, *Theodosian Code,* 19–44.

Mauss, Marcel. *A General Theory of Magic.* Translated by Robert Brain. London: Routledge & Kegan Paul, 1972.

Maxwell, Jaclyn L. *Christianization and Communication in Late Antiquity: John Chrysostom and His Congregation in Antioch.* Cambridge, MA: Cambridge University Press, 2006.

McCance, Dawne, ed. *Derrida on Religion: Thinker of Difference.* Key Thinkers in the Study of Religion. London: Routledge, 2009.

McCluskey, Stephen C. "Astronomies in the Latin West from the Fifth to the Ninth Centuries." In Butzer and Lohrmann, *Science in Western and Eastern Civilization,* 139–60.

———. "Gregory of Tours, Monastic Timekeeping, and Early Christian Attitudes to Astronomy." *Isis* 81, no. 1 (1990): 8–22.

McCormick, Michael. *Les annales de haut Moyen Âge.* Typologie des sources du Moyen Âge occidental 14. Turnhout, Belgium: Brepols, 1975.

McCready, William D. *Signs of Sanctity: Miracles in the Thought of Gregory the Great*. Studies and Texts 91. Toronto: Pontifical Institute of Mediaeval Studies, 1989.
McDaniel, Rhonda L. "Pride Goes before a Fall: Aldhelm's Practical Application of Gregorian and Cassianic Conceptions of *Superbia* and the Eight Principal Vices." In *The Seven Deadly Sins From Communities to Individuals*, edited by Richard Newhauser, 95–109. Studies in Medieval and Reformation Traditions: History, Culture, Religion, Ideas 123. Leiden: Brill, 2007.
McKitterick, Rosamond, ed. *Carolingian Culture: Emulation and Innovation*. Cambridge, MA: Cambridge University Press, 1994.
———. *The Carolingians and the Written Word*. Cambridge, MA: Cambridge University Press, 1989.
———. *Charlemagne: The Formation of a European Identity*. Cambridge, MA: Cambridge University Press, 2008.
———. "England and the Continent." In McKitterick, *New Cambridge Medieval History*, 64–84.
———. *The Frankish Church and the Carolingian Reforms, 789–895*. Royal Historical Society Studies in History 2. London: Royal Historical Society, 1977.
———. *The Frankish Kingdoms under the Carolingians, 751–987*. London: Longman, 1983.
———. "The Legacy of the Carolingians." In McKitterick, *Carolingian Culture: Emulation and Innovation*, 317–23.
———, ed. *The New Cambridge Medieval History, c. 700–c. 900*. Vol. 2. Cambridge: University of Cambridge Press, 1995.
McNamara, Jo Ann Kay. *Sisters in Arms: Catholic Nuns through Two Millennia*. Cambridge, MA: Harvard University Press, 1996.
McNamara, JoAnn Kay, and Suzanne F. Wemple. "Marriage and Divorce in the Frankish Kingdom." In *Women in Medieval Society*, edited by Susan M. Stuard, 95–124. Philadelphia: University of Pennsylvania Press, 1976.
Meaney, Audrey L. "Aelfric and Idolatry." *Journal of Religious History* 13 (1984): 119–35.
———. "Aethelweard, Aelfric, and the Norse Gods." *Journal of Religious History* 6, no. 2 (1970): 105–32.
———. *Anglo-Saxon Amulets and Curing Stones*. BAR British Series 96. Oxford: BAR, 1981.
———. "The Anglo-Saxon View of the Causes of Illness." In *Health, Disease, and Healing in Medieval Culture*, edited by Sheila D. Campbell, Bert S Hall, and David N. Klausner, 12–33. New York: St. Martin's Press, 1992.
———. "Variant Versions of Old English Medical Remedies and the Compilation of Bald's *Leechbook*." *Anglo-Saxon England* 13 (1984): 235–68.
———. "Women, Witchcraft and Magic in Anglo-Saxon England." In *Superstition and Popular Medicine in Anglo-Saxon England*, edited by D. G. Scragg, 9–40. Manchester: Centre for Anglo-Saxon Studies, University of Manchester, 1989.
Meens, Rob. "The Frequency and Nature of Early Medieval Penance." In *Handling Sin: Confession in the Middle Ages*, edited by Peter Biller and A. J. Minnis, 35–61. York Studies in Medieval Theology 2. Woodbridge, UK: York Medieval Press, 1998.
———. "The Historiography of Early Medieval Penance." In Firey, *New History of Penance*, 73–95.

———. "Magic and the Early Medieval World View." In Hill and Swan, *Community, the Family and the Saint*, 285–95.

———. *Penance in Medieval Europe, 600–1200*. Cambridge, MA: Cambridge University Press, 2014.

———. "Pollution in the Early Middle Ages: The Case of Food Regulations in Penitentials." *EME* 4, no. 1 (1995): 3–19.

———. "Thunder Over Lyon: Agobard, The Tempestarii and Christianity." In *Paganism in the Middle Ages: Threat and Fascination*, edited by Carlos Steel, John Marenbon, and Werner Verbeke. Leuven, Belgium: Leuven University Press, 2012.

Meens, Rob, Dorine van Espelo, Bram van den Hoven van Genderen, Janneke Raaijmakers, Irene van Renswoude, and Carine van Rhijn, eds. *Religious Franks: Religion and Power in the Frankish Kingdoms: Studies in Honour of Mayke de Jong*. Manchester: Manchester University Press, 2016.

Meerson, Michael. "Secondhand Homer." In Luijendijk and Klingshrin, *My Lots are in Thy Hands*, 138–53.

Melville, Gert. *The World of Medieval Monasticism: Its History and Forms of Life*. Translated by James D. Mixson. Cistercian Studies Series 263. Collegeville, MN: Liturgical Press, 2016.

Meslin, Michel. *La fête des kalendes de janvier dans l'empire romain: Étude d'un rituel de Nouvel An*. Collection Latomus 115. Brussels: Latomus, 1970.

Meyer, Marc Anthony. "Queens, Convents and Conversion in Early Anglo-Saxon England." *Revue bénédictine* 109, nos. 1–2 (1999): 90–116.

Milanezi, Silvia. "Pratiques et censures du rire et de la comédie en Grèce ancienne." *Revue européenne d'histoire* 2, no. 1 (1995): 7–18.

Mistry, Zubin. *Abortion in the Early Middle Ages, c. 500–900*. Woodbridge, UK: York Medieval, 2015.

Mitchell, David C. *The Songs of Ascents: Psalms 120 to 134 in the Worship of Jerusalem's Temples*. Newton Mearns, UK: Campbell Publications, 2015.

Momigliano, Arnaldo, ed. *The Conflict between Paganism and Christianity in the Fourth Century*. Oxford-Warburg Studies. Oxford: Clarendon, 1963.

———. "Pagan and Christian Historiography in the Fourth Century A.D." In Momigliano, *Conflict between Paganism and Christianity*, 79–99.

———. "Popular Religious Beliefs and the Late Roman Historians." In *Popular Belief and Practice: Papers Read at the Ninth Summer Meeting and the Tenth Winter Meeting of the Ecclesiastical History Society*, edited by G. J. Cuming and D. Baker, 1–18. Cambridge, MA: Cambridge University Press, 1972.

Monter, E. William. "The Historiography of European Witchcraft: Progress and Prospects." *Journal of Interdisciplinary History* 2, no. 4 (1972): 435–51.

Mordek, Hubert. "Kapitularien und Schriftlichkeit." In *Schriftkultur und Reichsverwaltung unter den Karolingern: Referate des Kolloquiums der Nordrhein–Westfälischen Akademie der Wissenschaften am 17.–18. Februar 1994 in Bonn*, edited by Rudolf Schieffer, 34–66. Abhandlungen der Nordrhein-Westfälischen Akademie der Wissenschaften 97. Opaden: Westdeutscher Verlag, 1996.

———. *Kirchenrecht und Reform im Frankenreich: Die Collectio vetus Gallica, die älteste systematische Kanonessammlung des fränkischen Gallien: Studien und Edition*. Beiträge zur Geschichte und Quellenkunde des Mittelalters 1. Berlin: De Gruyter, 1975.

———. "Recently Discovered Capitulary Texts Belonging to the Legislation of Louis the Pious." In Godman and Collins, *Charlemagne's Heir*, 437–53.
Moreira, Isabel. *Dreams, Visions, and Spiritual Authority in Merovingian Gaul*. Ithaca, NY: Cornell University Press, 2000.
Morse, Ruth. *Truth and Convention in the Middle Ages: Rhetoric, Representation, and Reality*. Cambridge, MA: Cambridge University Press, 1991.
Muhlberger, Steven. *The Fifth-Century Chroniclers: Prosper, Hydatius, and the Gallic Chronicler of 452*. ARCA Classical and Medieval Texts, Papers and Monographs 27. Leeds: Francis Cairns, 1990.
Muir, Edward. *Ritual in Early Modern Europe*. 2nd ed. New Approaches to European History 33. Cambridge, MA: Cambridge University Press, 2005.
Müller, Jörg. "Die Kirchenrechtssammlung des Bischofs Burchard I. von Worms." In Müller, Pinkert, and Seeboth, *Bischof Burchard I*, 162–81.
Müller, Thomas T., Maik Pinkert, and Anja Seeboth, eds. *Bischof Burchard I. in seiner Zeit: Tagungsband zum biographisch–landeskundlichen Kolloquium vom 13. bis 15. Oktober 2000 in Heilbad Heiligenstadt*. Beiträge aus den Archiven im Landkreis Eichsfeld 1. Heiligenstadt: Cordier, 2001.
Munn, Nancy D. "Symbolism in a Ritual Context: Aspects of Symbolic Action." In *Handbook of Social and Cultural Anthropology*, edited by John J. Honingmann, 579–612. Rand McNally Anthropology Series. Chicago: Rand McNally, 1973.
Murray, Alexander Callander. "Immunity, Nobility, and the Edict of Paris." *Speculum* 69, no. 1 (1994): 18–39.
———. "Missionaries and Magic in Dark-Age Europe." *Past and Present* 136 (August 1992): 186–205.
Murray, Margaret Alice. *The Witch-Cult in Western Europe*. Oxford: Clarendon, 1962. First published in 1921.
Muschiol, Gisela. "Men, Women and Liturgical Practice in the Early Medieval West." In Brubaker and Smith, *Gender in the Early Medieval World*, 198–216.
Myerhoff, Barbara G. "A Death in Due Time: Construction of Self and Culture in Ritual Drama." In MacAloon, *Rite, Drama, Festival, Spectacle*, 149–78.
Nadel, S. F. "Malinowski on Magic and Religion." In *Man and Culture: An Evaluation of the Work of Bronisław Malinowski*, edited by Raymond Firth, 189–208. London: Routledge & Kegan Paul, 1957.
Neidorf, Leonard, and Rafael J. Pascual. "The Language of *Beowulf* and the Conditioning of Kaluza's Law." *Neophilologus* 98, no. 4 (2014): 657–73.
Nelson, Janet L. "Carolingian Royal Funerals." In Theuws and Nelson, *Rituals of Power*, 131–84.
———. *Charles the Bald*. The Medieval World. London: Longman, 1992.
———. "Dispute Settlement in Carolingian West Francia." In Davies and Fouracre, *Settlement of Disputes*, 45–64.
———. *The Frankish World, 570–900*. London: Hambledon Press, 1996.
———. "Gendering Courts in the Early Medieval West." In Brubaker and Smith, *Gender in the Early Medieval World*, 185–97.
———. "Kingship and Empire in the Carolingian World." In McKitterick, *Carolingian Culture: Emulation and Innovation*, 52–87.
———. "Les femmes et l'évangélisation au IXe siècle." *Revue du Nord* 68, no. 269 (1986): 471–85.

———. "Organic Intellectuals in the Dark Ages?" *History Workshop Journal* 66 (Autumn 2008): 1–17.

———. "Public *Histories* and Private History in the Work of Nithard." *Speculum* 60, no. 2 (1985): 251–93.

———. "Queens as Jezebels: Brunhild and Balthild in Merovingian History." In *Politics and Ritual in Early Medieval Europe*, 1–48. London: Hambledon, 1986.

———. Review of *The Dangers of Ritual: Between Early Medieval Texts and Social Scientific Theory*, by Philippe Buc. *Speculum* 78, no, 3 (2003): 847–51.

———. "Society, Theodicy and the Origins of Heresy: Towards a Reassessment of the Medieval Evidence." In *Schism, Heresy and Religious Protest: Papers Read at the Tenth Summer Meeting and the Eleventh Winter Meeting of the Ecclesiastical History Society*, edited by Derek Baker, 65–77. Studies in Church History 9. Cambridge, MA: Cambridge University Press, 1972.

———. "Women at the Court of Charlemagne: A Case of Monstrous Regiment?" In *Medieval Queenship*, edited by John Carmi Parsons, 43–61. New York: St. Martin's, 1993.

Newlands, Carole E. "The Metamorphosis of Ovid's *Medea*." In Clauss and Johnston, *Medea*, 178–208.

Nickelsburg, George W. E. *1 Enoch 1: A Commentary on the Book of 1 Enoch, Chapters 1–36; 81–108*. Minneapolis, MN: Augsburg Fortress, 2001.

Nielsen, Svend, Jan Holme Andersen, Joel A. Baker, Charlie Christensen, Jens Glastrup, Pieter M. Grootes, Matthias Hüls, et al. "The Gundestrup Cauldron: New Scientific and Technical Investigations." *Acta Archaeologica* 76 (2005): 1–58.

Niermeyer, J. F., ed. *Mediae latinitatis lexicon minus: Lexique latin médiéval–français/anglais*. Leiden: Brill, 1997. First published in 1976.

Nisbet, Robert A. *Social Change and History: Aspects of the Western Theory of Development*. New York: Oxford University Press, 1969.

Noble, Thomas F. X. "Pope Nicholas I and the Franks: Politics and Ecclesiology in the Ninth Century." In Meens et al., *Religious Franks*, 472–88.

Noble, Thomas F. X., and Julia M. H. Smith, eds. *Early Medieval Christianities, c. 600–c. 1100*. Vol. 3 of *The Cambridge History of Christianity*. Cambridge, MA: Cambridge University Press, 2008.

Nock, Arthur Darby. "Paul and the Magus." *Essays on Religion and the Ancient World* 1 (1972): 308–30.

Nokes, Richard Scott. "The Several Compilers of Bald's 'Leechbook.'" *Anglo-Saxon England* 33 (2004): 51–76.

Nolte-Wolf, Cordula. "*Conversio* und *Cristianitas*: Frauen in der Christianisierung vom 5. bis 8. Jahrhundert." PhD diss., Freien Universität Berlin, 1993.

Noth, W. "Semiotics of the Old English Charm." *Semiotica* 19, nos. 1–2 (1977): 59–83.

Nussbaum, Martha C. "Serpents in the Soul: A Reading of Seneca's *Medea*." In Clauss and Johnston, *Medea*, 219–49.

O'Gorman, Ellen. "Detective Fiction and Historical Narrative." *Greece and Rome* 46 (1999): 19–26.

O'Hara, Alexander, ed. *Columbanus and the Peoples of Post-Roman Europe*. Oxford Studies in Late Antiquity. Oxford: Oxford University Press, 2018.

Olesiejko, Jacek. "Wealhtheow's Peace-Weaving: Diegesis and Genealogy of Gender in *Beowulf.*" *Studia Anglica Posnaniensia* 49, no. 1 (2014): 103–23.

Olsan, Lea. "The Inscription of Charms in Anglo-Saxon Manuscripts." *Oral Tradition* 14, no. 2 (1999): 401–19.

Olsen, Glenn W. "Marriage in Barbarian Kingdom and Christian Court: Fifth through Eleventh Centuries." In *Christian Marriage: A Historical Study*, edited by Glenn W. Olsen, 146–212. New York: Crossroad, 2001.

O'Malley, John W. "Introduction: Medieval Preaching." In Amos, Green, and Kienzle, *De ore domini*, 1–11.

Osborn, Marijane. "Anglo-Saxon Ethnobotany: Women's Reproductive Medicine in *Leechbook III*." In *Health and Healing from the Medieval Garden*, edited by Peter Dendle and Alain Touwaide, 145–61. Woodbridge, UK: Boydell, 2008.

Owen-Crocker, Gale R. "Beast Men: Wulf and Eofor and the Mythic Significance of Names in Beowulf." In Glosecki, *Myth in Early Northwest Europe*, 257–80.

Pagels, Elaine. *Adam, Eve, and the Serpent*. New York: Vintage Books, 1989. First published in 1988.

———. *Beyond Belief: The Secret Gospel of Thomas*. New York: Vintage Books, 2003.

———. *The Gnostic Gospels*. New York: Random House, 1979.

———. "The Social History of Satan, Part Three: John of Patmos and Ignatius of Antioch: Contrasting Visions of 'God's People.'" *Harvard Theological Review* 99, no. 4 (2006): 487–505.

Palmer, James T. *Anglo-Saxons in a Frankish World 690–900*. Studies in the Early Middle Ages 19. Turnhout, Belgium: Brepols, 2009.

———. "Defining Paganism in the Carolingian World." *EME* 15, no. 4 (2007): 402–25.

Parisse, Michel. *Les nonnes au Moyen Âge*. Le Puy, France: Bonneton, 1983.

———. "Noblesse et monastères en Lotharingie du IXe au XIe siècle." In Kottje and Maurer, *Monastische Reformen im 9. und 10. Jahrhundert*, 167–96.

Patai, Raphael. *The Hebrew Goddess*. 3rd ed. Jewish Folklore and Anthropology. Detroit: Wayne State University Press, 1990.

Patlagean, Evelyne. "Ancient Byzantine Hagiography and Social History." In *Saints and Their Cults: Studies in Religious Sociology, Folklore and History*, edited by Stephen Wilson, 101–21. Cambridge, MA: Cambridge University Press, 1983.

Paxton, Frederick S. *Christianizing Death: The Creation of a Ritual Process in Early Medieval Europe*. Ithaca, NY: Cornell University Press, 1990.

Payer, Pierre J. *Sex and the Penitentials: The Development of a Sexual Code, 550–1150*. Toronto: University of Toronto Press, 1984.

Peirce, Charles S. *Philosophical Writings of Peirce*. Edited by Justus Buchler. New York: Dover Books, 1955. First published in 1940.

Pelikan, Jaroslav. *Mary through the Centuries: Her Place in the History of Culture*. New Haven, CT: Yale University Press, 1996.

———. *The Shape of Death: Life, Death, and Immortality in the Early Fathers*. Westport, CT: Greenwood, 1978. First published in 1961.

Pestell, Tim. *Landscapes of Monastic Foundation: The Establishment of Religious Houses in East Anglia, c. 650–1200*. Anglo-Saxon Studies 5. Woodbridge, UK: Boydell, 2004.

Peters, Edward. *The Magician, the Witch, and the Law*. The Middle Ages. Philadelphia: University of Pennsylvania Press, 1978.

Petersen, Nils Holger. "Carolingian Music, Ritual, and Theology." In Petersen et al., *Appearances of Medieval Rituals*, 13–31.

Petersen, Nils Holger, Mette Birkedal Bruun, Jeremy Llewellyn, and Eyolf Østrem, eds. *The Appearances of Medieval Rituals: The Play of Construction and Modification*. Disputatio 3. Turnhout, Belgium: Brepols, 2004.

Petkov, Kiril. "The Cultural Career of a 'Minor' Vice: Arrogance in the Medieval Treatise on Sin." In *Sin in Medieval and Early Modern Culture: The Tradition of the Seven Deadly Sins,* edited by Richard G. Newhauser and Susan J. Ridyard, 43–64. York: York Medieval Press, 2012.

Petts, David. *Pagan and Christian: Religious Change in Early Medieval Europe*. Debates in Archeology. London: Bristol Classical, 2011.

Petzoldt, Leander. "Magie und Religion." In *Volksreligion im hohen und späten Mittelalter*, edited by Peter Dinzelbacher and Dieter R. Bauer, 467–85. Quellen und Forschungen aus dem Gebiet der Geschichte 13. Paderborn, DE: Schöningh, 1990.

Peyroux, Catherine. Review of *Matrology: A Bibliography of Writings by Christian Women from the First to the Fifteenth Centuries*, by Andrew Kadel. *Speculum* 72, no. 3 (1997): 844–45.

Phillips, L. Edward. "Prayer in the First Four Centuries A.D." In *A History of Prayer: The First to the Fifteenth Century*, edited by Roy Hammerling, 31–58. Brill's Companions to the Christian Tradition 13. Leiden: Brill, 2008.

Pierce, Rosamond. "The Frankish Penitentials." *Studies in Church History* 11 (1975): 31–39.

Pintel-Ginsberg, Idit. "Lilith." In *Encyclopedia of Jewish Folklore and Traditions*, edited by Raphael Patai and Haya Bar–Itzhak; 332–35. Armonk, NY: M. E. Sharpe, 2013.

Pössel, Christina. "The Magic of Early Medieval Ritual." *EME* 17, no. 2 (2009): 111–25.

Poulin, Joseph-Claude. *Entre magie et religion: Recherches sur les utilisations marginales de l'écrit dans la culture populaire du Haut Moyen Âge*. Montréal: L'Aurore, 1997.

———. *L'idéal de sainteté dans l'Aquitaine carolingienne: D'après les sources hagiographiques 750–950*. Québec: Les Presses de l'Université Laval, 1975.

Rajak, Tessa. "Talking at Trypho: Christian Apologetic as Anti-Judaism in Justin's *Dialogue with Trypho the Jew*." In Edwards et al., *Apologetics in the Roman Empire*, 59–80.

Rampton, Martha. "Burchard of Worms and Female Magical Ritual." In *Medieval and Early Modern Ritual: Formalized Behavior in Europe, China and Japan*, edited by Joelle Rollo-Koster, 7–34. Leiden: Brill, 2002.

———. "Frankish Holy Women as Makers of Miracles." In *Earthly Love, Spiritual Love, Love of the Saints*, edited by Susan J. Ridyard, 243–68. Sewanee Medieval Studies 8. Sewanee, TN: University of the South Press, 1999.

———. "The Gender of Magic in the Early Middle Ages." PhD diss., University of Virginia, 1998.

———. "Love and the Divorce of Lothar II." In *On the Shoulders of Giants: Essays in Honor of Glenn W. Olsen*. Edited by Teresa Olsen Pierre and David F. Appleby, 91–115. Papers in Mediaeval Studies 27. Toronto: Pontifical Institute of Mediaeval Studies, 2015.

———. "Mary the Virgin." In *Women in World History: A Biographical Encyclopedia*, edited by Anne Commire and Deborah Klezmer, 561–75. Vol. 10. Waterford, CT: Yorkin, 2001.

———. Review of *"Charms," Liturgies, and Secret Rites in Early Medieval England*, by Ciaran Arthur. *The Medieval Review* (September 2018).

———. "Up from the Dead: Magic and Miracle." In *Death and Dying in the Middle Ages*, edited by Edelgard E. DuBruck and Barbara I. Gusick, 7–34. New York: Peter Lang, 1999.

Rappaport, Roy A. *Ecology, Meaning and Religion*. Richmond, CA: North Atlantic Books, 1979.

Reed, Annette Yoshiko. "The Trickery of the Fallen Angels and the Demonic Mimesis of the Divine: Aetiology, Demonology, and Polemics in the Writings of Justin Martyr." *Journal of Early Christian Studies* 12, no. 2 (2004): 141–71.

Reimitz, Helmut. *History, Frankish Identity and the Framing of Western Ethnicity, 550–850*. Cambridge Studies in Medieval Life and Thought 101. 4th ser. Cambridge, MA: Cambridge University Press, 2015.

Rembold, Ingrid. *Conquest and Christianization: Saxony and the Carolingian World, 772–888*. Cambridge Studies in Medieval Life and Thought 108, 4th ser. Cambridge: Cambridge University Press, 2018.

Renehan, Robert. "The Staunching of Odysseus' Blood: The Healing Powers of Magic." *American Journal of Philology* 113, no. 1 (1992): 1–4.

Rezeanu, Ca?ta?lina-Ionela. "The Relationship between Domestic Space and Gender Identity: Some Signs of Emergence of Alternative Domestic Femininity and Masculinity." *Journal of Comparative Research in Anthropology and Sociology* 6, no. 2 (2015): 9–29.

Riché, Pierre. *The Carolingians: A Family Who Forged Europe*. Translated by Michael Idomir Allen. The Middle Ages. Philadelphia: University of Pennsylvania Press, 1993.

———. *Daily Life in the World of Charlemagne*. Translated by Jo Ann McNamara. The Middle Ages. Philadelphia: University of Pennsylvania Press, 1988. First published in 1973.

———. *Education and Culture in the Barbarian West, Sixth through the Eighth Centuries*. Translated by John J. Contreni. Columbia: University of South Carolina Press, 1976.

Ricoeur, Paul. "The Model of the Text: Meaningful Action Considered as a Text." *New Literary History* 5 (What is Literature?), no. 1 (1973): 91–117.

———. "The Symbol Gives Rise to Thought." In *Ways of Understanding Religion*, edited by Walter H. Capps, 309–17. New York: Macmillan, 1972.

Riddle, John M. *Contraception and Abortion from the Ancient World to the Renaissance*. Cambridge, MA: Harvard University Press, 1992.

———. "Theory and Practice in Medieval Medicine." *Viator* 5 (Summer 1974): 157–84.

Rider, Catherine. *Magic and Impotence in the Middle Ages*. Oxford: Oxford University Press, 2006.

Ristuccia, Nathan J. *Christianization and Commonwealth in Early Medieval Europe: A Ritual Interpretation*. Oxford: Oxford University Press, 2018.

Roach, Levi. *Kingship and Consent in Anglo-Saxon England, 871–978: Assemblies and the State in the Early Middle Ages*. Cambridge Studies in Medieval Life and Thought. 4th ser. Cambridge: Cambridge University Press, 2013.

Robinson, Thomas A. *Who Were the First Christians?: Dismantling the Urban Thesis.* Oxford: Oxford University Press, 2017.
Rollo-Koster, Joelle. Review of *The Dangers of Ritual: Between Early Medieval Texts and Social Scientific Theory,* by Philippe Buc. *The Medieval Review* (February 2001).
Rose, Els. *Ritual Memory: The Apocryphal Acts and Liturgical Commemoration in the Ealry Medieval West (c. 500–1215).* Mittellateinische Studien und Texte 40. Leiden: Brill, 2009.
Rousseau, Philip. "Late Roman Christianities." In Noble and Smith, *Early Medieval Christianities,* 21–45.
Rubin, Miri. *Mother of God: A History of the Virgin Mary.* New Haven, CT: Yale University Press, 2009.
Russell, James. "The Archaeological Context of Magic in the Early Byzantine Period." In Maguire, *Byzantine Magic,* 35–50.
Russell, Jeffrey Burton. *Lucifer: The Devil in the Middle Ages.* Ithaca, NY: Cornell University Press, 1984.
———. *Witchcraft in the Middle Ages.* Ithaca, NY: Cornell University Press, 1972.
Russom, Geoffrey. "At the Center of *Beowulf.*" In Glosecki, *Myth in Early Northwest Europe,* 225–40.
Salzman, Michele Renee. *The Making of a Christian Aristocracy: Social and Religious Change in the Western Roman Empire.* Cambridge, MA: Harvard University Press, 2002.
———. "'Superstitio' in the Codex Theodosianus and the Persecution of Pagans." *Vigiliae Christianae* 41, no. 2 (1987): 172–88.
Sax, William S. "Ritual and the Problem of Efficacy." In *The Problem of Ritual Efficacy,* edited by William S. Sax, Johannes Quack, and Jan Weinhold, 3–16. Oxford Ritual Studies. Oxford: Oxford University Press, 2010.
Scarborough, John. *Roman Medicine.* Aspects of Greek and Roman Life. Ithaca, NY: Cornell University Press, 1969.
Scarre, Geoffrey. *Witchcraft and Magic in Sixteenth- and Seventeenth-Century Europe.* Basingstoke, UK: Palgrave, 2001. First published in 1987.
Schäfer, Peter. *The Hidden and Manifest God: Some Major Themes of Early Jewish Mysticism.* Translated by Aubrey Pomerance. Albany: State University of New York Press, 1992.
———. "Jewish Magic Literature in Late Antiquity and Early Middle Ages." *Journal of Jewish Studies* 41, no. 4 (1990): 75–91.
Scharer, Anton. "La conversion des rois anglo-saxons." In *Clovis histoire et mémoire: Le baptême de Clovis, l'événement,* edited by Michel Rouche, 881–98. Paris: Presses de l'Université de Paris-Sorbonne, 1997.
Schieffer, Rudolf. *Die Karolinger.* 4th edition. Stuttgart: W. Kohlhammer, 2006. First published in 1992.
———. "Neue Bonifatius-Literatur." *Deutsches Archiv für Erforschung des Mittelalters* 63, no. 1 (2007): 111–23.
Schilderman, Hans, ed. *Discourse in Ritual Studies.* Empirical Studies in Theology 14. Leiden: Brill, 2007.
Schmitt, Jean-Claude. *Les revenants: Les vivants et les morts dans la société médiévale.* Paris: Gallimard, 1994.

Schmitz, Gerhard. "The Capitulary Legislation of Louis the Pious." In Godman and Collins, *Charlemagne's Heir*, 425–36.

Schneidmüller, Bernd. "Widukind von Corvey, Richer von Reims und der Wandel politischen Bewusstseins im 10. Jahrhundert." In *Beiträge zur mittelalterlichen Reichs- und Nationsbildung in Deutschland und Frankreich*, edited by Carlrichard Brühl and Bernd Schneidmüller, 83–102. Historische Zeitschrift 24. Munich: Oldenbourg, 1997.

Schulenburg, Jane Tibbetts. *Forgetful of Their Sex: Female Sanctity and Society ca. 500–1100*. Chicago: University of Chicago Press, 1998.

——. "Strict Active Enclosure and Its Effects on the Female Monastic Experience (ca. 500–1100)." In *Medieval Religious Women*. Vol. 1 *Distant Echoes*, edited by John A. Nichols and Lillian Thomas Shank, 51–86. Cistercian Studies Series 71. Kalamazoo, MI: Cistercian, 1984.

——. "Women's Monastic Communities, 500–1100: Patterns of Expansion and Decline." In Bennett et al., *Sisters and Workers in the Middle Ages*, 208–39.

Schoolman, Edward M. *Rediscovering Sainthood in Italy: Hagiography and the Late Antique Past in Medieval Ravenna*. New Middle Ages. New York: Palgrave Macmillan, 2016.

Searle, John. *Speech Acts: An Essay in the Philosophy of Language*. Cambridge, MA: Cambridge University Press, 1969.

Segal, Alan F. "Hellenistic Magic: Some Questions of Definition." In *Studies in Gnosticism and Hellenistic Religions: Presented to Gilles Quispel on the Occasion of his 65th Birthday*, edited by R. Van den Broek and M. J. Vermaseren, 349–75. Études préliminaires aux religions orientales dans l'Empire Romain 91. Leiden: Brill, 1981.

Semmler, Josef. "Das Erbe der karolingischen Klosterreform im 10. Jahrhundert." In Kottje and Maurer, *Monastische Reformen im 9. und 10. Jahrhundert*, 29–77.

Shaw, Gregory. "Neoplatonic Theurgy and Dionysius the Areopagite." *Journal of Early Christian Studies* 7, no. 4 (1999): 573–99.

——. *Theurgy and the Soul: The Neoplatonism of Iamblichus*. Hermeneutics: Studies in the History of Religions. University Park: Pennsylvania State University Press, 1995.

——. "Theurgy: Rituals of Unification in the Neoplatonism of Iamblichus." *Traditio* 41 (1985): 1–28.

Shaw, Patrick A. *Pagan Goddesses in the Early Germanic World: Eostre, Hreda and the Cult of Matrons*. Studies in Early Medieval History. London: Bristol Classical, 2011.

Shoemaker, Stephen J. "Epiphanius of Salamis, the Kollyridians, and the Early Dormition Narratives: The Cult of the Virgin in the Fourth Century." *Journal of Early Christian Studies* 16, no. 3 (2008): 371–401.

Sigerist, Henry E. *A History of Medicine*. 2 vols. Yale Medical Library. Historical Library 27. Yale University. Department of the History of Medicine 38. New York: Oxford University Press, 1967. First published in 1951.

Singer, Charles. *From Magic to Science: Essays on the Scientific Twilight*. New York: Dover, 1958. First published in 1928.

Siraisi, Nancy G. *Medieval and Early Renaissance Medicine: An Introduction to Knowledge and Practice*. Chicago: University of Chicago Press, 1990.

Sirks, Boudewijn. "The Sources of the Code." In Harries and Wood, *Theodosian Code*, 45–67.
Skinner, Patricia. "A Cure for a Sinner: Sickness and Healthcare in Medieval Southern Italy." In Hill and Swan, *Community, the Family and the Saint*, 297–309.
Smith, Jonathan Z. *To Take Place: Toward Theory in Ritual*. Chicago Studies in the History of Judaism. Chicago: University of Chicago Press, 1987.
Smith, Julia M. H. "Did Women Have a Transformation of the Roman World?" *Gender and History* 12, no. 3 (2002): 552–71.
———. *Europe after Rome: A New Cultural History, 500–1000*. Oxford: Oxford University Press, 2005.
———. "Gender and Ideology in the Early Middle Ages." *Studies in Church History* 34 (1998): 51–73.
———. "The Problem of Female Sanctity in Carolingian Europe, c. 780–920." *Past and Present* 146, no. 1 (1995): 3–37.
Smith, Julie Ann. *Ordering Women's Lives: Penitentials and Nunnery Rules in the Early Medieval West*. Aldershot, UK: Ashgate, 2001.
Smith, Morton. *Jesus the Magician*. San Francisco: Harper & Row, 1978.
Smith, Rowland. *Julian's Gods: Religion and Philosophy in the Thought and Action of Julian the Apostate*. London: Routledge, 1995.
Sowerby, Richard. *Angels in Early Medieval England*. Oxford Theology and Religion Monographs. Oxford: Oxford University Press, 2016.
Spickermann, Wolfgang. "Interpretatio Romana? Zeugnisse der Religion von Römern, Kelten und Germanen im Rheingebiet bis zum Ende des Bataveraufstandes." In *Die frühe römische Kaiserzeit im Ruhrgebiet*, edited by Detlef Hopp, 94–106. Essen: Klartext, 2001.
Stafford, Pauline. *Queens, Concubines, and Dowagers: The King's Wife in the Early Middle Ages*. Women, Power and Politics. London: Leicester University Press, 1998.
Stanley, Christopher D. "Paul and Asklepios: The Greco-Roman Quest for Healing and the Mission of Paul." *Journal for the Study of the New Testament* 41, no. 3 (2019): 279–309.
Staubach, Nikolaus. "'Des grossen Kaisers kleiner Sohn': Zum Bild Ludwigs des Frommen in der älteren deutschen Geschichtsforschung." In Godman and Collins, *Charlemagne's Heir*, 701–21.
Stevens, Wesley. "Alternatives to Ptolemy: Astronomy in Carolingian Schools." In *Dimensions of Time*, edited by Maureen Muldoon, 1–22. Working Papers in the Humanities 8. Windsor, Canada: University of Windsor, 1999.
Stock, Brian. *The Implications of Literacy: Written Language and Models of Interpretation in the Eleventh and Twelfth Centuries*. Princeton, NJ: Princeton University Press, 1983.
Story, Joanna. "Cathwulf, Kingship, and the Royal Abby of Saint-Denis." *Speculum* 74, no. 1 (1999): 1–21.
———. "Charlemagne and the Anglo-Saxons." In *Charlemagne: Empire and Society*, edited by Joanna Story, 195–210. Manchester: Manchester University Press, 2005.
Stratton, Kimberly B., and Dayna S. Kalleres, eds. *Daughters of Hecate: Women and Magic in the Ancient World*. Oxford: Oxford University Press, 2014.

Strayer, Joseph R., ed. *Dictionary of the Middle Ages*. New York: Scribner, 1982–89.
Struck, Peter T. "The Poet as Conjurer: Magic and Literary Theory in Late Antiquity." In *Magic and Divination in the Ancient World*, edited by Leda Ciraolo and Jonathan Seidel, 119–31. Ancient Magic and Divination 2. Leiden: Brill, 2002.
Summers-Effler, Erika. *Laughing Saints and Righteous Heroes: Emotional Rhythms in Social Movement Groups*. Morality and Society. Chicago: University of Chicago Press, 2010.
Tambiah, Stanley Jeyaraja. *Culture, Thought, and Social Action: An Anthropological Perspective*. Cambridge, MA: Harvard University Press, 1985.
——. "The Magic Power of Words." *Man*, n.s., 3, no. 2 (1968): 175–208.
——. *Magic, Science, Religion, and the Scope of Rationality*. Lewis Henry Morgan Lectures 1984. Cambridge, MA: Cambridge University Press, 1990.
——. "A Performative Approach to Ritual." Radcliffe-Brown Lecture in SocialAnthropology. *Proceedings of the British Academy* 65 (1979): 113–69. London: British Academy, 1981.
Thee, Francis C. R. *Julius Africanus and the Early Christian View of Magic*. Hermeneutische Untersuchungen zur Theologie 19. Tübingen: Mohr Siebeck, 1984.
Theuws, Frans. "Introduction: Rituals in Transforming Societies." In Theuws and Nelson, *Rituals of Power*, 1–13.
Theuws, Frans, and Janet L. Nelson, eds. *Rituals of Power from Late Antiquity to the Early Middle Ages*. The Transformation of the Roman World 8. Leiden: Brill, 2000.
Thomas, Keith. "The Relevance of Social Anthropology to the Historical Study of English Witchcraft." In Douglas, *Witchcraft Confessions and Accusations*, 47–79.
——. *Religion and the Decline of Magic: Studies in Popular Beliefs in Sixteenth- and Seventeenth-Century England*. New York, Oxford University Press, 1997. First published in 1971.
Thorndike, Lynn. *A History of Magic and Experimental Science: During the First Thirteen Centuries of Our Era*. 8 vols. New York: Columbia University Press, 1923–58.
Thurston, H., ed. *The Catholic Encyclopedia*. New York: Robert Appleton Company, 1912.
Timmermann, Josh. "An Authority Among Authorities: Knowledge and Use of Augustine in the Wider Carolingian World." *EME* 28, no. 4 (2020), 532–59.
Trahern, J. B., Jr. "Caesarius of Arles and Old English Literature." *Anglo-Saxon England* 5 (1976): 105–19.
Treffort, Cécile. "Consécration de cimetière et contrôle épiscopal des lieux d'inhumation au Xe siècle." In Kaplan, *Le sacré et son inscription*, 285–99.
Tremp, Ernst. "Thegan und Astronomus, die beiden Geschichtsschreiber Ludwigs des Frommen." In Godman and Collins, *Charlemagne's Heir*, 691–700.
Trevett, Christine. *Montanism: Gender, Authority and the New Prophecy*. Cambridge, MA: Cambridge University Press, 1996.
Trevor-Roper, H. R. *The European Witch-Craze of the Sixteenth and Seventeenth Centuries*. London: Penguin, 1990. First published in 1967.
Truitt, E. R. *Medieval Robots: Mechanism, Magic, Nature, and Art*. The Middle Ages. Philadelphia: University of Pennsylvania Press, 2015.

Turner, Victor W. *Dramas, Fields, and Metaphors: Symbolic Action in Human Society*. Symbol, Myth, and Ritual Series. Ithaca, NY: Cornell University Press, 1974.
———. *The Forest of Symbols: Aspects of Ndembu Ritual*. Ithaca, NY: Cornell University Press, 1967.
———. "Liminality and the Performative Genres." In MacAloon, *Rite, Drama, Festival, Spectacle*, 19–41.
———. *The Ritual Process: Structure and Anti-Structure*. Symbol, Myth, and Ritual Series. Ithaca, NY: Cornell University Press, 1977. First published in 1969.
———. *Schism and Continuity in an African Society: A Study of Ndembu Village Life*. Classic Reprints in Anthropology. Oxford: Berg. 1996. Originally published in 1957.
Turpin, W. "The Law Codes and Late Roman Law." *Revue internationale des droits de l'antiquité* 32, no. 3 (1985): 339–53.
Tylor, Edward Burnett. *Primitive Culture: Researches into the Development of Mythology, Philosophy, Religion, Language, Art and Custom*. 3rd American ed. Vol. 1. New York: Holt, 1889.
Ubl, Karl. *Inzestverbot und Gesetzgebung: Die Konstruktion eines Verbrechens (300–1100)*. Millennium-Studien zu Kultur und Geschichte des ersten Jahrtausends n. Chr. 20. Berlin: De Gruyter, 2008.
Uhalde, Kevin. "Juridical Administration in the Church and Pastoral Care in Late Antiquity." In Firey, *New History of Penance*, 97–120.
Uszkalo, Kirsten C. "Rage Possession: A Cognitive Science Approach to Early English Demon Possession." In Crawford and Lee, *Bodies of Knowledge*, 5–17.
Van Dam, Raymond. *Saints and Their Miracles in Late Antique Gaul*. Princeton, NJ: Princeton University Press, 1993.
van der Horst, Pieter W. "Pious Long-Sleepers in Greek, Jewish, and Christian Antiquity." In *Tradition, Transmission, and Transformation from Second Temple Literature through Judaism and Christianity in Late Antiquity: Proceedings of the Thirteenth International Symposium of the Orion Center for the Study of the Dead Sea Scrolls and Associated Literature, Jointly Sponsored by the Hebrew University Center for the Study of Christianity, 22–24 February, 2011*, edited by Menahem Kister, Hillel I. Newman, Michael Segal, and Ruth A. Clements, 93–111. Studies on the Texts of the Desert of Judah 113. Leiden: Brill, 2015.
VanderKam, James C. "1 Enoch, Enochic Motifs, and Enoch in Early Christian Literature." In *The Jewish Apocalyptic Heritage in Early Christianity*, edited by James C. VanderKam and William Adler, 33–101. Jewish Traditions in Early Christian Literature 4. Minneapolis, MN: Fortress, 1996.
Van Straten, F. T. "Gifts for the Gods." In *Faith, Hope and Worship: Aspects of Religious Mentality in the Ancient World*, edited by H. S. Versnel, 61–151. Studies in Greek and Roman Religion 2. Leiden: Brill, 1981.
Veenstra, Jan. R. "The Ever-Changing Nature of the Beast: Cultural Change, Lycanthropy and the Question of Substantial Transformation (from Petronius to Del Rio)." In Bremmer and Veenstra, *Metamorphosis of Magic*, 133–66.
Venarde, Bruce L. *Women's Monasticism and Medieval Society: Nunneries in France and England, 890–1215*. Ithaca, NY: Cornell University Press, 1997.
Versnel, H. S. "Some Reflections on the Relationship: Magic-Religion." *Numen* 38, no. 2 (1991): 177–97.

Vogel, Cyrille. *La discipline pénitentielle en Gaule des origines à la fin du VIIe siècle*. Paris: Letouzey et Ané, 1952.

———. *Les "Libri paenitentiales."* Typologie des sources du Moyen Âge occidental 27. Turnhout, Belgium: Brepols, 1978.

———. "Pratiques superstitieuses au début du XIe siècle d'après le *Corrector sive medicus* de Burchard, évêque de Worms (925–1025)." In *Études de civilisation médiévale (IXe–XIIe siècles): Mélanges offerts à Edmond-René Labande à l'occasion de son départ à la retraite et du XX*, 751–61. Poitiers: CÉSCM, 1974.

Voigts, Linda E. "Anglo-Saxon Plant Remedies and the Anglo-Saxons." *Isis* 70, no. 2 (1979): 250–68.

Vollrath, Hanna. *Die Synoden Englands bis 1066*. Konziliengeschichte. Paderborn, Germany: Schöningh, 1985.

Vos, Nienke. "Demons Without and Within: The Representation of Demons, the Saint, and the Soul in Early Christian Lives, Letters and Sayings." In *Demons and the Devil in Ancient and Medieval Christianity*, edited by Nienke Vos and Willemien Otten, 159–82. Supplements to *Vigiliae Christianae*. Texts and Studies of Early Christian Life and Language 108. Leiden: Brill, 2011.

Wagner, Karen. "*Cum aliquis venerit ad sacerdotem*: Penitential Experience in the Central Middle Ages." In Firey, *New History of Penance*, 201–18.

Walker, P. W. L. *Holy City, Holy Places?: Christian Attitudes to Jerusalem and the Holy Land in the Fourth Century*. Oxford Early Christian Studies. Oxford: Clarendon Press, 1990.

Wallis, Faith. "Medicine in Medieval Calendar Manuscripts." In *Manuscript Sources of Medieval Medicine: A Book of Essays*, edited by Margaret R. Schleissner, 105–43. Garland Medieval Casebooks 8. Garland Reference Library of the Humanities 1576. New York: Garland, 1995.

Walsham, Alexandra. Review of *The Dangers of Ritual: Between Early Medieval Texts and Social Scientific Theory*, by Philippe Buc. *Past & Present* 180, no. 1 (2003): 277–87.

Van Uytfanghe, Marc. "L'hagiographie et son public à l'époque mérovingienne." Papers Presented to the Seventh International Conference on Patristic Studies held in Oxford 1975, edited by Elizabeth A. Livingstone, 54–62. Studia Patristica 16. Texte und Untersuchungen zur Geschichte der altchristlichen Literatur 129. Berlin: Akademie, 1985.

Ward, Elizabeth. "Agobard of Lyons and Paschasius Radbertus as Critics of the Empress Judith." *Studies in Church History* 27 (1990): 15–25.

———. "Caesar's Wife: The Career of the Empress Judith, 819–829." In Godman and Collins, *Charlemagne's Heir*, 205–27.

Ward-Perkins, Bryan. "Reconfiguring Sacred Space: From Pagan Shrines to Christian Churches." *Die spätantike Stadt und ihre Christianisierung: Symposion vom 14. Bis 16. Februar 2000 in Halle/Saale*, 285–90. Wiesbaden: Reichert, 2003.

Warner, David A. "Ritual and Memory in the Ottonian *Reich*: The Ceremony of *Adventus*." *Speculum* 76, no. 2 (2001): 255–83.

Weiss, Hans-Friedrich. *Frühes Christentum und Gnosis: Eine rezeptionsgeschichtliche Studie*. Wissenschaftliche Untersuchungen zum Neuen Testament 225. Tübingen: Mohr Siebeck, 2008.

Weltin, E. G. "The Concept of *Ex-Opere-Operato* Efficacy in the Fathers as an Evidence of Magic in Early Christianity." *Greek, Roman, and Byzantine Studies* 3, no. 2/3 (1960): 74–100.

Wemple, Suzanne Fonay. *Women in Frankish Society: Marriage and the Cloister, 500 to 900*. The Middle Ages. Philadelphia: University of Pennsylvania Press, 1981.

Werblowsky, R. J. Zwi, and Geoffrey Wigoder, eds. *The Oxford Dictionary of the Jewish Religion*. New York: Oxford University Press, 1997.

Weston, L. M. C. "Women's Medicine, Women's Magic: The Old English Metrical Childbirth Charms." *Modern Philology* 92, no. 3 (1995): 279–93.

Whitehouse, Harvey, and James Laidlaw, eds. *Ritual and Memory: Toward a Comparative Anthropology of Religion*. Cognitive Science of Religion Series. Walnut Creek, CA: AltaMira, 2004.

Wickham, Chris. *Framing the Early Middle Ages: Europe and the Mediterranean, 400–800*. Oxford: Oxford University Press, 2005.

Wilken, Robert Louis. *The First Thousand Years: A Global History of Christianity*. New Haven, CT: Yale University Press, 2012.

———. *The Land Called Holy: Palestine in Christian History and Thought*. New Haven, CT: Yale University Press, 1992.

Williams, Craig. "Perpetua's Gender: A Latinist Reads the *Passio Perpetuae et Felicitatis*." In *Perpetua's Passions: Multidisciplinary Approaches to the "Passio Perpetuae et Felicitatis,"* edited by Jan N. Bremmer and Marco Formisano, 54–77. Oxford: Oxford University Press, 2012.

Wils, Jean-Pierre. "From Ritual to Hermeneutics. An Exploration with Ethical Intent." In Schilderman, *Discourse in Ritual Studies*, 257–75.

Wilson, Monica Hunter. "Witch Beliefs and Social Structure." *American Journal of Sociology* 56, no. 4 (1951): 307–13.

Wiśniewski, Robert. "Pagan Temples, Christians, and Demons in the Late Antique East and West." *Sacris Erudiri* 54 (2015): 111–28.

Wittgenstein, Ludwig. *Remarks on Frazer's "Golden Bough."* Edited by Rush Rhees. Translation by A. C. Miles. Doncaster, UK: Brynmill, 1979.

Wood, Ian. "Administration, Law, and Culture in Merovingian Gaul." In *The Uses of Literacy in Early Medieval Europe*, edited by Rosamond McKitterick, 63–81. Cambridge, MA: University of Cambridge Press, 1990.

———. "The Code in Merovingian Gaul." In Harries and Wood, *Theodosian Code*, 161–77.

———. "Disputes in Late Fifth- and Sixth-Century Gaul: Some Problems." In Davies and Fouracre, *Settlement of Disputes*, 7–22.

———. "Gregory of Tours and Clovis." *Revue belge de philologie et d'histoire* 63, no. 2 (1985): 249–72.

———. *The Merovingian Kingdoms, 450–751*. London: Longman, 1994.

———. *The Missionary Life: Saints and the Evangelisation of Europe, 400–1050*. The Medieval World. Harlow, UK: Longman, 2001.

———. "The Northern Frontier: Christianity Face to Face with Paganism." In Noble and Smith, *Early Medieval Christianities*, 230–46.

———. "Pagan Religion and Superstitions East of the Rhine from the Fifth to the Ninth Century." In *After Empire: Towards an Ethnology of Europe's Barbarians*, edited by G. Ausenda, 253–79. Studies in Historical Archaeoethnology 1. Woodbridge, UK: Boydell, 1995.

———. "Reform and the Merovingian Church." In Meens et al., *Religious Franks*, 95–111.

———. "The Use and Abuse of Latin Hagiography in the Early Medieval West." In *East and West: Modes of Communication. Proceedings of the First Plenary Conference at Merida*, edited by Euangelos K. Chrysos and I. Wood, 93–109. Leiden: Brill, 1999.

Wood, Michael. "'Stand Strong against the Monsters': Kingship and Learning in the Empire of King Æthelstan." In Wormald and Nelson, *Lay Intellectuals in the Carolingian World*, 192–217.

Wormald, Patrick. "The Age of Offa and Alcuin." In *The Anglo-Saxons*, edited by James Campbell, Eric John, and Patrick Wormald, 101–31. London: Penguin, 1991. First published in 1982.

———. "*Lex scripta* and *verbum regis*: Legislation and Germanic Kingship, from Euric to Cnut." In *Early Medieval Kingship*, edited by P. H. Sawyer and I. N. Wood, 105–38. Leeds: University of Leeds and Contributors, 1977.

———. *The Making of English Law: King Alfred to the Twelfth Century*. Vol. 1, *Legislation and Its Limits*. Oxford: Blackwell, 1999.

———. "Pre-modern 'State' and 'Nation': Definite or Indefinite?" In Airlie, Pohl, and Reimitz, *Staat im frühen Mittelalter*, 179–89.

Wormald, Patrick, and Janet L. Nelson, eds. *Lay Intellectuals in the Carolingian World*. Cambridge, MA: Cambridge University Press, 2007.

Zambelli, Paola. *White Magic, Black Magic in the European Renaissance: From Ficino, Pico, Della Porta to Trithemius, Agrippa, Bruno*. Studies in Medieval and Reformation Traditions 125. Leiden: Brill, 2007.

Zeddies, Nicole. *Religio et Sacrilegium: Studien zur Inkriminierung von Magie, Häresie und Heidentum (4.–7. Jahrhundert)*. Europäische Hochschulschriften, Reihe 3: Geschichte und ihre Hilfswissenschaften 964. Frankfurt am Main: Peter Lang, 2003.

Index

Aachen, Council of (862), 356n53
abortion. *See* love and birth magic
Abydus, mysteries of, 148
Acacius, 83, 96
Acca of Hexham, 53
Achilles, 142, 156
Acts of Barnabas, 138
Acts of John, 171–72
Acts of John in Ephesus, 167
Acts of Paul and Thecla, 171
Adalard (Carolingian courtier), 344
Adam and Eve, 68n25, 127, 166–68, 365n17
Adamnan, 228, 253, 254
Adelaide of Italy, 14
Adelbert (false prophet/heretic), 299, 309
Aelfric of Eynsham, 72n41, 259n34, 279, 303, 317, 369; *On Auguries,* 380; *Passion of St. Bartholomew,* 362–63, 367
Aeluis Aristides, 139
Æthelbald of Mercia (king), 13
Æthelbert of Kent (king), 12, 49, 200
Æthelhild (abbess), 76
Æthelred (king of Northumbria), 81
Agde, Council of (506), 226
Agiluf (Lombard king), 299
Agobard of Lyon, 345, 391; *On Hail and Thunder,* 286–88, 292n54; *Liber apologeticus,* 346–47, 350
Aidan of Lindisfarne, 191, 211
Alammanic code *(Lex Alamannorum),* 339
Alban (saint), 229
Albruna (prophetess), 176
Alcinous, *Handbook of Platonism,* 64n3, 66
Alcuin, 81, 277n13, 297, 392; *De virtutibus,* 69n28; *Epistolae,* 343; *Life of Willibrord,* 78–79
Alfred the Great (Anglo-Saxon ruler), 13, 57n119
Almond, Philip, 69
Amand (bishop of Tongeren-Maastricht), 196, 197
Ambrose of Milan, 103, 104n56

Ammianus Marcellinus, 65–66, 66n11, 98n38, 108–9, 118n28, 122, 146–47, 148, 152n23, 176, 184
amulets, 19, 29, 129, 131, 216, 236–38, 307–8, 368
Anatolian Ma (deity), 101, 103
Anaxagoras, 108
Ancyra, Council of (314), 180–81, 335, 366
angels, 28, 65, 68n25, 69, 78, 81n69, 82, 230, 308–9, 373. *See also* fallen angels; *specific archangels*
animal masquerades/transmogrification, 201–5, 206–7, 265, 285
Annales Xantenses, 352n35
Annals of Fulda, 76, 78, 279n21, 300, 301n20, 318–19, 354n44, 362n6
Annals of Saint Bertin, 350, 351n32, 352nn35–36, 354n44, 356n56
Anstrude, *vita* of, 362
Antichrist, 17, 46, 135, 219
Antony of the Desert, 53, 63, 79, 117n34, 124, 225, 227
apocrypha, pseudepigrapha, and intertestamental writings, 46, 68. *See also* Enoch corpus; *specific texts*
Apollo (deity), 80, 139, 142, 170, 176
Apollonius of Tyana, 134, 156, 157, 166
Apronian, 146–47
Apuleius of Madaura, 230; *Apologia,* 64, 66, 133, 136n102, 147, 182; *Herbarius* attributed to, 142, 259, 263, 363–64, 368, 375; *Metamorphoses (The Golden Ass),* 101, 108, 151, 152, 155, 165–66, 169, 182, 252, 328
Arabic Gospel of the Infancy of Jesus, 141
Arbesmann, Rudolph, 202, 204
Aredius (abbot), 210–11, 220
arioli, 216
Aristophanes, *Vespae,* 164–65
Aristotle, 65; *Politics,* 56n115
Arnulf (Carolingian ruler), 318–319

451

Artemis. *See* Diana
Arthur, Ciaran, 264, 373; *"Charms," Liturgies, and Secret Rites*, 367
Asclepius and Asclepieia, 139–42, 156, 166, 184, 229, 364
Asterius of Amasea, 201
astrology: in Carolingian era, 296–98; in late antiquity/early Christian era, 65, 82–83, 113–16; in post-Roman Europe/Merovingian era, 205–6n45, 222–25
Astronomer, *Vita Hludowici imperatoris*, 297, 300n15, 344, 345, 350
Atargatis (deity), 101
Athanasius of Alexandria, 104; *De incarnatione*, 89, 156–57; *Life of Antony*, 63, 79, 80, 82, 113, 117n34, 124, 155n28, 161n46
Audoin of Rouen, *Vita Eligii*, 132n87, 195, 203, 208n53, 209n55, 214, 217–18, 226, 235n57
Augustine of Canterbury, 12, 200
Augustine of Hippo: Aelfric and Wulfstan, influence on, 259n34; on astrology, 115, 297; Christian understanding of magic and, 27–28, 385; on curiosity, 135, 136; on demons, 69, 82–83, 190; on divination and theurgy, 112, 215; on dream analysis, 119, 230, 301n18; on healing magic, 367–68, 369; on Kalends of January, 201; on *maleficium*, 149; on moon magic, 205–6; on music and dance, 103–4; on necromancy/revivification, 157, 161; in post-Roman/Merovingian era, 190; on ritual, 4; *sortilegium*, use of, 117, 225, 227; on superstition, 95, 107, 121, 122, 231, 301–2, 310; on suspensions and ligatures, 129–31, 310; on sympathetic magic, 122–23, 129, 260
Augustine of Hippo, works: *Confessions*, 104n60, 117n34; *Contra Julianum Pelagianum*, 82n72; *De civitate Dei*, 4n14, 27–28nn15–17, 64nn3–5, 66n12, 68n23, 69n28, 72n41, 73, 77n57, 82, 83n74, 84, 89, 102n51, 112n18, 115n29, 119nn42–43, 120n46, 135nn98–99, 136n101, 142n120, 149n12, 174n33, 206nn46–47, 331n57, 331n59; *De cura pro mortuis gerenda*, 119n43, 161n47; *De diversis quaestionibus*, 161n47; *De divinatione daemonum*, 27n15, 66n13, 82n72, 149n15; *De doctrina Christiana*, 27n15, 75n47, 107, 115n28, 122–23nn51–53, 122n47, 126n64, 129, 130nn81–83, 136n100, 140n114, 141–42n120, 206n46, 231, 365n17; *De utilitate credendi*, 27n16; *Enarrationes in Psalmos*, 70n30; *In Iohannis evangelium tractatus*, 126, 130n83; *Letters*, 117, 157; *Quaestionum in Heptateuchum*, 68n25; *Sermones*, 103n55, 201n33, 302
Augustus Caesar, 109, 142, 176n38
Aurelius (bishop of Carthage), 220
Austin, J. L., 126
Austraberta, *vita* of, 242–43
Auxerre, Council of (578–603), 203, 226
Avitus of Vienne, 198n20

Baader, Gerhard, 363
Bacchanalia, 148
Balaam and the ass, 110, 113
Bald's Leechbook, 334, 364, 365n16, 368–69, 375, 376, 392n7
Balthildis (Frankish queen), 245
baptism, 89, 91, 92n17, 93, 114–15, 124–25, 127, 129, 132, 145, 191, 236–37, 276–78, 303, 304
Baraquiel/Baraqijal (demon), 90n10, 114
Barontus, 71, 79–80
Barth, Fredrik, 26n13
Bartlett, Robert, 54
Basil of Caesarea, 72, 103, 115n29, 358
Bavarian code *(Lex Baiwariorum)*, 339, 353
Bede: *De temporum ratione liber*, 205–6; *Ecclesiastical History*, 5n18, 49n93, 71, 76, 189, 191, 197n17, 197n19, 200, 208n53, 211, 224, 233, 242, 245n78, 387n5; *Expositio actum apostolorum*, 226–27; *Life of St. Cuthbert*, 244–45. *See also Penitential of Pseudo-Bede;* Pseudo-Bede
Bell, Catherine, 5, 8, 30n25, 32, 38n57, 90
Bellona (deity), 100
Benedict of Nursia, 10n31, 80, 196, 197, 243, 244
Benko, Stephen, 5n19, 175n35
Beowulf, 193, 205, 234–35, 268
Bernard of Septimania, 345–51
Bertilla (wife of Berengar I), 347n17
Bethlehem, star of, 110, 113, 114, 298
Bigotian Penitential, 241
binding and loosing, 131–33, 232–36, 260, 305–8
birth magic. *See* love and birth magic
Blair, John, 373–74
Blickling Homilies, 198–99
Bobbio Penitential, 257, 261n43
Boniface (saint), 18–19, 71–72, 275, 277–79, 282, 284, 296, 299, 303, 310–11. *See also* Pseudo-Boniface

Book of David, 254
Book of Nicodemus, 69–70
Book of the Watchers, 68n25, 69, 90n10, 99n39, 206n48
Booker, Courtney M., 38n57
Bourdieu, Pierre, 4, 33
Braga, First Council of (561), 212, 223
Braga, Second Council of (572), 194, 203, 206
Brakke, David, 79
Breviarium Alaricianum, 258
Bridget (saint), 10n31
Brown, Peter, 27n15, 52, 53n106, 62, 65n10, 97, 114, 154n27, 213, 387
Buc, Philippe, 30–31n26, 91; *Dangers of Ritual*, 36–38
Burchard of Worms, 2, 8, 44, 70–71, 320, 323, 333, 393–94; *Corrector sive medicus*, 44, 303–5, 317, 322, 324–26, 328–29, 335; *Decretum*, 1, 28n18, 43n71, 44, 70n31, 263n49, 288–89, 299, 302, 305, 306–7, 311, 313, 317nn14–15, 322n26, 325–32, 335–36, 337n73, 338, 362, 369, 381
Burgundian law code, 250, 252, 253
Burgundian Penitential, 203, 212, 217, 227, 249, 257, 261n43
burials. *See* the dead
Burke, Kenneth, *Grammar of Motives*, 35
Bynum, Caroline Walker, 329n50

Caecilius Natalis, 148
Caesarius of Arles: Augustinian precepts filtered through, 302n22; convent for sister established by, 10n31; at Council of Agde, 226
Caesarius of Arles, *Sermones*: on amulets, 236–38; on astrology, 223; on binding as magical procedure, 233; on birth magic, 261, 262–63, 338, 341, 353; on demons, 74–75, 82, 201, 217; on healing/healing magic, 240–41, 243–44, 245; on idolatry and nature worship, 195, 199n23, 217; on Kalends of January, 203–5; on Rogationtide, 198; on singing and dancing, 209–10, 290; as source, 45; on suspensions, 310, 370n34; on veneration of the moon, 84, 269n66; on weather magic, 210
Calcidius, 301n18; *Commentary on Plato's Timaeus*, 119
calendar's importance in Christianity, 207–8
Cameron, M. L., 263n49, 371, 375

Canon episcopi, 322, 324, 325, 327, 376
Canones Hibernenses, 261n43
canons, as source, 49–50. *See also specific councils*
capitularies, as source, 48–49. *See also specific capitularies*
Carneades, 113n20
Carolingian era, 11–14, 15, 273–74, 390–94; astrology in, 296–98; binding, loosing, and suspensions in, 305–8; changes in understanding of magic in, 2–3, 309–12, 313–15, 358–59, 390–94; conciliar activity in, 50; core lands and margins of Europe in, 273–74, 299, 391; demons in, 74–84, 276, 277, 279, 282–84, 286, 309; Diana in, 323–27, 331, 332, 337, 339, 340, 374–76, 394; divination and theurgy in, 296–99, 311–12; dreams in, 301; gender and magic in, 7–8, 300, 303–7, 311, 312, 313–59, 391–94 (*see also* gender and magic); history writing in, 51–52; idols/idolatry, 274–85, 290, 291; *lamiae* and *striae* in, 320–32, 339–40, 357; law codes of, 47–48; *maleficium* in, 283, 286, 291, 308; necromancy/revivification in, 315–18; pagan culture in, 274–85, 291–92; poison, female use of, 318–20; prophecy in, 299–300, 312; sacred space and nature worship in, 274–85; Saxony, expansion into, 276–78, 322–23; singing, dancing, and juggling (ecstatic celebration) in, 289–91; *sortilegium* in, 298–99, 306n44; standardization as watchword of, 295, 308; superstition in, 276, 301–5, 308, 310–11; unauthorized saints and angels, veneration of, 308–9; weather magic in, 285–89. *See also* healing/healing magic in Carolingian era; love and birth magic in Carolingian era
Carolingian reforms, 11–12, 14, 279–80, 292–93, 295, 360–61, 368, 369
Cassius Felix, 58n123
Cathwulf, 286, 316, 322
Cato the Elder, *On Agriculture*, 143n124
Celsus, 27n15, 133, 134, 148, 156n29. *See also* Origen, *Contra Celsus*
Chad (bishop of Mercia), 210
Chaldean Oracles, 109, 127, 129, 152n22, 173
Chance, Jane, 268
Charibert (Frankish ruler), 220
Charlemagne, 11, 13, 44, 55, 205, 276–80, 286, 297, 309, 316, 322, 340, 342–44, 354, 392

Charles the Bald (Carolingian ruler), 13, 319, 344, 345, 349, 354–55
Charles the Fat (Carolingian ruler), 76
Charles Martel, 11
Charles-Edwards, Thomas, 43
Childebert I (Frankish ruler), 228, 229n38
Childebert II (Frankish ruler), 254, 255
Chilperic I (Frankish ruler), 221, 229
Chiron (centaur), 142, 375
Chlotar I (Frankish ruler), 229n38
Christianity, 1–2, 385–87; on astrology, 113–16; calendar's importance in, 207–8; Carolingian healing magic incorporating Christian symbols or utterances, 370–71; competition between magical behavior and, 2–4, 31; deaconesses, 98; death, the grave, and necromancy in, 97, 154–62; definition of magic in, 27–28; demons in, 67–74; on divination and theurgy, 110–12; dream analysis in, 118–19; in England, 10n31; graves in, 97; on healing and medicine, 137–43; late antiquity, rise in, 9; legalization, effects of, 94–95; on *maleficium*, 148–50; Mary and Mariology, 158, 167–68, 174–75, 186; masculinization of sacred space in, 98; monasticism, 9, 11; multiple forms of, 2n2; pagan culture in late antiquity and, 6, 30, 34–35, 39, 81, 87–94, 139–43; pagan culture in post-Roman Europe and, 189–91, 197; prophecy and women in, 177–79; ritual and, 4–6, 90–95; "Saxon problem" in Carolingian era, 276–78; on singing, dancing, and juggling (ecstatic celebration), 102–5; on *sortilegium*, 116–18; transactional exchanges resembling magic in, 24. *See also* late antiquity/early Christian era
Chronicon Gothanum, 300n16
Cicero: *De divinatione*, 109n9, 176n37; *De natura deorum*, 64n3, 67, 113n20; *De senectute*, 109n9, 176n37
Circe, 168, 169, 179–80, 181n58, 185, 256, 257n27, 265, 269
1 and 2 Clement, 49n79, 132, 138
Clement I (bishop of Rome), 45n79, 69n26, 177. *See also* Pseudo-Clement
Clement of Alexandria, 93, 104–5; *Exhortation to the Heathen*, 84, 103
Clothar II (Merovingian ruler), 10
Clovis I (Merovingian ruler), 9–10, 198, 315
Cockayne, Oswald, 379
Columbanus, 11. See also *Penitential of Columbanus*

computus, 297n5
Confessional of (pseudo) *Egbert*, 382
Constantine I the Great (emperor), 9, 96, 97, 111, 157, 180, 279
Constantius II (emperor), 65–66, 75, 112, 122, 146
contraria contrariis sanantur, 138–39, 240, 383
Contreni, John, 57, 362n4
councils: canons of, as sources, 49–50; in late antiquity/early Christian era, 144. *See also* specific councils, *e.g.* Agde, Council of
Cousser, Jonathan, 196n16
creative/fictional texts, as sources, 54–55
cross, sign of the, 123–24, 303, 334, 363
cross-dressing, 101, 201, 285, 290–91
curiosity, 135–37
curse tablets and *defixiones*, 132–33, 149–50, 173n28, 183, 184–85, 233
Cuthbert (saint), 197, 242, 244–45
Cybele (deity), 100, 101, 102n49, 103, 321n22
Cyril of Jerusalem, 89, 93, 96n31, 125; *Catecheses*, 124

Dagobert I (Merovingian ruler), 10–11
dance. *See* singing, dancing, and juggling
David (biblical king), 105
De medicina, 381
De taxone liber, 363, 364, 371
De Vriend, Hubert, 364
deaconesses, 98
the dead: Christian attitudes toward, 97, 154–62; grave robbing, prohibitions of, 252–53; staking certain dead bodies, 304; trafficking with (*see* necromancy/revivification)
Delos, ecstatic worship at, 101
demons, 15–16, 63–84, 384; in Carolingian era, 74–84, 276, 277, 279, 282–84, 286, 309; Christian definition of magic as trafficking with, 27–28, 72–73; in Christianity, 67–74; churches repelling, 97; curiosity, as satisfiers of, 135–36; divination and theurgy believed to rely on, 215; dreams troubled by, 75–76; as evil, 68–69, 77, 83; human ability to dominate, 79–81; illness, as cause of, 366, 378; as independent agents, 77–79; in late antiquity/early Christian era, 63–67; *maleficium*, as agents of, 163; nature of, 79–84; necromancy and, 157, 161–62; "of the lower air," 3, 65, 66, 69, 70, 73, 83, 148, 157, 163, 192, 248, 331; "of the middle air," 68, 71; as the other, 77, 79; possession by, 75–77, 125–26; in post-Roman Europe/

INDEX 455

Merovingian era, 74–84, 196, 197–99, 201, 207–8, 217; practitioners of magic drawing on powers of, 29; sin versus trafficking with, 74
Derrida, Jacques, 3, 165, 325
Desiderius (magician), 219–20, 310
the Devil. *See* Satan
Diana (deity): in Carolingian era, 323–27, 331, 332, 337, 339, 340, 374–76, 394; Ephesus, temple of Artemis in, 170–72; in healing magic, 374–76; in late antiquity/early Christian era, 101, 142, 169–73, 174, 175; moon, connection to, 170, 174, 206, 268, 324, 325; in post-Roman Europe/Merovingian era, 206, 259, 265, 268, 269
Didache (The Teaching of Twelve Apostles), 90, 178
Dionysian worship practices, 102
Dionysius the Areopagite, 111
Dioscorides, *De materia medica*, 58. *See also* Pseudo-Dioscorides
divination and theurgy, 16; in Carolingian era, 296–99, 311–12; Christianity on, 110–12; demons, reliance on, 215; in late antiquity/early Christianity, 108–12; male domination of, 119–20; *maleficium* compared, 148–49; pagan culture, 16, 108–12; poisoning as, 181; in post-Roman Europe/Merovingian era, 214–18. *See also* astrology; dreams; prophecy; *sortilegium*
Dobbie, Elliott Van Kirk, 378
Donatists, 103n55
Dorotheus of Dison, *Carmen astrologicum*, 206n45
double monasteries, 313–14
Douglas, Mary, 34n43
"drawing children through the earth," 380–83
dreams: Asclepius and Asclepieia, 140, 229; in Carolingian era, 301; demons disturbing, 75–76; in late antiquity/early Christian era, 118–20; in post-Roman Europe/Merovingian era, 229–31; *sortilegium* compared, 231
Drew, Katherine Fischer, 40
Dungal of Bobbio, 297
Durkheim, Émile, 24, 32, 36n52
Dutton, Paul, 45n80, 97, 205, 288, 301
dwarfs, 193, 365, 366, 377–78

Eanswith (daughter of Eadbald of Kent), 10n31
early Christian era. *See* Christianity; late antiquity/early Christian era
Ebbo of Reims, 42n70, 283n32
ecstatic celebration. *See* singing, dancing, and juggling
Edict of Milan (313), 94
Edictum Rothari, 250, 267, 366
Edington, battle of (878), 13
Egbert (archbishop of York), 203n38
Eighth Book of Moses, 133
Eigil, *Vita S. Strumi*, 57n119, 278
Einhard, 301; *Vita Karoli Magni*, 55, 276, 343, 345
Eligius of Noyon, 195, 203, 208, 209, 214, 217–18, 226, 231, 235
elves and elf disease, 70, 193, 328, 329, 332, 334, 365, 371–72, 376, 378, 390
Empedocles, 160
Endor, witch/pythoness of, 159–61, 166, 251, 316–17, 392
England: Anglo-Saxons in, 12, 191, 205; Christianity and pagan culture in, 10n31, 11–13, 191, 197, 200, 279; healing/healing magic in, 363–64, 369, 373–74, 394n7; law codes, 47, 49; monasticism in, 10n31; Rogationtide in, 198–99; unnatural female entities in, 268; Viking invasions of, 13
Enoch Corpus, 46, 65n7, 68, 69, 90n10, 99, 112n17, 113n21, 118n37, 119, 206n48, 268
Enright, Michael, 234, 382; *Lady with a Mead Cup*, 215–16
Ephesus, First Council of (341), 174–75
Ephesus, temple of Artemis in, 170–72
Epiphanius of Salamis, *Panarion*, 98n35, 124, 138, 150n18, 175n35, 181
Epistola de litteris colendis, 362n4
Erictho, 152–55, 159, 162–63, 166, 168–69, 180–81, 252, 265, 317
Ermengard (empress of Louis the Pious), 344
Eulalius (count), 255, 260
Eusebius of Caesarea, 128, 129, 138, 184; *Commentary on Psalms*, 105; *Historia ecclesiastica*, 128n74, 279; *Life of Constantine*, 87, 96; *Preparation for the Gospel*, 112, 129n77; *Reply to Hierocles*, 134, 157
Eustathius, *On the Belly-Myther Against Origen*, 161
Eustemia (niece of Gregory of Tours), 242
Euthymius (saint), 150
Evans-Pritchard, E. E., 28–29, 33
Eve, 68n25, 69, 166–68, 174, 186, 365n17
exorcism, 125–26

INDEX

Faileuba (Frankish Queen), 254
the fall, 127, 135–36, 166–68
fallen angels, 68n25, 69, 70, 80, 195, 384
false prophecy. *See* prophecy
familiar spirits/guardian angels, 65
Fastrada (wife of Charlemagne), 343, 344
Fates, 304, 329–30
Faulker, Thomas, 48
Favorinus, 113n20
feasting, in late antiquity/early Christian era, 93
female magic. *See* gender and magic
Ferngren, Gary, 371
Filotas, Bernadette, 16, 17n48, 39, 59, 202, 289
Finnian of Clonard, 240. See also *Penitential of Finnian*
fire, passing children through, 381–83
First Saxon Capitulary, 276–77, 322
Flint, Valerie, 67–68, 252, 287, 304, 355, 356n53
Fortunatus of Todi, 243
Foucault, Michel, 5, 31n29; *The Order of Things*, 232
Fouracre, Paul, 309
Frankfurt Council (794), 280
Frankfurter, David, 70, 77, 183
Frankish Council (747), 296
Frazer, James, *The Golden Bough*, 24, 33
Fredegund (Frankish queen), 255–56, 315, 349, 353, 359
Fredegund (Merovingian ruler), 57n119
Freising, Council of (early 9th century), 362
Frisian code, 228
Frymer-Kensky, Tikva, 385–86
Fursa (saint), 71

Gabriel (archangel), 301, 309, 345
Gager, John, 132
galdor/galdru, 367, 373n44
Galen, 58
Gambara (sibyl), 300
Garver, Valerie L., 7n23
Gaul. *See* Carolingian era; post-Roman Europe/Merovingian era
Geertz, Clifford, 5n16, 31, 32–33, 37, 38n57, 88, 144, 204, 207, 274n3; *Interpretation of Cultures*, 384
gender and magic, 6–8, 185–86; association of women with magic, 6–8; binding and loosing, 234–35, 305–7; in Carolingian era, 7–8, 300, 303–7, 311, 312, 313–59,

391–94; clandestine nature of women's magic, 148, 180, 234; dancing, post-Roman change in gender associations of, 210; divination, male domination of, 119; dreams and dream analysis, 120, 230; ecstatic worship, women associated with, 100–101, 102; in Enoch corpus, 69; female monastic communities, 9, 10n31; female principle of deity, 320–21; *gynaecea* or women's communal textile workshops, 260, 305–6; healing/healing magic in Carolingian era, 374–83, 391–92; in history writing, 51; Judith (empress of Louis the Pious), case study of, 342–51, 359; in late antiquity/early Christian era, 164–86, 386; liminality and, 152; male virility, aids for, 259–60; *maleficium* and, 148, 150, 248, 249, 250; Mary and Mariology, 158, 167–68, 174–75, 186; masculinization of Christian sacred space and, 98; monasticism and, 9, 10, 312, 313–15; moon's association with female magic, 206; necromancy/revivification and, 152–54, 155, 162; poison, female use of, 179–81, 253–56, 318–20; in post-Roman Europe/Merovingian era, 199, 215–16, 220–22, 234–35, 248–70, 389; prophecy, 120, 144, 175–79, 220–22, 300; public space, male domination of magic in, 6–7; sources, gender assumptions in, 60–61; superstitions, domestic persistence of, 303–5, 311; Theutberga and Waldrada (wife and mistress of Lothar II), case study of, 351–58. *See also* Diana; Hekate; *lamiae* and *striae*; love and birth magic; *specific women by name*
General Admonition (789), 280, 286, 298, 301, 305n38, 308n51, 309, 323, 392, 393
Genovefa, *vita* of, 53, 199
Gerberga (sister of Bernard of Septimania), 350
German Council (742), 275, 307, 309
Germanus of Auxerre, 211, 229
Ghaerbald of Liège, 333
Gibson, Kelly, 54n109
Gieryn, Thomas, *Truth-Spots*, 192, 275
Gillmeister, Andrzej, 176n37
Glosecki, Steven, 205, 325n37
Gnostics and Gnosticism, 65n7, 67, 102, 127, 129, 167, 177, 184, 321n22
Gospel of Nicodemus, 119
Gospel of the Lots of Mary, 118n36

grain, burning, as healing cure, 382
Gratian (emperor), 58n123
Grattan, J. H. G., 373, 377
graves. *See* the dead
great chain of being, 3, 64–65, 83, 384
Green, Monica, 336n70
Gregorian reform movement, 2n3
Gregory I the Great (pope), *Dialogues*, 5, 12, 80n65, 119, 196n16, 197, 198, 208, 211, 229–30, 243, 244, 249, 252n11, 301, 387
Gregory the Miracle-Worker, 97
Gregory of Nyssa, 124n58, 128n76, 158, 161, 174
Gregory of Tours: *De beata Monegunde*, 52n104, 210, 321; *De cursu stellarum*, 224–25; *Decem libri historiarum*, 45n80, 57n119, 193–94, 205, 209n55, 211, 219–23, 227–29, 232–33, 239, 244, 251n7, 254–56, 260, 269, 299, 300, 310, 353, 359, 366–67, 370; *Gloria confessorum*, 208–9, 210, 229–30, 234; *Gloria martyrum*, 211n60; *Liber vitae patrum*, 228n33; *Miracles of St. Martin*, 242
Grig, Lucy, 202, 204, 238n63
guardian angels/familiar spirits, 65
Gundestrup Cauldron, 382
Gundowald (king), 366, 370
Guntram Boso (king), 220, 227, 229, 366
gynaecea or women's communal textile workshops, 260, 305–6

Hadrian (emperor), 96
hagiography: demons in, 79; healing magic in, 242–43; pagan/Christian contestation in, 196; prophecy in, 177; revivifications in, 252, 316; as source, 52–54; weather magic in Carolingian era and, 286
Halitgar of Cambrai: letter of Ebbo to, 42n70; *Pseudo-Roman Penitential (Poenitentiale Romanum)*, 43n71, 283–84, 286, 297–98, 307–8, 333, 337n73, 338
Hall, Alaric, 332, 379
Harris-Stoertz, Fiona, 336n70
harrowing of hell, 69–70
Hausmann, Chris, 38–39n58
healing/healing magic, 17; Asclepius and Asclepieia, 139–42, 156, 166, 184, 229, 364; in late antiquity/early Christianity, 137–43; looking around or looking backward, 303; in post-Roman Europe/Merovingian era, 240–46, 259; sources, medical materials as, 55–58

healing/healing magic in Carolingian era, 360–83, 391–92; Carolingian reform program and, 360–61, 369; Christian symbols and utterances, incorporation of, 370–71; demons as cause of illness, 366, 378; disease, concept of, 364–66, 378; gender and, 374–83, 391–92; herbal texts, magic and ritual in, 363–74; liberal arts, medicine incorporated into, 57, 361; magical nature of cures and treatments, discerning, 366–73; mental/psychic disorders and "arcane diseases," 371–72, 375–276, 381; practitioners of, 372–74, 379–83; spiritual and physical health, relationship between, 361–63
Hekate (deity), 101, 152, 169, 170n20, 173–74, 175, 184, 327
Helena (mother of Constantine), 96, 97, 279
Hen, Yitzak, 59–60, 274n3
Henry II (Emperor), 44
Heraclides of Pontus, 160
Herard of Tours, 309
Herbariencorpus, 363
Herbarius Apulei Platonici Maudaurenses (Pseudoapulei herbarius), 142, 259, 263, 363–64, 368, 375
Hercules, 142
Herlihy, David, 6
Herodias (wife of Herod Antipas), 327
Hierocles, 134
Hilarion (saint), 75, 79, 80, 99n40, 129, 138, 140
Hilary of Poitiers, 127
Hincmar of Reims, 393; *De divortio Lotharii regis*, 43n72, 72nn40–41, 76n53, 306, 316–17, 322, 331–32n59, 351n34, 352–58, 393; *De nuptiis Stephani*, 358n65
Hippolytus, *On the Apostolic Tradition*, 93n21, 96n28, 104, 117, 124n58, 125n59
histories and history writing, as sources, 50–52
Homer, 65, 110, 142, 162, 168, 179–80
Homeromanteion, 116
Homilia de sacrilegiis, 278, 281, 285, 286, 290, 297, 298, 302, 308, 316, 322
homilies and sermons, as sources, 44–45
Horace, 166n9, 182, 375
hot water/hot iron, ordeal by, 78, 228–29, 353
Hrabanus Maurus. *See* Raban Maur
Hubert Boso, 352, 355

Hugh of Tours, 345–46
Hulda (deity), 324n36, 325–28

Iamblichus, 109
idolatry/idol worship, 16; in Carolingian era, 274–85, 290, 291; in late antiquity/early Christian era, 90; in post-Roman Europe/Merovingian era, 192–208, 213, 258
Ignatius of Antioch, 98, 113, 138
incest, 352–58
incubatio, 140
incubi and succubi, 331, 334
Indiculus superstitionum et paganiarum, 275, 280–81, 286, 302, 305, 307, 308, 309, 322
indoors and outdoors. *See* nature worship/worship outdoors; sacred space
Infancy Gospel of Matthew, 336n70
infanticide. *See* love and birth magic
Innes, Matthew, 51
Innocent I (pope), 138
intertestamental writings, pseudepigrapha, and apocrypha, 46, 68. *See also* Enoch corpus; *specific texts*
Irenaeus of Lyon, *Adversus haereses*, 65n7, 103, 129n78, 177n43, 184
Irene (empress), 343
Irminsul (tree shrine), destruction of, 278
Isidore of Seville, 298, 316; *De natura rerum*, 205–6; *Differences*, 77–78; *Etymologies*, 28n18, 46, 56n116, 70n31, 73–74, 192, 215n1, 216–17, 223–24, 226, 233, 251, 257n27, 258, 265, 297, 331n57, 334; *Quaestiones in Vetus Testamentum*, 251
Isis (deity), 101, 118

Janowitz, Naomi, 23n1, 25–26; *Icons of Power*, 127
Jerome, 158, 174, 241; *On Illustrious Men*, 72n40; *Life of St. Hilarion*, 75, 79, 80, 99n40, 138n111, 140–41, 183, 184
Jerusalem, as Christian model of sacred space, 96–97, 279
Jews and Judaism, 67, 68, 88–92, 114, 118, 126, 166, 170–71, 175, 209, 265n54
Jezebel (biblical queen), 346, 347
John XII (pope), 14
John the Baptist, 93, 196, 208, 219, 327
John of Beverley, 245
John Cassian, 9, 72n41, 75, 139
John Chrysostom, 72, 81, 103, 114, 125n60, 125n61, 129, 200–201

Jolly, Karen, 39, 264, 367, 371, 373
Jonas of Orléans, 392; *De institutione regia*, 305
Jonason, Amy, 38–39n58
Jubilees, Book of, 68
Judgment of Clement, 77, 290
Judith (empress of Louis the Pious), 342–51, 359
juggling. *See* singing, dancing, and juggling
Julian (emperor), 56, 65, 109n10, 118, 122
Julius Caesar, 152; *Gallic Wars*, 176
Jupiter's Oak, felling of, 277–78
Jurasinki, Stefan, 279n19
Justin Martyr, 128, 190, 195, 386; *Dialogue with Trypho*, 91–92, 140, 156–57; *First Apology (Apology on Behalf of Christians)*, 52n105, 65nn8–9, 70n30, 88, 89, 91n15, 92, 93, 102n49, 118, 140, 158, 160, 166–67, 176; *Second Apology*, 68–69, 386n2
Juvenal, *Satires*, 100–101, 185n74

Kadel, Andrew, *Matrology*, 379
Kahlos, Maijastina, 40n64
Kalends of January, 34–35, 200–205, 206, 207, 213, 284–85, 305–6, 307
Karlomann (Frankish ruler), 307
Keller, Hagen, 347n17
Kempten, demon of, 78–79
Kieckhefer, Richard, 6, 39, 390
King, Karen, 177, 178
King, Margot, 53
Klingshirn, William, 204, 225
Kokabel (fourth fallen angel), 90n10, 114
Kollyridians, 175
Koziol, Geoffrey, 31n27
Künzel, Rudi, 59, 60

Lacnunga, 250n4, 336–38, 364, 365, 366, 375, 376, 378, 392n7
Lactantius, *Divine Institutes*, 72n41, 75, 119, 157, 158
lamiae and *striae*, 17; in Carolingian era, 320–32, 339–40, 357; in late antiquity/early Christianity, 162, 164–69; in post-Roman Europe/Merovingian era, 265–69
Laodicea, Council of (363–364), 102n50, 131
Larner, Christina, 28n20
late antiquity/early Christian era, 8–9, 15, 87–95, 384–87; astrology in, 65, 82–83, 113–16; binding and loosing, 131–33; councils of the church in, 144;

cultural tensions between paganism and Christianity, 6, 30, 34–35, 39, 81, 87–94, 139–43; curiosity in, 135–37; demons in, 63–67; Diana in, 101, 142, 169–73, 174, 175; divination and theurgy in, 108–12; dreams in, 118–20; gender and magic in, 164–86, 386 (see also gender and magic); healing/healing magic in, 137–43; *lamiae* and *striae* in, 162, 164–69; legalization of Christianity, 94–95, 96; *mageia* in, 107–8; *maleficium* in, 120, 146–50, 162–63; necromancy/revivification in, 151–62; ritual and Christianity in, 90–95, 144–45; sacred space and nature worship in, 95–100; singing, dancing, and juggling (ecstatic celebration), 100–105; superstition in, 107, 120–21, 122, 126, 144; suspensions and ligatures, 129–31; sympathetic magic (signs, symbols, and names), 121–29; tricks and trickery in, 121, 133–35; weather magic in, 98–99. *See also* Christianity; divination and theurgy; pagan culture

law codes, as sources, 46–48. *See also specific law codes*

Law of Adamnán (Law of the Innocents), 228

Lazarus, raising of, 155–56, 162

Leach, Edmund, 36, 147

Leander of Seville, 209, 210

learned treatises, as sources, 46

Lefebvre, Henri, 199

legal texts, as sources, 46–50

Leges Visigothorum, 250n5, 252n14, 253–54, 262n47

Leja, Meg, 361

Leo III (pope), 13, 198n20

Leo IV (pope), 303

Letter of Barnabas, 91n15, 97n34

letters, as sources, 44–45

Lévy-Bruhl, Lucien, 34

Lex Alamannorum, 262

Lex Cornelia de sicariis et veneficiis, 180

Lex Ribuaria (Ripuarian code), 228, 318

Life of Saint Wilfred, 336n70

Lifshitz, Felice, 53n106

ligatures and suspensions, 129–31, 307–8, 310, 368–69

Lilith, 265n54

liminality, 35–36, 152–54, 164, 173–74, 182, 207

Liuzza, Roy Michael, 193n7

Livy, *History of Rome*, 148

Lombard Laws (*Lex Longobardum*), 23, 40, 47, 250, 254n18, 267, 366–67

looking around or looking backward, 302–3

Lorica, 365–66, 379

Lorsch Abbey pharmaceutical text, 361

Lorsch Annals, 343

Lothar I (Carolingian ruler), 344, 345, 346, 350

Lothar II (Carolingian ruler), 13, 276n10, 316, 351–58, 391

lots (*sortes*), divination by drawing. *See sortilegium*

Louis II of Italy, 352

Louis the German (Carolingian ruler), 13, 301

Louis the Pious (Carolingian ruler), 13, 297, 299–300, 301, 339, 342–51, 391

love and birth magic, 17; in late antiquity/early Christian era, 181–85; male involvement in, 341n79; in post-Roman Europe/Merovingian era, 256–65

love and birth magic in Carolingian era, 332–39, 340–41; birth magic, 336–39; Judith (empress of Louis the Pious), case study of, 342–51, 359; love magic, 332–36; Theutberga and Waldrada (wife and mistress of Lothar II), case study of, 351–58

Lucan, *The Civil War*, 146, 152–53, 169, 180, 252, 317, 375n48

Lucian of Samosata, 113n20; *Passing of Peregrinus*, 90, 154n27; *On the Syrian Goddess* and *On Dance*, 101

Lupus of Troyes, 211

MacAloon, John, 204

MacMullen, Ramsey, 94, 100, 104, 192n5

Macrobius, 64–65, 65n6, 301n18; *Commentary on the Dream of Scipio*, 119

maeres, 329, 365, 379

magi, 107, 110, 114, 133

magic, 1–19, 384–94; "black" versus "white," inapplicable to early Middle Ages, 137; categories of, 16–17 (*see also specific types*); changes in understanding of, 2–3, 14; concepts of, 14–15, 18–19; defined, 23–28; egregiousness of, 83–84; modern scholarly attention to, 23–26; ordinariness of, 81; possession versus, 75–76; practitioners of, 18, 28–30; secrecy associated with, 147–48, 149, 180, 248–49; sinful behavior versus, 74; terms related

magic: (*continued*)
to, 3n6, 18; time frame for study of, 8–14, 15–16; as trafficking with demons, 27–28, 72–73. *See also* Carolingian era; Christianity; demons; gender and magic; late antiquity / early Christian era; pagan culture; post-Roman Europe / Merovingian era
male magic. *See* gender and magic
maleficium, 17; in Carolingian era, 283, 286, 291, 308; Christian interpretation of, 148–50; demons as agents of, 163; divination and theurgy compared, 148–49; gender and, 148, 150, 248, 249, 250; in late antiquity / early Christianity, 120, 146–50, 162–63; in pagan culture, 146–48; poison, women's use of, 179–81, 253–56; in post-Roman Europe / Merovingian era, 192, 248–50; practitioners of, 146–47; ritual of, 147. *See also* necromancy / revivification
Malinowski, Bronisław, 33, 34, 147
Mamertus of Vienne, 198
Mamre, oak at, 83, 96
Marcellus Empiricus of Bordeaux, 58n123
Marcus (Valentinian leader), 184
Marcus Manilius, *Astronomica*, 66–67
Markus, Robert A., 39–40n63, 96n31
Martianus Capella, 57
Martin of Braga: *Canones ex orientalum patrum synodi* 75, 230n41, 234; *De correctione rusticorum*, 193–94, 195, 203, 206, 208, 217–18, 230, 233, 235, 277, 280n23; Polemius of Astorga, letter to, 193–94, 208, 217, 235, 280; *Pride*, 69n28; translation of *Sayings of the Egyptian Fathers*, 136n101
Martin of Tours, 196, 197, 209, 218–19, 221, 227–28, 242, 251–52, 277, 310
Mary and Mariology, 158, 167–68, 174–75, 186, 321
materia medica. *See* healing / healing magic
Matfrid of Orléans, 345–46
Mauss, Marcel, 24
Maximus of Turin, 203, 269
McCluskey, Stephen, 224
McKitterick, Rosamund, 48, 51, 274n2
Meaney, Audrey, 234, 279
Medea, 168–69, 173, 180, 185, 256, 265
medicine and medical matters. *See* healing / healing magic
Medusa, 166n9
Meens, Rob, 42n69
Mellitus (abbot and first bishop of London), 5, 197, 211

Meroe, 165–66, 168, 169, 328
Merovech (son of Chilperic I), 220–21, 222, 227–28
Merovingians. *See* post-Roman Europe / Merovingian era
Methodist school of medicine, 139
Michael (archangel), 69, 166, 200, 309
Minucius Felix, *Octavius*, 66n13, 72n41, 88n3, 147–48, 154
miracles, 134, 135
Mistry, Zubin, 353
Mithra, cult of, 89
Momigliano, Arnaldo, 51
monasticism, 9, 10, 312, 313–15
Monegund of Tours, 321
Montanists, 129, 177, 321n22
Monte Cassino, monastery of, 10n31, 80
Monte Gargano, sanctuary of, 200
moon: "calling down" or "calling out," 135n97, 165, 169n18, 170, 173, 205–7, 268, 281–82; Diana, Hekate, and Mary connected to, 170, 174, 206, 268, 324, 325; healing magic in Carolingian era and, 374–76; poison from, 180; space between earth and, 3, 65, 157; veneration of, 84, 133, 205–6, 269, 275, 280–81; women, association with, 206, 268–69
Moses, as sorcerer or wizard, 133–34
mother earth (deity), 173, 376–77
Mummolus, 255, 260, 353
music. *See* singing, dancing, and juggling
Myerhoff, Barbara, 90–91, 92, 197, 245, 281, 318

Nadel, S. F., 30
names, signs, and symbols. *See* sympathetic magic
Nanaia, ecstatic worship at, 101
nature worship / worship outdoors: in Carolingian era, 274–85; in late antiquity / early Christian era, 95–100; in post-Roman Europe / Merovingian era, 192–208
necromancy / revivification: in Carolingian era, 315–18; Christian attitudes toward death and, 154–62; defined, 151, 251; Endor, witch / pythoness of, 159–61, 166, 251, 316–17, 392; gender and, 152–54, 155, 162, 315–18; in late antiquity / early Christian era, 151–62; Lazarus, raising of, 155–56, 162; liminality and, 152–54; in pagan culture, 151–54, 156, 160; in post-Roman Europe / Merovingian era, 251–53
Nelson, Janet L., 2n4, 343, 344–45

INDEX

Neoplatonism, 64, 65–67, 109–12, 127, 128–29, 149, 162, 173
Nephilim, 68n25, 69
Nestorius, 174
Nicaea, Second Council of (787), 314
Nicholas I (pope), 354
Nichomachus of Gerasa, 108n6
Nicolaitans, 301
Niermeyer, J. E., 165
Nine Herbs Charm, 360, 376, 378–79
Nisbet, Robert, 96–97, 387
Nithard, *Historiarum*, 344, 345, 350
Notker the Stammerer, 351

Octavius Januarius, 148
Odysseus/Ulysses, 162, 168, 179–80, 181n58, 265
Offa (king of Mercia), 13, 49n93
Olbert of Gembloux, 44
Old English Herbarium, 368, 369n30, 370, 375n49, 375n51
Old Irish Table of Commutations, 61
ordeal, trials by, 78, 228–29, 353
Ordinatio imperii, 344
Oribasius, 56, 58
Origen of Alexandria, 128, 190, 386; *Contra Celsum*, 27n15, 66n13, 70n30, 72n41, 73, 88–89, 90, 92, 113, 127, 133n91, 134, 137, 138, 149n13, 156–58, 160–61, 386n2; Eustathius, *On the Belly-Myther Against Origen*, 161; *Exhortation to Martyrdom*, 71, 128n75; *Peri Archôn*, 83
Orléans, First Council of (511), 198, 226
Otto I (Emperor), 14
Otto III (Emperor), 44
outdoors and indoors. *See* nature worship/worship outdoors; sacred space
Ovid: *Amores*, 180, 182; *Metamorphoses*, 166n9, 169
Owen-Crocker, Gale, 205

Pacian of Barcelona, *Cervulus*, 202
Pactus legis Alamannorum, 253, 262, 266
pagan culture, 384–85; in Carolingian era, 274–85, 291–92; concept of magic and, 3n6, 6, 18–19; demons in, 63–67; divination and theurgy in, 108–10; early Christianity and, 6, 30, 34–35, 39, 81, 87–94, 139–43; gender and magic, relationship between, 7–8; graves in, 97, 154; on *maleficium*, 146–48; medicine and healing in, 139–43; necromancy/revivification in, 151–54, 156, 160; in post-Roman Europe/Merovingian era, 189–91, 196, 197; prophecy and women in, 175–76; ritual as means of defusing, 4–5; on singing, dancing, and juggling (ecstatic celebration), 100–102. *See also* Diana; Hekate; nature worship
Palmer, James T., 40n64
Parcae, 330
Paris, Council of (829), 286, 392–93
Paschasius of Dumium, 74
Paschasius Radbert of Corbie, 343, 345; *Epitaphium Arsenii*, 346, 347–49
Patrick (saint), 10n31, 11, 200, 217, 265–66
Patroclus (saint), 227
Paul and Pauline writings, 93, 104, 134, 170–72, 283
Paul the Deacon, *History of the Lombards*, 47, 299–300
Pelagianism, 211
Penitential of Columbanus, 241, 249, 257
Penitential of Cummean, 61, 240
Penitential of Egbert, 318
Penitential of Finnian (Poenitentiale Vinniai), 61, 240, 257, 261–62, 365n17
Penitential of Pseudo-Bede, 203, 206, 212n63, 217, 227, 261n43, 268, 381
Penitential of Pseudo-Egbert, 253
Penitential of Silos, 285, 287–88, 290, 297, 298, 303, 305–6, 307, 369, 382
Penitential of Theodore, 43, 61n131, 76–77, 203n38, 230n42, 233, 249, 257–58, 333–34, 335, 353, 370, 381, 382
Penitential of Vigilanus, 338
penitentials, as sources, 41–44, 60–61. *See also specific penitentials*
Perpetua (saint), 132, 177–78, 321
Peter (apostle), 65n10, 79–80, 132, 134, 158, 174, 177, 238
Peter Chrysologus of Ravenna, 201, 203
Peters, Edward, 30n23
Peyroux, Catherine, 379
Philostratus, 134, 156, 166, 331
Pippin III (Carolingian ruler), 11
Pippin of Italy (king), 300n16
Pirmin of Reichenau, *De singulis libris*, 203
planets, as demons, 65
Plato and Platonism, 66, 69, 119, 142n122, 160. *See also* Neoplatonism
Pliny the Elder, *Natural History*, 56n115, 98, 133, 143n124, 146–47, 176n37, 375n51
Plutarch, *Moralia*, 100–101, 172
poison, female use of, 179–81, 253–56, 318–20

Poitiers, rebellion at convent of, 254
Polemius of Astorga, 193–94, 208, 217, 235, 280
Pompey, 152, 180
Porphyry of Tyre, 110, 128–29, 149
Pössel, Christina, 30n25, 31n30, 36n52
possession by demons, 75–77, 125–26
post-Roman Europe/Merovingian era, 9–11, 15, 189–92, 387–90; astrology in, 205–6n45, 222–25; binding and loosing in, 232–36, 260; demons in, 74–84, 196, 197–99, 201, 207–8, 217; Diana in, 206, 259, 265, 268, 269; divination and theurgy in, 214–18; dreams in, 229–31; gender and magic in, 199, 215–16, 220–22, 234–35, 248–70, 389 (*see also* gender and magic); healing/healing magic in, 240–46, 259; idolatry/idol worship, 192–208, 213, 258; *lamiae* and *striae* in, 265–69; love and birth magic, 256–65; *maleficium* in, 192, 248–50; necromancy/revivification in, 251–53; pagan culture and Christianity in, 189–91, 197; poison, women's use of, 253–56; prophecy in, 218–22; ritual in, 214–18; sacred space and nature worship in, 192–208; singing, dancing, and juggling (ecstatic celebration) in, 208–10; *sortilegium* in, 225–29; *striae* in, 165; superstition in, 190, 192, 231–32; sympathetic magic (signs, symbols, names, and words) in, 232–38, 259, 260; tricks and trickery in, 121, 133–35; weather magic in, 210–12
practitioners of magic, 18; demons as agents independent of, 77–79; drawing on powers of demons, 29; healing magic in Carolingian era, 372–74, 379–83; *maleficium*, 146–47; sorcerers and witches, 28–30; *tempestarii* (weather magicians), 212, 286–89, 328, 391, 392n8. *See also* gender and magic
Prior Metz Annals, 344
Priscillianists, 287
Proclus, 109–10
Programmatic Capitulary (802), 323
prophecy: in Carolingian era, 299–300, 312; gender and, 120, 144, 175–79, 220–22, 300; in late antiquity/early Christian era, 120, 144, 175–79; in post-Roman Europe/Merovingian era, 218–22
prostitution, 102, 103, 267
Proterius, daughter of, 357–58
Prudentius, *Origin of Sin*, 71

pseudepigrapha, apocrypha, and intertestamental writings, 46, 68. *See also* Enoch corpus; *specific texts*
Pseudo-Antonius Musa, *De herba vettonica*, 363, 364
Pseudo-Apuleius, *Herbarius*, 142, 259, 263, 363–64, 368, 375
Pseudo-Bede, *Expositio in Evangelium S. Matthaei*, 298
Pseudo-Boniface, *Sermones*, 18–19
Pseudo-Clement, *Recognitions*, 69n26, 75n48, 83, 93–94n23, 102–3, 113, 115n29, 124n58, 132, 135, 137, 141, 158, 160–61, 205n45
Pseudo-Dioscorides, *Ex herbis femininis*, 363, 364
public/private, concept of, 2n4, 215

Quierzy, capitulary of (873), 319–20

Raban Maur, 394; *De magicis artibus*, 28n18, 74, 82, 295, 297, 298, 301, 302, 316, 331n57; *De universo*, 361; *Homily 142*, 273, 281, 292; *Poenitentiale ad Heribaldum Antissiodorensem*, 43n71, 258, 299, 333–34, 335, 381–82; *Poenitentium liber ad Otgarium*, 43n71
Radegund (Frankish queen), 10n31
rainmaking. *See* weather magic
Raphael (archangel), 71, 309
Rappaport, Roy, 4
Recceswinth (Visigothic ruler), 50n98, 258, 262
Reed, Annette, 69n25
Regino of Prüm, 333, 335–36; *Canon episcopi*, 322, 324–27, 376; *Chronicon*, 342, 351n32, 354n44, 355n50; *De synodalibus causis*, 28n18, 299, 306, 319, 322n26, 323–24, 325, 334, 353, 381, 382
relics, powers of, 5, 78, 126, 199, 211, 237, 244, 251
Rembold, Ingrid, 40n64
Reuter, Timothy, 319
revivification. *See* necromancy/revivification
Riché, Pierre, 6
Ricoeur, Paul, 4, 38n57, 321
Riddle, John, 56
Riesbach, Council of (early 9th century), 362
Ripuarian code (*Lex Ribuaria*), 228, 318
ritual, 4–6; Christianity and, 4–6, 90–95; defined, 30–38; healing magic and, 372; in late antiquity/early Christian era, 90–95,

144–45; liminality and, 35–36, 207; of *maleficium*, 147; in post-Roman Europe/Merovingian era, 214–18; rationality of, 33–35; Rogationtide, 197–99; as "social drama," 32, 204; symbols/symbolism and, 4, 32–33, 34
Rivers, Theodore John, 266, 339
Roach, Levi, 36n52
Robinson, Thomas A., 102n50, 192n5
Rogationtide, 197–99, 211–12, 240–41, 286n37
Royal Frankish Annals, 344
Rudolph of Bourges, 43n72, 306
Ruodpurc (poisoner), 318–19
Russell, Jeffrey, 6, 25, 75, 327
Russom, Geoffrey, 193

sacred space: in Carolingian era, 274–85; Jerusalem, as Christian model of, 96–97, 279; in late antiquity/early Christian era, 95–100; in post-Roman Europe/Merovingian era, 192–208
Saint Gall sacramentary, 361–62
Saint Hubert Penitential, 285, 291, 298, 334, 337n73
saints: Christianity and cult of, 154; relics, powers of, 5, 78, 126, 199, 211, 237, 244, 251; veneration of unauthorized saints and angels, 308–9. *See also* hagiography; *specific saints by name*
Salic law code (*Pactus legis Salicae* and *Lex Salica emendata*), 228, 248, 250, 252, 253, 262, 266–67, 322–23, 339
Salomon of Mainz, 300
Salzburg, Council of (early 9th century), 362
Satan, 1, 3n6, 29, 42, 69, 70, 72, 75, 79, 80, 125, 135, 136, 166–68, 243–44, 306, 365, 384
Saxony, Carolingian expansion into, 276–78, 322–23
Scarre, Geoffrey, 256
Schäfer, Peter, 25
Schmitt, Jean-Claude, 282
screech owl figures (*striae*). *See lamiae* and *striae*
Second Synod of Saint Patrick, 200
secrecy and magic, 147–48, 149, 180, 248–49
Seneca, 100; *Epistles*, 56n115; *Medea*, 168–69, 180; *Natural Questions*, 98
Septimima, 254–55
sermons and homilies, as sources, 44–45

sex and sexuality, 61, 100, 106, 148, 173n28, 175, 177, 186, 254n21, 259–60, 267, 268, 270, 321, 329, 331–32n59, 343, 358, 385. *See also* gender and magic; *lamiae* and *striae*; love and birth magic
Sextus Empiricus, 113n20
Sextus Placitus, *De medicina de quadrupedibus (Liber medicinae ex animalibus)*, 58n123, 142, 259, 260, 263–64, 363, 368
Shepherd of Hermas, 65n10
sibyl and *Sibylline Books*, 176, 300
Sidonius Apollinaris, 198n20
Sigerist, Henry, 143
sign of the cross, 123–24, 303, 334, 363
signs, symbols, and names. *See* sympathetic magic
Simon Magus, 132, 134–35, 158, 160–61, 238
sin versus magic, 74
Singer, Charles, 373, 377
singing, dancing, and juggling (ecstatic celebration): in Carolingian era, 289–91; in late antiquity/early Christianity, 100–105; in post-Roman Europe/Merovingian era, 208–10
Smith, Jonathan, 96
Smith, Julia (J. M. H.), 2n2, 48, 182–83, 189n1
snakes, 166, 364–65
"social drama," ritual as, 32, 204
Socrates, 92
Sol Invictus, 67
Somniale Danielis, 301
Sophronius of Jerusalem, *The Account of the Miracles of Saints Cyrus and John*, 140, 150
sorcerers and witches, 28–30. *See also* practitioners of magic
sortes biblicae, 226, 227, 228
Sortes Sanctorum, 225–27, 301
sortilegium: in Carolingian era, 298–99, 306n44; dream analysis compared, 231; in late antiquity/early Christianity, 116–18; ordeal by lot, 228–29; in post-Roman Europe/Merovingian era, 225–29
sources, 39–62; gender assumptions in, 60–61; legal texts, 46–50; medical materials, 55–58; narrative texts, 50–55; pastoral, polemic, and didactic works, 41–46; textual borrowing in, 58–60
Sowerby, Richard, 373
Sozomen, *Ecclesiastical History*, 96n29, 132n87

speech acts, 6, 127
spell-binders, 216
star of Bethlehem, 110, 113, 114, 298
Stellinga revolt, 276n10
Stephen of Auvergne, 354–55, 357
Stock, Brian, 39n60
striae. See *lamiae* and *striae*
Sturm (saint), 278
sub dio (open air). See nature worship/worship outdoors; sacred space
succubi and incubi, 331, 334
Suetonius, 109n10, 176n38, 277n12
Sulla, 180
Sulpicius Severus, *Vita Martini*, 196n16, 209, 218–19, 227–28, 251–52
Summers-Effler, Erika, 38–39n58
superstition, 17; amorphousness of concept, 301–2; in Carolingian era, 276, 301–5, 308, 310–11; in late antiquity/early Christian era, 107, 120–21, 122, 126, 144; in post-Roman Europe/Merovingian era, 190, 192, 231–32
suspensions and ligatures, 129–31, 307–8, 310, 368–69
sylvaticas, 330–31
symbols/symbolism, 4, 6, 32–33, 34, 88, 96–97, 321, 325
sympathetic magic (signs, symbols, names, and words): in late antiquity/early Christian era, 121–29; in post-Roman Europe/Merovingian era, 232–38, 259, 260

Tacitus, *Germania/De origine*, 116, 176, 223
Tambiah, Stanley, 31–32
tempestarii (weather magicians), 212, 286–89, 328, 391, 392n8
Tertullian, 22, 125, 230; *Ad nationes*, 137; *Apologeticum*, 66n13, 72n41, 102–3, 128, 140n118, 156–57; *De anima*, 161; *De baptismo*, 129n78; *De corona*, 123; *De cultu feminarum*, 69n27, 150n18; *De idolatria*, 69n27, 90n10, 113, 114, 128n75, 161n47
textiles and textile production, 260, 305–6
textual borrowing in medieval writings, 58–60
Thegan, *Life the Emperor Louis*, 350
Theodore of Canterbury, 224
Theodorus Priscian, 58n123
Theodosian Code, 46–47, 95, 99, 110–11, 115–16, 149–50, 151n19, 180nn53–54, 183, 212, 250, 252, 254n21, 258

Theodosius I (emperor), 161
Theodosius II (emperor), 46–47, 95
Theodulf of Orléans, 42, 43n72
Thesmophoria, 175
theurgy. See divination and theurgy
Theutberga (wife of Lothar II), 351–58
thick description, 274
Thiota (false prophetess), 300
Tiberius (emperor), 180
tombs. See the dead
Tours, Council of (813), 44–45n75, 362
Trevor-Roper, Hugh, 25
tricks and trickery, 17; in late antiquity/early Christian era, 121, 133–35; in post-Roman Europe/Merovingian era, 121, 133–35
Trier: demon of, 78–79; Diana statue, destruction of, 269
"truth-spots," 192, 275
Turner, Victor, 35, 37, 173, 321, 329; *The Ritual Process*, 164
Twelve Tables, 147n6
Tylor, Edward Burnett, 24, 33

"vacuous observances," 107, 121, 231, 301
Valens (emperor), 147, 148, 184
Valentinian I (emperor), 109, 111, 166n7
Valentinians, 184
Valerian (bishop of Cimelium), 139
Valerius Maximus, 139n115
Vallicellian Penitential, 335, 337n73, 338
vampiric figures *(lamiae)*. See *lamiae* and *striae*
Vannes, Council of (465), 225n27, 226
vaticination (poisoning), 179–81, 253–56, 318–20
Velaeda (prophetess), 176
Vercelli Homily XII, 198
Vergil, *Aeneid*, 116, 170n20, 182
Vikings, 13, 215
Visigoths and Visigothic law, 47, 49, 50n98, 55, 216, 250, 252n14, 253–54, 258, 262, 262n47
Vos, Nienke, 79n62
Vulcanalia, 208
Vulfolaic (saint), 269

Wala of Corbie, 344, 345, 346, 348–49
Walafrid Strabo, 297, 361

Waldrada (mistress of Lothar II), 351–58
Walker, P.W. L., 96n31
Walter of Aquitaine, 55
Walter of Speyer, 44
Waltharius, 55
Ward, Elizabeth, 346
weather magic: in Carolingian era, 210–12, 285–89; in late antiquity/early Christianity, 98–99; in post-Roman Europe/Merovingian era, 210–12; *tempestarii* (weather magicians), 212, 286–89, 328, 391, 392n8
Wickham, Chris, 212
Wilfrid of Northumbria, 13, 336n70
Willibald, *Vita Bonifati*, 278
Wils, Jean-Pierre, 30n58
Wiśniewski, Robert, 196n16

witches and sorcerers, 28–30. *See also* practitioners of magic
Wittgenstein, Ludwig, 35
women's magic. *See* gender and magic
Wood, Ian, 53, 256n25
words, signs, symbols, and names. *See* sympathetic magic
Wormald, Patrick, 48
Wulfstan (bishop of London), 259n34; "Canons of Edgar," 380–81

Zacharias (pope), 11, 279, 303n28, 309, 310–11
Zatchlas, 151–53, 155, 252
Zeddies, Nicole, 30n23, 228n35
zodiac, 205–6n45, 223
Zoroaster, 223

www.ingramcontent.com/pod-product-compliance
Lightning Source LLC
Chambersburg PA
CBHW022059300426
44117CB00007B/518